Checklist for Revising Paragraphs

- Can a reader understand and follow my ideas?
- Is the topic sentence clear?
- Have I fully supported the topic sentence with details and facts?
- Does the paragraph have unity? Does every sentence relate to the main idea?
- Does the paragraph have coherence? Does it follow a logical order and guide the reader from point to point?
- Have I varied the length and type of my sentences?
- Is my language exact, concise, and fresh?
- Have I proofread carefully for grammatical and spelling errors?

Checklist for Revising Essays

- Is the thesis statement clear?
- Does the body of the essay fully support the thesis statement?
- Does the essay have unity? Does every paragraph relate to the thesis statement?
- Does the essay have coherence? Do the paragraphs follow a logical order?
- Are the topic sentences clear?
- Does each paragraph provide good details and well-chosen examples?
- Does the essay conclude, not just leave off?

Five Useful Ways to Join Ideas

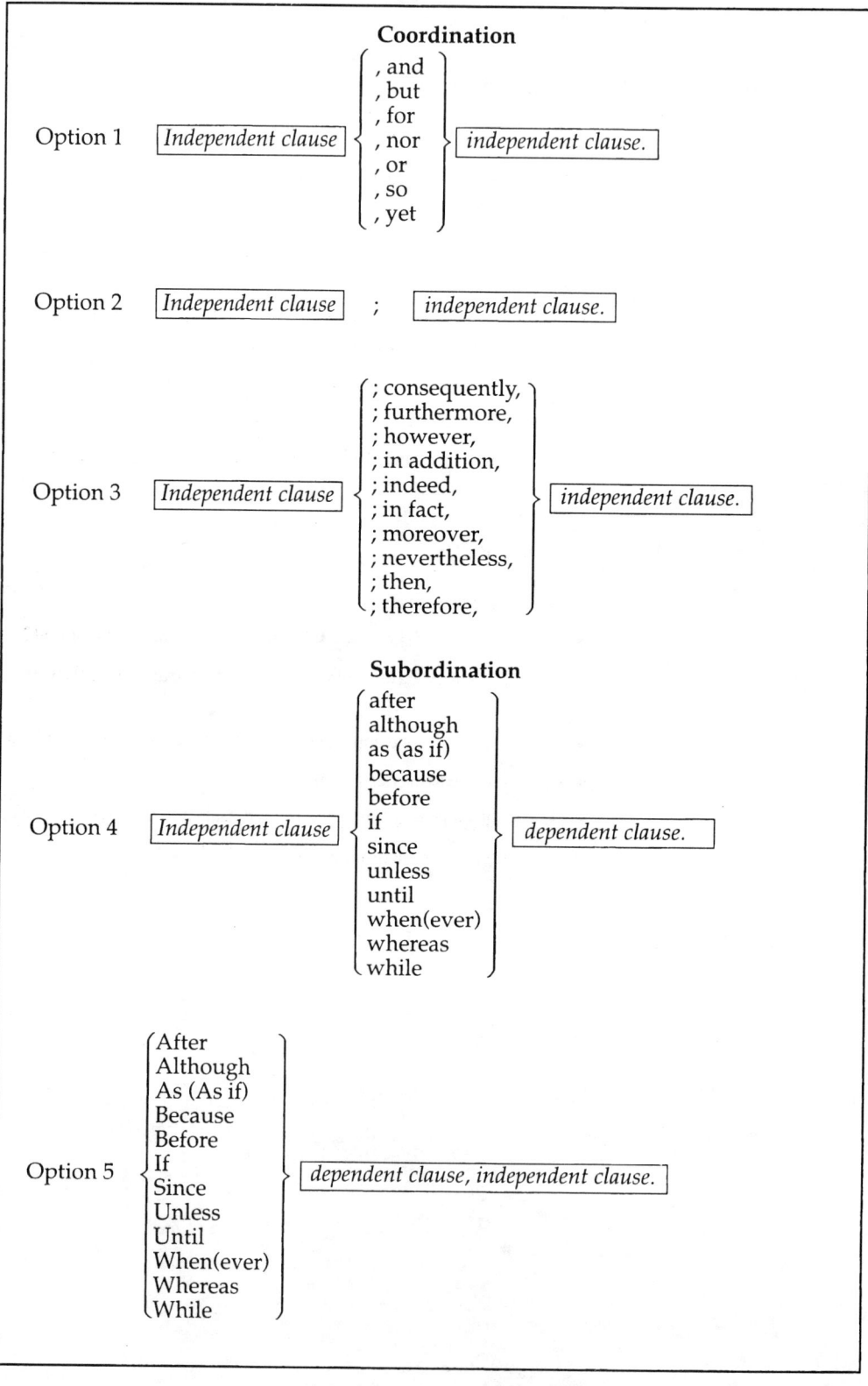

7 Evergreen

Seventh Edition

A Guide to Writing With Readings

Susan Fawcett

Houghton Mifflin Company | Boston New York

Custom Publishing Editor: Kyle Henderson
Custom Publishing Production Manager: Kathleen McCourt
Custom Publishing Project Coordinator: Kim Gavrilles

Cover Designer: Kyle Sarofeen

Vice President and Publisher: Patricia A. Coryell
Senior Sponsoring Editor: Mary Jo Southern
Development Editor: Kellie Cardone
Editorial Assistant: Peter Mooney
Project Editor: Cecilia Molinari
Editorial Assistant: Celeste Ng
Senior Production/Design Coordinator: Sarah Ambrose
Senior Manufacturing Coordinator: Priscilla Bailey
Marketing Manager: Annamarie Rice

Photo and Art Credits: We are grateful to the following individuals for permission to reproduce their photographs in this text. Page 7: Partnership for a Drug-Free America. Page 42: © Lloyd Wolf. Page 50: © Stephen Rice. Page 59: © Jessie Cohen, Smithsonian's National Zoo. Page 82: © James Carroll. Page 90: 50.23. George Tooker. *The Subway*, 1950. Egg tempera on composition board. Sight: 18.125" X 36.125" (46.04 X 91.76 cm). Frame 26" X 44" Whitney Museum of American Art, New York; Purchase, with funds from the Juliana Force Purchase Award. Page 95: Grant Heilman. Page 104: © Anne-Marie Webert/Corbis. Page 105: Corbis-Bettmann. Page 124: © Jeff Greenburg/Stock Boston. Page 130: Original Artwork by Ian Falconer. Copyright © 2002 Condé Nast Publications, Inc. Reprinted by permission. All Rights Reserved. Page 162: Dave Anderson (ANDY), Cartoonists & Writers Syndicate/cartoonweb.com. Page 163: Image courtesy of www.adbusters.org. Page 220: The Florida Anti-Tobacco Campaign. Page 311: © James Carroll. Page 327: *Crocodile Village* by Milan Kunc, 1985, oil on canvas, 120 X 120cm. Page 356: © 2002 The new Yorker Collection from cartoonbank.com. All Rights Reserved. Page 444: *Half-Dome, Winter*, photograph by Ansel Adams. © 1999 by the trustees of the Ansel Adams Publishing Rights Trust. All rights reserved.

Text Credits: Page 63: Reprint courtesy of SPORTS ILLUSTRATED "A New Dawn" by Same Moses, *SPORTS ILLUSTRATED*, April 23, 1990. Copyright © 1990, Time Inc. All rights reserved. Page 270: "Animal Passions" from Susan Schindehette and Terry Smith/People Weekly © 1994. All Rights Reserved Time Inc. Reprinted by permission. Page 542-547: "Beauty: When the Other Dancer is the Self" from IN SEARCH OF OUR MOTHERS' GARDENS: WOMANIST PROSE, copyright © 1983 by Alice Walker, reprinted by permission of Harcourt, Inc. *Text credits continued on page A7.*

This work was produced by Houghton Mifflin Custom Publishing and contains material not subject to Houghton Mifflin Company editorial review. The author is responsible for editing, accuracy, and content.

Copyright © 2004 by Houghton Mifflin Company. 2004 Impression. All rights reserved

All rights reserved. No part of this publication may be reproduced in any form whatsoever, by photograph or xerography or by any other means, by broadcast or transmission, by translation into any kind of language, nor by recording electronically or otherwise, without permission in writing from the publisher, except by a reviewer, who may quote brief passages in critical articles and reviews.

Printed in the United States of America.

ISBN: 0-618-44321-X
N02888

1 2 3 4 5 6 7 8 9 – CC – 05 04 03

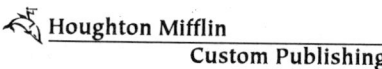
Houghton Mifflin
Custom Publishing

222 Berkeley Street • Boston, MA 02116

Address all correspondence and order information to the above address.

Contents

Preface xiii

Unit 1 — Getting Started 2

1 Exploring the Writing Process 3
- Part A   The Writing Process 3
- Part B   Subject, Audience, and Purpose 4

2 Prewriting to Generate Ideas 8
- Part A   Freewriting 8
- Part B   Brainstorming 11
- Part C   Clustering 12
- Part D   Asking Questions 13
- Part E   Keeping a Journal 15

Unit 1 Writers' Workshop: Using Just One of Your Five Senses, Describe a Place 18

Unit 2 — Discovering the Paragraph 20

3 The Process of Writing Paragraphs 21
- Part A   Defining and Looking at the Paragraph 21
- Part B   Narrowing the Topic and Writing the Topic Sentence 26
- Part C   Generating Ideas for the Body 31
- Part D   Selecting and Dropping Ideas 32
- Part E   Arranging Ideas in a Plan or an Outline 33
- Part F   Writing and Revising the Paragraph 34

4 Achieving Coherence 44
- Part A   Coherence Through Order 44
- Part B   Coherence Through Related Sentences 53
- Exploring Online 56
- Exploring Online 59

Unit 2 Writers' Workshop: Discuss the Pressures to Grow Up Fast 64

Unit 3 — Developing the Paragraph 66

5 Illustration 67
Thinking and Writing Together 74
Exploring Online 74
Checklist: The Process of Writing an Illustration Paragraph 74
Suggested Topic Sentences for Illustration Paragraphs 75

6 Narration 76
Thinking and Writing Together 81
Exploring Online 82
Checklist: The Process of Writing a Narrative Paragraph 83
Suggested Topics for Narrative Paragraphs 83

7 Description 84
Thinking and Writing Together 89
Exploring Online 90
Checklist: The Process of Writing a Descriptive Paragraph 91
Suggested Topics for Descriptive Paragraphs 91

8 Process 92
Thinking and Writing Together 100
Exploring Online 100
Checklist: The Process of Writing a Process Paragraph 100
Suggested Topics for Process Paragraphs 101

9 Definition 102
Part A Single-Sentence Definitions 102
Part B The Definition Paragraph 107
Thinking and Writing Together 112
Exploring Online 113
Checklist: The Process of Writing a Definition Paragraph 113
Suggested Topics for Definition Paragraphs 114

10 Comparison and Contrast 115
Part A The Contrast and Comparison Paragraphs 115
Thinking and Writing Together 125
Exploring Online 125
Checklist: The Process of Writing a Contrast or Comparison Paragraph 125
Suggested Topics for Contrast or Comparison Paragraphs 126
Part B The Comparison-Contrast Paragraph 126
Working Through the Comparison-Contrast Paragraph 130
Suggested Topics for Comparison-Contrast Paragraphs 131

11 Classification 132
Thinking and Writing Together 138
Exploring Online 138
Checklist: The Process of Writing a Classification Paragraph 139
Suggested Topics for Classification Paragraphs 139

12 Cause and Effect 141

Thinking and Writing Together 148
Exploring Online 148
Checklist: The Process of Writing a Cause and Effect Paragraph 148
Suggested Topics for Cause and Effect Paragraphs 149

13 Persuasion 150

Thinking and Writing Together 162
Exploring Online 163
Checklist: The Process of Writing a Persuasive Paragraph 164
Suggested Topics for Persuasive Paragraphs 165
Unit 3 Writers' Workshop: Give Advice to College Writers 166

Unit 4 — Writing the Essay 168

14 The Process of Writing an Essay 169

Part A Looking at the Essay 169
Part B Writing the Thesis Statement 173
Part C Generating Ideas for the Body 177
Part D Ordering and Linking Paragraphs in the Essay 184
Part E Writing and Revising Essays 190
Checklist: The Process of Writing an Essay 196
Suggested Topics for Essays 196
Exploring Online 197

15 Types of Essays 198

Part A The Illustration Essay 198
Part B The Narrative Essay 201
Part C The Descriptive Essay 203
Part D The Process Essay 205
Part E The Definition Essay 208
Part F The Comparison or Contrast Essay 210
Part G The Classification Essay 212
Part H The Cause and Effect Essay 215
Part I The Persuasive Essay 217

16 The Introduction, the Conclusion, and the Title 222

Part A The Introduction 222
Part B The Conclusion 225
Part C The Title 227

17 Special College Skills: Summary and Quotation 230

Part A Avoiding Plagiarism 230
Part B Writing a Summary 231
Checklist: The Process of Writing a Summary 234
Part C Using Direct and Indirect Quotation 235

18 Strengthening an Essay with Research 240

- Part A Improving an Essay with Research 240
- Part B Finding and Evaluating Outside Sources: Library and Internet 243
- Part C Adding Sources to Your Essay and Documenting Them Correctly 246

19 Writing Under Pressure: The Essay Examination 253

- Part A Budgeting Your Time 253
- Part B Reading and Understanding the Essay Question 255
- Part C Choosing the Correct Paragraph or Essay Pattern 258
- Part D Writing the Topic Sentence or the Thesis Statement 260
- Checklist: The Process of Answering an Essay Question 263

Unit 4 Writers' Workshop: Analyze a Social Problem 264

Unit 5 Improving Your Writing 266

20 Revising for Consistency and Parallelism 267

- Part A Consistent Tense 267
- Part B Consistent Number and Person 272
- Part C Parallelism 277
- Exploring Online 282

21 Revising for Sentence Variety 283

- Part A Mix Long and Short Sentences 283
- Part B Use a Question, a Command, or an Exclamation 285
- Part C Vary the Beginnings of Sentences 287
- Part D Vary Methods of Joining Ideas 291
- Part E Avoid Misplaced and Confusing Modifiers 306
- Part F Review and Practice 308

22 Revising for Language Awareness 312

- Part A Exact Language: Avoiding Vagueness 312
- Part B Concise Language: Avoiding Wordiness 318
- Part C Fresh Language: Avoiding Triteness 321
- Part D Figurative Language: Similes and Metaphors 323

23 Putting Your Revision Skills to Work 328

Unit 5 Writers' Workshop: Examine the Bright (or Dark) Side of Family Life 334

Unit 6 Reviewing the Basics 336

24 The Simple Sentence 337

- Part A Defining and Spotting Subjects 337
- Part B Spotting Prepositional Phrases 338
- Part C Defining and Spotting Verbs 340
- Exploring Online 342

25 Coordination and Subordination 343

Part A Coordination 343
Part B Subordination 346
Part C Semicolons 350
Part D Conjunctive Adverbs 351
Part E Review 353
Exploring Online 357

26 Avoiding Sentence Errors 358

Part A Avoiding Run-Ons and Comma Splices 358
Part B Avoiding Fragments 362
Exploring Online 373

27 Present Tense (Agreement) 374

Part A Defining Subject-Verb Agreement 374
Part B Three Troublesome Verbs in the Present Tense: *To Be, To Have, To Do* 376
Part C Special Singular Constructions 378
Part D Separation of Subject and Verb 380
Part E Sentences Beginning with *There* and *Here* 381
Part F Agreement in Questions 381
Part G Agreement in Relative Clauses 382
Exploring Online 384

28 Past Tense 385

Part A Regular Verbs in the Past Tense 385
Part B Irregular Verbs in the Past Tense 386
Part C A Troublesome Verb in the Past Tense: *To Be* 389
Part D Troublesome Pairs in the Past Tense: *Can/Could, Will/Would* 390
Exploring Online 393

29 The Past Participle 394

Part A Past Participles of Regular Verbs 394
Part B Past Participles of Irregular Verbs 396
Part C Using the Present Perfect Tense 400
Part D Using the Past Perfect Tense 401
Part E Using the Passive Voice (*To Be* and the Past Participle) 402
Part F Using the Past Participle as an Adjective 403
Exploring Online 406

30 Nouns 407

Part A Defining Singular and Plural 407
Part B Signal Words: Singular and Plural 409
Part C Signal Words with *Of* 410
Exploring Online 412

31 Pronouns 413

Part A   Defining Pronouns and Antecedents   413
Part B   Making Pronouns and Antecedents Agree   414
Part C   Referring to Antecedents Clearly   417
Part D   Special Problems of Case   420
Part E   Using Pronouns with *-Self* and *-Selves*   424
Exploring Online   426

32 Prepositions 427

Part A   Working with Prepositional Phrases   427
Part B   Prepositions in Common Expressions   429
Exploring Online   434

33 Adjectives and Adverbs 435

Part A   Defining and Using Adjectives and Adverbs   435
Part B   The Comparative and the Superlative   437
Part C   A Troublesome Pair: *Good/Well*   440
Exploring Online   442

34 The Apostrophe 443

Part A   The Apostrophe for Contractions   443
Part B   The Apostrophe for Ownership   445
Part C   Special Uses of the Apostrophe   447
Exploring Online   449

35 The Comma 450

Part A   Commas for Items in a Series   450
Part B   Commas with Introductory Phrases, Transitional Expressions, and Parentheticals   451
Part C   Commas for Appositives   453
Part D   Commas with Nonrestrictive and Restrictive Clauses   454
Part E   Commas for Dates and Addresses   455
Part F   Minor Uses of the Comma   457
Exploring Online   459

36 Mechanics 460

Part A   Capitalization   460
Part B   Titles   462
Part C   Direct Quotations   464
Part D   Minor Marks of Punctuation   466
Exploring Online   468

37 Putting Your Proofreading Skills to Work 469

Exploring Online   477

Unit 6 Writers' Workshop: Adopt a New Point of View   478

Unit 7 — Strengthening Your Spelling 480

38 Spelling 481
- Part A Suggestions for Improving Your Spelling 481
- Part B Computer Spell Checkers 482
- Part C Spotting Vowels and Consonants 483
- Part D Doubling the Final Consonant (in Words of One Syllable) 484
- Part E Doubling the Final Consonant (in Words of More Than One Syllable) 485
- Part F Dropping or Keeping the Final *E* 486
- Part G Changing or Keeping the Final *Y* 487
- Part H Adding *-S* or *-ES* 488
- Part I Choosing *IE* or *EI* 488
- Part J Spelling Lists 490

Exploring Online 492

39 Look-Alikes/Sound-Alikes 493
Exploring Online 505

Unit 7 Writers' Workshop: Discuss a Time When Diverse People Were United 506

Unit 8 — Reading Selections 508

Reading Strategies for Writers 509
How Sunglasses Spanned the World 510
Homeward Bound Janet Wu 512
Cell Yell: Thanks for (Not) Sharing Eric A. Taub 514
A Brother's Murder Brent Staples 517
Only Daughter Sandra Cisneros 520
The Case for Torture Michael Levin 523
Let's Get Vertical Beth Wald 526
On the Rez Ian Frazier 529
Bam! Crash! Kapow! Girls Are Heroes Now Susan Hopkins 532
My Outing Arthur Ashe 534
Build Yourself a Killer Bod with Killer Bees Dave Barry 537
Follow the Leader to the Next Fad Karen Castellucci Cox 540
Beauty: When the Other Dancer Is the Self Alice Walker 542
A Smoker's Right Mario Vargas Llosa 548
Some Thoughts About Abortion Anna Quindlen 550
Road Rage Andrew Ferguson 553

Quotation Bank A1
Acknowledgments A7
ESL Reference Guide A9
Index A11
Rhetorical Index A17

Preface

"*Evergreen* works." Again and again, I hear this comment from instructors and students alike, and I consider it the greatest possible compliment. Based on my years of classroom experience at Bronx Community College of the City University of New York, *Evergreen* is designed for students who need to improve the writing skills so necessary to success in college and in most careers. The text's clear, paced lessons, inspiring student and professional models, high-interest practices, and varied writing assignments have guided nearly two million students through the process of writing effectively, from prewriting to final draft. In 2000, the Sixth Edition of *Evergreen with Readings* won the McGuffey Award for sustained excellence—a prize given by the Text and Academic Authors Association.

In this exciting Seventh Edition, I have thoroughly reviewed and updated the text, guided by the thoughtful suggestions of faculty across the country and by the kinds of academic and job-related challenges our students face. My goal has been to take an excellent book and make it more motivating, useful, and engaging than ever before.

Specifically, I have added a critical-thinking group assignment to every rhetorical paragraph chapter and placed web sites selectively throughout the text for further review, practice, and exploration. *Evergreen's* reading selections have been significantly freshened with nine provocative contemporary essays, now combined with favorites retained from the last edition. As always, I have replaced numerous models and content-based practices with new subject matter intended to spark and hold students' interest as they learn. Other improvements include a livelier and more engaging Chapter 1; a new section on misplaced modifiers; a clearer sentence fragment review chart; more mixed-error proofreading exercises in Chapter 37; more humor throughout; and upgraded photographs, cartoons, and other visuals. An important change is the addition of a new chapter on research.

Instructors who use *Evergreen* divide—passionately—on whether or not to teach research in this course. After much thought, I have created a flexible, two-chapter approach that allows instructors to bypass research altogether, teach some research skills, or teach an essay enriched with one or more sources. I have revised Chapter 17 on summarizing and quoting to include more practice on avoiding plagiarism. A new brief Chapter 18, "Strengthening an Essay with Research," guides students through the process of improving an essay with research—bolstered by interesting practices.

xiii

Special Features of *Evergreen with Readings*, Seventh Edition

- **New Critical-Thinking Activity for Every Rhetorical Mode.** A collaborative feature—*Thinking and Writing Together*—is now the final practice in every chapter of Unit 3, *Developing the Paragraph.* Here students apply the rhetorical strategy just learned to a problem, set of facts, or visual image. They might narrate an experience of stereotyping, contrast gender-targeted toys, illustrate random acts of kindness, or evaluate the persuasive humor in a spoof Big Mac ad.

- **New *Exploring Online* feature.** Selected web sites provide an option for online review, practice, or discovery. For example, one or two top OWL (online writing lab) sites conclude each grammar chapter. Quality web sites also follow each *Thinking and Writing Together* activity and selected practices, on such topics as endangered species, how movies are classified, Van Gogh's *Starry Night*, and qualities of a team player.

- **Flexible New Research Coverage.** Now instructors may include as little or as much research instruction as they wish. Chapter 17, "Special College Skills: Summary and Quotation," has been revised with more instruction and practice on avoiding plagiarism. In addition, a new, friendly Chapter 18, "Strengthening an Essay with Research," builds on these research "sub-skills," applying them to library and Internet research. Chapter 18 guides students through the basics of finding and evaluating outside sources, adding them to an essay, and documenting them correctly. Enjoyable practices, boxes showing one student's research process, and her sample essay on campus credit card debt all help students master useful research skills.

- **60 Percent New Reading Selections.** Based on feedback from faculty and students, Unit 8 has been extensively freshened with nine strong and eloquent readings. New to this edition are Eric Taub on obnoxious cell-phone users, Janet Wu on reuniting with her grandmother, Mario Vargas Llosa on smokers' lawsuits, Beth Wald on rock climbing, Dave Barry on fitness, Susan Hopkins on "girl heroes," Michael Levin on the controversial case for torture, Karen Castellucci Cox on consumer fads, and Ian Frazier on a young athlete's social courage. Readers' favorite selections from the last edition—those rated most thought-provoking and appealing—have been kept.

- **75 New High-Interest Models and Practices.** Engaging models and content-based practice sets are vital to *Evergreen's* effectiveness. Fresh subjects include the birth of video games, Dr. Seuss, pet cloning, the growth of *Monster.com*, writer Oscar Hijuelos, birth order and personality, online versus traditional courses, actress Lea Salonga, flashbulb memories, CEO Maria Elena Ibanez, the Youth Orchestra of Venezuela, Cirque du Soleil, the first African American woman in space, humor as a career asset, a Chinese wedding banquet, athletic dolls that rival Barbie, the American Freshman survey, and Dominican baseball stars.

- **Other Enriched Instruction.** Chapter 1 has been revised to engage students more quickly—through new practices, an emphasis on writing as a means to job success, humor, and a contemporary visual to analyze for subject, audience, and purpose. As requested by instructors, a section on misplaced and confusing modifiers has been added as Part E of Chapter 21, "Revising for Sentence Variety," and more mixed-error proofreading exercises are offered in Chapter 37.

Six types of sentence fragments are now discussed, and a clear new review chart has been added.

- **More Humor and More Contemporary Visuals.** Humor can lighten the composition classroom and serve an instructional purpose. For example, Internet dating disasters, the comedians of *Saturday Night Live*, and real-life bloopers from résumés and job-application letters form the subject matter of new proofreading exercises. Students are invited to analyze and write about a number of new cartoons on contemporary topics, photos, paintings, and a witty *New Yorker* cover.

Extensive Ancillary Package

Available on adoption of the text, the following ancillaries expand the instructor's teaching options. New with this edition are several exciting offerings designed specifically for use with *Evergreen*. *EverWrite* is a CD-ROM with hundreds of uniquely practical writing-process, rhetorical, and grammatical exercises, providing students with lots of extra support. In addition, PowerPoint slides are provided to enhance classroom presentations and create key student handouts. Now two *Evergreen* web sites are available—one for faculty and one for students. The popular, updated *Evergreen Community* (a resource allowing users to exchange ideas about teaching with *Evergreen*) can be accessed online through the faculty site and in a new print edition.

- **Instructor's Annotated Edition**
- **New!** *EverWrite* **CD-ROM** created for *Evergreen*, with 120 interactive writing-process and rhetorical exercises, plus 350 grammar practices to hone students' skills
- **New! Extensive PowerPoint Slide Package** for classroom use
- **Evergreen Web Site for Faculty,** with additional Mastery and Diagnostics tests, links, plus the Evergreen Community, a resource for sharing teaching ideas
- **New! Evergreen Web Site for Students,** with writing tips, links to OWLs, and other resources
- **Evergreen Community,** a print compendium of successful classroom strategies contributed by instructors who use the text—also available online.

Organization of the Text

Evergreen's self-contained chapters and units can be taught in any order. Unit 1 provides an overview of the writing process, audience, and purpose and then introduces five prewriting techniques. Unit 2 guides students through the paragraph-writing process: planning, writing topic sentences, generating ideas, organizing, making smooth transitions, and revising. Unit 3 moves on to the rhetorical modes most often required in college writing (illustration, narration, description, process, definition, comparison/contrast, classification, cause/effect, and persuasion). In Unit 4, the techniques of paragraph writing are applied step by step to the process of writing essays, summarizing and quoting from sources, strengthening an essay with research, and answering essay examination questions. Unit 5 covers the more subtle skills of revising for consistency, sentence variety, and language awareness. Unit 6 thoroughly reviews basic grammar, highlighting such major problem areas as verbs, sentence boundaries, punctuation, and mechanics; Unit 7 covers spelling and homonyms. In Unit 8, the instructor can choose from fifteen richly varied, thought-provoking reading selections by such authors as Sandra Cisneros, Brent Staples, Anna Quindlen, and Alice Walker. Each selection is accompanied by a headnote, glosses, critical-thinking questions, and writing assignments, some of them collaborative. A Quotation Bank—a mini-reader of great short quotations for student use—concludes the text.

Evergreen with Reading's full range of materials and flexible organization adapt easily to almost any course design and to a wide range of student needs. Because each chapter is self-contained, the text also works well for tutorials, laboratory work, and self-teaching.

Acknowledgments

Sincerest thanks to these people whose thoughtful comments and suggestions helped to develop this Seventh Edition.

Kathleen Beauchene of Community College of Rhode Island
Michelle J. Biferie of Palm Beach Community College
Larry Bohlender of Glendale (AZ) Community College
Nicole Cortz of Long Beach City College
Christopher B. Crumlish of Montgomery County Community College
Ray Foster of Scottsdale Community College
Carmen Hall of St. Petersburg Community College
Teresa S. Irvin of Columbus State University
Lisa Kekaha of Butte-Glenn Community College
Jim Kolsky of Western Nevada Community College
Irma Luna of San Antonio College
Patricia A. Malinowski of Finger Lakes Community College
David Merves of Miami-Dade Community College
Libby Miller of Merritt College
Nancy Schneider of the University of Maine at Augusta
Linda J. Whisnant of Guilford Technical Community College
David Winner of Hudson County Community College
Cody Yeager of Central Oregon Community College

I am indebted to the editors at Houghton Mifflin who have worked so hard to make *Evergreen* quite simply the best book of its kind in the country. Special thanks to my friend and Senior Sponsoring Editor, Mary Jo Southern, who has long championed *Evergreen* and its mission; to Kellie Cardone, Development Editor, who solved the inevitable problems of a major revision with dedication and aplomb—even when it seemed that we were always out of time; to Harriett

Prentiss, Development Editor, who leant her keen editing eye and assembled manuscript when my back rebelled; to Cecilia Molinari, Project Editor, whose artistry turned messy manuscript and unpleasant surprises into beautiful pages; and to Maria Maimone for expertly securing permissions.

In addition, Ann Marie Radaskiewicz helped with high-quality research, writing, and troubleshooting, always with her characteristic professionalism and good cheer. Karen Castellucci Cox of City College of San Francisco generously shared her instructional ideas, research approaches, and love of teaching; her entertaining essay on the consumers who fuel popular trends appears in this edition. Sandra K. Hall of Corning Community College and Linda Perry contributed the useful visual, "Building Blocks to Effective Persuasion," that augments instruction in Chapter 14.

To the English Department faculty—in particular, Chair Frederick De Naples—and to the students of Bronx Community College, I owe a debt of gratitude. Many of the excellent student paragraphs and essays in this book were written in BCC classrooms.

My husband, Richard Donovan, contributed at every level to *Evergreen*—suggesting topics and readings, making sure my sports references are up-to-date, discussing (for the third time, with absolute focus) which of two approaches would better help our students, and even copying and collating pages at midnight when a deadline loomed.

Finally, I dedicate this edition of *Evergreen* to the dear friends who believe in my writing but lovingly remind me to take care of myself. Without them, life would lose so much joy, juice, luster, and love—in particular, Maggie Smith, Pamela Tudor, Sondra Zeidenstein, Trisha Nelson, Colleen Fix, Stuart Huff, Bryan Hoffman, Eleanor Caracciolo, Doris Rudnick, Carole Stone, my mother Harriet Fawcett, and my brother David Fawcett.

S.F.

Evergreen:

A Guide to Writing With Readings

Seventh Edition

UNIT 1

Getting Started

CHAPTER 1 Exploring the Writing Process

CHAPTER 2 Prewriting to Generate Ideas

CHAPTER 1
Exploring the Writing Process

PART A   The Writing Process
PART B   Subject, Audience, and Purpose

Did you know that the ability to write well characterizes the most successful college students and employees—in fields from education to medicine to computer science? Skim the job postings in career fields that interest you and notice how many stress "excellent writing and communication skills." Furthermore, reading and writing enrich our daily lives; in surveys, adults always rate reading, writing, and speaking well as the most important life skills a person can possess.

The goal of this book is to help you become a more skilled, powerful, and confident writer. You will see that writing is not a magic ability only a few are born with, but a life skill that can be learned. The first chapter presents a brief overview of the writing process, explored in greater depth throughout the book. Now I invite you to decide to excel in this course. Let *Evergreen* be your guide, and enjoy the journey.

Part A
The Writing Process

Many people have the mistaken idea that good writers simply sit down and write out a perfect letter, paragraph, or essay from start to finish. In fact, writing is a **process** consisting of a number of steps:

The Writing Process

Prewriting
- Thinking about possible subjects
- Freely jotting ideas on paper or computer
- Narrowing the subject and writing your main idea in one sentence
- Deciding which ideas to include
- Arranging ideas in a plan or outline

2 Writing — Writing the first draft

3 Revising
- Rethinking, rearranging, and revising as necessary
- Writing one or more new drafts
- Proofreading for grammar and spelling errors

Not all writers perform all the steps in this order, but most **prewrite, write,** and **revise.** Actually, writing can be a messy process of thinking, writing, reading what has been written, and rewriting. Sometimes steps overlap or need to be repeated. The important thing is that writing the first draft is just one stage in the process. "I love being a writer," jokes Peter De Vries. "What I can't stand is the paperwork."

Good writers take time at the beginning to **prewrite**—to think, jot ideas, and plan the paper—because they know it will save time and avoid frustration later. Once they write the first draft, they let it "cool off." Then they read it again with a fresh, critical eye and **revise**—crossing out, adding, and rewriting for more clarity and punch. Good writers are like sculptors, shaping and reworking their material into something more meaningful. Finally, they **proofread** for grammar and spelling errors so that their writing seems to say, "I am proud to put my name on this work." As you practice writing, you will discover your own most effective writing process.

PRACTICE 1 Think of something that you wrote recently—and of which you felt proud—for college, work, or your personal life. Now on paper or with classmates, discuss the *process* you followed in writing it. Did you do any *planning* or *prewriting*—or did you just sit down and start writing? How much time did you spend rewriting and *revising* your work? What one change in your writing process do you think would most improve your writing? Taking more time to prewrite? Taking more time to revise? Improving your grammar and spelling?

PRACTICE 2 Bring in several newspaper help-wanted sections. In a group with four or five classmates, study the ads in career fields that interest you. How many fields require writing and communication skills? Which job ad requiring these skills most surprised you or your group? Be prepared to present your findings to the class. Or, if your class has Internet access, visit *Monster.com, HotJobs.com,* or other job-search web sites and perform the same exercise.

Exploring Online

http://www.pbs.org/literacy/wes/description.html/ How does this site rank communication and writing as skills essential to career success in all fields?

Part B

Subject, Audience, and Purpose

Early in the prewriting phase, writers should give some thought to their **subject, audience,** and **purpose.**

In college courses, you may be assigned a broad **subject** by your instructor. First, make sure you understand the assignment. Then focus on one aspect of the subject that intrigues you. Whenever possible, choose something that you know and care about: life in Cleveland, working with learning-disabled children, repairing motorcycles, overcoming shyness, watching a friend struggle with drug addiction, playing soccer. You may not realize how many subjects you do know about.

> To find or focus your subject, ask yourself:
> - What special experience or expertise do I have?
> - What inspires, angers, or motivates me? What do I love to do?
> - What story in the news affected me recently?
> - What campus, job, or community problem do I have ideas about solving?

Your answers will suggest good subjects to write about. Keep a list of all your best ideas.

How you approach your subject will depend on your **audience**—your readers. Are you writing for your professor, classmates, boss, closest friend, youngsters in the community, or the editor of a newspaper?

> To focus on your audience, ask yourself:
> - For whom am I writing? Who will read this?
> - How much do they know about the subject? Are they beginners or experts?
> - Will they likely agree or disagree with my ideas?

Keeping your audience in mind helps you know what information to include and what to leave out. For example, if you are writing about women's college basketball for readers who think that hoops are big earrings, you will approach your subject in a basic way, perhaps discussing the recent explosion of interest in women's teams. But an audience of sports lovers will already know about this; for them, you would write in more depth, perhaps comparing the technique of two point guards.

Finally, keeping your **purpose** in mind will help you write more effectively. Do you want to explain something to your readers, persuade them that a certain view is correct, entertain them, tell a good story, or some combination of these?

PRACTICE 3 List five subjects that you might like to write about. Consider your audience and purpose: For whom are you writing? What do you want them to know about your subject? Notice how the audience and purpose will help shape your paper. For ideas, reread the boxed questions on this page.

	Subject	**Audience**	**Purpose**
Example	my recipe for seafood gumbo	inexperienced cooks	to show how easy it is to make seafood gumbo
1.	_____	_____	_____
2.	_____	_____	_____
3.	_____	_____	_____
4.	_____	_____	_____
5.	_____	_____	_____

PRACTICE 4 Jot ideas for the two assignments below, by yourself or in a group with four or five classmates. Notice how your ideas and details differ, depending on the audience and purpose.

1. You have been asked to write a description of your college for local high school students. Your purpose is to explain what advantages the college offers its students. What kinds of information should you include? What will your audience want to know? What information should you leave out?

2. You have been asked to write a description of your college for the governor of your state. Your purpose is to persuade her or him to spend more money to improve your college. What information should you include? What will your audience want to know? What information should you leave out?

PRACTICE 5 Study the public service advertisement on the following page and then answer these questions: What *subject* is the ad addressing? Who is the target *audience*? What is the intended *purpose*? In your view, how successful is this ad in achieving its purpose?

PRACTICE 6 In a group with three or four classmates, read these sentences from real job-application letters and résumés, published in *Forbes Magazine*. Each writer's *subject* was his or her job qualifications; the *audience* was an employer, and the *purpose* was to get a job. How did each person undercut his or her own purpose? What writing advice would you give each of these job seekers?

1. I have lurnt Word and computer spreasheet programs.

2. Please don't misconstrue my 14 jobs as "job-hopping." I have never quit a job.

3. I procrastinate, especially when the task is unpleasant.

4. Let's meet, so you can "ooh" and "aah" over my experience.

5. It is best for employers that I not work with people.

6. Reason for leaving my last job: maturity leave.

7. As indicted, I have over five years of analyzing investments.

8. References: none. I have left a path of destruction behind me.

CHAPTER 2 Prewriting to Generate Ideas

- PART A Freewriting
- PART B Brainstorming
- PART C Clustering
- PART D Asking Questions
- PART E Keeping a Journal

This chapter presents five effective prewriting techniques that will help you get your ideas onto paper (or onto the computer). These techniques can help you overcome the "blank-page jitters" that many people face when they first sit down to write. You also can use them to generate new ideas at any point in the writing process. Try all five to see which ones work best for you.

In addition, if you write on a computer, try prewriting in different ways: on paper and on computer. Some writers feel they produce better work if they prewrite by hand and only later transfer their best ideas onto the computer. Every writer has personal preferences, so don't be afraid to experiment.

Part A

Freewriting

Freewriting is an excellent method that many writers use to warm up and to generate ideas. These are the guidelines: for five, ten, or fifteen minutes, write rapidly, without stopping, about anything that comes into your head. If you feel stuck, just repeat or rhyme the last word you wrote, but *don't stop writing*. And don't worry about grammar, logic, complete sentences, or grades.

The point of freewriting is to write so quickly that ideas can flow without comments from your inner critic. The *inner critic* is the voice inside that says, every time you have an idea, "That's dumb; that's no good; cross that out." Freewriting helps you tell this voice, "Thank you for your opinion. Once I have lots of ideas and words on paper, I'll invite you back for comment."

After you freewrite, read what you have written, underlining or marking any parts you like.

Here is one student's first freewriting, with his own underlinings:

> Boy I wish this class was over and I could go home and get out of this building, boy was my day miserable and this sure is a crazy thing to do <u>if a shrink could see us now.</u> My I just remember I've got to buy that CD my my my I am running out of stuff to write but dont worry teach because this is really the nuttiest thing but lots of fun you probably like reading this mixed up thing That girl's remark sounded dumb but impressing. You know <u>this writing sure puts muscles in your fingers</u> if I stop writing oh boy <u>this is the most incredible assignment in the world</u> think and write without worrying about sentence structure and other English garbage to stall you down boy that guy next to me is writing like crazy so he looks crazy you know this is outrageous I'm writing and writing I never realized the extent of mental and physical concentration it takes to do this constantly <u>dont mind the legibility of my hand my hand oh my hand is ready to drop off</u> please this is crazy crazy and too much work for a poor guy like myself. Imagine me putting on paper all I have to say and faster than a speeding bullet.

■ This example has the lively energy of many freewritings. Why do you think the student underlined what he did? Would you have underlined other words or phrases? Why?

Freewriting is a powerful tool for helping you turn thoughts and feelings into words, especially when you are unsure about what you want to say. Sometimes freewriting produces only nonsense; often, however, it can help you zoom in on possible topics, interests, and worthwhile writing you can use later.

If you are freewriting on a computer, try turning off the monitor and writing "blind." Some students find that this helps them forget about making mistakes and concentrate on getting words and ideas out fast.

PRACTICE 1

1. Set a timer for ten minutes or have someone time you. Freewrite without stopping for the full ten minutes. If you get stuck, repeat or rhyme the last word you wrote until words start flowing again but *don't stop writing*!

2. When you finish, write down one or two words that describe how you felt while freewriting.

_____

_____

3. Next, read your freewriting. Underline any words or lines you like—anything that strikes you as interesting, thoughtful, or funny. If nothing strikes you, that's okay.

PRACTICE 2

Try three more freewritings at home—each one ten minutes long. Do them at different times of day or night when you have a quiet moment. If possible, use a timer. Set it for ten minutes; then write quickly and freely until it rings. Later, read over your freewritings and underline any striking lines or ideas.

Focused Freewriting

In **focused freewriting**, you simply try to focus your thoughts on one subject as you freewrite. The subject might be one assigned by your instructor, one you choose, or one you have discovered in unfocused freewriting. The goal of most writing is a polished, organized piece of writing; focused freewriting can help you generate ideas or narrow a topic to one aspect that interests you.

Here is one student's focused freewriting on the topic *someone who strongly influenced you:*

> Mr. Martin, the reason I'm interested in science. Wiry, five-foot-four-inch, hyperactive guy. A darting bird in the classroom, a circling teacher-bird, now jabbing at the knee bone of a skeleton, now banging on the jar with the brain in it. Like my brain used to feel, pickled, before I took his class. I always liked science but everything else was too hard. I almost dropped out of school, discouraged, but Martin was fun, crazy, made me think. Encouragement was his thing. Whacking his pencil against the plastic model of an eyeball in his office, he would bellow at me, "Taking too many courses! Working too many hours in that restaurant! Living everyone else's life but your own!" Gradually, I slowed down, got myself focused. Saw him last at graduation, where he thwacked my diploma with his pencil, shouting, "Keep up the good work! Live your own life! Follow your dreams!"

- This student later used this focused freewriting—its vivid details about Mr. Martin and his influence—as the basis for an effective paper. Underline any words or lines that you find especially striking or appealing. Be prepared to explain why you like what you underline.

PRACTICE 3 Do a three-minute focused freewriting on three of these topics:

beach	body piercing
friendship	parent (or child)
news	tests

Underline as usual. Did you surprise yourself by having so much to say about any one topic? Perhaps you would like to write more about that topic.

PRACTICE 4
1. Read over your earlier freewritings and notice your underlinings. Would you like to write more about any underlined words or ideas? Write two or three such words or ideas here:

   _____

   _____

   _____

2. Now choose one word or idea. Focus your thoughts on it and do a ten-minute focused freewriting. Try to stick to the topic as you write but don't worry too much about keeping on track; just keep writing.

Part B
Brainstorming

Another prewriting technique that may work for you is **brainstorming** or freely jotting down ideas about a topic. As in freewriting, the purpose is to generate lots of ideas so you have something to work with and choose from. Write everything that comes to you about a topic—words and phrases, ideas, details, examples.

After you have brainstormed, read over your list, underlining interesting or exciting ideas you might develop further. As with freewriting, many writers brainstorm on a general subject, underline, and then brainstorm again as they focus on one aspect of that subject.

Here is one student's brainstorm list on the topic *email:*

> everyone has it—really neat
>
> can send mail day or night
>
> not like snail mail—so slow
>
> I hate to write letters but I love to email
>
> I email my friends at their colleges all the time
>
> I even email my little brother at home
>
> more intimate than phone calls—you can share inner thoughts
>
> Mom's always sending me emails
>
> she emails her old college friends, too
>
> people are more in touch with each other now

With brainstorming, this writer generated many ideas and started to move toward a more focused topic: *People are more in touch with each other now because of email.* With a narrowed topic, brainstorming once more can help the writer generate details and reasons to support the idea.

PRACTICE 5 Choose one of the following topics that interests you and write it at the top of your paper or computer screen. Then brainstorm. Write anything that comes into your head about the topic. Just let ideas pour out fast!

1. a place I want to go back to
2. dealing with difficult people
3. an unforgettable person in politics, sports, or religious life
4. growing up
5. my best/worst job
6. a first or blind date

Once you fill a page with your list, read it over, marking the most interesting ideas. Draw arrows or highlight and move text on your screen to connect related ideas. Is there one idea that might be the subject of a paper?

Part C

Clustering

Some writers use still another method—called **clustering** or **mapping**—to get their ideas on paper. To begin clustering, simply write an idea or a topic, usually one word, in the center of a piece of paper. Then let your mind make associations, and write these associations branching out from the center.

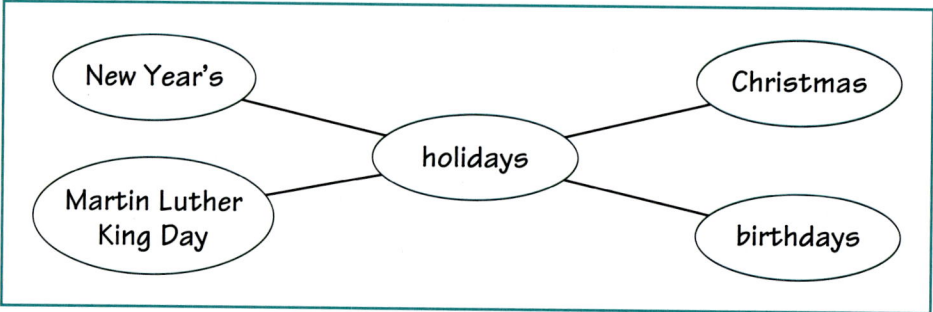

When one idea suggests other ideas, details, and examples, write these around it in a "cluster." After you finish, pick the cluster that most interests you. You may wish to freewrite for more ideas.

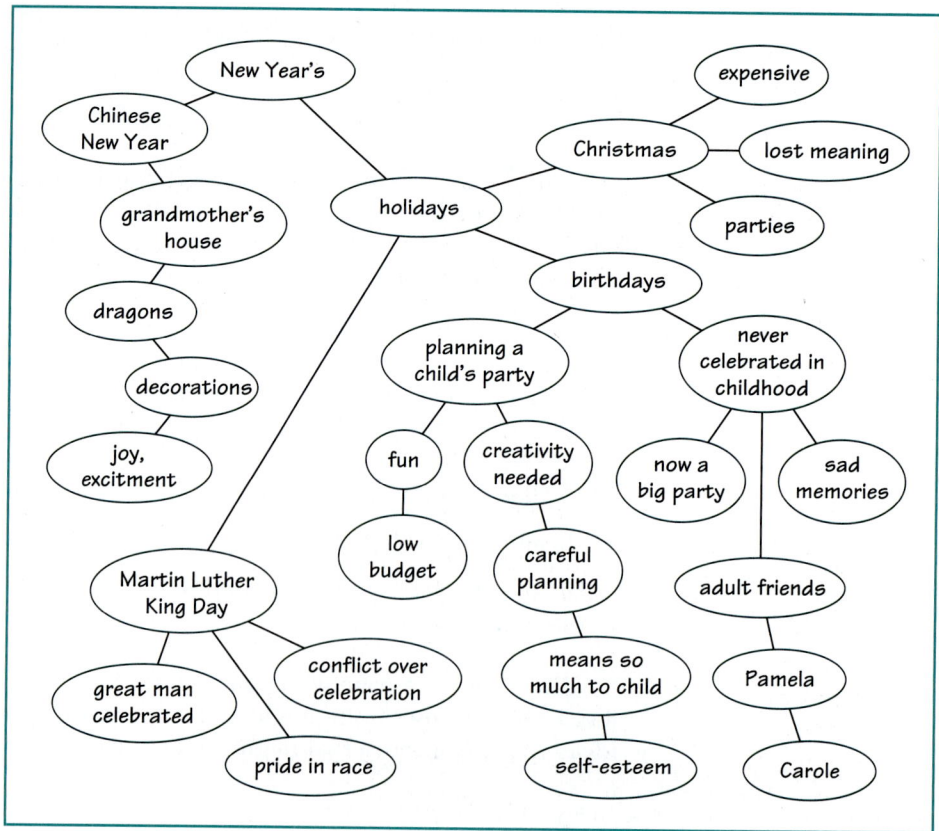

PRACTICE 6 Choose one of these topics or another topic that interests you. Write it in the center of a piece of paper and then try clustering. Keep writing down associations until you have filled most of the page.

1. heroes
2. holidays
3. food
4. inspiration
5. a dream
6. movies

Part D

Asking Questions

Many writers get ideas about a subject by asking questions and trying to answer them. This section describes two ways of doing this.

The Reporter's Six Questions

Newspaper reporters often answer six basic questions at the beginning of an article: **Who? What? Where? When? Why? How?** Here is the way one student used these questions to explore the general subject of *sports* assigned by his instructor:

Who?	Players, basketball and football players, coaches, fans. Violence—I'm tired of that subject. Loyal crazy screaming fans—Giants fans.
What?	Excitement. Stadium on the day of a game. Tailgate parties. Cookouts. Incredible spreads—Italian families with peppers, stuff to spread on sandwiches. All-day partying. Radios, TVs, grills, Giants caps.
Where?	Giants Stadium parking lot. People gather in certain areas—meet me in 10-B. Stadiums all over the country, same thing. People party on tailgates, in cars, on cars, plastic chairs, blankets.
When?	People arrive early morning—cook breakfast, lunch. After the game, many stay on in parking lot, talking, drinking beer. Year after year they come back.
Why?	Big social occasion, emotional outlet.
How?	They come early to get space. Some stadiums now rent parking spaces. Some families pass on season tickets in their wills!

Notice the way this writer uses the questions to focus his ideas about tailgate parties at Giants Stadium. He has already come up with many interesting details for a good paper.

Ask Your Own Questions

If the reporter's six questions seem too confining, just ask the questions *you* want answered about a subject. Let each answer suggest the next question.

Here is how one student responded to the subject of *teenage pregnancy:*

> **What do I know about teenage pregnancy?** My sister's plans for her future were cut short by pregnancy. She won a high-school fashion design award, was spunky, full of fun. Now, with a child to raise, she works in a diner. The father of the child disappeared two years ago.
>
> **What would I like to know?** Why do teenagers get pregnant? Teenage girls think they can't get pregnant. Teenage boys think it's macho to get a girl pregnant. Lack of knowledge of birth control methods. Teenage girls think that having a baby will keep their boyfriends from leaving them. They think that babies are fun to have around, to play with.
>
> **Where can I get more information?** Guidance counselors at my old school. Planned Parenthood. Interview my friends who had babies when they were still teenagers. Talk to my sister. Conduct an Internet search.
>
> **What would I like to focus on?** What interests me? I would like to know what pressures, fears, and hopes teenage girls feel that would allow them to take the chance of becoming pregnant.
>
> **What is my point of view?** I would like teenagers to be aware of how their lives will be forever changed by a pregnancy.
>
> **Who is my audience?** I would like to write for teenagers—primarily girls—to help them understand the problems of teenage pregnancy.

PRACTICE 7 Answer the reporter's six questions on one of the following topics or on a topic of your own choice.

1. career goals
2. sports
3. stress among students
4. neighbors/neighborhood
5. music
6. family get-togethers
7. living a simple life
8. choosing a major or concentration

PRACTICE 8 Ask and answer at least five questions of your own about one of the topics in Practice 7. Use these questions if you wish: What do I know about this subject? What would I like to know? Where can I find answers to my questions? What would I like to focus on? What is my point of view about this subject? Who is my audience?

Part E

Keeping a Journal

Keeping a journal is an excellent way to practice your writing skills and discover ideas for further writing. Your journal is mostly for you—a private place where you record your experiences and your inner life; it is the place where, as one writer says, "I discover what I really think by writing it down."

You can keep a journal in a notebook or on a computer. If you prefer handwriting, get yourself an attractive notebook with 8½-by-11-inch paper. If you prefer to work on a computer, just open a "Journal" folder or keep a "Journal" disk. Then every morning or night, or several times a week, write for at least fifteen minutes in this journal. Don't just record the day's events. ("I went to the store. It rained. I came home.") Instead, write in detail about what most angered, moved, or amused you that day.

Write about what you really care about—motorcycles, loneliness, building web sites, working in a doughnut shop, family relationships, grades, ending or starting a relationship. You may be surprised by how much you know. Write, think, and write some more. Your journal is private, so don't worry about grammar or correctness. Instead, aim to capture your truth so exactly that someone reading your words might experience it too.

You might also carry a little 3-by-5-inch pad with you during the day for "fast sketches," jotting down things that catch your attention: a man playing drums in the street; a baby wearing a bib that reads *Spit Happens;* a compliment you receive at work; something your child just learned to do.

Every journal is unique—and usually private—but here is a sample journal entry to suggest possibilities. The student links a quotation he has just learned to a disturbing "lesson of love":

> Apr. 11. Two weeks ago, our professor mentioned a famous quote: "It is better to have loved and lost than never to have loved at all." The words had no particular meaning for me. How wrong I was. Last Sunday I received some very distressing news that will change my life from now on.
>
> My wife has asked me why I never notified any family members except my mother of the birth of our children. My reply has been an argument or an angry stare. Our daughter Angelica is now two months shy of her second birthday, and we were also blessed with the birth of a son, who is five months old. I don't know whether it was maturity or my conscience, but last Sunday I decided it was time to let past grievances be forgotten. Nothing on this green earth would shelter me from what I was to hear that day.
>
> I went to my father's address, knocked on his door, but got no response. Nervous but excited, I knocked again. Silence. On leaving the building, I bumped into his neighbor and asked for the possible whereabouts of my father. I couldn't brace myself for the cold shock of hearing from him that my father had died. I was angry as well as saddened, for

> my father was a quiet and gentle man whose love of women, liquor, and good times exceeded the love of his son.
>
> Yes, it would have been better to have loved my father as he was than never to have gotten the opportunity to love such a man. A lesson of love truly woke me up to the need to hold dearly the ones you care for and overcome unnecessary grudges. "I love you, Pop, and may you rest in peace. Qué Dios te guíe."
>
> —Anthony Falu (Student)

The uses of a journal are limited only by your imagination. Here are some ideas:

- Write down your career goals and dreams; then brainstorm steps you can take to make them reality. (Notice negative thoughts—"I can't do that. That will never work." Focus on positive thoughts—"Of course I can! If X can do it, so can I.")
- Write about a problem you are having and creative ways in which you might solve it.
- Analyze yourself as a student. What are your strengths and weaknesses? What can you do to build on the strengths and overcome the weaknesses?
- What college course do you most enjoy? Why?
- Who believes in you? Who seems not to believe in you? How do these attitudes make you feel?
- If you could spend time with one famous person, living or dead, who would it be? Why?
- If you could change one thing about yourself, what would it be? What might you do to change it?
- List five things you would love to do if they didn't seem so crazy.
- Do you have an important secret? Kept from whom? How do you feel about keeping this secret?
- Name three people you are supposed to admire; then name three you really do admire. Do the differences teach you anything about yourself?
- Use your journal as a place to think about material that you have read in a textbook, newspaper, magazine, or the Internet.
- What news story most upset you or made you laugh out loud in the past month? Why?
- Write down facts that impress you—the average American child watches 200,000 acts of violence before graduating from high school! Analyzing that one fact could produce a good paper.
- Read through the Quotation Bank at the end of this book, and copy your five favorite quotations into your journal.

PRACTICE 9 Get a notebook or set up your computer journal. Write for at least fifteen minutes three times a week.

   At the end of each week, reread what you have written or typed. Underline sections or ideas you like and put a check mark next to subjects you might like to write more about.

PRACTICE 10 Choose one passage in your journal that you would like to rewrite and let others read. Mark the parts you like best. Now rewrite and polish the passage so you would be proud to show it to someone else.

Writers' Workshop

Using Just One of Your Five Senses, Describe a Place

Readers of a finished paper can easily forget that they are reading the *end result* of someone else's writing process. The writer has already thought about audience and purpose, zoomed in on a subject, and prewritten to get ideas.

Here is one student's response to the following assignment: "Using just one of the five senses—smell, hearing, taste, touch, or sight—describe a special place." In your class or group, read the paper, aloud if possible. As you read, underline words or lines that strike you as especially well written or powerful.

Noises in My Village

Orlu, my village in Nigeria, has a population of about five hundred sounds. The sounds range from the clucking of the rooster in the morning to the rumbling of people getting ready for market. You hear the shrill cry of the widow and the squeaking of the rats. At the farm, two men start a fight over land and slam each other on the ground with great thuds. Water flows with a rushing sound from the rocks into the river, and the trees whisper themselves. People fill their earthen pots with water while children splash into the water after washing their clothes. From a distance, a lost goat bleats, "Meeee, meee." At the village square, bamboo drums sound, "Drooom, drooom." This signifies a curfew for the women. A young man tells how his friend bought a car that sounded "Vrooom, vrooom." At dusk people return from the market. One woman shouts at the top of her voice, "I forgot my palm oil keg!" and rushes to get it. After supper children gather at the village square. They clap their hands and listen to folk tales. From distance, the town crier announces the arrival of the new moon.

—Chinwe Okorie (Student)

---

1. How effective is Ms. Okorie's paper?

   _____ Good topic for a college audience?   _____ Clear main idea?

   _____ Rich supporting details?   _____ Logical organization?

2. Does the first sentence make you want to read on? Why or why not?

3. Which of the five senses does the writer emphasize? What words reveal this?

4. Discuss your underlinings with the group or class. Try to explain why a particular word or sentence is effective. For instance, the fourth sentence contains such precise words that we can almost hear the two men "*slam* each other *on the ground* with great *thuds*."

5. Would you suggest that the writer make any improvements? For instance, does the word *cluck* accurately describe the sound roosters make?

6. Last, proofread for grammar, spelling, and omitted words. Do you spot any error patterns (the same type of error made two or more times) that this student should watch out for?

> Of her prewriting process, Chinwe Okorie writes: "I decided to write about my village in Africa because I thought my American classmates (my audience) would find that more interesting than the local neighborhood. This paper also taught me the importance of brainstorming. I filled two whole pages with my brainstorming list, and then it was easy to pick the best details."

Group Work

Imagine that you have been given this assignment: *Using just one of the five senses, describe a special place.* Your audience will be your college writing class. Working as a group, plan a paper and prewrite. First, choose a place that your group will describe; if it is a place on campus, your instructor might even want you to go there. Second, decide whether you will emphasize sound, smell, taste, touch, or sight. Choose someone to write down the group's ideas, and then brainstorm. List as many sounds (or smells, etc.) as your group can think of. Fill at least one page. Now read back the list and put a check next to the best details; does your group agree or disagree about which ones are best?

You are well on your way to an excellent paper. Each group member can now complete the assignment, based on the list. If necessary, prewrite again for more details.

Writing and Revising Ideas

1. Using one of your five senses, describe a place. You might use a first sentence like this:

   _____ has a population of about five hundred _____.
      (place)   (smells, tastes, etc.)

2. List unusual experiences you have had that your classmates and professor might like to read about (a job, time in another country, and so on). Choose one of these and prewrite; use the prewriting method of your choice and fill at least a page with ideas.

UNIT 2
Discovering the Paragraph

CHAPTER 3 The Process of Writing Paragraphs

CHAPTER 4 Achieving Coherence

CHAPTER 3
The Process of Writing Paragraphs

PART A   Defining and Looking at the Paragraph

PART B   Narrowing the Topic and Writing the Topic Sentence

PART C   Generating Ideas for the Body

PART D   Selecting and Dropping Ideas

PART E   Arranging Ideas in a Plan or an Outline

PART F   Writing and Revising the Paragraph

This chapter will guide you step by step from examining basic paragraphs to writing them. The paragraph makes a good learning model because it is short yet contains many of the elements found in longer compositions. Therefore, you easily can transfer the skills you gain by writing paragraphs to longer essays, reports, and letters.

In this chapter, you will first look at finished paragraphs and then move through the process of writing paragraphs of your own.

PART A
Defining and Looking at the Paragraph

A **paragraph** is a group of related sentences that develops one main idea. Although there is no definite length for a paragraph, it is often from five to twelve sentences long. A paragraph usually occurs with other paragraphs in a longer piece of writing—an essay, an article, or a letter, for example. Before studying longer compositions, however, we will look at single paragraphs.

A paragraph looks like this on the page:

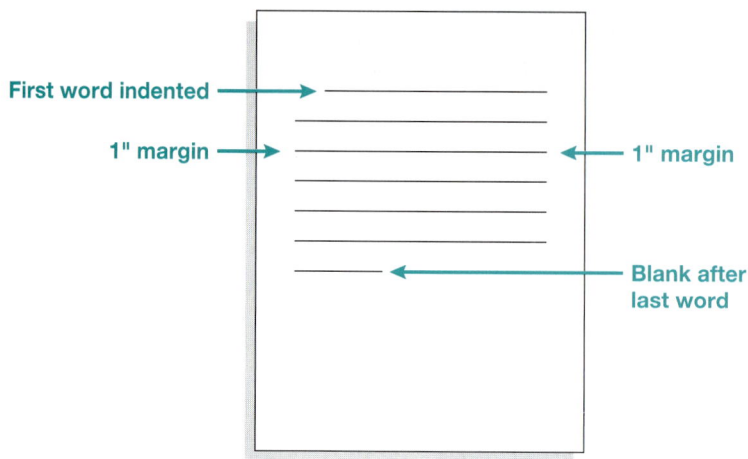

- Clearly **indent** the first word of every paragraph about 1 inch (five spaces on the computer).
- Extend every line of a paragraph as close to the right-hand margin as possible.
- However, if the last word of the paragraph comes before the end of the line, leave the rest of the line blank.

Topic Sentence and Body

Most paragraphs contain one main idea to which all the sentences relate.
　　The **topic sentence** states this main idea.
　　The **body** of the paragraph develops and supports this main idea with particular facts, details, and examples:

> 　　I allow the spiders the run of the house. I figure that any predator that hopes to make a living on whatever smaller creatures might blunder into a four-inch-square bit of space in the corner of the bathroom where the tub meets the floor needs every bit of my support. They catch flies and even field crickets in those webs. Large spiders in barns have been known to trap, wrap, and suck hummingbirds, but there's no danger of that here. I tolerate the webs, only occasionally sweeping away the very dirtiest of them after the spider itself has scrambled to safety. I'm always leaving a bath towel draped over the tub so that the big, haired spiders, who are constantly getting trapped by the tub's smooth sides, can use its rough surface as an exit ramp. Inside the house the spiders have only given me one mild surprise. I washed some dishes and set them to dry over a plastic drainer. Then I wanted a cup of coffee, so I picked from the drainer my mug, which was still warm from the hot rinse water, and across the rim of the mug, strand after strand, was a spider web.
>
> —Annie Dillard, *Pilgrim at Tinker Creek*

- The first sentence of Dillard's paragraph is the **topic sentence.** It states the main idea of the paragraph: that *the spiders are allowed the run of the house.*

- The rest of the paragraph, the **body,** fully explains and supports this statement. The writer first gives a reason for her attitude toward spiders and then gives particular examples of her tolerance of spiders.

The topic sentence is more *general* than the other sentences in the paragraph. The other sentences in the paragraph provide specific information relating to the topic sentence. Because the topic sentence tells what the entire paragraph is about, *it is usually the first sentence,* as in the example. Sometimes the topic sentence occurs elsewhere in the paragraph, for example, as the sentence after an introduction or as the last sentence. Some paragraphs contain only an implied topic sentence but no stated topic sentence at all.

As you develop your writing skills, however, it is a good idea to write paragraphs that *begin* with the topic sentence. Once you have mastered this pattern, you can try variations.

PRACTICE 1 Find and underline the **topic sentence** in each of the following paragraphs. Look for the sentence that states the **main idea** of the entire paragraph. Be careful: the topic sentence is not always the first sentence.

Paragraph a

The summer picnic gave ladies a chance to show off their baking hands. On the barbecue pit, chickens and spareribs sputtered in their own fat and in a sauce whose recipe was guarded in the family like a scandalous affair. However, every true baking artist could reveal her prize to the delight and criticism of the town. Orange sponge cakes and dark brown mounds dripping Hershey's chocolate stood layer to layer with ice-white coconuts and light brown caramels. Pound cakes sagged with their buttery weight and small children could no more resist licking the icings than their mothers could avoid slapping the sticky fingers.

—Maya Angelou, *I Know Why the Caged Bird Sings*

Paragraph b

These people often stay late at the office even if they are not paid extra to do so. On weekends, they think about their jobs—trying to solve a problem, worrying about a client, or planning for Monday. If you ask them to explain, they will probably tell you that they love working, that many aspects of the job are fun. It doesn't matter whether they are the heads of companies or clerks at a local flower shop. What matters is the match between their passion, interests, personalities, and the work they do. A few lucky people have found for themselves what many seek—the perfect job.

—Jared Barnes, *Job Watch*

Paragraph c

Eating sugar can be worse than eating nothing. Refined sugar provides only empty calories. It contributes none of the protein, fat, vitamins, or minerals needed for its own metabolism in the body, so these nutrients must be obtained elsewhere. Sugar tends to replace nourishing food in the diet. It is a thief that robs us of nutrients. A dietary emphasis on sugar can deplete the body of nutrients. If adequate nutrients are not supplied by the diet—and they tend not to be in a sugar-rich diet—they must be leached from other body tissues before sugar can be metabolized. For this reason, a U.S. Senate committee labeled sugar as an "antinutrient."

—Janice Fillip, "The Sweet Thief," *Medical Self-Care*

UNIT 2 Discovering the Paragraph

PRACTICE 2 Each group of sentences below could be unscrambled and written as a paragraph. Circle the letter of the **topic sentence** in each group of sentences. Remember: The topic sentence should state the main idea of the entire paragraph and should be general enough to include all the ideas in the body.

Example
- a. Rubies were supposed to stimulate circulation and restore lost vitality.
- b. Clear quartz was believed to promote sweet sleep and good dreams.
- (c.) For centuries, minerals and precious stones were thought to possess healing powers.
- d. Amethysts were thought to prevent drunkenness.

(Sentence c includes the ideas in all the other sentences.)

1.
   - a. Invited to join the space program, she trained as an astronaut and flew on the space shuttle *Endeavor* in 1992.
   - b. The young Dr. Jemison headed to West Africa, where she worked in the Peace Corps for two years.
   - c. Though a childhood teacher urged her to be a nurse, Mae Jemison knew she wanted to be a scientist and doctor.
   - d. After eight years at NASA, she became a professor at Dartmouth College and started a company to help poor countries use solar energy.
   - e. The life of Dr. Mae Jemison, the first African-American female astronaut, is characterized by daring achievements and a strong desire to give back.
   - f. A fine student, Jemison entered Stanford University at sixteen and later earned her M.D. degree from Cornell in 1981.

2.
   - a. The left side of the human brain controls spoken and written language.
   - b. The right side, on the other hand, seems to control artistic, musical, and spatial skills.
   - c. Emotion is also thought to be controlled by the right hemisphere.
   - d. The human brain has two distinct halves, or hemispheres, and in most people, each one controls different functions.
   - e. Logical reasoning and mathematics are left-brain skills.
   - f. Interestingly, the left brain controls the right hand and vice versa.

3.
   - a. As a Bronx Community College student, Oscar Hijuelos showed his gift for writing.
   - b. He researched the Cuban music scene of New York in the '50s for his second novel, *Mambo Kings Play Songs of Love*.
   - c. After one year at Bronx Community, he transferred to City College, earning his B.A. in creative writing.
   - d. Step by step, Oscar Hijuelos, the son of Cuban immigrants, has become a very successful writer.

e. While crafting his first two books, Hijuelos earned money selling shoes and writing ad copy for subway cars.

f. After *Mambo Kings* won the Pulitzer Prize and was made into a film, Hijuelos wrote three more novels and inspired many young writers.

4. a. Male and female insects are attracted to each other by visual, auditory, and chemical means.

   b. Through its chirping call, the male cricket attracts a mate and drives other males out of its territory.

   c. Butterflies attract by sight, and their brightly colored wings play an important role in courtship.

   d. Some female insects, flies among them, release chemicals called *pheromones* that attract males of the species.

5. a. Albert Einstein, whose scientific genius awed the world, did not speak until he was four and could not read until he was nine.

   b. Inventor Thomas Edison had such severe problems reading, writing, and spelling that he was called "defective from birth," taken out of school, and taught at home.

   c. Many famous people have suffered from learning disabilities.

   d. Actor Tom Cruise battles dyslexia, yet he has mastered the scripts of many movies and won awards for his performances.

6. a. This college student from Los Angeles could not find pastel nail polish in the stores, so she started mixing her own.

   b. When Mohajer took samples to a trendy shop in 1995, one customer snapped up four bottles at $18 apiece.

   c. Celebrities like Alicia Silverstone started buying the polish in colors like pea green and black, with offbeat names like "Geek," "Tantrum," and "Trailer Trash."

   d. Mohajer received so many compliments that she decided to start selling her product.

   e. Soon the business was so big that Mohajer hired someone to handle the finances.

   f. With only a fine sense of style and a knack for mixing colors, twenty-two-year-old Dineh Mohajer created a $10-million company.

7. a. The better skaters glided in wide circles, playing tag or crack the whip.

   b. Every winter, the lake was the center of activity.

   c. People talked and shoveled snow, exposing the dark, satiny ice.

   d. Children on double runners skated in the center of the cleared area.

   e. Dogs raced and skidded among the skaters.

8.
   a. Believe it or not, the first contact lens was drawn by Leonardo da Vinci in 1508.
   b. However, not until 1877 was the first thick glass contact actually made by a Swiss doctor.
   c. The journey of contact lenses from an idea to a comfortable, safe reality took nearly five hundred years.
   d. In 1948, smaller, more comfortable plastic lenses were introduced to enthusiastic American eyeglass wearers.
   e. These early glass lenses were enormous, covering the whites of the eyes.
   f. Today, contact lens wearers can choose ultra-thin, colored, or even disposable lenses.

PART B

Narrowing the Topic and Writing the Topic Sentence

A writer can arrive at the goal—a finished paragraph—in several ways. However, before writing a paragraph, most writers go through a process that includes these important steps:

1. Narrowing the topic
2. Writing the topic sentence
3. Generating ideas for the body
4. Selecting and dropping ideas
5. Arranging ideas in a plan or an outline

The rest of this chapter will explain these steps and guide you through the process of writing basic paragraphs.

Narrowing the Topic

As a student, you may be assigned broad writing topics by your instructor—success, cheating in schools, a description of a person. Your instructor is giving you the chance to cut the topic down to size and choose one aspect of the topic *that interests you.*

Suppose, for example, that your instructor gives this assignment: "Write a paragraph describing a person you know." The challenge is to pick someone you would *like* to write about, someone who interests you and also would probably interest your readers.

Thinking about your *audience* and *purpose* may help you narrow the topic. In this case, your audience probably will be your instructor and classmates; your purpose is to inform or perhaps to entertain them by describing a person you want to write about.

Many writers find it useful at this point—on paper or on computer—to brainstorm, freewrite, or ask themselves questions: "What person do I love or hate or admire? Is there a family member I would enjoy writing about? Who is the funniest, most unusual, or most talented person I know?"

Let's suppose you choose Pete, an unusual person and one about whom you have something to say. But Pete is still too broad a subject for one paragraph; you could probably write pages and pages about him. To narrow the topic further, you might ask yourself, "What is unusual about him? What might interest others?" Pete's room is the messiest place you have ever seen; in fact, Pete's whole life is sloppy, and you decide that you could write a good paragraph about that. You have now narrowed the topic to just one of Pete's qualities: *his sloppiness*.

Writing the Topic Sentence

The next important step is to state your topic clearly *in sentence form*. Writing the topic sentence helps you further narrow your topic by forcing you to make a statement about it. The simplest possible topic sentence about Pete might read *Pete is sloppy*, but you might wish to strengthen it by saying, for instance, *Pete's sloppiness is a terrible habit*.

Writing a good topic sentence is an important step toward an effective paragraph because the topic sentence controls the direction and scope of the body. A topic sentence should have a clear *controlling idea* and should be a *complete sentence*.

You can think of the topic sentence as having two parts, a **topic** and a **controlling idea.** The controlling idea states the writer's point of view or attitude about the topic.

                    topic   controlling idea

Topic sentence: Pete's sloppiness is a terrible habit.

The controlling idea helps you focus on just one aspect or point. Here are three possible topic sentences about the topic *a memorable job.*

> 1. My job in the complaint department taught me how to calm down angry people.
> 2. Two years in the complaint department persuaded me to become an assistant manager.
> 3. Working in the complaint department persuaded me to become a veterinarian.

- These topic sentences all explore the same topic—working in a complaint department—but each controlling idea is different. The controlling idea in 1 is *taught me how to calm down angry people.*

- What is the controlling idea in 2?

_____

What is the controlling idea in 3?

_____

- Notice the way in which the controlling idea lets the reader know what the paragraph will be about. There are many possible topic sentences for any topic, depending on the writer's interests and point of view. If you were assigned the topic *a memorable job,* what would your topic sentence be?

_____

_____

PRACTICE 3 Read each topic sentence below. Circle the topic and underline the controlling idea.

1. A low-fat diet provides many health benefits.
2. *Animal Planet* is both entertaining and educational.
3. Our football coach works to build players' self-esteem.
4. This campus offers many peaceful places where students can relax.
5. My cousin's truck looks like something out of *Star Wars.*

As a rule, the more specific and clearer your topic and controlling idea, the better the paragraph; in other words, your topic sentence should not be so broad that it cannot be developed in one paragraph. Which of these topic sentences do you think will produce the best paragraphs?

> 4. Five wet, bug-filled days at Camp Nirvana made me a fan of the great indoors.
> 5. This town has problems.
> 6. Road rage is on the rise for three reasons.

- Topic sentences 4 and 6 are both specific enough to write a good paragraph about. In each, the topic sentence is carefully worded to suggest clearly what ideas will follow. From topic sentence 4, what do you expect the paragraph to include?

_____

- What do you expect paragraph 6 to include?

_____

- Topic sentence 5, on the other hand, is so broad that a paragraph could include almost anything. Just what problems does the town have? Strained relations between police and the community? Litter in public parks? Termites? The writer needs to rewrite the controlling idea, focusing on just one problem for an effective paragraph.

The topic sentence also must be a **complete sentence.** It must contain a subject and a verb, and express a complete thought.* Do not confuse a topic with a topic sentence. For instance, *a celebrity I would like to meet* cannot be a topic sentence because it is not a sentence; however, it could be a title† because topics and titles need not be complete sentences. One possible topic sentence might read, *A celebrity I would like to meet is writer Julia Alvarez.*

Do not write *This paragraph will be about . . .* or *In this paper I will write about. . . .* Instead, craft your topic sentence carefully to focus the topic and let your reader know what the paragraph will contain. Make every word count.

PRACTICE 4 Put a check beside each topic sentence that is focused enough to allow you to write a good paragraph. If a topic sentence is too broad, narrow the topic according to your own interests and write a new topic sentence with a clear controlling idea.

Examples

✓ Keeping a journal can improve a student's writing.

Rewrite: _____

___ This paper will be about my family.

Rewrite: My brother Mark has a unique sense of humor.

1. ___ Eugene's hot temper causes problems at work.

   Rewrite: _____
   _____

2. ___ This paragraph will discuss study techniques.

   Rewrite: _____
   _____

3. ___ Many beer commercials on TV imply that people need to drink in order to have a good time.

   Rewrite: _____
   _____

4. ___ Child abuse is something to think about.

   Rewrite: _____
   _____

---

* For practice in correcting fragments, see Chapter 26, "Avoiding Sentence Errors," Part B.

† For practice in writing titles, see Chapter 16, "The Introduction, the Conclusion, and the Title," Part C.

5. ____ Company officials should not read employees' email.

Rewrite: _____

_____

PRACTICE 5 Here is a list of broad topics. Choose three that interest you from this list or from your own list in Chapter 1, page 5. Narrow each topic, choose your controlling idea, and write a topic sentence focused enough to write a good paragraph about. Make sure that each topic sentence has a clear controlling idea and is a complete sentence.

Overcoming fears	Insider's tour of your community
Popular music	Balancing work and play
Credit cards	A person you like or dislike
An act of cowardice or courage	A time when you were (or were not) in control

1. Narrowed topic: _____

   Controlling idea: _____

   Topic sentence: _____

   _____

   _____

2. Narrowed topic: _____

   Controlling idea: _____

   Topic sentence: _____

3. Narrowed topic: _____

   Controlling idea: _____

   Topic sentence: _____

   _____

PRACTICE 6 Many writers adjust the topic sentence after they have finished drafting the paragraph. In a group of three or four classmates, study the body of each of these paragraphs to find the main, or controlling, idea. Then, working together, write the most exact and interesting topic sentence you can for each paragraph.

Paragraph a _____

_____

In 1981, fewer than 300 computers were linked to the Internet. By 1989, the number of Internet users was fewer than 90,000. However, by 1993, more than 1 million computer users had logged on and were sending email, doing research, working, and shopping in cyberspace. According to a survey conducted by *Business Week* magazine in 1997, about 60 million people in the United States alone were hooked up to the Internet. As the twenty-first century dawned, that number topped 200 million, with no end to the explosive growth in sight.

Paragraph b _____

_____

A pet parrot recently saved his owner's life. Harry Becker was watching TV in his living room when he suddenly slumped over with a heart attack. The parrot screamed loudly until Mr. Becker's wife awoke and called 911. In another reported case of animal rescue, a family cat saved six-week-old Stacey Rogers. When the cat heard the baby gasping for breath in her crib, it ran howling to alert the baby's mother, who called paramedics. Even more surprising was an event reported in newspapers around the world. In 1996 in a Chicago zoo, a female gorilla rushed to save a three-year-old boy who fell accidentally into the gorilla enclosure. Still carrying her own baby on her back, the 150-pound gorilla gently picked up the unconscious child and carried him to the cage door to be rescued. Though we might not understand why, animals sometimes help and even save us.

Part C

Generating Ideas for the Body

One good way to generate ideas for the body of a paragraph is **brainstorming**—freely jotting on paper or computer anything that relates to your topic sentence: facts, details, examples, little stories. This step might take just a few minutes, but it is one of the most important elements of the writing process. Brainstorming can provide you with specific ideas to support your topic sentence. Later you can choose from these ideas as you compose your paragraph.

Here, for example, is a possible brainstorm list for the topic sentence *Pete's sloppiness is a terrible habit*:

1. His apartment is full of dirty clothes, books, candy wrappers
2. His favorite candy—M&Ms
3. He is often a latecomer or a no-show
4. He jots time-and-place information for dates and appointments on scraps of paper that are soon forgotten
5. Stacks of old newspapers sit on chair seats
6. Socks are on the lampshades
7. Papers for classes are wrinkled and carelessly scrawled
8. I met Pete for the first time in math class
9. His sister is just the opposite, very neat

10. Always late for classes, out of breath

11. He is one messy person

12. Papers are stained with coffee or M&Ms

Instead of brainstorming, some writers freewrite or ask themselves questions to generate ideas for their paragraphs. Some like to perform this step on paper whereas others use a computer. Do what works best for you. The key is to write down lots of ideas during prewriting. If you need more practice in any of these methods, reread Chapter 2, "Prewriting to Generate Ideas."

PRACTICE 7 Now choose the topic from Practice 5 that most interests you. Write your narrowed topic, controlling idea, and topic sentence here.

Narrowed topic: _____

Controlling idea: _____

Topic sentence: _____

_____

Next, brainstorm. On paper or on computer, write anything that comes to you about your topic sentence. Just let your ideas pour out. Try to fill at least one page.

Part D

Selecting and Dropping Ideas

Next, simply read over what you have written, **selecting** those ideas that relate to and support the topic sentence and **dropping** those that do not. That is, keep the facts, examples, or little stories that provide specific information about your topic sentence. Drop ideas that just **repeat** the topic sentence but that add nothing new to the paragraph.

If you are not sure which ideas to select or drop, underline the **key word(s)** of the topic sentence, the ones that indicate the real point of your paragraph. Then make sure that the ideas that you select are related to those key words.

Here again is the brainstorm list for the topic sentence *Pete's sloppiness is a terrible habit*. The key word in the topic sentence is *sloppiness*. Which ideas would you keep? Why? Which would you drop? Why?

1. His apartment is full of dirty clothes, books, candy wrappers

2. His favorite candy—M&Ms

3. He is often a latecomer or a no-show

4. He jots time-and-place information for dates and appointments on scraps of paper that are soon forgotten

5. Stacks of old newspapers sit on chair seats

6. Socks are on the lampshades

7. Papers for classes are wrinkled and carelessly scrawled
8. I met Pete for the first time in math class
9. His sister is just the opposite, very neat
10. Always late for classes, out of breath
11. He is one messy person
12. Papers are stained with coffee or M&Ms

You probably dropped ideas 2, 8, and 9 because they do not relate to the topic—Pete's sloppiness. You should also have dropped idea 11 because it merely repeats the topic sentence.

PRACTICE 8 Read through your own brainstorm list from Practice 7. Select the ideas that relate to your topic sentence and drop those that do not. In addition, drop any ideas that just repeat your topic sentence. Be prepared to explain why you drop or keep each idea.

Part E

Arranging Ideas in a Plan or an Outline

After you have selected the ideas you wish to include in your paragraph, you can begin to make a **plan** or an **outline**. A plan briefly lists and arranges the ideas you wish to present in your paragraph. An outline does the same thing a bit more formally, but in an outline, letters or numbers indicate the main groupings of ideas.

First, group together ideas that have something in common, that are related or alike in some way. Then order your ideas by choosing which one you want to present first, which one second, and so on.

Below is a plan for a paragraph about Pete's sloppiness:

Topic sentence: Pete's sloppiness is a terrible habit.

- His apartment is full of dirty clothes, books, candy wrappers
- Stacks of old newspapers sit on chair seats
- Socks are on the lampshades

- He jots time-and-place information for dates and appointments on scraps of paper that are soon forgotten
- He is often a latecomer or a no-show
- Always late for classes, out of breath

- Papers for classes wrinkled and carelessly scrawled
- Papers stained with coffee or M&Ms

- Do you see the logic in this arrangement? How are the ideas in each group above related? _____

_____

_____

- Does it make sense to discuss Pete's apartment first, his lateness second, and his written work third? Why? _____

_____

_____

- Once you have finished arranging ideas, you should have a clear **plan** from which to write your paragraph.*

PRACTICE 9 On paper or on computer, arrange the ideas from your brainstorm list according to some plan or outline. First, group together related ideas; then decide which ideas will come first, which second, and so on.

Keep in mind that there is more than one way to group ideas. Think about what you want to say; then group ideas according to what your point is.

Part F

Writing and Revising the Paragraph

Writing the First Draft

The first draft should contain all the ideas you have decided to use in the order you have chosen in your plan. Be sure to start with your topic sentence. Try to write the best, most interesting, or most amusing paragraph you can, but avoid getting stuck on any one word, sentence, or idea. If you are unsure about something, put a check in the margin and come back to it later. Writing on every other line or double spacing if you write on computer will leave room for later corrections.

Once you have included all the ideas from your plan, think about adding a concluding sentence that summarizes your main point or adds a final idea. Not all paragraphs need concluding sentences. For example, if you are telling a story, the paragraph can end when the story does. Write a concluding sentence only if it will help to bring your thoughts to an end for your reader.

If possible, once you have finished the first draft, set the paper aside for several hours or several days.

PRACTICE 10 Write a first draft of the paragraph you have been working on.

---

* For more work on order, see Chapter 4, "Achieving Coherence," Part A.

Revising

Revising means rethinking and rewriting your first draft and then making whatever changes, additions, or corrections are necessary to improve the paragraph. You may cross out and rewrite words or entire sentences. You may add, drop, or rearrange details.

As you revise, keep the *reader* in mind. Ask yourself these questions:

- Is my topic sentence clear?
- Can a reader understand and follow my ideas?
- Does the paragraph follow a logical order and guide the reader from point to point?
- Will the paragraph keep the reader interested?

In addition, check your paragraph for adequate support and unity, characteristics that we'll consider in the following pages.

Revising for Support

As you revise, make sure your paragraph contains excellent **support**—that is, specific facts, details, and examples that fully explain your topic sentence.

Be careful, too, that you have not simply repeated ideas—especially the topic sentence. Even if they are in different words, repeated ideas only make the reader suspect that your paragraph is padded and that you do not have enough facts and details to support your main idea properly.

Which of the following paragraphs contains the most convincing support?

Paragraph a
(1) Our run-down city block was made special by a once-vacant lot called The Community Garden. (2) The lot was planted with all sorts of plants, vegetables, and flowers. (3) There was a path curving through it. (4) We went there to think. (5) The Community Garden made our block special. (6) Though our neighborhood was known as "tough," no one ever vandalized the garden.

Paragraph b
(1) Our run-down city block was made special by a once-vacant lot called The Community Garden. (2) I'm not sure who first had the idea, but the thin soil had been fertilized, raked, and planted with a surprising assortment of vegetables and flowers. (3) Anyone interested in gardening could tend green pepper plants, string beans, fresh herbs, even corn. (4) Others planted flowers, which changed with the seasons—tall red dahlias, white and purple irises, and taxi-yellow marigolds to discourage the insects. (5) Paved with bricks no doubt left over from the building that once stood here, a narrow path curved gracefully among the plants. (6) The Community Garden was our pride, the place we went to think and to be still. (7) Though the neighborhood was known as "tough," no one ever vandalized the garden.

- *Paragraph a* contains general statements but little specific information to support the topic sentence.

- *Paragraph a* also contains needless repetition. What is the number of the sentence or sentences that just repeat the topic sentence? _____

- *Paragraph b*, however, supports the topic sentence with specific details and examples: *thin soil, fertilized, raked and planted, green pepper plants, string beans, fresh herbs, corn, red dahlias*. What other specific support does it give?

_____

_____

_____

_____

_____

PRACTICE 11 Check the following paragraphs for adequate support. As you read each one, decide which places need more or better support—specific facts, details, and examples. Then rewrite the paragraphs, inventing facts and details whenever necessary and dropping repetitious words and sentences.

Paragraph a   (1) My uncle can always be counted on when the family faces hardship. (2) Last year, when my mother was very ill, he was there, ready to help in every way. (3) He never has to be called twice. (4) When my father became seriously depressed, my uncle's caring made a difference. (5) Everyone respects him for his willingness to be a real "family man." (6) He is always there for us.

Paragraph b   (1) Lending money to a friend can have negative consequences. (2) For example, Ashley, a student at Tornado Community College, agreed to lend $200 to her best friend, Jan. (3) This was a bad decision even though Ashley meant well. (4) The results of this loan were surprising and negative for Ashley, for Jan, and for the friendship. (5) Both women felt bad about it but in different ways. (6) Yes, lending money to a friend can have very negative consequences, like anger and hurt.

Paragraph c   (1) Many television talk shows don't really present a discussion of ideas. (2) Some people who appear on these shows don't know what they are talking about; they just like to sound off about something. (3) I don't like these shows at all. (4) Guests shout their opinions out loud but never give any proof for what they say. (5) Guests sometimes expose their most intimate personal and family problems before millions of viewers—I feel embarrassed. (6) I have even heard hosts insult their guests and guests insult them back. (7) Why do people watch this junk? (8) You never learn anything from these dumb shows.

Revising for Unity

It is sometimes easy, in the process of writing, to drift away from the topic under discussion. Guard against doing so by checking your paragraph for unity; that is, make sure the topic sentence, every sentence in the body, and the concluding sentence all relate to one main idea.*

This paragraph lacks unity:

> (1) A new rival to the Barbie doll aims to provide children with more realistic role models. (2) Named Get Real Girls by their creator, Julz Chavez, the new dolls have pretty faces like Barbie; but more realistic

_____

* For more work on revising, see Chapter 23, "Putting Your Revision Skills to Work."

measurements and flat, not "high-heeled," feet. (3) Each doll plays a different sport, like soccer or basketball, and comes with realistic equipment. (4) For example, the scuba diving doll has fins, mask, spear gun, and oxygen tank. (5) Chavez patterned the dolls after her real-life friends, so each one is a different ethnicity—Caucasian, African-American, Latina, or Asian. (6) Chavez grew up in California with ten brothers and sisters. (7) To inspire children to achieve, each doll has a "life story," including educational goals and personal interests. (9) Chavez hopes to answer complaints from parents all over the world that Barbie seems to care more about shopping and partying than fitness and education.

- What is the number of the topic sentence in this paragraph?

- Which sentence in the paragraph does not clearly relate to the topic sentence?

This paragraph also lacks unity:

(1) Quitting smoking was very difficult for me. (2) When I was thirteen, my friend Janice and I smoked in front of a mirror. (3) We practiced holding the cigarette in different ways and tried French inhaling, letting the smoke roll slowly out of our mouths and drawing it back through our noses. (4) I thought this move, when it didn't incite a fit of coughing, was particularly sexy. (5) At first I smoked only to give myself confidence on dates and at parties. (6) Soon, however, I was smoking all the time.

- Here the topic sentence itself, sentence 1, does not relate to the rest of the paragraph. The main idea in sentence 1, that quitting smoking was difficult, is not developed by the other sentences. Since the rest of the paragraph *is* unified, a more appropriate topic sentence might read, *As a teenager, I developed the bad habit of smoking.*

PRACTICE 12 Check the following paragraphs for unity. If a paragraph has unity, write U in the blank. If not, write the number of the sentence that does not belong in the paragraph.

Paragraph a ____ (1) The first batch of one of the world's most popular soft drinks was mixed in a backyard kettle over a hundred years ago. (2) On May 6, 1886, Dr. John Styth Pemberton heated a mixture of melted sugar, water, coca leaves, kola nuts, and other ingredients. (3) He planned to make one of the home-brewed medical syrups so popular at that time. (4) However, this one tasted so good that Dr. Pemberton decided to sell it as a soda fountain drink for five cents a glass. (5) The first glass of this new drink was sold at Jacob's Pharmacy in Atlanta, Georgia. (6) Atlanta was and still is a wonderful place to live. (7) Pemberton's tasty invention, Coca-Cola, caught on. (8) Today, Coca-Cola is consumed by 140,000 people every minute.

Paragraph b ___ (1) Technology enables people like the famous physicist Dr. Stephen Hawking to continue working despite serious physical disabilities. (2) For thirty-five years, Dr. Hawking has lived with Lou Gehrig's disease, which attacks the muscles, but his brilliant mind works perfectly. (3) He can no longer walk, speak, or feed himself. (4) Nevertheless, a high-tech wheelchair with computer attachments allows him to continue his research and stay in touch with friends and colleagues around the world. (5) His computer is hooked up full-time to the Internet. (6) To speak, he chooses words displayed on the computer screen, and then an electronic voice machine pronounces each word. (7) A pressure-sensitive joystick even lets Dr. Hawking make his way through traffic. (8) In his home, infrared remote control operates doors, lights, and his personal entertainment center. (9) He had two children with his first wife, Jane. (10) Dr. Hawking continues to search for new ways to overcome his problems through technology.

Paragraph c ___ (1) At Paradise Produce, attractive displays of fruit and vegetables caught my eye. (2) On the left, oranges, lemons, and apples were stacked in neat pyramids. (3) In the center of the store, baskets of ripe peaches, plums, and raspberries were grouped in a kind of still life. (4) Many nutritionists believe that berries help prevent certain diseases. (5) On the right, the leafy green vegetables had been arranged according to intensity of color: dark green spinach, then romaine lettuce and parsley, next the lighter iceberg lettuce, and finally the nearly white Chinese cabbage. (6) On the wall above the greens hung braided ropes of garlic.

Revising with Peer Feedback

You may wish to show or read your first draft to a respected friend. Ask this person to give an honest response, *not* to rewrite your work. Ask specific questions of your own or use this peer feedback sheet.

PEER FEEDBACK SHEET

To _____ From _____ Date _____

1. What I like about this piece of writing is _____

   _____

2. Your main point seems to be _____

   _____

3. These particular words or lines struck me as powerful:

   Words or lines   I like them because

   _____   _____

   _____   _____

   _____   _____

> 4. Some things aren't clear to me. These lines or parts could be improved (meaning not clear, supporting points missing, order seems mixed up, writing not lively):
>
> Lines or parts   Need improving because
>
> _____   _____
>
> _____   _____
>
> _____   _____
>
> _____   _____
>
> 5. The one change you could make that would make the biggest improvement in this piece of writing is _____
>
> _____

Writing the Final Draft

When you are satisfied with your revisions, recopy your paper or print a fresh copy. If you are writing in class, the second draft will usually be the last one. Be sure to include all your corrections, writing neatly and legibly.

The first draft of the paragraph about Pete, showing the writer's changes, and the revised, final draft follow. Compare them.

First Draft with Revisions

Pete's sloppiness is a terrible habit. He lives by him-

Add details to show his sloppiness!

self in a small apartment with dirty clothes, books, and *[carpeted]*   *how small?—better word needed*

candy wrappers. Stacks of papers cover the chair seats.

Socks ~~are~~ *[bake!]* on the lampshades. When Pete makes a date or

an appointment, he may jot down the time and place on a

scrap of paper that is soon forgotten, or—more likely— *[tucked into a pocket and]*

he doesn't jot down the information at all. Pete often ar- *[As a result,]*   *Show consequences*

rives late, or he completely forgets to appear. His grades

have suffered, too, Few instructors will put up with a stu- *[because]*

Add more details—better support

dent who arrives out of breath and whose messy papers *[ten minutes after class has begun]* *[wrinkled, scrawled]*

arrive (late of course) with stains on them. ~~Pete's sloppi-~~ *[punctuated with coffee stains and melted M&Ms.]*   *This repeats t.s. Better conclusion needed.*

~~ness really is a terrible habit.~~

Final Draft

> Pete's sloppiness is a terrible habit. He lives by himself in a one-room apartment carpeted with dirty clothes, books, and crumpled candy wrappers. Stacks of papers cover the chair seats. Socks bake on the lampshades. When Pete makes a date or an appointment, he may jot down the time and place on a scrap of paper that is soon tucked into a pocket and forgotten, or—more likely—he doesn't jot down the information at all. As a result, Pete often arrives late, or he completely forgets to appear. His grades have suffered, too, because few instructors will put up with a student who arrives out of breath ten minutes after the class has begun and whose wrinkled, carelessly scrawled papers arrive (late, of course) punctuated with coffee stains and melted M&Ms. The less Pete controls his sloppiness, the more it seems to control him.

- Note that the paragraph contains good support—specific facts, details, and examples that explain the topic sentence.
- Note that the paragraph has unity—every idea relates to the topic sentence.
- Note that the final sentence provides a brief conclusion, so that the paragraph *feels finished*.

Proofreading

Whether you write by hand or on computer, be sure to **proofread** your final draft carefully for grammar and spelling errors. Pointing to each word as you read it will help you catch errors or words you might have left out, especially small words like *to, the,* or *a*. If you are unsure of the spelling of a word, consult a dictionary and run spell check if you work on a computer.* Make neat corrections in pen or print a corrected copy of your paper. Chapter 37, "Putting Your Proofreading Skills to Work," and all of Units 6 and 7 in this book are devoted to improving your proofreading skills.

PRACTICE 13 Now read the first draft of your paragraph with a critical eye. Revise and rewrite it, checking especially for a clear topic sentence, strong support, and unity.

PRACTICE 14 Exchange *revised* paragraphs with a classmate. Ask specific questions or use the Peer Feedback Sheet displayed earlier.
   When you *give* feedback, try to be as honest and specific as possible; saying a paper is "good," "nice," or "bad" doesn't really help the writer. When you *receive* feedback, think over your classmate's responses; do they ring true?
   Now **revise** a second time, with the aim of writing a fine paragraph. Proofread carefully for grammar errors, spelling errors, and omitted words.

---

*For tips and cautions on using a computer spell checker, see Chapter 38, Part B.

 **Writing Assignments**

The assignments that follow will give you practice in writing basic paragraphs. In each, aim for (1) a topic sentence with a clear controlling idea and (2) a body that fully supports and develops the topic sentence.

Remember to **narrow the topic, write the topic sentence, freewrite or brainstorm, select,** and **arrange ideas** in a plan or an outline before you write. Rethink and **revise** as necessary before composing the final version of the paragraph. As you work, refer to the checklist at the end of this chapter.

Paragraph 1 *Discuss an important day in your life*

Think back to a day when you learned something important. In the topic sentence, tell what you learned. Freewrite or brainstorm to gather ideas. Then describe the lesson in detail, including only the most important steps or events in the learning process. Conclude with an insight.

Paragraph 2 *Examine campus fashion*

What clothing and hairstyles are currently in fashion on your campus? Update your readers on the look—or looks—of the moment. Focus your topic: You might write about a certain group of students who share one look, hair only, clothing styles only, and so forth. Use humor if you wish. Vivid supporting details, descriptions, and examples will help make your point. Revise your work for good support, unity, and all-around excellent writing.

Paragraph 3 *Interview a classmate about an achievement*

Write about a time when your classmate achieved something important, like winning an award for a musical performance, getting an *A* in a difficult course, or helping a friend through a hard time. To gather interesting facts and details, ask your classmate questions like these and take notes: *Is there one accomplishment of which you are very proud? Why was this achievement so important?* Keep asking questions until you feel you can give the reader a vivid sense of your classmate's triumph. In your first sentence, state the person's achievement—for instance, *Being accepted in the honors program improved Gabe's self-esteem.* Then explain specifically why the achievement was so meaningful.

Paragraph 4 *Choose an ideal job*

Decide what kind of job you are best suited for and, in your topic sentence, tell what this job is. Then give three or four reasons that will convince readers of the wisdom of your choice. Discuss any special qualifications, talents, skills, or attitudes that would make you an excellent _____. Revise your work, checking for support and unity.

Paragraph 5 *Discuss a quotation*

Look through the quotations in the Quotation Bank before the indexes in this book. Pick a quotation you especially agree or disagree with. In your topic sentence, state how you feel about the quotation. Then explain why you feel the way you do, giving examples from your own experience to support or contradict the quotation. Make sure your reader knows exactly how you feel.

Paragraph 6 *Explain a sports or music fanatic*

Do you know a sports or music fan who takes his or her loyalty and enthusiasm to an extreme? Explain this person's behavior to your readers. You might choose several details or actions that best capture his or her fanatic behavior. Or you might wish to discuss why you think a team or musical group is so important to this person. Use humor if you wish. State your controlling idea in the topic sentence and support this idea fully with details, facts, and examples.

Paragraph 7   *Discuss a childhood experience*

Choose an experience that deeply affected you. First tell exactly what happened, giving important details. Then explain the meaning this experience had for you.

Paragraph 8   *Describe a portrait*

Look closely at this portrait of a young man, Dion Johnson, taken by photographer Lloyd Wolf. Study the young man in the picture—his eyes, expression, hands, clothing, and other important details. What is he holding? What does the viewer learn or guess about Dion from this photo? Now write a paragraph in which you describe the photograph for a reader who has never seen it. In your topic sentence, state your overall impression of the young man. Support this impression with details.

✔ Checklist

The Process of Writing Basic Paragraphs

Refer to this checklist of steps as you write a basic paragraph.

___ 1. Narrow the topic in light of your audience and purpose.

___ 2. Write a topic sentence that has a clear controlling idea and is a complete sentence. If you have trouble, freewrite or brainstorm first; then narrow the topic and write the topic sentence.

___ 3. Freewrite or brainstorm, generating facts, details, and examples to develop your topic sentence.

___ 4. Select and drop ideas for the body of the paragraph.

___ 5. Arrange ideas in a plan or an outline, deciding which ideas will come first, which will come second, and so forth.

___ 6. Write the best first draft you can.

___ 7. Conclude. Don't just leave the paragraph hanging.

___ 8. Revise as necessary, checking your paragraph for support and unity.

___ 9. Proofread for grammar and spelling errors.

CHAPTER 4

Achieving Coherence

PART A   Coherence Through Order
PART B   Coherence Through Related Sentences

Every composition should have **coherence.** A paragraph *coheres*—holds together—when the sentences are arranged in a clear, logical *order* and when the sentences are *related* like links in a chain.

Part A
Coherence Through Order

An orderly presentation of ideas within the paragraph is easier to follow and more pleasant to read than a jumble. *After* jotting down ideas but *before* writing the paragraph, the writer should decide which ideas to discuss first, which second, which third, and so on, according to a logical order.

There are many possible orders, depending on the subject and the writer's purpose. This section will explain three basic ways of ordering ideas: **time order, space order,** and **order of importance.**

Time Order

One of the most common methods of ordering sentences in a paragraph is through **time,** or **chronological, order,** which moves from present to past or from past to present. Most stories, histories, and instructions follow the logical order of time.* The following paragraph employs time order:

---

*For work on narrative paragraphs, see Chapter 6, "Narration," and for work on process paragraphs, see Chapter 8, "Process."

> (1) Most Westerners are fascinated by Japanese sumo wrestling, but few understand the elaborate ritual that begins every bout. (2) *First*, the two *rikishi* (the Japanese term for "sumo wrestlers") step to the edge of the ring opposite each other, squat on their haunches, extend their arms, and clap once. (3) *Then* they go to the center of the ring; each lifts one leg sideways and stomps down on the mat. (4) *Next*, each opponent returns to his side of the ring and receives a dipper of "power-water" to rinse his mouth. (5) *At this point*, an attendant offers each a basket of unrefined salt. (6) The wrestlers walk toward the center of the ring, scattering salt to purify the ring. (7) They stop in the center, squat on their haunches with their fists on their knees, and lean toward each other, eyeball to eyeball. (8) As the fans scream and shout, the wrestlers return to the edge of the ring *one more time*. (9) The referee raises his war fan. (10) *Finally*, the fighters approach each other and begin fighting.

- The events in this paragraph are clearly arranged in the order of time. They are presented as they happen, *chronologically*.

- Throughout the paragraph, key words like *first, then, next,* and *at this point* emphasize time order and guide the reader from event to event.

Careful use of time order helps prevent confusing writing like this: *Oops, I forgot to mention that before the wrestlers scatter salt, they rinse their mouths.*

Occasionally, when the sentences in a paragraph follow a very clear time order, the topic sentence is only implied, not stated directly, as in this example:

> (1) In 1905, a poor washerwoman with a homemade hair product started a business—with $1.50! (2) In just five years, Madame C. J. Walker established offices and manufacturing centers in Denver, Pittsburgh, and Indianapolis. (3) The Madame C. J. Walker Manufacturing Company specialized in hair supplies, but Madame Walker specialized in independence for herself and for others. (4) Although she was not formally educated, she developed an international sales force, teaching her African-American agents the most sophisticated business skills. (5) Eight years after starting her business, Madame Walker was the first African-American woman to become a self-made millionaire. (6) In addition, she drew thousands of former farm and domestic workers into the business world. (7) One of her most original ideas was to establish "Walker Clubs," and she awarded cash prizes to the clubs with the most educational and philanthropic projects in their African-American communities. (8) When she died in 1919, Madame Walker left two-thirds of her fortune to schools and charities. (9) Another of her contributions also lived on. (10) After her death, many of her former employees used their experience to start businesses throughout the United States and the Caribbean.

- Time order gives coherence to this paragraph. Sentence 1 tells us about the beginning of Madame Walker's career as a businessperson. However, it does not express the main idea of the entire paragraph.

- What is the implied topic sentence or main idea developed by the paragraph?

  _____

  _____

  _____

- The implied topic sentence or main idea of the paragraph might read, *With nothing but natural business ability and vision, Madame C. J. Walker achieved history-making success for herself and others.*

- Because the writer arranges the paragraph in chronological order, the reader can easily follow the order of events in Madame Walker's life. What words and phrases indicate time order? Underline them and list them here:

  _____

  _____

  _____

PRACTICE 1   Arrange each set of sentences in logical time order, numbering the sentences 1, 2, 3, and so on, as if you were preparing to write a paragraph. Underline any words and phrases, like *first, next,* and *in 1692,* that give time clues.

1. ___ First, lie on your back with your knees comfortably bent.

   ___ Next, put your hands at your sides or fold them over your chest.

   ___ Finally, focus on your abs and do your crunches slowly, three sets of 10 each.

   ___ Lift your torso until the shoulder blades leave the floor, and then slowly roll back down.

   ___ The perfect crunch should be done slowly and deliberately, working the whole abdominal wall.

2. ___ In 1957, *The Cat in the Hat* made famous both its hat-wearing tomcat with terrible manners and its author.

   ___ Before he died in 1991, Seuss inspired millions to love language with such creations as the Grinch, Nerds, Wockets, Bar-ba-loots, bunches of Hunches, and fox in sox.

   ___ *Green Eggs and Ham* came out in 1960 and told a memorable story, using only 55 different words.

   ___ In his long career, Theodor Geisel, better known as Dr. Seuss, wrote 46 wildly imaginative children's books, now read all over the world.

   ___ His first book was rejected by 28 publishers, who found it "too strange for children."

   ___ In 1937, when it finally was published, readers loved the rhythmic march of tongue-twisting, invented words and the wacky characters.

- Transitional phrases like *just inside the door* and *all around the walls* guide the reader from sentence to sentence. What phrases in sentences 4 and 6 help guide the reader?

_____

PRACTICE 2 Following are topic sentences followed by supporting details. Arrange each group of details according to space order, numbering them 1, 2, 3, and so on, as if you were preparing to write a descriptive paragraph. On the line after each topic sentence, tell what kind of space order you used: *left to right, back to front,* and so forth.

1. Describe a firefighter's uniform. _____
   - ___ fire-retardant pants, called "turnouts"
   - ___ black, hard plastic helmet with flashlight attached
   - ___ steel-reinforced black rubber bunker boots
   - ___ bright yellow, fireproof Kevlar jacket
   - ___ compressed-air face mask

2. Describe a city scene. _____
   - ___ dented trash cans in the alley
   - ___ a bird riding the wind in blue sky
   - ___ rusty metal fire escape zigzagging up from the ground
   - ___ laundry flapping on a line near the eighth floor
   - ___ glimpse of the old wooden rooftop water tower

3. Describe a gift. _____
   - ___ white rectangular box
   - ___ big blue bow
   - ___ flannel nightgown with Minnie Mouse design
   - ___ white tissue paper, the innermost wrapping
   - ___ flowered wrapping paper

Writing Assignment 2

Use **space order** to give coherence to one of the following paragraphs. Compose a topic sentence, freewrite or brainstorm for more details, and then arrange them in space order. Use transitional words and phrases like these if you wish:*

on the left	above	next to
on the right	below	behind
in the middle	beside	farther out

_____

* For a more complete list of transitional expressions, see p. 60.

Paragraph 1   *Describe a firefighter's uniform, a city scene, or a gift*

Choose one group of details from Practice 2, formulate a topic sentence that sets the scene for them all, and use them as the basis of a paragraph. Convert the details into complete sentences, adding words if you wish.

Paragraph 2   *Describe a photograph*

Describe this unusual house and its setting as clearly and exactly as you can. First, jot down the five or six most important or striking details. Then, before writing your paragraph, arrange these details according to space order—moving from bottom to top, perhaps, or from left to right. Why do you think an adult might want to build a tree house? If you wish, answer this question in a second paragraph.

Order of Importance

Ideas in a paragraph can also be arranged in the **order of importance.** You may start with the most important ideas and end with the least, or you may begin with the least important idea and build to a climax with the most important one. If you wish to persuade your reader with arguments or examples, beginning with the most important points impresses the reader with the force of your ideas and persuades him or her to continue reading.*

On essay examinations and in business correspondence, be especially careful to begin with the most important idea. In those situations the reader definitely wants your important points first.

Read the following paragraph and note the order of ideas.

> (1) Louis Pasteur is revered as a great scientist for his three major discoveries. (2) Most important, this Frenchman created vaccines that have saved millions of human and animal lives. (3) The vaccines grew out of his discovery that weakened forms of a disease could help the person or animal build up antibodies that would prevent the disease. (4) The vaccines used today to protect children from serious illnesses owe their existence to Pasteur's work. (5) Almost as important was Pasteur's brilliant idea that tiny living beings, not chemical reactions, spoiled beverages. (6) He developed a process, pasteurization, that keeps milk, wine, vinegar, and beer from spoiling. (7) Finally, Pasteur found ways to stop a silkworm disease that threatened to ruin France's profitable silk industry. (8) Many medical researchers regard him as "the father of modern medicine."

■ The ideas in this paragraph are explained in the **order of importance,** from the *most important to the least important:*

What was Pasteur's most important discovery? _____

What was his next most important discovery? _____

What was his least important one? _____

■ Note how the words *most important, almost as important,* and *finally* guide the reader from one idea to another.

Sometimes, if you wish to add drama and surprise to your paragraphs, you may want to begin with the least important idea and build toward a climax by saving the most important idea for last. This kind of order can help counter the tendency of some writers to state the most important idea first and then let the rest of the paragraph dwindle away.

Read the following paragraph and note the order of ideas.

> (1) El Niño, an unusual flow of warm ocean water in the Pacific, has many destructive effects. (2) Peruvian fishermen usually are the first to know that El Niño is back. (3) The warm currents prevent plankton—tiny plants and animals on which fish feed—from forming on the surface of the ocean. (4) When the plankton supply goes down, so does the fish supply.

---

*See Chapter 5, "Illustration," and Chapter 13, "Persuasion."

> (5) Even more devastating, however, are the rainstorms that are caused by the change in water temperature. (6) Rains that normally move west "follow" the warm water east, bringing severe storms—and flooding—to North and South America. (7) But the most destructive effects of El Niño are unrelenting heat and drought. (8) Some areas in the United States, for example, have suffered temperatures of more than a hundred degrees for several months at a time. (9) Crops have been ruined, herds have been destroyed, and hundreds of people have died of heat-related causes.

- The destructive effects of El Niño that develop the topic sentence in this paragraph are discussed in the **order of importance:** *from the least to the most harmful.*
- The effects of the rainstorms are more destructive than the effects of the lessened fish supply. However, the destructive effects of heat and drought—which result in lost crops and the deaths of animals and people—are the most destructive effects of all.
- Transitional words like *more* and *most* help the reader follow clearly from one set of destructive effects to the next.

PRACTICE 3 Arrange the ideas that develop each topic sentence in their **order of importance,** numbering them 1, 2, 3, and so on. *Begin with the most important* (or largest, most severe, most surprising) and continue to the *least* important. Or reverse the order if you think that the paragraph would be more dramatic by beginning with the *least* important ideas and building toward a climax, with the most important last.

1. Cynthia Lopez's first year of college brought many unexpected expenses.
   - ___ Her English professor wanted her to own a college dictionary.
   - ___ All those term papers to write required a computer.
   - ___ She had to spend $90 for textbooks.
   - ___ Her solid geometry class required various colored pencils and felt-tipped pens.

2. Alcoholic beverages should not be sold at sporting events.
   - ___ Injuries and even deaths caused by alcohol-induced crowd violence would be eliminated.
   - ___ Fans could save money by buying soft drinks instead of beer.
   - ___ Games and matches would be much more pleasant without the yelling, swearing, and rudeness often caused by alcohol.

3. The apartment needed work before the new tenants could move in.
   - ___ The handles on the kitchen cabinets were loose.
   - ___ Every room needed plastering and painting.
   - ___ Grime marred the appearance of the bathroom sink.
   - ___ Two closet doors hung off the hinges.

 **Writing Assignment 3**

Use **order of importance** to give coherence to one of the paragraphs that follow. Use transitional words and phrases like these to guide the reader along:*

first	even more	another
next	last	least of all
above all	especially	most of all

Paragraph 1 *Describe a day in which everything went right (or wrong)*

Freewrite or brainstorm to generate ideas. Choose three or four of the day's best (or worst) events and write a paragraph in which you present them in order of importance—either from the most to the least important, or from the least to the most important.

Paragraph 2 *Describe an unusual person*

Choose a person you know whose looks or actions are unusual. Write your topic sentence and generate ideas; choose three to five details about the person's looks or behavior. Arrange the details according to the order of importance—either from the most to the least important or from the least to the most important.

Part B

Coherence Through Related Sentences

In addition to arranging ideas in a logical order, the writer can ensure paragraph coherence by linking one sentence to the next. This section will present four basic ways to link sentences: **repetition of important words, substitution of pronouns, substitution of synonyms,** and **transitional expressions.**

Repetition of Important Words and Pronouns

Link sentences within a paragraph by *repeating important words and ideas.*

> (1) A grand jury is an investigative body composed of members elected from the community. (2) It serves as a buffer between the state and the citizen. (3) The prosecutor, in many cases, brings before the grand jury the evidence gathered on a particular case. (4) The grand jury must then decide if sufficient evidence exists to hand down an indictment—the indictment being a formal charge against an accused person written by the prosecutor and submitted to a court by the grand jury. (5) With the indictment issued, the prosecutor can proceed to the arraignment.
> —Ronald J. Waldron et al., *The Criminal Justice System: An Introduction*

*For a more complete list of transitional expressions, see page 60.

- What important words are repeated in this paragraph?

- The words *grand jury* appear four times, in sentences 1, 3, and 4. The word *indictment*, introduced near the end of the paragraph, appears three times, in sentences 4 and 5. The word *prosecutor* appears three times, in sentences 3, 4, and 5.

- Repetition of these key words helps the reader follow from sentence to sentence as these terms are defined and the relationships between them are explained.

Although repetition of important words can be effective, it can also become boring if overused.* To avoid *unnecessary* repetition, substitute *pronouns* for words already mentioned in the paragraph, as this author does:

> (1) The first time a student walked into class wearing a "blue jay," *it* did startle me. (2) Royal-blue slabs of hair were brushed and sprayed straight up along the sides of *his* head, a long jelly roll of white hair fell forward over *his* eyebrows, and the back was shiny black, brushed straight up and plastered close to the head. (3) I didn't dislike *it*; *it* just seemed like a lot to fuss with each day.
>
> —Dianne Ackerman, *Natural History of the Senses*

- The use of pronouns in this paragraph avoids unnecessary repetition. In sentence 1, the pronoun *it* refers to the antecedent,† "blue jay."

- In sentence 2, the pronoun *his* gives further coherence to the paragraph by referring to what antecedent? _____

- The pronoun *it* in sentence 3 refers to what antecedent? _____

Use pronoun substitution together with the repetition of important words or a smooth presentation of ideas.

PRACTICE 4

What important words are repeated in the following paragraph? Underline them. Circle any pronouns that replace them. Notice the varied pattern of repetitions and pronoun replacements.

I have always considered my father a very intelligent person. His intelligence is not the type usually tested in schools; perhaps he would have done well on such tests, but the fact is that he never finished high school. Rather, my father's intelligence is his ability to solve problems creatively as they arise. Once when I was very young, we were driving through the desert at night when the oil line broke. My father improvised a light, squeezed under the car, found the break, and

---

* For practice in eliminating wordiness (repetition of unimportant words), see Chapter 22, "Revising for Language Awareness," Part B.

† For more work on pronouns and antecedents, see Chapter 31, "Pronouns," Parts A, B, and C.

managed to whittle a connection to join the two severed pieces of tubing; then he added more oil and drove us over a hundred miles to the nearest town. Such intelligent solutions to unforeseen problems were typical of him. In fact, my father's brand of brains—accurate insight, followed by creative action—is the kind of intelligence that I admire and most aspire to.

Writing Assignment 4

Paragraph 1 *Explain success*

How do you measure *success*? By the money you make, the number or quality of friends you have? Freewrite or brainstorm for ideas. Then answer this question in a thoughtful paragraph. Give the paragraph coherence by repeating important words and using pronouns.

Paragraph 2 *Discuss a public figure*

Choose a public figure whom you admire—from the arts, politics, media, or sports—and write a paragraph discussing *one quality* that makes that person special. Name the person in your topic sentence. Vary repetition of the person's name with pronouns to give the paragraph coherence.

Synonyms and Substitutions

When you do not wish to repeat a word or use a pronoun, give coherence to your paragraph with a **synonym** or **substitution. Synonyms** are two or more words that mean nearly the same thing. For instance, if you do not wish to repeat the word *car*, you might use the synonym *automobile* or *vehicle*. If you are describing a sky and have already used the word *bright*, try the synonym *radiant*.

Or instead of a synonym, **substitute** other words that describe the subject. If you are writing about Manny Ramirez, for example, refer to him as *this powerful slugger* or *this versatile athlete*. Such substitutions provide a change from constant repetition of a person's name or a single pronoun.*

Use synonyms and substitutions together with repetition and pronouns to give coherence to your writing:

> (1) *The main building of Ellis Island* in New York Harbor reopened as a museum in 1990. (2) Millions of people visit *the huge brick and limestone structure* every year. (3) From 1892 to 1954, *this famous immigrant station* was the first stop for millions of newcomers to American shores. (4) In fact, the ancestors of nearly 40 percent of American citizens passed through *this building*. (5) Abandoned in 1954, *it* deteriorated so badly that snow and rain fell on its floor. (6) Today visitors can follow the path of immigrants from a ferryboat, through the great arched doorway, into the room where the weary travelers left their baggage, up the stairway

---

*For more work on exact language, see Chapter 22, "Revising for Language Awareness," Part A.

> where doctors kept watch, and into the registry room. (7) Here questions were asked that determined if each immigrant could stay in the United States. (8) *This magnificent monument to the American people* contains exhibits that help individuals search for their own relatives' names and that tell the whole immigration history of the United States.

- This paragraph effectively mixes repetition, pronouns, and substitutions. The important word *building* is stated in sentence 1 and repeated in sentence 4.
- Sentence 5 substitutes the pronoun *it*.
- In sentence 2, *the huge brick and limestone structure* is substituted for *building*, and a second substitution, *this famous immigrant station*, occurs in sentence 3. Sentence 8 refers to the building as *this magnificent monument to the American people* and concludes the paragraph.

Exploring Online

http://www.ellisisland.com/ This site has links to Ellis Island immigration records; however, your name or a family story might be fine writing topics, wherever you are from.

To find synonyms, check a **dictionary**. For instance, the entry for *smart* might list *clever, witty, intelligent*. An even better source of synonyms is the **thesaurus**, a book of synonyms. For example, if you are describing a city street and cannot think of other words meaning "noisy," look in the thesaurus. The number of choices will amaze you.

PRACTICE 5 Read each paragraph carefully. Then write on the lines any synonyms and substitutions that the writer has used to replace the word(s) in italics.

Paragraph 1   According to sports writer Ian Stafford, the British hold the record for winning the world's *oddest competitions*. In one of these bizarre events, contestants contort their faces and are judged on their ugliness. One competitor removed half his dentures and reversed the other half, rolled his eyes, and tucked his nose into his mustache and upper lip to achieve prize-winning ugliness. Another of these eccentric contests is snail racing. Opponents in this case are, of course, snails, which are placed in the center of a thirteen-inch cloth circle. The first to reach the edge of the circle wins. The race often takes four to five minutes, although the all-time champion (owned and trained by an English seven-year-old) finished the course in two minutes. Toe wrestling, bog snorkeling, worm charming—the British have emerged as unconquered rivals in all of these so-called sports. Perhaps you think that sports writer Ian Stafford should win first prize in the Biggest Liar in the World Competition. No, every one of these outlandish games exists. You can check them all out on the Internet.

Oddest competitions are also referred to as _____, _____, _____, and _____.

Paragraph 2   When Lewis and Clark made their way through what is now North Dakota, the Shoshone Indian woman named *Sacajawea* and her French-Canadian husband joined the team of explorers. Because the expedition was traveling with a Native American, other tribes did not attack the group. In fact, one tribe even supplied horses to help the explorers and their interpreter cross the Rocky Mountains. This invaluable team member taught the men how to find medicine and food in the wilderness and once even saved the records of the journey when a canoe overturned during a storm. Sacajawea reached the Pacific Ocean with Lewis and Clark in 1805. Her fame eventually spread; one of the best-known monuments to her is a statue in Portland, Oregon.

Sacajawea is also referred to as _____,

_____, and _____.

PRACTICE 6   Give coherence to the following paragraphs by thinking of appropriate synonyms or substitutions for the words in italics. Then write them in the blanks.

Paragraph 1   Christopher Reeve's story includes an extraordinary twist of fate. This *star* played Superman, the fictional hero who inspired fans with his ability to overcome obstacles and save others from harm. How ironic that this _____ was paralyzed from the neck down in a horse-jumping accident in 1995 and now personifies that superhuman perseverance himself. Before his accident, Reeve was not only a(n) _____ but a pianist, an athlete who performed his own film stunts, a pilot, and an all-round outdoorsman. Now he depends on a ventilator to breathe and operates his wheelchair by sipping or puffing on a straw. Since his accident, however, this _____ has directed and narrated award-winning films, written the best-selling autobiography *Still Me*, and inspired thousands of people through speeches and interviews. He also has raised millions of dollars for research on spinal cord injuries. Christopher Reeve has become a(n) _____ of a different kind; his heroism depends not on physical strength but on courage, optimism, and a sense of purpose.

Paragraph 2   Much evidence shows that the urge to take a midafternoon *nap* is natural to humans. Sleep researchers have found that volunteer subjects, kept in underground rooms where they cannot tell the time, need a _____ about twelve hours after the halfway point of their main sleep. For example, if people sleep from midnight till 6:00 A.M., they'll be ready for a _____ at 3:00 the next afternoon. Other studies show that people have less trouble taking a _____ in midafternoon than at any other daylight time. In many countries with warm climates, citizens take their daily _____ in the afternoon. Even stressed Americans take an average of two afternoon naps a week.

Writing Assignment 5

As you do the following assignments, try to achieve paragraph coherence by using repetition, pronouns, synonyms, and substitutions.

Paragraph 1 *Discuss your favorite form of relaxation*

Tell what you like to do when you have free time. Do you like to get together with friends? Do you like to go to a movie or to some sporting event? Or do you prefer to spend your time alone, perhaps listening to music, reading or going fishing? Whatever your favorite free-time activity, name it in your topic sentence. Be sure to tell what makes your activity *relaxing*. Then give your paragraph coherence by using pronouns and synonyms such as *take it easy, unwind* and *feel free*.

Paragraph 2 *Describe your ideal mate*

Decide on three or four crucial qualities that your ideal husband, wife, or friend would possess, and write a paragraph describing this extraordinary person. Use repetition, pronouns, and word substitutions to give coherence to the paragraph. For example, *My ideal husband . . . he . . . my companion.*

Paragraph 3 *React to a quotation*

Choose a quotation from the Quotation Bank before the indexes in this book, one you strongly agree or disagree with. Write a paragraph explaining why you feel that way. As you write, refer to the quotation as a *wise insight* or *an absurd idea*—depending on what you think of it. Use other substitutions to refer to the quotation without repeating it or calling it *the quotation*.

Transitional Expressions

Skill in using transitional expressions is vital to coherent writing. **Transitional expressions** are words and phrases that point out the exact relation between one idea and another, one sentence and another. Words like *therefore, however, for example,* and *finally* are signals that guide the reader from sentence to sentence. Without them, even orderly and well-written paragraphs can be confusing and hard to follow.

The transitional expressions in this paragraph are italicized:

> (1) Zoos in the past often contributed to the disappearance of animal populations. (2) Animals were cheap, and getting a new gorilla, tiger, or elephant was easier than providing the special diet and shelter needed to keep captive animals alive. (3) *Recently, however,* zoo directors have realized that if zoos themselves are to continue, they must help save many species now facing extinction. (4) *As a result,* some zoos have redefined

themselves as places where endangered animals can be protected and even revived. (5) The National Zoo, in Washington, D.C., *for example*, has successfully bred rare Asian rhinos, and the San Diego Zoo has bred giant pandas. (6) The births of these endangered-species babies made international news. (7) If zoos continue such work, perhaps they can, like Noah's ark, save some of earth's wonderful creatures from extinction.

- Each transitional expression in the previous paragraph links, in a precise way, the sentence in which it appears to the sentence before. The paragraph begins by explaining the destructive policies of zoos in the past.

- In sentence 3, two transitional expressions of contrast—*recently* (as opposed to the past) and *however*—introduce the idea that zoo policies have *changed*.

- The phrase *as a result* makes clear that sentence 4 is a *consequence* of events described in the previous sentence(s).

- In sentence 5, *for example* tells us that the National Zoo is *one particular illustration* of the previous general statement, and the San Diego Zoo is another.

Baby Chitwan and her mother, National Zoo   Jessie Cohen

 Exploring Online

On Altavista, Google, or another search engine, type the words, "endangered species, zoos." Take notes on writing ideas, and bookmark web sites that intrigue you.

As you write, use various transitional expressions, together with the other linking devices, to connect one sentence to the next. Well-chosen transitional words also help stress the purpose and order of the paragraph.

Particular groups of transitional expressions are further explained and demonstrated in each chapter of Unit 3. However, here is a combined partial list for handy reference as you write.

Transitional Expressions at a Glance

Purpose	Transitional Expressions
to add	also, and, and then, as well, besides, beyond that, first (second, third, last, and so on), for one thing, furthermore, in addition, moreover, next, what is more
to compare	also, as well, both (neither), in the same way, likewise, similarly
to contrast	although, be that as it may, but, even though, however, in contrast, nevertheless, on the contrary, on the other hand, whereas, yet
to concede (a point)	certainly, granted that, of course, no doubt, to be sure
to emphasize	above all, especially, indeed, in fact, in particular, most important, surely
to illustrate	as a case in point, as an illustration, for example, for instance, in particular, one such, yet another
to place	above, below, beside, beyond, farther, here, inside, nearby, next to, on the far side, opposite, outside, to the east (south, and so on)
to qualify	perhaps, maybe
to give a reason or cause	as, because, for, since
to show a result or effect	and so, as a consequence, as a result, because of this, consequently, for this reason, hence, so, therefore, thus
to summarize	all in all, finally, in brief, in other words, lastly, on the whole, to sum up
to place in time	after a while, afterward, at last, at present, briefly, currently, during, eventually, finally, first (second, and so on), gradually, immediately, in the future, later, meanwhile, next, now, recently, soon, suddenly, then

PRACTICE 7 Carefully determine the *exact relationship* between the sentences in each pair below. Then choose from the list a **transitional expression** that clearly expresses this relationship and write it in the blank. Pay attention to punctuation and capitalize the first word of every sentence.*

1. No one inquired about the money found in the lobby. _____, it was given to charity.

2. First, cut off the outer, fibrous husk of the coconut. _____ poke a hole through one of the dark "eyes" and sip the milk through a straw.

3. The English Department office is on the fifth floor. _____ to it is a small reading room.

4. Some mountains under the sea soar almost as high as those on land. One underwater mountain in the Pacific, _____, is only 500 feet shorter than Mount Everest.

5. All citizens should vote. Many do not, _____.

6. Mrs. Dalworth enjoys shopping in out-of-the-way thrift shops. _____, she loves bargaining with the vendors at outdoor flea markets.

7. In 1887, Native Americans owned nearly 138 million acres of land. By 1932, _____, 90 million of those acres were owned by whites.

8. Kansas corn towered over the fence. _____ the fence, a red tractor stood baking in the sun.

9. Most street crime occurs between 2:00 and 5:00 A.M. _____, do not go out alone during those hours.

10. Dr. Leff took great pride in his work at the clinic. _____, his long hours often left him exhausted.

11. Few scientists have worked so creatively with a single agricultural product. _____ peanut oil and peanut butter, George Washington Carver developed literally hundreds of uses for the peanut.

12. We waited in our seats for over an hour. _____ the lights dimmed, and the Fabulous String Band bounded on stage.

PRACTICE 8 Add **transitional expressions** to this essay to guide the reader smoothly from sentence to sentence. To do so, consider the relationship between sentences (shown in parentheses). Then write the transitional word or phrase that best expresses this relationship.

---

* For practice using conjunctions to join ideas, see Chapter 25, "Coordination and Subordination."

Oldest Child, Youngest Child—Does It Matter?

A number of studies show that birth order—whether a person is the first-born, middle, or last-born child in the family—can affect both personality and career choice. _____ (illustration), first-borns carry the weight of their parents' expectations and _____ (time) are urged to be responsible and set a good example for their younger siblings. _____ (result) they may develop leadership skills and a strong motivation to achieve. Many eldest children _____ (time) become leaders. High percentages of U.S. presidents and CEOs, _____ (illustration) are first-borns.

Middle children, _____ (contrast), get less attention and applause in childhood. _____ (result), they tend to become flexible and good at resolving conflicts. _____ (addition), some middle children become rebellious or creative as they make their place in the world. _____ (time), many choose careers as entrepreneurs, negotiators, or businesspeople. _____ (addition), later-born or last-born children, in order to compete with their older siblings, may become rule-breakers or family clowns. Professionally, babies of the family tend to become musicians, adventurers, and comedians. _____ (conceding a point), there are countless exceptions to these general trends, _____ (contrast), it is interesting to ponder the evidence that our birth order _____ (emphasis) helps shape who we are.

PRACTICE 9 REVIEW

Most paragraphs achieve coherence through a variety of linking devices: repetition, pronouns, substitutions, and transitional expressions. Read the following paragraphs with care, noting the kinds of linking devices used by each writer. Answer the questions after each paragraph.

Paragraph 1

(1) The blues is the one truly American music. (2) Born in the Mississippi Delta, this twelve-bar cry of anguish found its durable, classic form in the searing soliloquies of poor black men and women who used it to ventilate all the aches and pains of their condition—the great Bessie Smith, Robert Johnson, Ma Rainey, Lightnin' Hopkins and Son House, Mississippi John Hurt, John Lee Hooker and Blind Lemon Jefferson. (3) And, ever since, the blues has served as the wellspring of every major movement in this country's popular music.

—Paul D. Zimmerman with Peter Barnes et al., "Rebirth of the Blues," *Newsweek*

1. What important words appear in both the first and the last sentence? _____

2. In sentence 2, *the blues* is referred to as _____

3. What transitional expressions are used in sentence 3? _____

Paragraph 2   (1) In the annals of great escapes, the flight by seventeen-year-old Lester Moreno Perez from Cuba to the United States surely must rank as one of the most imaginative. (2) At 8:30 on the night of Thursday, March 1, Lester crept along the beach in Varadero, a resort town on the north coast of Cuba. (3) Working quickly, he launched his sailboard—a surfboard equipped with a movable sail—into the shark-haunted waters off the Straits of Florida. (4) At first guided by the stars and later by the hazy glow from electric lights in towns beyond the horizon, Lester sailed with 20-knot winds toward the Florida Keys, 90 miles away. (5) All night he balanced on the small board, steering through black waters. (6) Just past daybreak on Friday, Lester was sighted 30 miles south of Key West by the Korean crew of the freighter *Tina D.* (7) The boom on his tiny craft was broken. (8) The astonished sailors pulled him aboard, fed him chicken and rice, and finally radioed the U.S. Coast Guard.

—Adapted from Sam Moses, "A New Dawn," *Sports Illustrated*

1. Underline the transitional expressions in this paragraph.

2. What *order* of ideas does the paragraph employ? _____

Paragraph 3   (1) Mrs. Zajac seemed to have a frightening amount of energy. (2) She strode across the room, her arms swinging high and her hands in small fists. (3) Taking her stand in front of the green chalkboard, discussing the rules with her new class, she repeated sentences, and her lips held the shapes of certain words, such as "homework," after she had said them. (4) Her hands kept very busy. (5) They sliced the air and made karate chops to mark off boundaries. (6) They extended straight out like a traffic cop's, halting illegal maneuvers yet to be perpetrated. (7) When they rested momentarily on her hips, her hands looked as if they were in holsters. (8) She told the children, "One thing Mrs. Zajac expects from each of you is that you do *your* best." (9) She said, "Mrs. Zajac gives homework. (10) I'm sure you've all heard. (11) The old meanie gives homework." (12) *Mrs. Zajac.* (13) It was in part a role. (14) She worked her way into it every September.

—Tracy Kidder, *Among Schoolchildren*

1. What important words are repeated in this paragraph? _____

2. What word does *they* in sentences 5 and 6 refer to? _____

UNIT 2

Writers' Workshop

Discuss the Pressures to Grow Up Fast

In this unit, you learned that most good paragraphs have a clear topic sentence, convincing support, and an order that makes sense. In your group or class, read this student's paragraph, aloud if possible. Underline any parts you find especially well written. Put a check next to anything that might be improved.

> **Young Immigrant Translators**
>
> ~~This paper will discuss children as translators.~~ When immigrant children become translators for their parents, this can change the normal relationship between parent and child. Many immigrant parents do not have the time or opportunity to develop their English skills, even though they know that speaking English is the most important part of surviving in the United States. When they need to understand or speak English, they often ask their school-age children for help. The children must act like little adults, helping their parents with all kinds of problems. They end up taking time away from school and their friends because they are responsible for everything related to English. For example, they might have to answer the phone, fill out forms, pay bills, or shop for groceries. Even in more serious situations, like medical or financial problems, the children might have to translate for the doctor or accountant. Eventually, some children can start to resent their parents for relying on them so much. Instead of turning to their parents for help with homework or personal worries, they might turn instead to friends or teachers who understand the culture better. Although most immigrant children know their parents love them and want a better life for them, the role reversal of being child translators can make them become adults too soon.
>
> —Mandy Li (Student)

1. How effective is this paragraph?

    _____ Clear topic sentence?   _____ Good supporting details?

    _____ Logical organization?   _____ Effective conclusion?

2. Which sentence, if any, is the topic sentence? Is sentence 1 as good as the rest of the paragraph? If not, what revision advice would you give the writer?

3. Does this student provide adequate support for her main idea? Why or why not?

4. Discuss your underlinings with the group or class. Which parts or ideas in this essay did you find most powerful? As specifically as you can, explain

why. For example, the list of possible tasks a child translator must handle vividly supports the main idea of the paragraph.

5. Do you agree with Ms. Li that children being asked to translate for their parents makes children grow up too soon? Have you experienced or witnessed other situations in which children must become adults too soon? What are those situations?

6. Do you see any error patterns (one error made two or more times) that this student needs to watch out for)?

Group Work

In your group or class, make a plan of Ms. Li's paragraph. How many points does she use to support her topic sentence? How can a writer know whether a paragraph has good support or needs better support? List three ways. Did this paragraph make you think? How would you rate the ideas in this paragraph? Extremely interesting? Interesting? Not very interesting? Be prepared to explain your rating to the full class.

Writing and Revising Ideas

1. Discuss the ways in which a child you know had to grow up too soon.

2. What is the most important tool for surviving in the United States, in your view?

UNIT 3

Developing the Paragraph

CHAPTER 5　Illustration
CHAPTER 6　Narration
CHAPTER 7　Description
CHAPTER 8　Process
CHAPTER 9　Definition
CHAPTER 10　Comparison and Contrast
CHAPTER 11　Classification
CHAPTER 12　Cause and Effect
CHAPTER 13　Persuasion

CHAPTER 5 Illustration

To **illustrate** is to explain a general statement by means of one or more specific examples.

Illustration makes what we say more vivid and more exact. Someone might say, "My math professor is always finding crazy ways to get our attention. Just yesterday, for example, he wore a high silk hat to class." The first sentence is a general statement about this professor's unusual ways of getting attention. The second sentence, however, gives a specific example of something he did that *clearly shows* what the writer means.

Writers often use illustration to develop a paragraph. They explain a general topic sentence with one, two, three, or more specific examples. Detailed and well-chosen examples add interest, liveliness, and power to your writing.

Topic Sentence

Here is the topic sentence of a paragraph that is later developed by examples:

> Great athletes do not reach the top by talent alone but by pushing themselves to the limit and beyond.

- The writer begins an illustration paragraph with a topic sentence that makes a general statement.
- This generalization may be obvious to the writer, but if he or she wishes to convince the reader, some specific examples would be helpful.

Paragraph and Plan

Here is the entire paragraph:

> Great athletes do not reach the top by talent alone but by pushing themselves to the limit and beyond. For instance, golf legend Tiger Woods keeps striving for perfection. Long after dark—even during tournaments—he practices at the driving range, hitting ball after ball. Even after winning his first Masters Tournament in 1997, Tiger spent 18 months refining his swing. Recently, he added twenty pounds of muscle to his lean frame with a secret training plan. Another example is hard-working tennis star Serena Williams, who practices on the court for hours each day with her sister Venus. Serena builds her speed and strength with yoga, running, weight-lifting, and boxing. By studying videotapes of all her matches, she constantly improves her game. Perhaps no player in any sport, however, can match the work ethic of Lance Armstrong. In 1996, this bicycle racer was diagnosed with testicular cancer that had spread to his brain and lungs. After surgery and chemotherapy left him weak and exhausted, Armstrong began a brutal training regimen, following a strict diet and cycling up to six hours a day. His commitment paid off when, in 1999 and every year through 2002, he won the Tour de France, cycling's toughest race. Like many top athletes, he turned his talent into greatness through sheer hard work.

- How many examples does the writer use to develop the topic sentence?

_____

- Who are they?

_____

Before completing this illustration paragraph, the writer probably made an outline or **plan** like this:

Topic Sentence: Great athletes do not reach the top by talent alone but by pushing themselves to the limit and beyond.

Example 1: Tiger Woods

—practices after dark—even during tournaments
—after first Masters, 18 months improving swing
—added 20 pounds of muscle—secret plan

Example 2: Serena Williams

—practices hours a day with Venus
—yoga, running, weights, boxing
—studies videos of her matches

Example 3: Lance Armstrong

—1996, cancer diagnosis
—after surgery and chemo, strict training (diet, cycling)
—won Tour de France, 1999–2002

Conclusion: Like many top athletes, he turned talent into greatness through sheer hard work.

- Note that each example clearly relates to and supports the topic sentence.

Instead of using three or four examples to support the topic sentence, the writer may prefer instead to discuss one single example:

> Many schools in the twenty-first century will look more like elegant shopping malls than like old-fashioned school buildings. The new Carl Sandburg High School in Chicago is just one example. Now being redesigned, the school will feature a main library with the comfortable, open layout of a super-bookstore like Barnes & Noble or Borders. The physical education facilities will include rock-climbing walls and other features now seen in health clubs. Carl Sandburg's cafeteria will be laid out like a food court, not only giving students more choices, but eliminating the long lunch lines that caused delays in the old high school. Retailers have learned how to create attractive, practical public spaces, and many modern school planners think it's time that school officials learned the same lessons.

- What is the general statement? _____

_____

_____

- What specific example does the writer give to support the general statement?

_____

The single example may also be a **narrative,*** a *story* that illustrates the topic sentence.

> Aggressive drivers not only are stressed out and dangerous, but often they save no time getting where they want to go. Recently I was driving south from Oakland to San Jose. Traffic was heavy but moving. I noticed an extremely aggressive driver jumping lanes, speeding up and slowing down. Clearly, he was in a hurry. For the most part, I remained in one lane for the entire forty-mile journey. I was listening to a new audiotape and daydreaming. I enjoyed the trip because driving gives me a chance to be alone. As I was exiting off the freeway, the aggressive driver crowded up behind me and raced on by. Without realizing it, I had arrived in San Jose ahead of him. All his weaving, rapid acceleration, and putting families at risk had earned him nothing except perhaps some high blood pressure and a great deal of wear and tear on his vehicle.
>
> —Adapted from Richard Carlson, *Don't Sweat the Small Stuff*

---

* For more on narrative, see Chapter 6, "Narration," and Chapter 15, "Types of Essays," Part B.

- What general statement does the aggressive driver story illustrate?

  _____

  _____

- Note that this narrative follows time order.*

Transitional Expressions

The simplest way to tell your reader that an example is going to follow is to say so: *"For instance,* Tiger Woods . . ." or "The new Carl Sandburg High School is *just one example."* This partial list should help you vary your use of **transitional expressions** that introduce an illustration:

Transitional Expressions for Illustration	
for instance	another instance of
for example	another example of
an illustration of this	another illustration of
a case in point is	here are a few examples
to illustrate	(illustrations, instances)

- Be careful not to use more than two or three of these transitional expressions in a single paragraph.†

PRACTICE 1 Read each of the following paragraphs of illustration. Underline each topic sentence. Note in the margin how many examples are provided to illustrate each general statement.

Paragraph 1

Random acts of kindness are those little sweet or grand lovely things we do for no reason except that, momentarily, the best of our humanity has sprung . . . into full bloom. When you spontaneously give an old woman the bouquet of red carnations you had meant to take home to your own dinner table, when you give your lunch to the guitar-playing beggar who makes music at the corner between your two subway stops, when you anonymously put coins in someone else's parking meter because you see the red "Expired" medallion signaling to a meter maid—you are doing not what life requires of you, but what the best of your human soul invites you to do.

—Daphne Rose Kingma, *Random Acts of Kindness*

---

*For more work on time order, see Chapter 4, "Achieving Coherence," Part A.
†For a complete essay developed by illustration, see "Libraries of the Future—Now," Chapter 15, Part A.

Paragraph 2   There are many quirky variations to lightning. A "bolt from the blue" occurs when a long horizontal flash suddenly turns toward the earth, many miles from the storm. "St. Elmo's Fire," often seen by sailors and mountain climbers, is a pale blue or green light caused by weak electrical discharges that cling to trees, airplanes, and ships' masts. "Pearl lightning" occurs when flashes are broken into segments. "Ball lightning" can be from an inch to several feet in diameter. <u>Pearls and balls are often mistaken for flying saucers or UFOs, and many scientists believe they are only optical illusions.</u>

—Reed McManus, *Sierra Magazine*

PRACTICE 2   Each example in a paragraph of illustration must clearly relate to and support the general statement. Each general statement in this practice is followed by several examples. Circle the letter of any example that does *not* clearly illustrate the generalization. Be prepared to explain your choices.

Example   The museum contains many fascinating examples of African art.

a. It houses a fine collection of Ashanti fertility dolls.

b. Drums and shamans' costumes are displayed on the second floor.

(c.) The museum building was once the home of Frederick Douglass. (The fact that the building was once the home of Frederick Douglass is *not an example* of African art.)

1. The International Space Station is designed for efficient use of limited space.

    a. Food has been dehydrated so it can be stored in tiny packages.

    b. Special science laboratories onboard are the size of clothes closets.

    (c.) Daily life in the space station can be observed by 90 percent of the world's population.

    d. Each little "bedroom" can be folded and stored in a single sleeping bag.

2. Today's global companies sometimes find that their product names and slogans can translate into embarrassing bloopers.

    a. Pepsi's slogan "Come alive with the Pepsi Generation" didn't work in Taiwan, where it meant "Pepsi will bring your ancestors back from the dead."

    b. When General Motors introduced its Chevy Nova in South America, company officials didn't realize that *no va* in Spanish means "it won't go."

    c. In Chinese, the Kentucky Fried Chicken slogan "finger-lickin' good" means "eat your fingers off."

    (d.) Nike runs the same ad campaign in several countries, changing the ad slightly to fit each culture.

3. Natural remedies are now widely used to treat common ailments.

    (a.) Asthma is more common than ever and has become a serious problem among children.

    b. Many people take the vitamin niacin to lower high cholesterol.

    c. Thousands claim that the herb St. John's Wort lifts their depression, without the side effects of antidepressant medications.

4. Some writers use strange tricks to overcome writer's block and keep their ideas flowing.

   a. To help himself choose the right word, the German playwright and poet Schiller sniffed rotten apples that he kept inside his desk.

   b. Benjamin Franklin believed that he had to write in the nude to do his best work, and he often wrote in the bathtub.

   (c.) Argentinian writer Jorge Luis Borges went blind, but he kept creating brilliant stories packed with learning, philosophy, and magic.

   d. To inspire herself before she started writing, Dame Edith Sitwell would lie for a while each morning in an open coffin.

5. In the Arizona desert, one sees many colorful plants and flowers.

   a. Here and there are patches of pink clover.

   b. Gray-green saguaro cacti rise up like giant candelabra.

   (c.) Colorful birds dart through the landscape.

   d. Bright yellow poppies bloom by the road.

6. Many important inventions were rejected when they were first introduced.

   a. Chester Carlson was laughed at for his dry copy process, xerography, but it later made him rich and gave a company its name, Xerox.

   (b.) The invention of NutraSweet happened accidentally in 1965 when a chemist noticed that a chemical he had spilled tasted sweet.

   c. When John Holland first invented the submarine in the late 1800s, the Navy saw no use for it and treated him like a kook.

7. The United States offers many unusual tourist attractions for those who venture off the beaten path.

   a. Visitors to Mitchell, South Dakota, can stop at the Mitchell Corn Palace, a castle covered with murals made of corn, grass, and grain.

   (b.) One of the most popular tourist stops in the country is the Washington Monument in Washington, D.C.

   c. Hard-core Elvis fans can visit the Elvis Museum in Pigeon Forge, Tennessee, to see Elvis's razor, hair dryer, and nasal spray applicator.

   d. On Route 115 in Colorado, drivers can gawk at the World's Largest Hercules Beetle, a giant bug made of plaster.

8. Many months in our calendar take their names from Roman gods or heroes.

   a. Mars, the Roman war god, gave his name to March.

   b. January was named for Janus, the god of doorways, whose two faces looked both forward and back.

   c. August honors Augustus, the first Roman emperor and the second Caesar.

   (d.) December took its name from *decem*, the Latin word meaning "ten," and was the tenth month in the Roman calendar.

PRACTICE 3 The secret of good illustration lies in well-chosen, well-written examples. Think of one example that illustrates each of the following general statements. Write out the example in sentence form (one to three sentences) as clearly and exactly as possible.

1. A few contemporary singers work hard to send a positive message.

   Example _____

   _____

   _____

2. In a number of ways, this college makes it easy for working students to attend.

   Example By having weekend and evening classes while providing distant learning.

   _____

3. Believing in yourself is 90 percent of success.

   Example _____

   _____

   _____

4. Many teenagers believe they must have expensive designer clothing.

   Example _____

   _____

   _____

5. Growing up in a large family can teach the value of compromise.

   Example _____

   _____

   _____

6. A number of shiny classic cars cruised up and down Ocean Drive.

   Example _____

   _____

   _____

7. Children say surprising things.

   Example _____

   _____

   _____

8. Sadly, rudeness seems more and more common in America.

   Example _____

   _____

   _____

PRACTICE 4 **Thinking and Writing Together**
Illustrate Acts of Kindness

In the news, we often hear the phrase "random acts of violence"—acts whose unlucky victims are in the wrong place at the wrong time. The phrase "random acts of kindness" reverses this idea in a wonderful way—kind acts whose recipients are often perfect strangers. In a group with four or five classmates, read about random acts of kindness (Practice 1, Paragraph 1, page 70). Now think of one good example of a real-life random act of kindness, performed by you or someone else—either at college or work, or in everyday life. Share and discuss these examples with your group. Which examples are the most striking or moving? Why?

Write up your example in one paragraph. Begin with a clear topic sentence and present the act of kindness as movingly as you can. Refer to the checklist, and ask your group mates for feedback.

Exploring Online

http://www.actsofkindness.org/ Click "Inspiration" to read about acts of kindness that people have sent in; click "Contact Us" to submit your group's best writing for possible publication.

✔ Checklist

The Process of Writing an Illustration Paragraph

Refer to this checklist of steps as you write an illustration paragraph of your own.

____ 1. Narrow the topic in light of your audience and purpose.

____ 2. Compose a topic sentence that can honestly and easily be supported by examples.

> ___ 3. Freewrite or brainstorm to find six to eight examples that support the topic sentence. If you wish to use only one example or a narrative, sketch out your idea. (You may want to freewrite or brainstorm before you narrow the topic.)
>
> ___ 4. Select only the best two to four examples and drop any examples that do not relate to or support the topic sentence.
>
> ___ 5. Make a plan or an outline for your paragraph, numbering the examples in the order in which you will present them.
>
> ___ 6. Write a draft of your illustration paragraph, using transitional expressions to show that an example or examples will follow.
>
> ___ 7. Revise as necessary, checking for support, unity, logic, and coherence.
>
> ___ 8. Proofread for errors in grammar, punctuation, sentence structure, spelling, and mechanics.

Suggested Topic Sentences for Illustration Paragraphs

1. The car a person drives (or the way a person dresses) often makes a statement about him or her.
2. Most people have special places where they go to relax or find inspiration.
3. In my family, certain traditions (or values or beliefs) are very important.
4. Some lucky people love their jobs.
5. Painful experiences can sometimes teach valuable lessons.
6. Many enjoyable activities in this area are inexpensive or even free.
7. Celebrities who have overcome illness or tragedy can inspire others.
8. A sense of humor can make difficult times easier to bear.
9. Sexual harassment is a fact of life for some employees.
10. Eating disorders are a serious problem.
11. College students face a number of pressures.
12. Some unusual characters live in my neighborhood.
13. A true friend is one who sees and encourages the best in us.
14. Choose a quotation from the Quotation Bank at the end of this book. First, state whether you think this saying is true; then use an example from your own or others' experience to support your view.
15. Writer's choice: _____

CHAPTER 6 Narration

To **narrate** is to tell a story that explains what happened, when it happened, and who was involved.

A news report may be a narrative telling how a man was rescued from icy flood waters or how a brave whistle blower risked her career and perhaps her life to expose an employer's harmful practices. When you read a bedtime story to a child, you are reading a narrative. In a college paper on campus drug use, telling the story of a friend who takes ecstacy would help bring that subject to life. In an email or letter, you might entertain a friend by narrating your failed attempts to wind surf during a seaside vacation.

We tell stories to teach a lesson, illustrate an idea, or make someone laugh, cry, or get involved. No matter what your narrative is about, every narrative should have a clear **point**: It should reveal what you want your reader to learn or take away from the story.

Topic Sentence

Here is the topic sentence of a **narrative** paragraph:

> The crash of a Brinks truck on a Miami overpass still raises disturbing questions.

- The writer begins a narrative paragraph with a topic sentence that tells or sets up the point of the narrative.
- What is the point of this narrative? _____

_____

Paragraph and Plan

Here is the entire paragraph:

> The crash of a Brinks truck on a Miami overpass still raises disturbing questions. January 8, 1997 was just another crowded, rude, and crazy day in Miami traffic until an armored Brinks truck flipped and broke open, sending nearly a million dollars in cash swirling over the highway. Hundreds of motorists screeched to a stop, grabbing whatever money they could. People in nearby houses raced outside, shouting and scooping up bills. When it was over, a tiny handful of people returned some money. Firefighter Manny Rodriguez turned in a huge bale of bills worth $330,000, and one teenager returned some quarters. However, nearly half a million dollars was missing—stolen by everyday people like you and me. In the following days, some rationalized the mass theft as a kind of Robin Hood action because the truck had crashed in a poor area of town. Most people claimed to be shocked. Now we are all left with hard questions: *Why did a few people "do the right thing"? Why did the majority do the "wrong thing"? What causes people to act virtuously, even if no one is watching? What would you or I have done?*

- The body of a narrative paragraph is developed according to time, or chronological, order.* That is, the writer explains the narrative—the entire incident—as a series of small events or actions in the order in which they occurred. By keeping to strict chronological order, the writer helps the reader follow the story more easily and avoids interrupting the narrative with *But I forgot to mention that before this happened....*

- What smaller events make up this paragraph? _____

- What strong verbs or details help the writing come alive? _____

- The writer ends the paragraph with some "hard questions." Do these questions express the point of the story? _____

---

*For more work on time, see Chapter 4, "Achieving Coherence," Part A.

Before writing this narrative paragraph, the writer may have brainstormed or freewritten to gather ideas, and then she may have made an **outline** or a **plan** like this:

Topic Sentence: The crash of a Brinks truck on a Miami overpass still raises disturbing questions.

- **Event 1:** Brinks truck flips, spilling cash on the highway.
- **Event 2:** Hundreds of motorists stop, grab money.
- **Event 3:** People race out of houses, grabbing money.
- **Event 4:** Later, firefighter Rodriguez returns $330,000.
- **Event 5:** Just a few others give anything back; half million is gone.
- **Event 6:** Days after, some call it "Robin Hood" action.
- **Event 7:** Some say they are shocked.

Conclusion: Now we are all left with hard questions. (Some questions are listed.)

- Note that all of the events occur in chronological order.
- Note also that the conclusion provides a strong and thought-provoking ending.
- Finally, note that the specific details of certain events (like events 2 and 4) make the narrative more vivid.

Transitional Expressions

Because narrative paragraphs tell a story in **chronological** or **time order**, transitional expressions that indicate time can be useful.*

Transitional Expressions for Narratives		
after	finally	soon
as (soon as)	later	then
before	meanwhile	upon
during	next	when
first	now	while

PRACTICE 1 Read the following narrative paragraph carefully and answer the questions.

---

* For a complete essay developed by narration, see "Maya Lin's Vietnam War Memorial," Chapter 15, "Types of Essays," Part B.

> A birthday gift I received years ago has become a lasting symbol of love. It was a cold day during my first year in college. My birthday had just passed, and I hadn't heard from my best friend, Linda, who had moved away two years before. A card and a present would have been nice, but what I really wanted from her was a hug. Suddenly the doorbell rang. I ran downstairs and signed the receipt that the letter carrier held out—in return for a package from Linda! I pulled off all the wrappings—and stared. Then, because I didn't know whether to laugh or cry, I ended up doing some of each. Linda's gift was a sweater, but this sweater had something extra. Attached to each cuff was a cutout of one of Linda's hands, and the hands in the box were arranged in a hug around the sweater. I loved the sweater, but I didn't wear it for months because I couldn't bear to unpin the hands, which would have looked pretty silly just dangling from my cuffs. Then I got an idea. I'm not an artist, but I decided to make a collage. I got hours of pleasure painting a background and then cutting, arranging, and pasting photographs and magazine pictures, along with the hands, into what is surely a unique piece of artwork. I eventually wore out the sweater, but the collage has hung in every place I've ever lived. Every time I look at it, I feel hugged, loved, and comforted.

1. What is the point of the narrative? _____

2. What events make up this narrative paragraph? _____

PRACTICE 2 Here are three plans for narrative paragraphs. The events in the plans are not in correct chronological order. The plans also contain events that do not belong in each story. Number the events in the proper time sequence and cross out any irrelevant ones.

1. Aesop's fable about a dog and his reflection teaches a lesson about greed.

    ___ He thought he saw another dog with another piece of meat in his mouth, so he decided to get that one too.

    ___ Now the dog had nothing at all to eat.

    ___ A dog was happily carrying a piece of meat in his mouth.

    ___ The dog was brown with white spots.

    ___ While crossing a bridge, he saw his reflection in the water of a running brook.

_____ When he snapped at the reflection, the meat dropped from his mouth into the water and sank.

2. Through talent and fortunate timing, Vera Wang has become one of the world's top designers of women's gowns.

_____ In 1971, after college, Wang became a fashion editor at *Vogue,* a job she held for 15 years.

_____ Soon stars like Halle Berry, Uma Thurman, and Meg Ryan began wearing Vera Wang gowns, and Wang's reputation soared.

_____ In 1990, Wang made her dream a reality, opening a high-style bridal and evening gown business.

_____ Every year, 2.4 million couples get married in the United States, spending an average of $19,000 per wedding.

_____ The world took note when Wang designed elegant costumes for skater Nancy Kerrigan during the much-watched 1994 Winter Olympics.

3. The Civil War battle between two iron-covered ships, on March 9, 1862, changed sea warfare forever.

_____ Two hours into the battle, the *Monitor* ran out of ammunition and moved into shallow water to reload.

_____ After four hours, the *Merrimack,* her hull leaking and her smokestack broken, escaped from the scene of battle.

_____ When the *Monitor* returned with guns loaded, the *Merrimack* lured her into deep water and then suddenly swung around and rammed her, leaving barely a dent.

_____ The Civil War lasted from 1861 to 1865.

_____ At the end of the conflict, neither ironclad ship had really won, but the wooden fighting ship was a thing of the past.

_____ At first, the two ships—the North's *Monitor* and the South's *Merrimack*—just circled each other like prehistoric monsters, firing at close range but causing no damage.

PRACTICE 3   Here are topic sentences for three narrative paragraphs. Make a plan for each paragraph, placing the events of the narrative in the proper time sequence.

1. When I had trouble with _____, help came from an unexpected source.

_____

_____

_____

_____

2. The accident (or performance) lasted only a few moments, but I will never forget it.

_____

_____

_____

_____

_____

_____

3. Last year, _____ learned something surprising about himself/herself.

_____

_____

_____

_____

_____

_____

PRACTICE 4 Study the photo on page 82 and tell the story behind it. That is, you must invent a brief narrative that explains this mysterious picture. What are these people looking at so intently and why? Your narrative can be serious, funny, or otherworldly. First, list the main events and include them in chronological order. State the point of your narrative in the topic sentence, which you may wish to place last rather than first in your paragraph.

PRACTICE 5 Thinking and Writing Together
Narrate an Experience of Stereotyping

Good narratives have a *point;* they bring to life a moral, lesson, or idea. In a group with four of five classmates, read this narrative passage about "The Latina Stereotype" by Judith Ortiz Cofer and then discuss and answer the questions.

> My first public poetry reading took place at a restaurant where a luncheon was being held before the event. I was nervous and excited as I walked in with a notebook in hand. An older woman motioned me to her table, and thinking (foolish me) that she wanted me to autograph a copy of my newly published slender volume of verse, I went over. She ordered a cup of coffee from me, assuming that I was the waitress. (Easy enough to mistake my poems for menus, I suppose.) I know it wasn't an intentional act of cruelty. Yet of all the good things that happened later, I remember that scene most clearly, because it reminded me of what I had to overcome before anyone would take me seriously.

- What is the point of this story? Exactly what *stereotype* did the writer encounter? What did the woman assume about her and why?

- Have you ever been stereotyped? That is, has anyone ever treated you a certain way based only on your age, clothing, race, gender, major, accent, piercings or other decoration, or even things you are carrying, like books or a beeper? Share a story with the group. What stereotype was imposed on you, and how did you react? Now narrate vividly in writing your experience of stereotyping. You might wish to place your topic sentence, stating the meaning or point, last. Refer to the checklist, and ask your group mates for feedback.

 Exploring Online

http://www.tolerance.org/ Explore this interesting site about increasing tolerance.

> ✓ **Checklist**
>
> **The Process of Writing a Narrative Paragraph**
>
> Refer to this checklist of steps as you write a narrative paragraph of your own.
>
> ___ 1. Narrow the topic in light of your audience and purpose.
>
> ___ 2. Compose a topic sentence that tells the point of the story.
>
> ___ 3. Freewrite or brainstorm for all of the events and details that might be part of the story. (You may want to freewrite or brainstorm before you narrow the topic.)
>
> ___ 4. Select the important events and details; drop any that do not clearly relate to the point in your topic sentence.
>
> ___ 5. Make a plan or an outline for the paragraph, numbering the events in the correct time (chronological) sequence.
>
> ___ 6. Write a draft of your narrative paragraph, using transitional expressions to indicate time sequence.
>
> ___ 7. Revise as necessary, checking for support, unity, logic, and coherence.
>
> ___ 8. Proofread for errors in grammar, punctuation, sentence structure, spelling, and mechanics.

Suggested Topic Sentences for Narrative Paragraphs

1. A favorite family story
2. A lesson in tolerance
3. A fulfilled ambition
4. A few moments that changed someone's life
5. A laugh at yourself
6. A breakthrough (emotional, physical, or spiritual)
7. An experience in a new country
8. A memorable experience at work
9. A triumphant (or embarrassing) moment
10. The first time you met an important friend
11. A serious choice or decision
12. A visit to the ER (or other interesting place)
13. Something you or another person dared to do
14. An incident that made you happy (or proud)
15. Writer's choice: _____

CHAPTER 7 Description

To **describe** something—a person, a place, or an object—is to capture it in words so others can imagine it or see it in their mind's eye.

The best way for a writer to help the reader get a clear impression is to use language that appeals to the senses: sight, sound, smell, taste, and touch. For it is through the senses that human beings experience the physical world around them, and it is through the senses that the world is most vividly described.

Imagine, for instance, that you have just gone boating on a lake at sunset. You may not have taken a photograph, yet your friends and family can receive an accurate picture of what you have experienced if you *describe* the pink sky reflected in smooth water, the creak of the wooden boat, the soothing drip of water from the oars, the occasional splash of a large bass jumping, the faint fish smells, the cool and darkening air. Writing down what your senses experience will teach you to see, hear, smell, taste, and touch more acutely than ever before.

Description is useful in English class, the sciences, psychology—anywhere that keen observation is important.

Topic Sentence

Here is the topic sentence of a descriptive paragraph:

> On November 27, 1922, when archaeologist Howard Carter unsealed the door to the ancient Egyptian tomb of King Tut, he stared in amazement at the fantastic objects heaped all around him.

- The writer begins a descriptive paragraph by pointing out what will be described. What will be described in this paragraph?

_____

- The writer can also give a general impression of this scene, object, or person. What overall impression of the tomb does the writer provide?

_____

_____

_____

Paragraph and Plan

Here is the entire paragraph:

> On November 27, 1922, when archaeologist Howard Carter unsealed the door to the ancient Egyptian tomb of King Tut, he stared in amazement at the fantastic objects heaped all around him. On his left lay the wrecks of at least four golden chariots. Against the wall on his right sat a gorgeous chest brightly painted with hunting and battle scenes. Across from him was a gilded throne with cat-shaped legs, arms like winged serpents, and a back showing King Tut and his queen. Behind the throne rose a tall couch decorated with animal faces that were half hippopotamus and half crocodile. The couch was loaded with more treasures. To the right of the couch, two life-sized statues faced each other like guards. They were black, wore gold skirts and sandals, and had cobras carved on their foreheads. Between them was a second sealed doorway. Carter's heart beat loudly. Would the mummy of King Tut lie beyond it?

- The overall impression given by the topic sentence is that the tomb's many objects were amazing. List three specific details that support this impression.

_____

_____

_____

- Note the importance of words that indicate richness and unusual decoration in helping the reader visualize the scene.* List as many of these words as you can:

_____

_____

_____

_____

- This paragraph, like many descriptive paragraphs, is organized according to space order.† The author uses transitional expressions that show where things are. Underline the transitional expressions that indicate place or position.

---

*For more work on vivid language, see Chapter 22, "Revising for Language Awareness."

†For more work on space order and other kinds of order, see Chapter 4, "Achieving Coherence," Part A.

Before composing this descriptive paragraph, the writer probably brainstormed and freewrote to gather ideas and then made an **outline** or a **plan** like this:

Topic sentence: On November 27, 1922, when archaeologist Howard Carter unsealed the door to the ancient Egyptian tomb of King Tut, he stared in amazement at the fantastic objects heaped all around him.

1. To the left: chariots
   —wrecked
   —golden

2. To the right: a gorgeous chest
   —brightly painted with hunting and battle scenes

3. Across the room: a throne
   —gilded
   —cat-shaped legs
   —arms like winged serpents

4. Behind the throne: a couch
   —decorated with faces that were half hippopotamus and half crocodile

5. To the right of the couch: two life-sized statues
   —black
   —gold skirts and sandals
   —cobras carved on foreheads

6. Between the two statues: a second sealed doorway

Conclusion: expectation that King Tut's mummy was beyond the second door

---

- Note how each detail supports the topic sentence.

Transitional Expressions

Since space order is often used in description, **transitional expressions** indicating place or position can be useful:

Transitional Expressions Indicating Place	
next to, near	on top, beneath
close, far	toward, away
up, down, between	left, right, center
above, below	front, back, middle

Of course, other kinds of order are possible. For example, a description of a person might have two parts: details of physical appearance and details of behavior.*

PRACTICE 1 Read the following paragraph carefully and answer the questions.

The woman who met us had an imposing beauty. She was tall and large-boned. Her face was strongly molded, with high cheekbones and skin the color of mahogany. She greeted us politely but did not smile and seemed to hold her head very high, an effect exaggerated by the abundant black hair slicked up and rolled on the top of her head. Her clothing was simple, a black sweater and skirt, and I remember thinking that dressed in showier garments, this woman would have seemed overwhelming.

1. What overall impression does the writer give of the woman? _____

   _____

2. What specific details support this general impression? _____

   _____

   _____

3. What kind of order does the writer use? _____

PRACTICE 2 It is important that the details in a descriptive paragraph support the overall impression given in the topic sentence. In each of the following plans, one detail has nothing to do with the topic sentence; it is merely a bit of irrelevant information. Find the irrelevant detail and circle its letter.

1. Leo's dormitory room is uniquely decorated.
   a. dozens of cartoons taped on the door
   b. Leo's car painted with Spider Man designs
   c. lime green junk-shop chair in corner
   d. silver robotic dog guarding the door
   e. bookshelves crammed with computer books
   f. monitor glows with shifting pictures of Einstein

2. A large pitcher of iced tea sat on the tray.
   a. ice maker humming in the refrigerator
   b. clear glass of the pitcher frosted with cold
   c. large drops running downward, pooling on the tray

---

*For a complete essay developed by description, see "The Day of the Dead," Chapter 15, Part C.

d. clear ice cubes gleaming in rust-brown tea

e. orange and lemon slices among the ice cubes

3. The Calle Ocho Festival, named after S.W. 8th Street in Little Havana, is a giant Latino street party.

    a. as far as the eye can see on S.W. 8th Street, thousands of people stroll, eat, and dance

    b. on the left, vendors sell hot pork sandwiches, *pasteles* (spiced meat pies), and fried sweets dusted with powdered sugar

    c. up close, the press of bare-limbed people, blaring music, and rich smells

    d. during the 1980s, Dominican merengue music hit the dance clubs of New York

    e. on the right, two of many bands play mambo or merengue music

4. In the photograph from 1877, Chief Joseph looks sad and dignified.

    a. long hair pulled back, touched with gray

    b. dark eyes gaze off to one side, as if seeing a bleak future

    c. strong mouth frowns at the corners

    d. ceremonial shell necklaces cover his chest

    e. Nez Percé tribe once occupied much of the Pacific Northwest

5. An illegal dump site has spoiled the field near the edge of town.

    a. fifty or more rusting metal drums, some leaking

    b. pools of green-black liquid on the ground

    c. in the distance, view of the mountains

    d. wildflowers and cottonwood trees dead or dying

    e. large sign reading "Keep Out—Toxic Chemicals"

PRACTICE 3 Here are three topic sentences for descriptive paragraphs. Give five specific details that would support the overall impression given in each topic sentence. Appeal to as many of the senses as possible. Be careful not to list irrelevant bits of information.

Example | Stopped in time by the photographer, my mother appears confident.

Details: a. her hair swept up in a sophisticated pompadour

b. a determined look in her young eyes

c. wide, self-assured smile

d. her chin held high

e. well-padded shoulders

(These five details support *confident* in the topic sentence.)

1. This was clearly a music lover's room.

   a. _____

   b. _____

   c. _____

   d. _____

   e. _____

2. The buildings on that street look sadly rundown.

   a. _____

   b. _____

   c. _____

   d. _____

   e. _____

3. The beach on a hot summer day presented a constant show.

   a. _____

   b. _____

   c. _____

   d. _____

   e. _____

PRACTICE 4 Pick the description you like best from Practice 3. Prewrite for more details if you wish. Choose a logical order in which to present the best details, make a plan or an outline, and then write an excellent descriptive paragraph.

PRACTICE 5 **Thinking and Writing Together**
Describe a Painting

In a group with four or five classmates, study the painting on page 90. Your task is to write one paragraph describing this painting so that someone who has never seen it can visualize it. As a group, craft a good topic sentence that gives an *overall impression* of the scene. Your topic sentence might take this form:

"George Tooker's 1950 painting, *Subway*, shows (or captures) _____

_____."

Have one person take notes as you brainstorm important details, using rich language to capture the scene. Now decide the best order in which to present your details—right to left, center to sides, or some other. Use transitional expressions to guide the reader's eye from detail to detail. Revise the writing to make it as exact and fresh as possible. Be prepared to read your work to the full class.

Detail of *Subway* by George Tooker

Exploring Online

http://www.artic.edu/aic/ Art Museum of Chicago: Find a work of art that intrigues you and describe it.

http://www.moma.org/ Museum of Modern Art: Find a work of art that intrigues you and write about it.

✔ Checklist

The Process of Writing a Descriptive Paragraph

Refer to this checklist of steps as you write a descriptive paragraph of your own.

____ 1. Narrow the topic in light of your audience and purpose.

____ 2. Compose a topic sentence that clearly points to what you will describe or gives an overall impression of the person, object, or scene.

____ 3. Freewrite or brainstorm to find as many specific details as you can to capture your subject in words. Remember to appeal to your readers' senses. (You may want to freewrite or brainstorm before you narrow the topic.)

____ 4. Select the best details and drop any irrelevant ones.

____ 5. Make a plan or an outline for the paragraph, numbering the details in the order in which you will present them.

____ 6. Write a draft of your descriptive paragraph, using transitional expressions wherever they might be helpful.

____ 7. Revise as necessary, checking for support, unity, logic, and coherence.

____ 8. Proofread for errors in grammar, punctuation, sentence structure, spelling, and mechanics.

Suggested Topics for Descriptive Paragraphs

1. An unusual man or woman: for example, an athlete, an entertainer, someone with amazing hair or clothing, or a teacher you won't forget
2. A food, object, or scene from another country
3. The face of someone in the news
4. A tool or machine you use at work
5. An animal, a bird, or an insect you have observed closely
6. Someone or something you found yourself staring at
7. A photograph of yourself as a child
8. A scene of peace (or of conflict)
9. A room that reveals something about its owner
10. An intriguing outdoor scene
11. A shop that sells only one type of item: cheese, computer software, Western boots, car parts, flowers
12. An interesting person you have seen on campus
13. A public place: emergency room, library, fast-food restaurant, town square, or theater lobby
14. A neighborhood personality
15. Writer's choice: _____

CHAPTER 8 Process

Two kinds of **process paragraphs** will be explained in this chapter: the how-to paragraph and the explanation paragraph.

The **how-to paragraph** gives the reader directions on how he or she can do something: how to install a software program, how to get to the airport, or how to make tasty barbecued ribs. The goals of such directions are the installed software, the arrival at the airport, or the great barbecued ribs. In other words, the reader should be able to do something after reading the paragraph.

The **explanation paragraph,** on the other hand, tells the reader how a particular event occurred or how something works. For example, an explanation paragraph might explain how an internal combustion engine works or how palm trees reproduce. After reading an explanation paragraph, the reader is not expected to be able to do anything, just to understand how it happened or how it works.

Process writing is useful in history, business, the sciences, psychology, and many other areas.

Topic Sentence

Here is the topic sentence of a **how-to paragraph:**

> Careful preparation before an interview is the key to getting the job you want.

- The writer begins a how-to paragraph with a topic sentence that clearly states the goal of the process—what the reader should be able to do.

- What should the reader be able to do after he or she has read the paragraph following this topic sentence?

___

Paragraph and Plan

Here is the entire paragraph:

> "Luck is preparation meeting opportunity," it has been said, and this is true for a job interview. Careful preparation before an interview is the key to getting the job you want. The first step is to learn all you can about the employer. Read about the company in its brochures or in newspaper and magazine articles. A reference librarian can point you to the best sources of company information. You can also find company web sites and other useful material on the Internet. Second, as you read, think about the ways your talents match the company's goals. Third, put yourself in the interviewer's place, and make a list of questions that he or she will probably ask. Employers want to know about your experience, training, and special skills, like foreign languages. Remember, every employer looks for a capable and enthusiastic team player who will help the firm succeed. Fourth, rehearse your answers to the questions out loud. Practice with a friend or a tape recorder until your responses sound well prepared and confident. Finally, select and prepare a professional-looking interview outfit well in advance to avoid the last-minute panic of a torn hem or stained shirt. When a job candidate has made the effort to prepare, the interviewer is much more likely to be impressed.

- The topic sentence is the second sentence. In the first sentence, the writer has used a quotation to open the paragraph and spark the reader's interest.

- The body of the how-to paragraph is developed according to time, or chronological, order.* That is, the writer gives directions in the order in which the reader is to complete them. Keeping to a strict chronological order avoids the necessity of saying, *By the way, I forgot to tell you . . . ,* or *Whoops, a previous step should have been to. . . .*

- How many steps are there in this how-to paragraph and what are they?

___

* For more work on order, see Chapter 4, "Achieving Coherence," Part A.

Before writing this how-to paragraph, the writer probably brainstormed or freewrote to gather ideas and then made an **outline** or a **plan** like this:

Topic sentence: Careful preparation before an interview is the key to getting the job you want.

Step 1:	Learn about the employer —read company brochures, papers, magazines —reference librarian can help —check company web site
Step 2:	Think how your talents match company goals
Step 3:	List interviewer questions —think about experience, training, special skills —employers want capable team players
Step 4:	Rehearse your answers out loud —practice with friend or tape recorder
Step 5:	Select your interview outfit —avoid last-minute panic —avoid torn hem, stained shirt

Conclusion: Interviewer more likely to be impressed

- Note that each step clearly relates to the goal stated in the topic sentence.

The second kind of process paragraph, the **explanation paragraph,** tells how something works, how it happens, or how it came to be:

> Many experts believe that recovery from addiction, whether to alcohol or other drugs, has four main stages. The first stage begins when the user finally admits that he or she has a substance abuse problem and wants to quit. At this point, most people seek help from groups like Alcoholics Anonymous or treatment programs because few addicts can "get clean" by themselves. The next stage is withdrawal, when the addict stops using the substance. Withdrawal can be a painful physical and emotional experience, but luckily, it does not last long. After withdrawal comes the most challenging stage—making positive changes in one's life. Recovering addicts have to learn new ways of spending their time, finding pleasure and relaxation, caring for their bodies, and relating to spouses, lovers, family, and friends. The fourth and final stage is staying off drugs. This open-ended part of the process often calls for ongoing support or therapy. For people once defeated by addiction, the rewards of self-esteem and a new life are well worth the effort.

- What process does the writer explain in this paragraph? _____

_____

- How many stages or steps are explained in this paragraph? _____

CHAPTER 8   Process   95

- What are they? _____
  _____

- Make a plan of the paragraph in your notebook.

Just as the photographs on this page show each stage in the process of a chick hatching, so your process paragraph should clearly describe each step or stage for the reader. Before you write, try to visualize the process as if it were a series of photographs.*

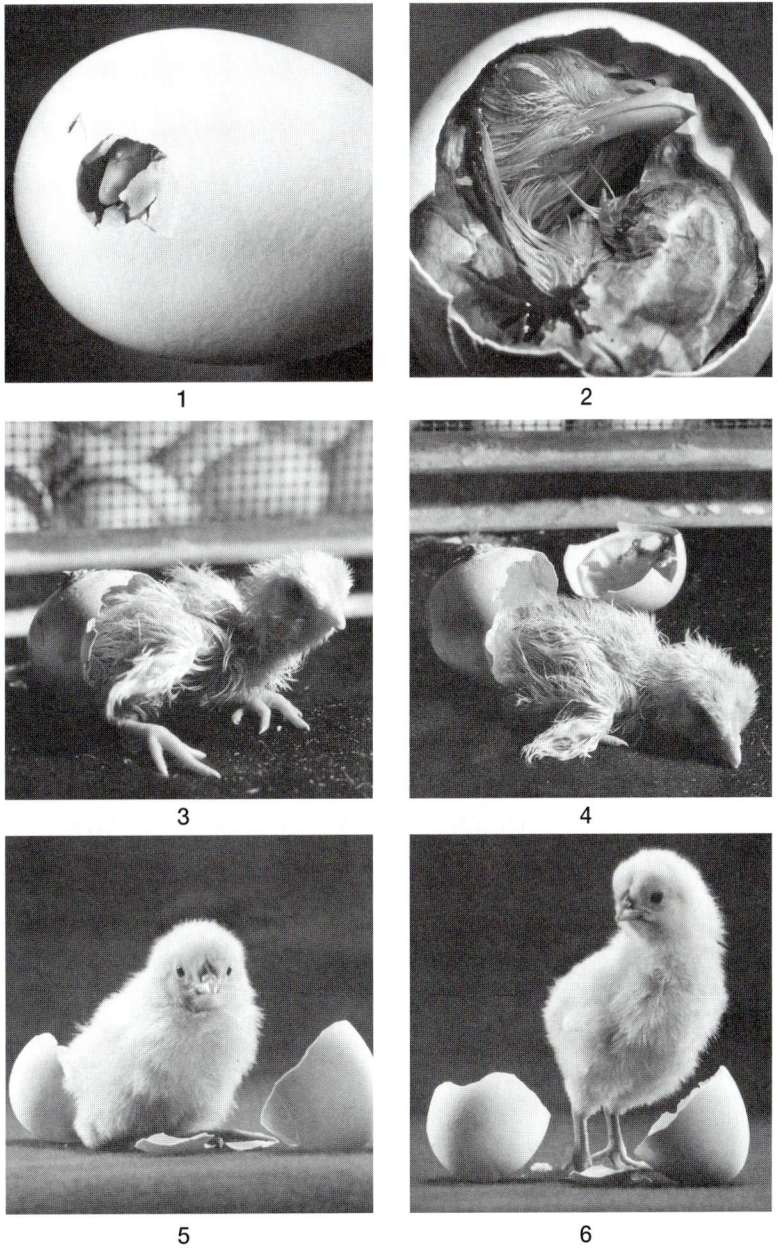

1   2
3   4
5   6

---

*For complete essays developed by process, see "How to Prepare for a Final Exam," Chapter 15, Part D, and "Bottle Watching," page 172.

Transitional Expressions

Since process paragraphs rely on **chronological order,** or **time sequence,** words and expressions that locate the steps of the process in time are extremely helpful.

Transitional Expressions for Process

Beginning a Process	Continuing a Process		Ending a Process
(at) first	second, third step	when	finally
initially	until	while	at last
begin by	after(ward)	as soon as	
	then	as	
	next	upon	
	later	during	
	before	meanwhile	

PRACTICE 1 Read the following how-to paragraph carefully and answer the questions.

If your dog barks too much, the Humane Society recommends an easy way to solve the problem. All you need is a plant mister—a small spray bottle—filled with water and kept handy. First and most important, respond immediately every time your dog barks unnecessarily. Instantly say, "Quiet, Pluto," or whatever the dog's name is, giving one or two squirts of water in the dog's face. Be sure to do this while the dog is barking. Waiting until the dog stops barking may confuse it. If the dog moves away, say, "Quiet" again as you move toward the dog and give it one more squirt of water. Second, repeat this procedure every time the dog barks without a good reason. The dog will soon learn that your saying "Quiet" comes with a squirt of water. Usually two days—about five to ten water treatments—are enough. Third, as time goes by, use the spray bottle only if the dog forgets—that is, rarely. Throughout the training process, remember to be consistent, using the spray technique every single time, and don't forget to reassure your dog that you two are still friends by petting it when it is quiet.

—Eleanor Steiger (Student)

1. What should you be able to do after reading this paragraph?

   _____

   _____

2. Are any "materials" necessary for this process? _____

   _____

3. How many steps are there in this paragraph? List them.

_____

_____

_____

4. What order does the writer employ? _____

PRACTICE 2 Here are five plans for process paragraphs. The steps for the plans are not in the correct chronological order. The plans also contain irrelevant details that are not part of the process. Number the steps in the proper time sequence and cross out any irrelevant details.

1. Monster.com grew quickly into a popular resource for both job seekers and employers.

   ___ In 1994, before the Internet was used much by the public, Taylor launched the Monster Board to post jobs online.

   ___ Businessman Jeff Taylor was looking for a way to help his customers find good staff.

   ___ So many people used the Monster Board that the company soon expanded from 24 to 2000 employees.

   ___ One night in a dream, he had a "monster idea"—to use the Internet as a job-search tool.

   ___ Monsters have always been popular in films, from Frankenstein and Dracula to the frightening creatures in the *Alien* series.

   ___ In 1999, Monster.com joined with Online Career Center, adding free help with résumé writing and other career skills.

2. Stress, which is your body's response to physical or mental pressures, occurs in three stages.

   ___ In the resistance stage, your body works hard to resist or handle the threat, but you may become more vulnerable to other stressors, like flu or colds.

   ___ If the stress continues for too long, your body uses up its defenses and enters the exhaustion stage.

   ___ Trying to balance college courses, parenthood, and work is sure to cause stress.

   ___ During the alarm stage (also called *fight or flight*), your body first reacts to a threat by releasing hormones that increase your heart rate and blood pressure, create muscle tension, and supply quick energy.

3. Chewing gum is made entirely by machine.

   ___ Then the warm mass is pressed into thin ribbons by pairs of rollers.

   ___ First, the gum base is melted and pumped through a high-speed spinner that throws out all impurities.

   ___ The gum base makes the gum chewy.

   ___ Huge machines mix the purified gum with sugar, corn syrup, and flavoring, such as spearmint, peppermint, or cinnamon.

   ___ Finally, machines wrap the sticks individually and then package them.

   ___ Knives attached to the last rollers cut the ribbons into sticks.

4. Many psychologists claim that marriage is a dynamic process consisting of several phases.

   ___ Sooner or later, romance gives way to disappointment as both partners really see each other's faults.

   ___ Idealization is the first phase, when two people fall romantically in love, each thinking the other is perfect.

   ___ The last phase occurs as the couple face their late years as a twosome once again.

   ___ The third phase is sometimes called the productivity period, when two people work at parenting and career development.

   ___ Men and women may have different expectations in a marriage.

   ___ As the children leave home and careers mature, couples may enter a stage when they rethink their lives and goals.

5. Helping to save rare stranded sea turtles, our service learning project, was a rewarding series of steps.

   ___ Inside, we rubbed Vaseline on each turtle's shell and put saline in its eyes; the sickest turtles needed IV fluids.

   ___ We gently loaded each tired giant in the front seat of a pickup truck and hurried back to the sanctuary.

   ___ In the fall, when temperatures dropped, we volunteers at the Wellfleet Wildlife Sanctuary raced to the beaches to find any giant sea turtles that had not swum south.

   ___ Two volunteers so loved working with endangered turtles that they are now pursuing careers in marine biology.

   ___ Within 12 hours, we drove our patients to the aquarium in Boston, to spend the winter and get well before their release in warm Florida seas.

PRACTICE 3 Here are topic sentences for three process paragraphs. Make a plan for each paragraph, listing in proper time sequence all the steps that would be necessary to complete the process. Now choose one plan and write an excellent process paragraph.

1. Although I'm still not the life of the party, I took these steps to overcome my shyness at parties.

   _____

   _____

   _____

   _____

   _____

   _____

   _____

2. Good kids turning bad: it is a process occurring all over the country.

   _____

   _____

   _____

   _____

   _____

   _____

   _____

3. _____ is/was a very complicated (or simple) process.

   _____

   _____

   _____

   _____

   _____

PRACTICE 4   Thinking and Writing Together
Explain the Process of Intoxication

In a group with four or five classmates, study and discuss these percentages that show rising blood alcohol content (BAC), a measure of intoxication. Now plan and write a paragraph that describes what happens as BAC rises. Your purpose is to inform the public about this process. Write a topic sentence that gives an overview; in the body, include three or four percentages if you wish. In your concluding sentence or sentences, you might wish to emphasize the dangerous human meaning of these numbers. Be prepared to read your paragraph to the full class.

BAC	Effect
0.03%	relaxation, mood change
0.05%	decrease in motor skills; legal driving limit in New York
0.07%	legal driving limit in 16 states
0.09%	delayed reaction time, decreased muscle control, slurred speech
0.15%	blurred vision, unsteadiness, impaired coordination
0.18%	difficulty staying awake
0.30%	semi-stupor
0.50%	coma and risk of death

Now assume your purpose is to write another paragraph convincing young people not to binge drink. Would BAC percentages help persuade your audience, or would you take another approach? What might that approach be?

Exploring Online

http://www.hsph.harvard.edu/cas/ College Alcohol Study
http://www.dui.com/duieducation/LegalDefinition.html Defining drunk driving

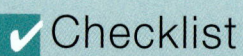

The Process of Writing a Process Paragraph

Refer to this checklist of steps as you write a process paragraph of your own.

____ 1. Narrow the topic in light of your audience and purpose.

____ 2. Compose a topic sentence that clearly states the goal or end result of the process you wish to describe.

____ 3. Freewrite or brainstorm to generate steps that might be part of the process. (You may want to freewrite or brainstorm before you narrow the topic.)

_____ 4. Drop any irrelevant information or steps that are not really necessary for your explanation of the process.

_____ 5. Make an outline or a plan for your paragraph, numbering the steps in the correct time (chronological) sequence.

_____ 6. Write a draft of your process paragraph, using transitional expressions to indicate time (chronological) sequence.

_____ 7. Revise as necessary, checking for support, unity, logic, and coherence.

_____ 8. Proofread for errors in grammar, punctuation, sentence structure, spelling, and mechanics.

Suggested Topics for Process Paragraphs

1. How to relax or meditate
2. How to establish credit
3. How to break up with (or attract) someone
4. How an important discovery was made
5. How to find information in the library's electronic card catalogue (or reference book section)
6. How to be a good friend
7. How someone landed a wonderful job
8. How to prepare your favorite dish
9. How to shop on a budget for a computer (or clothes, school supplies, and so on)
10. How to appear smarter than you really are
11. How to break an unhealthy habit
12. How a team won an important game
13. How to get the most out of a visit to the doctor
14. How to choose a major
15. Writer's choice: _____

CHAPTER 9 Definition

PART A Single-Sentence Definitions
PART B The Definition Paragraph

To **define** is to explain clearly what a word or term means.

As you write, you will sometimes find it necessary to explain words or terms that you suspect your reader may not know. For example, *net profit* is the profit remaining after all deductions have been taken; a *bonsai* is a dwarfed, ornamentally shaped tree. Such terms can often be defined in just a few carefully chosen words. However, other terms—like *courage, racism,* or *a good marriage*—are more difficult to define. They will test your ability to explain them clearly so that your reader knows exactly what you mean when you use them in your writing. They may require an entire paragraph for a complete and thorough definition.

In this chapter, you will learn to write one-sentence definitions and then whole paragraphs of definition. The skill of defining clearly will be useful in such courses as psychology, business, the sciences, history, and English.

Part A

Single-Sentence Definitions

There are many ways to define a word or term. Three basic ways are **definition by synonym, definition by class,** and **definition by negation.**

Definition by Synonym

The simplest way to define a term is to supply a **synonym,** a word that means the same thing. A good synonym definition always uses an easier and more familiar word than the one being defined.

1. *Gregarious* means *sociable.*
2. *To procrastinate* means *to postpone needlessly.*

> 3. A *wraith* is a *ghost* or *phantom.*
> 4. *Adroitly* means *skillfully.*

Although you may not have known the words *gregarious, procrastination, wraith,* and *adroitly* before, the synonym definitions make it very clear what they mean.

A synonym should usually be the same part of speech as the word being defined, so it could be used as a substitute. *Gregarious* and *sociable* are both adjectives; *to procrastinate* and *to postpone* are verb forms; *wraith, ghost,* and *phantom* are nouns; *adroitly* and *skillfully* are adverbs.

> 5. Quarterback Payton Manning *adroitly* moved his team up the field.
> 6. Quarterback Payton Manning *skillfully* moved his team up the field.

- In this sentence *skillfully* can be substituted for *adroitly.*

Unfortunately, it is not always possible to come up with a good synonym definition.

Definition by Class

The **class** definition is the one most often required in college and formal writing—in examinations, papers, and reports.

The class definition has two parts. First, the writer places the word to be defined into the larger **category,** or **class,** to which it belongs.

> 7. *Lemonade* is a *drink* . . .
> 8. An *orphan* is a *child* . . .
> 9. A *dictatorship* is a *form of government* . . .

Second, the writer provides the **distinguishing characteristics** or **details** that make this person, object, or idea *different* from all others in that category. What the reader wants to know is what *kind* of drink is lemonade? What *specific* type of child is an orphan? What *particular* form of government is a dictatorship?

> 10. *Lemonade* is a drink *made of lemons, sugar, and water.*
> 11. An *orphan* is a child *without living parents.*
> 12. A *dictatorship* is a form of government *in which one person has absolute control over his or her subjects.*

Here is a class definition for the action pictured: A slam-dunk is a basket that is scored when the shooter leaps high, forcefully throwing the basketball through the rim from above.

Think of class definitions as if they were in chart form:

Word	Category or Class	Distinguishing Facts or Details
lemonade	drink	made of lemons, sugar, and water
orphan	child	without living parents
dictatorship	form of government	one person has absolute control over his or her subjects

When you write a class definition, be careful not to place the word or term in too broad or vague a category. For instance, saying that lemonade is a *food* or that an orphan is a *person* will make your job of zeroing in on a distinguishing detail more difficult.

Besides making the category or class as limited as possible, be sure to make your distinguishing facts as specific and exact as you can. Saying that lemonade is a drink *made with water* or that an orphan is a child *who has lost family members* is not specific enough to give your reader an accurate definition.

Definition by Negation

A definition by **negation** means that the writer first says what something is not, and then says what it is.

> 13. A *good parent* does not just feed and clothe a child but loves, accepts, and supports that child for who he or she is.
>
> 14. *College* is not just a place to have a good time but a place to grow intellectually and emotionally.
>
> 15. *Liberty* does not mean having the right to do whatever you please but carries the obligation to respect the rights of others.

Definitions by negation are extremely helpful when you think that the reader has a preconceived idea about the word you wish to define. You say that *it is not* what the reader thought, but that *it is* something else entirely.

Here is a definition by negation: The fax machine is not the revolutionary new office machine that people think but an invention patented in 1863 and used to send words and pictures between the United States and France.

PRACTICE 1 Write a one-sentence definition by **synonym** for each of the following terms. Remember, the synonym should be more familiar than the term being defined.

1. *irate:* _____

2. *to elude:* _____

3. *pragmatic:* _____

4. *fiasco:* _____

5. *elated:* _____

PRACTICE 2 Here are five **class definitions.** Circle the category and underline the distinguishing characteristics in each. You may find it helpful to make a chart.

1. A *haiku* is a Japanese poem that has seventeen syllables.

2. A *homer* is a referee who unconsciously favors the home team.

3. An *ophthalmologist* is a doctor who specializes in diseases of the eye.

4. The *tango* is a ballroom dance that originated in Latin America and is in 2/4 or 4/4 time.

5. *Plagiarism* is stealing writing or ideas that are not one's own.

PRACTICE 3 Define the following words by **class definition.** You may find it helpful to use this form: "A _____ is a _____
   (noun)   (class or category)
that _____."
        (distinguishing characteristic)

1. *hamburger:* _____
_____
_____

2. *bikini:* _____
_____
_____

3. *snob:* _____
_____
_____

4. *mentor:* _____

5. *adolescence:* _____

PRACTICE 4 Write a one-sentence definition by **negation** for each of the following terms. First say what each term is not; then say what it is.

1. *hero:* _____

2. *final exam:* _____

3. *self-esteem:* _____

4. *intelligence:* _____

5. *freedom of speech:* _____

Part B

The Definition Paragraph

Sometimes a single-sentence definition may not be enough to define a word or term adequately. In such cases, the writer may need an entire paragraph in which he or she develops the definition by means of examples, descriptions, comparisons, contrasts, and so forth.

Topic Sentence

The topic sentence of a definition paragraph is often one of the single-sentence definitions discussed in Part A: definition by synonym, definition by class, definition by negation.

Here is the topic sentence of a definition paragraph:

> A *flashbulb memory* can be defined as a vivid, long-lasting memory that is formed at the moment a person learns of a highly emotional event.

- What kind of definition does the topic sentence use? _____

- To what larger category or class does a *flashbulb memory* belong? _____

_____

- What are the distinguishing details about a *flashbulb memory* that make it different from other kinds of memories? _____

_____

Paragraph and Plan

Here is the entire paragraph:

> A *flashbulb memory* can be defined as a vivid and long-lasting memory formed at the moment a person experiences a highly emotional event. It is as though a mental flashbulb pops, preserving the moment in great detail. Although flashbulb memories can be personal, they often are triggered by public events. For example, many older Americans recall exactly what they were doing when they learned that Pearl Harbor was bombed in 1941. Time froze as people crowded around their radios to find out what would happen next. Many more people recall in detail the shocking moment on November 11, 1963 when they heard that President John F. Kennedy had been assassinated. Considered the most widely shared flashbulb memory of our time, the image of Kennedy's death is burned into the minds of people the world over. More recently, the terrorist attack on the World Trade Center became a flashbulb memory for millions. Whether they heard the terrible news on their morning commute or were awakened by a panicked voice on the phone telling them to turn on the television, research into memory suggests that they will never forget that day. As these examples show, flashbulb memories mark some of our most permanent and haunting experiences, moments that were scored into our hearts.

- One effective way for a writer to develop the body of a definition paragraph is to provide examples.*
- What three examples does this writer give to develop the definition in the topic sentence? _____

- By repeating the word being defined—or a form of it—in the context of the definition paragraph, the writer helps the reader understand the definition better: "Although *flashbulb memories* can be personal . . . ," "Considered the most widely shared *flashbulb memory* of our time . . . ," ". . . on the World Trade Center became a *flashbulb memory* for millions."
- Before writing the paragraph, the writer probably brainstormed or freewrote to gather ideas and then made an **outline** or **plan** like this:

Topic sentence: A flashbulb memory is a vivid and long-lasting memory formed at the moment a person experiences a highly emotional event.

Example 1:	Pearl Harbor —older Americans recall what they were doing in 1941 —people crowded around radios
Example 2:	J. F. Kennedy's assassination —most widely shared flashbulb memory of our time —image of Kennedy's death burned into minds all over the world
Example 3:	World Trade Center attack —more recent flashbulb memory for millions —whether on morning commute or phone, will never forget

Conclusion: Flashbulb memories mark our most permanent and haunting experiences.

- Note that each example in the body of the paragraph clearly relates to the definition in the topic sentence.

Although examples are an excellent way to develop a definition paragraph, other methods of development are also possible. For instance, you might compare and contrast† *love* and *lust*, *assertiveness* and *aggressiveness*, or *the leader* and *the follower*. You could also combine definition and persuasion.‡ Such a paragraph might begin *College is a dating service* or *Alcoholism is not a moral weakness but a disease*. The rest of the paragraph would have to persuade readers that this definition is valid.

---

*For more work on examples, see Chapter 5, "Illustration."
†For more work on contrast, see Chapter 10, "Comparison and Contrast."
‡For more work on persuasion, see Chapter 13, "Persuasion."

There are no transitional expressions used specifically for definition paragraphs. Sometimes phrases like *can be defined as* or *can be considered* or *means that* can help alert the reader that a definition paragraph will follow.*

Here cartoonist Gary Larson takes a somewhat lighter look at flashbulb memory.

More facts of nature: All forest animals, to this very day, remember exactly where they were and what they were doing when they heard that Bambi's mother had been shot.

PRACTICE 5 Read the following paragraph carefully and then answer the questions.

A feminist is *not* a man-hater, a masculine woman, a demanding shrew, or someone who dislikes housewives. A feminist is simply a woman or man who believes that women should enjoy the same rights, privileges, opportunities, and pay as men. Because society has deprived women of many equal rights, feminists have fought for equality. For instance, Susan B. Anthony, a famous nineteenth-century feminist, worked to get women the right to vote. Today, feminists want women to receive equal pay for equal work. They support a woman's right to pursue her goals and dreams, whether she wants to be an astronaut, athlete, banker, or full-time homemaker. On the home front, feminists believe that two partners who work should equally share the housework and child care. Because the term is often misunderstood, some people don't call themselves feminists even though they share feminist values. But courageous feminists of both sexes continue to speak out for equality.

---

*For an entire essay developed by definition, see "Winning," Chapter 15, Part E.

1. The definition here spans two sentences. What kind of definition does the writer use in sentence 1? _____

2. What kind of definition appears in sentence 2? _____

3. The paragraph is developed by describing some key beliefs of feminists. What are these? _____

4. Which point is supported by an example? _____

5. Make a plan or an outline of the paragraph.

PRACTICE 6 Read the following paragraphs and answer the questions.

Induction is reasoning from particular cases to general principles; that is, the scientific method: you look at a number of examples, then come to a general conclusion based on the evidence. For instance, having known twenty-five people named Glenn, all of whom were men, you might naturally conclude, through induction, that all people named Glenn are men. The problem with inductive reasoning here, however, is Glenn Close, the movie actress.

Deduction is reasoning from the general to the particular. One starts from a statement known or merely assumed to be true and uses it to come to a conclusion about the matter at hand. Once you know that all people have to die sometime and that you are a person, you can logically deduce that you, too, will have to die sometime.

—Judy Jones and William Wilson, "100 Things Every College Graduate Should Know," *Esquire*

1. What two terms are defined? _____

_____

2. What kind of definition is used in both topic sentences? _____

_____

3. In what larger category do the writers place both induction and deduction? _____

_____

4. What example of induction do the writers give? _____

_____

5. What example shows the *problem* with induction? _____

_____

6. What example of deduction do the writers give? _____

_____

PRACTICE 7 Here are some topic sentences for definition paragraphs. Choose one that interests you and make a plan for a paragraph, using whatever method of development seems appropriate.

1. An optimist is someone who usually expects the best from life and from people.
2. Prejudice means prejudging people on the basis of race, creed, age, or sex—not on their merits as individuals.
3. A wealthy person does not necessarily have money and possessions, but he or she might possess inner wealth—a loving heart and a creative mind.
4. Registration is a ritual torture that students must go through before they can attend their classes.
5. Bravery and bravado are very different character traits.

PRACTICE 8 **Thinking and Writing Together**
Define a Team Player

Whether or not we play sports, most of us know what it means to be a *team player* on a basketball or soccer team. But these days, many employers also want to hire "team players." What, exactly, are they looking for? What qualities does a team player bring to the job?

In a group with four or five classmates, discuss the meaning of *team player*, listing all the qualities that you think a team player has. List at least eight qualities. Now craft a topic sentence of definition; have a group member write it down, using the form, "A team player is a/an _____ who _____." Choose the three or four most important qualities and write a paragraph defining *team player*. Use examples or details to bring your paragraph to life. Be prepared to share your paragraph with the full class.

Exploring Online

http://content.monster.com/tools/quizzes/teamplayer/ Take the team player quiz; write about your results.

http://web.cba.neu.edu/~ewertheim/teams/ovrvw2.htm Resources for "Surviving the Group Project"

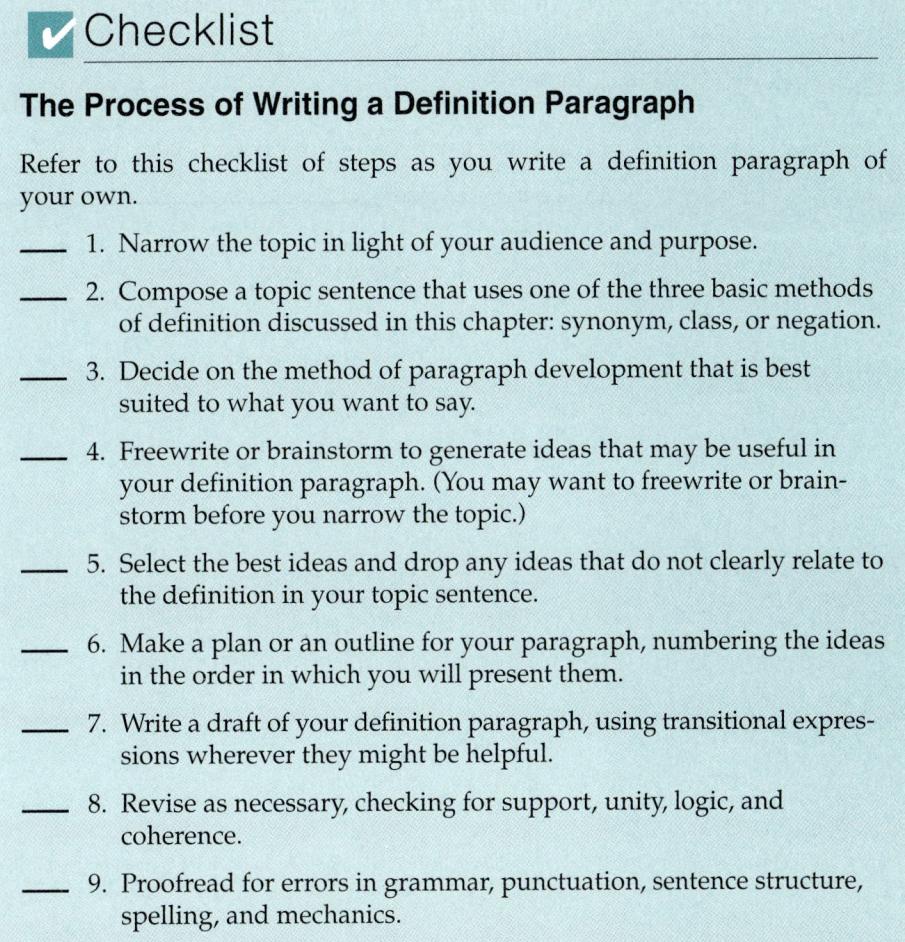

✔ Checklist

The Process of Writing a Definition Paragraph

Refer to this checklist of steps as you write a definition paragraph of your own.

____ 1. Narrow the topic in light of your audience and purpose.

____ 2. Compose a topic sentence that uses one of the three basic methods of definition discussed in this chapter: synonym, class, or negation.

____ 3. Decide on the method of paragraph development that is best suited to what you want to say.

____ 4. Freewrite or brainstorm to generate ideas that may be useful in your definition paragraph. (You may want to freewrite or brainstorm before you narrow the topic.)

____ 5. Select the best ideas and drop any ideas that do not clearly relate to the definition in your topic sentence.

____ 6. Make a plan or an outline for your paragraph, numbering the ideas in the order in which you will present them.

____ 7. Write a draft of your definition paragraph, using transitional expressions wherever they might be helpful.

____ 8. Revise as necessary, checking for support, unity, logic, and coherence.

____ 9. Proofread for errors in grammar, punctuation, sentence structure, spelling, and mechanics.

Suggested Topics for Definition Paragraphs

1. A self-starter
2. The loner (or life of the party, perfectionist, big mouth, Internet addict)
3. Country and western music (or rock, gospel, Celtic, or some other type of music)
4. A term from popular culture (email *spam*, *sampling* in music, *Spanglish*, and so on)
5. A dead-end job
6. A good marriage (or a good partner, parent, or friend)
7. The racing-car (or fashion, football, shopping, computer-game, or other) fanatic
8. An interesting term you know from reading (*placebo, UFO, apartheid, surrealism,* and so forth)
9. Spring break
10. A racist (terrorist, sexist, artist, philanthropist, or other *-ist*)
11. The night person (or morning person)
12. Integrity
13. A technical term you know from work or a hobby
14. A slang term you or your friends use
15. Writer's choice: _____

CHAPTER 10 Comparison and Contrast

PART A   The Contrast and the Comparison Paragraphs

PART B   The Comparison-Contrast Paragraph

To **contrast** two persons, places, or things is to examine the ways in which they are different. To **compare** them is to examine the ways in which they are similar.

Contrast and comparison are useful skills in daily life, work, and college. When you shop, you often compare and contrast. For instance, you might compare and contrast two dishwashers to get the better value. In fact, the magazine *Consumer Reports* was created to help consumers compare and contrast different product brands.

Your employer might ask you to compare and contrast two computers, two telephone services, or two shipping crates. Your job is to gather information about the similarities and differences to help your employer choose one over the other. In nearly every college course, you will be expected to compare and contrast—two generals, two types of storm systems, two minerals, or two painters of the same school.

Part A

The Contrast and the Comparison Paragraphs

Topic Sentence

Here is the topic sentence of a **contrast** paragraph:

> Although soul and hip-hop both spring from African-American roots, they are very different musical expressions.

- The writer begins a contrast paragraph with a topic sentence that clearly states what two persons, things, or ideas will be contrasted.
- What two things will be contrasted?

_____

115

- What word or words in the topic sentence make it clear that the writer will contrast soul and hip-hop?

_____

Paragraph and Plan

Here is the entire paragraph:

> Although soul and hip-hop both spring from African-American roots, they are very different musical expressions. Soul music borrows from gospel and rhythm and blues. The singer's voice, backed up by live instruments, soars with emotion, with soul. This music captures the optimism of its time—the civil rights movement of the 1960s and hope for social change. There are two types of soul—the smooth Detroit style of the Supremes, Stevie Wonder, and The Temptations and the more gritty, gospel-driven Memphis style of Otis Redding and Booker T and the MGs. Soul music is upbeat and often joyful; its subjects are love and affirmation of the human condition. On the other hand, hip-hop (or rap) draws on hard rock, funk, and techno. The rapper chants rhymes against a driving instrumental background that may be prerecorded. Rap grew out of the New York ghettos in the late 1970s and the 1980s, when crack and guns flooded "the hood" and many dreams seemed broken. Of the rival East and West Coast rappers, New Yorkers include Grandmaster Flash, LL Cool J, and the murdered Biggie Smalls, while Los Angeles rappers include Ice Cube and the murdered Tupac Shakur. The subjects of hip-hop are racism, crime, and poverty. Both soul and hip-hop claim to "tell it like it is." Hip-hop's answer to the soulful Four Tops is the Furious Four. What's in a name? Perhaps the way the listener experiences reality.
>
> —Maurice Bosco (Student)

- The writer first provides information about (A) soul music and then gives contrasting parallel information about (B) hip-hop.

- What information about (A) soul does the writer provide in the first half of the paragraph? _____

_____

_____

- What contrasting parallel information does the writer provide about (B) hip-hop in the second half of the paragraph? _____

_____

_____

- Why do you think the writer chose to present the points of contrast in this order? _____

- Note that the last four sentences provide a thoughtful conclusion. What final point does the writer make? _____

Before composing the paragraph, the writer probably brainstormed or freewrote to gather ideas and then made an **outline** or a **plan** like this:

Topic sentence: Although soul and hip-hop both spring from African-American roots, they are very different musical expressions.

Points of Contrast	A. Soul	B. Hip-Hop
1. influences	gospel, R&B	hard rock, funk, techno
2. sound	soaring voice, live instruments	chanted rhymes; instrumentals may be prerecorded
3. time period	1960s, civil rights, hope for change	1970s–80s, crack, guns
4. types	Detroit, Memphis	New York, Los Angeles
5. subjects	love, affirmation	racism, crime, poverty

Organized in this manner, the plan for this contrast paragraph helps the writer make sure that the paragraph will be complete. That is, if the historical period of soul is discussed, that of hip-hop must also be discussed, and so on, for every point of contrast.

Here is another way to write the same paragraph:

> Although soul and hip-hop both spring from African-American roots, they are very different musical expressions. Soul music borrows from gospel and rhythm and blues, whereas hip-hop (or rap) draws on hard rock, funk, and techno. The soul singer's voice, backed up by live instruments, soars with emotion, with soul; however, the rapper chants rhymes against a driving instrumental background that may be prerecorded. Soul music captures the optimism of its time—the civil rights movement of the 1960s and hope for social change. On the other hand,

> hip-hop grew out of the New York ghettos in the late 1970s and the 1980s, when crack and guns flooded "the hood" and many dreams seemed broken. There are two types of soul—the smooth Detroit style of the Supremes, Stevie Wonder, and The Temptations and the more gritty, gospel-driven Memphis style of Otis Redding and Booker T and the MGs. Of the rival East and West Coast rappers, New Yorkers include Grandmaster Flash, LL Cool J, and the murdered Biggie Smalls, while Los Angeles rappers include Ice Cube and the murdered Tupac Shakur. Whereas soul music's subjects are love and affirmation of the human condition, the subjects of hip-hop are racism, crime, and poverty. Both soul and hip-hop claim to "tell it like it is." Hip-hop's answer to the soulful Four Tops is the Furious Four. What's in a name? Perhaps the way the listener experiences reality.

- Instead of giving all the information about soul music and then going on to hip-hop, this paragraph moves back and forth between soul and hip-hop, dealing with *each point of contrast separately.*

Use either one of these **two patterns** when writing a contrast or a comparison paragraph:

> 1. Present all the information about **A** and then provide parallel information about **B**:
>
> **First all A:**   point 1
>   point 2
>   point 3
>
> **Then all B:**   point 1
>   point 2
>   point 3

- This pattern is good for paragraphs and for short compositions. The reader can easily remember what was said about A by the time he or she gets to B.

> 2. Move back and forth between **A** and **B**. Present one point about **A** and then go to the parallel point about **B**. Then move to the next point and do the same:
>
> **First A,** point 1;   **then B,** point 1
>
> **First A,** point 2;   **then B,** point 2
>
> **First A,** point 3;   **then B,** point 3

- The second pattern is better for longer papers, where it might be hard for the reader to remember what the writer said about A by the time he or she gets to B a few paragraphs later. By going back and forth, the writer makes it easier for the reader to keep the contrasts or comparisons in mind.

What you have learned so far about planning a contrast paragraph holds true for a comparison paragraph as well. Just remember that *contrast stresses differences* whereas *comparison stresses similarities.*

Here is a **comparison** paragraph:

> In my family, personality traits are said to skip generations, so that might explain why my grandfather and I have so much in common. My grandfather arrived in the United States at sixteen, a penniless young man from Italy looking for a new life and ready to earn it. He quickly apprenticed himself to a shoe cobbler and never stopped working until he retired fifty-three years later. Similarly, when I was fourteen, I asked permission to apply for my first job as a bank teller. My parents smiled and said, "She's just like Grandpa." Though everyone else in my family spends money the minute it reaches their hands, my habit of saving every penny does not seem strange to them. My grandfather also was careful with money, building his own shoe repair business out of nothing. He loved to work in his large vegetable garden and brought bags of carrots and tomatoes to our house on Saturday mornings. Like him, I enjoy the feeling of dirt on my fingers and the surprise of seedlings sprouting overnight. Though I raise zinnias instead of zucchinis, I know where I inherited a passion to make things grow. Only in opportunities, we differed. Although my grandfather's education ended with third grade, I am fortunate to attend college—and hope that education will be my legacy to the generations that come after me.
>
> —Angela De Renzi (Student)

- What words in the topic sentence does the writer use to indicate that a comparison will follow? _____

- In what ways are the writer and her grandfather similar? _____

- What transitional words stress the similarities? _____

- What pattern of presentation does the writer use? _____

- What one point of *contrast* serves as a strong punch line for the paragraph? _____

- Make a plan or an outline of this comparison paragraph.

Transitional Expressions

Transitional expressions in contrast paragraphs stress opposition and difference:

Transitional Expressions for Contrast	
although	on the other hand
whereas	in contrast
but	while
however	yet
conversely	unlike

Transitional expressions in comparison paragraphs stress similarities:

Transitional Expressions for Comparison	
in the same way	just as . . . so
and, also, in addition	similarly
as well as	like
both, neither	too
each of	the same

As you write, avoid using just one or two of these transitional expressions. Learn new ones from the list and practice them in your paragraphs.*

PRACTICE 1 Read the following paragraph carefully and answer the questions.

Certain personality traits, like whether a person is more reactive or proactive, can predict success or its opposite. In his book *The Seven Habits of Highly Effective People,* Steven Covey writes that reactive people tend to sit back and wait for life or circumstances to bring them opportunities. They react instead of act. When good things happen, they are happy, but when bad things happen, they feel like victims. Reactive people often say things like, "There's nothing I can do," "I can't because . . . ," and "If only." In the short term, reactive people might feel comfortable playing it safe, holding back, and avoiding challenges; in the long term, though, they are often left dreaming. On the other hand, proactive people know that they have the power to choose their responses to whatever life brings. They act instead of react: If things aren't going their way, they take action to help create the outcome they desire. Proactive people can be recognized by their tendency to say things like "Let's consider the alternatives," "I prefer," "We can," and "I will." In the short term, proactive people might face the discomfort of failing because they take on challenges, set goals, and work toward them. But in the long term, Covey says, proactive people are the ones who achieve their dreams.

---

*For an entire essay developed by comparison-contrast, see "E-Notes from an Online Learner," Chapter 15, Part F.

1. Can you tell from the topic sentence whether a contrast or comparison will follow? _____

2. What two personality types are being contrasted? _____

3. What information does the writer provide about reactive people? _____

4. What parallel information does the writer provide about proactive people?

5. What pattern does the writer of this paragraph use to present the contrasts?

6. What transitional expression does the writer use to stress the shift from A to B? _____

PRACTICE 2 This paragraph is hard to follow because it lacks transitional expressions that emphasize contrast. Revise the paragraph, adding transitional expressions of contrast. Strive for variety.

Either a cold or the flu can make you miserable, so does it really matter which one you have? Experts say it does because a cold will go away by itself. The flu can lead to pneumonia and other serious or even deadly problems. A cold usually comes on gradually, accompanied by little or no fever. The flu comes on suddenly, and its fever can spike as high as 104 degrees and linger for three or four days. Someone with a cold might experience mild body aches and fatigue. The flu often brings severe body aches, deep fatigue, chills, and a major headache. In general, a cold is wet, with much congestion, a runny nose and even runny eyes. The flu is far drier, marked by a dry cough. Because both are caused by viruses, little can be done to cure them except rest, fluids, zinc lozenges perhaps, and a good, long book.

PRACTICE 3 Below are three plans for contrast paragraphs. The points of contrast in the second column do not follow the same order as the points in the first column. In addition, one detail is missing. First, number the points in the second column to match those in the first. Then fill in the missing detail.

1. **Shopping at a Supermarket** **Shopping at a Local Grocery**

    1. carries all brands ___ personal service

    2. lower prices ___ closed on Sundays

    3. open seven days a week ___ prices often higher

    4. little personal service ___ _____

    5. no credit ___ credit available for steady customers

2. **My Son** **My Daughter**

    1. fifteen years old ___ good at making minor household repairs

    2. likes to be alone ___ likes to be with friends

    3. reads a lot ___ doesn't like to read

    4. is an excellent cook ___ expects to attend a technical college

    5. wants to go to chef school ___ _____

3. **Job A** **Job B**

    1. good salary ___ three-week vacation

    2. office within walking distance ___ work on a team with others

    3. two-week vacation ___ one-hour bus ride to office

    4. work alone ___ health insurance

    5. lots of overtime ___ no overtime

    6. no health insurance ___ _____

PRACTICE 4 Here are three topics for either contrast or comparison paragraphs. Compose two topic sentences for each topic, one for a possible contrast paragraph and one for a possible comparison paragraph.

	Topic		Topic Sentences
Example	Two members of my family	A.	My brother and sister have different attitudes toward exercise.
		B.	My parents are alike in that they're easygoing.
1.	Two friends or coworkers	A.	
		B.	
2.	You as a child and you as an adult	A.	
		B.	
3.	Two vacations	A.	
		B.	

PRACTICE 5   Here are four topic sentences for comparison or contrast paragraphs. For each topic sentence, think of one supporting point of comparison or contrast and explain that point in one or two sentences.

1. When it comes to movies (TV shows, books, entertainment), Demetrios and Arlene have totally different tastes.

   _____

   _____

2. My mother and I have few personality traits in common. _____

   _____

3. Although there are obvious differences, the two neighborhoods (blocks, homes) have much in common.

   _____

   _____

4. Paying taxes is like having a tooth pulled.*

   _____

   _____

* For more work on this kind of comparison, see Chapter 22, "Revising for Language Awareness," Part D.

PRACTICE 6 Study the photograph on page 124 of a sunbather at the Indiana Dunes National Lakeshore. Then write a paragraph *contrasting* the man and his rather unusual surroundings. Notice the man's posture, clothing, and apparent mood. How do these differ from the scene on the dunes behind him? In your topic sentence, state your overall impression. Then support this main idea with details. Remember to conclude your paragraph; don't just stop abruptly.

PRACTICE 7 **Thinking and Writing Together**
Contrast Toys for Boys and Toys for Girls

Stores like Toys-R-Us frequently recommend toys for different age groups, often dividing their suggestions into "toys for boys" and "toys for girls." In a group with four or five classmates, examine and discuss these typical "great gift ideas" for six-year-olds, made by Etoys.com in 2000:

Boys	Girls
Pro Pitcher baseball-pitching machine	Patty Playground Interactive doll
Wild Planet wrist walkie-talkies	Barbie Dream Bed and Bath
Fisher-Price pirate ship	My First Phonebook
Nerf Triple Strike arrow shooter	Yoga Kit for Kids
Hot Wheels X-V Racers Daytona 500 Superspeedway Set	Baskin-Robbins ice cream maker

Based on these lists, what contrasting messages are being sent about what boys and girls supposedly like to do? Is one list more active or passive? More indoors or out? More fun? Do these lists put unfair limits on children of either sex? Now plan and write a comparison-contrast paragraph based on your discussion.

Exploring Online

http://www.google.com/ or your favorite search engine; search, "toys, gender roles."

 Checklist

The Process of Writing a Contrast or Comparison Paragraph

Refer to this checklist of steps as you write a contrast or comparison paragraph of your own.

____ 1. Narrow the topic in light of your audience and purpose.

____ 2. Compose a topic sentence that clearly states that a contrast or a comparison will follow.

____ 3. Freewrite or brainstorm to generate as many points of contrast or comparison as you can think of. (You may want to freewrite or brainstorm before you narrow the topic.)

> _____ 4. Choose the points you will use, and drop any details that are not really part of the contrast or the comparison.
>
> _____ 5. List parallel points of contrast or of comparison for both *A* and *B*.
>
> _____ 6. Make a plan or an outline, numbering all the points of contrast or comparison in the order in which you will present them in the paragraph.
>
> _____ 7. Write a draft of your contrast or comparison paragraph, using transitional expressions that stress either differences or similarities.
>
> _____ 8. Revise as necessary, checking for support, unity, logic, and coherence.
>
> _____ 9. Proofread for errors in grammar, punctuation, sentence structure, spelling, and mechanics.

Suggested Topics for Contrast or Comparison Paragraphs

1. Compare or contrast two attitudes toward money (the spendthrift and the miser) or dating (the confirmed single and the committed partner).
2. Compare or contrast two young children parented in different ways.
3. Compare or contrast a job you hated and a job you loved.
4. Compare or contrast two athletes in the same sport.
5. Compare or contrast the same scene at two times of day.
6. Compare or contrast two high schools or colleges that you have attended (perhaps one in the United States and one in a different country).
7. Compare or contrast two ways to treat an illness or headache—Western medicine and some alternative.
8. Compare or contrast your *expectations* of a person, place, or situation and *reality*.
9. Compare or contrast your best friend and your spouse or partner.
10. Writer's choice: _____

Part B

The Comparison-Contrast Paragraph

Sometimes an assignment will ask you to write a paragraph that both compares and contrasts, one that stresses both similarities and differences.

Here is a comparison-contrast paragraph:

> Although contemporary fans would find the game played by the Knickerbockers—the first organized baseball club—similar to modern baseball, they would also note some startling differences. In 1845, as now, the four bases of the playing field were set in a diamond shape, ninety feet from one another. Nine players took the field. The object of the game was to score points by hitting a pitched ball and running around the bases. The teams changed sides after three outs. However, the earlier game was also different. The umpire sat at a table along the third base line instead of standing behind home plate. Unlike the modern game, the players wore no gloves. Rather than firing the ball over the plate at ninety miles an hour, the pitcher gently tossed it underhand to the batter. Since there were no balls and strikes, the batter could wait for the pitch he wanted. The game ended, not when nine innings were completed, but when one team scored twenty-one runs, which were called "aces."

- How are the Knickerbockers' game and modern baseball similar?

　

- How are these two versions of the game different?

　

- What transitional expressions in the paragraph emphasize similarities and differences?

Before composing this comparison-contrast paragraph, the writer probably brainstormed or freewrote to gather ideas and then made a plan like this:

Topic sentence: Although contemporary fans would find the game played by the Knickerbockers—the first organized baseball club—similar to modern baseball, they would also note some startling differences.

Comparisons	Knickerbockers	Modern Game
Point 1	four bases, ninety feet apart, in diamond shape	
Point 2	nine players	
Point 3	scoring points	
Point 4	three outs	
Contrasts		
Point 1	umpire sat at third base line	umpire at home plate
Point 2	no gloves	gloves
Point 3	pitcher gently tossed ball	pitcher fires ball at plate
Point 4	no balls and strikes	balls and strikes
Point 5	twenty-one "aces" to win, no innings	most runs to win, nine innings

---

- A plan such as this makes it easier for the writer to organize a great deal of material.
- The writer begins by listing all the points of comparison—how the Knickerbockers' game and modern baseball are similar. Then the writer lists all the points of contrast—how they are different.

PRACTICE 8 Here is a somewhat longer comparison and contrast (two paragraphs). Read it carefully and answer the questions.

No meal eaten in the Middle East ends without coffee or tea, but coffee takes precedence most of the time. Coffee is a social beverage, offered to guests by housewives and to customers by merchants; to refuse it borders upon insult. There are two distinct but similar ways of preparing it, Turkish and Arabic. Both are served black, in cups the size of a demitasse or smaller. And both are brewed by starting with green beans, roasting them to a chocolate brown color, pulverizing them at once, either with mortar and pestle or in a handsome cylindrical coffee mill of chased brass, and quickly steeping them in boiling water.

The Turkish version is made in a coffee pot that has a long handle to protect the fingers from the fire and a shape narrowing from the bottom to the open neck to intensify the foaming action as the coffee boils up. Water, sugar and coffee are stirred together to your taste; then, at the first bubbling surge, the pot is whisked from the fire. It is returned briefly one or two more times to build up the foamy head, which is poured into each cup in equal amounts, to be followed by the rest of the brew, grounds and all. The dregs soon settle to the bottom, and the rich, brown coffee that covers them is ready to be enjoyed, with more sugar if you like. The Arabs prepare coffee in a single boil; they almost never use sugar; they pour the liquid into a second pot, leaving the sediment in the first, and then add such heady spices as cloves or cardamon seeds.

—*Foods of the World/Middle Eastern Cooking,* Time-Life Books

1. What two things does this writer contrast and compare? _____

_____

_____

2. What words indicate that both contrast *and* comparison will follow?

_____

3. How are Arabic and Turkish coffee similar? _____

_____

_____

_____

_____

4. How are Arabic and Turkish coffee different? _____

_____

_____

_____

5. On a separate sheet of paper, make a plan or an outline for these paragraphs.

PRACTICE 9 On page 130 you will find a cartoon showing two women in a department store. Study the two women in detail: their clothing, ages, facial expressions, and so forth. Notice the name of the perfume the taller one is holding. For a paragraph that compares and contrasts the women, jot down similarities and differences. Ask yourself, "What is going on here? What is my impression of each woman? Do the similarities or differences between them add to the humor of the cartoon?" Then plan and write your paragraph.

Original Artwork by Ian Falconer. Copyright © 2002 Condé Nast Publications, Inc. Reprinted by permission. All Rights Reserved.

Working Through the Comparison-Contrast Paragraph

You can work through the comparison-contrast paragraph in the same way that you do a comparison or a contrast paragraph. Follow the steps in the earlier checklist, but make certain that your paragraph shows both similarities and differences.

Suggested Topics for Comparison-Contrast Paragraphs

1. Compare and contrast calling on a cell phone and a regular phone.
2. Compare and contrast the requirements for two jobs or careers.
3. Compare and contrast your life now with your life five years ago.
4. Compare and contrast two films on similar subjects.
5. Compare and contrast learning something from experience and learning something from books.
6. Compare and contrast two singers or musicians.
7. Compare and contrast parties, weddings, or funerals in two different cultures.
8. Compare and contrast two popular television programs of the same type (newscasts, situation comedies, talk shows, and so on).
9. Compare and contrast two attitudes toward one subject (firearms, education, immigration, and so forth).
10. Writer's choice: _____

CHAPTER 11 Classification

To **classify** is to gather into types, kinds, or categories according to a single basis of division.

Mailroom personnel, for example, might separate incoming mail into four piles: orders, bills, payments, and inquiries. Once the mail has been divided in this manner—according to which department should receive each pile—it can be efficiently delivered.

The same information can be classified in more than one way. The Census Bureau collects a variety of data about the people living in the United States. One way to classify the data is by age group—the number of people under eighteen, between eighteen and fifty-five, over fifty-five, and over seventy. Such information might be useful in developing programs for college-bound youth or for the elderly. Other ways of dividing the population are by geographic location, occupation, family size, level of education, and so on.

Whether you classify rocks by their origin for a geology course or children by their stages of growth for a psychology course, you will be organizing large groups into smaller, more manageable units that can be explained to your reader.

Topic Sentence

Here is the topic sentence for a classification paragraph:

> Gym-goers can be classified according to their priorities at the gym as sweaty fanatics, fashionites, busybodies, or fit normals.

- The writer begins a classification paragraph with a topic sentence that clearly states what group of people or things will be classified.
- What group of people will be classified? _____
- Into how many categories will they be divided? What are the categories?

_____

_____

Paragraph and Plan

Here is the entire paragraph:

> Gym-goers can be classified according to their priorities at the gym as sweaty fanatics, fashionites, busybodies, and fit normals. Sweaty fanatics take gym-going to the extreme. They hog the machines, drip sweat everywhere, and barely look up if someone falls off the treadmill beside them. Occasionally, they will stare at the mirror, admiring the muscle group they are working on. The fashionites also admire their own reflections, but they barely break a sweat. For them, the gym is just another excuse to buy clothes. They wear perfectly matched workout clothes with color-coordinated sport watches and gym shoes. The third group, the busybodies, can't stop talking. Whether it's making idle chitchat or correcting another exerciser's form on a machine, they seem unable to shut up. Not even headphones and one-word answers can stop the busybodies from babbling. Luckily, the fit normals keep things from getting too far out of control. They come to the gym to work out, stay healthy, and go home, but they remember that basic good manners apply in every setting.
>
> —Laurie Zamot (Student)

- On what basis does the writer classify gym-goers? *Priorities*

- What information does the writer provide about the first type, sweaty fanatics?
  They take going to the gym to the extreme

- What information does the writer provide about the second type, fashionites?
  Their clothing is more important

- What information does the writer provide about the third type, busybodies?
  They talk to much

- What information does the writer provide about the fourth type, the fit normals?
  They keep the gym normal

- Why do you think the writer discusses fit normals last? *Because they use the gym for what it is there for.*

Before composing the paragraph, the writer probably brainstormed or free-wrote to gather ideas and then made an **outline** or **plan** like this:

Topic sentence: Gym-goers can be classified according to their priorities at the gym as sweaty fanatics, fashionites, busybodies, or fit normals.

> **Type 1:** Sweaty fanatics
> —hog machines; drip sweat
> —barely look if someone falls
> —stare in mirror, admiring muscles
>
> **Type 2:** Fashionites
> —admire themselves but don't sweat
> —excuse to buy clothes
> —matched workout clothes
> —coordinating sport watches and gym shoes
>
> **Type 3:** Busybodies
> —can't stop talking, advising
> —headphones, short answers don't work
>
> **Type 4:** Fit normals
> —keep things from going out of control
> —work out, go home
> —remember good manners even in gym

- Note that the body of the paragraph discusses all four types of gym-goers mentioned in the topic sentence and does not add any new ones.

This classification paragraph sticks to a single method of classification: *the priorities of gym-goers at the gym*. If the paragraph had also discussed a fourth category—*left-handed gym-goers*—the initial basis of classification would fall apart because *left-handedness* has nothing to do with *the priorities of different gym-goers*.

The topic sentence of a classification paragraph usually has two parts: the *topic* and the *basis of classification*. The basis of classification is the controlling idea: it *controls* how the writer will approach the topic. Stating it in writing will help keep the paragraph on track.

There is no set rule about which category to present first, second, or last in a classification paragraph. However, the paragraph should follow some kind of **logical sequence** from the most to least outrageous, least to most expensive, from the largest to the smallest category, and so on.*†

---

* For more work on order, see Chapter 4, "Achieving Coherence," Part A.
† For a complete essay developed by classification, see "The Potato Scale," Chapter 15, Part G.

Transitional Expressions

Transitional expressions in classification paragraphs stress divisions and categories:

Transitional Expressions for Classification	
can be divided	the first type
can be classified	the second kind
can be categorized	the last category

PRACTICE 1 Read the following paragraph carefully and answer the questions.

Judges can be divided, on the basis of their written opinions, into three categories: conservative, liberal, and centrist. Although all judges respect the law, conservative judges have an especially strong belief in the importance of the law and the history surrounding it. They believe that real justice comes only from strictly applying the law to the facts of a case, whether or not the outcome seems fair to an individual. On the other hand, liberal judges look beyond a rigid reading to the "spirit of the law" in their search for real justice in a case. They might broadly interpret the law in order to champion individual rights. The outcome of the case matters more to them than the letter of the law. Finally, centrist judges walk the middle ground between conservative and liberal. They do not apply the law as rigidly as conservative judges, yet they are not as willing as liberal judges to apply the law loosely. Having different types of judges helps balance our legal system; their differing views help protect both the law and individual rights.

1. How many categories are there, and what are they?

   3, conservative, liberal, centrist

2. On what basis does the writer classify judges?

   written opinions

3. Make a plan of the paragraph on a separate sheet of paper.

PRACTICE 2 Each group of things or persons on the following page has been divided according to a single basis of classification. However, one item in each group does not belong—it does not fit that single basis of classification.

Read each group of items carefully; then circle the letter of the one item that does *not* belong. Next write the single basis of classification that includes the rest of the group.

Example Shirts
a. cotton
b. suede
(c.) short-sleeved
d. polyester
material they are made of

1. Shoes
   a. flat heels
   b. 2-inch heels
   c. *(circled)* patent leather heels
   d. 3-inch heels

   Sizes of heels

2. Dates
   a. *(circled)* very good-looking
   b. sometimes pay
   c. always pay
   d. expect me to pay

   _____

3. Students
   a. *(circled)* talkative in class
   b. very hard-working
   c. goof-offs
   d. moderately hard-working

   How hard they work

4. Contact lenses
   a. *(circled)* soft
   b. green
   c. brown
   d. lavender

   Colors

5. Milk
   a. 2 percent fat
   b. whole
   c. *(circled)* chocolate
   d. 1 percent fat

   Types of ~~(crossed out)~~

6. Drivers
   a. obey the speed limit
   b. *(circled)* teenage drivers
   c. speeders
   d. creepers

   _____

PRACTICE 3 Any group of persons, things, or ideas can be classified in more than one way, depending on the basis of classification. For instance, students in your class can be classified on the basis of height (short, average, tall) or on the basis of class participation (often participate, sometimes participate, never participate). Both of these groupings are valid classifications of the same group of people.

Think of two ways in which each of the following groups could be classified.

Example	Group		Basis of Classification
	Bosses	(A)	how demanding they are
		(B)	how generous they are
	1. Members of my family	(A)	_____
		(B)	_____
	2. Hurricanes	(A)	_____
		(B)	_____
	3. Fans of a certain sport	(A)	_____
		(B)	_____
	4. Vacations	(A)	_____
		(B)	_____
	5. Fitness magazines	(A)	_____
		(B)	_____

PRACTICE 4 Listed below are three groups of people or things. Decide on a single basis of classification for each group and the categories that would develop from your basis of classification. Finally, write a topic sentence for each of your classifications.

Example

Group	Basis of Classification	Categories
Professors at Pell College	methods of instruction	1. lectures 2. class discussions 3. both

Topic Sentence: Professors at Pell College can be classified according to their methods of instruction: those who lecture, those who encourage class discussions, and those who do both.

Group	Basis of Classification	Categories
1. Car owners	_____	_____

Topic Sentence: _____

Group	Basis of Classification	Categories
2. Credit-card users	_____	_____

Topic Sentence: _____

3. Ways of reacting   how much
   to crisis

                         emotions

Topic Sentence: _____

_____

_____

_____

PRACTICE 5 Now choose the classification in Practice 4 that most interests you and make a plan or outline for a paragraph on a separate sheet of paper. As you work, make sure that you have listed all possible categories for your basis of classification. Remember, every car owner or credit-card user should fit into one of your categories. Finally, write your paragraph, describing each category briefly and perhaps giving an example of each.

PRACTICE 6 **Thinking and Writing Together**
Classify Students on Campus

In a group with four or five classmates, discuss some interesting ways in which you might classify the students at your college. List at least five possible ways. You might focus on students in just one place—like the computer lab, swimming pool, coffee stand, library, or an exam room during finals week. Then come up with one basis of classification, either serious or humorous. For example, you could classify swimmers according to their level of expertise or splashing; students during finals week according to their fashion statements; or students standing in line for coffee according to their degree of impatience.

Now choose the most interesting basis of classification. Name three or four categories that cover the group, and write a paragraph classifying your fellow students. You might wish to enrich your categories with details and examples. Be prepared to read your paragraph to the full class.

Exploring Online

http://www.filmratings.com/ Click "ratings guide" for movie classifications.
http://sln.fi.edu/tfi/units/life/classify/classify.html Introduction to the classification of plants and animals.

✓ Checklist

The Process of Writing a Classification Paragraph

Refer to this checklist of steps as you write a classification paragraph.

____ 1. Narrow the topic in light of your audience and purpose. Think in terms of a group of people or things that can be classified easily into types or categories.

____ 2. Decide on a single basis of classification. This basis will depend on what information you wish to give your audience.

____ 3. Compose a topic sentence that clearly shows what you are dividing into categories or types. If you wish, your topic sentence can state the basis on which you are making the classification and the types that will be discussed in the paragraph.

____ 4. List the categories into which the group is being classified. Be sure that your categories cover all the possibilities. Do not add any new categories that are not logically part of your original basis of classification.

____ 5. Freewrite, cluster, or brainstorm to generate information, details, and examples for each of the categories. (You may want to prewrite before you narrow the topic.)

____ 6. Select the best details and examples, and drop those that are not relevant to your classification.

____ 7. Make a plan or an outline for your paragraph, numbering the categories in the order in which you will present them.

____ 8. Write a draft of your classification paragraph, using transitional expressions wherever they may be helpful.

____ 9. Revise as necessary, checking for support, unity, logic, and coherence.

____ 10. Proofread for errors in grammar, punctuation, sentence structure, spelling, and mechanics.

Suggested Topics for Classification Paragraphs

1. Shoppers
2. Jobs
3. Women or men you date
4. Clothing in your closet

5. Friends
6. Dancers at a party
7. Problems facing college freshmen or someone new to a job
8. College classes or instructors
9. Ways to prevent school violence
10. Neighbors or coworkers
11. Kinds of success
12. Performers of one type of music
13. Kinds of marriages
14. Brands of jeans, backpacks, cola drinks, or some other product
15. Writer's choice: _____

CHAPTER 12   Cause and Effect

The ability to think through **causes and effects** is a key to success in many college courses, jobs, and everyday situations. Daily we puzzle over the **causes** of, or reasons for, events: What caused one brother to drop out of school and another to succeed brilliantly? What causes Jenine's asthma attacks? Why did the stock market plunge 300 points?

Effects are the *results* of a cause or causes. Does playing violent computer games affect a child's behavior? What are the effects of being a twin, keeping a secret, or winning the lottery?

Most events worth examining have complex, not simple, causes and effects. That is, they may have several causes and several effects. Certainly, in many fields, questions of cause and effect challenge even the experts: *What will be the long-term effects of the breakup of the former Soviet Union? What causes the HIV virus to disappear from the blood of some infected babies?* (This one answer could help save millions of lives.)

Topic Sentence

Here is the topic statement of a cause and effect paragraph; the writer has chosen to break the information into two sentences.

> What killed off the dinosaurs—and 70 percent of life on earth—65 million years ago? According to recent research, this massive destruction had three causes.

- The writer begins a cause and effect paragraph by clearly stating the subject and indicating whether causes or effects will be discussed. What is the subject of this paragraph? Will causes or effects be the focus? _____

_____

141

- The writer states the topic in two sentences rather than one. Is this effective? Why or why not? (A single sentence might read, "According to recent research, the massive destruction of dinosaurs and other creatures 65 million years ago had three causes.") _____

- Words like *causes, reasons,* and *factors* are useful to show causes. Words like *effects, results,* and *consequences* are useful to show effects.

Paragraph and Plan

Here is the entire paragraph:

> What killed off the dinosaurs—and 70 percent of life on earth—65 million years ago? According to recent research, this massive destruction had three causes. Dr. Peter Ward of the University of Washington reports that the first cause was simple "background extinction." This is the normal disappearance of some animals and plants that goes on all the time. Second, a drop in sea level during this period slowly destroyed about 25 percent more of the world's species. Last and most dramatic, a comet as big as Manhattan smashed into the earth near Mexico's Yucatan peninsula, literally shaking the world. The huge buried crater left by this comet was found in 1991. Now Dr. Ward has proved that ash and a rare metal from that fiery crash fell around the globe. This means that the impact, fires, smoke, and ash quickly wiped out the dinosaurs and much of life on earth. This great "die-off" cleared the way for mammals to dominate the earth.

- How many causes does this writer give for the destruction of the dinosaurs and other species? What are they? _____

- Did the writer make up these ideas? If not, who or what is the source of the information? _____

- What transitional words introduce each of the three causes? _____

- What kind of order is used in this paragraph?* _____

---

*For more work on order, see Chapter 4, "Achieving Coherence," Part A.

Before writing the paragraph, the writer probably jotted an outline or plan like this:

Topic sentence: According to recent research, this massive destruction had three causes.
      —write a catchy introductory sentence?
      —mention time, 65 million years ago

Cause 1: "background extinction"
      —normal disappearance of animals and plants
      —give credit to Dr. Ward

Cause 2: drop in sea level
      —25 percent more species destroyed

Cause 3: giant comet hit earth
      —big as Manhattan
      —crater found in 1991 near Yucatan peninsula
      —now Ward proves ash and rare metal circled globe
      —this comet destroyed dinosaurs and others

Conclusion: "die-off" cleared way for mammals—OR tie to current news and films about comet danger

---

Other paragraphs examine *effects*, not causes. Either they try to predict future effects of something happening now, or they analyze past effects of something that happened earlier, as does this paragraph:

    For Christy Haubegger, the lack of Latina role models had life-changing consequences. As a Mexican-American girl adopted by Anglo parents, Christy found no reflection of herself in teen magazines or books. One result of seeing mostly blonde, blue-eyed models was an increase in her adolescent insecurities. A more damaging effect was Christy's confusion as she wondered what career to pursue; there were no Hispanic role models in schoolbooks to suggest possible futures for this excellent student. Even at Stanford Law School, Christy and her friends missed the inspiration and encouragement of professional Latina role models. At Stanford, Christy began to see this problem as an opportunity. She decided to start a national magazine that would showcase talented and successful Latinas. The 27-year-old made a detailed business plan and, incredibly, won the financial backing of the CEO of *Essence* magazine. In 1996, the first issue of *Latina* hit the newstands—the very positive consequence of an old loneliness.

- Underline the topic sentence in this paragraph.

- For Ms. Haubegger, the lack of Latina role models caused "life-changing consequences." What effects are discussed? _____

- What order does the writer follow? _____

- Notice that the paragraph first discusses negative effects and then a positive one.

Before you write about causes or effects, do some mental detective work. First, search out the three most important causes or effects. For example, if you are trying to understand the causes of a friend's skiing accident, you might consider the snow conditions that day, whether he took unnecessary risks, and whether he had been drinking.

Causes	Effect	Further Effects
ice on the ski slope		can't drive
J. took steep course	J. breaks his leg	can't play sports
had two beers		decides to read more

In exploring the effects of something, consider both short-term and long-term effects and both negative and positive effects. (Although Jay could *not* do many things, perhaps he took advantage of his recovery time to read more or to learn a new computer program.)

Avoiding Problems in Cause and Effect Writing

1. **Do not oversimplify.** Avoid the trap of naming one cause for a complex problem: *Why did they divorce? Because she is a hothead.* Or *The reason that reading scores have fallen in the school is television.* Searching for the three most important causes or effects is a good way to avoid oversimplifying.

2. **Do not confuse time order with causation.** If your eye starts watering seconds after the doorbell rings, you cannot assume that the doorbell made your eye water. Were you peeling onions? Is it allergy season? Do you need to wet your contact lenses?

3. **Do not confuse causes and effects.** This sounds obvious, but separating causes and effects can be tricky. (Is Rita's positive attitude the cause of her success in sales or the result of it?)

Transitional Expressions

These transitional expressions are helpful in cause and effect paragraphs, which often imply order of importance or time order:*

---

*To read an essay of cause and effect, see "Why I Stayed and Stayed," Chapter 15, Part H.

Transitional Expressions	
To Show Causes	**To Show Effects**
the first cause (second, third)	one important effect
the first reason (second, third)	another result
yet another factor	a third outcome
because	as a result
is caused by	consequently
results from	then, next, therefore, thus, so

PRACTICE 1 Read this paragraph and answer the questions.

   Sadly, this college is part of a national trend: Date rape is on the rise. To stop date rape, college administrators and students must understand and deal with its possible causes. First, some fraternities and male peer groups on campus promote an attitude of disrespect toward women. This mentality sets the stage for date rape. Second, alcohol and drugs erode good judgment and self-control. The kegs, barrels, and bags consumed at many parties here put students at risk, including the risk of date rape. A third cause of date rape is miscommunication between men and women. Men and women often have different ideas of what date rape is or even if it exists. We need campus workshops in which we can discuss this issue openly and come to some understanding between the sexes. Date rape is a serious problem that can ruin lives. We can make a difference by addressing the causes of date rape: the male mentality of disrespect, heavy campus use of alcohol and drugs, and the differing views of men and women.

   —Michael White Moon (Student)

1. Underline the topic sentence. Does this paragraph discuss the causes or effects of date rape? _____

2. Do you agree with this student's analysis of the problem? Would you name other causes, and if so, which? _____

3. On a separate sheet of paper, make a plan of this paragraph.

4. Does Mr. White Moon discuss the three causes in a logical order? Why or why not? _____

UNIT 3 Developing the Paragraph

PRACTICE 2 To practice separating cause from effect, write the cause and the effect contained in each item below.

Example Fewer people are attending concerts at the Boxcar Theater because ticket prices have nearly doubled.

Cause: *ticket prices nearly doubled*

Effect: *fewer people attending concerts*

1. A thunderstorm was approaching, so we moved our picnic into the van.

   Cause: _____

   Effect: _____

2. Seeing my father suffer because he could not read motivated me to excel in school.

   Cause: _____

   Effect: _____

3. One study showed that laughter extended the lives of cancer patients.

   Cause: _____

   Effect: _____

4. Americans are having fewer children and doing so later in life. Some experts believe this is why they are spending more money every year on their pets.

   Cause: _____

   Effect: _____

5. According to NBA coach Phil Jackson, what turns talent into greatness is hard work.

   Cause: _____

   Effect: _____

6. Many doctors urged that trampolines be banned because of an "epidemic" of injuries to children playing on them.

   Cause: _____

   Effect: _____

7. I bought this glow-in-the-dark fish lamp for one reason only: it was on sale.

   Cause: _____

   Effect: _____

8. As more people spend time surfing the Internet, television viewing is declining for the first time in fifty years.

   Cause: _____

   Effect: _____

9. Wild animals in South African game parks can bring in millions of tourist dollars; consequently, the government is trying to save many species.

   Cause: _____

   Effect: _____

10. For years, Charboro cigarettes outsold all competitors as a result of added ammonia. This ammonia gave smokers' brains an extra "kick."

    Cause: _____

    First Effect: _____

    Second Effect: _____

PRACTICE 3 List three causes *or* three effects to support each topic sentence below. First, read the topic sentence to see whether causes or effects are called for. Then think, jot, and list your three best ideas.

1. The huge success of Barbie (or some other toy, game, or product) has a number of causes. _____

   _____

   _____

2. There are several reasons why AIDS continues to spread among teenagers, despite widespread knowledge about the deadly nature of the disease.

   _____

   _____

   _____

3. Reading books by authors of many nationalities, instead of just American and English authors, has many positive (or negative) effects on American students. _____

_____

_____

_____

PRACTICE 4 Now choose one topic from Practice 3 that interests you and write a paragraph of cause or effect on notebook paper. Before you write a draft, think and make a plan. Have you chosen the three most important causes or effects and decided on an effective order in which to present them? As you write, use transitional expressions to help the reader follow your ideas.

PRACTICE 5 **Thinking and Writing Together
Analyze the Causes of Leadership**

In a group of four or five classmates, read this passage aloud. Then follow the directions below.

Creative risk takers are often high achievers who tend to start their own businesses or become leaders in some other way. Researchers have identified two different types of home environments that tend to produce creative risk takers: (1) "high expectation families" that enthusiastically support the child and expect great things from him or her and (2) very poor, alcoholic, or broken homes where the child receives almost no support and few positive expectations.

Your group should analyze possible reasons why households of the *second* type tend to produce creative risk takers. Write down your three best reasons. Your instructor might wish to have you report your theories to the class.

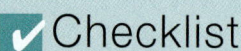

Exploring Online

http://www.nsba.org/sbot/toolkit/LeadQual.html Qualities of a leader
http://www.plainfield.k12.in.us/hschool/webq/webq57/adverse.htm Leaders who faced adversity

✔**Checklist**

The Process of Writing a Cause and Effect Paragraph

Refer to this checklist of steps as you write a paragraph.

___ 1. Narrow the topic in light of your audience and purpose. Think of a subject that can be analyzed for clear causes or effects.

____ 2. Decide whether you will emphasize causes or effects. What information would be most interesting to your audience?

____ 3. Compose a topic sentence that states the subject and indicates whether causes or effects will be discussed.

____ 4. Now freewrite, brainstorm, or cluster to find at least three possible causes or effects. Do your mental detective work. At this stage, think of all possible causes; think of short- and long-term effects, as well as positive and negative effects.

____ 5. Select the best causes or effects with which to develop your paragraph. Drop those that are not relevant.

____ 6. Make a plan or an outline for your paragraph, numbering the causes or effects in the order in which you will present them.

____ 7. Write a first draft of your cause and effect paragraph, explaining each point fully so that your reader understands just how X caused Y. Use transitional expressions to emphasize these relationships.

____ 8. Revise as necessary, checking for good support, unity, logic, and coherence. Does your paragraph have an interesting opening sentence?

____ 9. Proofread for errors in grammar, punctuation, sentence structure, spelling, and mechanics. Especially watch for your personal error patterns.

Suggested Topics for Cause and Effect Paragraphs

1. Reasons why someone made an important decision
2. Reasons why some people cheat in college
3. Causes of an act of courage or cowardice
4. Causes of a marriage or divorce (friendship or end of a friendship)
5. Reasons for doing volunteer work
6. Causes or effects of membership in a group (choir, band, sports team, church, or gang)
7. Causes or effects of dropping out of school (or attending college)
8. Effects of email or a computer on a person's life
9. Effects of having a certain boss (or teacher, parent, or leader)
10. Effects of a superstition or prejudice
11. Effects of the death of a loved one
12. Effects (positive or negative) of a habit or practice
13. Effects of living in a repressive country or home
14. Effects of living in a rural (or urban, mountainous, flat, rich, poor, or ethnically diverse) place
15. Writer's choice: _____

CHAPTER 13 Persuasion

To persuade is to convince someone that a particular opinion or point of view is the correct one.

Any time you argue with a friend, you are each trying to persuade, to convince, the other that your opinion is the right one. Commercials on television are another form of persuasion. Advertisers attempt to convince viewers that the product they sell—whether a deodorant, a soft drink, or an automobile—is the best one to purchase.

You will often have to persuade in writing. For instance, if you want a raise, you will have to write a persuasive memo to convince your employer that you deserve one. You will have to back up, or support, your request with proof, listing important projects you have completed, noting new responsibilities you have taken upon yourself, or showing how you have increased sales.

Once you learn how to persuade logically and rationally, you will be less likely to accept the false, misleading, and emotional arguments that you hear and read every day. Persuasion is vital in daily life, in nearly all college courses, and in most careers.

Topic Sentence

Here is the topic sentence of a **persuasive** paragraph:

> Passengers should refuse to ride in any vehicle driven by someone who has been drinking.

- The writer begins a persuasive paragraph by stating clearly what he or she is arguing for or against. What will this persuasive paragraph argue against?

_____

_____

- Words like *should, ought,* and *must* (and the negatives *should not, ought not,* and *must not*) are especially effective in the topic sentence of a persuasive paragraph.

Paragraph and Plan

Here is the entire paragraph:

> Passengers should refuse to ride in any vehicle driven by someone who has been drinking. First and most important, such a refusal could save lives. The National Council on Alcoholism reports that drunk driving causes 25,000 deaths and 50 percent of all traffic accidents each year. Not only the drivers but the passengers who agree to travel with them are responsible. Second, riders might tell themselves that some people drive well even after a few drinks, but this is just not true. Dr. Burton Belloc of the local Alcoholism Treatment Center explains that even one drink can lengthen the reflex time and weaken the judgment needed for safe driving. Other riders might feel foolish to ruin a social occasion or inconvenience themselves or others by speaking up, but risking their lives is even more foolish. Finally, by refusing to ride with a drinker, one passenger could influence other passengers or the driver. Marie Furillo, a student at Central High School, is an example. When three friends who had obviously been drinking offered her a ride home from school, she refused, despite the driver's teasing. Hearing Marie's refusal, two of her friends got out of the car. Until the laws are changed and a vast re-education takes place, the bloodshed on American highways will probably continue. But there is one thing people can do: They can refuse to risk their lives for the sake of a party.

- The first reason in the argument **predicts the consequence.** If passengers refuse to ride with drinkers, what will the consequence be?

  _____

- The writer also supports this reason with **facts.** What are the facts?

  _____
  _____

- The second reason in the argument is really an **answer to the opposition.** That is, the writer anticipates the critics. What point is the writer answering?

  _____
  _____

- The writer supports this reason by **referring to an authority.** That is, the writer gives the opinion of someone who can provide unbiased and valuable information about the subject. Who is the authority and what does this person say?

  _____
  _____

- The third reason in the argument is that risking your life is foolish. This reason is really another **answer to the opposition.** What point is the writer answering?

  _____
  _____

- The final reason in the argument is that one passenger could influence others. What **example** does the writer supply to back up this reason?

  _____

  _____

- Persuasive paragraphs either can begin with the most important reason and then continue with less important ones, or they can begin with the least important reasons, saving the most important for last.* This paragraph begins with what the author considers *most* important. How can you tell?

  _____

Before composing this persuasive paragraph, the writer probably brainstormed or freewrote to gather ideas and then made an **outline** or a **plan** like this:

Topic sentence: Passengers should refuse to ride in any vehicle driven by someone who has been drinking.

Reason 1: Refusal could save lives **(predicting a consequence)**.
—statistics on deaths and accidents **(facts)**
—passengers are equally responsible

Reason 2: Riders might say some drinkers drive well—not true **(answering the opposition)**.
—Dr. Belloc's explanation **(referring to authority)**

Reason 3: Others might feel foolish speaking up, but risking lives is more foolish **(answering the opposition)**.

Reason 4: One rider might influence other passengers.
—Marie Furillo **(example)**

Conclusion: Bloodshed will probably continue, but people can refuse to risk their lives.

- Note how each reason clearly supports the topic sentence.

Transitional Expressions

The following transitional expressions are helpful in persuasive paragraphs:

Transitional Expressions for Persuasion

Give Reasons	Answer the Opposition	Draw Conclusions
first (second, third)	of course	therefore
another, next	some may say	thus
last, finally	nevertheless	hence
because, since, for	on the other hand	consequently
although		

---

* For work on order of importance, see Chapter 4, "Achieving Coherence," Part A.

Methods of Persuasion

The drinking-and-driving example showed the basic kinds of support used in persuasive paragraphs: **facts, referring to an authority, examples, predicting the consequences,** and **answering the opposition.** Although you will rarely use all of them in one paragraph, you should be familiar with them all. Here are some more details:

1. **Facts: Facts** are simply statements of *what is*. They should appeal to the reader's mind, not just to the emotions. The source of your facts should be clear to the reader. If you wish to prove that children's eyesight should be checked every year by a doctor, you might look for supporting facts in appropriate books and magazines, or you might ask your eye doctor for information. Your paper might say, "Many people suffer serious visual impairment later in life because they received insufficient or inadequate eye care when they were children, according to an article in *Better Vision*."*

    Avoid the vague "everyone knows that" or "it is common knowledge that" or "they all say." Such statements will make your reader justifiably suspicious of your "facts."

2. **Referring to an authority:** An **authority** is an expert, someone who can be relied on to give unbiased facts and information. If you wish to convince your readers that asthma is a far more serious illness than most people realize, you might speak with an emergency-room physician about the numbers of patients treated for asthma attacks, or you might quote experts from the literature of national organizations like the Asthma and Allergy Foundation of America or the American Lung Association. These are all excellent and knowledgeable authorities whose opinions on medical matters would be considered valid and unbiased.

    Avoid appealing to "authorities" who are interesting or glamorous but who are not experts. A basketball player certainly knows about sports, but probably knows little about cameras or cookware.

3. **Examples:** An **example** should clearly relate to the argument and should be typical enough to support it.† If you wish to convince your reader that high schools should provide more funds than they do for women's sports, you might say, "Jefferson High School, for instance, has received inquiries from sixty female students who would be willing to join a women's basketball or baseball team if the school could provide the uniforms, the space, and a coach."

    Avoid examples that are not typical enough to support your general statement. That your friend was once bitten by a dog does not adequately prove that all dogs are dangerous pets.

4. **Predicting the consequence: Predicting the consequence** helps the reader visualize what will occur if *something does or does not happen*. To convince your readers that a college education should be free to all qualified students, you might say, "If bright but economically deprived students cannot attend college because they cannot afford it, our society will be robbed of their talents."

    Avoid exaggerating the consequence. For instance, telling the reader, "If you don't eat fresh fruit every day, you will never be truly healthy," exaggerates the consequences of not eating fresh fruit and makes the reader understandably suspicious.

---

* For more work on summarizing and quoting outside sources, see Chapter 18.

† For more work on examples, see Chapter 5, "Illustration."

5. **Answering the opposition:** *Answering possible critics* shows that you are aware of the opposition's argument and are able to respond to it. If you wish to convince your readers that your candidate is the best on the ballot, you might say, "Some have criticized him for running a low-key campaign, but he feels that the issues and his stand on them should speak for themselves."

Avoid calling the opposition "fools" or "crooks." Attack their ideas, not their character.

Considering the Audience

In addition to providing adequate proof for your argument, pay special attention to the **audience** as you write persuasively. In general, we assume that our audience is much like us—reasonable people who wish to learn the truth. But because argument can evoke strong feelings, directing your persuasive paper toward a particular audience can be helpful. Consider just *what kind of evidence* this audience would respond to. For instance, if you were attempting to persuade parents to volunteer their time to establish a local Scout troop, you might explain to them the various ways in which their children would benefit from the troop. In other words, show these parents how the troop is important to *them*. You might also say that you realize how much time they already spend on family matters and how little spare time they have. By doing so, you let them know that you understand their resistance to the argument and that you are sympathetic to their doubts. When you take your audience into consideration, you will make your persuasive paragraph more convincing.*†

Building Blocks To Effective Persuasive Writing

Topic: Students should acquire computer skills.

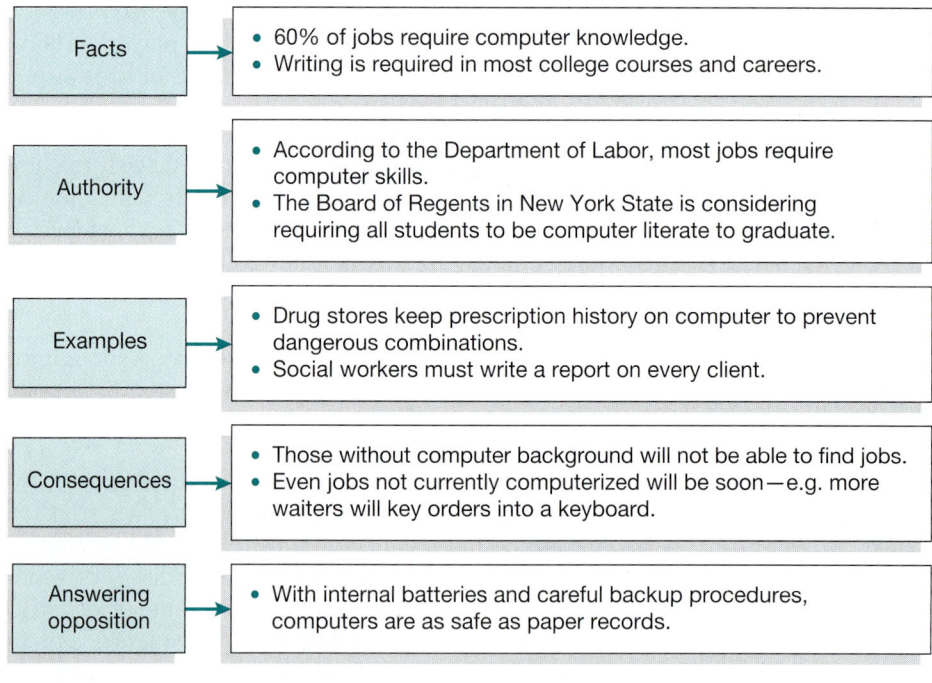

Facts	• 60% of jobs require computer knowledge. • Writing is required in most college courses and careers.
Authority	• According to the Department of Labor, most jobs require computer skills. • The Board of Regents in New York State is considering requiring all students to be computer literate to graduate.
Examples	• Drug stores keep prescription history on computer to prevent dangerous combinations. • Social workers must write a report on every client.
Consequences	• Those without computer background will not be able to find jobs. • Even jobs not currently computerized will be soon—e.g. more waiters will key orders into a keyboard.
Answering opposition	• With internal batteries and careful backup procedures, computers are as safe as paper records.

---

* For more work on audience, see Chapter 1, "Exploring the Writing Process," Part B.

† For a complete essay developed by persuasion, see "Stopping Youth Violence: An Inside Job," Chapter 15, Part I.

PRACTICE 1 Read the following persuasive paragraph carefully and answer the questions.

  American women should stop buying so-called women's magazines because these publications lower their self-esteem. First of all, publications like *Glamour* and *Cosmo* appeal to women's insecurities and make millions doing it. Topics like "Ten Days to Sexier Cleavage" and "How to Attract Mr. Right" lure women to buy seven million copies a month, reports Claire Ito in *The Tulsa Chronicle*, May 4, 2002. The message: women need to be improved. Second, although many people—especially magazine publishers—claim these periodicals build self-esteem, they really do the opposite. One expert in readers' reactions, Deborah Then, says that almost all women, regardless of age or education, feel worse about themselves after reading one of these magazines. Alice, one of the women I spoke with, is a good example: "I flip through pictures of world-class beauties and six-foot-tall skinny women, comparing myself to them. In more ways than one, I come up short." Finally, if women spent the money and time these magazines take on more self-loving activities—studying new subjects, developing mental or physical fitness, setting goals and daring to achieve them—they would really build self-worth. Sisters, seek wisdom, create what you envision, and above all, know that you can.

—Rochelle Revard (Student)

1. What is this paragraph arguing for or against? _____

   _____

2. What audience is the writer addressing? _____

3. Which reason is supported by facts? _____

   What are the facts, and where did the writer get them? _____

   _____

   _____

4. Which reason answers the opposition? _____

5. Which reason is supported by an example? _____

   What is the example? _____

   _____

6. Which reason appeals to an authority? _____

   Who is the authority? _____

   _____

PRACTICE 2 Read the following paragraph carefully and answer the questions.

  This state should offer free parenting classes, taught by experts, to anyone who wishes to become a parent. First and most important, such parenting classes could save children's lives. Every year, over two million American children are hurt, maimed, or killed by their own parents, according to the National Physicians Association. Some of these tragedies could be prevented by showing parents how to recognize and deal with their frustration and anger. Next, good parenting skills do not come naturally, but must be learned. Dr. Phillip Graham, chairman of England's National Children's Bureau, says that most parents have "no good role models" and simply parent the way they were parented. The courses would not only improve parenting skills but might also identify people at high risk of abusing their children. Third, critics might argue that the state has no business getting involved in parenting, which is a private responsibility. However, the state already makes decisions about who is a fit parent—in the courts, child-protection services, and adoption agencies—but often this is too late for the well-being of the child. Finally, if we do nothing, the hidden epidemic of child abuse and neglect will continue. We train our children's teachers, doctors, day-care workers, and bus drivers. We must also educate parents.

1. What is this paragraph arguing for or against? _____

2. Which reason appeals to an authority for support? _____

   Who is the authority? _____

3. Which reason answers the opposition? _____

4. Which reason includes facts? What is the source of these facts? _____

5. What consequence does the writer predict if parenting classes are not offered? _____

6. Does this writer convince you that parenting classes might make a difference? If you were writing a persuasion paragraph to oppose or support this writer, what would your topic sentence be? _____

PRACTICE 3 So far you have learned five basic methods of persuasion: **facts, referring to an authority, examples, predicting the consequence,** and **answering the opposition.** Ten topic sentences for persuasive paragraphs follow. Write one reason in support of each topic sentence, using the method of persuasion indicated.

Facts

1. A stop sign should be placed at the busy intersection of Hoover and Palm streets.

   Reason: _____

   _____

   _____

   _____

2. People should not get married until they are at least twenty-five years old.

   Reason: _____

   _____

   _____

   _____

Referring to an Authority

(If you cannot think of an authority offhand, name the kind of person who would be an authority on the subject.)

3. These new Sluggo bats will definitely raise your batting average.

   Reason: _____

   _____

   _____

   _____

4. Most people should get at least one hour of vigorous exercise three times a week.

   Reason: _____

   _____

   _____

   _____

Examples

5. Pet animals should be allowed in children's hospital rooms because they speed healing.

Reason: _____

_____

_____

_____

6. Mace and pepper spray should be legalized because they can prevent crime without causing permanent injury.

Reason: _____

_____

_____

_____

Predicting the Consequence

7. Companies should (should not) be allowed to conduct random drug testing on employees.

Reason: _____

_____

_____

_____

8. The federal government should (should not) prohibit the sale of handguns through the mail.

Reason: _____

_____

_____

_____

Answering the Opposition

(State the opposition's point of view and then refute it.)

9. This college should (should not) drop its required-attendance policy.

Reason: _____

_____

_____

_____

10. Teenagers should (should not) be required to get their parents' permission before being allowed to have an abortion.

    Reason: _____

    _____

    _____

    _____

PRACTICE 4 Each of the following sentences tells what you are trying to persuade someone to do. Beneath each sentence are four reasons that attempt to convince the reader that he or she should take this particular course of action. Circle the letter of the reason that seems *irrelevant, illogical,* or *untrue*.

1. If you wanted to persuade someone to do holiday shopping earlier, you might say that
   a. shopping earlier saves time.
   b. more gifts will be in stock.
   c. stores will not be overly crowded.
   d. Ja Rule shops early.

2. If you wanted to persuade someone to buy a particular brand of cereal, you might say that
   a. it is inexpensive.
   b. it contains vitamins and minerals.
   c. it comes in an attractive box.
   d. it makes a hearty breakfast.

3. If you wanted to persuade someone to move to your town, you might say that
   a. two new companies have made jobs available.
   b. by moving to this town, he or she will become the happiest person in the world.
   c. there is a wide selection of housing.
   d. the area is lovely and still unpolluted.

4. If you wanted to persuade someone to vote for a particular candidate, you might say that
   a. she has always kept her promises to the voters.
   b. she has lived in the district for thirty years.
   c. she has substantial knowledge of the issues.
   d. she dresses very fashionably.

5. If you wanted to persuade someone to learn to read and speak a foreign language, you might say that
   a. knowledge of a foreign language can be helpful in the business world.
   b. he or she may want to travel in the country where the language is spoken.
   c. Enrique Iglesias sings in two languages.
   d. being able to read great literature in the original is a rewarding experience.

6. If you wanted to persuade someone to quit smoking, you might say that
   a. smoking is a major cause of lung cancer.
   b. smoking stains teeth and softens gums.
   c. ashtrays are often hard to find.
   d. this bad habit has become increasingly expensive.

PRACTICE 5 As you write persuasive paragraphs, make sure that your reasons can withstand close examination. Here are some examples of *invalid* arguments. Read them carefully. Decide which method of persuasion is being used and explain why you think the argument is invalid. Refer to the list on pages 153–154.

1. Men make terrible drivers. That one just cut right in front of me without looking.

   Method of persuasion: _____

   Invalid because _____

   _____

2. Many people have become vegetarians during the past ten or fifteen years, but such people have lettuce for brains.

   Method of persuasion: _____

   Invalid because _____

   _____

3. Candy does not really harm children's teeth. Tests made by scientists at the Gooey Candy Company have proved that candy does not cause tooth decay.

   Method of persuasion: _____

   Invalid because _____

   _____

4. Stealing pens and pads from the office is perfectly all right. Everyone does it.

   Method of persuasion: _____

   Invalid because _____

   _____

5. We don't want _____ in our neighborhood. We had a _____ family once, and they made a lot of noise.

   Method of persuasion: _____

   Invalid because _____

6. If our city doesn't build more playgrounds, a crime wave will destroy our homes and businesses.

   Method of persuasion: _____

   Invalid because _____

7. Studying has nothing to do with grades. My brother never studies and still gets *A*'s all the time.

   Method of persuasion: _____

   Invalid because _____

8. Women bosses work their employees too hard. I had one once, and she never let me rest for a moment.

   Method of persuasion: _____

   Invalid because _____

9. The Big Deal Supermarket has the lowest prices in town. This must be true because the manager said on the radio last week, "We have the lowest prices in town."

   Method of persuasion: _____

   Invalid because _____

10. If little girls are allowed to play with cars and trucks, they will grow up wanting to be men.

   Method of persuasion: _____

   Invalid because _____

   _____

PRACTICE 6 In a group of four or five classmates, discuss the meaning of this cartoon. Like many cartoons, this one expresses a strong point of view. What issue is this cartoonist commenting on? What point is he making? Working together, write down the cartoon's "topic sentence" and argument. How effective—how persuasive—is this cartoon? Do you agree or disagree with the cartoonist?

PRACTICE 7 **Thinking and Writing Together**
Persuade Through Humor

Advertisements bombard us every day—through TV, newspapers, magazines, billboards, store windows, and the labels on people's clothing and possessions. The billions of dollars that Americans spend on brandname products tell us that ads are very persuasive, usually making their argument with a strong visual image and a few catchy words. To expose the great power of advertising, a group called Adbusters creates stylish spoof ads for real products. The goal is to expose the truth that real-life ads often hide. In a group of four or five classmates, study the ad below and then answer the questions.

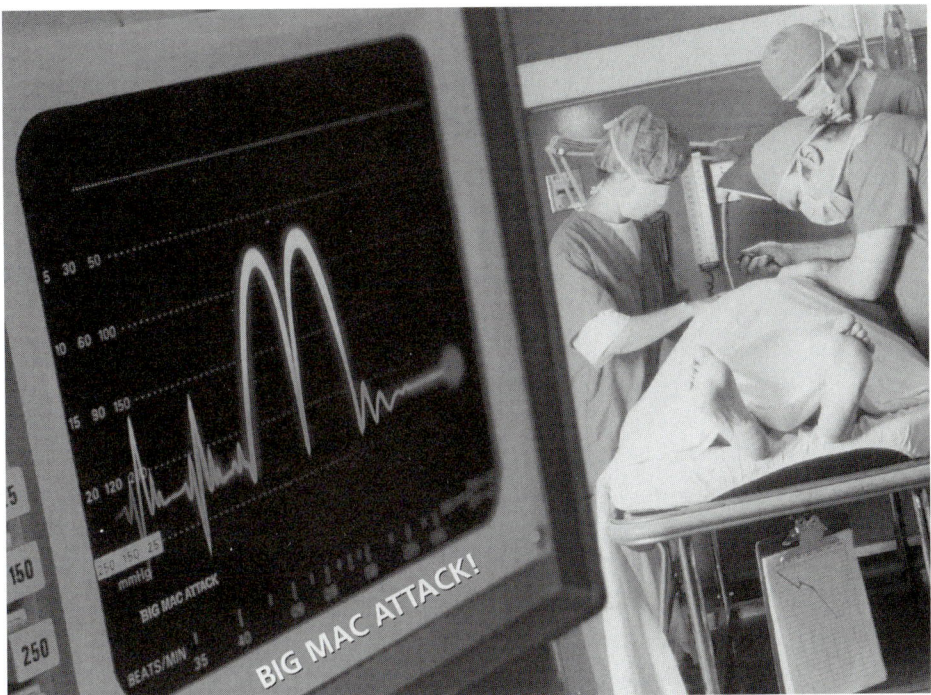

What hugely popular product is being "busted" by this Adbusters spoof? What is the persuasive message of this ad? Working together, write down the ad's "topic sentence" and argument. How effective is Adbuster's ad? Does it successfully answer the "opposition"—that is, McDonald's worldwide campaign to convince us to buy more Big Macs?

 Exploring Online

http://www.adbusters.org/spoofads/ Study other Adbuster spoof ads, especially those for fashion, alcohol, and tobacco. Pick the funniest and write about its persuasive message. Or click "Create your own print ad." In your group, create a persuasive ad, perhaps using the slogan, "Got_____?"

 Writing Assignment

To help you take a stand for a persuasive paragraph of your own, try the following exercises on notebook paper:

1. List five things you would like to see changed at your college.

2. List five things you would like to see changed in your home *or* at your job.

3. List five things that annoy you or make you angry. What can be done about them?

4. Imagine yourself giving a speech on national television. What message would you like to convey?

From your lists, pick one topic you would like to write a persuasive paragraph about and write the topic sentence here:

_____

_____

Now make a plan or an outline for a paragraph on a separate sheet of paper. Use at least two of the five methods of persuasion. Arrange your reasons in a logical order, and write the most persuasive paragraph you can.

Checklist

The Process of Writing a Persuasive Paragraph

Refer to this checklist of steps as you write a persuasive paragraph of your own.

____ 1. Narrow the topic in light of your audience and purpose. What do you wish to persuade your reader to believe or do?

____ 2. Compose a topic sentence that clearly states your position for or against. Use *should*, *ought*, *must*, or their negatives.

____ 3. Freewrite or brainstorm to generate all the reasons you can think of. (You may want to freewrite or brainstorm before you narrow the topic.)

____ 4. Select the best three or four reasons and drop those that do not relate to your topic sentence.

____ 5. If you use *facts*, be sure that they are accurate and that the source of your facts is clear. If you use an *example*, be sure that it is a valid one and adequately supports your argument. If you *refer to an authority*, be sure that he or she is really an authority and *not biased*. If one of your reasons *predicts the consequence*, be sure that the consequence flows logically from your statement. If one of your reasons *answers the opposition*, be sure to state the opposition's point of view fairly and refute it adequately.

____ 6. Make a plan or an outline for the paragraph, numbering the reasons in the order in which you will present them.

____ 7. Write a draft of your persuasive paragraph, using transitional expressions wherever they may be helpful.

____ 8. Revise as necessary, checking for support, unity, logic, and coherence.

____ 9. Proofread for errors in grammar, punctuation, sentence structure, spelling, and mechanics.

Suggested Topics for Persuasive Paragraphs

A list of possible topic sentences for persuasive paragraphs follows. Pick one statement and decide whether you agree or disagree with it. Modify the topic sentence accordingly. Then write a persuasive paragraph that supports your view, explaining and illustrating from your own experience, your observations of others, or your reading.

1. Companies should not be allowed to read their employees' email.
2. Occasional arguments are good for friendship.
3. A required course at this college should be _____ (Great American Success Stories, Survey of World Art, How to Use the Internet, or another).
4. The families of AIDS patients are the hidden victims of AIDS.
5. Condom machines should be permitted on campus.
6. People should laugh more because laughter heals.
7. Expensive weddings are an obscene waste of money.
8. Gay people should be allowed to adopt children.
9. Some college football (soccer, basketball, and so on) programs send the message that academic excellence is not important.
10. TV talk shows trivialize important social issues.
11. _____ is the most _____ (hilarious, educational, mindless, racist) show on television.
12. To improve academic achievement, this town should create same-sex high schools (all boys, all girls).
13. No one under the age of 21 should be allowed to have body piercing (tattoos, cosmetic surgery, or other).
14. _____ (writer, singer, or actor) has a message that more people need to hear.
15. Writer's choice: _____

UNIT 3

Writers' Workshop

Give Advice to College Writers

When you are assigned a writing task, take a few minutes to think about the different types of paragraphs you have studied in this unit. Could a certain type of paragraph help you present your ideas more forcefully? You might ask yourself, "Would a paragraph developed by examples work well for this topic? How about a paragraph of cause and effect?"

When he received the assignment "Give advice to other college writers," this student not only made use of one paragraph pattern he had learned, but he added something of his own—humor. In your class or group, read his work, aloud if possible, underlining any lines that you find especially funny or effective.

English Students, Listen Up!

You may think that years of school have taught you how to put off writing a paper; however, true procrastination is an art form, and certain steps must be followed to achieve the status of Master Procrastinator. The first step is to come up with a good reason to put off writing the paper. Reasons prevent others from hassling you about your procrastination. A reason should not be confused with an excuse. An excuse would be, "I am too tired." A reason would be, "It is important that I rest in order to do the best possible job." The second step is to come up with a worthwhile task to do before starting the paper. If you put off writing your paper by watching *Baywatch*. You will feel guilty. On the other hand, if you put off writing your paper by helping your child do his or her homework or by doing three weeks' worth of laundry or by organizing your sock drawer, there will be no guilt. After completing your worthwhile task. You will be hungry. In order to have the energy necessary to write the paper, you will need to eat something. The true artist can make this third step last even longer by either cooking a meal or going out for food. It is important not to risk your energy level by simply eating a bowl of cereal or a ketchup sandwich. After you eat, the fourth step is to prepare the space in which you will write the paper. This includes cleaning all the surfaces, sharpening pencils. And making sure the lighting is exactly right. You may think that after this fourth step is completed, you will have no choice but to start your paper, but you do if you have done the other steps correctly. It is now too late in the day to start your paper. The fifth step is, of course, to go to bed and start over with step one in the morning.

—Thomas Capra (Student)

1. How effective is this paragraph?

_____ Clear topic sentence?   _____ Good supporting details?

_____ Logical organization?   _____ Effective conclusion?

2. What type of paragraph development does Mr. Capra use here? How do you know? Does the topic sentence indicate what kind of paragraph will follow?

3. One step in the process of becoming a Master Procrastinator contains a *contrast*. Which step? What two things are contrasted?

4. Discuss your underlinings with the group or class. Tell what parts of the paragraph you like best, explaining as specifically as possible why. For example, the mention of a ketchup sandwich in step three adds an extra dash of humor.

5. Although this writer is having fun, procrastination is a serious problem for some people. Do you think Mr. Capra is writing from experience? Why or why not?

6. This otherwise excellent writer makes the same grammar error three times. Can you spot and correct the error pattern that he needs to avoid?

Group Work

In your group or class, make a chart like the one below, listing all the types of paragraph development that you have studied. Now suppose that you have been assigned the topic *procrastination*. Discuss how different paragraphs could be developed on the subject of procrastination, each one using a different paragraph pattern. For instance, you could *illustrate* procrastination by discussing examples of procrastinators you have known. Fill in the chart with one idea per paragraph type. Then share your group's ideas with the whole class.

Topic: Procrastination

Method of development:	A paragraph could
Illustration	
Narration	
Description	
Process	
Definition	
Comparison and Contrast	
Classification	
Cause and Effect	
Persuasion	

Writing and Revising Ideas

1. Give advice to college writers. Use humor if you wish.

2. Discuss procrastination, using one kind of paragraph development that you studied this term.

UNIT 4
Writing the Essay

CHAPTER 14 The Process of Writing an Essay
CHAPTER 15 Types of Essays
CHAPTER 16 The Introduction, the Conclusion, and the Title
CHAPTER 17 Special College Skills: Summary and Quotation
CHAPTER 18 Strengthening an Essay with Research
CHAPTER 19 Writing Under Pressure: The Essay Examination

CHAPTER 14: The Process of Writing an Essay

PART A Looking at the Essay
PART B Writing the Thesis Statement
PART C Generating Ideas for the Body
PART D Ordering and Linking Paragraphs in the Essay
PART E Writing and Revising Essays

Although writing effective paragraphs will help you complete short-answer exams and do brief writing assignments, much of the time—in college and in the business world—you will be required to write essays and reports several paragraphs long. Essays are longer and contain more ideas than the single paragraphs you have practiced so far, but they require many of the same skills that paragraphs do.

This chapter will help you apply the skills of paragraph writing to the writing of short essays. It will guide you from a look at the essay and its parts through the planning and writing of essays.

Part A

Looking at the Essay

An **essay** is a group of paragraphs about one subject. In many ways, an essay is like a paragraph in longer, fuller form. Both have an introduction, a body, and a conclusion. Both explain one main, or controlling, idea with details, facts, and examples. An essay is not just a padded paragraph, however. An essay is longer because it contains more ideas.

The paragraphs in an essay are part of a larger whole, so each one has a special purpose.

- The **introductory paragraph*** opens the essay and tries to catch the reader's interest. It usually contains a **thesis statement,** one sentence that states the main idea of the entire essay.
- The **body** of an essay consists of one, two, three, or more paragraphs, each one making a different point about the main idea.
- The **conclusion**† brings the essay to a close. It might be a sentence or a paragraph long.

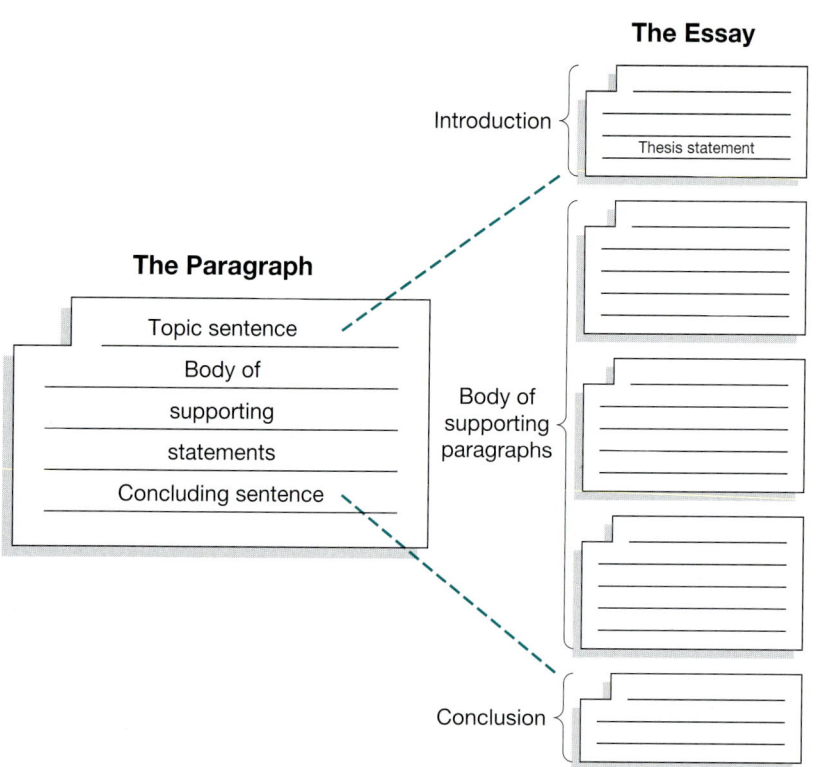

Here is a student essay:

Sunlight

(1) An old proverb says, "He who brings sunlight into the lives of others cannot keep it from himself." Students who volunteer through the Center for Community Service often experience this wisdom firsthand. By giving their time and talents to the local community, these students not only enrich the lives of others, but they receive many surprising benefits for themselves.

---

*For more work on introductions, see Chapter 16, "The Introduction, the Conclusion, and the Title."
†For more work on conclusions, see Chapter 16, "The Introduction, the Conclusion, and the Title."

(2) Most important, volunteering can bring a sense of empowerment, a knowledge that we can make a difference. This is significant because many students feel passive and hopeless about "the way things are." My first volunteer assignment was working with a group of troubled teenagers. Together we transformed a dismal vacant lot into a thriving business. The three-acre lot in the South Bronx, surrounded by abandoned buildings, was full of junk and heaps of wood. One teenager kicked a piece of wood and said, "Why don't we chop this up and sell it?" We surprised him by taking his idea seriously. We helped these young men, some of whom already had rap sheets, to chop up the wood, bundle it, contact restaurants with wood-burning ovens, and make deliveries. The restaurants, most of them very elegant, were happy to get cheap firewood, and the teenagers were thrilled to be treated like businesspeople. Most rewarding for me was seeing the changes in Raymond, "Mr. Apathy," as he took on a leading role in our project.

(3) Second, the volunteer often gains a deeper understanding of others. Another student, Shirley Miranda, worked with SHARE, a food cooperative that distributes bulk food once a month to its members. SHARE does not give food as charity; rather, each person does a job like unloading trucks at 5 A.M. on delivery day or packing boxes in exchange for healthy, inexpensive food. For Shirley, SHARE was a lesson in human relationships. Reflecting on her service, she wrote: "I learned that people may sometimes need guidance with dignity rather than total dependency on others. I saw that true teamwork is based on people's similarities, not their differences." SHARE so impressed Shirley that she worked in the program through her graduation.

(4) Finally, volunteering can be a way to "try on" a work environment. Sam Mukarji, an engineering student, volunteers on Saturdays as a docent, or guide, at the Museum of Science and Industry, which he describes as "my favorite place on the planet." Sam admires the creative uses of science in this museum, such as the virtual-reality experience of piloting an airplane. When many visitors asked Sam how the exhibit was put together, he suggested that the museum include signs explaining the technology. His idea was accepted, and he was asked to help implement it. Struggling to explain the exhibit in a clear way taught Sam how important writing skills are, even for an engineering major. Now he is paying closer attention to his English assignments and has discovered that working in a science museum would be his "dream job."

(5) Stories like these are not unusual at the Center for Community Service. Whenever the volunteers meet there, we always seem to end up talking about the positive ways in which volunteering has changed our lives. The Center is in a cinder-block basement without a single window, but it is filled with sunlight.

- The last sentence in the introduction is the *thesis statement*. Just as a topic sentence sets forth the main idea of a paragraph, so the thesis statement sets forth the main idea of the whole essay. It must be *general enough to include the topic sentence of every paragraph in the body.*

- Underline the topic sentence of each supporting paragraph. Each topic sentence introduces one *benefit* that volunteers receive.

- Note that the thesis and topic sentences of paragraphs 2, 3, and 4 make a rough *plan* of the entire essay:

1. INTRODUCTION and Thesis statement:		By giving their time and talents to the local community, these students not only enrich the lives of others, but they receive many surprising benefits for themselves.
2. Topic sentence:		Most important, volunteering can bring a sense of empowerment, a knowledge that we can make a difference.
3. Topic sentence:		Second, the volunteer often gains a deeper understanding of others.
4. Topic sentence:		Finally, volunteering can be a way to "try on" a work environment.
5. CONCLUSION		

- Note that every topic sentence supports the thesis statement. Every paragraph in the body discusses in detail one *benefit* that students receive from volunteering. Each paragraph also provides an *example* to explain that benefit.

- The last paragraph *concludes* the essay by mentioning sunlight, a reference to the proverb in paragraph 1.

PRACTICE 1 Read this student essay carefully and then answer the questions.

Bottle Watching

(1) Every time I see a beer bottle, I feel grateful. This reaction has nothing to do with beer. The sight reminds me of the year I spent inspecting bottles at a brewery. That was the most boring and painful job I've ever had, but it motivated me to change my life.

(2) My job consisted of sitting on a stool and watching empty bottles pass by. A glaring light behind the conveyor belt helped me to spot cracked bottles or bottles with something extra—a dead grasshopper, for example, or a mouse foot. I was supposed to grab such bottles with my hooked cane and break them before they went into the washer. For eight or nine hours a day that was all I did. I got dizzy and sore in the eyes. I longed to fall asleep. I prayed that the conveyor would break down so the bottles would stop.

(3) After a while, to put some excitement into the job, I began inventing little games. I would count the number of minutes that passed before a broken bottle would come by, and I would compete against my own past record. Or I would see how many broken bottles I could spot in one minute. Once, I organized a contest for all the bottle watchers with a prize for the best dead insect or animal found in a bottle—anything to break the monotony of the job.

(4) After six months at the brewery, I began to think hard about my goals for the future. Did I want to spend the rest of my life looking in beer bottles? I realized that I wanted a job I could believe in. I wanted to use my mind for better things than planning contests for bleary-eyed bottle watchers. I knew I had to hand in my hook and go back to school.

(5) Today I feel grateful to that terrible job because it motivated me to attend college.

—Pat Barnum (Student)

1. Which sentence in the introductory paragraph is the thesis statement? _____

2. Did Mr. Barnum's introduction catch and hold your interest? Why or why not?

3. Underline the topic sentences in paragraphs 2, 3, and 4.

4. What is the controlling idea of paragraph 2? _____

5. What is the controlling idea of paragraph 3? What examples support this idea?

6. What do you like best about this essay? What, if anything, would you change?

Part B

Writing the Thesis Statement

The steps in the essay-writing process are the same as those in the paragraph-writing process: **narrow the topic, write the thesis statement, generate ideas for the body,** and **organize them.** However, in essay writing, planning on paper and prewriting are especially important because an essay is longer than a paragraph and more difficult to organize.

Narrowing the Topic

The essay writer usually starts with a broad subject and then narrows it to a manageable size. An essay is longer than a paragraph and gives the writer more room to develop ideas; nevertheless, the best essays, like the best paragraphs, are often quite specific. For example, if you are assigned a 400-word essay titled "A Trip I Won't Forget," a description of your recent trip to Florida would be too broad a subject. You would need to *narrow* the topic to just one aspect of the trip. Many writers list possible narrowed subjects on paper or on computer:

1. huge job of packing, more tiring than the trip
2. how to pack for a trip with the children without exhausting yourself

3. Disney World, more fun for adults than for children
4. our afternoon of deep-sea fishing: highlight of the trip
5. terrible weather upsetting many of my sightseeing plans

Any one of these topics is narrow enough and specific enough to be the subject of a short essay. If you had written this list, you would now consider each narrowed topic and perhaps freewrite or brainstorm possible ways to support it. Keeping your audience and purpose in mind may also help you narrow your topic. Your audience here might be your instructor and classmates; your purpose might be to inform (by giving tips about packing) or to entertain (by narrating a funny or a dramatic incident). Having considered your topic, audience, and purpose, you would then choose the topic that you could best develop into a good essay.

If you have difficulty with this step, reread Chapter 2, "Prewriting to Generate Ideas."

Writing the Thesis Statement

The **thesis statement**—like the topic sentence in a paragraph—further focuses the narrowed subject because it must clearly state, in sentence form, the writer's **controlling idea**—the main point, opinion, or angle that the rest of the essay will support and discuss.

Narrowed subject:	My job at the brewery
Controlling idea:	So bad it changed my life
Thesis statement:	That was the most boring and painful job I've ever had, but it motivated me to change my life.

■ This thesis statement has a clear controlling idea. From it, we expect the essay to discuss specific ways in which this job was boring and painful and how it motivated a change.

The thesis statement and its controlling idea should be as **specific** as possible. By writing a specific thesis statement, you focus the subject and give yourself and your readers a clear idea of what will follow. Here are three ways to make a vague thesis statement more specific.

1. As a general rule, replace vague words with more exact words* and replace vague ideas with more exact information:

Vague thesis statement:	My recent trip to Florida was really bad.
Revised thesis statement:	My recent trip to Florida was disappointing because the weather upset my sightseeing plans.

---

*For more practice in choosing exact language, see Chapter 22, "Revising for Language Awareness," Part A.

- The first thesis statement above lacks a clear controlling idea. The inexact words *really bad* do not say specifically enough *why* the trip was bad or what the rest of the essay might discuss.

- The second thesis statement is more specific. The words *really bad* are replaced by the more exact word *disappointing.* In addition, the writer has added more complete information about why the trip was disappointing. From this thesis statement, it is clear that the essay will discuss how the weather upset the writer's plans.

2. **Sometimes you can make the thesis statement more specific by stating the natural divisions of the subject.** If a subject naturally has two, three, or four divisions, stating these in the thesis can set up an outline for your entire essay:

Vague thesis statement:	The movie *Southern Smoke* seemed phony.
Revised thesis statement:	The costumes, the dialogue, and the plot of the movie *Southern Smoke* all seemed phony.

- The first thesis statement above gives little specific direction to the writer or the reader.

- The second thesis statement, however, actually sets up a plan for the whole essay. The writer has divided the subject into three parts—the costumes, the dialogue, and the plot—and he or she will probably devote one paragraph to discussing the phoniness of each one, following the order in the thesis statement.

3. **Avoid a heavy-handed thesis statement that announces, "Now I will write about . . ." or "This essay will discuss. . . ."** Don't state the obvious. Instead, craft a specific thesis statement that will capture the reader's interest and control what the rest of your essay will be about. Make every word count.

PRACTICE 2 Revise each vague thesis statement, making it more specific. Remember, a good thesis statement should have a clear controlling idea and indicate what the rest of the essay will be about.

Example | Watching TV news programs has its good points.
Watching news programs on TV can make one a more informed and responsible citizen.

1. The library at this college is bad.

_____

_____

2. A visit to the emergency room can be interesting.

   _____

   _____

3. There are many unusual people in my family.

   _____

   _____

4. School uniforms are a good idea.

   _____

   _____

5. I will write about my job, which is very cool.

   _____

   _____

6. Professors should teach better.

   _____

   _____

7. You can learn a lot by observing children.

   _____

   _____

8. Sketching caricatures is a great hobby.

   _____

   _____

PRACTICE 3 Eight possible essay topics follow. Pick three that interest you. For each one, **narrow** the topic, choose your **controlling idea,** and then compose a specific **thesis statement.**

an addictive habit	a problem on campus or at work
when parents work	a story or issue in the news now
a volunteer experience	handling anger (or other emotion)
the value of pets	advantages or disadvantages of Internet Research

CHAPTER 14   The Process of Writing an Essay   177

Example   Subject: _handling anger_

Narrowed subject: _my angry adolescence_

Controlling idea: _channeling adolescent anger into art_

Thesis statement: _In a photography workshop for "at-risk" teenagers, I learned that anger can be channeled positively into art._

1. Subject: _____

   Narrowed subject: _____

   Controlling idea: _____

   Thesis statement: _____

2. Subject: _____

   Narrowed subject: _____

   Controlling idea: _____

   Thesis statement: _____

3. Subject: _____

   Narrowed subject: _____

   Controlling idea: _____

   Thesis statement: _____

Part C

Generating Ideas for the Body

The thesis statement sets forth the main idea of the entire essay, but it is the **body** of the essay that must fully support and discuss that thesis statement. In composing the thesis statement, the writer should already have given some thought to what the body will contain. Now he or she should make a **plan** or an **outline** that includes the following:

1. Two to four main ideas to support the thesis statement
2. Two to four topic sentences stating these ideas

3. A plan for each paragraph in the body (developed in any of the ways explained earlier in this book)

4. A logical order in which to present these paragraphs

Different writers create such plans in different ways. Some writers brainstorm or freewrite ideas and then find paragraph groups. Others first write topic sentences and then plan paragraphs.

1. Brainstorm ideas and then find paragraph groups. Having written the thesis statement, some writers brainstorm on paper or on the computer—they jot down any ideas that develop the thesis statement, including main ideas, specific details, and examples, all jumbled together. Only after creating a long list do they go back over it, drop any ideas that do not support the thesis statement, and then look for "paragraph groups."

Suppose, for instance, that you have written this thesis statement: *Although people often react to stress in harmful ways, there are many positive ways to handle stress.* By brainstorming and then dropping ideas that do not relate, you might eventually produce a list like this:

work out

dig weeds or rake leaves

call a friend

talking out problems relieves stress

jogging

many sports ease tension

go to the beach

take a walk

taking breaks, long or short, relieves stress

talk to a shrink if the problem is really bad

escape into a hobby—photography, bird watching

go to a movie

talk to a counselor at the college

talk to a minister, priest, rabbi, etc.

many people harm themselves trying to relieve stress

they overeat or smoke

drinking too much, other addictions

do vigorous household chores—scrub a floor, beat the rugs, pound pillows

doing something physical relieves stress

some diseases are caused by stress

take a nap

some people blow up to help tension, but this hurts their relationships

Now read over the list, looking for groups of ideas that could become paragraphs. Some ideas might become topic sentences; others might be used to support a topic sentence. How many possible paragraphs can you find in this list?

_____

PRACTICE 4 From the list, make a **plan** or an **outline** for an essay that supports the thesis statement *Although people often react to stress in harmful ways, there are many positive ways to handle stress.*

Plan four paragraphs for the body of the essay. Find four paragraph groups in the list and determine the main idea of each paragraph; then write a topic sentence stating this main idea.

Now arrange the topic sentences in an order that makes sense. Under each topic sentence, list supporting examples or details.

1. INTRODUCTION and Thesis statement: Although people often react to stress in harmful ways, there are many positive ways to handle stress.

2. Topic sentence: _____

   _____

   (examples) _____

   _____

3. Topic sentence: _____

   _____

   (examples) _____

   _____

4. Topic sentence: _____

   _____

   (examples) _____

   _____

5. Topic sentence: _____

   _____

   (examples) _____

   _____

6. CONCLUSION: _____

_____

_____

_____

- Does every topic sentence support the thesis statement?
- Have you arranged the paragraphs in a logical order?

2. Write topic sentences and then plan paragraphs. Sometimes a writer can compose topic sentences directly from the thesis statement without extensive jotting first. This is especially true if the thesis statement itself shows how the body will be divided or organized. Such a thesis statement makes the work of planning paragraphs easy because the writer has already broken down the subject into supporting ideas or parts:

Thesis statement:	Because the student cafeteria has many problems, the college should hire a new administrator to see that it is properly managed in the future.

- This thesis statement contains two main ideas: (1) that the cafeteria has many problems and (2) that a new administrator should be hired. The first idea states the problem and the second offers a solution.

From this thesis statement, a writer could logically plan a two-paragraph body, with one paragraph explaining each idea in detail. He or she might compose two topic sentences as follows:

Thesis statement:	Because the student cafeteria has many problems, the college should hire a new administrator to see that it is properly managed in the future.
Topic sentence:	Foremost among the cafeteria's problems are unappetizing food, slow service, and high prices.
Topic sentence:	A new administrator could do much to improve these terrible conditions.

These topic sentences might need to be revised later, but they will serve as guides while the writer further develops each paragraph.

The writer might develop the first paragraph in the body by giving **examples*** of the unappetizing foods, slow service, and high prices.

He or she could develop the second paragraph through **process**,[†] by describing the **steps** that the new administrator could take to solve the cafeteria's problems. The completed essay **plan** might look like this:

---

* For more work on developing paragraphs with examples, see Chapter 5, "Illustration."
† For more work on developing paragraphs by process, see Chapter 8, "Process."

1. **INTRODUCTION and Thesis statement:**	Because the student cafeteria has many problems, the college should hire a new administrator to see that it is properly managed in the future.
2. **Topic sentence:**	Foremost among the cafeteria's problems are unappetizing food, slow service, and high prices.

Problem 1: Food is unappetizing

—sandwiches with tough meat, stale bread
—salads with wilted lettuce, tasteless tomatoes
—hot meals often either overcooked or undercooked

Problem 2: Service is slow

—students wait 30 minutes for sandwiches
—students wait 15 minutes just for a cup of coffee
—have to gulp meals to get to class on time

Problem 3: Prices too high

—sandwiches overpriced
—coffee or tea costs $1.50

3. **Topic sentence:**	A new administrator could do much to improve these terrible conditions.

Step 1. Set minimum quality standards

—personally oversee purchase of healthful food
—set and enforce rules about how long food can be left out
—set cooking times for hot meals

Step 2. Reorganize service lines

—study which lines are busiest at different times of the day
—shift cooks and cashiers to those lines
—create a separate beverage line

Step 3. Lower prices

—better food and faster service would attract more student customers
—cafeteria could then lower prices

4. **CONCLUSION**

Note that the order of paragraphs logically follows the order in the thesis statement, discussing first the problem and then the solution.

The writer now has a clear **outline** or **plan** from which to write the first draft of the essay.

PRACTICE 5 Write from two to four topic sentences to support *three* of the thesis statements that follow. (First you may wish to brainstorm or freewrite on paper or on computer.) Make sure that every topic sentence really supports the thesis statement and that every one could be developed into a good paragraph. Then arrange your topic sentences in an **outline** or **plan** in the space provided.

Example | Before you buy a computer, do these three things.

Topic sentence: *Decide how much you can spend, and determine your price range.*

Topic sentence: *Examine the models that are within your price range.*

Topic sentence: *Shop around; do not assume that all computer dealers are created equal.*

1. I vividly recall the sights, smells, and tastes of _____

   Topic sentence: _____

   Topic sentence: _____

   Topic sentence: _____

   Topic sentence: _____

2. Living alone has both advantages and disadvantages.

   Topic sentence: _____

   Topic sentence: _____

   Topic sentence: _____

   Topic sentence: _____

3. Doing well at a job interview requires careful planning.

   Topic sentence: _____

   _____

   Topic sentence: _____

   _____

   Topic sentence: _____

   _____

   Topic sentence: _____

   _____

4. _____ is a fascinating and profitable hobby.

   Topic sentence: _____

   _____

   Topic sentence: _____

   _____

   Topic sentence: _____

   _____

   Topic sentence: _____

   _____

5. My three children have individual techniques for avoiding housework.

   Topic sentence: _____

   _____

   Topic sentence: _____

   _____

   Topic sentence: _____

   _____

   Topic sentence: _____

   _____

PRACTICE 6 Now choose *one* thesis statement you have written, or write one now, and develop a plan for an essay of your own. (For ideas, reread the thesis statements you wrote for Practice 3, p. 177.) Your plan should include your thesis statement, two to four topic sentences, and supporting details, facts, and examples. Brainstorm or freewrite every time you need ideas; revise the thesis statement and the topic sentences until they are sharp and clear.

Part D

Ordering and Linking Paragraphs in the Essay

An essay, like a paragraph, should have **coherence.** That is, the paragraphs in an essay should be arranged in a clear, logical order and should follow one another like links in a chain.

Ordering Paragraphs

It is important that the paragraphs in your plan, and later in your essay, follow a **logical order.** The rule for writers is this: Use your common sense and plan ahead. *Do not* leave the order of your paragraphs to chance.

The types of order often used in single paragraphs—**time order, space order,** and **order of importance***—can sometimes be used to arrange paragraphs within an essay. Essays about subjects that can be broken into stages or steps, with each step discussed in one paragraph, should be arranged according to *time. Space order* is used occasionally in descriptive essays. A writer who wishes to save the most important or convincing paragraph for last would use *order of importance.* Or he or she might wish to reverse this order and put the most important paragraph first.

Very often, however, the writer simply arranges paragraphs in whatever order makes sense in the particular essay. Suppose, for example, that you have written the thesis statement *Photographers Cindy Sherman and Nikki S. Lee have much in common,* and you plan three paragraphs with these topic sentences:

Each photographer uses elaborate costumes, wigs, and props to become other people.

In her photos, Sherman poses as movie or magazine images of the 1950s, 60s, and 70s, while Lee actually enters groups in disguise and becomes a skateboarder, senior citizen, yuppie, or biker chick.

Each woman is her own model and photographs herself role-playing different characters.

Because each woman photographs herself role-playing other people, this point might be a logical starting point for the essay. How each does this—with costumes, wigs, and so on—follows logically as the second paragraph. Once the reader has heard in detail about how these two interesting photographers change their identities, it would make sense to end with one way in which they differ, with Sherman posing in a studio and Lee actually joining groups in disguise. A logical order of paragraphs, then, might be the following:

---

*For more work on time order, space order, and order of importance, see Chapter 4, "Achieving Coherence," Part A.

1. **INTRODUCTION** and thesis statement:		Photographers Cindy Sherman and Nikki S. Lee have much in common.
2. **Topic sentence:**		Each woman is her own model and photographs herself role-playing different characters.
3. **Topic sentence:**		Each photographer uses elaborate costumes, wigs, and props to become other people.
4. **Topic sentence:**		In her photos, Sherman poses as movie or magazine images of the 1950s, 60s, and 70s, while Lee actually enters groups in disguise and appears in photos as a skateboarder, senior citizen, yuppie, or biker chick.
5. **CONCLUSION**		

Finally, if your thesis statement is divided into two, three, or four parts, the paragraphs in the body should follow the order in the thesis; otherwise, the reader will be confused. Assume, for instance, that you are planning three paragraphs to develop the thesis statement *Using a CD-ROM encyclopedia for the first time can be overwhelming, exciting, and educational.*

Paragraph 2 should discuss _____.

Paragraph 3 should discuss _____.

Paragraph 4 should discuss _____.

PRACTICE 7 Plans for three essays follow, each containing a thesis statement and several topic sentences in scrambled order. Number the topic sentences in each group according to an *order that makes sense*. Be prepared to explain your choices.

1. **Thesis statement:** The practice of tai chi can improve one's concentration, health, and peace of mind.

   Topic sentences:
   ___ In several ways, tai chi boosts physical health.

   ___ Peace of mind increases gradually as one becomes less reactive.

   ___ Concentrating on the movements of tai chi in practice promotes better concentration in other areas of life.

2. **Thesis statement:** The fastest-growing job markets through the year 2008 will be in the computer and medical fields.

   Topic sentences:
   ___ Numerous job openings will also exist for nurses, home health aides, and nurse's aides.

   ___ The sources of these career opportunities are the rapid growth of the Internet and a generation of aging baby boomers needing more medical care.

	____ Skilled computer engineers, systems analysts, and technical support personnel will find many job opportunities to choose from.
3. Thesis statement:	The history of European contact with the Karaja Indians of Brazil is one of violence and exploitation.
Topic sentences:	____ The Karaja, exposed to European diseases during the nineteenth century, were reduced in numbers by 90 percent.
	____ During the eighteenth century, the *bandeirantes* led attacks on Karaja villages to get slaves.
	____ Since the turn of the twentieth century, Brazilian pioneers have increasingly used Indian territory as grazing land.

PRACTICE 8   Now, go over the essay plan that you developed in Practice 6 and decide which paragraphs should come first, which second, and so forth. Does time order, space order, or order of importance seem appropriate to your subject? Number your paragraphs accordingly.

Linking Paragraphs

Just as the sentences within a paragraph should flow smoothly, so the paragraphs within an essay should be clearly **linked** one to the next. As you write your essay, do not make illogical jumps from one paragraph to another. Instead, guide your reader. Link the first sentence of each new paragraph to the thesis statement or to the paragraph before. Here are four ways to link paragraphs:

1. Repeat key words or ideas from the thesis statement.
2. Refer to words or ideas from the preceding paragraph.
3. Use transitional expressions.
4. Use transitional sentences.

   1. Repeat key words or ideas from the thesis statement.* The topic sentences in the following essay plan repeat key words and ideas from the thesis statement.

Thesis statement:	Spending time in nature can promote inner peace and a new point of view.
Topic sentence:	A stroll in the woods or a picnic by the sea often brings feelings of inner peace and well-being.
Topic sentence:	Natural places can even give us a new point of view by putting our problems in perspective.

---

* For more work on repetition of key words, see Chapter 4, "Achieving Coherence," Part B. See also "Synonyms and Substitutions" in the same section.

- In the first topic sentence, the words *feelings of inner peace* repeat, in slightly altered form, words from the thesis statement. The words *a stroll in the woods or a picnic by the sea* refer to the idea of *spending time in nature*.
- Which words in the second topic sentence repeat key words or ideas from the thesis statement?

___

2. Refer to words or ideas from the preceding paragraph. Link the first sentence of a new paragraph to the paragraph before, especially by referring to words or ideas near the end of the paragraph. Note how the two paragraphs are linked in the following passage:

> (1) Would you rather take the risk of starting your own business than work for someone else? Would you prefer an insecure job with a large income over a secure job with an average income? Do you have a high energy level? If you answered yes to these questions, you might have some of the traits of what Dr. Frank Farley calls the "Type T" personality.
>
> (2) According to Farley, Type T people ("T" stands for "Thrill") are creative risk takers. He believes that as much as 30 percent of the American public falls into this category. "They are the great experimenters of life," declares Farley. "They break the rules."
>
> —Ira Peck and Larry F. Krieger, *Sociology: The Search for Social Patterns*

- What words and groups of words in paragraph 2 clearly refer to paragraph 1?

___

3. Use transitional expressions.* Transitional expressions—words like *for example, therefore,* and *later on*—are used within a paragraph to show the relationship between sentences. Transitional expressions can also be used within an essay to show the relationships between paragraphs:

> (1) The house where I grew up was worn out and run-down. The yard was mostly mud, rock hard for nine months of the year but wet and swampy for the other three. Our nearest neighbors were forty miles away, so it got pretty lonely. Inside, the house was shabby. The living room furniture was covered in stiff, nubby material that had lost its color over the years and become a dirty brown. Upstairs in my bedroom, the wooden floor sagged a little farther west every year.
>
> (2) *Nevertheless*, I love the place for what it taught me. There I learned to thrive in solitude. During the hours I spent alone, when school was over and the chores were done, I learned to play the guitar and sing. Wandering in the fields around the house or poking under stones in the creek bed, I grew to love the natural world. Most of all, I learned to see and to appreciate small wonders.

___

* For a complete list of transitional expressions, see Chapter 4, "Achieving Coherence," Part B. See also the chapters in Unit 3 for ways to use transitional expressions in each paragraph and essay pattern.

- The first paragraph describes some of the negative details about the writer's early home. The second paragraph *contrasts* the writer's attitude, which is positive. The transitional expression *nevertheless* eases the reader from one paragraph to the next by pointing out the exact relationship between the paragraphs.

- Transitional expressions can also highlight the *order* in which paragraphs are arranged.* Three paragraphs arranged in time order might begin: *First . . . , Next . . . , Finally. . . .* Three paragraphs arranged in order of importance might begin: *First . . . , More important . . . , Most important. . . .* Use transitional expressions alone or together with other linking devices.

   4. Use transitional sentences. From time to time, you may need to write an entire sentence of transition to link one paragraph to the next, as shown in this passage:

> (1) Dee Kantner and Violet Palmer were hardly radicals, but they helped bring about a revolution in sports. In 1995, both were experienced referees in women's college basketball and in the newly created Women's National Basketball Association, the WNBA. Although they were the top women in their profession, they wanted the prize all great referees want—to work in the NBA. In 1997, they won that prize, becoming the first women to referee regular-season games in the NBA and in professional football, hockey, and baseball.
>
> (2) *Achieving this goal, however, created a new challenge.* The two women now faced the criticism and even taunts of male players and coaches. Former Chicago Bulls coach Phil Jackson stated publicly that gender got them into NBA, not qualifications. Dennis Rodman shouted negative comments on the court. Kenny Anderson responded to a foul call by telling Kantner to keep her eyes on the game and off his pants. Yet Kantner and Palmer kept their cool, above all, focusing on the game. When asked how they could curb the behavior of quick-tempered players like Rodman, Charles Barkley, and Anthony Mason, Palmer told a reporter, "Confrontation is part of being a referee. If they cross a line, they get a technical foul."

- In paragraph 1, Kantner and Palmer achieve their goal. In paragraph 2, they face the reaction of the all-male NBA. The topic sentence of paragraph 2 is the second sentence: *The two women now faced the criticism and even taunts of male players and coaches.*

- The first sentence of paragraph 2 is actually a **sentence of transition** that eases the reader from success to a new challenge. (Note that it includes a transitional expression of contrast, *however*.)

Use all four methods of linking paragraphs as you write your essays.

PRACTICE 9 Read the essay that follows, noting the paragraph-to-paragraph *links*. Then answer the questions.

Skin Deep

(1) What do Johnny Depp, Lady Randolph Churchill, Whoopi Goldberg, and Charles Manson all have in common? Perhaps you guessed tattoos: body decorations made by piercing the skin and inserting colored pigments. In fact, tattoos

---

* For more work on transitional expressions of time, space, and importance, see Chapter 4, "Achieving Coherence," Part A.

have a long and nearly worldwide history, ranging from full-body art to a single heart, from tribal custom to pop-culture fad.

(2) The earliest known tattoo was found on the mummy of an Egyptian priestess dating back to 2200 B.C. Tattoos were also used in the ancient world to decorate Japanese noblemen, mark Greek spies, and hide expressions of fear on Maori tribesmen in New Zealand. Full-body tattooing was practiced for centuries in the South Seas; in fact, the word *tattoo* comes from the Tahitian word *tattaw*. In medieval times, small tattoos were common in Europe. For instance, in 1066, after the famous Battle of Hastings, the only way that the body of the Anglo Saxon King Harold could be identified was by the word *Edith* tattooed over his heart.

(3) For the next 600 years, however, Europeans lost interest in tattoos. Then, in the 1700s, explorers and sailors rekindled public excitement. Captain Cook, returning from a trip to Tahiti in 1761, described the wonders of tattoos. Cook enthusiastically paraded a heavily tattooed Tahitian prince named Omai through England's finest drawing rooms. People were intrigued by the colorful flowers, snakes, and geographical maps covering Omai's body. Although large tattoos were too much for the British, the idea of a pretty little bee or royal crest on the shoulder was very appealing. Tattooing remained popular with Europe's royalty and upper classes through the nineteenth century. The Prince of Wales, the Duke of York, Tsar Nicholas of Russia, and Winston Churchill's mother all had tattoos.

(4) When tattooing first reached America, on the other hand, its image was definitely not refined. American soldiers and sailors, feeling lonely and patriotic during World War II, visited tattoo parlors in South Pacific ports and came home with *Mother* or *Death Before Dishonor* inked into their arms. Soon motorcyclists started getting tattoos as part of their rebellious, macho image. The process was painful, with a high risk of infection, so the more elaborate a cyclist's bloody dagger or skull and crossbones, the better.

(5) Tattooing did not remain an outlaw rite of passage for long. Safer and less painful methods developed in the 1970s and 1980s brought tattooing into the American mainstream, especially among the young. Designs ranged from one butterfly to black-and-white patterns like Native American textiles to flowing, multicolored, stained-glass designs. With the media documenting the tattoos of the rich and famous, tattooing became a full-blown fad by the 1990s. Now the onetime symbols of daring have become so common that many rebels are having their tattoos removed. About one-third of all the work performed by tattoo artists in the United States is "erasing" unwanted tattoos.

1. What transitional expressions does this writer use to link paragraphs? (Find at least two.) _____

2. How does the writer link paragraphs 1 and 2? _____

3. How does the writer link paragraphs 4 and 5? _____

Part E

Writing and Revising Essays

Writing the First Draft

Now you should have a clear plan or outline from which to write your first draft. This plan should include your thesis statement, two to four topic sentences that support it, details and facts to develop each paragraph, and a logical order. Write on every other line to leave room for later corrections, including all your ideas and paragraphs in the order you have chosen to present them. Explain your ideas fully, but avoid getting stuck on a particular word or sentence. When you have finished the draft, set it aside, if possible, for several hours or several days.

PRACTICE 10 Write a first draft of the essay you have been working on in Practices 6 and 8.

Revising and Proofreading

Revising is perhaps the most important step in the essay-writing process. Revising an essay involves the same principles as revising a paragraph.* Read your first draft slowly and carefully to yourself—aloud if possible. Imagine you are a reader who has never seen the paper before. As you read, underline trouble spots, draw arrows, and write in the margins, if necessary, to straighten out problems.

Here are some questions to keep in mind as you revise:

1. Is my thesis statement clear?
2. Does the body of the essay fully support my thesis statement?
3. Does the essay have unity; does every paragraph relate to the thesis statement?
4. Does the essay have coherence; do the paragraphs follow a logical order?
5. Are my topic sentences clear?
6. Does each paragraph provide good details, well-chosen examples, and so on?
7. Is the language exact, concise, and fresh?
8. Are my sentences varied in length and type?
9. Does the essay conclude, not just leave off?

If possible, ask a **peer reviewer**—a trusted classmate or friend—to read your paper and give you feedback. Of course, this person should not rewrite or correct the essay but should simply tell you which parts are clear and which parts are confusing.

To guide your peer reviewer, you might ask him or her to use the Peer Feedback Sheet on pages 38–39 or to answer these questions in writing:

---

*For more work on revising, see Chapter 3, "The Process of Writing Paragraphs," Part F, and Chapter 23, "Putting Your Revision Skills to Work."

1. What do you like about this piece of writing?
2. What seems to be the main point?
3. Which parts could be improved (meaning unclear sentences, supporting points missing, order mixed up, writing not lively, and so forth)? Please be specific.
4. What one change would most improve this essay?

Proofreading and Writing the Final Draft

Next, carefully **proofread** the draft for grammar and spelling. Check especially for those errors you often make: verb errors, comma splices, and so forth.* If you are unsure about the spelling of a word, check a dictionary or use the spellcheck on your computer.

Finally, neatly recopy your essay or print out a final copy on $8\frac{1}{2}$-by-11-inch paper. Write on one side only. When you finish, proofread the final copy.

The following sample essay by a student shows his first draft, the revisions he made, and the revised draft. Each revision has been numbered and explained to give you a clear idea of the thinking process involved.

First Draft

Portrait of a Bike Fanatic

(1) I first realized how serious Diane was when I joined her on a long trip one Sunday afternoon. Her bike looked new, so I asked her if it was. When she told me she had bought it three years ago, I asked her how she kept it looking so good. She showed me how she took good care of it.

(2) Diane had just about every kind of equipment I've ever seen. She put on her white crash helmet and attached a tiny rearview mirror on it—the kind the dentist uses to check out the backs of your teeth. She put a warning light on her left leg. She carried a whole bag full of tools. When I looked into it, I couldn't believe how much stuff was in there (wrenches, inner tubes, etc.)—tools to meet every emergency. I was tempted to see if it had a false bottom.

(3) I had no idea she was such a bike nut. We rode thirty miles and I was exhausted. Her equipment was something else, but useful because she had a flat and was able to fix it, saving our trip.

(4) She doesn't look like a bike fanatic, just a normal person. You'd never guess that her bike has more than 10,000 miles on it.

(5) As we rode, Diane told me about her travels throughout the Northeast (Cape Cod, Vermont, Penn., New York). Riding to work saved her money, kept her in shape. Her goal for the next summer was a cross-country tour over the Rockies!

(6) Our trip was no big deal to her but to me it was something. I might consider biking to work because it keeps you in shape. But basically I'm lazy. I drive a car or take the bus. I do like to walk though.

---

*For practice proofreading for individual errors, see chapters in Unit 6; for mixed-error proofreading, see Chapter 37.

Revisions

Portrait of a Bike Fanatic

① Add intro and thesis

② about bicycling

I first realized how serious Diane was when I joined her on a ~~long~~ ③ thirty-mile trip one Sunday afternoon. Her bike looked new, so I asked her if it was. When she told me she had bought it three years ago, I asked her how she kept it looking so good. ~~She showed me how she took good care of it.~~

④ Describe in detail

Diane had just about every kind of equipment I've ever seen. ⑤ For example, She put on her white crash helmet and attached a tiny rearview mirror on it—the kind the dentist uses to ~~check out~~ ⑥ examine the backs of your teeth. She ~~put~~ ⑦ strapped a warning light ~~on~~ to her leg, just below the knee.

⑧ Mention trip location

⑨ New ¶ on tools, flat tire

She carried a whole bag full of tools. When I looked into it, I couldn't believe how much stuff was in there (wrenches, inner tubes, etc.)—tools to meet every emergency. I was tempted to see if it had a false bottom.

⑩ ~~I had no idea she was such a bike nut. We rode thirty miles and I was exhausted.~~ Her equipment was something else, but useful because she had a flat and was able to fix it, saving our trip.

⑪ Combine into one ¶ on tools

⑫ Move to intro?

She doesn't look like a bike fanatic, just a normal person. You'd never guess that her bike has more than 10,000 miles on it.

⑬ Describe in detail. Make interesting!

As we rode, Diane told me about her travels throughout the Northeast (Cape Cod, Vermont, Penn., New York). Riding to work saved her money, kept her in shape. Her goal for the next summer was a cross-country tour over the Rockies!

(14) Better conclusion needed

Our trip was no big deal to her, but to me it was something. ~~I might consider biking to work because it keeps you in shape. But basically I'm lazy. I drive a car or take the bus. I do like to walk though.~~

(15) Drop. Irrelevant

Reasons for Revisions

1. No thesis statement. Add catchy introduction. (introduction and thesis statement)
2. Add *bicycling*. What she is serious *about* is not clear. (exact language)
3. Tell *how* long! (exact language)
4. Expand this; more details needed. (support, exact language)
5. Add transition. (transitional expression)
6. Wrong tone for college essay. (exact language)
7. Find more active verb; be more specific. (exact language)
8. Conclude paragraph; stress time order. (order)
9. This section is weak. Add one paragraph on tools. Tell story of flat tire? (paragraphs, support)
10. Drop! Repeats thesis. Not really a paragraph. (unity, paragraphs)
11. Put this in tools paragraph. Order is mixed up. (order)
12. Put this in introduction? (order)
13. Add details; make this interesting! (support, exact language)
14. Write a better conclusion. (conclusion)
15. Drop! Essay is about Diane and biking, not my bad exercise habits. (unity)

Final Draft

Portrait of a Bike Fanatic

(1) You'd never guess that the powder-blue ten-speed Raleigh had more than 10,000 miles on it. And you'd never guess that the tiny woman with the sweptback hair and the suntanned forearms had ridden those miles over the last two years, making trips through eleven states. But Diane is a bicycle fanatic.

(2) I first realized how serious Diane was about bicycling when I joined her on a thirty-mile trip one Sunday afternoon. Her bike looked new, so I asked her if it was. When she told me she had bought it three years ago, I asked her how she

kept it looking so good. From her saddlebag she took the soft cloth that she wiped the bike down with after every long ride and the plastic drop cloth that she put over it every time she parked it outdoors overnight.

(3) Diane had just about every kind of bike equipment I've ever seen. For example, she put on her white crash helmet and attached a tiny rearview mirror to it—the kind the dentist uses to examine the backs of your teeth. She strapped a warning light to her left leg, just below the knee. Then we set off on our trip, starting at Walden Pond in Concord and planning to go to the Wayside Inn in Sudbury and back again before the sun set.

(4) We were still in Concord when Diane signaled me to stop. "I think I have a flat," she said. I cursed under my breath. I was sure that would mean the end of our trip; we'd have to walk her bike back to the car and she'd have to take it to the shop the next day. But she reached into her saddlebag again, and out came a wrench and a new tube. Before I knew it, she took the rear wheel off the bike, installed the new tube, and put the wheel back on. I began to wonder what else was in that saddlebag. When I asked, she showed me two sets of wrenches, another spare inner tube, two brake pads, a can of lubricating oil, two screwdrivers, a roll of reflective tape, extra bulbs for her headlight and taillight, and an extra chain. She had so much in the bag, I was tempted to see if it had a false bottom. Diane is one of those bicyclists who have tools to meet any emergency and know how to use them.

(5) As we rode along, Diane told me about her travels throughout the Northeast. She had taken her bike on summer vacations on Cape Cod and fall foliage tours in Vermont. She had ridden all over Pennsylvania and upstate New York, covering as much as seventy miles in a single day. She also rode to and from work every day, which she said saved money, kept her in shape, and helped her start each day feeling good. Her goal for the next summer, she said, was a cross-country tour. "All the way?" I asked. "What about the Rockies?" "I know," she said. "What a challenge!"

(6) Our trip took a little less than three hours, but I'm sure Diane was slowing down to let me keep up with her. When we got back to the parked car, I was breathing hard and had worked up quite a sweat. Diane was already there waiting for me, looking as if she did this every day—which she does. For Diane, riding a bike is as easy and natural as walking is for most people. Look out, Rockies.

PRACTICE 11 Now, carefully read over the first draft of your essay from Practice 10 and **revise** it, referring to the checklist of questions on page 190. You might wish to ask a peer reviewer for feedback before you revise. Ask specific questions or use the peer feedback sheet on pages 38–39. Take your time and write the best essay you can. Once you are satisfied, **proofread** your essay for grammar and spelling errors. Neatly write the final draft or print a final copy.

Writing Assignments

The assignments that follow will give you practice in writing essays. In each, concentrate on writing a clear thesis statement and a full, well-organized body. Because introductions and conclusions are not discussed until Chapter 16, you may wish to begin your essay with the thesis statement and conclude as simply as possible.

Before you write, make a plan or an outline that includes

- a clear thesis statement
- two to four topic sentences that support the thesis statement
- details, facts, and examples to develop each paragraph
- a logical order of paragraphs

1. Some college students cheat on their papers and exams; some people cheat on the job. Why do people cheat? What are the advantages and disadvantages of cheating? Does cheating pay off? Does it achieve the end that the cheater desires? Focus on cheating at college or at work, and choose one main idea to write about. You might wish to use examples to support your thesis. Plan your essay carefully on paper—before you write it.

2. Interview a classmate (or, if you do this assignment at home, someone with an unusual skill). As you talk to the person, look for a thesis: ask questions, take notes. What stands out about the person? Is there an overall impression or idea that can structure your essay? Use your descriptive powers. Notice the person's looks, clothes, typical expressions, and gestures. Later, formulate a thesis statement about the person, organize your ideas, and write.

3. Do you feel that certain television programs (or music videos) show stereotypical women, African Americans, Hispanics, or members of any other group instead of believable people? Examine and discuss just one such program (or video) and one group of people. What situations, words, and actions by the characters are stereotypical, not real? Focus your subject, make a plan, and write a well-organized essay.

    You might wish to construct a thesis statement divided in this way: On the television program ___(name show)___, ___(name group)___ are often portrayed as being ___(name stereotype)___.

4. Give advice to the weary job hunter. Describe the most creative job-hunting strategies you have ever tried or heard about. Support your thesis statement with examples, or consider using time order to show a successful job-hunting day in the life of the expert, you.

5. For better or worse, sex education begins at home—whether or not parents speak about the subject, whether parents' words reinforce or contradict the message of their own behavior. How do you think a parent should handle this responsibility? Be as specific as possible, including details from your own and your friends' experiences to make your point.

6. Draw upon your romantic misfortunes to give dating advice to others. Think back to the two, three, or four most disastrous dates you ever had. Relive the unhappy details, the disappointment, the shock, and take notes; look for a pattern, a thesis, that can pull these isolated bad times together. Now write an excellent paper in which you tell what happened to you and share your hard-earned wisdom with those seeking love—or at least, a first-run movie and popcorn.

7. Have you ever had a close call with death? Describe the experience and its effect, if any, on your attitudes and actions since. If it has had little or no effect

on you, try to explain why. Be sure to unify your essay with a clear thesis statement.

8. Many children have working parents; in fact, mothers of young children make up 45 percent of the American work force. How do you think children are affected when both parents work or when their single parent works? Focus your discussion on one aspect of this topic that you can discuss fully in a short essay—on the positive and/or negative emotional effects on children, on the way day care affects children, and so forth.

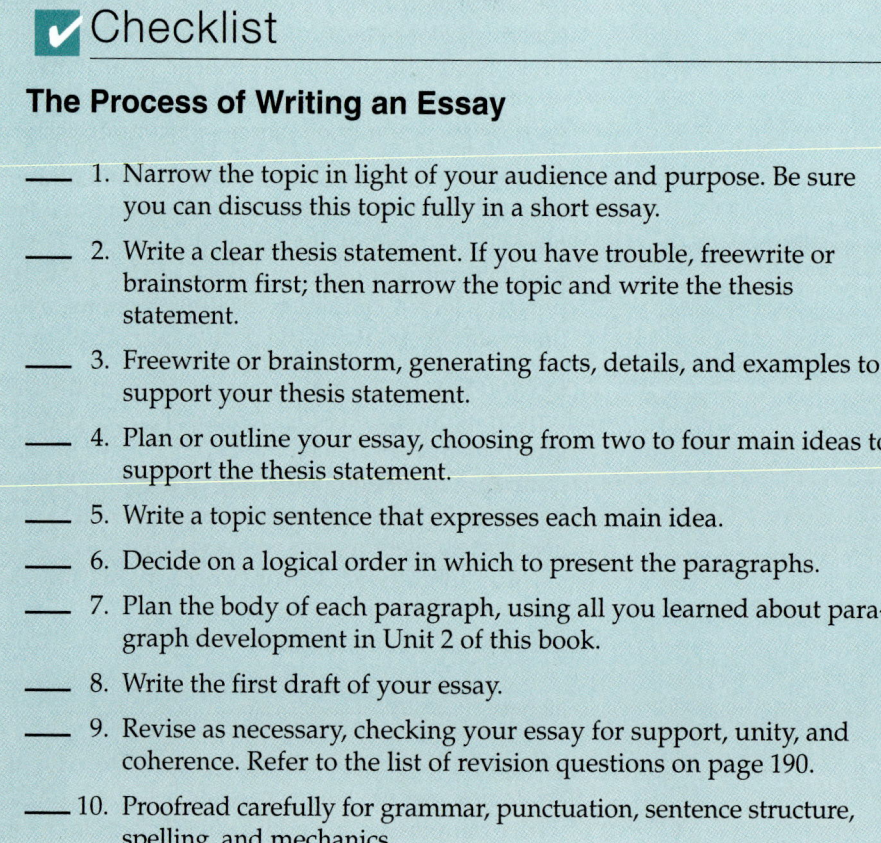

✔ Checklist

The Process of Writing an Essay

___ 1. Narrow the topic in light of your audience and purpose. Be sure you can discuss this topic fully in a short essay.

___ 2. Write a clear thesis statement. If you have trouble, freewrite or brainstorm first; then narrow the topic and write the thesis statement.

___ 3. Freewrite or brainstorm, generating facts, details, and examples to support your thesis statement.

___ 4. Plan or outline your essay, choosing from two to four main ideas to support the thesis statement.

___ 5. Write a topic sentence that expresses each main idea.

___ 6. Decide on a logical order in which to present the paragraphs.

___ 7. Plan the body of each paragraph, using all you learned about paragraph development in Unit 2 of this book.

___ 8. Write the first draft of your essay.

___ 9. Revise as necessary, checking your essay for support, unity, and coherence. Refer to the list of revision questions on page 190.

___ 10. Proofread carefully for grammar, punctuation, sentence structure, spelling, and mechanics.

Suggested Topics for Essays

1. The career for which I am best suited
2. This college's worst problem (propose a solution)
3. A special or unusual person
4. A valuable discipline or practice (lifting weights, rock climbing, meditating, or other)
5. Why many Americans don't read the newspaper (vote, value education, give their all at work, or read poetry)

6. The best (or worst) teacher I ever had
7. Music videos (choose one performer or group, one type of music, or one TV show)
8. A lesson in diversity, race, or difference
9. The joys of homework (or housework or some other supposedly unpleasant task)
10. How to resolve a disagreement peacefully
11. An important film (book, magazine, or program)
12. The best gift I ever gave (or received)
13. Three ways that cigarette ads hook kids
14. Should courts require a one-year "cooling-off" period before a divorce?
15. Writer's choice: _____

Exploring Online

Review the essay writing process.
http://www.powa.org
http://web.uvic.ca/wguide/Pages/StartHere.html (click "essays")

CHAPTER 15: Types of Essays

PART A   The Illustration Essay
PART B   The Narrative Essay
PART C   The Descriptive Essay
PART D   The Process Essay
PART E   The Definition Essay
PART F   The Comparison or Contrast Essay
PART G   The Classification Essay
PART H   The Cause and Effect Essay
PART I   The Persuasive Essay

Because an essay is like an expanded paragraph, the methods for developing and organizing a paragraph that you learned in Unit 3—illustration, process, and so forth—can also be used to develop an entire essay. The rest of this chapter will show you how.

Part A

The Illustration Essay

The **illustration** essay is one of the most frequently used in college writing and in business. For papers and exams in history, psychology, health, English, and other subjects, you will often be asked to develop a main point with examples. In a letter of job application, you might wish to give examples of achievements that demonstrate your special skills.

Here is an illustration essay:

Libraries of the Future—Now

(1) When you think of the word *library,* do you picture an old-fashioned building, dusty books, and stern librarians? Think instead of an electronic theme park for readers, where people from tots to seniors can not only read books from the stacks around them, but explore cyberspace from one of many computer terminals. Imagine yourself calling up documents from libraries around the world or working with other students on multimedia projects. In fact, the future has arrived in a few pioneering libraries that are using technology to offer more resources to library users than ever before.

(2) For instance, the San Francisco Public Library is helping its diverse community enter the information age. At San Francisco's many branch libraries, visitors can now surf the Internet from public terminals, but the hub of the system is the $140 million San Francisco Main Public Library building, which opened in 1996. The seven-story building features 300 computer terminals where users can access catalogues, databases, and the World Wide Web. Another 1,100 users can plug their own laptops into the library's outlets. The huge children's book room has many more computers on child-sized tables. The San Francisco Library appears to be achieving its goal. In its first year, library visits jumped from 1.1 million to 2.1 million, and the number of library-card holders tripled.

(3) A second example of today's high-tech libraries is the private Vatican Library in Rome. The Vatican, headquarters of the Roman Catholic Church, has one of the finest collections of manuscripts and books in the world. The entire catalogue of this collection is now available on the Internet. Yet until recently, only about 2,000 scholars a year could come to Rome and examine such costly treasures as an ancient text handwritten on antelope skin or a perfect Gutenberg Bible. Now, with help from IBM, the Vatican is making digital images of these documents. In an underground, atom bomb-proof vault where the originals are kept, two technicians are scanning one page at a time with a special camera. Soon anyone will be able to see 20,000 rare, perfectly colored images and to enlarge the tiniest details on his or her computer screen.

(4) An even more futuristic library is the University of Michigan's new Media Union. Besides holding the University's art and architecture libraries, the 225,000-square-foot Media Union contains 500 computer workstations, computer training areas, four interactive multimedia classrooms, video and sound production facilities, a theater, a virtual reality and animation lab, a gallery, and, last but not least, books. Students can experience virtual worlds in dance, engineering, art, architecture, and computer science. Imagine two engineering students playing with 3-D designs of a century-old bridge to come up with a dynamic new form or a dance student moving with a virtual dance performance in real time. This exciting library lets people in many fields work together on new creations.

(5) These three unique libraries are helping to adapt the printed past to a digital future. However, they are still the exception, not the rule. Transforming our libraries requires millions of private and public dollars. As citizens, we can urge our elected officials to support the efforts of libraries as they help move all our

citizens into the information age. When many of us were children, libraries opened the door to a world of dreams through books. The high-tech libraries of the future will open doors we cannot yet imagine.

- The **thesis statement** of an illustration essay states the writer's central point—a general statement that the rest of the essay will develop with examples.

- Which sentence in the introductory paragraph is the thesis statement?

  _____

  _____

- How many **examples** does the writer use to develop the thesis statement? What are they?

  _____

  _____

- Underline the topic sentence of each supporting paragraph.

- The thesis statement and topic sentences setting forth the three examples create an **outline** for this essay. The writer no doubt made such a plan or an outline before she wrote the first draft.

   Before writing an illustration essay, you may wish to reread Chapter 5, "Illustration." As you pick a topic and plan your illustration essay, make sure your thesis statement can be richly developed by examples. Then brainstorm or freewrite, jotting down as many possible examples as you can think of; choose the best two or three examples. If you devote one paragraph to each example, each topic sentence should introduce the example to be developed. As you revise, make sure you have fully discussed each example, including all necessary details and facts.

PRACTICE 1 Choose a topic from the following list or use a topic that you or your instructor has chosen. Write an illustration essay, referring to the essay checklist at the end of Chapter 14.

Suggested Topics: The Illustration Essay

1. Good deeds that backfired
2. Inventions that probably will shape the twenty-first century
3. Failure as the best teacher
4. TV talk show hosts who send a positive message (or who _____)
5. Small events that changed lives
6. Memorable neighbors (professors, friends, and so on)
7. Currently cool hairstyles or clothing styles
8. Unusual places to go on dates (or to study, de-stress, get married, and so on)
9. Successful (or unsuccessful) college students

10. Musicians or artists of a particular group (R&B, tropical Latin, surrealist, French impressionist, and so on)

11. Writer's choice: _____

Part B

The Narrative Essay

The narrative essay is used frequently in college writing. For instance, in a history course you might be assigned a paper on the major battles of World War I or be given an essay examination on the story of women's struggle to gain the right to vote. An English teacher may ask you to write a composition in which you retell a meaningful incident or personal experience. In all of these instances, your ability to organize facts and details in clear chronological, or time, order—to tell a story well—will be a crucial factor in the success of your paper.

Here is a narrative essay:

Maya Lin's *Vietnam War Memorial*

(1) The Vietnam War was the longest war in United States history, lasting from 1965 until 1975. Also our most controversial war, it left a deep wound in the nation's conscience. The creation of the Vietnam War Memorial helped heal this wound and put an unknown architecture student into the history books.

(2) In 1980, when the call went out for designs for a Vietnam War Memorial, no one could have predicted that as many as 14,000 entries would be submitted. The rules were clear. The memorial had to be contemplative, harmonize with its surroundings, list the names of those dead or missing, and—most important—make no political statement about the war. When the judges, all well-known architects and sculptors, met in April 1981, they unanimously chose entry number 1026. The winner was Maya Lin, a twenty-one-year-old Asian American architecture student who, ironically, was too young to have had any direct experience of the war.

(3) Lin envisioned shining black granite slabs embedded in a long V-shaped trench, with one end pointing toward the Lincoln Memorial and the other toward the Washington Monument. She defined the trench as a cut in the earth, "an initial violence that in time would heal." Names would be carved into the granite in the order of the dates on which the soldiers had died or disappeared. Lin felt that finding a name on the memorial with the help of a directory would be like finding a body on a battlefield.

(4) Although her design satisfied all the contest criteria and was the judges' clear favorite, it aroused much controversy. Some critics called it a "black gash of shame and sorrow," labeling it unpatriotic, unheroic, and morbid. They were upset that the memorial contained no flags, no statues of soldiers, and no inscription other than the names. Privately, some complained that Lin was too young to win the contest—and that she was female besides. She fought back. She claimed that a flag would make the green area around the memorial look like a golf course and that a traditional statue on her modern structure would be like a mustache drawn

on someone else's portrait. At last, a compromise was reached: A flag and a statue were added to the memorial, and the critics withdrew their complaints. On Veterans Day, November 11, 1982, the Vietnam War Memorial was finally dedicated.

(5) Since then, the memorial has become the most popular site in Washington, D.C. Some visit to see the monument and pay tribute to those who died in the war. Others come to locate and touch the names of loved ones. As they stand before the wall, they also learn the names of those who served and died with their relatives and friends. When the rain falls, all the names seem to disappear. Visitors often leave memorials of their own—flowers, notes to the departed, bits of old uniforms. A place of national mourning and of love, Maya Lin's monument has helped heal the wounds of the Vietnam War.

- The **thesis statement** of a narrative essay gives the point of the essay.
- What is the thesis statement of the essay?

_____

_____

- Paragraphs 2, 4, and 5 of this essay tell in chronological order the incidents of the narrative.
- What are the incidents?

_____

_____

- What is the main idea of paragraph 3?

_____

- Paragraph 1 provides background information that helps the reader understand the narrative.
- What background material is given in this paragraph?

_____

_____

Before writing a narrative essay, you may wish to reread Chapter 6, "Narration." Make sure that your thesis statement clearly states the point of your narrative. Organize all the incidents and details in chronological, or time, order, in general beginning with the earliest event and ending with the latest. Be sure to supply any necessary background information. As you plan your essay, pay careful attention to paragraphing; if your narrative consists of just a few major incidents, you may wish to devote one paragraph to each one. Use transitional expressions that indicate time order to help your reader follow the narrative easily.

PRACTICE 2 Choose a topic from the following list or use a topic that you or your instructor has chosen. Write a narrative essay, referring to the essay checklist at the end of Chapter 14.

Suggested Topics: The Narrative Essay

1. A risk that paid off
2. How someone chose his or her career
3. The story behind a key scientific discovery or invention
4. An event that changed your view of yourself
5. An unforgettable incident you witnessed
6. An important historical event
7. A time someone acted with courage or cowardice
8. The plot line of a movie or TV show you would like to produce
9. Learning a new language (or other subject or skill)
10. Someone's battle with a serious illness
11. Writer's choice: _____

Part C

The Descriptive Essay

Although paragraphs of **description** are more common than whole essays, you will sometimes need to write a descriptive essay. In science labs, you may need to describe accurately cells under a microscope or a certain kind of rock. In business, you might have to describe a product, piece of equipment, or the behavior of consumers in a test group. Travel writers frequently use description, and personal letters often call on your descriptive powers.

Here is a descriptive essay:

The Day of the Dead

(1) The most important holiday in Mexico is the Day of the Dead, *El Día de Los Muertos*. Surprisingly, this holiday is anything but depressing. In the weeks before, Mexicans excitedly prepare to welcome the souls of the dead, who come back each year to visit the living. From October 31 through November 2 this year, I attended this fiesta with my roommate Manuel. By sharing Day of the Dead activities in his family's home, in the marketplace, and in a cemetery, I have observed that Mexicans, unlike other North Americans, accept and celebrate death as a part of life.

(2) For this holiday, the home altar, or *ofrenda,* lovingly celebrates the dead. In the Lopez home, a trail of marigold petals and the rich smell of incense led us from the front door to the altar. The bright orange marigold blooms, the flowers of the dead, also trimmed a card table overflowing with everything the dead would need to take up their lives again. For Manuel's Uncle Angel there was a fragrant bowl of *mole,** a glass of tequila, cigars, playing cards, and two Miles Davis jazz CDs. For

---
mole: a spicy sauce made with unsweetened chocolate

Manuel's cousin Lucia, who died at eighteen months, there was a worn stuffed puppy, a coral blanket, and a bowl of the rice pudding she loved. Heavy black and yellow beeswax candles threw a soft glow on photos of Angel and Lucia. It was as if the dead had never left and would always have a place of honor.

(3) While death is given an honored place in the home, it is celebrated with humor and mockery in the marketplace. Here the skeleton, or *calavera*, rules. Shops sell sugar skulls, humorous bone figures, and even skeletons made of flowers. At the candy store, Manuel's niece picked out a white chocolate skull decorated with blue icing and magenta sequins in the eye sockets. In many bakeries, skull-and-crossbones designs decorated the delicious "bread of the dead." Most impressive were the stalls filled with *calacas*, handmade wooden skeletons, some no bigger than my thumb. The shelves showed a lively afterlife where skeleton musicians played in a band, skeleton writers tapped bony fingers on tiny typewriters, and teenage skeletons hoisted boom boxes on their matchstick-sized shoulder bones.

(4) On the evening of November first, reverence and fun combined in an all-night vigil at the cemetery. On a path outside the cemetery gate, rows of vendors sold soft drinks and cotton candy as if it were a sporting event. Men drank a strong fermented cactus beverage called *pulque* and played cards at picnic tables. The loud music of a mariachi band serenaded the dead, who would come back to eat the food laid out for them on the graves. Old grandmothers wearing hand-woven shawls mourned and wept while children chased each other around the pink- and blue-painted graves. Nobody scolded the children. Life and death did not seem so separate.

(5) While I have always felt fearful in cemeteries at home, there I felt excited and hopeful. When a soft breeze made the rows of candles flicker, I wondered if the souls of the children, the *angelitos*, had come back, laughing and giggling. Or was it the real children I heard laughing? I really didn't know. But I felt more alive than ever, waiting for the dead to arrive in a dusty cemetery in Mexico.

—Jason Eady (Student)

- The **thesis statement** of a descriptive essay says what will be described and sometimes gives an overall impression of it or tells how the writer will approach the subject. Which sentence in the introductory paragraph is the thesis statement?

_____

_____

_____

- Each paragraph in the body of this essay describes one scene or aspect of the topic. How many scenes or aspects are described, and what are they?

_____

_____

- What kind of **order** does the writer follow in organizing paragraph 2?

_Space_____

_____

- Paragraph 5 completes and **concludes** the essay. How effective is this student's conclusion?

  _____

  _____

  _____

- Note that the thesis statement and topic sentences make an **outline** for the whole essay.

  Before writing an essay of description, you may wish to reread Chapter 7, "Description." Make sure that your thesis statement clearly sets forth the precise subject your essay will describe. Use your senses—sight, smell, hearing, taste, and touch—as you jot down ideas for the body. As you plan, pay special attention to organizing details and observations; space order is often the best way to organize a description. As you revise, pay special attention to the richness and exactness of your language and details; these are what make good descriptions come alive.

PRACTICE 3 Choose a topic from the following list or use a topic that you or your instructor has chosen. Write an essay of description, referring to the essay checklist at the end of Chapter 14.

Suggested Topics: The Descriptive Essay

1. The decorations and rituals of a holiday you know
2. A person or animal you have closely observed
3. The scene of a historic event or battle as you imagine it
4. A school, landfill, church, prison, store, health club, or other public place
5. A tourist attraction or a place of natural beauty
6. College classrooms in the late twenty-first century
7. A computer, motorcycle, or piece of equipment from your job
8. A place you know from travel or reading
9. Your family portrait
10. A scene you will never forget
11. Writer's choice: _____

Part D

The Process Essay

The **process** essay is frequently used in college and business. In psychology, for example, you might describe the stages of personality development. In history, you might explain the process of electing a president or how a battle was won or lost, while in business, you might set forth the steps of an advertising campaign. In science labs, you will often have to record the stages of an experiment.

Here is a process essay:

How to Prepare for a Final Exam

(1) At the end of my first semester at college, I postponed thinking about final examinations, desperately crammed the night before, drank enough coffee to keep the city of Cincinnati awake, and then got C's and D's. I have since realized that the students who got A's on their finals weren't just lucky; they knew how to *prepare*. There are many different ways to prepare for a final examination, and each individual must perfect his or her own style, but over the years, I have developed a method that works for me.

(2) First, when your professor announces the date, time, and place of the final—usually at least two weeks before—ask questions and take careful notes on the answers. What chapters will be covered? What kinds of questions will the test contain? What materials and topics are most important? The information you gather will help you study more effectively.

(3) Next, survey all the textbook chapters the test will cover, using a highlighter or colored pen to mark important ideas and sections to be studied later. Many textbooks emphasize key ideas with boldface titles or headlines; others are written so that key ideas appear in the topic sentences at the beginning of each paragraph. Pay attention to these guides as you read.

(4) Third, survey your class notes in the same fashion, marking important ideas. If your notes are messy or disorganized, you might want to rewrite them for easy reference later.

(5) Fourth, decide approximately how many hours you will need to study. Get a calendar and clearly mark off the hours each week that you will devote to in-depth studying. If possible, set aside specific times: Thursday from 1 to 2 P.M., Friday from 6 to 8 P.M., and so on. If you have trouble committing yourself, schedule study time with a friend; but pick someone as serious as you are about getting good grades.

(6) Fifth, begin studying systematically, choosing a quiet place free from distractions in which to work—the library, a dorm room, whatever helps you concentrate. One of my friends can study only in his attic; another, in her car. As you review the textbook and your notes, ask yourself questions based on your reading. From class discussions, try to spot the professor's priorities and to guess what questions might appear on the exam. Be creative; one friend of mine puts important study material on cassette tapes, which he plays walking to and from school.

(7) Finally, at least three days before the exam, start reviewing. At the least opportunity, refer to your notes, even if you are not prepared to digest all the material. Use the moments when you are drinking your orange juice or riding the bus; just looking at the material can promote learning. By the night before the exam, you should know everything you want to know—and allow for a good night's sleep!

(8) By following these simple procedures, you may find, as I do, that you are the most prepared person in the exam room, confident that you studied thoroughly enough to do well on the exam.

—Mark Reyes (Student)

- The **thesis statement** in a process essay tells the reader what process the rest of the essay will describe.
- What is the thesis statement in this essay?

  _____

  _____

  _____

- What **process** will be described?

  _____

- How many steps make up this process, and what are they?

  _____

  _____

  _____

- What kind of **order** does the writer use to organize his essay?

  _____

  Before writing a process essay, you may wish to reread Chapter 8, "Process." The thesis statement should clearly set forth the process you intend to describe. As you plan your essay, jot down all the necessary steps or stages and put them in logical order. As you revise, make sure you have fully and clearly explained each step so that a reader who may not be familiar with the subject matter can follow easily. Clear language and logical organization are the keys to good process writing. Pay special attention to paragraphing; if the process consists of just three or four steps, you may wish to devote one paragraph to each step. If the steps are short or numerous, you will probably wish to combine two or three steps in each paragraph.

PRACTICE 4 Choose a topic from the list below or use a topic that you or your instructor has chosen. Write a process essay, referring to the essay checklist at the end of Chapter 14.

Suggested Topics: The Process Essay

1. How someone achieved success
2. How to build a web site
3. How to get in shape
4. How a cell phone can ruin a date (or other social occasion)
5. How to get action on a community problem
6. How to teach a child a skill or value
7. The yearly cycle of a crop (corn, wheat, oranges, cocoa, and so on)

8. How to impress the boss
9. A process you learned in another course (stages of human moral development, how a lake becomes a meadow, and so on)
10. How to get an A in _____
11. Writer's choice: _____

Part E

The Definition Essay

Although paragraphs of **definition** are more common in college writing than essays are, you may at some time have to write a definition essay. In a computer course, for example, you might be called on to define *Internet* and *intranet*. In psychology, you might need to define the *Oedipus complex,* or in biology, the terms *DNA* or *spontaneous remission.* Sometimes defining at length a term people think they know can be illuminating.

Here is a definition essay:

Winning

(1) The dictionary defines winning as "achieving victory over others in a competition, receiving a prize or reward for achievement." Yet some of the most meaningful wins of my life were victories over no other person, and I can remember winning when there was no prize for performance. To me, winning means overcoming obstacles.

(2) My first experience of winning occurred in elementary school gym. Nearly every day, after the preparatory pushups and squat-thrusts, we had to run relays. Although I had asthma as a child, I won many races. My chest would burn terribly for a few minutes, but it was worth it to feel so proud—not because I'd beaten others or won a prize, but because I'd overcome a handicap. (By the way, I "outgrew" my asthma by age eleven.)

(3) In high school, I had another experience of winning. Although I loved reading about biology, I could not bring myself to dissect a frog in lab. I hated the smell of the dead animals, and the idea of cutting them open disgusted me. Every time I tried, my hands would shake and my stomach would turn. Worst of all, my biology teacher reacted to my futile attempts with contempt. After an upsetting couple of weeks, I decided to get hold of myself. I realized that I was overreacting. "The animals are already dead," I told myself. With determination, I swept into my next lab period, walked up to the table, and with one swift stroke, slit open a frog. After that, I excelled in biology. I had won again.

(4) I consider the fact that I am now attending college winning. To get here, I had to surmount many obstacles, both outside and inside myself. College costs money, and I don't have much of it. College takes time, and I don't have much of that either with a little son to care for. But I overcame these obstacles and a bigger one still—lack of confidence in myself. I had to keep saying, "I won't give up." And here I am, winning!

(5) These examples should clarify what winning means to me. I don't trust anything that comes too easily. In fact, I expect the road to be rocky, and I appreciate a win more if I have to work, sacrifice, and overcome. This is a positive drive for me, the very spirit of winning.

—Audrey Holmes (Student)

- The **thesis statement** of a definition essay tells the reader what term will be defined and usually defines it as well.
- Which sentence in the introductory paragraph is the thesis statement?

_____

_____

- What is the writer's **definition** of *winning*?

_____

_____

- Underline the topic sentences of paragraphs 2, 3, and 4.
- How do paragraphs 2, 3, and 4 develop the thesis statement?

_____

_____

- What **order** does the writer follow in paragraphs 2, 3, and 4?

_____

_____

Before writing a definition essay, you may wish to reread Chapter 9, "Definition." Choose a word or term that truly interests you, one about which you have something to say. Decide what type of definition you will use and write the thesis statement, which should state and define your term. Then brainstorm ideas to explain your definition. Consider using two or three examples to develop the term—the way the writer does in the preceding essay—devoting one paragraph to each example. As you revise, make sure your writing is very clear, so the reader knows exactly what you mean.

PRACTICE 5 Choose a topic from the following list or one that you or your instructor has chosen. Write a definition essay, referring to the essay checklist at the end of Chapter 14.

Suggested Topics: The Definition Essay

1. A special term from sports, music, art, science, or technology
2. Tolerance
3. A friend

4. An environmental term (*endangered species, biodiversity, wind chill, global warming,* and so on)

5. A breed of dog or other animal

6. Sexual harassment

7. Maturity

8. A slang term in current use

9. A term from another language (*salsa, joie de vivre, machismo, zeitgeist,* and so on)

10. A disease or medical condition

11. Writer's choice: _____

Part F

The Comparison or Contrast Essay

Essays of **comparison** or **contrast** are frequently called for in college courses. In an English or a drama class, you might be asked to contrast two of Shakespeare's villains—perhaps Iago and Claudius. In psychology, you might have to contrast the training of the clinical psychologist and that of the psychiatrist, or in history, to compare ancient Greek and Roman religions.

Does the following essay compare or contrast?

E-Notes from an Online Learner

(1) This year I attended my first U.S. history class at midnight, clad in my dancing cow pajamas and fluffy slippers. No, I was not taking part in some bizarre campus ritual. I am enrolled in two courses in the University of Houston's Distance Education Program. Although I took classes on campus at the same college last year, my experiences in the traditional classroom and in the virtual classroom have been vastly different.

(2) Attending online courses has proved more convenient for me than traveling to regular classes each day. Because I live over an hour away from campus, I was often stalled in traffic when my 8:00 A.M. psychology lecture was beginning. Then I spent the last half hour of my afternoon English class praying that the discussion—however lively and interesting—would not go past 4:00 P.M. and make me late to pick up my son at day care. In contrast, my online classes are always convenient to attend because I set my own schedule. Lectures for my history survey course are posted to the class web site, so I can log on whenever I want to read new material or review. My writing seminar is "asynchronous." This means that students and instructors communicate at their convenience on an electronic bulletin board. I can email my questions, file homework, and respond to other students' work at night or on weekends without ever leaving my apartment.

(3) Though some students miss the human energy of a real classroom, the online format actually encourages me to participate more in discussions. As a shy

woman who is older than many of my peers, I used to hide in the back row to avoid having to speak. I only answered questions when called upon. On the other hand, writing online, I am more confident. I have time to think about what I want to say, and I know people are not judging me by anything except my ideas. Even though bulletin board discussions can be painfully slow and disjointed compared to the back-and-forth of a great classroom discussion, I like the equality in a virtual classroom. Surprisingly, there I feel freer to be the real me.

(4) The biggest difference in moving from a regular classroom to a virtual one, in my view, is learning to be self-motivated. Attending classes on campus, I was motivated by the personal involvement of my instructors. I also caught that group adrenaline rush, seeing other students hunched over their notebooks in a lecture hall or coffeehouse. While my online courses still require papers to be written each week and tests to be completed within a certain time, now no instructor is prodding me to get busy. Instead, only the soft bubbling noise of my computer's aquarium screen saver reminds me to tap the keyboard and dive into my coursework. Fortunately, I am self-motivated and focused. As a returning student with a job and a child, I have to be. Honestly, however, I have already seen some of my online classmates post homework assignments later and later until they drop off the screen entirely.

(5) Overall, my experience with online classes has been more positive than my experience on campus, but online learning is not for everyone. So far I find online classes convenient, welcoming for self-expression, and well-suited to my particular personality, which is organized, shy, and prone to bouts of midnight energy. In fact, it's 12:14 A.M. now as I input the final draft of this essay assignment. My son is asleep in the next room and my cat, Miss Fleason, is nuzzling my hot pink fluffy slippers.

—Brenda Wilson (Student)

- The **thesis statement** of a comparison or contrast essay tells what two persons or things will be compared or contrasted.

- What is the thesis statement of this essay?

  _____

  _____

  _____

- Will this essay **compare** or **contrast** the two kinds of classrooms? What word or words in the thesis indicate this?

  _____

- Does the writer discuss all points about A and then all points about B, or skip back and forth from A to B?

  _____

- Note that the thesis statement and topic sentences make an **outline** for this essay.

Before you plan or outline your essay, you may wish to reread Chapter 10, "Comparison and Contrast." Bear in mind, as you choose a subject, that the most interesting essays usually compare two things that are different or contrast two things that are similar. Otherwise, you run the risk of saying the obvious ("Cats and dogs are two different animals").

Here are a few tips to keep in mind as you write your thesis statement: Don't just say that A and B are similar or different; instead, say *in what way* A and B are similar or different, as the writer does on pages 210–211. You may wish to use this form for a contrast thesis: *Although A and B have this similarity, they are different in these ways.* And for a comparison: *Although A and B are unlike in this way, they are similar in these ways.*

As you plan the body of your essay, you may wish to make a chart of all your points of comparison or contrast. In any case, if you discuss the food, service, price, and atmosphere of Restaurant A, you must discuss the food, service, price, and atmosphere of Restaurant B as well.

In your essay, you can first discuss A (one paragraph), then discuss B (one paragraph), or you can skip back and forth between A and B (one paragraph on point one, A and B, one paragraph on point two, A and B, and one paragraph on point three, A and B). Refer to the charts in Chapter 10, page 118.

PRACTICE 6 Choose a topic from the list below or use a topic that you or your instructor has chosen. Write either a comparison or a contrast essay, referring to the essay checklist at the end of Chapter 14.

Suggested Topics: The Comparison or Contrast Essay

1. Shopping at a mall and shopping online
2. Your mother's or father's childhood and your own
3. Two cultural attitudes about one subject
4. A neighborhood store and a chain store (bookstore, restaurant, music store, and so on)
5. Two entertainers, athletes, philosophers, politicians, or other public figures
6. Two views on a controversial issue
7. Two houses or apartments that you know well
8. A traditional doctor and an alternative healer
9. A book and a movie made from that book
10. Two pets
11. Writer's choice: _____

Part G

The Classification Essay

The **classification** essay is useful in college and business. In music, for example, you might have to classify Mozart's compositions according to the musical periods of his life. A retail business might classify items in stock according to popularity—how frequently they must be reordered. All plants, animals, rocks, and stars are classified by scientists. A recent book even classified L.A. gangs and their tattoos.

Although the classification essay is usually serious, the pattern ca good humorous essay, as this essay shows:

The Potato Scale

(1) For years, television has been the great American pastime. Nearly every household has at least one TV, which means that people are spending time watching it, unless, of course, they bought it to serve as a plant stand. Television viewers can be grouped in many ways—by the type of shows they watch (but there is no accounting for taste) or by hours per week of watching (but that seems unfair since a working, twelve-hour-a-week viewer could conceivably become a fifty-hour-a-week viewer if he or she were out of a job). So I have developed the Potato Scale. The four major categories of the Potato Scale rank TV viewers on a combination of leisure time spent watching, intensity of watching, and the desire to watch versus the desire to engage in other activities.

(2) First, we have the True Couch Potatoes. They are diehard viewers who, when home, will be found in front of their televisions. They no longer eat in the dining room, and if you visit them, the television stays on. *TV Guide* is their Bible. They will plan other activities and chores around their viewing time, always hoping to accomplish these tasks in front of the tube. If a presidential address is on every channel but one, and they dislike the president, they will tune in that one channel, be it Bugs Bunny reruns or Polynesian barge cooking. These potatoes would never consider turning off the box.

(3) The second group consists of the Pseudo Couch Potatoes. These are scheduled potatoes. They have outside interests and actually eat at the table, but for a certain period of time (let's say from seven to eleven in the evening), they will take on the characteristics of True Couch Potatoes. Another difference between True and Pseudo Potatoes deserves note. The True Potato must be forced by someone else to shut off the television and do something different; however, if the Pseudo Potato has flipped through all the channels and found only garbage, he or she still has the capacity to think of other things to do.

(4) Third, we have the Selective Potatoes. These more discriminating potatoes enjoy many activities, and TV is just one of them. They might have a few shows they enjoy watching regularly, but missing one episode is not a world-class crisis. After all, the show will be on next week. They don't live by *TV Guide*, but use it to check for interesting specials. If they find themselves staring at an awful movie or show, they will gladly, and without a second thought, turn it off.

(5) The fourth group consists of Last Resort Potatoes. These people actually prefer reading, going to the theater, playing pickup basketball, walking in the woods, and many other activities to watching television. Only after they have exhausted all other possibilities or are dog tired or shivering with the flu, will they click on the tube. These potatoes are either excessively choosy or almost indifferent to what's on, hoping it will bore them to sleep.

(6) These are the principal categories of the Potato Scale, from the truly vegetable to the usually human. What type of potato are you?

—Helen Petruzzelli (Student)

- The **thesis statement** in a classification essay tells the reader what group will be classified and on what basis.

- This entire essay **classifies** people on the basis of their television viewing habits. Which sentence is the thesis statement?

_____

_____

- Into how many categories are TV viewers divided?

  _____

- Each paragraph in the body of the essay discusses one of four categories, which the writer names. What are they?

  1. _____
  2. _____
  3. _____
  4. _____

- The thesis statement and the topic sentences setting forth the four categories create an **outline** for the essay. The writer no doubt made the outline before she wrote the first draft.

- Can you see the logic in the writer's *order* of paragraphs? That is, why does she present True Couch Potatoes first, Pseudo Potatoes second, Selective Potatoes third, and Last Resort Potatoes last?

  _____

  _____

Before writing your classification essay, you may wish to reread Chapter 11, "Classification." Choose a topic that lends itself to classification and carefully determine your basis of classification. Your thesis statement should state clearly the group you will classify and your basis of classification. As you plan, make sure that all your categories (three or four is a good number) reflect that basis of classification. Discuss one category per paragraph, including enough examples, details, and facts to let the reader completely understand your ideas.

PRACTICE 7 Choose a topic from the following list or use a topic that you or your instructor has chosen. Write a classification essay, referring to the essay checklist at the end of Chapter 14.

Suggested Topics: The Classification Essay

1. Members of your family
2. People studying in the library
3. Stories on the front page of the newspaper
4. Drivers
5. Music videos
6. Teenagers whom you interview about their hopefulness or the lack of it (or their belief in education, thoughts about intolerance, and so on)
7. Restaurants, clothes stores, or shoe stores in your neighborhood
8. Shoplifters

9. Your coworkers
10. People in a movie theater or mall
11. Writer's choice: _____

Part H

The Cause and Effect Essay

Essays of **cause and effect** are among the most important kinds of essays to master because knowing how to analyze the causes and consequences of events will help you succeed in college, at work, and in your personal life. What *caused* a historic battle, an increase in urban homelessness, or two friends' breaking apart? How will a certain child be *affected* by owning a computer, spending time at Sunshine Day Care, or being teased because he loves to dance? In business, the success of every company and product relies on a grasp of cause and effect in the marketplace. Why does this brand of athletic shoe outsell all others? What causes employees to want to work hard? How will the Internet affect business in 2015?

Here is an essay of cause and effect. As you will see, this writer's eventual understanding of causes and effects might have saved her life.

Why I Stayed and Stayed

(1) It has been proven that about 1.8 million women are battered each year, making battery the single largest cause of injury to women in the United States. Domestic violence can be physical, emotional, verbal, financial, or sexual abuse from a partner you live with. I suffered from most of these abuses for almost ten years. I have had black eyes, busted lips, bruises, and scars on my face. He had affairs with other women, yet he claimed that he loved me. People ask, "Why did you wait so long to leave him?" I stayed for many reasons.

(2) First, I was born in a country that is male-dominated. Many of my people accept violence against women as a part of life. I grew up seeing hundreds of women staying in violent relationships for the sake of their children. They wanted their children to grow up with a father at home. Relatives convinced these women to try to make their marriages work. This was all I knew.

(3) Another reason I stayed was that I was afraid to make changes in my life. I had been with him so long that I thought I had nowhere to go. I depended on him to provide me and my child with food and shelter. How could I manage on my own? Of course, the longer I believed these things, the more my self-confidence withered.

(4) Finally, I stayed because I was isolated. I felt ashamed to talk about the problem, believing it was somehow my fault. Fear was isolating, too. Living in a violent home is very frightening. Like many women, I was afraid to say anything to anyone, thinking he would get upset. If I just kept quiet, maybe he wouldn't hurt me. But nothing I did made any difference.

(5) When I finally realized that the abuse was not going to stop, I decided to do something about it. I was finally ready to end my pain. I began to talk to people and learn about ways to get help.

(6) On April 24 of this year, I fought back. When he punched me in the eye, I called 911. Thank God for changes in the way domestic violence cases are now being handled. The police responded quickly. He was arrested and taken to jail, where he waited for two days to go to court. The next day, I went to the courthouse to press charges. I spoke to the district attorney in charge, asking for an order of protection. This order forbids him from having any verbal or physical contact with me.

(7) It is very hard to see someone you love being taken away in handcuffs, but I had to put my safety and my child's well-being first. Although he is now out of jail, I feel safe with my order of protection; however, I understand that court orders sometimes do not stop abusers. These are very difficult days for me, but I pray that time will heal my wounds. I cry often, which helps my pain. But an innocent life depends on me for guidance, and I cannot let her down.

(8) Every case is different, and you know your partner better than anyone, but help is out there if you reach for it. Most cities have a twenty-four-hour hotline. There is help at this college at the PASS Center and the Department of Student Development. You can go to a shelter, to a friend, to your family. These people will not fail you. You too can break the chain.

—Student, name withheld by request

- The **thesis statement** in a cause and effect essay identifies the subject and tells whether causes or effects will be emphasized. What is this writer's thesis statement? Will she emphasize causes or effects?

  _____

- How many **causes** does the writer discuss, and what are they?

  _____

- Although some essays discuss either causes or effects, this one does both. Paragraph 5 marks a turning point, her decision to take action. What positive effects of this new decision does she discuss? Are there any negative effects?

  _____

  _____

  _____

- Before she wrote this essay, the writer probably made a **plan** or **outline** like this:

  Introduction and thesis statement
  Reasons for staying with abusive partner ⟵ upbringing / fear of change / isolation
  Decision to leave
  Effects of leaving abusive partner ⟵ reached out for help / fought back (911, order of protection) / acted for daughter / sadness, guilt
  Advice for women in the same situation

- What order does this essay follow?

  _____

- Do you think paragraph 8 makes an effective **conclusion**?

___

Before writing an essay of cause or effect, reread Chapter 12, "Cause and Effect," especially the section called "Avoiding Problems in Cause and Effect Writing." Choose a subject that lends itself to analysis of causes or effects; see the topic lists in Chapter 12 and this chapter for ideas. Think on paper or on computer, listing many possible causes or effects; then choose the best three or four. Don't forget to consider short- and long-term effects, as well as positive and negative effects. Decide on a logical order—probably time order or order of importance.

PRACTICE 8 Choose a topic from the following list or one that your instructor has chosen. Write a cause and effect essay, referring to the checklist at the end of Chapter 14.

Suggested Topics: The Cause and Effect Essay

1. What are the reasons for the popularity of a product, musical group, or game?
2. What caused you to do something you are not proud of?
3. Analyze the main causes of a serious problem in society.
4. Analyze the effects of shyness on someone's life (or anger, pride, curiosity or the lack of it, and so on).
5. What are the effects of a divorce, death, or other loss?
6. What are the effects of a new experience (a trip, military service, living in another country, dorm life)?
7. What causes a hurricane, tornado, or other natural disaster?
8. Choose an event in history that interests you and analyze its causes.
9. What effects did an early failure or success (in public speaking, sports, and so on) have on someone you know?
10. How does being unusual looking affect one's daily life?
11. Writer's choice: _____

Part I

The Persuasive Essay

Persuasive essays are the essay type most frequently called for in college, business, and daily life. That is, you will often be asked to take a stand on an issue—censorship on the Internet, capital punishment, whether a company should invest in on-site child care—and then try to persuade others to agree with you. Examination questions asking you to "agree or disagree" are really asking you to take a stand and make a persuasive case for that stand—for example, "The 9-11 terrorist attacks marked a new kind of war. Agree or disagree." You are asked to muster factual evidence to support your stand.

Here is a persuasive essay:

Stopping Youth Violence: An Inside Job

(1) Every year, nearly one million twelve- to nineteen-year-olds are murdered, robbed, or assaulted—many by their peers—and teenagers are more than twice as likely as adults to become the victims of violence, according to the Children's Defense Fund. Although the problem is far too complex for any one solution, teaching young people conflict-resolution skills—that is, nonviolent techniques for resolving disputes—seems to help. To reduce youth violence, conflict-resolution skills should be taught to all children before they reach junior high school.

(2) First and most important, young people need to learn nonviolent ways of dealing with conflict. In a dangerous society where guns are readily available, many youngsters feel they have no choice but to respond to an insult or an argument with violence. If they have grown up seeing family members and neighbors react to stress with verbal or physical violence, they may not know that other choices exist. Robert Steinback, a *Miami Herald* columnist who works with at-risk youth in Miami, writes that behavior like carrying a weapon or refusing to back down gives young people "the illusion of control," but what they desperately need is to learn real control—for example, when provoked, to walk away from a fight.

(3) Next, conflict-resolution programs have been shown to reduce violent incidents and empower young people in a healthy way. Many programs and courses around the country are teaching teens and preteens to work through disagreements without violence. Tools include calmly telling one's own side of the story and listening to the other person without interrupting or blaming—skills that many adults don't have! Conflict Busters, a Los Angeles public school program, starts in the third grade; it trains students to be mediators, helping peers find their own solutions to conflicts ranging from "sandbox fights to interracial gang disputes," according to *Youthwatch: Statistics on Violence,* May, 2003. Schools in Claremont, Connecticut, run a conflict-resolution course written by Dr. Luz Rivera, who said in a phone interview that fewer violent school incidents have been reported since the course began. Although conflict resolution is useful at any age, experts agree that students should first be exposed before they are hit by the double jolts of hormones and junior high school.

(4) Finally, although opponents claim that this is a "Band-Aid" solution that does not address the root causes of teen violence—poverty, troubled families, bad schools, and drugs, to name a few—in fact, conflict-resolution training saves lives now. The larger social issues must be addressed, but they will take years to solve, whereas teaching students new attitudes and "people skills" will empower them immediately and serve them for a lifetime. For instance, fourteen-year-old Verna, who once called herself Vee Sinister, says that Ms. Rivera's course has changed her life: "I learned to stop and think before my big mouth gets me in trouble. I use the tools with my mother, and guess what? No more screaming at home."

(5) The violence devastating Verna's generation threatens everyone's future. One proven way to help youngsters protect themselves from violence is conflict-resolution training that begins early. Although it is just one solution among many, this solution taps into great power: the hearts, minds, and characters of young people.

- The **thesis statement** in a persuasive essay clearly states the issue to be discussed and the writer's position on it. What is the thesis statement?

  _____

  _____

- This introduction includes *facts*. What is the source of these facts and why does the writer include them here?

  _____

  _____

- Sometimes a writer needs to define terms he or she is using. What term does the writer define?

  _____

- How many reasons does this writer give to back up the thesis statement?

  _____

- Notice that the writer presents one reason per paragraph.
- Which reasons refer to an *authority*?

  _____

- Who are these authorities?

  _____

  _____

  _____

- How is the second reason supported?

  _____

- What is the source of information on Conflict Busters?

  _____

- Which reason is really an *answer to the opposition*?

  _____

- This reason also uses an *example*. What or who is the example?

  _____

- Note that the thesis statement and topic sentences make up a **plan** or an **outline** for the whole essay.

Before writing an essay of persuasion, reread Chapter 13, "Persuasion." Craft your thesis statement carefully. Devote one paragraph to each reason, developing each paragraph fully with facts and discussion. Use some of the methods of persuasion discussed in Chapter 13: *facts, referring to an authority, examples, predicting* *the consequence*, and *answering the opposition*. Revise for clarity and support, and remember, ample factual support is the key to successful persuasion. An excellent way to find interesting factual support is to do some basic **research**—for example, to find books or magazine articles by or about experts on your subject or even to conduct your own interviews, as does the author of "Stopping Youth Violence: An Inside Job."*

PRACTICE 9 In a group of four or five classmates, study this billboard. It is part of a campaign to persuade young people in Florida *not to smoke*.

Now have someone record your group's answers to these questions:

1. How effective—how persuasive—is the antismoking message of this billboard? Why?

2. Do you think the intended audience of teens and young people will get the message? Why or why not?

3. The tobacco industry spends billions for ads that make smoking seem glamorous and grown-up. Does this picture successfully *oppose the tobacco industry's claim* that smoking is glamorous?

4. If your group were designing a billboard to persuade young people *not to smoke*, what would your message be?

---

*For information on summarizing and quoting outside sources and on using research in an essay, see Chapter 17, "Special College Skills: Summary and Quotation" and Chapter 18, "Strengthening an Essay with Research."

PRACTICE 10 Choose a topic from the list below or one that your instructor has chosen. Make sure your thesis statement takes a clear stand. Write a persuasive essay, referring to the checklist at the end of Chapter 14.

Suggested Topics: The Persuasive Essay

1. Parents should routinely test their children's urine for evidence of drug use.
2. Computer and Internet classes should be given to every child in this state.
3. All animal testing of medicines should be banned, even if it will save human lives.
4. Every college student should be required to give three credit hours' worth of community service a year.
5. Only minority police should patrol minority neighborhoods.
6. A college education is (not) worth the time and money.
7. Gay couples should be allowed to adopt children.
8. Naturalized citizens should be allowed to run for president.
9. To better prepare students for the world of work, this college should do three things.
10. The United States must find and deport all illegal aliens, including students with expired visas.
11. Writer's choice: _____

CHAPTER 16: The Introduction, the Conclusion, and the Title

PART A   The Introduction
PART B   The Conclusion
PART C   The Title

Part A

The Introduction

An **introduction** has two functions in an essay. First, it contains the **thesis statement** and, therefore, tells the reader what central idea will be developed in the rest of the paper. Since the reader should be able to spot the thesis statement easily, it should be given a prominent place—for example, the first or the last sentence in the introduction. Second, the introduction has to interest the reader enough that he or she will want to continue reading the paper.

Sometimes the process of writing the essay will help clarify your ideas about how best to introduce it. So once you have completed your essay, you may wish to revise and rewrite the introduction, making sure that it clearly introduces the essay's main idea.

There is no best way to introduce an essay, but you should certainly avoid beginning your work with "I'm going to discuss" or "This paper is about." You needn't tell the reader you are about to begin; just begin!

Here are six basic methods for beginning your composition effectively. In each example, the thesis statement is italicized.

1. **Begin with a single-sentence thesis statement.** A single-sentence thesis statement can be effective because it quickly and forcefully states the main idea of the essay:

> *Time management should be a required course at this college.*

- Note how quickly and clearly a one-sentence thesis statement can inform the reader about what will follow in the rest of the essay.

2. **Begin with a general idea and then narrow to a specific thesis statement.** The general idea gives the reader background information or sets the scene. Then the topic narrows to one specific idea—the thesis statement. The effect is like a funnel, from wide to narrow.

> Few Americans stay put for a lifetime. We move from town to city to suburb, from high school to college in a different state, from a job in one region to a better job elsewhere, from the home where we raise our children to the home where we plan to live in retirement. *With each move we are forever making new friends, who become part of our new life at that time.*
> —Margaret Mead and Rhoda Metraux, "On Friendship," in *A Way of Seeing*

- What general idea precedes the thesis statement and then leads the reader to focus on the specific main point of the essay?

_____

_____

3. **Begin with an illustration.** One or more brief illustrations in the introduction of an essay make the thesis statement more concrete and vivid:

> Lisette Flores-Nieves, a thirty-three-year-old consumer affairs representative for Colgate-Palmolive in New York City, was turned down when she first applied for a job at the company. But she was undaunted. "The original job was filled, but I believe in convincing people and letting them know where I stand." She decided to keep phoning the human resources staff, and as it turned out, a new position opened up and Flores-Nieves was hired. "This is all because I'm very assertive and persistent. After all, what can you lose?"
> *As job openings with America's top corporations continue to decrease in number and recruiters become more selective, entry-level job seekers need to be more creative and aggressive in their planning and hunting.*
> —Irene Middleman Thomas, "First Steps: Advice for Creating Your Own Opportunities," *Hispanic*

- What example does the writer provide to make the thesis statement more concrete?

_____

_____

4. **Begin with a surprising fact or idea.** A surprising fact or idea arouses the reader's curiosity about how you will support this initial startling statement.

> *Millions of law-abiding Americans are physically addicted to caffeine—and most of them don't even know it.* Caffeine is a powerful central nervous system stimulant with substantial addiction potential. When deprived of their caffeine, addicts experience often severe withdrawal symptoms, which may include a throbbing headache, disorientation, constipation, nausea, sluggishness, depression, and irritability. As with other addictive drugs, heavy users develop a tolerance and require higher doses to obtain the expected effect.
>
> —Tom Ferguson and Joe Graedon, "Caffeine," *Medical Self-Care*

- Why are the facts in this introduction likely to startle or surprise the reader?

_____

_____

5. **Begin with a contradiction.** In this type of introduction, your thesis statement contradicts what many or most people believe. In other words, your essay will contrast your opinion with the widely held view.

> Millions of parents take it as an article of faith that putting a bicycle helmet on their children, or themselves, will keep them out of harm's way.
>
> But new data on bicycle accidents raise questions about that. The number of head injuries has increased 10 percent since 1991, even as bicycle helmet use has risen sharply, according to figures compiled by the Consumer Product Safety Commission. But given that ridership has declined over the same period, the rate of head injuries per active cyclist has increased 51 percent just as bicycle helmets have become widespread. What is going on here?
>
> —Julian E. Barnes, "A Bicycling Mystery: Head Injuries Piling Up," *New York Times*

- What widely held view does the author open with?

_____

- How does he contradict this idea?

_____

_____

6. **Begin with a direct quotation.** A direct quotation is likely to catch your reader's attention and to show that you have explored what others have to say about the subject. You can then proceed to agree or to disagree with the direct quotation.

> "Speech is silver; silence is golden," according to an old Swiss saying. In a close relationship, however, silence often loses value. If we speak about certain issues, we may endanger the relationship; but if we do not speak, the relationship may become static and tense until the silence takes on a life of its own. Such silences are corrosive. They eat at the innards of intimacy until, often, *the silence itself causes the very rupture or break-up that we've tried to avoid by keeping silent.*
>
> —Adapted from Michael Ventura,
> "Don't Even Think About It," *Psychology Today*

- Does the author agree or disagree with the Swiss saying?

_____

_____

Of course, definitions, comparisons, or any of the other kinds of devices you have already studied can also make good introductions. Just make sure that the reader knows exactly which sentence is your thesis statement.

Writing Assignment 1

Here are five statements. Pick three that you would like to write about and compose an introduction for each one. Use any of the methods for beginning compositions discussed in this chapter thus far.

1. Cell phones in cars can be dangerous.
2. Noise is definitely a form of pollution.
3. Serious illness—our own or a loved one's—sometimes can bring surprising blessings.
4. Studying with someone else can pay off in better grades.
5. The college cafeteria should offer vegetarian meals.

Part B

The Conclusion

A conclusion signals the end of the essay and leaves the reader with a final thought. As with the introduction, you may wish to revise and rewrite the conclusion once you have completed your essay. Be certain your conclusion flows logically from the body of the essay.

Like introductions, conclusions can take many forms, and the right one for your essay depends on how you wish to complete your paper—with what thought you wish to leave the reader. However, never conclude your paper with "As I said in the beginning," and try to avoid the overused "In conclusion" or "In summary." Don't end by saying you are going to end; just end!

Here are three ways to conclude an essay.

1. **End with a call to action.** The call to action says that in view of the facts and ideas presented in this essay, the reader should *do something*.

> Single-gender schools work. As we have seen, boys-only and girls-only middle and high schools help steer young people toward academic achievement and higher self-esteem. Showing off for the opposite sex, dating too early, and, especially in the case of girls, failing to raise their hands for fear of outshining the boys, are problems avoided altogether in single-gender environments. Parents and concerned citizens must contact their representatives and school boards to demand the option of single-gender schools. We owe it to our children to fight for the schools that truly serve them.

■ What does the writer want the reader to do?

_____

_____

2. **End with a final point.** The final point can tie together all the other ideas in the essay; it provides the reader with the sense that the entire essay has been leading up to this one final point.

> Some estimate that millions of Earth-like planets may be in our Milky Way galaxy alone. The Milky Way is just one of about 100 billion galaxies in the universe. So chances are, plenty of not-too-big, not-too-small, not-too-hot, not-too-cold planets are out there, with water and sunshine—and, perhaps, life.
> —Kathy Wollard, "Millions of Unseen Planets May Hide in Galaxies," *Milwaukee Journal Sentinel*

■ With what final point does Wollard end her article?

_____

_____

3. **End with a question.** By ending with a question, you leave the reader with a final problem that you wish him or her to think about.

> Illness related to chemical dumping is increasing in Larkstown, yet only a handful of citizens have joined the campaign to clean up the

> chemical dump on the edge of town and to stop further dumping. Many people say that they don't want to get involved, but with their lives and their children's futures at stake, can they afford not to?

- What problem does the writer's final question point to?

Writing Assignment 2

Review two or three essays that you have written recently. Do the conclusions bring the essays to clear ends? Are those conclusions interesting? How could they be improved? Using one of the three strategies taught in this section, write a new conclusion for one of the essays.

Part C

The Title

If you are writing just one paragraph, chances are that you will not need to give it a title, but if you are writing a multiparagraph essay, a title is definitely in order.

The title is centered on the page above the body of the composition and separated from it by several blank lines (about 1 inch of space), as shown here.

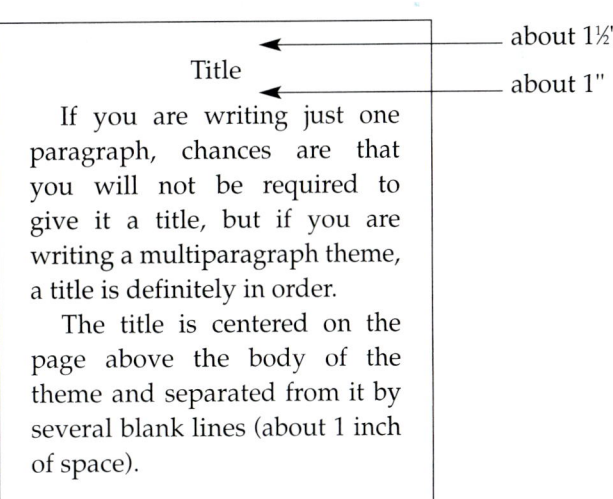

- *Do not* put quotation marks around the title of your own paper.
- *Do not* underline or italicize the title of your own paper.
- Remember, unlike the topic sentence, the title is not part of the first paragraph; in fact, it is usually only four to five words long and is rarely an entire sentence.

A good title has two functions: to suggest the subject of the essay and to spark the reader's interest. Although the title is the first part of your essay the reader sees, the most effective titles are usually written *after* the essay has been completed.

To create a title, reread your essay, paying special attention to the **thesis statement** and the **conclusion.** Try to come up with a few words that express the main point of your paper.

Here are some basic kinds of titles.

1. **The most common title used in college writing is the no-nonsense descriptive title.** In this title, stress key words and ideas developed in the essay:

   > Anger in the Work of Jamaica Kincaid
   >
   > Advantages and Disadvantages of Buying on Credit

2. **Two-part titles are also effective.** Write one or two words stating the general subject, and then add several words that narrow the topic:

   > Rumi: Poet and Mystic
   >
   > Legal Gambling: Pro and Con

3. **Write the title as a rhetorical question.** Then answer the question in your essay:

   > What Can Be Done About the High Price of Higher Education?
   >
   > Are Athletes Setting Bad Examples?

4. **Relate the title to the method of development used in the essay** (see Unit 3 and Chapter 15):

Illustration:	Democracy in Action
	Three Roles I Play
Narration:	The Development of Jazz
	Amy Tan: The Making of a Storyteller
Description:	Portrait of a Scientist
	A Waterfront Scene
Process:	How to Start a Book Group
	How to Get in Shape Fast
Definition:	What It Means to Be Unemployed
	A Definition of Respect

Comparison:	Two Country Stars Who Crossed Over
	Strange Realities: *Star Wars* and *X Files*
Contrast:	Pleasures and Problems of Owning a Home
	Montreal: City of Contrasts
Classification:	Three Types of Soap Operas
	What Kind of Email User Are You?
Cause and Effect:	What Causes Whales to Beach Themselves?
	The Effects of Divorce on Children
Persuasion:	Internet Pornography Should Be Banned
	The Need for Metal Detectors in Our Schools

Use this list the next time you title a paper.*

Writing Assignment 3

Review two or three essays that you have written recently. Are the titles clear and interesting? Applying what you've learned in this chapter, write a better title for at least one paper.

---

*For more on how to capitalize in titles, see Chapter 36, *Mechanics*, Part B.

CHAPTER 17
Special College Skills: Summary and Quotation

PART A Avoiding Plagiarism
PART B Writing a Summary
PART C Using Direct and Indirect Quotation

Welcome to the Information Age! Now more than ever before, it is important for you to know how to find, evaluate, and use information from **outside sources**—that is, sources outside yourself (for example, books, articles, Internet sites, or other people). In some college courses, you will write papers with no outside sources. However, many courses and jobs will require you to refer to outside sources as you write reports, essays, and research papers. Besides, information from outside sources can vastly enrich your writing with facts, statistics, experts' ideas, and more.

In this chapter, you will learn what **plagiarism** is and how to avoid it. You will also learn and practice three excellent ways to use outside sources in your writing: **summarizing, quoting directly,** and **quoting indirectly.**

Part A

Avoiding Plagiarism

Before we discuss how to summarize or quote from an outside source, it is all-important that you understand—so you can avoid—**plagiarism.** Plagiarism is failing to give proper credit to an author whose words or ideas you have used. That is, plagiarism means passing off someone else's words or ideas as your own. Whether intentional or careless, plagiarism is stealing. A college student who plagiarizes a paper may be expelled from the course or from college. In the business world, publishing material copied from someone else is a crime.

To avoid plagiarism, you must give proper credit to the original author, as this chapter and the next will explain. Meanwhile, keep this simple rule in mind: **Always tell your reader the source of any words and ideas not your own. Give enough information so that a reader who wants to find your original source can do so.**

PRACTICE 1 What is your college's policy on plagiarism? That is, what consequences or penalties follow if a student is found to have plagiarized a paper or other work? The reference librarian can help you find this information.

Part B
Writing a Summary

A **summary** presents the main idea and supporting points of a longer work *in much shorter form*. A summary might be one sentence, one paragraph, or several paragraphs long, depending on the length of the original and the nature of your assignment.

Summarizing is important both in college and at work. In a persuasive essay, you might summarize the ideas of an expert whose views support one of your points. A professor might ask you to summarize a book, a market survey, or even the plot of a film—that is, to condense it in your own words, presenting only the highlights. Of course, many essay exams also call for written summaries.

Compare this short newspaper article—the *source*—with the *summary* that follows:

Source

> Fido may be cute, cuddly, and harmless. But in his genes, he's a wolf.
> Researchers tracing the genetic family tree of man's best friend have confirmed that domestic dogs, from petite poodles to huge elkhounds, descended from wolves that were tamed 100,000 years ago.
> "Our data show that the origin of dogs seems to be much more ancient than indicated in the archaeological record," said Robert K. Wayne of UCLA, the leader of a team that tested the genes from 67 dog breeds and 62 wolves on four continents.
> Wayne said the study showed so many DNA changes that dogs had to have diverged genetically from wolves 60,000 to more than 100,000 years ago.
> The study suggests that primitive humans living in a hunting and gathering culture tamed wolves and then bred the animals to create the many different types of dogs that now exist.
>
> Recer, Paul. "Dogs Tamed 100,000 Years Ago." <u>The Herald</u> 13 June 1997: 9A

Summary

> Dogs began evolving from wolves between 60,000 and 100,000 years ago, reports Paul Recer in *The Herald*. Apparently, humans tamed wolves far earlier than was previously thought. Researchers at UCLA, led by Robert K. Wayne, came to these conclusions after studying the genes of 67 breeds of dogs and 62 wolves on four continents (9A).

- Notice that sentence 1 states the author and source of the original article. Sentence 1 also states the main idea of the article. What is its main idea?

- What evidence supports this idea?

- The original is short, so the summary is very short—just three sentences long.
- The summary writer does not add his own opinions about dogs or evolution but simply states the main ideas of the source. Unlike many kinds of writing, a summary should not contain your personal opinions and feelings.
- Note that the page number of the original source appears in parentheses at the end of the summary.*

Preparing to Write a Summary

The secret of writing a good summary is clearly understanding the original. If you doubt this, try to summarize out loud Chapter 3 of your biology book. To summarize well, you have to know the subject matter.

Before you summarize a piece of writing, notice the title and subtitle (if there is one); these often state the main idea. Read quickly for meaning; then carefully read the work again, underlining or jotting down notes for yourself. What is the author's thesis or main point? What points does he or she offer in support? Be careful to distinguish between the most and least important points; your summary should include only the most important ones.

To help you understand *what the author thinks is important,* notice which ideas get the most coverage. Read with special care the topic sentence of each paragraph and the first and last paragraphs of the work. If you are summarizing a magazine article or a textbook chapter, the subheads (often in boldface type) point out important ideas.

> Your written summary should include the following:
> 1. The author, title, and source of the original
> 2. The main idea or thesis of the original, in your own words
> 3. The most important supporting ideas or points of the original, in your own words

Try to present the ideas in your summary in proportion to those in the original. For instance, if the author devotes one paragraph to each of four ideas, you might give one sentence to each idea. To avoid plagiarism, when you finish, compare your summary with the original; that is, make sure you have not just copied the phrasing and sentences of the original.

A summary differs from much other writing in that it *should not* contain your feelings or opinions—just the facts. Your job is to capture the essence of the original, with nothing added.

Following are two summaries of the student essay in Chapter 15, Part F, of this book. Which do you think is the better summary, A or B? Be prepared to say specifically why.

---

*For more precise information on how to cite sources, see Chapter 18, Part C.

CHAPTER 17 Special College Skills: Summary and Quotation

Summary A

(1) In the essay "E-Notes from an Online Learner," printed in Fawcett, *Evergreen,* 7th Edition, student and mother Brenda Wilson contrasts her learning experiences in traditional and online classrooms. (2) Whereas Wilson's long commute to campus once made her late to class or anxious, she finds online classes more convenient because she can read lectures or submit coursework any time, from home. (3) Next, Ms. Wilson says that other students might prefer the energy of live class discussion, but she feels freer online, writing her thoughts with less self-consciousness. (4) Finally, she stresses that online students must be self-motivated, unlike regular students who can rely on professors to prod them or on the "group adrenaline rush of seeing other students hunched over their notebooks." (5) Less focused students might procrastinate and drop out. (6) Overall, Wilson prefers distance learning (210–211).

Summary B

(1) This excellent essay is by Brenda Wilson, student. (2) I enjoyed reading about online learning because I have never taken a course online. (3) This year Ms. Wilson attended her history class dressed in dancing cow pajamas and fluffy slippers. (4) This was not a bizarre college ritual but part of the University of Houston's Distance Education Program. (5) Virtual courses are very different. (6) She has a job and a son, so she is very busy, like many students today. (7) Online classes are great for this type of student, more convenient. (8) Students have to motivate themselves, and Ms. Wilson has only the soft bubbling noise of her aquarium screen saver to remind her to work. (9) She ends by saying it is 12:14 A.M. and her cat is nuzzling her fluffy pink slippers. (10) I also liked her cat's name.

- The test of a good summary is how well it captures the original. Which better summarizes Ms. Wilson's essay, A or B?

- If you picked A, you are right. Sentence 1 states the author and title of the essay, as well as the name and edition of the book in which it appears. Sentence 1 also states the main idea of the original, which *contrasts* the author's experience of traditional classes and virtual classes. Does any sentence in B state the main idea of the original essay? _____

- Compare the original with the two summaries. How many points of contrast does A include? B? _____

- Does each writer summarize the essay *in his or her own words*? If not, which sentences might seem plagiarized? _____

- Writer A once quotes Ms. Wilson directly. How is this shown? Why do you think the summary writer chose this sentence to quote? _____

- Do both summaries succeed in keeping personal opinion out? If not, which sentences contain the summary writer's opinion? _____

- Note that summary writer A includes the source page number in parenthesis at the end of the summarized material. On the other hand, writer B refers to Brenda Wilson but does not name her essay or the source in which it appears.

PRACTICE 2 In a group with three or four other classmates, choose just one of the following essays to summarize: "Libraries of the Future—Now" (Chapter 15, Part A); "The Day of the Dead" (Chapter 15, Part C); "Stopping Youth Violence: An Inside Job" (Chapter 15, Part I); or "Skin Deep" (Chapter 14, Part D). Read your chosen essay in the group, aloud if possible. Then each person should write a one-paragraph summary of it, referring to the following checklist (15–20 minutes).

Now read your finished summaries aloud to your group. How well does each writer briefly capture the meaning of the original? Has he or she kept out personal opinion? What suggestions for improvement can you offer? Your instructor may wish to have the best summary in each group read aloud to the whole class.

PRACTICE 3 Flip through a copy of a current magazine: *Newsweek, People, Essence, Wired,* or another. Pick one article that interests you, read it carefully, and write a one- to three-paragraph summary of the article, depending on the length of the article. The points you include in your summary should reflect the emphasis of the original writer. Try to capture the essence of the article. Remember to give your source at the beginning, to keep out personal opinion, and to check your summary for plagiarism. Refer to the checklist.

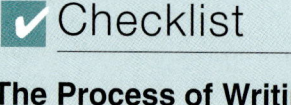

Checklist

The Process of Writing a Summary

____ 1. Notice the title and subtitle of the original; do these state its main idea?

____ 2. Read the original quickly for meaning; then carefully read it again, underlining important ideas and jotting down notes for yourself.

____ 3. Determine the author's thesis or main idea.

____ 4. Now find the main supporting points. Subheads (if any), topic sentences, and the first and last paragraphs of the original may help you find key points.

___ 5. Write your topic sentence or thesis statement, stating the author's thesis, title, source, and date of the original.

___ 6. In your own words, give the author's most important supporting points, in the same order in which the author gives them. Keep the same proportion of coverage as the original.

___ 7. Write your summary, skipping lines so you will have room to make corrections.

___ 8. Now revise, asking yourself, "Will my summary convey to someone who has never read the original the author's main idea and key supporting points?"

___ 9. Proofread, making neat corrections above the lines.

___ 10. Compare your final draft with the original to avoid plagiarism.

Part C

Using Direct and Indirect Quotation

Sometimes you will want to quote an outside source directly. A quotation might be part of a summary or part of a longer paper or report. Quoting the words of others can add richness and authority to your writing; in fact, that is why we include a Quotation Bank at the end of this book—a kind of minireader of great thoughts. Use short quotations in these ways:

- Use a quotation to stress a key idea.
- Use a quotation to lend expert opinion to your argument.
- Use a quotation to provide a catchy introduction or conclusion.
- Use a quotation about your topic that is wonderfully written and "quotable" to add interest.

However, avoid using very long quotations or too many quotations. Both send the message that you are filling up space because you don't have enough to say. Of course, to avoid plagiarism, you always must credit the original author or speaker.

Here are some methods for introducing quotations:

Ways to Introduce Quotations

Mr. Taibi says, . . .	Ms. Luboff writes, . . .
One expert had this to say:	. . . , one authority reported.
In a recent *Times* column, Maureen Dowd observes . . .	According to Dr. Haynes, . . .

Following are a passage from a well-known book and two ways that students quoted the author:

Source

> On film or videotape, violence begins and ends in a moment. "Bang bang, you're dead." Then the death is over. This sense of action-without-consequences replicates and reinforces the dangerous "magical" way many children think. Do the twelve- and fourteen-year-olds who are shooting each other to death in Los Angeles, Chicago, or Washington, D.C., really understand that death is permanent, unalterable, final, tragic? Television certainly is not telling them so.
>
> Prothrow-Stith, Deborah. <u>Deadly Consequences</u>.
> New York: Harper Perennial, 1991: 34

Two students who wrote about the effects of TV violence correctly quoted Dr. Prothrow-Stith as follows:

Direct Quotation

> "This sense of action-without-consequences replicates and reinforces the dangerous 'magical' way many children think," writes Dr. Deborah Prothrow-Stith in <u>Deadly Consequences</u> (34).

Indirect Quotation

> In <u>Deadly Consequences</u>, Prothrow-Stith points out that TV and movie violence, which has no realistic consequences, harms children by reinforcing the magical way in which they think (34).

- The first sentence gives Dr. Prothrow-Stith's exact words inside quotation marks. This is **direct quotation.** Note the punctuation.

- The second sentence uses the word *that* and gives the *meaning* of Prothrow-Stith's words without quotation marks. This is **indirect quotation,** or **paraphrase.** Note the punctuation.

- Both students correctly quote the writer and credit the source. Both include the page number in parentheses after the quoted material and before the period. (See Chapter 18, Part C, for more information on this style of citing sources.)

Now read this passage from a third student's paper:

Plagiarism

> On film and television, violence begins and ends in a minute, and then the death is over. Teenagers killing each other across the country don't realize that death is "unalterable, final, and tragic" because they do not see its consequences on TV.

- Can you see why this passage is plagiarized (and why the student received a failing grade)?

- Both the ideas and many of the words are clearly Prothrow-Stith's, yet the student never mentions her or her book. Four words from the original are placed in quotation marks, but the reader has no idea why. Instead, the student implies that all the ideas and words are his own. What exact words are plagiarized from the source? What ideas are plagiarized?

- Revise this passage as if it were your own, giving credit to the original author and avoiding plagiarism.

PRACTICE 4 Following are passages from two sources. Read each one, and then, as if you were writing a paper, quote two sentences from each, one directly quoting the author's words and one indirectly quoting the author's ideas. Review the boxed ways to introduce quotations and try several methods. Finally, write a brief summary of each passage. Check your work to avoid plagiarism.

Source 1

In most cultures throughout history, music, dance, rhythmic drumming, and chanting have been essential parts of healing rituals. Modern research bears out the connection between music and healing. In one study, the heart rate and blood pressure of patients went down when quiet music was piped into their hospital coronary care units. At the same time, the patients showed greater tolerance for pain and less anxiety and depression. Similarly, listening to music before, during, or after surgery has been shown to promote various beneficial effects—from alleviating anxiety to reducing the need for sedation by half. When researchers played Brahms' "Lullaby" to premature infants, these babies gained weight faster and went home from the hospital sooner than babies who did not hear the music. Music may also affect immunity by altering the level of stress chemicals in the blood. An experiment at Rainbow Babies and Children's Hospital found that a single thirty-minute music therapy session could increase the level of salivary IgA, an immunoglobulin that protects against respiratory infections.

Institute of Noetic Sciences with William Poole. The Heart of Healing. Atlanta: Turner Publishing, 1993: 134

Direct quotation: _____

Indirect quotation: _____

Summary:

Source 2   The television commercial is not at all about the character of products to be consumed. It is about the character of the consumers of products. Images of movie stars and famous athletes, of serene lakes and macho fishing trips, of elegant dinners and romantic interludes, of happy families packing their station wagons for a picnic in the country—these tell nothing about the products being sold. But they tell everything about the fears, fancies and dreams of those who might buy them.

Postman, Neil. <u>Amusing Ourselves to Death.</u>
New York: Viking Penguin, 1985: 128

Direct quotation: _____

_____

Indirect quotation: _____

_____

Summary:

_____

_____

_____

_____

_____

_____

PRACTICE 5   Following are four sources and four quotations from student papers. If the student has summarized, directly quoted, or indirectly quoted the source correctly, write C. If you believe the source is plagiarized, write P; then revise the student's work as if it were your own to avoid plagiarism.

- Does each student clearly distinguish between his or her ideas and the source's?
- Does each student give enough information so that a reader could locate the original source?

Source 1   "Binge drinking, according to criteria used in periodic surveys by the Harvard researchers, is defined as five or more drinks on one occasion for a man or four or more drinks on one occasion for a woman. Students who reported one or two such episodes in the two weeks preceding the survey were classified as occasional binge drinkers; those reporting three or more were considered frequent binge drinkers."

Okie, Susan. "Survey: 44% of College Students Are Binge Drinkers."
<u>The Washington Post</u> 25 Mar. 2002: A6

CHAPTER 17   Special College Skills: Summary and Quotation   239

Student's Version   _____   Binge drinking is a dangerous problem on campuses, but college administrators are not doing enough to stop it. An amazing 44 percent of college students are binge drinkers. Let us define binge drinking as five or more drinks on one occasion for a man or four or more drinks on one occasion for a woman. College officials need to ask why so many students are drinking dangerously.

Source 2   "The image of the Kitchen God (alternatively known as the Hearth God) usually stood above the family stove, from where he would observe the household. Every New Year he was said to visit heaven to give an account of the behavior of the family in the past year."

Willis, Roy. <u>Dictionary of World Myth</u>. London: Duncan Baird Publishers, 1995: 116

Student's Version   _____   My Chinese grandmother has a Kitchen God above her stove. It says in the dictionary that this is a special god who observes the household and then visits heaven every New Year to report on the behavior of the family in the past year.

Source 3   "Although astronomers often speak of the 'solar surface,' the Sun actually has no surface at all. The Sun is gaseous throughout its volume because of its high internal temperature. If you were somehow able to enter the Sun without vaporizing, you would encounter only denser and denser gases as you went to greater depths."

Kaufmann, William J., and Roger A. Freedman. <u>Universe</u>. 5th ed.
New York: W.H. Freeman and Co., 1999: 422

Student's Version   _____   As Kaufmann and Freedman explain in <u>Universe</u>, the sun is too hot to have a solid surface but is made up instead of very dense gases (422).

Source 4   "As alpine glaciers around the world succumb to warming, scientists are reaping grand harvests of frozen organic objects—and with them previously unavailable information on past wildlife, human culture, genetics, climate and more. Tissues with intact DNA and archaeological objects of wood and bone provide pictures that stone tools only hint at, and because they can all be radio-carbon dated, there is little guessing about chronology."

Krajick, Kevin. "Melting Glaciers Release Ancient Relics."
<u>Science</u> 19 Apr. 2002: 454–456

Student's Version   _____   There might be a positive side to global warming after all. Kevin Krajick reports in <u>Science</u>, April 19, 2002, that melting glaciers are providing scientists with many objects and tissue samples that will give them "previously unavailable information on past wildlife, human culture, genetics, climate and more."

CHAPTER 18

Strengthening an Essay with Research

PART A	Improving an Essay with Research
PART B	Finding and Evaluating Outside Sources: Library and Internet
PART C	Adding Sources to Your Essay and Documenting Them Correctly

You will have opportunities in college to prepare formal research papers with many outside sources. However, you should not limit your definition of "research" to just such assignments. Whenever you have a question and seek an answer from a source outside yourself, you are doing **research.** Most of us research every day, whether or not we call it that—when we gather facts and opinions about the cheapest local restaurant, the college with the best fire science program, the safest new cars, or various medical conditions. In this chapter, you will learn skills valuable both in college and at work: how to improve your writing with interesting information from outside sources.

Part A

Improving an Essay with Research

Almost any essay, particularly one designed to *persuade* your reader, can benefit from the addition of outside material. In fact, even one outside source—a startling statistic or a memorable quote—can enrich your essay. Supporting your main points with outside sources can be an excellent way to establish your credibility, strengthen your argument, and add power to your words. Compare two versions of this student's paragraph

> Inexperienced hikers often get in trouble because they worry about rare dangers like snakebites, but they minimize the very serious dangers of dehydration and exposure to cold. For example, my brother-in-law once hiked into the Grand Canyon with only a granola bar and a small bottle of water. He became severely dehydrated and was too weak to climb back up without help.

- This paragraph makes an important point about the dangers that inexperienced hikers can face. The example of the brother-in-law supports the main point, but the paragraph needs more complete support.

Now read the paragraph strengthened by some relevant facts from an outside source.

> Inexperienced hikers often get in trouble because they worry about rare dangers like snakebites, but they minimize the very serious dangers of dehydration and exposure to cold. For example, my brother-in-law once hiked into the Grand Canyon with only a granola bar and a small bottle of water. He became severely dehydrated and was too weak to climb back up without help. He was lucky. According to the National Park Service (NPS) web site, over a hundred hikers die every year because they are not properly prepared for the environment. In addition, the NPS reports that over $1.7 million was spent last year to perform 5,843 search-and-rescue operations to save poorly prepared hikers like my brother-in-law ("Search and Rescue Report 1998").

- What facts from the National Park Service web site support the main point and add to the persuasive power of this paragraph?

- What sentence of transition does the writer use to connect his example of the brother-in-law with facts from the outside source? What transitional words connect the fact about hikers' deaths each year?

- Remember that just one well-chosen outside source can improve and enliven a paper.

Consider the facts in this chart:

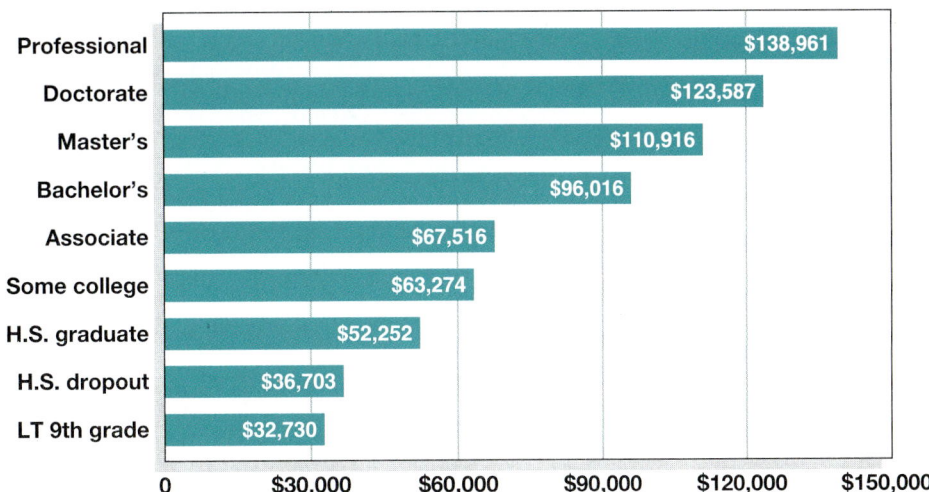

- What patterns do you see in this chart?
- How might you use this information in an essay?

Facts and statistics can make a strong statement, but there are many other ways to enhance your writing. Consider adding a good quotation to emphasize one of your key points. You can begin by looking through the Quotation Bank at the end of this book or an online version of *Bartlett's Quotations* at http://www.bartleby.com/100/. Or find and quote an expert on the subject you are writing about. For example, if your subject is the lack of recycling receptacles on your campus, an opinion from a Sierra Club official would give authority to your essay. And don't forget experts closer to home; details about a student you know who has begun a recycling campaign on campus would add life and emotion to your work. If your essay is about your family history or the school's registration system, you could interview a relative or a school administrator and use that material to add authority to your paper.

A good way to begin using research is to pick an essay you have recently written. Reread it, marking any places where outside sources might make it even better. Write down any questions you want answers to or information that you would like to find:

- What would I like to know more about?
- What outside source might make my essay more interesting?
- What information—fact, statistic, detail, or quotation—would make my essay more convincing?
- What people are experts on this topic? Where can I find them or their opinions?

Carmen's Research Process

Student Carmen Gevana is learning to use outside sources. She plans to add research support to a favorite essay. She selects a cause-and-effect paper that examines the reasons her best friend went into credit card debt and the devastating effects this debt had on her friend's life. In her paper, Carmen named two causes: credit card companies using gifts to encourage students to apply for cards and students getting higher credit lines than they can realistically handle. The consequences Carmen discussed were unmanageable debt and ruined credit. Now Carmen wants to add two or three sources to support her own ideas. Her first question is whether heavy credit card debt is a problem unique to her friend or more widespread among college students. She also wonders how much debt a typical college student carries. Finally, she hopes to find an expert opinion about the effects on college students.

PRACTICE 1 Choose one of the following: either your favorite paper written this term or a paper on a topic assigned by your instructor. Then read through your paper, marking any spots where an outside source—fact, statistic, expert opinion, or quotation—might strengthen your essay. Write down any questions that you want to answer.

Part B

Finding and Evaluating Outside Sources: Library and Internet

The next step is finding the information you seek—or something even better. This section will show you how to find sources in the library and on the Internet.

Doing Research at the Library

Visit your college library, with your notes from Practice 1 in hand. Ask about any print guides, workshops, or web sites that show you how to use the library facilities. Introduce yourself to the reference librarian, tell him or her what subject you are exploring, and ask for help finding and using any of these resources in your search:

> 1. **Online Catalog or Card Catalog.** This will show you what books are available on your topic. For every book that looks like it might be interesting, jot down its title, author, and call number (the number that lets you find the book in the library).
> 2. **Periodical Indexes.** The more current your topic, the more likely you are to find interesting information in periodicals—magazines, journals, and newspapers—rather than books. *The Readers' Guide to Periodical Literature* is a print resource, listing articles by subject. The library will also have computerized indexes like *InfoTrac*, *EBSCOhost*, and *Lexis-Nexus*. Ask the librarian to help you explore these exciting resources.
> 3. **Statistical Sources.** If you are looking for statistics and facts, the library has volumes like *The Statistical Abstract of the United States* with fascinating information on population, education, immigration, crime, economic issues, and so on.
> 4. **Encyclopedias and Reference Books.** General books on subjects like geology or psychology can be helpful. Special reference books and encyclopedias exist for almost every area—for example, world soccer statistics, terrorism, or the birds of South America.

As you explore, you might see why experienced researchers often love what they do. They never know what they will find, and they learn the darnedest, most interesting things. However, they must **evaluate** each source. If you are writing about the space shuttle, a current article in *The Chicago Tribune* would more likely impress readers as a truthful source than, say, a story in *The National Enquirer* called "Space Aliens Ate My Laundry." Look at the date of a book or article; if your subject is current, your sources should be too. Is the author a respected expert on this subject? Is the information balanced and objective? The librarian can help you find strong sources.

Once you discover good information that will strengthen your essay, take clear and careful notes, using 4 × 6 note cards or your notebook. Use the techniques you learned in Chapter 17 to summarize and quote directly and indirectly; these will help you avoid accidental plagiarism. Write down everything you might need later. Print or buy copies of an article or book pages that are important. Don't leave the library without this information:

Book: Author name(s), title and subtitle, year of publication, publisher and location of publisher, exact pages of material quoted or summarized.

Magazine: Author name(s), title of article, title of magazine or journal, year, month, day of publication, volume and number, page numbers.

Carmen's Research Process

Carmen visits her college library and gets help from the librarian using the computerized database *EBSCOhost.* Because Carmen's topic—student credit card debt—is current, she assumes that newspapers and magazines will give her the most up-to-date information. Searching "credit card debt," she finds a recent *Business Week* article called "Congratulations, Grads—You're Bankrupt." She is surprised and excited to learn that credit problems like her friend's are a growing national problem. She copies the article and adds it to her source folder.

PRACTICE 2 In your college or local library, find the answers to the following questions; write the answers and the complete source for each piece of information. Your instructor might wish to have you work in competing teams.

1. List the full titles of five novels by Toni Morrison. What major prize did she win and in what year?
2. How many acres of rain forest are destroyed every day in Brazil?
3. What is the average hourly wage of men in the United States? Of women?
4. How many murders were committed in your town or city last year? Is the number up or down from ten years ago?
5. What was the newspaper headline in your hometown or city on the day and year of your birth? What stories dominated page 1?

PRACTICE 3 In your college or local library, find at least two excellent additions from outside sources that will improve your essay: a fact, statistic, example, quotation, or expert opinion. Write the information from each source precisely on 4 × 6 note cards, using quotation marks as you learned in Chapter 17, Part C, or make copies. Write down everything you will need later to cite the source: the book or magazine, article name, author name(s), and so on. Spell everything perfectly; copy exact punctuation of titles, and don't forget page numbers.

Doing Research on the Internet

The Internet is a wonderful source of information on just about everything—a great place to brainstorm, get ideas as you research, and find certain facts. However, it is harder to evaluate information on the web than in print, as this section will explain, so be careful.

If you have Internet access at the library or at home, use one of the search engines below. Type in search words that narrow your subject the same way you narrow a topic in writing—for example, *credit card debt, college students*. Spell correctly, and try different words if necessary. Chances are, you will have too many "hits," rather than too few.

Google	http://google.com
AltaVista	http://www.altavista.com
Northern Light	http://www.northernlight.com
HotBot	http://www.hotbot.com
All the Web	http://www.alltheweb.com

Evaluate each web site carefully. Who sponsors the site? How balanced and unbiased is the information? Notice also the date of the site and article; many web sites come and go in the night. With practice, web researchers get better at spotting good and not-so-good sources of information. One tip is the web address, or URL (Uniform Resource Locator) of each site. The last part of a URL says who owns the site:

.com	=	company (aims to sell something and make a profit)
.org	=	non-profit organization (aims to promote a cause)
.gov	=	government (provides many public information sites)
.edu	=	college or educational institution (aims to inform the public and promote itself)

For instance, if you are researching *asthma in children, treatments,* a government-sponsored health site might give more unbiased information than a company that sells asthma medications or a personal web site called *Troy's Asthma Story*. For more help evaluating web sites, see http://www.lib.vt.edu/research/evaluate/evalbiblio.html.

As in the library—to avoid plagiarism later—take good notes, clearly marking words and ideas taken from your sources. Before you leave a web site you wish to quote, cut and paste or print the material you want, and make sure you have full information to cite the source later in your paper:

Web site: URL address, owner of site, author name(s), title of article, date written (if available), and date you accessed the web site.

Carmen's Research Process

Carmen chooses the Google search engine and types the search words, "college students, credit card debt." The search engine returns several thousand sources! Carmen scrolls quickly through many different "hits," until she finds one that looks promising. It's the web site for Nellie Mae, a federal loan provider for college students. Carmen takes notes on a number of useful statistics and makes sure she has the URL address and other pertinent information before she logs off the computer.

PRACTICE 4 Go to www.fedstats.gov and learn how to find statistics quickly and easily. Answer these questions:

1. How many people live in the United States?
2. What is the leading cause of death in American men? Women?
3. What is the leading export from your state?
4. How many different ethnic groups live in your state?
5. How many new AIDS cases were reported in your state last year? What groups were most hard-hit?

PRACTICE 5 Using one of the suggested search engines, find at least two good pieces of information to strengthen your essay—facts, statistics, expert opinions, and so on. Hone your search words and see what you find. Take careful notes, and cut and paste or print the information you need. Did you find any good material that you were not expecting? (Did you find exciting information on another subject that you might use in another paper? Be sure to take down any information you might use in the future.)

Part C

Adding Sources to Your Essay and Documenting Them Correctly

Now, reread your original essay and the new material you found in your research process. Did you find other or better material than you looked for? Where in the paper will your outside sources be most effective? The next step is to use any of the three methods you learned in Chapter 17, Parts B and C—summary, direct quotation, or indirect quotation (paraphrase)—as you revise your essay and add your outside sources. This section will show you how.

The **MLA style** (named after the Modern Language Association) is one of the easiest methods for documenting sources quickly and clearly. MLA style is also called *parenthetical* documentation because it puts source information in the body of the essay, in parentheses, rather than in cumbersome footnotes or endnotes.

A correct citation does two things:

- It tells your reader that the material is from an outside source.
- It gives your reader enough information to find the original source.

A correct citation appears in *two places* in your essay:

- **inside** the essay in parentheses
- **at the end** in a Works Cited list

Inside Your Essay: Summarize or Quote and Give Credit

When you quote an outside source in an essay, indicate that the material is not yours by introducing the quote with one of the phrases that you practiced in Part C of Chapter 17. If you use the author's name in this phrase, you will put only the page number in parentheses. If you leave the author unnamed, be sure to include both the author's last name and the page number in parentheses. If your source is a web site, no page number is needed—just the author or first word of the title.

Here is the introductory paragraph from Carmen's original essay about credit card debt.

> In her second year of college, when she was supposed to declare her major, my best friend Maya almost had to declare bankruptcy. In just two years, she had racked up $7,000 in credit card debt. Starting with necessities such as textbooks and car repairs, Maya soon began charging everything from midnight pizza parties to shopping sprees at the mall. It didn't take long before she had accrued a debt far greater than her part-time campus job could cover. What caused this intelligent student and perhaps others like her to get into so much debt?

- This is a catchy introduction on a good topic. You can probably see why Carmen chose to do more with this paper.

Now read the same paragraph, strengthened and expanded by facts that Carmen found on the Internet:

> In her second year of college, when she was supposed to declare her major, my best friend Maya almost had to declare bankruptcy. In just two years, she had racked up $7,000 in credit card debt. Starting with necessities such as textbooks and car repairs, Maya soon began charging everything from midnight pizza parties to shopping sprees at the mall. It didn't take long before she had accrued a debt far greater than her part-time campus job could cover. Yet Maya's is not an isolated case of bad financial management. According to a 2001 report on the web site of Nellie Mae, the student loan provider, 78 percent of all college students had credit cards in 2000, and the typical student's credit card balance grew 46 percent, to $2,748, just from 1998 to 2000 ("Credit"). What has caused this jump in credit card debt among college students nationwide and what can be done about it?

- Through her research online, Carmen learned that students all over the country are carrying higher credit card balances. This information adds power to Maya's story.

- What transitional sentence moves the paragraph from Maya's personal story to the bigger picture? _____

- What transitional expression introduces the Nellie Mae report?

_____

- Because this article has no listed author, the first word of the title, "Credit," is shown in parentheses. The full title and web site will be listed in Works Cited.

Note: Electronic resources do not have set page numbers because everyone's printer is different, so no page number is shown in parentheses as it would be with a book or article.

At the End of Your Essay: List Works Cited

The last page of your essay will be a list of all the sources you summarized, directly quoted, or indirectly quoted in your essay, in alphabetical order by the author's last name. If there is no named author, list the entry alphabetically by its title (in quotation marks). Title the page *Works Cited,* and center the title. Use the models below to format each source properly. (Don't worry about memorizing the forms; even experienced writers often have to check an MLA manual for the correct form.) If a citation goes beyond one line, indent any following lines five spaces to make it clear that the information belongs together.

Books

One author:

Erdrich, Louise. The Last Report on the Miracles at Little No Horse. New York: HarperCollins, 2001.

More than one author:

McClelland, Deke and Katrin Eismann. Real World Digital Photography. Berkeley, CA: Peachpit Press, 1999.

Encyclopedia:

"Geneva Convention." Encyclopedia Britannica. 15th ed. 2002.

Periodicals

Article in a newspaper:

Asimov, Eric. "Peruvian Cuisine Takes On the World." New York Times 26 May 1999, late ed.: F1.

Article in a magazine:

Alexander, Charles P. "Death Row: Our Relatives in Peril: an Exclusive Look at the 25 Most Endangered Primates." Time 17 Jan. 2000: 76+.

Article in a journal:

Lockwood, C. J. "Predicting Premature Delivery—No Easy Task." New England Journal of Medicine 346 (2002): 299–300.

Electronic Sources

Because the World Wide Web is a rapidly changing environment, include the date the source was published or updated, as well as the date you accessed the information.

Web site:

Links to Advertising Resources. 2002. Department of Advertising, University of Texas, Austin. 3 Jan. 2003 <http://advertising.utexas.edu/world/Ads.html>.

Article in an online periodical:

Thurer, Shari. "The Working Mom Myth." Salon.com 6 April 1999. 12 August 2002 <http://www.salon.com/mwt/feature/1999/04/06/childcare_study/index.html>.

Work from a subscription service (give the name of the library you used):

Schacter, Daniel. "The Seven Sins of Memory: How the Mind Forgets and Remembers." Psychology Today May 2001: 90–99. Expanded Academic ASAP. InfoTrac. City College of San Francisco Lib., San Francisco, CA. 22 Jan. 2002.

Multimedia

Film or video:

Dancing in One World. Dir. Mark Obenhaus. Perf. Raoul Trujillo, Peter Sellars, Falakika Mauvaka, Judy Mitoma, and Little Crow. Videocassette. RM Arts, 1993.

Radio or television program:

"Machismo." Sixty Minutes. Narr. Morley Safer. CBS. WCBS, New York. 6 Aug. 1993.

Personal interview:

Santos, Mariela. Personal Interview. Mar. 31, 2003.

These models cover the most common outside sources you will encounter in your research. If you need assistance with another source, you can find other models in one of the many web sites that publish MLA guidelines. Try Purdue's Online Writing Lab at http://owl.english.purdue.edu/handouts/research/r_mla.html. (If your instructor requires APA style instead of MLA, click *APA* at the site above or try http://www.wisc.edu/writing/Handbook/DocAPA.html.)

Carmen's Research Process

During her library and Internet research, Carmen had carefully copied the quotes and facts that she wanted to use in her essay onto index cards or copied relevant pages. Now, as she revises her essay to add these sources, she makes sure that she quotes her sources accurately and avoids unintentional plagiarism. As she rewrites her essay, she refers to Chapters 17 and 18. She uses transitional expressions to weave the outside sources smoothly into her essay. Then she prepares a Works Cited list, referring to the models above, as the last page of her paper.

Read Carmen's completed essay with research, "Drastic Plastic: Credit Card Debt on Campus," at the end of this chapter.

PRACTICE 6 Below are five sources a student has compiled for a research essay on the history of the Olympics. Using the models above to guide you, prepare a Works Cited list for the paper that includes all five sources, properly formatted and in alphabetical order.

- A book by Susan Wels called The Olympic Spirits: 100 Years of the Games that was published in Del Mar, California by Tehabi Books in 1995

- An article in the February 25, 2002 issue of Newsweek called "Going Extreme: Snowboarding and Moguls" written by Devin Gordon and T. Trent Gegax and appearing on page 48

- A web site called The Ancient Olympic Games Virtual Museum that was presented by Dartmouth College and last updated on January 11, 2002 (the student viewed it on March 12, 2003 at http://minbar.cs.Dartmouth.edu/greecom/olympics/)

- A book by Allen Guttman titled The Olympics: A History of the Modern Games published by the University of Illinois Press in the city of Champaign in 2002, 248 pages long

- An article from the New York Times called "15,000-Mile Olympic Torch Route Gives Lots of People Reasons to Feel Good" that was written by Dirk Johnson and appeared on page 12 of section 1 on May 26, 1996

Works Cited

_____

_____

_____

_____

_____

_____

_____

_____

PRACTICE 7 Now, using two of the three methods—summary, direct quotation, or indirect quotation—add your research findings to your essay. Review Chapters 17 and 18 if you need to. Aim to achieve two things: First try to add the new material gracefully, using introductory phrases so that it relates clearly to your ideas in the essay. Second, be careful to avoid plagiarism by documenting your sources correctly, both inside the essay and in your Works Cited list.

Following is Carmen's final essay strengthened by research.

Gevana 1

Carmen Gevana
Professor Fawcett
English 100
10 May 2001

Drastic Plastic: Credit Card Debt on Campus

> **Introduction**

In her second year of college, when she was supposed to declare her major, my best friend Maya almost had to declare bankruptcy. In just two years, she had racked up $7,000 in credit card debt. Starting with necessities such as textbooks and car repairs, Maya soon began charging everything from midnight pizza parties to shopping sprees at the mall. It didn't take long before she had accrued a debt far greater than her part-time campus job could cover. Yet Maya's is not an isolated case of bad financial management. According to a 2001 report on the web site of Nellie Mae, the student loan provider, 78 percent of all college students had credit cards in 2000, and the typical student's credit card balance grew 46 percent to $2,748, just from 1998 to 2000 ("Credit"). What has caused this jump in credit card debt among college students nationwide and what can be done about it?

> **Indirectly quoted facts from Nellie Mae expand the topic; short title given, no page for web site.**

> **Thesis statement, phrased as a question**

> **Topic sentence: cause #1**

A major cause of growing student debt is that credit card companies bombard college students the minute they step on campus. Targeting a profitable market of young consumers, these credit companies use many tactics to lure new college students into applying for their cards. Smiling salespeople stand behind tables offering free goodies like candy bars, school sweatshirts, and even airline tickets. They flood students' mailboxes with credit card offers and pay the college bookstore to stuff applications into every plastic book bag. For my friend Maya, the temptation was too great. Before she had been in college a week, she had already applied for two cards, each with a large credit limit.

> **Developed by author's ideas, observations**

> **Topic sentence: cause #2**

Maya's credit card behavior illustrates the second cause for the widespread crisis in college debt—most college students spend more than they can repay. Companies that extend credit typically offer higher limits than their customers can handle. After all, the company makes its profit through charging interest, and interest only accrues if the customer cannot pay off the full balance every month. New credit card users, especially college students who don't have a lot of extra cash and often lack training in how to handle money responsibly, may rapidly build a balance beyond their means. When this occurs, students may be able to cover little more than the minimum monthly payment of $15 to $25. With high average interest rates, the outstanding balance can grow quickly until the student ends up paying more interest than she originally charged.

> **Developed by author's ideas, observations**

> **Topic sentence: effects of heavy debt**

The drastic effects of a reliance on plastic are clear. Some students end up with debts in the thousands that trail them for years. If they have to default on their cards or declare bankruptcy, a bad credit report can follow them into adulthood, hurting their chances to rent an apartment or purchase a home or car. Some students have even fallen into depression and, in one or two extreme cases, suicide. At my cousin's college, the University of Oklahoma, a student committed suicide after being overwhelmed by a $3,000 credit card debt. Thankfully, Maya avoided such serious consequences; however, her dependence on credit seriously affected

> **Developed by author's ideas; suicide case source is author's cousin**

Gevana 2

her education. To avoid bankruptcy, she had to leave college for a semester to work full-time and pay off her debt.

Fortunately, the consequences of students' ever-increasing credit card debt are gaining more widespread attention. Lawmakers and colleges are taking action. A May 21, 2001, article in Business Week entitled "Congratulations, Grads—You're Bankrupt," reports that over a dozen schools have simply banned all credit card marketers from campuses (48). Yet, students should not wait for others to act on their behalf. Financial expert Beth Kobliner, in her book Get a Financial Life, advises, "Limiting your access to credit is a smart move whether you're a binge shopper or a model of self-control" (49). In short, any student can practice self-discipline with credit by following three simple rules: 1) carry just one card, 2) use it only for emergencies; and 3) pay your entire balance every month.

Gevana 3

Works Cited

"Congratulations, Grads—You're Bankrupt." Business Week 21 May 2001: 48.

Credit Card Usage Continues among College Students. Nellie Mae. 2001. 26 Apr. 2002 <http://www.nelliemae.com/library/cc_use.html>.

Kobliner, Beth. Get a Financial Life. New York: Fireside/Simon & Schuster, 1996.

CHAPTER 19
Writing Under Pressure: The Essay Examination

PART A	Budgeting Your Time
PART B	Reading and Understanding the Essay Question
PART C	Choosing the Correct Paragraph or Essay Pattern
PART D	Writing the Topic Sentence or the Thesis Statement

Being able to write under pressure is a key skill both in college and in the workplace. Throughout your college career, you will be asked to write **timed papers** in class and to take **essay examinations.** In fact, many English programs base placement and passing on timed essay exams. Clearly, the ability to write under pressure is crucial.

An **essay question** requires the same writing skills that a student uses in composing a paragraph or an essay. Even in history and biology, how well you do on an essay test depends partly on how well you write; yet many students, under the pressure of a test, forget or fail to apply what they know about good writing. This chapter will improve your ability to write under pressure. Many of the sample exam questions on the following pages were taken from real college examinations.

Part A
Budgeting Your Time

To do well on a timed essay or an essay test, it is not enough to know the material. You must also be able to call forth what you know, organize it, and present it in writing—all under pressure in a limited time.

Since most essay examinations are timed, it is important that you learn how to **budget** your time effectively so that you can devote adequate time to each question *and* finish the test. The following six tips will help you use your time well.

1. **Make sure you know exactly how long the examination lasts.** A one-hour examination may really be only fifty minutes; a two-hour examination may last only one hour and forty-five minutes.

2. **Note the point value of all questions and allot time accordingly to each question.** That is, allot the most time to questions that are worth the most points and less time to ones that are worth fewer.

3. **Decide on an order in which to answer the questions.** You do not have to begin with the first question on the examination and work, in order, to the last. Instead, you may start with the questions worth the most points. Some students prefer to begin with the questions they feel they can answer most easily, thereby guaranteeing points toward the final grade on the examination. Others combine the two methods. No matter which system you use, be sure to allot enough time to the questions that are worth the most points—whether you do them first or last.

4. **Make sure you understand exactly what each question asks you to do; then quickly prewrite and plan your answer.** It is all-important to take a breath, study the question, and make a quick scratch outline or plan of your answer *before you start to write.* Parts B through D of this chapter will guide you through these critical steps.

5. **Time yourself.** As you begin a particular question, calculate when you must be finished with that question in order to complete the examination, and note that time in the margin. As you write, check the clock every five minutes so that you remain on schedule.

6. **Finally, do not count on having enough time to recopy your work.** Skip lines and write carefully so that the instructor can easily read your writing as well as any neat corrections you might make.

PRACTICE 1 Imagine that you are about to take the two-hour history test shown below. Read the test carefully, noting the point value of each question, and then answer the questions that follow the examination.

Part I   Answer both questions. 15 points each.

1. Do you think that the Versailles Peace Treaty was a "harsh" one? Be specific.

2. List the basic principles of Karl Marx. Analyze them in terms of Marx's claim that they are scientific.

Part II Answer two of the following questions. 25 points each.

3. Describe the origins of, the philosophies behind, and the chief policies of either Communist Russia or Fascist Italy. Be specific.

4. What were the causes of Nelson Mandela's presidential victory in South Africa in 1994?

5. European history of the nineteenth and twentieth centuries has been increasingly related to that of the rest of the world. Why? How? With what consequences for Europe?

Part III Briefly identify ten of the following. 2 points each.

a. John Locke
b. Franco-Prussian War
c. Stalingrad
d. Cavour
e. Manchuria, 1931
f. Entente Cordiale
g. Existentialism
h. Jacobins
i. The Opium Wars
j. Social Darwinism
k. The Reform Bill of 1832
l. The most interesting reading you have done this term (from the course list)

1. Which part would you do first and why? _____

   _____

   How much time would you allot to the questions in this part and why?

   _____

2. Which part would you do second and why? _____

   _____

   How much time would you allot to the questions in this part and why?

   _____

   _____

3. Which part would you do last and why? _____

   _____

   How much time would you allot to the questions in this part and why?

   _____

   _____

Part B

Reading and Understanding the Essay Question

Before you begin writing, carefully examine each question to decide exactly what your purpose is: that is, what the instructor expects you to do.

- This question contains three sets of instructions.

> *Question:* Using <u>either</u> Communist China or Nazi Germany as a model, (a) <u>describe</u> the characteristics of a totalitarian <u>state</u>, and (b) <u>explain</u> how such a state was <u>created</u>.

- First, you must use "either Communist China or Nazi Germany as a model." That is, you must **choose** *one or the other* as a model.

- Second, you must **describe,** and third, you must **explain.**

- Your answer should consist of two written parts, a **description** and an **explanation.**

It is often helpful to underline the important words, as shown in the previous box, to make sure you understand the entire question and have noted all its parts.

> *The student must* (1) <u>choose</u> to write about either Communist China or Nazi Germany, not both; (2) <u>describe</u> the totalitarian state; (3) <u>explain</u> how such a state was created.

PRACTICE 2 Read each essay question and underline key words. Then, on the lines beneath the question, describe in your own words exactly what the question requires: (1) What directions does the student have to follow? (2) How many parts will the answer contain?

Example What were the <u>causes</u> of the Cold War? What were its chief <u>episodes</u>? <u>Why</u> has there <u>not</u> been a "hot" war?

Student must *(1) tell what caused the Cold War (two or more causes), (2) mention main events of Cold War, (3) give reasons why we haven't had a full-scale war. The essay will have three parts: causes, main events, and reasons.*

1. State Newton's First Law and give examples from your own experience.

   Student must _____

2. Choose one of the following terms. Define it, give an example of it, and then show how it affects *your* life: (a) freedom of speech, (b) justice for all, (c) equal opportunity.

   Student must _____

3. Shiism and Sunni are the <u>two great branches of Islam</u>. Discuss the <u>religious beliefs</u> and the <u>politics</u> of each branch.

   Student must 1. How does each branche treat women
   2. does these branche believe in democra
   Politics Are they democrates or Republics
   Compare the (2) branches

4. Name and explain four types of savings institutions. What are three factors that influence one's choice of a savings institution?

   Student must ① When deciding on a Saving inst. what are the advantages. ② How does a Saving account differ from Mutal funds,

5. Steroids: the athlete's "unfair advantage." Discuss.

   Student must _____

6. Discuss the causes and consequences of the Broad Street cholera epidemic in mid-nineteenth-century London. What was the role of Dr. John Snow?

   Student must _____

7. Define the Monroe Doctrine of the early nineteenth century and weigh the arguments for and against it.

   Student must _____

8. The sixteenth century is known for the Renaissance, the Reformation, and the Commercial Revolution. Discuss each event, showing why it was important to the history of Western civilization.

   Student must _____

258 UNIT 4 Writing the Essay

9. Erik Erikson has theorized that adult actions toward children may produce either (a) trust or mistrust, (b) autonomy or self-doubt, (c) initiative or guilt. Choose one of the pairs above and give examples of the kinds of adult behavior that might create these responses in a child.

   Student must _____

   _____

   _____

   _____

   _____

   _____

10. Simón Bolívar may not have been as great a hero as he was believed to be. Agree or disagree.

    Student must _____

    _____

    _____

    _____

    _____

    _____

Part C

Choosing the Correct Paragraph or Essay Pattern

Throughout this book, you have learned how to write various types of paragraphs and compositions. Many examinations will require you simply to **illustrate, define, compare,** and so forth. How well you answer questions may depend partly on how well you understand these terms.

> 1. *Illustrate* "behavior modification."
> 2. *Define* "greenhouse effect."
> 3. *Compare* Agee and Nin as diarists.

■ The key words in these questions are *illustrate, define,* and *compare*—**instruction words** that tell you what you are supposed to do and what form your answer should take.

Here is a review list of some common instruction words used in college examinations.

1. **Classify:** Gather into categories, types, or kinds according to a single basis of division (see Chapter 11).

2. **Compare:** Point out similarities (see Chapter 10). Instructors often use *compare* to mean point out both *similarities* and *differences*.

3. **Contrast:** Point out differences (see Chapter 10).

4. **Define:** State clearly and exactly the meaning of a word or term (see Chapter 9). You may be required to write a single-sentence definition or a full paragraph. Instructors may use *identify* as a synonym for *define* when they want a short definition.

5. **Discuss:** (analyze, describe, or explain) Often an instructor uses these terms to mean "thoughtfully examine a subject, approaching it from different angles." These terms allow the writer more freedom of approach than many of the others.

6. **Discuss causes:** Analyze the reasons or causes for something; answer the question *Why?* (see Chapter 12).

7. **Discuss effects:** Analyze the effects, consequences, or results of something (see Chapter 12).

8. **Evaluate:** Weigh the pros and cons, advantages and disadvantages (see Chapters 10 and 13).

9. **Identify:** Give a capsule who-what-when-where-why answer. Sometimes *identify* is a synonym for *define*.

10. **Illustrate:** Give one or more examples (see Chapter 5).

11. **Narrate:** (trace) Follow the development of something through time, event by event (see Chapters 6 and 8).

12. **Summarize:** Write the substance of a longer work in condensed form (see Chapter 17, Part B).

13. **Take a stand:** Persuade; argue for a particular position (see Chapter 13).

PRACTICE 3 You should have no trouble deciding what kind of paragraph or composition to use if the question uses one of the terms just defined—*contrast, trace, classify,* and so on. However, questions are often worded in such a way that you have to discover what kind of paragraph or essay is required. What kind of paragraph or essay is required by each of the following questions?

Example | What is *schizophrenia*? (Write a paragraph to. . . .) _____*define*_____

1. In one concise paragraph, give the main ideas of Simone de Beauvoir's famous book *The Second Sex*. _____

2. What is the difference between veins and arteries? _____

3. Follow the development of Wynton Marsalis's musical style. _____

4. How do jet- and propeller-driven planes differ? _____

5. Who or what is each of the following: the Gang of Four, Ho Chi Minh, Tiananmen Square? _____

6. Explain the causes of the American Civil War. _____

7. Explain what is meant by "magical realism." _____

8. Take a stand for or against legalizing marijuana in this country. Give reasons to support your stand. _____

9. Give two recent instances of military hazing that you consider "out of control." _____

10. Divide into groups the different kinds of web sites giving out medical information. _____

Part D

Writing the Topic Sentence or the Thesis Statement

A good way to ensure that your answer truly addresses itself to the question is to compose a topic sentence or a thesis statement that contains the key words of the question.

> *Question:* How do fixed-rate and adjustable-rate mortgages differ?

- The key words in this question are *fixed-rate* and *adjustable-rate mortgages,* and *differ.*

- What kind of paragraph or essay would be appropriate for this question?

> *Topic sentence* or *thesis statement of answer:* Fixed-rate and adjustable-rate mortgages differ in three basic ways.

- The answer repeats the key words of the question: *fixed-rate, adjustable-rate, mortgages,* and *differ.*

PRACTICE 4 Here are eight examination questions. Write a topic sentence or thesis statement for each question by using the question as part of the answer. Pretend that you know all the material. Even though you may not know anything about the subjects, you should be able to formulate a topic sentence or thesis statement based on the question.

1. Contrast high school requirements in Jamaica with those in the United States.

   Topic sentence or thesis statement: _____

2. Do you think that the terrorist attacks of September 11, 2001, had any positive effects on Americans?

   Topic sentence or thesis statement: _____

3. What steps can a busy person take to reduce the destructive impact of stress in his or her life?

   Topic sentence or thesis statement: _____

4. Gay couples should be allowed to adopt children. Agree or disagree with this statement.

   Topic sentence or thesis statement: _____

   _____

   _____

5. Assume that you manage a small shop that sells men's apparel. What activities would you undertake to promote the sale of sportswear?

   Topic sentence or thesis statement: _____

   _____

   _____

6. The U.S. government should cover the medical costs of AIDS. Agree or disagree with this statement.

   Topic sentence or thesis statement: _____

   _____

   _____

7. The state should subsidize students in medical school because the country needs more doctors. Agree or disagree with this statement.

   Topic sentence or thesis statement: _____

   _____

   _____

8. Does religion play a more vital role in people's lives today than it did in your parents' generation?

   Topic sentence or thesis statement: _____

   _____

   _____

✔ Checklist

The Process of Answering an Essay Question

___ 1. Survey the test and note the point value for each question.

___ 2. Calculate how much time you need for each question. Then check the clock as you write so that you complete all the questions.

___ 3. Read each question carefully, underlining important words.

___ 4. Determine how many parts the answer should contain.

___ 5. Considering your audience (usually the teacher) and purpose, choose the paragraph or essay pattern that would best answer the question.

___ 6. Write a topic sentence or a thesis statement that repeats the key words of the question.

___ 7. Quickly freewrite or brainstorm ideas on scrap paper and arrange them in a logical order, making a scratch outline or plan.

___ 8. Write your paragraph or essay neatly, skipping lines so you will have enough room to make corrections.

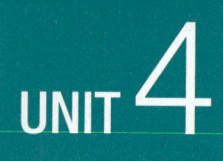

Writers' Workshop

Analyze a Social Problem

Because essays are longer and more complex than paragraphs, organizing an essay can be a challenge, even for experienced writers. Techniques like having a clear *controlling idea*, a good *thesis statement*, and a *plan or an outline* all help an essay writer manage the task. Another useful approach is dividing the subject into three parts, as one student does here. In your group or class, read the essay, aloud if possible, underlining the parts you find most powerful and paying special attention to organization.

It's Great to Get Old

(1) I knock at the door and patiently await an answer. I listen and hear the thump of a cane on the hard wood floor, edging slowly toward the door. "It's great to get old," my grandmother says facetiously[1] as she opens the door, apologizing for making me wait. Through her I learn firsthand the problems of the aged. Loneliness, lack of money, and ailing health are just some of the problems old people must deal with.

(2) For one thing, loneliness seems endemic[2] among old people in America. With difficulty getting around, many spend most of their time confined to their apartments, awaiting visits from family or friends. Through my grandmother, I realize that as much as old people's families may care about them, the family members obviously have lives of their own and cannot visit as much as old persons would like. And when people are very old, most of their friends have already died, so they spend most of their time alone.

(3) Poor health is also a major problem. Any number of physical ailments create a problem. Cataracts, for example, are a common eye problem among old people. Health problems can make life very difficult for an old person.

(4) Last but not least is the financial burden old people must cope with. The rising costs of basic necessities such as food, housing, and health care are especially difficult for old people to meet. Sadly, most are forced to compromise what they need for what they can afford. Take, for example, an old person who buys pounds of inexpensive pasta for dinner every night. While the person may need other nutrients, the person forfeits this need for what the person can afford. Financial problems also make life very difficult for an old person.

(5) There is no easy way to ease the problems of the aged. Simply being aware of them is an important step in the right direction. If we turn our attention and compassion toward the elderly, we can begin to help them find solutions.

—Denise Nelley (Student)

[1]facetiously: humorously
[2]endemic: typical in a certain place or population

1. How effective is Ms. Nelley's essay?

   _____ Strong thesis statement?   _____ Good supporting details?

   _____ Logical organization?   _____ Effective conclusion?

2. Did the introductory paragraph catch your interest? Explain why or why not.

3. What is the controlling idea of the essay? What is the thesis statement?

4. This writer has skillfully organized her ideas. Her thesis names three problems facing the elderly. What are they? Does the body of the essay discuss these three problems in the same order that the thesis names them? If not, what changes would you suggest?

5. Are the three problems fully explained in paragraphs 2, 3, and 4? That is, does Ms. Nelley provide enough support for each problem? If not, what revision suggestions would you give the writer, especially for paragraph 3?

6. This student movingly presents some problems of the elderly. Do you think she should have included solutions? Why or why not?

7. Can you spot any error patterns (the same error two or more times) that this student should watch out for?

Group Work

In your group or class, evaluate (or grade) Ms. Nelley's essay. Then, based on your evaluation, decide what changes or revisions would most improve the essay, and revise it accordingly, as if it were your own. If your group wishes to add any new ideas or support, brainstorm together and choose the strongest ideas. Rewrite as needed.

When you are done, evaluate the essay again, with your changes.

Writing and Revising Ideas

1. Discuss the ways in which a loved one's experience has taught you about a problem (addiction, AIDS, disability, and so on).
2. Analyze a social problem (racial profiling or shoplifting, for example).

Improving Your Writing

CHAPTER 20 Revising for Consistency and Parallelism
CHAPTER 21 Revising for Sentence Variety
CHAPTER 22 Revising for Language Awareness
CHAPTER 23 Putting Your Revision Skills to Work

CHAPTER 20 Revising for Consistency and Parallelism

PART A Consistent Tense
PART B Consistent Number and Person
PART C Parallelism

All good writing is **consistent.** That is, each sentence and paragraph in the final draft should move along smoothly without confusing shifts in **tense, number,** or **person.** In addition, good writing uses **parallel structure** to balance two or more similar words, phrases, or clauses.

Although you should be aware of consistency and parallelism as you write the first draft of your paragraph or essay, you might find it easier to **revise** for them—that is, to write your first draft and then, as you read it again later, check and rewrite for consistency and parallelism.

Part A

Consistent Tense

Consistency of tense means using the same verb tense whenever possible throughout a sentence or an entire paragraph. Do not shift from one verb tense to another—for example, from present to past or from past to present—unless you really mean to indicate different times.

1.	Inconsistent tense:	We *stroll* down Bourbon Street as the jazz bands *began* to play.
2.	Consistent tense:	We *strolled* down Bourbon Street as the jazz bands *began* to play.
3.	Consistent tense:	We *stroll* down Bourbon Street as the jazz bands *begin* to play.

267

- Sentence 1 begins in the present tense with the verb *stroll* but then slips into the past tense with the verb *began*. The tenses are inconsistent since both actions (strolling and beginning) occur at the same time.
- Sentence 2 is consistent. Both verbs, *strolled* and *began*, are now in the past tense.
- Sentence 3 is also consistent, using the present tense forms of both verbs, *stroll* and *begin*. The present tense here gives a feeling of immediacy, as if the action is happening now.*

Of course, you should use different verb tenses in a sentence or paragraph if they convey the meaning that you wish to convey:

> 4. Last fall I *took* English 02; now I *am taking* English 13.

- The verbs in this sentence accurately show the time relationship between the two classroom experiences.†

PRACTICE 1 Read the following sentences carefully for meaning. Then correct any inconsistencies of tense by changing the verbs that do not accurately show the time of events.

Example | I took a deep breath and opened the door; there stands a well-dressed man with a large box.

Consistent: I took a deep breath and opened the door; there ~~stands~~ *stood* a well-dressed man with a large box.

or

Consistent: I ~~took~~ *take* a deep breath and ~~opened~~ *open* the door; there stands a well-dressed man with a large box.

1. Two seconds before the buzzer sounded, Kevin Garnett sank a basket from midcourt, and the crowd goes wild.

2. Nestlé introduced instant coffee in 1938; it takes eight years to develop this product.

3. We expand our sales budget, doubled our research, and soon saw positive results.

4. For twenty years, Dr. Dulfano observed animal behavior and seeks clues to explain the increasing violence among human beings.

5. I knew how the system works.

---

* For more work on spotting verbs, see Chapter 24, "The Simple Sentence," Part C.
† For more work on particular verb tenses and forms, see Chapters 27, 28, and 29.

6. I was driving south on Interstate 90 when a truck approaches with its high beams on.

7. Two brown horses graze quietly in the field as the sun rose and the mist disappeared.

8. Lollie had a big grin on her face as she walks over and kicked the Coke machine.

9. Maynard stormed down the hallway, goes right into the boss's office, and shouts, "I want curtains in my office!"

10. The nurses quietly paced the halls, making sure their patients rest comfortably.

PRACTICE 2 Inconsistencies of tense are most likely to occur within paragraphs and longer pieces of writing. Therefore, it is important to revise your writing for tense consistency. Read this paragraph for meaning. Then revise, correcting inconsistencies of tense by changing incorrect verbs.

It was 1850. A poor German-born peddler named Levi Strauss came to San Francisco, trying to sell canvas cloth to tent makers. By chance he met a miner who complained that sturdy work pants are hard to find. Strauss had an idea, measures the man, and makes him a pair of canvas pants. The miner loved his new breeches, and Levi Strauss goes into business. Although he ordered more canvas, what he gets is a brown French cloth called *serge de Nîmes*, which Americans soon called "denim." Strauss liked the cloth but had the next batch dyed blue. He became successful selling work pants to such rugged men as cowboys and lumberjacks. In the 1870s, hearing about a tailor in Nevada adding copper rivets to a pair of the pants to make them stronger, Strauss patents the idea. When he died in 1902, Levi Strauss was famous in California, but the company keeps growing. In the 1930s, when Levi's jeans became popular in the East, both men and women wear them. By 2000, people all over the world had purchased 2.5 billion pairs of jeans.

PRACTICE 3 The following paragraph is written in the past tense. Rewrite it in consistent present tense; make sure all verbs agree with their subjects.*

In the late afternoon light on the plains of Botswana, Dereck and Beverly Joubert spotted what appeared to be a gray boulder a thousand yards away. It was a bull elephant, about 40 years old, in his prime. Dereck grabbed his movie camera while Beverly swooped up her Nikon. They barely began to shoot when the five-ton bull became enraged, trumpeted, spread his ears, and charged full-speed. The Jouberts continued filming—even as the elephant suddenly dug both front legs into the ground, skidded forward in a cloud of dust, and came to a halt within yards of the couple. Later, in their Land Cruiser, the Jouberts admitted that while danger sometimes came a bit too close, they loved their lives as documentary filmmakers in Africa. Together they lived in tents in the wild, wrote, produced, shot, and edited award-winning films. By educating the public, they helped stop the poaching of lions, elephants, and other big game.

Based on Susan Schindehette and Terry Smith, "Animal Passions," *People*

_____

_____

_____

_____

_____

_____

_____

_____

_____

_____

PRACTICE 4 The following paragraph is written in the present tense. Rewrite it in consistent past tense.†

On the night of December 2, 1777, in Philadelphia, a woman stands breathlessly at a closed door in her house. While she listens at the keyhole, the British soldiers inside plan a surprise attack on George Washington's army. On the morning of December 4, carrying an empty flour sack, Lydia Darragh sets out. As she passes the British soldiers who occupy the town, she tells them she is on her way to buy flour. She walks five miles to the miller's, leaves her sack to be filled, and then heads toward the American camp. On the road, she meets American Colonel

_____

* For more work on agreement, see Chapter 27, "Present Tense (Agreement)."
† For more work on the past tense, see Chapter 28, "Past Tense."

Thomas Craig and gives him her message. Craig gallops off to warn Washington of the danger—and Darragh goes back to pick up her flour. When British General Howe marches his army out of Philadelphia that night, the American troops are ready for the attack. Although Lydia Darragh's actions help the Americans win the Revolutionary War, she is never suspected.

_____
_____
_____
_____
_____
_____
_____
_____
_____
_____
_____

PRACTICE 5 Longer pieces of writing often use both the past tense and the present tense. However, switching correctly from one tense to the other requires care. Read the following essay carefully and note when a switch from one tense to another is logically necessary. Then revise verbs as needed.

A Quick History of Chocolate

Most of us now take solid chocolate—especially candy bars—so much for granted that we find it hard to imagine a time when chocolate didn't exist. However, this delicious food becomes an eating favorite only about 150 years ago.

The ancient peoples of Central America began cultivating cacao beans almost 3,000 years ago. A cold drink made from the beans is served to Hernando Cortés, the Spanish conqueror, when he arrives at the Aztec court of Montezuma in 1519. The Spaniards took the beverage home to their king. He likes it so much that he kept the formula a secret. For the next 100 years, hot chocolate was the private drink of the Spanish nobility. Slowly, it makes its way into the fashionable courts of France, England, and Austria. In 1657, a Frenchman living in London opened a shop where devices for making the beverage are sold at a high price. Soon chocolate houses appeared in cities throughout Europe. Wealthy clients met in them, sipped chocolate, conducted business, and gossip.

During the 1800s, chocolate became a chewable food. The breakthrough comes in 1828 when cocoa butter was extracted from the bean. Twenty years later, an English firm mixed the butter with chocolate liquor, which results in the first solid chocolate. Milton Hershey's first candy bar come on the scene in 1894, and Tootsie Rolls hit the market two years later. The popularity of chocolate bars soar during World War I when they are given to soldiers for fast energy. M&Ms gave the industry another boost during World War II; soldiers needed candy that wouldn't melt in their hands.

On the average, Americans today eat ten pounds of hard chocolate a year. Their number-one choice is Snickers, which sold more than a billion bars every year. However, Americans consume far less chocolate than many Western Europeans. The average Dutch person gobbled up more than fifteen pounds a year while a Swiss packed away almost twenty pounds. Chocolate is obviously an international favorite.

Part B

Consistent Number and Person

Just as important as verb tense consistency is consistency of **number** and **person**.

Consistency of Number

Consistency of number means avoiding confusing shifts from singular to plural or from plural to singular within a sentence or paragraph. Choose *either* singular *or* plural; then be *consistent*.

CHAPTER 20   Revising for Consistency and Parallelism

1. Inconsistent number:	*The wise jogger* chooses *their* running shoes with care.
2. Consistent number:	*The wise jogger* chooses *his or her* running shoes with care.
3. Consistent number:	*Wise joggers* choose *their* running shoes with care.

- Since the subject of sentence 1, *the wise jogger,* is singular, use of the plural pronoun *their* is *inconsistent*.
- Sentence 2 is *consistent*. The singular pronoun *his* (or *her*) now clearly refers to the singular *jogger*.
- In sentence 3, the plural number is used *consistently*. *Their* clearly refers to the plural *joggers*.

If you begin a paragraph by referring to a web site designer as *she,* continue to refer to *her* in the **third person singular** throughout the paragraph:

The web site designer _____; she _____

_____. The law may not protect *her* _____

_____. Therefore, *she* _____.

Do not confuse the reader by shifting unnecessarily to *they* or *you*.

PRACTICE 6   Correct any inconsistencies of **number** in the following sentences.* Also make necessary changes in verb agreement.

Example | A singer must protect ~~their~~ *his or her* voice.

1. An individual's self-esteem can affect their performance.

2. Jorge started drinking diet sodas only last November, but already he hates the taste of it.

3. The headlines encouraged us, but we feared that it wasn't accurate.

4. The defendant who wishes to do so may ask a higher court to overturn their conviction.

5. Dreams fascinate me; it is like another world.

---

*For more practice in agreement of pronouns and antecedents, see Chapter 31, "Pronouns," Part B.

6. If a person doesn't know how to write well, they will face limited job opportunities.

7. Oxford University boasts of the great number of ancient manuscripts they own.

8. Always buy corn and tomatoes when it is in season.

9. The average American takes their freedom for granted.

10. Women have more opportunities than ever before. She is freer to go to school, get a job, and choose the kind of life she wants.

Consistency of Person

Consistency of person—closely related to consistency of number—means using the same *person,* or indefinite pronoun form, throughout a sentence or paragraph whenever possible.

> *First person* is the most personal and informal in written work: (singular) *I,* (plural) *we*
>
> *Second person* speaks directly to the reader: (singular and plural) *you*
>
> *Third person* is the most formal and most frequently used in college writing: (singular) *he, she, it, one, a person, an individual, a student,* and so on; (plural) *they, people, individuals, students,* and so on

Avoid confusing shifts from one person to another. Choose one, and then be *consistent.* When using a noun in a general way—*a person, the individual, the parent*—be careful not to slip into the second person, *you,* but continue to use the third person, *he or she.*

4. Inconsistent person		A *player* collects $200 when *you* pass "Go."
5. Consistent person:		A *player* collects $200 when *he or she* passes "Go."
6. Consistent person:		*You* collect $200 when *you* pass "Go."

- In sentence 4, the person shifts unnecessarily from the third person, *a player,* to the second person, *you.* The result is confusing.

- Sentence 5 maintains consistent third person. *He or she* now clearly refers to the third person subject, *a player.*

- Sentence 6 is also consistent, using the second person, *you,* throughout.

Of course, inconsistencies of person and number often occur together, as shown in the next box.

> | | |
> |---|---|
> | 7. Inconsistent person and number: | Whether *one* enjoys or resents commercials, *we* are bombarded with them every hour of the day. |
> | 8. Consistent person and number: | Whether *we* enjoy or resent commercials, *we* are bombarded with them every hour of the day. |
> | 9. Consistent person and number: | Whether *one* enjoys or resents commercials, *he or she* (or *one*) is bombarded with them every hour of the day. |

- Sentence 7 shifts from the third person singular, *one,* to the first person plural, *we.*
- Sentence 8 uses the first person plural consistently.
- Sentence 9 uses the third person singular consistently.

PRACTICE 7 Correct the shifts in **person** in these sentences. If necessary, change the verbs to make them agree with any new subjects.

Example | One should eliminate saturated fats from ~~your~~ *one's* diet.

1. Sooner or later, most addicts realize that you can't just quit when you want to.

2. One problem facing students on this campus is that a person doesn't know when the library will be open and when it will be closed.

3. One should rely on reason, not emotion, when they are forming opinions about such charged issues as abortion.

4. I have reached a time in my life when what others expect is less important than what one really wants to do.

5. Members of the orchestra should meet after the concert and bring your instruments and music.

6. The wise mother knows that she is asking for trouble if you let a small child watch violent television shows.

7. The student who participates in this program will spend six weeks in Spain and Morocco. You will study the art and architecture firsthand, working closely with an instructor.

8. You shouldn't judge a person by the way they dress.

9. If you have been working that hard, one needs a vacation.

10. People who visit the Caribbean for the first time are struck by the lushness of the landscape. The sheer size of the flowers and fruit amazes you.

PRACTICE 8 The following paragraph consistently uses third person singular—*the job applicant, the job seeker, he or she*. For practice in revising for consistency, rewrite the paragraph in **consistent third person plural.** Begin by changing *the job applicant* to *job applicants*. Then change verbs, nouns, and pronouns as necessary.

In a job interview these days, the job applicant should stress his or her personal skills, rather than only technical skills. This strategy could increase his or her chances of getting hired. The job seeker should point out such skills as speaking and writing confidently, working well on a team, solving problems quickly, or managing people. These days, many employers assume that if an applicant has excellent "soft skills" like these, he or she can be trained in the technical fine points of the job.

_____
_____
_____
_____
_____
_____

PRACTICE 9 Revise the following essay for inconsistencies of person and number. Correct any confusing shifts (changing words if necessary) to make the writing clear and *consistent* throughout.

Immortality In Wax

"Madame Tussaud's. Come and find out who's in. And who's out." That's how English advertisers lure visitors to a most unusual show—a display of the rich, the famous, and the infamous in the form of lifelike wax statues. Nearly three million people line up each year to rub shoulders with the images of historic and contemporary celebrities. You make Madame Tussaud's the most popular paid tourist attraction in England.

Visitors can see and have one's photograph taken with more than 400 eerily lifelike statues of such people as Princess Di, Joan of Arc, Elvis Presley, Naomi

Campbell, the Dalai Lama, and Britney Spears. The popular Chamber of Horrors displays the most notorious criminals of all time.

Recently two new Tussaud Museums have opened. In New York, tourists now can mingle with the likes of Whoopi Goldberg, Nicolas Cage, Martin Luther King, Jr., and Buffalo Bill. In Las Vegas, we can pose with Muhammad Ali, Liberace, Gloria Estefan, Lenny Kravitz, and nearly 100 others.

Each month, a committee decides who is in and who is out of the collections. A celebrity is chosen for your fame, recognizability, and publicity potential. You are invited to sit for moldings, a process that takes six months and costs $45,000. Mother Teresa was one of the few persons ever to decline an invitation from Madame Tussaud's.

Part C

Parallelism

Parallelism, or **parallel structure,** is an effective way to add smoothness and power to your writing. **Parallelism** is a balance of two or more similar words, phrases, or clauses.

Compare the two versions of each of these sentences:

> 1. She likes dancing, swimming, and to box.
> 2. She likes *dancing, swimming,* and *boxing.*
>
> 3. The cable runs across the roof; the north wall is where it runs down.
> 4. The cable runs *across the roof* and *down the north wall.*
>
> 5. He admires people with strong convictions and who think for themselves.
> 6. He admires people *who have strong convictions* and *who think for themselves.*

- Sentences 2, 4, and 6 use **parallelism** to express parallel ideas.

- In sentence 2, *dancing, swimming,* and *boxing* are parallel; all three are the *-ing* forms of verbs, used here as nouns.

- In sentence 4, *across the roof* and *down the north wall* are parallel prepositional phrases, each consisting of a preposition and its object.

- In sentence 6, *who have strong convictions* and *who think for themselves* are parallel clauses beginning with the word *who.*

Sometimes two entire sentences can be parallel:

> In a democracy we are all equal before the law. In a dictatorship we are all equal before the police.
>
> —Millor Fernandes

- In what way are these two sentences parallel? _____

_____

Certain special constructions require parallel structure:

> 7. The fruit is *both* tasty *and* fresh.
> 8. He *either* loves you *or* hates you.
> 9. Yvette *not only* plays golf *but also* swims like a pro.
> 10. I would *rather* sing in the chorus *than* perform a solo.

- Each of these constructions has two parts:
   both . . . and
   (n)either . . . (n)or
   not only . . . but also
   rather . . . than
- The words, phrases, or clauses following each part must be parallel:
   tasty . . . fresh
   loves you . . . hates you
   plays golf . . . swims like a pro
   sing in the chorus . . . perform a solo

PRACTICE 10 Rewrite each of the following sentences, using parallel structure to accent parallel ideas.

Example | The summer in Louisiana is very hot and has high humidity.

The summer in Louisiana is very hot and humid.

1. Teresa is a gifted woman—a chemist, does the carpentry, and she can cook.

_____

_____

2. The shape of the rock, how big it was, and its color reminded me of a small turtle.

_____

_____

3. He is an affectionate husband, a thoughtful son, and kind to his kids.

4. Marvin was happy to win the chess tournament and he also felt surprised.

5. Dr. Tien is the kindest physician I know; she has the most concern of any physician I know.

6. Joe would rather work on a farm than spending time in an office.

7. Every afternoon in the mountains, it either rains or there is hail.

8. *Sesame Street* teaches children nursery rhymes, songs, how to be courteous, and being kind.

9. Alexis would rather give orders than taking them.

10. His writing reveals not only intelligence but also it is humorous.

PRACTICE 11 Write one sentence that is parallel to each sentence that follows, creating pairs of parallel sentences.

Example | On Friday night, she dressed in silk and sipped champagne.
On Monday morning, she put on her jeans and crammed for a history test.

1. When he was twenty, he worked seven days a week in a fruit store.

2. The child in me wants to run away from problems.

3. The home team charged enthusiastically onto the field.

4. "Work hard and keep your mouth shut" is my mother's formula for success.

5. The men thought the movie was amusing.

PRACTICE 12 The following paragraph contains both correct and faulty parallel structures. Revise the faulty parallelism.

During World War II, United States Marines who fought in the Pacific possessed a powerful weapon that was also unbeatable: Navaho Code Talkers. Creating a secret code, Code Talkers sent and were translating vital military information. Four hundred twenty Navahos memorized the code, and it was used by them. It consisted of both common Navaho words and there were also about 400 invented words. For example, Code Talkers used the Navaho words for *owl*, *chicken hawk*, and *swallow* to describe different kinds of aircraft. Because Navaho is a complex language that is also uncommon, the Japanese military could not break the code. Although Code Talkers helped the Allied Forces win the war, their efforts were not publicly recognized until the code was declassified in 1968. On August 14, 1982, the first Navaho Code Talkers Day honored these heroes, who not only had risked their lives but also been developing one of the few unbroken codes in history.

PRACTICE 13 The following essay contains both correct and faulty parallel structures. Revise the faulty parallelism.

Vincent Van Gogh

Vincent Van Gogh sold only one painting in his lifetime, but his oil paintings later influenced modern art and establishing him as one of the greatest artists of all time. Born in Holland in 1853, Van Gogh struggled to find an inspiring career. After failing as a tutor and being a clergyman, he began to paint. Van Gogh's younger brother Theo supported him with money and also sending art supplies. Eventually, Van Gogh went to live with Theo in Paris, where the young artist was introduced to Impressionism, a style of painting that emphasizes light at different times of day. Using vivid colors and also with broad brush strokes, Van Gogh made powerful pictures full of feeling. His favorite subjects were landscapes, still lifes, sunflowers, and drawing everyday people. Perhaps his most famous picture, "Starry Night," shows a wild night sky over a French village, with the moon and stars swirling in fiery circles.

When mental illness or feeling depressed clouded Van Gogh's spirit, Theo gentle and firmly urged him to keep painting. Gradually, however, the penniless Van Gogh sank into insanity and feeling despair. "Cornfield with Crows," completed shortly before his death, shows a darkening sky spattered black with crows. Van Gogh committed suicide in 1890; his devoted brother died six months later. Theo's widow Johanna took the paintings back to Holland and working hard to get recognition for her brother-in-law's genius. Thanks to Theo's encouragement during Vincent's lifetime and Johanna who made efforts after his death, the dynamic paintings of Van Gogh today are admired, studied, and receive love all over the world.

# Exploring Online

http://www.vangoghgallery.com/ Find "Starry Night" and "Cornfield with Crows."
http://www.vangoghmuseum.nl Visit the Van Gogh Museum in the Netherlands, click the Permanent Collection, then periods on the timeline of Van Gogh's life.

CHAPTER 21

Revising for Sentence Variety

PART A   Mix Long and Short Sentences
PART B   Use a Question, a Command, or an Exclamation
PART C   Vary the Beginnings of Sentences
PART D   Vary Methods of Joining Ideas
PART E   Avoid Misplaced and Confusing Modifiers
PART F   Review and Practice

Good writers pay attention to **sentence variety.** They notice how sentences work together within a paragraph, and they seek a mix of different sentence lengths and types. Experienced writers have a variety of sentence patterns from which to choose. They try not to overuse one pattern.

This chapter will present several techniques for varying your sentences and paragraphs. Some of them you may already know and use, perhaps unconsciously. The purpose of this chapter is to make you more conscious of the **choices** available to you as a writer.

Remember, you achieve sentence variety by practicing, by systematically **revising** your papers, and by trying out new types of sentences or combinations of sentences.

Part A

Mix Long and Short Sentences

One of the basic ways to achieve sentence variety is to use both long and short sentences. Beginning writers tend to overuse short, simple sentences, which quickly become monotonous. Notice the length of the sentences in the following paragraph:

> (1) There is one positive result of the rising crime rate. (2) This has been the growth of neighborhood crime prevention programs. (3) These programs really work. (4) They teach citizens to patrol their neighborhoods. (5) They teach citizens to work with the police. (6) They have dramatically reduced crime in cities and towns across the country. (7) The idea is catching on.

The sentences in the paragraph above are all nearly the same length, and the effect is choppy and almost childish. Now read this revised version, which contains a variety of sentence lengths.

> (1) One cause of the falling crime rate in some cities is the growth of neighborhood crime prevention programs. (2) These programs really work. (3) By patrolling their neighborhoods and working with the police, citizens have shown that they can dramatically reduce crime. (4) The idea is catching on.

This paragraph is more effective because it mixes two short sentences, 2 and 4, and two longer sentences, 1 and 3. Although short sentences can be used effectively anywhere in a paragraph or an essay, they can be especially useful as introductions or conclusions, like sentence 4 above. Note the powerful effect of short sentences used between longer ones in the paragraph that follows. Underline the short sentences.

> (1) I recall being told, when I first moved to Los Angeles and was living on an isolated beach, that the Indians would throw themselves into the sea when the bad wind blew. (2) I could see why. (3) The Pacific turned ominously glossy during a Santa Ana period, and one woke in the night troubled not only by the peacocks screaming in the olive trees but by the eerie absence of surf. (4) The heat was surreal. (5) The sky had a yellow cast, the kind of light sometimes called "earthquake weather." (6) My only neighbor would not come out of her house for days, and there were no lights at night, and her husband roamed the place with a machete. (7) One day he would tell me that he had heard a trespasser, the next a rattlesnake.
>
> —Joan Didion, *Slouching Towards Bethlehem*

PRACTICE 1 Revise and rewrite the following paragraph in a variety of sentence lengths. Recombine sentences in any way you wish. You may add connecting words or drop words, but do not alter the meaning of the paragraph. Compare your work with a fellow student's.

The park is alive with motion today. Joggers pound up and down the boardwalk. Old folks watch them from the benches. Couples row boats across the lake. The boats are green and wooden. Two teenagers hurl a Frisbee back and forth. They yell and leap. A shaggy white dog dashes in from nowhere. He snatches the red disk in his mouth. He bounds away. The teenagers run after him.

_____

_____

_____

_____

_____

_____

_____

Part B

Use a Question, a Command, or an Exclamation

The most commonly used sentence is the **declarative sentence,** which is a statement. However, an occasional carefully placed **question, command,** or **exclamation** is an effective way to achieve sentence variety.

The Question

> *Why did I become a cab driver?* First, I truly enjoy driving a car and exploring different parts of the city, the classy avenues and the hidden back streets. In addition, I like meeting all kinds of people, from bookmakers to governors, each with a unique story and many willing to talk to the back of my head. Of course, the pay isn't bad and the hours are flexible, but it's the places and the people that I love.

This paragraph begins with a question. The writer does not really expect the reader to answer it. Rather, it is a **rhetorical question,** one that will be answered by the writer in the course of the paragraph. A rhetorical question used as a topic sentence can provide a colorful change from the usual declarative sentences: *Is America really the best-fed nation in the world? What is courage? Why do more young people take drugs today than ever before?*

The Command and the Exclamation

> (1) Try to imagine using failure as a description of an animal's behavior. (2) Consider a dog barking for fifteen minutes, and someone saying, "He really isn't very good at barking, I'd give him a C." (3) How absurd! (4) It is impossible for an animal to fail because there is no provision for evaluating natural behavior. (5) Spiders construct webs, not successful or unsuccessful webs. (6) Cats hunt mice; if they aren't successful in one attempt, they simply go after another. (7) They don't lie there and whine, complaining about the one that got away, or have a nervous breakdown because they failed. (8) Natural behavior simply is! (9) So apply the same logic to your own behavior and rid yourself of the fear of failure.
>
> —Dr. Wayne W. Dyer, *Your Erroneous Zones*

The previous paragraph begins and ends with **commands,** or **imperative sentences.** Sentences 1, 2, and 9 address the reader directly and have as their implied subject *you.* They tell the reader to do something: *(You) try to imagine . . . , (you) consider . . . , (you) apply. . . .* Commands are most frequently used in giving directions,* but they can be used occasionally, as in the previous paragraph, for sentence variety.

Sentences 3 and 8 in the Dyer paragraph are **exclamations,** sentences that express strong emotion and end with an exclamation point. These should be used very sparingly. In fact, some writers avoid them altogether, striving for words that convey strong emotion instead.

Be careful with the question, the command, and the exclamation as options in your writing. Try them out, but use them—especially the exclamation—sparingly.

Writing Assignment 1

Write a paragraph that begins with a rhetorical question. Choose one of the questions below or compose your own. Be sure that the body of the paragraph really does answer the question.

1. How has college (or anything else) changed me?
2. Should people pamper their pets?
3. Is marriage worth the risks?

---

* For more work on giving directions, see Chapter 8, "Process."

Part C

Vary the Beginnings of Sentences

Begin with an Adverb

Since the first word of many sentences is the subject, one way to achieve sentence variety is by occasionally starting a sentence with a word or words other than the subject.

For instance, you can begin with an **adverb**:[†]

> 1. He *laboriously* dragged the large crate up the stairs.
> 2. *Laboriously,* he dragged the large crate up the stairs.
> 3. The contents of the beaker *suddenly* began to foam.
> 4. *Suddenly,* the contents of the beaker began to foam.

- In sentences 2 and 4, the adverbs *laboriously* and *suddenly* are shifted to the first position. Notice the difference in rhythm that this creates, as well as the slight change in meaning: Sentence 2 emphasizes *how* he dragged the crate—*laboriously;* sentence 4 emphasizes the *suddenness* of what happened.

- A comma usually follows an adverb that introduces a sentence; however, adverbs of time—*often, now, always*—do not always require a comma. As a general rule, use a comma if you want the reader to pause briefly.

PRACTICE 2 Rewrite the following sentences by shifting the adverbs to the beginning. Punctuate correctly.

Example | He skillfully prepared the engine for the race.

Skillfully, he prepared the engine for the race.

1. Two deer moved silently across the clearing.

   _____

2. The chief of the research division occasionally visits the lab.

   _____

3. Proofread your writing always.

   _____

[†] For more work on adverbs, see Chapter 33, "Adjectives and Adverbs."

4. Children of alcoholics often marry alcoholics.

   _____

5. Jake foolishly lied to his supervisor.

   _____

PRACTICE 3 Begin each of the following sentences with an appropriate adverb. Punctuate correctly.

1. _____ the detective approached the ticking suitcase.

2. _____ Jennifer Capriati powered a forehand past her opponent.

3. _____ she received her check for $25,000 from the state lottery.

4. _____ he left the beach.

5. _____ the submarine sank out of sight.

PRACTICE 4 Write three sentences of your own that begin with adverbs. Use different adverbs from those in Practices 2 and 3; if you wish, use *graciously, furiously, sometimes*. Punctuate correctly.

1. _____

2. _____

3. _____

Begin with a Prepositional Phrase

A **prepositional phrase** is a group of words containing a **preposition** and its **object** (a noun or pronoun). *To you, in the evening,* and *under the old bridge* are prepositional phrases.*

Preposition	Object
to	you
in	the evening
under	the old bridge

Here is a partial list of prepositions:

---

*For work on spotting prepositional phrases, see Chapter 32, "Prepositions."

Common Prepositions

about	beneath	into	throughout
above	beside	near	to
across	between	of	toward
against	by	on	under
among	except	onto	up
at	for	out	upon
behind	from	over	with
below	in	through	without

For variety in your writing, begin an occasional sentence with a prepositional phrase:

5. Charles left the room *without a word*.
6. *Without a word*, Charles left the room.
7. A fat yellow cat lay sleeping *on the narrow sill*.
8. *On the narrow sill*, a fat yellow cat lay sleeping.

- In sentences 6 and 8, the prepositional phrases have been shifted to the beginning. Note the slight shift in emphasis that results. Sentence 6 stresses that Charles left the room *without a word*, and 8 stresses the location of the cat, *on the narrow sill*.

- Prepositional phrases that begin sentences are usually followed by commas. However, short prepositional phrases need not be.

Prepositional phrases are not always movable; rely on the meaning of the sentence to determine whether they are movable:

9. The dress *in the picture* is the one I want.
10. Joelle bought a bottle *of white wine for dinner.*

- *In the picture* in sentence 9 is a part of the subject and cannot be moved. *In the picture the dress is the one I want* makes no sense.

- Sentence 10 has two prepositional phrases. Which one *cannot* be moved to the beginning of the sentence? Why?

_____

_____

PRACTICE 5 Underline the prepositional phrases in each sentence. Some sentences contain more than one prepositional phrase. Rewrite each sentence by shifting a prepositional phrase to the beginning. Punctuate correctly.

Example | A large owl with gray feathers watched us from the oak tree.

From the oak tree, a large owl with gray feathers watched us.

1. The coffee maker turned itself on at seven o'clock sharp.

   _____

   _____

2. A growling Doberman paced behind the chainlink fence.

   _____

   _____

3. A man and a woman held hands under the street lamp.

   _____

   _____

4. They have sold nothing except athletic shoes for years.

   _____

   _____

5. A group of men played checkers and drank iced tea beside the small shop.

   _____

   _____

PRACTICE 6 Begin each of the following sentences with a different prepositional phrase. Refer to the list and be creative. Punctuate correctly.

1. _____ we ordered potato skins, salad, and beer.

2. _____ a woman in horn-rimmed glasses balanced her checkbook.

3. _____ everyone congratulated Jim on his promotion.

4. _____ one can see huge sculptures in wood, metal, and stone.

5. _____ three large helium-filled balloons drifted.

PRACTICE 7 Write three sentences of your own that begin with prepositional phrases. Use these phrases if you wish: *in the dentist's office, under that stack of books, behind his friendly smile.* Punctuate correctly.

1. _____

2. _____

3. _____

Part D

Vary Methods of Joining Ideas*

Join Ideas with a Compound Predicate

A sentence with a **compound predicate** contains more than one verb, but the subject is *not* repeated before the second verb. Such a sentence is really composed of two simple sentences with the same subject:

> 1. The nurse entered.
> 2. The nurse quickly closed the door.
> 3. The nurse *entered* and quickly *closed* the door.

- *The nurse* is the subject of sentence 1, and *entered* is the verb; *the nurse* is also the subject of sentence 2, and *closed* is the verb.

- When these sentences are combined with a compound predicate in sentence 3, *the nurse* is the subject of both *entered* and *closed* but is not repeated before the second verb.

- No comma is necessary when the conjunctions *and, but, or,* and *yet* join the verbs in a compound predicate.

A compound predicate is useful in combining short, choppy sentences:

> 4. He serves elaborate meals.
> 5. He never uses a recipe.
> 6. He serves elaborate meals yet never uses a recipe.
> 7. Aviators rarely get nosebleeds.
> 8. They often suffer from backaches.
> 9. Aviators rarely get nosebleeds but often suffer from backaches.

- Sentences 4 and 5 are joined by *yet*; no comma precedes *yet*.

- Sentences 7 and 8 are joined by *but*; no comma precedes *but*.

---

*For work on joining ideas with coordination and subordination, see Chapter 25, "Coordination and Subordination."

PRACTICE 8 Combine each pair of short sentences into one sentence with a compound predicate. Use *and, but, or,* and *yet.* Punctuate correctly.

Example | Toby smeared peanut butter on a thick slice of white bread. He devoured the treat in thirty seconds.

Toby smeared peanut butter on a thick slice of white bread and devoured the treat in thirty seconds.

1. Americans eat more than 800 million pounds of peanut butter.
   They spend more than $1 billion on the product each year.

2. Peanut butter was first concocted in the 1890s.
   It did not become the food we know for thirty years.

3. George Washington Carver did not discover peanut butter.
   He published many recipes for pastes much like it.

4. The average American becomes a peanut butter lover in childhood.
   He or she loses enthusiasm for it later on.

5. Older adults regain their passion for peanut butter.
   They consume great quantities of the delicious stuff.

PRACTICE 9 Complete the following compound predicates. *Do not repeat* the subjects.

1. Three Korean writers visited the campus and _____

_____

2. The singer breathed heavily into the microphone but _____

_____

3. Take these cans to the recycling center or _____

_____

4. The newspaper printed the story yet _____

_____

5. Three men burst into the back room and _____

_____

PRACTICE 10 Write three sentences with compound predicates. Be careful to punctuate correctly.

1. _____

2. _____

3. _____

Join Ideas with an *-ing* Modifier

An excellent way to achieve sentence variety is by occasionally combining two sentences with an *-ing* **modifier.**

> 10. He peered through the microscope.
> 11. He discovered a squiggly creature.
> 12. *Peering through the microscope,* he discovered a squiggly creature.

- Sentence 10 has been converted to an *-ing* modifier by changing the verb *peered* to *peering* and dropping the subject *he*. *Peering through the microscope* now introduces the main clause, *he discovered a squiggly creature.*

- A comma sets off the *-ing* modifier from the word it refers to, *he*. To avoid confusion, the word referred to must appear in the immediately following clause.

An *-ing* modifier indicates that two actions are occurring at the same time. The main idea of the sentence should be contained in the main clause, not in the *-ing* modifier. In the preceding example, the discovery of the creature is the main idea, not the fact that someone peered through a microscope.

Be careful; misplaced *-ing* modifiers can result in confusing sentences: *He discovered a squiggly creature peering through the microscope.* (Was the creature looking through the microscope?)*

Convert sentence 13 into an *-ing* modifier and write it in the blank:

13. We drove down Tompkins Road.
14. We were surprised by the number of "for sale" signs.
15. _____, we were surprised by the number of "for sale" signs.

- The new *-ing* modifier is followed directly by the word to which it refers, *we*.

PRACTICE 11 Combine the following pairs of sentences by converting the first sentence into an *-ing* modifier. Make sure the subject of the main clause directly follows the *-ing* modifier. Punctuate correctly.

Example
Jake searched for his needle-nose pliers.
He completely emptied the tool chest.

Searching for his needle-nose pliers, Jake completely emptied the tool chest.

1. She installed the air conditioner.
   She saved herself $50 in labor.

2. The surgeons raced against time.
   The surgeons performed a liver transplant on the child.

3. They conducted a survey of Jackson Heights residents.
   They found that most opposed construction of the airport.

---

*For more work on avoiding confusing modifiers, see Part E of this chapter.

4. Three flares spiraled upward from the little boat.
   They exploded against the night sky.

   _____

   _____

5. Virgil danced in the Pennsylvania Ballet.
   Virgil learned discipline and self-control.

   _____

   _____

6. The hen squawked loudly.
   The hen fluttered out of our path.

   _____

   _____

7. The engineer made a routine check of the blueprints.
   He discovered a flaw in the design.

   _____

   _____

8. Dr. Jackson opened commencement exercises with a humorous story.
   He put everyone at ease.

   _____

   _____

PRACTICE 12 Add either an introductory *-ing* modifier *or* a main clause to each sentence. Make sure that each *-ing* modifier refers clearly to the subject of the main clause.

Example | Reading a book a week _____, Jeff increased his vocabulary.
Exercising every day, *I lost five pounds* _____.

1. _____, she felt a sense of accomplishment.

2. Growing up in Hollywood, _____
   _____.

3. _____, the father and son were reconciled.

4. Interviewing his relatives, _____
_____.

5. _____, the wrecking ball swung through the air and smashed into the brick wall.

PRACTICE 13 Write three sentences of your own that begin with *-ing* modifiers. Make sure that the subject of the sentence follows the modifier and be careful of the punctuation.

1. _____
_____

2. _____
_____

3. _____
_____

Join Ideas with a Past Participial Modifier

Some sentences can be joined with a **past participial modifier**. A sentence that contains a *to be* verb and a **past participle*** can be changed into a past participial modifier:

> 16. Judith *is trapped* in a dead-end job.
> 17. Judith decided to enroll at the local community college.
> 18. *Trapped in a dead-end job,* Judith decided to enroll at the local community college.

- In sentence 18, sentence 16 has been made into a past participial modifier by dropping the helping verb *is* and the subject *Judith*. The past participle *trapped* now introduces the new sentence.

- A comma sets off the past participial modifier from the word it modifies, *Judith*. To avoid confusion, the word referred to must directly follow the modifier.

---

*For more work on past participles, see Chapter 29, "The Past Participle."

Be careful; misplaced past participial modifiers can result in confusing sentences: *Packed in dry ice, Steve brought us some ice cream.* (Was Steve packed in dry ice?)†

Sometimes two or more past participles can be used to introduce a sentence:

> 19. The term paper *was revised* and *rewritten*.
>
> 20. It received an A.
>
> 21. *Revised and rewritten*, the term paper received an A.

- The past participles *revised* and *rewritten* become a modifier that introduces sentence 21. What word(s) do they refer to?

_____

PRACTICE 14 Combine each pair of sentences into one sentence that begins with a past participial modifier. Convert the sentence containing a form of *to be* plus a past participle into a past participial modifier that introduces the new sentence.

Example | Duffy was surprised by the interruption.
He lost his train of thought.

Surprised by the interruption, Duffy lost his train of thought.

1. My mother was married at the age of sixteen.
   My mother never finished high school.

   _____

   _____

2. The 2:30 flight was delayed by an electrical storm.
   It arrived in Lexington three hours late.

   _____

   _____

3. The old car was waxed and polished.
   It shone in the sun.

   _____

   _____

---

†For more work on avoiding confusing modifiers, see Part E of this chapter.

4. The house was built by Frank Lloyd Wright.
   It has become famous.

   _____

   _____

5. The Nineteenth Amendment was ratified in 1920.
   It gave women the right to vote.

   _____

   _____

6. The manuscript seems impossible to decipher.
   It is written in code.

   _____

   _____

7. Dr. Bentley will address the premed students.
   He has been recognized for his contributions in the field of immunology.

   _____

   _____

8. Mrs. Witherspoon was exhausted by night classes.
   She declined the chance to work overtime.

   _____

   _____

PRACTICE 15 Complete each sentence by filling in *either* the past participial modifier *or* the main clause. Remember, the past participial modifier must clearly refer to the subject of the main clause.

Example Wrapped in blue paper and tied with string, *the gift arrived* _____.

Chosen to represent the team _____, Phil proudly accepted the trophy.

1. Made of gold and set with precious stones, _____

   _____

2. Overwhelmed by the response to her ad in *The Star*, _____

   _____

3. _____, Tom left no forwarding address.

4. _____, we found a huge basket of fresh fruit on the steps.

5. Astonished by the scene before her, _____
_____

PRACTICE 16 Write three sentences of your own that begin with past participial modifiers. If you wish, use participles from this list:

| shocked | dressed | hidden | bent |
| awakened | lost | stuffed | rewired |

Make sure that the subject of the sentence clearly follows the modifier.

1. _____

2. _____

3. _____

Join Ideas with an Appositive

A fine way to add variety to your writing is to combine two choppy sentences with an appositive. An **appositive** is a word or group of words that renames or describes a noun or pronoun:

> 22. Carlos is the new wrestling champion.
> 23. He is a native of Argentina.
> 24. Carlos, *a native of Argentina,* is the new wrestling champion.

- *A native of Argentina* in sentence 24 is an appositive. It renames the noun *Carlos*.
- An appositive must be placed either directly *after* the word it refers to, as in sentence 24, or directly *before* it, as follows:

> 25. *A native of Argentina,* Carlos is the new wrestling champion.

- Note that an appositive is set off by commas.

Appositives can add versatility to your writing because they can be placed at the beginning, in the middle, or at the end of a sentence. When you join two ideas with an appositive, place the idea you wish to stress in the main clause and make the less important idea the appositive:

> 26. Naomi wants to become a fashion model.
> 27. She is the daughter of an actress.
> 28. *The daughter of an actress,* Naomi wants to become a fashion model.
>
> 29. FACT made headlines for the first time only a few years ago.
> 30. FACT is now a powerful consumer group.
> 31. FACT, *now a powerful consumer group,* made headlines for the first time only a few years ago.
>
> 32. Watch out for Smithers.
> 33. He is a dangerous man.
> 34. Watch out for Smithers, *a dangerous man.*

Using an appositive to combine sentences eliminates unimportant words and creates longer, more fact-filled sentences.

PRACTICE 17

Combine the following pairs of sentences by making the *second sentence* an appositive. Punctuate correctly.

These appositives should occur at the *beginning* of the sentences.

Example
My uncle taught me to use watercolors.
He is a well-known artist.

A well-known artist, my uncle taught me to use watercolors.

1. Dan has saved many lives.
   He is a dedicated fire fighter.

   _____

   _____

2. Acupuncture is becoming popular in the United States.
   It is an ancient Chinese healing system.

   _____

   _____

3. The Cromwell Hotel was built in 1806.
   It is an elegant example of Mexican architecture.

   _____

   _____

These appositives should occur in the *middle* of the sentences. Punctuate correctly.

Example

His American history course is always popular with students.
It is an introductory survey.

His American history course, an introductory survey, is always popular with students.

4. The Korean Ping-Pong champion won ten games in a row.
   She is a small and wiry athlete.

   _____

   _____

5. The pituitary is located below the brain.
   It is the body's master gland.

   _____

   _____

6. The elevator shudders violently and begins to rise.
   It is an ancient box of wood and hope.

   _____

   _____

These appositives should occur at the *end* of the sentences. Punctuate correctly.

Example

I hate fried asparagus.
It is a vile dish.

I hate fried asparagus, a vile dish.

7. Jennifer flaunted her new camera.
   It was a Nikon with a telephoto lens.

   _____

   _____

8. At the intersection stood a hitchhiker.
   He was a young man dressed in a tuxedo.

   _____

   _____

9. We met for pancakes at the Cosmic Cafe.
   It was a greasy diner on the corner of 10th and Vine.

   _____

   _____

PRACTICE 18 Write three sentences using appositives. In one sentence, place the appositive at the *beginning;* in one sentence, place the appositive in the *middle;* and in one sentence, place it at the *end*.

1. _____

   _____

2. _____

   _____

3. _____

   _____

Join Ideas with a Relative Clause

Relative clauses can add sophistication to your writing. A **relative clause** begins with *who, which,* or *that* and describes a noun or pronoun. It can join two simple sentences in a longer, more complex sentence:

> 35. Jack just won a scholarship from the Arts Council.
>
> 36. He makes wire sculpture.
>
> 37. Jack, *who makes wire sculpture,* just won a scholarship from the Arts Council.

- In sentence 37, *who makes wire sculpture* is a relative clause, created by replacing the subject *he* of sentence 36 with the relative pronoun *who*.

- *Who* now introduces the subordinate relative clause and connects it to the rest of the sentence. Note that *who* directly follows the word it refers to, *Jack*.

The idea that the writer wishes to stress is placed in the main clause, and the subordinate idea is placed in the relative clause. Study the combinations in sentences 38 through 40 and 41 through 43.

> 38. Carrots grow in cool climates.
>
> 39. They are high in vitamin A.
>
> 40. Carrots, *which* are high in vitamin A, grow in cool climates.
>
> 41. He finally submitted the term paper.
>
> 42. It was due six months ago.
>
> 43. He finally submitted the term paper *that* was due six months ago.

- In sentence 40, *which are high in vitamin A* is a relative clause, created by replacing *they* with *which*. Which word in sentence 40 does *which* refer to?

_____

- What is the relative clause in sentence 43?

_____

- Which word does *that* refer to?

_____

Punctuating relative clauses can be tricky; therefore, you will have to be careful:*

> 44. Claude, *who grew up in Haiti,* speaks fluent French.

- *Who grew up in Haiti* is set off by commas because it adds information about Claude that is not essential to the meaning of the sentence. In other words, the sentence would make sense without it: *Claude speaks fluent French.*

- *Who grew up in Haiti* is called a **nonrestrictive clause.** It does not restrict or provide vital information about the word it modifies.

> 45. People *who crackle paper in theaters* annoy me.

- *Who crackle paper in theaters* is not set off by commas because it is vital to the meaning of the sentence. Without it, the sentence would read, *People annoy me;*

---

* For more practice in punctuating relative clauses, see Chapter 35, "The Comma," Part D.

yet the point of the sentence is that people *who crackle paper in theaters* annoy me, not all people.

- *Who crackle paper in theaters* is called a **restrictive clause** because it restricts the meaning of the word it refers to, *people*.

Note that *which* usually begins a nonrestrictive clause and *that* usually begins a restrictive clause.

PRACTICE 19 Combine each pair of sentences by changing the second sentence into a relative clause introduced by *who, which,* or *that*. Remember, *who* refers to persons, *that* refers to persons or things, and *which* refers to things.
These sentences require **nonrestrictive relative clauses.** Punctuate correctly.

Example | My cousin will spend the summer hiking in the Rockies.
She lives in Indiana.
My cousin, who lives in Indiana, will spend the summer hiking in the Rockies.

1. Scrabble has greatly increased my vocabulary.
   It is my favorite game.

   _____

   _____

2. Contestants on game shows often make fools of themselves.
   They may travel thousands of miles to play.

   _____

   _____

3. Arabic is a difficult language to learn.
   It has a complicated verb system.

   _____

   _____

The next sentences require **restrictive relative clauses.** Punctuate correctly.

Example | He described a state of mind.
I have experienced it.
He described a state of mind that I have experienced.

4. The house is for sale.
   I was born in it.

   _____

   _____

5. My boss likes reports.
They are clear and to the point.

_____

_____

6. People know how intelligent birds are.
They have owned a bird.

_____

_____

PRACTICE 20 Combine each pair of sentences by changing one into a relative clause introduced by *who, which,* or *that*. Remember, *who* refers to persons, *that* refers to persons or things, and *which* refers to things.
   Be careful of the punctuation. (Hint: *Which* clauses are usually set off by commas and *that* clauses are usually not.)

1. Her grandfather enjoys scuba diving.
He is seventy-seven years old.

_____

_____

2. You just dropped an antique pitcher.
It was worth two thousand dollars.

_____

_____

3. Parenthood has taught me acceptance, forgiveness, and love.
It used to terrify me.

_____

_____

4. James Fenimore Cooper was expelled from college.
He later became a famous American novelist.

_____

_____

5. The verb *to hector* means "to bully someone."
It derives from a character in Greek literature.

_____

_____

PART E

Avoid Misplaced and Confusing Modifiers

As you practice varying your sentences, be sure that your modifiers say what you mean! Revise your work to avoid **misplaced, confusing,** or **dangling modifiers.**

> 1. Perching on a scarecrow in the cornfield, the farmer saw a large crow.

- Probably the writer did not mean that the farmer was perching on a scarecrow. Who or what, then, was *perching on a scarecrow in the cornfield?*
- *Perching* refers to the *crow,* of course, but the order of the sentence does not show this. This misplaced modifier can be corrected by turning the ideas around:

> The farmer saw a large crow perching on a scarecrow in the cornfield.

Do these sentences say what they mean? Are the modifiers misplaced or correct?

> 2. Covered with whipped cream, Tyrone carried a chocolate cake.
> 3. I sold the tin soldiers to an antique dealer that I found in the basement.
> 4. A homeless teenager, the nun helped the girl find a place to live.

- In sentence 2, does the past participial modifier *covered with whipped cream* refer to Tyrone or the cake? Rewrite the sentence so that the modifier is placed correctly:

  _____

- In 3, who or what does the relative clause *that I found in the basement* refer to? Rewrite the sentence so that the modifier is placed correctly:

  _____

- In 4, the misplaced appositive totally changes the meaning of the sentence. What did this writer mean to say?

  _____

Sometimes a modifier is confusing because it does not refer to anything in the sentence. This is called a **dangling modifier** and must be corrected by rewriting.

> 5. Drilling for oil in Alaska, acres of wilderness were destroyed.
> 6. Tired and proud, the web site was completed at midnight.

CHAPTER 21   Revising for Sentence Variety   307

- In sentence 5, who or what was *drilling for oil?* The sentence doesn't tell us.
- *Drilling for oil* is a dangling modifier. It can be corrected only by rewording the sentence:

> 7. Drilling for oil in Alaska, the EndRun Company destroyed acres of wilderness.

- In 6, tired and proud is a dangling modifier. Surely the web site isn't tired and proud, so who is? Rewrite the sentence to say what the writer probably intended.

_____

PRACTICE 21   Correct any confusing, misplaced, or dangling modifiers. Rearrange words or rewrite as necessary.

1. Plump sausages, the dinner guests looked forward to the main course.

_____

_____

2. Soaring over the treetops in a hot air balloon, the view was spectacular.

_____

_____

3. Powered by hydrogen, the engineers designed a new kind of car.

_____

_____

4. I introduced my boyfriend to my father, who wanted to marry me.

_____

_____

5. Revised to highlight his computer expertise, Marcelo was proud of his new résumé.

_____

_____

6. Jim, who loved to lick car windows, drove his dog to the vet.

_____

_____

7. Banging inside the dryer, Carla heard the lost keys.

_____

_____

8. We complained about the proposed building to the mayor, which we found ugly and too large for the neighborhood.

_____

_____

Part F

Review and Practice

Before practicing some of the techniques of sentence variety discussed in this chapter, review them briefly:

> 1. Mix long and short sentences.
> 2. Add an occasional question, command, or exclamation.
> 3. Begin with an adverb: *Unfortunately,* the outfielder dropped the fly ball.
> 4. Begin with a prepositional phrase: *With great style,* the pitcher delivered a curve.
> 5. Join ideas with a compound predicate: The fans *roared and banged* their seats.
> 6. Join ideas with an *-ing* modifier: *Diving chin first onto the grass,* Johnson caught the ball.
> 7. Join ideas with a past participial modifier: *Frustrated by the call,* the batter kicked dirt onto home plate.
> 8. Join ideas with an appositive: Beer, *the cause of much rowdiness,* should not be sold at games.
> 9. Join ideas with a relative clause: Box seats, *which are hard to get for important games,* are frequently bought up by corporations.

Of course, the secret of achieving sentence variety is practice. Choose one, two, or three of these techniques to focus on and try them out in your writing. Revise your paragraphs and essays with an eye to sentence variety.

PRACTICE 22 Revise and then rewrite this essay, aiming for sentence variety. Vary the length and pattern of the sentences. Vary the beginnings of some sentences. Join two sentences in any way you wish, adding appropriate connecting words or dropping unnecessary words. Punctuate correctly.

Little Richard, the King of Rock 'n' Roll

With "A Wop-Bop-A-Loo-Bop-A-Lop-Bam-Boom," Little Richard hit the U.S. music scene on September 14, 1955. It has never been the same since. He had almost insane energy. He wore flamboyant clothes. He defined the rebellious behavior at the heart of rock'n'roll. He has influenced countless performers. These performers include the Beatles, the Rolling Stones, Prince, and Michael Jackson.

Richard Wayne Penniman was born on December 5, 1932, in Macon, Georgia. He was the third of thirteen children. He sang gospel music with his siblings. Richard was a wild and independent child. He left home at fourteen. He traveled through Georgia with musical shows of all kinds. He sang with B. Brown and his orchestra. He was called "Little Richard" for the first time.

By 1955, Richard had developed his own musical style. It combined gospel with rhythm and blues. At its center was a wild scream of pure joy. He had developed a stage style as well. It combined outrageous costumes, a mile-high pompadour, thick mascara, manic piano-playing, and uninhibited hip-swinging. "Tutti Frutti" made him an overnight sensation. Over the next two years, he produced one hit after another. His hits included "Long Tall Sally," "Slippin' and Slidin'," "Lucille," and "Good Golly Miss Molly."

Richard's fans loved him. In 1957, he stopped performing. He had a spiritual awakening. He quit alcohol, drugs, and sexual promiscuity. In 1962, he resurfaced. He became a cult figure over the next thirteen years. He was called "The King of Rock'n'Roll." His behavior on and off-stage became more outrageous. He dressed as Queen Elizabeth or the pope. He once wore a suit completely covered with small mirrors. In 1986, Richard's contribution to music history was recognized. He was one of the first inductees to the Rock and Roll Hall of Fame and Museum.

Today Richard is still going strong. In 1993, he performed at the presidential inauguration. In 2000, he was the subject of a made-for-television biography. In 2001, his All-Time Greatest Hits CD was issued. It's easy to believe Richard when he proclaims, "Rock still lifts my spirit and gives me joy and an energy force."

Little Richard, the King of Rock'n'Roll

Writing Assignment 2

Study this photograph of a wedding; then write a paragraph explaining how this scene came about. Invent a story of how the couple met, their courtship, and their decision to marry.

In your topic sentence, state the general feeling or mood of the photograph. Then tell the story behind the picture. Revise your paragraph, paying special attention to sentence variety. Try to vary sentence types and lengths.

CHAPTER 22 Revising for Language Awareness

PART A   Exact Language: Avoiding Vagueness
PART B   Concise Language: Avoiding Wordiness
PART C   Fresh Language: Avoiding Triteness
PART D   Figurative Language: Similes and Metaphors

Although it is important to write grammatically correct English, good writing is more than just correct writing. Good writing has life, excitement, and power. It captures the attention of the reader and compels him or her to read further.

The purpose of this chapter is to increase your awareness of the power of words and your skill at making them work for you. The secret of effective writing is **revision.** *Do not settle* for the first words that come to you, but go back over what you have written, replacing dull or confusing language with exact, concise, fresh, and sometimes figurative language.

Part A

Exact Language: Avoiding Vagueness

Good writers express their ideas as *exactly* as possible, choosing *specific, concrete,* and *vivid* words and phrases. They do not settle for vague terms and confusing generalities.

Which sentence in each of the following pairs gives the more *exact* information? That is, which uses specific and precise language? Which words in these sentences make them sharper and more vivid?

1. A car went around the corner.
2. A battered blue Mustang careened around the corner.

312

> 3. Janet quickly ate the main course.
>
> 4. Janet devoured the plate of ribs in two and a half minutes.
>
> 5. The president did things that caused problems.
>
> 6. The president's military spending increased the budget deficit.

- Sentences 2, 4, and 6 contain language that is *exact*.

- Sentence 2 is more exact than sentence 1 because *battered blue Mustang* gives more specific information than the general term *car*. The verb *careened* describes precisely how the car went around the corner, fast and recklessly.

- What specific words does sentence 4 substitute for the more general words *ate, main course,* and *quickly* in sentence 3?

- _____, _____, and
  _____

  Why are these terms more exact than those in sentence 3?
  _____
  _____

- What words in sentence 6 make it clearer and more exact than sentence 5?
  _____
  _____

Concrete and detailed writing is usually exciting as well and makes us want to read on, as does this passage by Toni Morrison, who won the Nobel Prize for literature:

> It is called the suburbs now, but when black people lived there it was called the Bottom. One road, shaded by beeches, oaks, maples, and chestnuts, connected it to the valley. The beeches are gone now, and so are the pear trees where children sat and yelled down through the blossoms at passersby. Generous funds have been allotted to level the stripped and faded buildings that clutter the road from Medallion up to the golf course. They are going to raze the Time and a Half Pool Hall, where feet in long tan shoes once pointed down from chair rungs. A steel ball will knock to dust Irene's Palace of Cosmetology, where women used to lean their heads back on sink trays and doze while Irene lathered Nu Nile into their hair. Men in khaki work clothes will pry loose the slats of Reba's Grill, where the owner cooked in her hat because she couldn't remember the ingredients without it.
>
> —Toni Morrison, *Sula*

Now compare a similar account written in general and inexact language:

> It is called the suburbs now, but when black people lived there it was called the Bottom. One road, shaded by big trees, connected it to the valley. Many of the trees are gone now. Generous funds have been allotted to level the buildings on the road from Medallion up to the golf course. They are going to knock down the pool hall, the beauty parlor, and the restaurant.

You do not need a large vocabulary to write exactly and well, but you do need to work at finding the right words to fit each sentence. As you revise, cross out vague or dull words and phrases and replace them with more exact terms. When you are tempted to write *I feel good*, ask yourself exactly what *good* means in that sentence: *relaxed? proud? thin? in love?* When people walk by, do they *flounce, stride, lurch, wiggle,* or *sneak?* When they speak to you, do people *stammer, announce, babble, murmur,* or *coo?* Question yourself as you revise; then choose the right words to fit that particular sentence.

PRACTICE 1 Lively verbs are a great asset to any writer. The following sentences contain four overused general verbs—*to walk, to see, to eat,* and *to be.* In each case, replace the general verb in parentheses with a more exact verb *chosen to fit the context of the sentence.* Use a different verb in every sentence. Consult a dictionary or thesaurus* if you wish.

Examples In no particular hurry, we __strolled__ (walked) through the botanical gardens.

Jane __fidgets__ (is) at her desk and watches the clock.

1. With guns drawn, three police officers _____ (walked) toward the door of the warehouse.

2. As we stared in fascination, an orange lizard _____ (walked) up the wall.

3. The four-year-old _____ (walked) onto the patio in her mother's high-heeled shoes.

4. A furious customer _____ (walked) into the manager's office.

5. Two people who _____ (saw) the accident must testify in court.

6. We crouched for hours in the underbrush just to _____ (see) a rare white fox.

7. Three makeshift wooden rafts were _____ (seen) off the coast this morning.

---

*A thesaurus is a book of *synonyms*—words that have the same or similar meanings.

8. For two years, the zoologist _____ (saw) the behavior of bears in the wild.

9. There was the cat, delicately _____ (eating) my fern!

10. Senator Gorman astounded the guests by loudly _____ (eating) his soup.

11. All through the movie, she _____ (ate) hard candies in the back row.

12. Within seconds, Dan had bought two tacos from a street vendor and _____ (eaten) them both.

13. During rush hour, the temperature hit 98 degrees, and dozens of cars _____ (were) on the highway.

14. A young man _____ (is) on a stretcher in the emergency room.

15. Workers who _____ (are) at desks all day should make special efforts to exercise.

16. Professor Nuzzo _____ (was) in front of the blackboard, excited about this new solution to the math problem.

PRACTICE 2 The following sentences contain dull, vague language. Revise them using vivid verbs, specific nouns, and colorful adjectives. As the examples show, you may add and delete words.

Examples A dog lies down in the shade.
A mangy collie flops down in the shade of a parked car.

My head hurts.
My head throbs.
I have shooting pains in the left side of my head.

1. Everything about the man looked mean.

   _____

   _____

2. I feel good today for several reasons.

   _____

   _____

3. A woman in unusual clothes went down the street.

4. The sunlight made the yard look pretty.

5. What the company did bothered the townspeople.

6. The pediatrician's waiting room was crowded.

7. As soon as he gets home from work, he hears the voice of his pet asking for dinner.

8. The noises of construction filled the street.

9. When I was sick, you were helpful.

10. This college does things that make the students feel bad.

PRACTICE 3 A word that works effectively in one sentence might not work in another sentence. In searching for the right word, always consider the **context** of the sentence into which the word must fit. Read each of the following sentences for meaning. Then circle the word in parentheses that *most exactly fits* the context of the sentence.

Example | The alchemist cautiously (threw, (dripped), held) the liquid mercury onto copper in order to make it look like gold.

1. Alchemy, an early form of chemistry, was a (course, way, science) that flourished from ancient times until around 1700.

2. It was based on the (knowledge, belief, fact) that a metal could be converted into another element.

3. Alchemists considered gold the (perfect, nicest, shiniest) metal.

4. Therefore, their goal was to (transform, redo, make) base metals, like lead, into gold.

5. They searched (eagerly, high and low, lots) for the "philosopher's stone," the formula that would make this change possible.

6. All "philosopher's stones" consisted of sulfur and mercury; the trick was to discover the proper way to (combine, destroy, mix up) the two.

7. Over time, alchemy incorporated various (aspects, things, stuff) of astrology and magic.

8. For example, certain metals were (the same as, equated with, sort of like) specific heavenly bodies—gold with the sun or silver with the moon.

9. One famous alchemist proudly (said, muttered, boasted) that he could magically transform winter into summer.

10. Many alchemists went to work for greedy princes and kings, who always (liked, lusted for, thought about) more gold.

11. It was dangerous work though; more than one alchemist was (done away with, executed, knocked off) because he could not produce gold.

12. In their search for gold, however, some alchemists (foolishly, hopefully, accidentally) made valid scientific discoveries that led to the development of modern chemistry.

PRACTICE 4 The following paragraph begins a mystery story. Using specific and vivid language, revise the paragraph to make it as exciting as possible. Then finish the story; be careful to avoid vague language.

The weather was bad. I was in the house alone, with a funny feeling that something was going to happen. Someone knocked at the door. I got up to answer it and found someone outside. She looked familiar, but I didn't know from where or when. Then I recognized her as a person from my past. I let her in although I was not sure I had done the right thing.

_____

_____

_____

Part B

Concise Language: Avoiding Wordiness

Concise writing comes quickly to the point. It avoids **wordiness**—unnecessary and repetitious words that add nothing to the meaning.

Which sentence in each of the following pairs is more *concise*? That is, which does *not* contain unnecessary words?

> 1. Because of the fact that the watch was inexpensive in price, he bought it.
> 2. Because the watch was inexpensive, he bought it.
> 3. In my opinion I think that the financial aid system at Ellensville Junior College is in need of reform.
> 4. The financial aid system at Ellensville Junior College needs reform.
> 5. On October 10, in the fall of 2003, we learned the true facts about the Peruvian mummies.
> 6. On October 10, 2003, we learned the facts about the Peruvian mummies.

- Sentences 2, 4, and 6 are *concise* whereas sentences 1, 3, and 5 are *wordy*.

- In sentence 1, *because of the fact that* is really a *wordy* way of saying *because*. *In price* simply repeats information already given by the word *inexpensive*.

- The writer of sentence 3 undercuts the point with the wordy apology of *in my opinion I think*. As a general rule, leave out such qualifiers and simply state the opinion; but if you do use them, use either *in my opinion* or *I think*, not both! Sentence 4 replaces *is in need of* with one direct verb, *needs*.

- *In the fall of* in sentence 5 is *redundant*; it repeats information already given by which word?

_____

- Why is the word *true* also eliminated in sentence 6?

_____

Concise writing avoids wordiness, unnecessary repetition, and padding. Of course, conciseness *does not mean* writing short, bare sentences, but simply cutting out all deadwood and never using fifteen words when ten will do.

PRACTICE 5 The following sentences are *wordy*. Make them more *concise* by crossing out or replacing unnecessary words or by combining two sentences into one concise sentence. Rewrite each new sentence on the lines beneath, capitalizing and punctuating correctly.

Examples The U.S. Census uncovers many interesting facts that have a lot of truth to them.

The U.S. Census uncovers many interesting facts.

In the year 1810, Philadelphia was called the cigar capital of the United States. The reason why was because the census reported that the city produced sixteen million cigars each year.

In 1810, Philadelphia was called the cigar capital of the United States because the census

reported that the city produced sixteen million cigars each year.

1. The Constitution requires and says that the federal government of the United States must take a national census every ten years.

2. At first, the original function of the census was to ensure fair taxation and representation.

3. Since the first count in 1790, however, the census has been controversial. There have been several reasons why it has been controversial.

4. One reason why is because there are always some people who aren't included.

5. The 1990 census, for example, missed almost five million people, many of whom were homeless with no place to live.

6. For the 2000 census, the Census Bureau considered using statistical methods. The statistical methods would have been used instead of the traditional direct head count.

7. The Bureau would have directly counted about 90 percent of U.S. residents who live in the United States and then estimated the number and characteristics of the remainder of the rest of the people.

8. Those who opposed the idea believed that in their opinion statistical methods would have introduced new errors that were mistaken into the count.

9. The distribution of $100 billion in money, as well as the balance of power in the House of Representatives, depended on how and in which manner the census was conducted.

10. Despite controversy, the U.S. census still continues to serve a beneficial purpose that is for the good of the United States.

PRACTICE 6 Rewrite this essay *concisely*, cutting out all unnecessary words. Reword or combine sentences if you wish, but do not alter the meaning.

Dr. Alice Hamilton, Medical Pioneer

At the age of forty years old, Dr. Alice Hamilton became a pioneer in the field of industrial medicine. In 1910, the governor of Illinois appointed her to investigate rumors that people who were doing the work in Chicago's paint factories were dying from lead poisoning. The result of her investigation was the first state law that was passed to protect workers.

The following year, the U.S. Department of Labor hired this woman, Dr. Hamilton to study industrial illness throughout the country of the United States. In the next decade, she researched and studied many occupational diseases, including tuberculosis among quarry workers and silicosis—clogged lungs—among sandblasters. To gather information, Dr. Hamilton went to the workplace—deep in mines, quarries, and underwater tunnels. She also spoke to the workers in their homes where they lived.

With great zeal, Dr. Hamilton spread her message about poor health conditions on the job. What happened with her reports is that they led to new safety regulations, workmen's compensation insurance, and improved working conditions in many industries. She wrote many popular articles and spoke to groups of interested citizens. In the year of 1919, she became the first woman to hold courses and teach at Harvard University. Her textbook which she wrote, *Industrial Poisons in the U.S.*, became the standard book on the subject. By the time she died in 1970—she was 101—she had done much to improve the plight of many working people. The reason why she is remembered today is because she cared at a time when many others seemed not to care at all.

Part C

Fresh Language: Avoiding Triteness

Fresh writing uses original and lively words. It avoids **clichés,** those tired and trite expressions that have lost their power from overuse.

Which sentence in each pair that follows contains fewer expressions that you have heard or read many times before?

> 1. Some people can relate to the hustle and bustle of city life.
> 2. Some people thrive on the energy and motion of city life.
>
> 3. This book is worth its weight in gold to the car owner.
> 4. This book can save the car owner hundreds of dollars a year in repairs.

- You probably found that sentences 2 and 4 contained fresher language. Which words and phrases in sentences 1 and 3 have you heard or seen before, in conversation, on TV, or in magazines and newspapers? List them:

_____

_____

Clichés and trite expressions like the following have become so familiar that they have almost no impact on the reader. Avoid them. Say what you mean in your own words:

> Cliché: She is pretty as a picture.
>
> Fresh: Her amber eyes and wild red hair mesmerize me.

Or occasionally, play with a cliché and turn it into fresh language:

> Cliché: ...as American as apple pie.
>
> Fresh: ...as American as a Big Mac.
>
> Cliché: The grass is always greener on the other side of the fence.
>
> Fresh: "The grass is always greener over the septic tank."—Erma Bombeck

The following is a partial list of trite expressions to avoid. Add to it any others that you overuse in your writing.

Trite Expressions and Clichés

at this point in time	in this day and age
awesome	last but not least
better late than never	living hand to mouth
break the ice	one in a million
cold cruel world	out of this world
cool, hot	sad but true
cry your eyes out	tried and true
easier said than done	under the weather
free as a bird	work like a dog
hustle and bustle	green with envy

PRACTICE 7 Cross out clichés and trite expressions in the following sentences and replace them with fresh and exact language of your own.

1. In 1929, toy dealer Edwin S. Lowe came across people having more fun than a barrel of monkeys while playing a game at a carnival in rural Georgia.

2. A leader called out each and every number, and the players used beans to cover the matching numbers on their cards.

3. The winners yelled "Beano!" at the top of their lungs when they had filled in a row of numbers.

4. According to the carnival owner, a stranger had brought the game from Europe, so it went without saying that no one owned the game.

5. Quick as a wink, Lowe saw the game was a winner.

6. As soon as he returned home, the businessman, who was as sharp as a tack, began testing beano on friends.

7. One night, instead of "Beano!" a guest who was beside himself with excitement shouted out, "Bingo!"

8. Lowe went on to market the game as Bingo, and it sold like crazy.

9. Soon many nonprofit organizations were holding bingo tournaments as a tried and true method of raising funds.

10. Because Lowe had produced only twenty-four different cards, too many people were cleaning up.

11. Therefore, Lowe paid a mathematics professor an awesome amount to develop six thousand cards, each with a different combination of numbers.

12. By 1934, hundreds of thousands of Americans were playing bingo like there was no tomorrow.

Part D

Figurative Language: Similes and Metaphors

One way to add sparkle and exactness to your writing is to use an occasional simile or metaphor. A **simile** is a comparison of two things using the word *like* or *as*:

> "He was *as ugly as* a wart." —Anne Sexton
>
> "The frozen twigs of the huge tulip poplar next to the hill clack in the cold *like* tinsnips." —Annie Dillard

A **metaphor** is a similar comparison without the word *like* or *as*:

> "My soul is a dark forest." —D. H. Lawrence
>
> Love is a virus.

- The power of similes and metaphors comes partly from the surprise of comparing two apparently unlike things. A well-chosen simile or metaphor can convey a lot of information in very few words.

- To compare a person to a wart, as Sexton does, lets us know quickly just how ugly that person is. And to say that *twigs clack like tinsnips* describes the sound so precisely that we can almost hear it.

- What do you think D. H. Lawrence means by his metaphor? In what ways is a person's soul like a *dark forest*?

  _____

  _____

  _____

- The statement *love is a virus* tells us something about the writer's attitude toward love. What is it? In what ways is love like a virus?

  _____

  _____

  _____

Similes and metaphors should not be overused; however, once in a while, they can be a delightful addition to a paper that is also exact, concise, and fresh.

PRACTICE 8 The author of the following paragraph describes a lake as winter turns to spring. She uses at least two similes and two metaphors. Underline the similes and circle the metaphors.

Mornings, a transparent pane of ice lies over the meltwater. I peer through and see some kind of water bug—perhaps a leech—paddling like a sea turtle between green ladders of lakeweed. Cattails and sweetgrass from the previous summer are bone dry, marked with black mold spots, and bend like elbows into the ice.

—Gretel Erlich, "Spring," *Antaeus*

PRACTICE 9

Think of several similes to complete each sentence that follows. Be creative! Then underline your favorite simile, the one that best completes each sentence.

Example | My English class is like an orchestra.
the Everglades.
an action movie.
a vegetable garden.

1. Job hunting is like _____

2. My room looks like _____

3. Writing well is like _____

4. Marriage is like _____

PRACTICE 10

Think of several metaphors to complete each sentence that follows. Jot down three or four ideas, and then underline the metaphor that best completes each sentence.

Example | Love is a blood transfusion.
a sunrise.
a magic mirror.
a roller coaster ride.

1. The Internet is _____

2. Registration is _____

3. My car is _____

4. Courage is _____

Writing Assignments

1. Good writing can be done on almost any subject if the writer approaches the subject with openness and with "new eyes." Take a piece of fruit or a vegetable—a lemon, a green pepper, a cherry tomato. Examine it as if for the first time. Feel its texture and parts, smell it, weigh it in your palm.

    Now capture your experience of the fruit or vegetable in words. First jot down words and ideas, or freewrite, aiming for the most *exact* description possible. Don't settle for the first words you think of. Keep writing. Then go back over what you have written, underlining the most exact and powerful writing. Compose a topic sentence and draft a paragraph that conveys your unique experience of the fruit or vegetable.

2. In the paragraph that follows, Don DeLillo describes a "small" experience in such rich, exact detail that it becomes alive and intriguing to the reader. Read his paragraph, underlining language that strikes you as especially *exact* and *fresh*. Can you spot the two similes? Can you find any especially vivid adjectives or unusual verbs?

    You have to know the feel of a baseball in your hand, going back awhile, connecting many things, before you can understand why a man would sit in a chair at four in the morning holding such an object, clutching it—how it fits the palm so reassuringly, the corked center making it buoyant in the hand, and the rough spots on an old ball, the marked skin, how an idle thumb likes to worry the scuffed horsehide. You squeeze a baseball. You kind of juice it or milk it. The resistance of the packed material makes you want to press harder. There's an equilibrium, an agreeable animal tension between the hard leather object and the sort of clawed hand, veins stretching with the effort. And the feel of raised seams across the fingertips, cloth contours like road bumps under the knuckle joints—how the whorled cotton can be seen as a magnified thumbprint. . . . The ball was smudged green near the Spalding trademark; it was still wearing a small green bruise where it had struck a pillar, according to the history that came with it—flaked paint from a bolted column in the left-field stands embedded in the surface of the ball.

    —Don DeLillo, *Underworld*

    Write a paragraph or essay in which you also describe a brief but interesting experience (or event), perhaps a time you observed, admired, or truly studied an object or person. As you freewrite or brainstorm, try to capture the most precise and minute details of what you experienced or what happened. Now revise your piece of writing, making the language as *exact, concise,* and *fresh* as you can.

3. The figure above shows a painting by Milan Kunc called "Crocodile Village." Look closely at this painting, noting the small huts on the crocodile's back, the man in the boat, and the unusual position of the moon. What overall impression or mood does the painting communicate to you? Is it peaceful, threatening, magical?

   Now write a two-paragraph composition discussing the painting. In the first paragraph, describe the painting, very specifically pointing out important details. In the second paragraph, explain what you think the painter is trying to convey by creating this picture. As you revise, make your writing as *exact*, *concise*, and *fresh* as possible so that a reader who has not seen the painting has a clear sense of it.

CHAPTER 23 Putting Your Revision Skills to Work

In Units 2 and 3, you learned to **revise** basic paragraphs, and in Unit 4, you learned to revise essays. All revising requires that you rethink and rewrite with such questions as these in mind:

> Can a reader understand and follow my ideas?
>
> Is my topic sentence or thesis statement clear?
>
> Does the body of my paragraph or essay fully support the topic or thesis statement?
>
> Does my paragraph or essay have unity? That is, does every sentence relate to the main idea?
>
> Does my paragraph or essay have coherence? That is, does it follow a logical order and guide the reader from point to point?
>
> Does my writing conclude, not just leave off?

Of course, the more writing techniques you learn, the more options you have as you revise. Unit 5 has moved beyond the basics to matters of style: consistency and parallelism, sentence variety, and clear, exact language. This chapter will guide you again through the revision process, adding questions like the following to your list:

> Are my verb tenses and pronouns consistent?
>
> Have I used parallel structure to highlight parallel ideas?
>
> Have I varied the length and type of my sentences?
>
> Is my language exact, concise, and fresh?

Many writers first revise and rewrite with questions like these in mind. They do *not* worry about grammar and minor errors at this stage. Then in a separate, final process, they **proofread*** for spelling and grammatical errors.

---

* For practice in proofreading for particular errors, see individual chapters in Units 6 and 7. For practice in proofreading for mixed errors, see Chapter 37, "Putting Your Proofreading Skills to Work."

Writing Sample 1

First Draft

I like to give my best performance. I must relax completely before a show. I often know ahead of time what choreography I will use and what I'll sing, so I can concentrate on relaxing completely. I usually do this by reading, etc. I always know my parts perfectly. Occasionally I look through the curtain to watch the people come in. This can make you feel faint, but I reassure myself and say I know everything will be okay.

Revisions

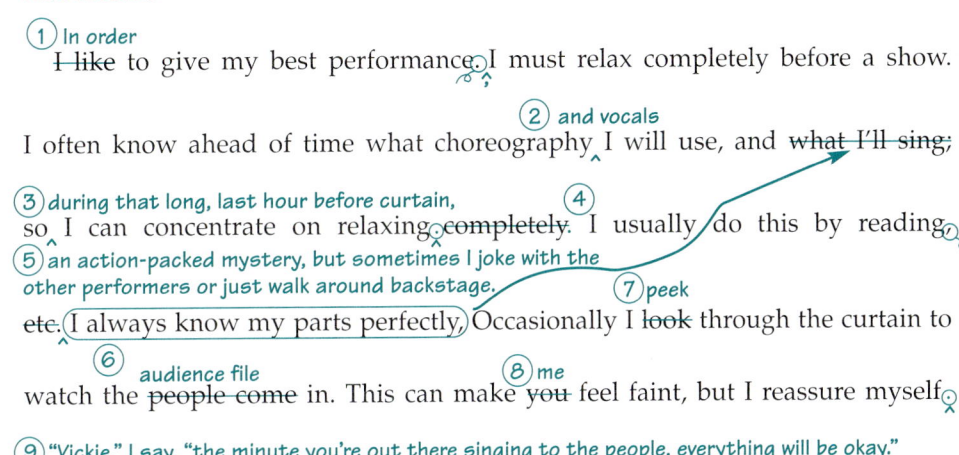

Reasons for Revisions

1. Combine two short sentences. (sentence variety)

2. Make *choreography* and *vocals* parallel and omit unnecessary words. (parallelism)

3. Make time order clear: First discuss what I've done during the days before the performance, and then discuss the hour before performance. (time order)

4. Drop *completely*, which repeats the word used in the first sentence. (avoid wordiness)

5. This is important! Drop *etc.*, add more details, and give examples. (add examples)

6. This idea belongs earlier in the paragraph—with what I've done during the days before the performance. (order)

7. Use more specific and interesting language in this sentence. (exact language)

8. Use the first person singular pronouns *I* and *me* consistently throughout the paragraph. (consistent person)

9. Dull—use a direct quotation, the actual words I say to myself. (exact language, sentence variety)

Revised Draft

In order to give my best performance, I must relax completely before a show. I often know ahead of time what choreography and vocals I will use, and I always know my parts perfectly, so during that long, last hour before curtain, I can concentrate on relaxing. I usually do this by reading an action-packed mystery, but sometimes I joke with the other performers or just walk around backstage. Occasionally I peek through the curtain to watch the audience file in. This can make me feel faint, but I reassure myself. "Vickie," I say, "the minute you're out there singing to the people, everything will be okay."

—Victoria DeWindt (Student)

Writing Sample 2

First Draft

My grandparents' house contained whole rooms that my parents' house did not (pantry, a parlor, a den where Grandpa kept his loot). The furniture and things always fascinated me. Best of all was the lake behind the house. Grandpa said that Evergreen Lake had grown old just like Grandma and him, that the game fish are gone and only a few bluegills remained. But one day he let me fish. No one thought I'd catch anything, but I caught a foot-long goldfish! Grandpa said it was a goddam carp, but it was a goldfish to me and I nearly fainted with ecstasy.

Revisions

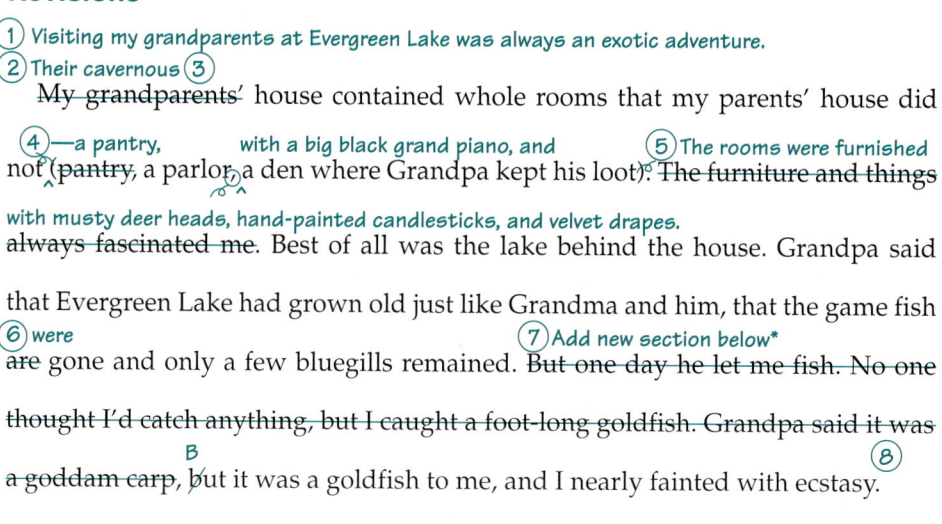

*Add: But one day he rigged up a pole for me and tossed my line into the water. I sat motionless for several hours, waiting for a miracle. Suddenly I felt a tug on my line. I screeched and yanked upward. By the time Grandpa arrived on the dock, there on the surface lazily moving its fins was the biggest goldfish I had ever seen, nearly a foot long! Grandpa reached down with the net and scooped the huge orange fish out of the water. "Bring down the pail," he shouted. "It's a goddam carp."

Reasons for Revisions

1. No topic sentence; add one. (topic sentence)

2. Now *grandparents'* repeats the first sentence; use *their*. (pronoun substitution)

3. Add a good descriptive word to give the feeling of the house. (exact language)

4. Expand this; add more details. (details, exact language)

5. More details and examples needed for support! Try to capture the "exotic" feeling of the house. (details, exact language)

6. Verb shifts to present tense; use past tense consistently. (consistent tense)

7. This section is weak. Tell the story of the goldfish; try to create the sense of adventure this had for me as a kid. Quote Grandpa? (details, exact language, direct quotation)

8. Revised paragraph is getting long. Consider breaking into two paragraphs, one on the house and one on the lake.

Revised Draft

Visiting my grandparents at Evergreen Lake was always an exotic adventure. Their cavernous house contained whole rooms that my parents' house did not—a pantry, a parlor with a big black grand piano, and a den where Grandpa kept his loot. The rooms were furnished with musty deer heads, hand-painted candlesticks, and velvet drapes.

Best of all was the lake behind the house. Grandpa said that Evergreen Lake had grown old just like Grandma and him, that the game fish were gone and only a few bluegills remained. But one day he rigged up a pole for me and tossed my line into the water. I sat motionless for several hours, waiting for a miracle. Suddenly I felt a tug on my line. I screeched and yanked upward. By the time Grandpa arrived on the dock, there on the surface lazily moving its fins was the biggest goldfish I had ever seen, nearly a foot long! Grandpa reached down with the net and scooped the huge orange fish out of the water. "Bring down the pail," he shouted. "It's a goddam carp." But it was a goldfish to me, and I nearly fainted with ecstasy.

PRACTICE Because revising, like writing, is a personal process, the best practice is to revise your own paragraphs and essays. Nevertheless, here is a first draft that needs revising.

Revise it *as if you had written it*. Mark your revisions on the first draft, using and building on the good parts, crossing out unnecessary words, rewriting unclear or awkward sentences, adding details, and perhaps reordering parts. Then, recopy your final draft on the lines. Especially, ask yourself these questions:

Are my verb tenses and pronouns consistent?

Have I used parallel structure?

Have I varied the length and type of my sentences?

Is my language exact, concise, and fresh?

First Draft

Breaking the Yo-Yo Syndrome

For years, I was a yo-yo dieter. I bounced from fad diets to eating binges when I ate a lot. This leaves you tired and with depression. Along the way, though, I learned a few things. As a result, I personally will never go on a diet again for the rest of my life.

First of all, diets are unhealthy. Some of the low carbohydrate diets are high in fat. Accumulating fat through meat, eggs, and the eating of cheese can raise blood levels of cholesterol and led to artery and heart disease. Other diets are too high in protein and can cause kidney ailments, and other things can go wrong with your body, too. Most diets also leave you deficient in essential vitamins and minerals that are necessary to health, such as calcium and iron.

In addition, diets are short-term. I lose about ten pounds. I wind up gaining more weight than I originally lost. I also get sick and tired of the restricted diet. On one diet, I ate cabbage soup for breakfast, lunch, and dinner. You are allowed to eat some fruit on day one, some vegetables on day two, and so on, but mostly you are supposed to eat cabbage soup. After a week, I never want to see a bowl of cabbage soup again. Because the diet was nutritionally unbalanced, I ended up craving bread, meat, and all the other foods I am not supposed to eat. Moreover, in the short-term, all one loses is water. You cannot lose body fat unless you reduce regularly and at a steady rate over a long period of time.

The last diet I try was a fat-free diet. On this diet I actually gained weight while dieting. I am surprised to discover that you can gain weight on a fat-free diet snacking on fat-free cookies, ice cream, and cheese and crackers. I also learn that the body needs fat—in particular, the unsaturated fat in foods like olive oil, nuts, avocados, and salad dressings. If a dieter takes in too little fat, you are constantly hungry. Furthermore, the body thinks it is starving, so it makes every effort to try to conserve fat, which makes it much harder for one to lose weight.

In place of fad diets, I now follow a long-range plan. It is sensible and improved my health. I eat three well-balanced meals, exercise daily, and am meeting regularly with my support group for weight control. I am much happier and don't weigh as much than I used to be.

Revised Draft

Breaking the Yo-Yo Syndrome

Writers' Workshop

Examine the Bright (or Dark) Side of Family Life

Revising is the key to all good writing—taking the time to sit down, reread, and rethink what you have written. In this unit, you have practiced revising for consistent verb tense, consistent person, parallelism, sentence variety, and language awareness.

In your group or class, read this student's essay, aloud if possible. Underline the parts that strike you as especially effective, and put a check by anything that might need revising.

Family Secrets: Don't You Go Talking

(1) Most families have secrets, but in some families, the secrets become too important. They shape the way people think about themselves and his or her relatives. What people are not supposed to talk about can seem more real than official family history. This was true in my family. Yet when I think about some of our secrets now, they don't seem much like secrets anymore.

(2) Psychologists say that "most secrets arise out of shame." The fact that my father drank excessively brought about a certain family shame. Quiet comments were made protesting his behavior, but no one dared discuss his drinking freely. In fact, I can remember "that look" my mother would give me, meaning "Don't you go talking about nothing that goes on in this house." I couldn't understand that. It was not as if he drank at home where no one but the family could see the staggering or hear the loud profanities. Yet because he was a member of the family, we were expected to turn a blind side.

(3) Secrets help create family history, and since history is said to repeat itself, I feel it safe to say that behavior kept hidden in family secrets may be hereditary. For instance, I have heard talk among family members of an aunt who loved to gamble. As the story goes, Aunt Sally loved to gamble so much that in her ninth month of pregnancy she left her home in California and traveled to Las Vegas by bus. She wanted to play the slot machines. Aunt Sally went into labor. She refused to stop gambling. The contractions were six minutes apart. She was heavily involved in a poker game. Still she refused to leave. The labor pains were four minutes apart. Aunt Sally continued to play. She was enjoying a winning streak. She intended to see it out.

(4) Four hours and $63,000 later, Aunt Sally gives birth to a baby boy. He weighs eight pounds, eight ounces. As luck would have it, her winning hand holds a pair of eights. Aunt Sally's left palm supposedly grips one particular chip so tightly during each contraction that the imprint drew blood. Today that baby born in Vegas is said to be a gambler

among gamblers. In the palm of his left hand is a birthmark, red in color and perfectly round in shape just like a poker chip. His name, by the way, is Chip. I don't see how that story can be a family secret, yet after years of not being able to talk freely about certain things, a discomfort remains when these things are in fact discussed.

(5) Shame over a particular event is defined by the values of the era in which the event takes place. Although it was an earlier generation that insisted years ago that certain things need not be openly discussed in my family, the shame lives on, outliving the people. The shame is inherited, if you will. Almost 115 years ago, my great grandfather supposedly stole a handful of rice. Because of shame, I was never supposed to know about it. The story is a family secret. I guess I understand why. After all, we don't want great granddad's picture showing up on "America's Most Wanted" anytime now.

—Jo-Ann Jenkins (Student)

1. How effective is Ms. Jenkins's essay?

    _____ Strong thesis statement? _____ Good supporting details?

    _____ Logical organization? _____ Effective conclusion?

2. What do you like best about this essay? What details or sections most command your attention or make you think?

3. Although this student writes about her personal family history, she is also *thinking about the meaning* of that experience and making sense of it for herself and the reader. What ideas about family secrets does this essay include? Do you agree or disagree?

4. Does your family have secrets? What effect does this have on you or other family members?

5. Do you spot any instance of inconsistent person (paragraph 1) or wordiness (paragraph 4)?

6. Are all the verb tenses correct, or do you notice any inconsistent tense?

7. Are there any places, especially in paragraph 3, where choppy sentences detracted from the excellent content?

8. Can you spot any error patterns (the same error two or more times) that this student should watch out for?

Group Work

In your group, revise Ms. Jenkins's essay as if it were your own. First, decide what problems need attention. Then rewrite those parts, sentence by sentence, aiming for a truly fine paper. Share your revision with the class, explaining why you made the changes you did.

Writing and Revising Ideas

1. Examine the bright (or dark) side of family life.
2. Discuss the effects of living with a secret or a lie.

UNIT 6

Reviewing the Basics

CHAPTER 24 The Simple Sentence

CHAPTER 25 Coordination and Subordination

CHAPTER 26 Avoiding Sentence Errors

CHAPTER 27 Present Tense (Agreement)

CHAPTER 28 Past Tense

CHAPTER 29 The Past Participle

CHAPTER 30 Nouns

CHAPTER 31 Pronouns

CHAPTER 32 Prepositions

CHAPTER 33 Adjectives and Adverbs

CHAPTER 34 The Apostrophe

CHAPTER 35 The Comma

CHAPTER 36 Mechanics

CHAPTER 37 Putting Your Proofreading Skills to Work

CHAPTER 24 The Simple Sentence

PART A Defining and Spotting Subjects
PART B Spotting Prepositional Phrases
PART C Defining and Spotting Verbs

Part A

Defining and Spotting Subjects

Every sentence must contain two basic elements: a **subject** and a **verb**.

A subject is the *who* or *what* word that performs the action or the *who* or *what* word about which a statement is made:

1. Three *hunters* tramped through the woods.
2. The blue *truck* belongs to Ralph.

- In sentence 1, *hunters*, the *who* word, performs the action—"tramped through the woods."
- In sentence 2, *truck* is the *what* word about which a statement is made—"belongs to Ralph."
- Some sentences have more than one subject, joined by *and*:

3. Her *aunt and uncle* love country music.

- In sentence 3, *aunt and uncle*, the *who* words, perform the action—they "love country music."
- *Aunt and uncle* is called a **compound subject**.

Sometimes an *-ing* word can be the subject of a sentence:

> 4. *Reading* strains my eyes.

- *Reading* is the *what* word that performs the action—"strains my eyes."

PRACTICE 1 Circle the subjects in these sentences.

1. Do you know the origin and customs of Kwanzaa?
2. This African-American holiday celebrates black heritage and lasts for seven days—from December 26 through January 1.
3. Maulana Karenga introduced Kwanzaa to America in 1966.
4. In Swahili, Kwanzaa means "first fruits of the harvest."
5. During the holiday, families share simple meals of foods from the Caribbean, Africa, South America, and the American South.
6. Specific foods have special meanings.
7. For instance, certain fruits and vegetables represent the products of group effort.
8. Another important symbol is corn, which stands for children.
9. At each dinner, celebrants light a black, red, or green candle and discuss one of the seven principles of Kwanzaa.
10. These seven principles are unity, self-determination, collective work and responsibility, cooperative economics, purpose, creativity, and faith.

Part B
Spotting Prepositional Phrases

One group of words that may confuse you as you look for subjects is the prepositional phrase. A **prepositional phrase** contains a **preposition** (a word like *at, in, of, from,* and so forth) and its **object.**

Preposition	Object
at	the beach
on	time
of	the students

The object of a preposition *cannot be* the subject of a sentence. Therefore, spotting and crossing out the prepositional phrases will help you find the subject.

1. The sweaters in the window look handmade.
2. The sweaters ~~in the window~~ look handmade.
3. ~~On Tuesday~~, a carton ~~of oranges~~ was left ~~on the porch~~.

- In sentence 1, you might have trouble finding the subject. But once the prepositional phrase is crossed out in sentence 2, the subject, *sweaters,* is easy to spot.
- In sentence 3, once the prepositional phrases are crossed out, the subject, *carton,* is easy to spot.

Here are some common prepositions that you should know:

Common Prepositions

about	before	in	through
above	behind	into	to
across	between	like	toward
after	by	near	under
along	during	of	until
among	for	on	up
at	from	over	with

PRACTICE 2 Cross out the prepositional phrases in each sentence. Then circle the subject of the sentence.

1. From 6 A.M. until 10 A.M., Angel works out.
2. Local buses for Newark leave every hour.
3. Three of my friends take singing lessons.
4. That man between Ralph and Cynthia is the famous actor Hank the Hunk.
5. Near the door, a pile of laundry sits in a basket.
6. Toward evening, the houses across the river disappear in the thick fog.
7. Before class, Helena and I meet for coffee.
8. In one corner of the lab, beakers of colored liquid bubbled and boiled.

Part C

Defining and Spotting Verbs

Action Verbs

In order to be complete, every sentence must contain a **verb.** One kind of verb, called an **action verb,** expresses the action that the subject is performing:

> 1. The star quarterback *fumbled.*
> 2. The carpenters *worked* all day, but the bricklayers *went* home early.

- In sentence 1, the action verb is *fumbled.*
- In sentence 2, the action verbs are *worked* and *went.**

Linking Verbs

Another kind of verb, called a **linking verb,** links the subject to words that describe or identify it:

> 3. Don *is* a fine mathematician.
> 4. This fabric *feels* rough and scratchy.

- In sentence 3, the verb *is* links the subject *Don* with the noun *mathematician.*
- In sentence 4, the verb *feels* links the subject *fabric* with the adjectives *rough* and *scratchy.*

Here are some common linking verbs:

Common Linking Verbs	
appear	feel
be (am, is, are, was, were, has been, have been, had been . . .)	look
become	seem

---

* For work on compound predicates, see Chapter 21, "Revising for Sentence Variety," Part D.

Verbs of More Than One Word—Helping Verbs

So far you have dealt with verbs of only one word—*fumbled, worked, is, feels,* and so on. But many verbs consist of more than one word:

> 5. He *should have taken* the train home.
> 6. *Are* Tanya and Joe *practicing* the piano?
> 7. The lounge *was painted* last week.

- In sentence 5, *taken* is the main verb; *should* and *have* are the **helping verbs.**
- In sentence 6, *practicing* is the main verb; *are* is the helping verb.
- In sentence 7, *painted* is the main verb; *was* is the helping verb.*

PRACTICE 3 Underline the verbs in these sentences.

1. She exposes insurance cheats and lying spouses.
2. She spies on suspected nannies with a tiny camera.
3. Theresa Coleman-Negast might have become a police officer.
4. However, wearing a uniform every day did not appeal to her.
5. Instead, she became a private investigator.
6. Only one of every ten private investigators is a woman.
7. Women in this business might face criticism or even sexual harassment.
8. On the other hand, many clients prefer a female P.I. and can talk more freely with her.
9. Theresa enjoys her lack of routine and even the spy equipment.
10. Thanks to technology, cameras and tape recorders have gotten small enough to fit into a Beanie Baby, a pair of sunglasses, or even a ballpoint pen.

PRACTICE 4 Circle the subjects and underline the verbs in the following sentences. First, cross out any prepositional phrases.

1. Do you think of baseball as America's oldest team sport?
2. In fact, lacrosse takes that honor.

---

*For more work on verbs in the passive voice, see Chapter 29, "The Past Participle," Part E.

3. Native Americans were playing the sport long before the arrival of Europeans.
4. A team scores by throwing a ball into the opposing team's goal.
5. The goal is ferociously guarded by a goalie.
6. Each player uses a curved racket with a mesh basket at its end.
7. Algonquin tribes in the valley of the St. Lawrence River invented the game.
8. The Hurons and Iroquois soon learned this demanding sport.
9. By 1500, the rough-and-tumble game was played by dozens of tribes in Canada and the United States.
10. Sometimes matches would require hundreds of players and might last for days.
11. Playing lacrosse trained young warriors for battle.
12. With this in mind, the Cherokees named lacrosse "little brother of war."
13. However, tribes often settled their differences peaceably with a lacrosse match.
14. French missionaries saw a resemblance between the racket and a bishop's cross.
15. They changed the name of the game from *boggotaway*, the native word, to *lacrosse*, French for *the cross*.

Exploring Online

http://webster.commnet.edu/grammar/quizzes/verbmaster.htm
Graded quiz: Find complete verbs in the sentences.

http://webster.commnet.edu/grammar/quizzes/preposition_quiz2.htm
Graded quiz: Find the prepositions in Hemingway's paragraph.

CHAPTER 25 Coordination and Subordination

PART A Coordination
PART B Subordination
PART C Semicolons
PART D Conjunctive Adverbs
PART E Review

Part A

Coordination

A **clause** is a group of words that includes a subject and a verb. If a clause can stand alone as a complete idea, it is an **independent clause** and can be written as a **simple sentence.***

Here are two independent clauses written as simple sentences:

1. The dog barked all night.
2. The neighbors didn't complain.

You can join two clauses together by placing a comma and a **coordinating conjunction** between them:

3. The dog barked all night, *but* the neighbors didn't complain.
4. Let's go to the beach today, *for* it is too hot to do anything else.

- The coordinating conjunctions *but* and *for* join together two clauses.
- Note that *a comma precedes each coordinating conjunction*.

---

* For more work on simple sentences, see Chapter 24, "The Simple Sentence."

Here is a list of the most common coordinating conjunctions:

Coordinating Conjunctions			
and	for	or	yet
but	nor	so	

Be sure to choose the coordinating conjunction that best expresses the *relationship* between the two clauses in a sentence:

5. It was late, *so* I decided to take a bus home.
6. It was late, *yet* I decided to take a bus home.

- The *so* in sentence 5 means that the lateness of the hour caused me to take the bus. (The trains don't run after midnight.)
- The *yet* in sentence 6 means that despite the late hour I still decided to take a bus home. (I knew I might have to wait two hours at the bus stop.)
- Note that a comma precedes the coordinating conjunction.

PRACTICE 1 Read the following sentences for meaning. Then fill in the coordinating conjunction that *best* expresses the relationship between the two clauses. Don't forget to add the comma.

1. Diners still dot the highways of the United States __but__ they are not as popular as they once were.

2. In 1872, Walter Scott of Providence, Rhode Island, decided to make prepared and cooked food easier to buy __so__ he started selling sandwiches and pies from a large horse-drawn wagon.

3. Customers flocked to this first "diner" __for__ the food was delicious, plentiful, and inexpensive.

4. Many did not like standing outside to eat __so__ another businessman, Sam Jones, redecorated the wagon and invited customers inside to dine.

5. In order to widen the appeal of their diners, some owners installed stained-glass windows __and__ other proprietors added elegant decorations.

6. In the 1920s, narrow booths began to replace stools __and__ diners were fixed permanently on the ground.

7. Stainless steel, efficient-looking diners were everywhere by the 1940s _But or yet_ even this style gave way to the fancy colonial and Mediterranean designs of the 1960s.

8. Diners are not as common as they were twenty years ago _nor_ can they compete with fast-food take-out chains like McDonald's and Wendy's.

9. Nonetheless, customers do have a choice; they can stand in line and wait for a quick hamburger _or_ they can sit and be waited on in a diner.

10. Most choose fast food _but or yet_ some find that the more leisurely diner still has its charm.

PRACTICE 2 Combine these simple sentences with a coordinating conjunction. Punctuate correctly.

1. My daughter wants to be a mechanic. She spends every spare minute at the garage.

2. Ron dared not look over the edge. Heights made him dizzy.

3. Tasha's living room is cozy. Her guests always gather in the kitchen.

4. Meet me by the bicycle rack. Meet me at Lulu's Nut Shop.

5. In 1969, the first astronauts landed on the moon. Most Americans felt proud.

Part B

Subordination

Two clauses can also be joined with a **subordinating conjunction.** The clause following a subordinating conjunction is called a **subordinate** or **dependent clause** because it depends on an independent clause to complete its meaning:

> 1. We will light the candles *when Flora arrives.*

- *When Flora arrives* is a subordinate or dependent clause introduced by the subordinating conjunction *when.*
- By itself, *when Flora arrives* is incomplete; it depends on the independent clause to complete its meaning.*

Note that sentence 1 can also be written this way:

> 2. *When Flora arrives,* we will light the candles.

- The meaning of sentences 1 and 2 is the same, but the punctuation is different.
- In sentence 1, because the subordinate clause *follows* the independent clause, *no comma* is needed.
- In sentence 2, however, because the subordinate clause *begins* the sentence, it is followed by a *comma*.

Here is a partial list of subordinating conjunctions:

Subordinating Conjunctions			
after	because	since	when(ever)
although	before	unless	whereas
as (if)	if	until	while

Be sure to choose the subordinating conjunction that *best expresses the relationship* between the two clauses in a sentence:

> 3. This course was excellent *because* Professor Green taught it.
> 4. This course was excellent *although* Professor Green taught it.

---

* For more work on incomplete sentences, or fragments, see Chapter 26, "Avoiding Sentence Errors," Part B.

CHAPTER 25 Coordination and Subordination 347

- Sentence 3 says that the course was excellent *because* Professor Green, a great teacher, taught it.
- Sentence 4 says that the course was excellent *despite the fact that* Professor Green, apparently a bad teacher, taught it.

PRACTICE 3 Read the following sentences for meaning. Then fill in the subordinating conjunction that *best* expresses the relationship between the two clauses.

1. We could see very clearly last night ___since___ the moon was so bright.

2. Violet read *Sports Illustrated* ___whereas___ Daisy walked in the woods.

3. ___When___ it is cold outside, our new wood-burning Franklin stove keeps us warm.

4. The students buzzed with excitement ___since___ Professor Hargrave announced that classes would be held at the zoo.

5. ___Unless___ or until his shoulder loosens up a bit, Ron will stay on the bench.

PRACTICE 4 Punctuate the following sentences by adding a comma where necessary. Put a C after any correct sentences.

1. Thousands of low-income children in Venezuela have been given a new life because Jose Antonio Abreu taught them to play classical music. C

2. While some people only talked about the poverty and drugs destroying many young Venezuelans, Abreu took action.

3. After he convinced government leaders that musical training builds self-worth, Abreu got funding to start children's orchestras. C

4. The results have been amazing as communities proudly support their young musicians. C

5. When the children practice their violins or oboes, they are also learning discipline, valuable skills, and the joys of musical teamwork.

6. The program ignores pop and tropical musicians like Christina Aguilera and Oscar de Leon because Abreu wants his students to master classical artists like Mozart and Beethoven. C

7. Since the program was launched, a generation of talented Venezuelan musicians is already performing, composing, and teaching classical music.

8. Because the program has been so successful it is the model for new youth orchestras now being formed throughout the world.

PRACTICE 5 Combine each pair of ideas below by using a subordinating conjunction. Write each combination twice, once with the subordinating conjunction at the beginning of the sentence and once with the subordinating conjunction in the middle of the sentence. Punctuate correctly.

Example
We stayed on the beach.
The sun went down.

We stayed on the beach until the sun went down.

Until the sun went down, we stayed on the beach.

1. This cactus has flourished.
2. I talk to it every day.

_____

_____

_____

_____

3. Ralph takes the train to Philadelphia.
4. He likes to sit by the window.

_____

_____

_____

_____

5. I had known you were coming.
6. I would have vacuumed the guest room.

_____

_____

_____

_____

7. He was the first person to eat a slice of meat between two pieces of bread.
8. The sandwich was named after the Earl of Sandwich.

CHAPTER 25 Coordination and Subordination 349

_____
_____
_____
_____

9. Akila was about to answer the final question.
10. The buzzer sounded.

_____
_____
_____
_____

11. Few soap operas remain on the radio.
12. Daytime television is filled with them.

_____
_____
_____
_____

13. She connected the speakers.
14. The room filled with glorious sound.

_____
_____
_____
_____

15. The chimney spewed black smoke and soot.
16. Nobody complained to the local environmental agency.

_____
_____
_____
_____

Part C

Semicolons

You can join two independent clauses by placing a **semicolon** between them. The semicolon takes the place of a conjunction:

> 1. She hopes to receive good grades this semester; her scholarship depends on her maintaining a 3.5 average.
> 2. Tony is a careless driver; he has had three minor accidents this year alone.

- Each of the sentences above could also be made into two *separate sentences* by replacing the semicolon with a period.
- Note that the first word after a semicolon is *not* capitalized (unless, of course, it is a word that is normally capitalized, like someone's name).

PRACTICE 6 Combine each pair of independent clauses by placing a semicolon between them.

1. Rush-hour traffic was worse than usual no one seemed to mind.
2. The senator appeared ill at ease at the news conference he seemed afraid of saying the wrong thing.
3. The new seed catalogue, a fifteen-hundred-page volume, was misplaced the volume weighed ten pounds.
4. On Thursday evening, Hector decided to go camping on Friday morning, he packed his bags and left.
5. In the early 1960s, the Beatles burst on the rock scene rock music has never been the same.
6. Ron Jackson has been promoted he will be an effective manager.
7. This stream is full of trout every spring men and women with waders and fly rods arrive on its banks.
8. Not a single store was open at that hour not a soul walked the streets.

PRACTICE 7 Each independent clause that follows is the first half of a sentence. Add a semicolon and a second independent clause. Make sure your second thought is also independent and can stand alone.

1. At 2 A.M. I stumbled toward the ringing telephone _____
_____

2. *People* magazine published my letter to the editor _____

3. The officer pulled over the speeding pickup truck _____

4. Faulkner's stories often depict life in the South _____

5. None of my friends can polka _____

6. During the Great Depression, millions of workers were unemployed _____

7. Cameras are not permitted in the museum _____

8. Bill's waiter recommended the vegetable soup _____

Part D
Conjunctive Adverbs

A **conjunctive adverb** placed after the semicolon can help clarify the relationship between two clauses:

1. I like the sound of that stereo; *however,* the price is too high.

2. They have not seen that film; *moreover,* they have not been to a theater for three years.

- Note that a comma follows the conjunctive adverb.

Here is a partial list of conjunctive adverbs.

Conjunctive Adverbs

consequently	in fact	nevertheless
furthermore	indeed	then → get rid of
however	moreover	therefore

PRACTICE 8 Punctuate each sentence correctly by adding a semicolon, a comma, or both, where necessary. Put a *C* after any correct sentences.

1. I hate to wash my car windows; nevertheless, it's a job that must be done.
2. Sonia doesn't know how to play chess; however, she would like to learn.
3. Dean Fader is very funny; in fact, he could be a professional comedian.
4. Deep water makes Maurice nervous; therefore, he does not want to join the scuba dive team.
5. I like this painting; the soft colors remind me of tropical sunsets.
6. The faculty approved of the new trimester system; furthermore, the students liked it too.
7. Bill has a cassette player plugged into his ear all day; consequently, he misses a lot of good conversations.
8. We toured the darkroom then we watched an actual photo shoot.

PRACTICE 9 Combine each pair of independent clauses by placing a semicolon and a conjunctive adverb between them. Punctuate correctly.

1. The lake is quite long we rowed from one end of it to the other.
2. I can still see the streaks under the fresh white paint we will have to give the room another coat.
3. Mr. Farrington loves bluegrass music he plays in a local bluegrass band.
4. Jay, a tall boy, has poor eyesight he was turned down for the basketball team.
5. Yesterday, hikers from the Nature-Walkers' Club made real progress in blazing a trail they managed to get as far as the foot of Mt. Lookout.
6. By midnight Tien had finished tuning his engine he still had enough time for a short nap before the race.
7. An arthroscope helps doctors examine the inside of an injured knee the use of this instrument can prevent unnecessary surgery.
8. Rhinoceroses live in protected animal preserves poachers still manage to kill a few of these magnificent beasts each year.

Part E

Review

In this chapter, you have combined simple sentences by means of a **coordinating conjunction,** a **subordinating conjunction,** a **semicolon,** and a **semicolon and conjunctive adverb.** Here is a review chart of the sentence patterns discussed in this chapter.*

Coordination

Option 1 Independent clause { , and / , but / , for / , nor / , or / , so / , yet } independent clause.

Option 2 Independent clause ; independent clause.   *did not do*

Option 3 Independent clause { ; consequently, / ; furthermore, / ; however, / ; in addition, / ; indeed, / ; in fact, / ; moreover, / ; nevertheless, / ; then, / ; therefore, } independent clause.

Subordination

Option 4 Independent clause { after / although / as (as if) / because / before / if / since / unless / until / when(ever) / whereas / while } dependent clause.

Option 5 { After / Although / As (As if) / Because / Before / If / Since / Unless / Until / When(ever) / Whereas / While } dependent clause, independent clause.

---

* For more ways to combine sentences, see Chapter 21, "Revising for Sentence Variety," Part D.

PRACTICE 10 Read each pair of simple sentences to determine the relationship between them. Then join each pair in three different ways, using the conjunctions or conjunctive adverbs in parentheses at the left. Punctuate correctly.

Example

The company picnic was canceled.
Rain started to fall in torrents.

(for) *The company picnic was canceled, for the rain started to fall in torrents.*

(because) *Because the rain started to fall in torrents, the company picnic was canceled.*

(therefore) *The rain started to fall in torrents; therefore, the company picnic was canceled.*

1. My grandmother is in great shape.
   She eats right and exercises regularly.

   (for) _____

   (because) _____

   (therefore) _____

2. We just put in four hours paving the driveway.
   We need a long break and a cold drink.

   (since) _____

   (because) _____

   (consequently) _____

3. The bus schedule was difficult to read.
   Penny found the right bus.

   (but) _____

(although) _____

(however) _____

4. Don is an expert mechanic.
   He intends to open a service center.

   (and) _____

   (because) _____

   (furthermore) _____

5. We haven't heard from her.
   We haven't given up hope.

   (but) _____

   (although) _____

   (nevertheless) _____

PRACTICE 11 In your writing, aim for variety by mixing coordination, subordination, and simple sentences.* Revise the following paragraphs to eliminate monotonous simple sentences. First, read the paragraph to determine the relationships between ideas; then choose the conjunctions that best express these relationships, making your corrections above the lines. Punctuate correctly.

Paragraph a Dating has always been a risky business. Television shows like *Blind Date* succeed. They let viewers leer at other people's embarrassing dates. Now the Internet is opening a whole new social frontier. It also is creating new dangers.

---

*For more work on sentence variety, see Chapter 21, "Revising for Sentence Variety."

Online, it is harder to spot nuts, flakes, and predators. We meet someone through e-mail. We lose our usual ways of judging people. According to Internet safety expert Parry Aftab, it is hard to gauge the truth of someone's statements. We cannot see, hear, and experience that person's eye contact, body language, dress, personal hygiene, and voice. Furthermore, most people lie. They begin to date online. Aftab says that men often fib about their income, fitness level, or amount of hair. Women shave pounds off their weight or years off their age. Cyber daters must remain skeptical, ask questions, and watch for red-flag comments. Your online love keeps calling herself Gilda, Bat Goddess of the Red Planet. It's probably time to log off.

"On the Internet, nobody knows you're a dog."

Paragraph b Languages are disappearing all over the world. North America has 200 Native American languages. Only about fifty have more than a thousand speakers.

Europe's Celtic languages have been declining for generations, language decline is most noticeable in tiny communities in Asia and Australia. Each isolated community speaks a different language. The population shrinks. The language begins to die out. In addition, a small community may make contact with a large one. The native language may start to fade. People use the "more important" language. It gives them better access to education, jobs, and new technology. A "powerful language" will almost always prevail over a native mother tongue.

Paragraph c   She was rich, brilliant, and descended from Alexander the Great. Cleopatra was nervous. She became Queen of Egypt at age 18. The young queen had a flair for ruling and was soon worshipped by her subjects. By 51 B.C. civil war in Egypt was bitter. Julius Caesar, the ruler of Rome, was sent to calm the battles. Cleopatra was in hiding. Caesar arrived. She directed her servants to roll her up inside a large rug and smuggle her into the palace. Julius Caesar was the most famous and powerful man in the world. He was amazed to receive a gift-wrapped queen. He was 52, much older than she. It was one of history's great love stories and lasted until Caesar's death. Later Marc Antony came to Egypt to add African lands to the Roman empire. He too fell in love with the spirited queen. One night, Cleopatra bet Marc Antony that she could spend $10 million on a single banquet. She owned two huge, valuable pearls. After dinner, she dropped one into a cup of vinegar. The pearl dissolved. She swallowed the vinegar, winning the bet.

Exploring Online

http://owl.english.purdue.edu/handouts/grammar/g_commacompEX1.html
Paper quiz: Combine clauses correctly.

CHAPTER 26

Avoiding Sentence Errors

PART A   Avoiding Run-Ons and Comma Splices
PART B   Avoiding Fragments

Part A

Avoiding Run-Ons and Comma Splices

Be careful to avoid **run-ons** and **comma splices**.

A **run-on sentence** incorrectly runs together two independent clauses without a conjunction or punctuation. This error confuses the reader, who cannot tell where one thought stops and the next begins:

> 1. Run-on: My neighbor Mr. Hoffman is seventy-five years old he plays tennis every Saturday afternoon.

A **comma splice** incorrectly joins two independent clauses with a comma but no conjunction:

> 2. Comma splice: My neighbor Mr. Hoffman is seventy-five years old, he plays tennis every Saturday afternoon.

The run-on and the comma splice can be corrected in five ways:

> Use two separate sentences.   My neighbor Mr. Hoffman is seventy-five years old. He plays tennis every Saturday afternoon.

358

CHAPTER 26   Avoiding Sentence Errors   359

Use a coordinating conjunction. (See Chapter 25, Part A.)		My neighbor Mr. Hoffman is seventy-five years old, but he plays tennis every Saturday afternoon.
Use a subordinating conjunction. (See Chapter 25, Part B.)		Although my neighbor Mr. Hoffman is seventy-five years old, he plays tennis every Saturday afternoon.
Use a semicolon. (See Chapter 25, Part C.)		My neighbor Mr. Hoffman is seventy-five years old; he plays tennis every Saturday afternoon.
Use a semicolon and a conjunctive adverb. (See Chapter 25, Part D.)		My neighbor Mr. Hoffman is seventy-five years old; however, he plays tennis every Saturday afternoon.

PRACTICE 1   Some of these sentences contain run-ons or comma splices; others are correct. Put a C next to the correct sentences. Revise the run-ons and comma splices in any way you choose. Be careful of the punctuation.

1. It was an astonishing exhibit, the Guggenheim Museum's recent show was called "The Art of the Motorcycle."

   Revised: *The Guggeheim museum's recent show was called "The Art of the Motorcycle." It was an astonishing exhibit*

2. Museumgoers sported leather vests and ponytails, their motorcycles jammed New York City streets.

   Revised: _____

3. Displayed were motorcycles through the years, including the earliest-known   *C*
   cycle.

   Revised: _____

4. That was the 1868 French velocipede, it looked more like a bicycle with a steam engine under the seat than a motorcycle.

   Revised: _____

5. The Italian MV Agusta F4 was the latest model on display, this one looked like a fantastic space machine.

   Revised: _____

6. A 1993 Harley-Davidson stole the show, it was a replica of Dennis Hopper's *Easy Rider* cycle.

   Revised: _____

7. The show attracted more visitors than any other Guggenheim exhibit, museum attendance was 45 percent higher than usual.

   Revised: _____

8. Tickets and gift-shop sales brought in more than $1 million, the exhibit catalog alone sold for $85.

   Revised: _____

9. Although Ducati leather jumpsuits cost $1,595, museumgoers could buy their kids red plastic BMW motorcycles for $120 each.

   Revised: _____

10. Whether motorcycles are art or not, "The Art of the Motorcycle" certainly brought many new visitors to the Guggenheim, the show was considered a huge success.

    Revised: _____

PRACTICE 2 Proofread the following paragraph for run-ons and comma splices. Correct them in any way you choose.

(1) College costs have risen dramatically in recent years, most students choose to work part-time to help cover their expenses. (2) Surprising new research reveals many benefits for college students who are employed a limited number of hours a week. (3) Part-time jobs can help students explore career fields and develop professional skills; they might even lead to permanent employment after graduation. (4) Another benefit is even more surprising students who work the ideal number of hours, between 15 and 20 per week, have higher grade point

averages and better retention rates than their peers. (5) However, working more than 20 hours can have negative consequences it may interfere with schoolwork and reduce financial aid eligibility. (6) Students who work 35 hours or more often have low grade point averages, they are also less likely to complete their degrees. (7) College students who can keep their working hours within the ideal range will enjoy the greatest benefits of part-time employment.

PRACTICE 3 Proofread the following essay for run-ons and comma splices. Correct them in any way you choose, writing your revised essay on a separate sheet of paper. Be careful of the punctuation.

Will K. Kellogg, Least Likely to Succeed

(1) Will Kellogg was an unlikely candidate for fame and fortune, he became one of America's great successes.

(2) The two Kellogg boys could not have been more different. (3) Will was a slow learner with few friends and interests. (4) His father pulled him from school at the age of thirteen he made Will a traveling broom salesman for the family company. (5) Eight years older than Will, John Harvey Kellogg was the family genius. (6) He became a noted surgeon and head of an exclusive health resort. (7) He treated his patients with exercise and a strict vegetarian diet, he wrote best-selling books about healthful living.

(8) In 1880, Will was twenty years old, Dr. John hired him to work at the resort. (9) For the next twenty-five years, Will served as his brother's flunky. (10) According to rumor, he shaved Dr. John every day and shined his shoes. (11) John bicycled to work, Will jogged alongside getting his daily work orders. (12) Dr. John was a wealthy man, he never paid Will more than eighty-seven dollars a month.

(13) One of the special foods at the resort was pressed wheat. (14) The brothers boiled wheat dough then they pressed it through rollers into thin sheets. (15) One night, they left the boiled dough out. (16) When they pressed it, it turned into flakes instead of forming sheets. (17) Will suggested that they toast the flakes.

(18) Resort guests loved the new cereal, former guests ordered it from their homes. (19) To meet the demand, the brothers opened a mail-order business, however, the snobbish Dr. John refused to sell the flakes to grocery stores.

(20) In 1906, Will finally bought out John's share of the cereal patents, struck out on his own. (21) Will turned out to be a business genius. (22) He invented advertising techniques that made his new product, Kellogg's Corn Flakes, a household word. (23) Will K. Kellogg quickly became one of the richest persons in America.

(24) Sadly, the two brothers never reconciled. (25) In 1943, ninety-one-year-old Dr. John wrote Will an apology John died before the letter reached his younger brother.

Part B

Avoiding Fragments

Another error to avoid is the **sentence fragment**. A **sentence** must contain a subject and a verb and must be able to stand alone as a complete idea. A **sentence fragment** is incomplete. It lacks a subject, a verb, or both—or it does not stand alone as a complete idea.

Here are six common fragments and ways to correct them. The first three are among the most frequently made errors in college and business writing.

Dependent Clause Fragments

A dependent clause fragment often starts with a subordinating conjunction like *although, because, if, when,* and so on.*

> Complete sentence: 1. Kirk decided to major in psychology.
> Fragment: 2. After his sister was diagnosed with anorexia.

- Example 1 is a complete sentence.
- Example 2 is a fragment because it is a dependent clause beginning with the subordinating conjunction *after*. Furthermore, it is not a complete idea.

---

*For a longer list of subordinating conjunctions and more work on dependent clauses, see Chapter 25, "Coordination and Subordination," Part B.

This fragment can be corrected in two ways:

> Corrected: 3. Kirk decided to major in psychology after his sister was diagnosed with anorexia.
>
> Corrected: 4. Kirk decided to major in psychology. His sister was diagnosed with anorexia.

- In sentence 3, the fragment is combined with the sentence before.
- In sentence 4, the fragment is changed into a complete sentence.

Relative Clause Fragments

A dependent clause fragment also can start with *who, whose, which,* or *that*.*

> Complete sentence: 5. Mrs. Costa is a popular history professor.
>
> Fragment: 6. Who never runs out of creative ideas.

- Example 5 is a complete sentence.
- Example 6 is a fragment because it is a relative clause beginning with *who*.* It is not a complete idea.

This fragment can be corrected in two ways:

> Corrected: 7. Mrs. Costa is a popular history professor who never runs out of creative ideas.
>
> Corrected: 8. Mrs. Costa is a popular history professor. She never runs out of creative ideas.

- In sentence 7, it is combined with the sentence before.
- In sentence 8, the fragment is changed into a complete sentence.

-ing Fragments

An *-ing* fragment starts with an *-ing* verb form.

> Complete sentence: 9. Joaquin can be seen on the track every morning.
>
> Fragment: 10. Running a mile or two before breakfast.

---

*For more work on relative clauses, see Chapter 21, "Revising for Sentence Variety," Part D, and Chapter 27, "Present Tense (Agreement), Part G.

- Example 9 is a complete sentence.
- Example 10 is a fragment because it lacks a subject and because an *-ing* verb form cannot stand alone without a helping verb.*

This fragment can be corrected in two ways:

> Corrected: 11. Joaquin can be seen on the track every morning, running a mile or two before breakfast.
>
> Corrected: 12. Joaquin can be seen on the track every morning. He runs a mile or two before breakfast.

- In sentence 11, the fragment is combined with the sentence before.
- In sentence 12, the fragment is changed into a complete sentence.

Watch out for fragments beginning with a subordinating conjunction; *who, which,* or *that;* or an *-ing* verb form. These groups of words cannot stand alone, but must be combined with another sentence or changed into a complete sentence.

PRACTICE 4 Some of these examples are fragments; others are complete sentences. Put a C next to the complete sentences. Revise the fragments any way you choose.

1. When Sandra completes her commercial jet training.

   Revised: _____

   _____

2. Loudly talking on his cell phone, Ivan strolled through the mall.

   Revised: _____

   _____

3. A city that I have always wanted to visit.

   Revised: _____

   _____

4. If she speaks Portuguese fluently, she will probably get the job.

   Revised: _____

   _____

---

*For more work on joining ideas with an *-ing* modifier, see Chapter 21, "Revising for Sentence Variety," Part D.

5. The comic strip Peanuts, which was created by Charles Schultz.

   Revised: _____

   _____

6. Interviewing divorced people for her research project.

   Revised: _____

   _____

7. Although some students bring laptop computers to class.

   Revised: _____

   _____

8. Frantically, the disc jockey flipping through stacks of CDs.

   Revised: _____

   _____

Prepositional Phrase Fragments

> Complete sentence: 13. A huge telescope in Green Bank, West Virginia, scans for signs of life.
>
> Fragment: 14. On stars 20 to 30 light years away.

- Sentence 13 is a complete sentence.
- Sentence 14 is a fragment because it is a prepositional phrase beginning with *on*. It lacks both a subject and a verb.

   This fragment can be corrected in two ways:

> Corrected: 15. A huge telescope in Green Bank, West Virginia, scans for signs of life on stars 20 to 30 light years away.
>
> Corrected: 16. A huge telescope in Green Bank, West Virginia, scans for signs of life. Its target is stars 20 to 30 light years away.

- Sentence 15 shows the easiest way to correct this fragment—by connecting it to the sentence before.
- In sentence 16, the fragment is changed into a complete sentence by adding a subject, *its target,* and a verb, *is*.

Appositive Phrase Fragments

> Fragment: 17. A fine pianist.
> Complete sentence: 18. Marsha won a scholarship to Juilliard.

- Example 17 is a fragment because it is an appositive—a noun phrase. It lacks a verb, and it is not a complete idea.*
- Example 18 is a complete sentence.

This fragment can be corrected in two ways:

> Corrected: 19. A fine pianist, Marsha won a scholarship to Juilliard.
> Corrected: 20. Marsha is a fine pianist. She won a scholarship to Juilliard.

- In sentence 19, the fragment is combined with the sentence after it.
- In sentence 20, the fragment is changed into a complete sentence by adding a verb, *is*, and a subject, *she* (to avoid repeating *Marsha*).

Infinitive Phrase Fragments

> Complete sentence: 21. Lauri has always wanted to become a biologist.
> Fragment: 22. To protect the environment.

- Example 21 is a complete sentence.
- Example 22 is a fragment because it lacks a subject and contains only the infinitive form of the verb—*to* plus the simple form of *protect*.

This fragment can be corrected in two ways:

> Corrected: 23. Lauri has always wanted to become a biologist and to protect the environment.
> Corrected: 24. Lauri has always wanted to become a biologist. Her goal is to protect the environment.

- In sentence 23, the fragment is combined with the sentence before it.
- In sentence 24, the fragment is changed into a complete sentence.

---

*For more work on appositives, see Chapter 21, "Revising for Sentence Variety," Part D.

Watch out for phrase fragments. A prepositional phrase, appositive phrase, or infinitive cannot stand alone, but must be combined with another sentence or changed into a complete sentence.

PRACTICE 5 Now, proofread for fragments. Some of these examples are fragments; others are complete sentences. Put a C next to the complete sentences. Revise the fragments any way you choose.

1. To earn money for college.

    Revised: _____

2. Terrence, a graphic designer at *Sports Illustrated*.

    Revised: _____

3. Across the railroad tracks and down the riverbank.

    Revised: _____

4. A born comedian.

    Revised: _____

5. To answer phones for the AIDS Education Network.

    Revised: _____

6. On a coffee plantation in Jamaica.

    Revised: _____

7. That silver razor scooter.

    Revised: _____

8. To find a job that you love.

    Revised: _____

Review Chart: Correcting Sentence Fragments

Type of Fragment	F *Fragment* C *Corrected*
1. Dependent clause	F After Jake moved to Colorado. C After Jake moved to Colorado, he learned to ski.
2. Relative clause	F Who loves computer games. C My niece, who loves computer games, repairs my computer.
3. *-ing* modifier	F Surfing the web. C Surfing the web, we visited European art museum sites.
4. Prepositional phrase	F Inside the cave. C They found mastodon bones inside the cave.
5. Appositive	F A slow student. C Einstein, a slow student, proved to be a genius.
6. Infinitive	F To go dancing tonight. C She wants to go dancing tonight.

PRACTICE 6 Fragments are most likely to occur in paragraphs or longer pieces of writing. Proofread the paragraph below for fragments. Correct them in any way you choose, either adding the fragments to other sentences or making them into complete sentences.

(1) The sinking of the *Titanic* in 1912 has inspired fifteen motion pictures over the years. (2) All of them requiring special effects. (3) What set James Cameron's *Titanic* apart, however, was his attention to detail. (4) Following the blueprints and plans for the original ship. (5) Cameron's team created scaled sets and models accurate down to the rivets. (6) Scenes of the ship in the water were made possible through the brilliant use of computer technology and a small model. (7) A larger model of the liner's huge cargo hold was needed. (8) To show the ocean rushing into the ship. (9) Although the model was only a quarter as large as the original. (10) It still had enough room for period luggage and a brand-new Renault. (11) The largest model was a 775-foot replica of the luxury ship. (12) Which reproduced every detail, from the ship's name lettered on the façade to the chairs on

the deck. (13) That set took almost a year to build. (14) And a good chunk of the $287 million that Cameron spent on the most expensive movie ever made.

PRACTICE 7 Proofread this essay for fragments. Correct them in any way you choose, either adding the fragments to other sentences or making them into complete sentences. Be careful of the punctuation.

Her Focus Is Success

(1) If the way we react to adversity reveals our true character. (2) Maria Elena Ibanez is extraordinary. (3) This successful computer engineer and businesswoman is a master at refusing to let obstacles keep her from a goal.

(4) In 1973, nineteen-year-old Maria Elena left Colombia and arrived alone in Miami. (5) Speaking just a few words of English. (6) Her goal was to learn 50 new words a day. (7) By talking to people and reading children's books. (8) Soon she spoke well enough to enroll at Florida International University, earn a computer science degree, and so impress college officials that they hired her as a programmer.

(9) In 1982, Maria Elena started her first company. (10) Because computers cost much more in South America than they did in the U.S. (11) She decided to sell reasonably priced computers to South American dealers. (12) When some dealers hesitated to do business with such a young woman, she won their respect with her expertise and willingness to teach them about the new technology. (13) Soon she sold International Micro Systems. (14) The nation's 55th fastest growing private company, at a huge profit.

(15) In spite of this success, people laughed out loud when Maria Elena announced her new goal. (16) To sell computers throughout Africa. (17) She paid no attention and returned from her first selling trip with handfuls of orders. (18) Then in 1992, disaster struck.

(19) Hurricane Andrew plowed into Miami, exploding Maria Elena's house. (20) As she and her two small children hid in a closet. (21) In the morning, dazed, she walked to the offices and warehouse of her new company. (22) The building

was a mangled mess of fallen walls, trees, wet paper, and smoking wires. (23) Sitting down on a curb, she cried, but as her employees began arriving. (24) She sprang into action.

(25) One worker said the company could set up in his home. (26) Which had electricity. (27) Working 24 hours a day and using cell phones, the employees called all their African customers. (28) To say everything was fine and their orders would be shipped on time. (29) International High Tech grew 700 percent that year. (30) Despite the most damaging hurricane in U.S. history.

(31) Maria Elena moved her company into its rebuilt offices. (32) Today she and the children live in an apartment. (33) Not a house. (34) Asked about losing every piece of clothing, every picture, every possession in her former home. (35) She laughs, says that most problems hide opportunities, and adds that now she has no lawn to mow.

PRACTICE 8 REVIEW

Proofread these paragraphs for run-ons, comma splices, and fragments. Correct the errors in any way you choose.

Paragraph a (1) Many experts believe that before the year 2020. (2) The moon will be a popular tourist destination. (3) Adventure travelers now might climb Mount Everest or take a canoe trip down the Amazon, soon they will be paying large sums for the adventure of a lifetime, in space. (4) After careful training and space suit drills, they will rocket out of Earth's orbit and spend a day at a fuel depot. (5) Circling Earth and playing in zero gravity. (6) Then they will board the space ship for the two-day flight to the moon. (7) Once they land near the hotel's main airlock and check in, guests will stare at Mother Earth in the black vastness of the sky, take tours in special buses through the dusty lunar landscape, and experience the thrill of moving at one-sixth the gravity of Earth. (8) This means they will jump six times higher and feel six times lighter. (9) The week will fly by. (10) As they pack for the return trip. (11) Many travelers will trade ten pounds of their baggage allowance for the moon rocks they've been collecting. (12) After an unforgettable final flight and decontamination, the space visitors will re-enter their lives on Earth, changed.

—Adapted from Gregory Bennett, "Your Vacation on the Moon"

Paragraph b   (1) Some teenagers seem to start the day tired, they are worn out even before they leave for school. (2) Once in class, they might doze off, even in the middle of an exciting lesson. (3) Are these students lazy, have they stayed out too late partying? (4) Medical research provides a different explanation for the exhaustion of these teens. (5) As children become adolescents, they develop an increased need for sleep, especially in the morning. (6) Unfortunately, most American high schools start around 7:30 A.M. many students have to get up as early as 5:00 A.M. (7) Scientists suggest that if students could start school later in the day. (8) They might get the extra sleep they need. (9) To test this theory, many schools have begun to experiment with later hours. (10) Congress is even paying the extra operating costs for schools that start after 9:00 A.M. (11) The hope is that teens will be less tired, furthermore, because schools that start later will end later, students will be off the streets and out of trouble during the late afternoon. (12) Which is prime mischief time.

PRACTICE 9   REVIEW

Proofread these two essays for run-ons, comma splices, and fragments. Correct the errors in any way you choose, writing the revised draft on a separate piece of paper.

Words for the Wise

(1) Everyone knows that Scrabble is America's favorite word game. (2) It was invented by Alfred Butts. (3) An architect who wanted to create a word game that required both luck and skill. (4) In 1938, Butts produced a board with 225 squares and 100 tiles with letters on them. (5) Each letter was worth a certain number of points, depending on how easy it was to use that letter in a word.

(6) Butts made fifty Scrabble sets by hand he gave them to his friends. (7) Who loved playing Scrabble. (8) Strangely enough, Butts could not interest a manufacturer in the game. (9) A friend of his, James Brunot, asked Butts for permission to manufacture and sell the game. (10) However, Brunot also had little success. (11) Selling only a few sets a year. (12) Then suddenly, in 1953, Scrabble caught on a million sets were sold that year.

(13) Butts and Brunot couldn't keep up with the demand, they sold the rights to a game manufacturer. (14) The rest is history today Scrabble is produced in half a dozen foreign languages it is also used as a learning tool. (15) To teach children spelling and vocabulary.

Humor as a Life Skill

(1) Do you love to laugh, can you find humor in daily life, even when things are going badly? (2) If so, you might be improving your health and your chances for success in life. (3) Recent studies are exploring the power of laughter to promote health and even improve performance in college and at work.

(4) Laughter improves health by lowering stress hormones and boosting the immune system. (5) Studies by Dr. Lee Berk and Dr. Stanley Tan of Loma Linda University in California show. (6) That belly laughter reduces at least four hormones associated with high levels of stress. (7) These researchers also found that laughter increases the body's natural ability to kill diseased cells. (8) Laughter seems to reduce pain, too, the *Journal of Holistic Nursing* reported. (9) That patients who were told jokes or watched comic videos after surgery perceived less pain than those who did not get a dose of humor. (10) Experts recommend taking time to laugh each day, especially during stressful times like finals week.

(11) In addition, laughter promotes productivity on the job, people who describe their work as fun perform better and have better relationships with their

coworkers, according to David Abramis. (12) A psychologist in the School of Business Administration at California State University-Long Beach who surveyed 382 people in various professions. (13) Another surprising study found that the most productive workplaces are those in which employees laugh ten minutes of every hour. (14) Writer Daniel Goleman believes that humor improves problem-solving skills and creativity. (15) Because many employers today recognize the value of humor to improve workers' loyalty, teamwork, and overall morale. (16) They are seeking employees who possess this valuable life skill—a sense of humor.

Exploring Online

http://webster.commnet.edu/grammar/quizzes/runons_quiz.htm
Interactive quiz: Correct run-on sentences and comma splices.

http://owl.english.purdue.edu/handouts/grammar/g_fragEX1.html
Paper quiz: Correct sentence fragments.

CHAPTER 27 Present Tense (Agreement)

PART A   Defining Subject-Verb Agreement
PART B   Three Troublesome Verbs in the Present Tense: *To Be, To Have, To Do*
PART C   Special Singular Constructions
PART D   Separation of Subject and Verb
PART E   Sentences Beginning with *There* and *Here*
PART F   Agreement in Questions
PART G   Agreement in Relative Clauses

PART A
Defining Subject-Verb Agreement

Subjects and verbs in the present tense must **agree** in number; that is, singular subjects take verbs with singular endings, and plural subjects take verbs with plural endings.

Verbs in the Present Tense
Sample Verb: *To Leap*

	Singular		Plural	
	If the subject is	the verb is	If the subject is	the verb is
1st person:	I	leap	we	leap
2nd person:	you	leap	you	leap
3rd person:	he, she, it	leaps	they	leap

■ Use an *-s* or *-es* ending on the verb only when the subject is *he, she,* or *it* or the equivalent of *he, she,* or *it.*

374

The subjects and verbs in the following sentences agree:

1. He *bicycles* to the steel mills every morning.
2. They *bicycle* to the steel mills every morning.
3. This student *hopes* to go to social work school.
4. The planets *revolve* around the sun.

- In sentence 1, the singular subject, *he*, takes the singular form of the verb, *bicycles*. *Bicycles* agrees with *he*.
- In sentence 2, the plural subject, *they*, takes the plural form of the verb, *bicycle*. *Bicycle* agrees with *they*.
- In sentence 3, the subject, *student*, is equivalent to *he* or *she* and takes the singular form of the verb, *hopes*.
- In sentence 4, the subject, *planets*, is equivalent to *they* and takes the plural form of the verb, *revolve*.

Subjects joined by the conjunction *and* usually take a plural verb:

5. Kirk and Quincy *attend* a pottery class at the Y.

- The subject, *Kirk and Quincy*, is plural, the equivalent of *they*.
- *Attend* agrees with the plural subject.*

PRACTICE 1 Underline the subject and circle the correct present tense verb.

1. A signed Green Bay Packers' helmet (brings, bring) in $2,000.
2. Bill Gates (pays, pay) $30.8 million for a notebook handwritten by Leonardo da Vinci.
3. Obviously, autographs (sells, sell)!
4. They (falls, fall) into three major categories—history, sports, and entertainment.
5. To a historian, an autograph (means, mean) a signed document, like a letter signed by President Lincoln.
6. For a sports fan, it (includes, include) anything signed, like a baseball or a cap.
7. In the entertainment field, collectors (associates, associate) an autograph with a signed photograph, like an eight-by-ten glossy of Jennifer Lopez.

---

*For work on consistent verb tense, see Chapter 20, "Revising for Consistency and Parallelism," Part A.

8. Some people (collects, <u>collect</u>) only specific items—for example, autographs of the signers of the Declaration of Independence or signed photographs of Bruce Willis.

9. Autograph shops (flourishes, flourish) in malls and airports.

10. However, technology and business (complicates, <u>complicate</u>) collecting.

11. For example, more and more public figures (uses, <u>use</u>) computers instead of pen and paper.

12. To make the situation even more complicated, an autopen sometimes (<u>confuses</u>, confuse) the unsuspecting buyer.

13. That pen, a perfect counterfeiter, automatically (<u>writes</u>, write) signatures for some celebrities.

14. Also, unlike their predecessors, athletes and movie stars sometimes (asks, <u>ask</u>) to be paid for their signatures.

15. Even with such problems, however, autograph hounds (continues, <u>continue</u>) to raise collecting to new heights.

PART B

Three Troublesome Verbs in the Present Tense: *To Be, To Have, To Do*

Choosing the correct verb form of *to be*, *to have*, and *to do* can be tricky. Study these charts:

Reference Chart—*To Be* Present Tense

	Singular		Plural	
	If the subject is	the verb is	If the subject is	the verb is
1st person:	I	am	we	are
2nd person:	you	are	you	are
3rd person:	he, she, it	is	they	are

CHAPTER 27 Present Tense (Agreement)

Reference Chart—To Have
Present Tense

	Singular		Plural	
	If the subject is	the verb is	If the subject is	the verb is
1st person:	I	have	we	have
2nd person:	you	have	you	have
3rd person:	he, she, it	has	they	have

Reference Chart—To Do
Present Tense

	Singular		Plural	
	If the subject is	the verb is	If the subject is	the verb is
1st person:	I	do	we	do
2nd person:	you	do	you	do
3rd person:	he, she, it	does	they	do

PRACTICE 2 Write the correct present tense form of the verb in the space at the right of the pronoun.

To be

I _____

we _____

he _____

you _____

it _____

they _____

she _____

To have

we _____

she _____

he _____

they _____

I _____

it _____

you _____

To do

it _____

they _____

she _____

you _____

he _____

we _____

I _____

UNIT 6 Reviewing the Basics

PRACTICE 3 Fill in the correct present tense form of the verb in parentheses.

1. Surfing __is__ (to be) an extreme sport that __has__ (to have) become very popular.

2. Most beginners __do__ (to do) basic moves on dry land—lying on the board, kneeling, and then rising to a hunched standing position.

3. An ocean beach with gentle, regular waves __is__ (to be) the ideal place to start surfing.

4. Expert surfers __have__ (to have) exceptional skills and __are__ (to be) at home in the monster waves off Hawaii or Australia.

5. An expert __does__ (to do) a "roller coaster" by soaring from the bottom to the top of a giant wave and down again.

6. "Riding a tube" __is__ (to be) a thrilling trip through the transparent green tunnel of a giant wave.

7. Hawaiian coastlines __have__ (to have) some of the world's best surfing.

8. Banzai Pipeline in Oahu __is__ (to be) a famous surfing break that __has__ (to have) excellent tubes and waves three stories high.

9. Oahu's Sunset Rip, a notorious break, __has__ (to have) several international surfing competitions.

10. For the surfer, wipeouts, flying boards, and sharks __are__ (to be) constant dangers.

11. Yet the sport __has__ (to have) new converts every year.

12. Many say that it __is__ (to be) a spiritual experience.

PART C

Special Singular Constructions

Each of these constructions takes a **singular** verb:

Special Singular Constructions		
either (of) . . .	each (of) . . .	every one (of) . . .
neither (of) . . .	one (of) . . .	which one (of) . . .

CHAPTER 27 Present Tense (Agreement)

> 1. *Neither* of the birds *has* feathers yet.
> 2. *Each* of the solutions *presents* difficulties.

- In sentence 1, *neither* means *neither one*. *Neither* is a singular subject and requires the singular verb *has*.
- In sentence 2, *each* means *each one*. *Each* is a singular subject and requires the singular verb *presents*.

However, an exception to this general rule is the case in which two subjects are joined by *(n)either . . . (n)or . . . .* Here, the verb agrees with the subject closer to it:

> 3. Neither the teacher nor the *pupils want* the semester shortened.
> 4. Either the graphs or the *map has* to be changed.

- In sentence 3, *pupils* is the subject closer to the verb. The plural subject *pupils* takes the verb *want*.
- In sentence 4, *map* is the subject closer to the verb. The singular subject *map* takes the verb *has*.

PRACTICE 4 Underline the subject and circle the correct verb in each sentence.

1. Each of these ferns (**needs**, need) special care.
2. One of the customers always (forget, **forgets**) his or her umbrella.
3. Which one of the flights (**goes**, go) nonstop to Dallas?
4. Every one of those cameras (**costs**, cost) more than I can afford.
5. Either you or Doris (**is**, are) correct.
6. Either of these computer diskettes (contain, **contains**) the information you need.
7. Do you really believe that one of these oysters (**holds**, hold) a pearl?
8. Neither of the twins (**resembles**, resemble) his parents.
9. One of the scientists (**believes**, believe) he can cure baldness.
10. Each of these inventions (**has**, have) an effect on how we spend our leisure time.

PART D

Separation of Subject and Verb

Sometimes a phrase or a clause separates the subject from the verb. First, look for the subject; then make sure that the verb agrees with the subject.

> 1. The economist's *ideas* on this matter *seem* well thought out.
> 2. *Radios* that were made in the 1930s *are* now collectors' items.

- In sentence 1, the *ideas* are well thought out. The prepositional phrase *on this matter* separates the subject *ideas* from the verb *seem*.*
- In sentence 2, *radios* are now collectors' items. The relative clause *that were made in the 1930s* separates the subject *radios* from the verb *are*.

PRACTICE 5 Read each sentence carefully for meaning. Cross out any phrase or clause that separates the subject from the verb. Underline the subject and circle the correct verb.

1. The plums in that bowl (tastes, taste) sweet.
2. The instructions on the package (is, are) in French and Japanese.
3. Our new community center, which has a swimming pool and tennis courts, (keeps, keep) everyone happy.
4. The lampshades that are made of stained glass (looks, look) beautiful at night.
5. All the CD players on that shelf (comes, come) with a remote control.
6. A movie that lasts more than three hours usually (puts, put) me to sleep.
7. The man with the dark sunglasses (looks, look) like a typical movie villain.
8. The two nurses who check blood pressure (enjoys, enjoy) chatting with the patients.
9. The function of these metal racks (remains, remain) a mystery to me.
10. The lizard on the wall (has, have) only three legs.

---

*For more work on prepositional phrases, see Chapter 24, "The Simple Sentence," Part B.

CHAPTER 27 Present Tense (Agreement) 381

PART E

Sentences Beginning with *There* and *Here*

In sentences that begin with **there** or **here,** the subject usually follows the verb:

> 1. There *seem* to be two *flies* in my soup.
> 2. Here *is* my *prediction* for the coming year.

- In sentence 1, the plural subject *flies* takes the plural verb *seem.*
- In sentence 2, the singular subject *prediction* takes the singular verb *is.*

You can often determine what the verb should be by reversing the word order: *two flies seem . . .* or *my prediction is. . . .*

PRACTICE 6 Underline the subject and circle the correct verb in each sentence.

1. There (goes, go) Tom Hanks.
2. There (is, are) only a few seconds left in the game.
3. Here (is, are) a terrific way to save money—make a budget and stick to it!
4. There (has, have) been robberies in the neighborhood lately.
5. Here (is, are) the plantains you ordered.
6. Here (comes, come) Jay, the television talk-show host.
7. There (is, are) no direct route to Black Creek from here.
8. There (seems, seem) to be something wrong with the doorbell.
9. Here (is, are) the teapot and sugar bowl I've been looking for.
10. There (is, are) six reporters in the hall waiting for an interview.

PART F

Agreement in Questions

In questions, the subject usually follows the verb:

> 1. What *is* the *secret* of your success?
> 2. Where *are* the *copies* of the review?

- In sentence 1, the subject *secret* takes the singular verb *is*.
- In sentence 2, the subject *copies* takes the plural verb *are*.

You can often determine what the verb should be by reversing the word order: *the secret of your success is* . . . or *the copies are*. . . .

PRACTICE 7 Underline the subject and circle the correct verb in each sentence.

1. How (<u>does</u>, do) the combustion engine actually work?
2. Why (is, <u>are</u>) Robert and Charity so suspicious?
3. Where (is, <u>are</u>) the new suitcases?
4. Which tour guide (have, <u>has</u>) a pair of binoculars?
5. (<u>Are</u>, Is) Dianne and Bill starting a mail-order business?
6. What (<u>seems</u>, seem) to be the problem here?
7. Why (is, <u>are</u>) those boxes stacked in the corner?
8. (<u>Is</u>, Are) the mattress factory really going to close in June?
9. How (does, <u>do</u>) you explain that strange footprint?
10. Who (is, <u>are</u>) those people on the fire escape?

PART G

Agreement in Relative Clauses

A **relative clause** is a subordinate clause that begins with *who*, *which*, or *that*. The verb in the relative clause must agree with the antecedent of the *who*, *which*, or *that*.*

> 1. People *who have a good sense of humor* make good neighbors.
> 2. Be careful of a scheme *that promises you a lot of money fast*.

- In sentence 1, the antecedent of *who* is *people*. *People* should take the plural verb *have*.
- In sentence 2, the antecedent of *that* is *scheme*. *Scheme* takes the singular verb *promises*.

---
* For more work on relative clauses, see Chapter 21, "Revising for Sentence Variety," Part D.

PRACTICE 8

Underline the antecedent of the *who, which,* or *that*. Then circle the correct verb.

1. Most patients prefer doctors who (spends, <u>spend</u>) time talking with them.
2. The gnarled oak that (<u>shades</u>, shade) the garden is my favorite tree.
3. Laptop computers, which (has, <u>have</u>) become very popular recently, are still fairly expensive.
4. My neighbor, who (<u>swims</u>, swim) at least one hour a day, is seventy years old.
5. Planning ahead, which (<u>saves</u>, save) hours of wasted time, is a good way to manage time effectively.
6. Employers often appreciate employees who (asks, <u>ask</u>) intelligent questions.
7. This air conditioner, which now (<u>costs</u>, cost) $800, rarely breaks down.
8. Everyone admires her because she is someone who always (<u>sees</u>, see) the bright side of a bad situation.
9. He is the man who (<u>creates</u>, create) furniture from scraps of walnut, cherry, and birch.
10. Foods that (contains, <u>contain</u>) artificial sweeteners may be hazardous to your health.

PRACTICE 9 REVIEW

Proofread the following essay for verb agreement errors. Correct any errors by writing above the lines.

Chimp Smarts

(1) Chimpanzees sometimes seem uncannily human, especially in their use of tools and language. (2) Neither the gorilla nor the orangutan, both close relatives of the chimp, exhibit such behavior.

(3) Chimps employs a number of tools in their everyday lives. (4) They dine by inserting sticks into insect nests and then licking their utensils clean. (5) Each of these intelligent animals also crack fruit and nuts with stones. (6) What's more, chimpanzees creates their own tools. (7) They make their eating sticks by cleaning

leaves from branches. (8) They even attaches small sticks together to make longer rods for getting at hard-to-reach insects. (9) Some of the other tools chimps make is fly-whisks, sponges of chewed bark, and leaf-rags to clean themselves with. (10) Scientists on safari has observed infant chimps imitating their parents' use of these tools.

(11) Recent experiments indicate that chimpanzees probably also understands language though they lack the physical ability to speak. (12) There are little doubt that they can comprehend individual words. (13) Using sign language and keyboards, some chimps in captivity use nearly 200 words. (14) This vocabulary include nouns, verbs, and prepositions. (15) Hunger and affection is needs that they have expressed by punching keyboard symbols. (16) Do chimps has the ability to string words into sentences? (17) Intriguingly, one chimp named Lucy has shown that she understand the difference between such statements as "Roger tickles Lucy" and "Lucy tickles Roger."

(18) Scientists still argue about just how much language a chimpanzee truly comprehend. (19) However, no one who have watched them closely doubt the intelligence of these remarkable beings.

Exploring Online

http://webster.commnet.edu/cgi-shl/quiz.pl/agreement_add3.htm
Choose the verb that agrees with each subject.

http://grammar.uoregon.edu/agreement/agreequiz1/lquizagree.html
Verb practice with pop-up answers.

CHAPTER 28　Past Tense

PART A　Regular Verbs in the Past Tense
PART B　Irregular Verbs in the Past Tense
PART C　A Troublesome Verb in the Past Tense: *To Be*
PART D　Troublesome Pairs in the Past Tense: *Can/Could, Will/Would*

Part A

Regular Verbs in the Past Tense

Regular verbs in the past tense take an *-ed* or *-d* ending:

1. The captain *hoisted* the flag.
2. They *purchased* a flat screen TV yesterday.
3. We *deposited* a quarter in the meter.

- *Hoisted, purchased,* and *deposited* are regular verbs in the past tense.
- Each verb ends in *-ed* or *-d*.

PRACTICE 1　Fill in the past tense of the regular verbs in parentheses.*

1. I _____ (raise) my arms in a move called "embrace the tiger."
2. Then I _____ (shift) my weight and _____ (walk) forward on my right foot to start the next move, "stroke the peacock's tail."

---

*If you have questions about spelling, see Chapter 38, "Spelling," Parts D, E, and F.

3. After stepping forward with my left foot, I _____ (reach) out my left hand and _____ (pull) back my right arm.

4. Unfortunately, my muscles _____ (clench), which _____ (result) in an awkward movement.

5. Talking calmly to myself, I _____ (relax) and _____ (start) again.

6. Then I _____ (move) fluidly to a new position.

7. These positions, which connect and flow into each other, _____ (evolve) over the centuries into what we now call tai chi.

8. Though tai chi _____ (develop) from the martial arts, today it emphasizes relaxation and stress reduction in addition to flexibility and fitness.

9. I chose to practice tai chi because it _____ (require) no special equipment, _____ (challenge) me physically, and _____ (promise) many benefits.

10. Tai chi is excellent exercise for all ages; a recent study _____ (show) that when older people _____ (perform) it regularly, they _____ (reduce) the likelihood of falling—and thus breaking bones—by almost 25 percent.

Part B

Irregular Verbs in the Past Tense

Irregular verbs do not take an *-ed* or *-d* ending in the past but change internally:

> 1. I *wrote* that letter in ten minutes.
> 2. Although the orange cat *fell* from a high branch, she escaped unharmed.
> 3. The play *began* on time but ended fairly late.

- *Wrote* is the past tense of *write*.
- *Fell* is the past tense of *fall*.
- *Began* is the past tense of *begin*.

Here is a partial list of irregular verbs:

Reference Chart
Irregular Verbs in the Past Tense

Simple Form	Past Tense	Simple Form	Past Tense
be	was, were	leave	left
become	became	let	let
begin	began	lie	lay
blow	blew	lose	lost
break	broke	make	made
bring	brought	mean	meant
build	built	meet	met
buy	bought	pay	paid
catch	caught	put	put
choose	chose	quit	quit
come	came	read	read
cut	cut	ride	rode
deal	dealt	rise	rose
dig	dug	run	ran
dive	dove (dived)	say	said
do	did	see	saw
draw	drew	seek	sought
drink	drank	sell	sold
drive	drove	send	sent
eat	ate	shake	shook
fall	fell	shine	shone (shined)
feed	fed	sing	sang
feel	felt	sit	sat
fight	fought	sleep	slept
find	found	speak	spoke
fly	flew	spend	spent
forbid	forbade	split	split
forget	forgot	spring	sprang
forgive	forgave	stand	stood
freeze	froze	steal	stole
get	got	stink	stank
give	gave	swim	swam
go	went	take	took
grow	grew	teach	taught
have	had	tear	tore
hear	heard	tell	told
hide	hid	think	thought
hold	held	throw	threw
hurt	hurt	understand	understood
keep	kept	wake	woke (waked)
know	knew	wear	wore
lay	laid	win	won
lead	led	write	wrote

PRACTICE 2 Fill in the past tense of the regular and irregular verbs in parentheses. If you are not sure of the past tense, use the chart on page 387. Do not guess.

Entrepreneurs Did It Their Way

(1) Beth Cross and Pam Parker _____ (work) in the same company. (2) After they _____ (become) friends, they _____ (discover) that they both _____ (love) to ride horses. (3) Both women also _____ (think) that their riding boots were extremely uncomfortable. (4) Eventually, they _____ (leave) their jobs, _____ (design) a new boot, and _____ (begin) their own company. (5) The boots _____ (catch) on, sales _____ (double) every year for the first four years, and they now sell boots in more than 2,000 outlets in the United States, Canada, Great Britain, and Australia.

(6) Cross and Parker _____ (go) from being employees to being entrepreneurs, individuals who start their own business. (7) These risk takers _____ (choose) to leave their job security so that they could try their hand at producing a new product.

(8) Duyen Le is a different type of entrepreneur, one who _____ (follow) his dream without ever joining a big company. (9) Le _____ (immigrate) to the United States from Vietnam. (10) Although he _____ (expect) to go into computer science, instead he _____ (open) a tiny Vietnamese restaurant in his neighborhood. (11) For years, he _____ (get) up at five each morning to search for the spices and vegetables he couldn't afford to have delivered.

(12) When customers almost _____ (pour) in, a rival _____ (challenge) him by opening a new Vietnamese restaurant around the corner. (13) Le simply _____ (buy) out his competitor. (14) Encouraged by his large number of non-Vietnamese customers, he very successfully _____ (start) many restaurants, first in local Boston neighborhoods and then in upscale areas of the city.

(15) Not every entrepreneur _____ (want) to become one. (16) However, when companies _____ (downsize) in recent years, thousands of employees _____ (lose) their jobs. (17) They _____ (have) to find new positions—or become entrepreneurs. (18) As it _____ (happen), thousands upon thousands of ordinary workers _____ (find) greater satisfaction—and sometimes _____ (make) far more money—when they _____ (do) it their way!

Part C

A Troublesome Verb in the Past Tense: *To Be*

To be is the only verb that in the past tense has different forms for different persons. Be careful of subject-verb agreement:

Reference Chart—*To Be* Past Tense

	Singular		Plural	
	If the subject is	the verb is	If the subject is	the verb is
1st person:	I	was	we	were
2nd person:	you	were	you	were
3rd person:	he, she, it	was	they	were

- Note that the first person singular form and the third person singular form are the same—*was*.

Be especially careful of agreement when adding *not* to *was* or *were* to make a contraction:

was + not = wasn't
were + not = weren't

UNIT 6 Reviewing the Basics

PRACTICE 3 Circle the correct form of the verb *to be* in the past tense. Do not guess. If you are not sure of the correct form, use the chart on page 389.

1. Ophrah Winfrey (was, were) always an avid reader.

2. In fact, books (was, were) sometimes her only comfort during her difficult childhood and painful adolescence.

3. When her producers (was, were) considering a TV book club, the world's most popular talk show host (was, were) sure she could get the whole country reading.

4. Her first book club selection (was, were) *The Deep End of the Ocean* by Jacquelyn Mitchard, the story of a kidnaped child.

5. The public's rush to buy books (wasn't, weren't) anticipated.

6. Mitchard's publishers (was, were) astonished to have to reprint the book nearly twenty times; all in all, 900,000 hardcovers and over 2 million paperbacks (was, were) sold.

7. Winfrey's next choice (was, were) *Song of Solomon* by Toni Morrison, a classic novel that (was, were) almost twenty years old.

8. About 300,000 copies (was, were) in print, but after Winfrey chose it, that figure (was, were) over 1,400,000.

9. Every book club pick (was, were) a huge success, and even people who didn't read much found they (was, were) eagerly awaiting Winfrey's next selection.

10. Between 1996 and 2002, the club's official close, millions (was, were) inspired to love reading, and many Winfrey-based book discussion groups continue to this day.

Part C

Troublesome Pairs in the Past Tense: Can/Could, Will/Would

Use **could** as the past tense of **can**.

> 1. Maria is extraordinary because she *can* remember what happened to her when she was three years old.
> 2. When I was in high school, I *could* do two sit-ups in an hour.

- In sentence 1, *can* shows the action is in the present.
- In sentence 2, *could* shows the action occurred in the past.

CHAPTER 28 Past Tense 391

PRACTICE 4 Fill in either the present tense *can* or the past tense *could*.

1. Tom is so talented that he __can__ play most music on the piano by ear.

2. He __can__ leave the hospital as soon as he feels stronger.

3. Last week we __could__ not find fresh strawberries.

4. When we were in Spain last summer, we __can__ see all of Madrid from our hotel balcony.

5. As a child, I __could__ perform easily in public, but I __can__ no longer do it.

6. Anything you __can__ do, he __could__ do better.

7. Nobody __could__ find the guard after the robbery yesterday.

6. These days, Fred __can__ usually predict the weather from the condition of his bunions.

Use **would** as the past tense of **will.**

> 3. Roberta says that she *will* arrive with her camera in ten minutes.
> 4. Roberta said that she *would* arrive with her camera in ten minutes.

- In sentence 3, *will* points to the future from the present.
- In sentence 4, *would* points to the future from the past.

PRACTICE 5 Fill in either the present tense *will* or the past tense *would*.

1. Sean expected that he __would__ arrive at midnight.

2. Sean expects that he __will__ arrive at midnight.

3. I hope the sale at the used car lot __will__ continue for another week.

4. I hoped the sale at the used car lot __would__ continue for another week.

5. When Benny had time, he __would__ color-code his computer disks.

6. When Benny has time, he __will__ color-code his computer disks.

7. The chefs assure us that the wedding cake __will__ be spectacular.

8. The chefs assured us that the wedding cake __would__ be spectacular.

PRACTICE 6 REVIEW

Proofread the following essay for past tense errors. Then write the correct past tense form above the line.

The Birth of Video Games

(1) With their vivid images, realistic sound effects, and imaginative characters, today's computer games look more like television and movies than like the simple electronic paddle-and-ball game that preceded them. (2) Yet only three decades ago, with the birth of Pong, the home entertainment industry change forever.

(3) As early as 1958, Willy Higinbotham, a New York physicist, invented an interactive version of table tennis with which he entertain visitors to his laboratory. (4) He used a 15-inch monitor to display his game, but he never patent it. (5) Three years later, students at MIT created another interactive game, Spacewar, but it required a powerful and expensive computer that (in those days before microchips) taken up several rooms in a building.

(6) Everything changed with Nolan Bushnell, the father of the video game industry. (7) He seen both Higinbotham's game and Spacewar and believed he could design a computer chip small enough to handle a single video game. (8) Bushnell name his new company Atari, hired some fellow engineers, and go to work. (9) In July 1972, Atari introduce Pong, the first electronic game for the mass market. (10) Little more than a black-and-white TV console with two wheels underneath to control the paddles, Pong became an overnight sensation in arcades and bars across the United States.

(11) People of all ages could play Pong, a simple game in which two players bounced a digital ball back and forth until one player miss. (12) Bushnell knowed that a home version using a television set was possible, but he needed financial backing. (13) Then Sears Roebuck offered to invest if its stores can be the sole distributor. (14) Soon Home Pong sweeped the country and outsold all other items in Sears's 1975 Christmas Catalogue.

(15) Within ten years, Atari grew into a major maker of home video games, including Breakout and Football. (16) The company introduce the joystick, which gave players more precise game control than the old knobs. (17) Ultimately, however, the arrival of the personal computer and strong overseas competition edge Atari out of the market. (18) Companies like Nintendo and Sega sent video game technology to new heights. (19) Yet Atari's Pong started it all—the humble beginning of a worldwide phenomenon.

Exploring Online

http://webster.commnet.edu/cgi-shl/par2_quiz.pl/irregular_quiz.htm
Type in the verbs; the machine checks you.

http://writesite.cuny.edu/grammar/general/irregverbs/practice.html
Graded practice: Change present tense to past.

CHAPTER 29 The Past Participle

PART A Past Participles of Regular Verbs
PART B Past Participles of Irregular Verbs
PART C Using the Present Perfect Tense
PART D Using the Past Perfect Tense
PART E Using the Passive Voice (*To Be* and the Past Participle)
PART F Using the Past Participle as an Adjective

Part A

Past Participles of Regular Verbs

The **past participle** is the form of the verb that can be combined with helping verbs like *have* and *has* to make verbs of more than one word:

Present Tense	Past Tense	Helping Verb plus Past Participle
1. They *skate*.	1. They *skated*.	1. They *have skated*.
2. Beth *dances*.	2. Beth *danced*.	2. Beth *has danced*.
3. Frank *worries*.	3. Frank *worried*.	3. Frank *has worried*.

- *Skated, danced,* and *worried* are all past participles of regular verbs.
- Note that both the *past tense* and the *past participle* of regular verbs end in *-ed* or *-d*.

PRACTICE 1 The first sentence of each pair that follows contains a regular verb in the past tense. Fill in *have* or *has* plus the past participle of the same verb to complete the second sentence.

1. Vance locked his keys in the car.

   Vance _____ _____ his keys in the car.

2. The carpenters gathered their tools from the littered floor.

   The carpenters _____ _____ their tools from the littered floor.

3. Clearly, you planned your vacation with care.

   Clearly, you _____ _____ your vacation with care.

4. Twice, Dianne and Carol visited the Dominican Republic.

   Twice, Dianne and Carol _____ _____ the Dominican Republic.

5. Detectives discovered the love letters in the garage.

   Detectives _____ _____ the love letters in the garage.

6. Mr. Yosufu carved this chess set out of wood.

   Mr. Yosufu _____ _____ this chess set out of wood.

7. My boss impressed everyone with her ability to read Chinese.

   My boss _____ _____ everyone with her ability to read Chinese.

8. Illness interrupted his work on the film.

   Illness _____ _____ his work on the film.

9. The windshields reflected the glow of the streetlights.

   The windshields _____ _____ the glow of the streetlights.

10. These three women studied with Madame Tebaldi.

    These three women _____ _____ with Madame Tebaldi.

Part B

Past Participles of Irregular Verbs

Most verbs that are irregular in the past tense are also irregular in the past participle, as shown in the box below.

Present Tense	Past Tense	Helping Verb plus Past Participle
1. We *sing*.	1. We *sang*.	1. We *have sung*.
2. Bill *writes*.	2. Bill *wrote*.	2. Bill *has written*.
3. I *think*.	3. I *thought*.	3. I *have thought*.

- Irregular verbs change from present to past to past participle in unusual ways.
- *Sung, written,* and *thought* are all past participles of irregular verbs.
- Note that the past tense and past participle of *think* are the same—*thought*.

Reference Chart
Irregular Verbs, Past and Past Participle

Simple Form	Past Tense	Past Participle
be	was, were	been
become	became	become
begin	began	begun
blow	blew	blown
break	broke	broken
bring	brought	brought
build	built	built
buy	bought	bought
catch	caught	caught
choose	chose	chosen
come	came	come
cut	cut	cut
deal	dealt	dealt
dig	dug	dug
dive	dove (dived)	dived
do	did	done
draw	drew	drawn
drink	drank	drunk
drive	drove	driven
eat	ate	eaten
fall	fell	fallen
feed	fed	fed

(continued)

Reference Chart
Irregular Verbs, Past and Past Participle
(continued)

Simple Form	Past Tense	Past Participle
feel	felt	felt
fight	fought	fought
find	found	found
fly	flew	flown
forbid	forbade	forbidden
forget	forgot	forgotten
forgive	forgave	forgiven
freeze	froze	frozen
get	got	got (gotten)
give	gave	given
go	went	gone
grow	grew	grown
have	had	had
hear	heard	heard
hide	hid	hidden
hold	held	held
hurt	hurt	hurt
keep	kept	kept
know	knew	known
lay	laid	laid
lead	led	led
leave	left	left
let	let	let
lie	lay	lain
lose	lost	lost
make	made	made
mean	meant	meant
meet	met	met
pay	paid	paid
put	put	put
quit	quit	quit
read	read	read
ride	rode	ridden
rise	rose	risen
run	ran	run
say	said	said
see	saw	seen
seek	sought	sought
sell	sold	sold
send	sent	sent
shake	shook	shaken
shine	shone (shined)	shone (shined)
sing	sang	sung
sit	sat	sat
sleep	slept	slept

(continued)

Reference Chart
Irregular Verbs, Past and Past Participle
(continued)

Simple Form	Past Tense	Past Participle
speak	spoke	spoken
spend	spent	spent
split	split	split
spring	sprang	sprung
stand	stood	stood
steal	stole	stolen
stink	stank	stunk
swim	swam	swum
take	took	taken
teach	taught	taught
tear	tore	torn
tell	told	told
think	thought	thought
throw	threw	thrown
understand	understood	understood
wake	woke (waked)	woken (waked)
wear	wore	worn
win	won	won
write	wrote	written

PRACTICE 2 The first sentence of each pair that follows contains an irregular verb in the past tense. Fill in *have* or *has* plus the past participle of the same verb to complete the second sentence.

1. Sean took plenty of time buying the groceries.

    Sean __has__ __taken__ plenty of time buying the groceries.

2. We sent our latest budget to the mayor.

    We __have__ __sent__ our latest budget to the mayor.

3. My daughter hid her diary.

    My daughter __has__ __hidden__ her diary.

4. The jockey rode all day in the hot sun.

    The jockey __has__ __ridden__ all day in the hot sun.

5. Hershey, Pennsylvania, became a great tourist attraction.

    Hershey, Pennsylvania, __has__ __become__ a great tourist attraction.

6. The company's managers knew about these hazards for two years.

   The company's managers __have__ __known__ about these hazards for two years.

7. Carrie floated down the river on an inner tube.

   Carrie __has__ __floated__ down the river on an inner tube.

8. At last, our team won the bowling tournament.

   At last, our team __has__ __won__ the bowling tournament.

9. Larry and Marsha broke their long silence.

   Larry and Marsha __has__ __broken__ their long silence.

10. Science fiction films were very popular this past year.

    Science fiction films __have__ __been__ very popular this past year.

PRACTICE 3 Complete each sentence by filling in *have* or *has* plus the past participle of the verb in parentheses. Some verbs are regular, some irregular.

1. Recently, soccer __has__ __gained__ (gain) in popularity in the United States.

2. Traditionally, most North Americans _____ _____ (consider) soccer much less exciting than basketball, football, or hockey.

3. Moreover, many North American players _____ _____ (find) it very difficult to compete at the highest levels of the game.

4. However, Canadian and U.S. interest in soccer _____ _____ (grow) ever since the 1994 World Cup, which was held in the United States.

5. Sports fans _____ _____ (see) the enormous enthusiasm and passionate emotion that soccer arouses in such countries as Argentina, Brazil, Italy, and Portugal.

6. Unexpected victories _____ _____ (add) even more excitement to the game, like France's defeat of Brazil in the 1998 World Cup.

7. The United States also _____ _____ (demonstrate) that it is able to win games in the biggest soccer competition in the world.

8. By advancing to the quarterfinals of the 2002 World Cup, the American soccer team _____ _____ (win) new respect worldwide.

9. However, Brazil _____ _____ (show) once again that it is soccer's international superstar.

10. Attention now _____ _____ (turn) to the 2006 World Cup competition, which should be exciting because Germany will host.

Part C

Using the Present Perfect Tense

The **present perfect tense** is composed of the present tense of *to have* plus the past participle. The present perfect tense shows that an action has begun in the past and is continuing into the present.

> 1. Past tense: Beatrice *taught* English for ten years.
> 2. Present perfect tense: Beatrice *has taught* English for ten years.

- In sentence 1, Beatrice *taught* English in the past, but she no longer teaches it. Note the use of the simple past tense, *taught*.

- In sentence 2, Beatrice *has taught* for ten years and is still teaching English *now*. *Has taught* implies that the action is continuing.

PRACTICE 4 Read these sentences carefully for meaning. Then circle the correct verb—either the **past tense** or the **present perfect tense.**

1. He (directed, has directed) the theater group for many years now.

2. Emilio lifted the rug and (has swept, swept) the dust under it.

3. She (went, has gone) to a poetry slam last night.

4. For the past four years, I (took, have taken) art classes in the summer.

5. We (talked, have talked) about the problem of your lateness for three days; it's time for you to do something about it.

6. While he was in Japan, he (took, have taken) many photographs of shrines.

7. She (won, has won) that contest ten years ago.

8. The boxers (fought, have fought) for an hour, and they look very tired.

9. He (applied, has applied) to three colleges and attended the one with the best sociology department.

10. The auto mechanics (had, have had) a radio show together for five years and are now extremely popular.

Part D

Using the Past Perfect Tense

The **past perfect tense** is composed of the past tense of *to have* plus the past participle. The past perfect tense shows that an action occurred further back in the past than other past action.

> 1. Past tense: Rhonda *left* for the movies.
> 2. Past perfect tense: Rhonda *had* already *left* for the movies by the time we *arrived*.

- In sentence 1, *left* is the simple past.
- In sentence 2, the past perfect *had left* shows that this action occurred even before another action in the past, *arrived*.

PRACTICE 5 Read these sentences carefully for meaning. Then circle the correct verb—either the **past tense** or the **past perfect tense**.

1. Tony came to the office with a cane last week because he (sprained, had sprained) his ankle a month ago.

2. As Janice (piled, had piled) the apples into a pyramid, she thought, "I should become an architect."

3. Juan (finished, had finished) his gardening by the time I (drove, had driven) up in my new convertible.

4. The man nervously (looked, had looked) at his watch and then walked a bit faster.

5. Roberto told us that he (decided, had decided) to enlist in the Marines.

6. The caller asked whether we (received, had received) our free toaster yet.

7. Last week he told me that he (forgot, had forgotten) to mail the rent check.

8. As the curtain came down, everyone (rose, had risen) and applauded the Brazilian dance troupe.

9. Scott (closed, had closed) his books and went to the movies.

10. The prosecutor proved that the defendant was lying; until then I (believed, had believed) he was innocent.

Part E

Using the Passive Voice (*To Be* and the Past Participle)

The **passive voice** is composed of the past participle with some form of *to be* (*am, is, are, was, were, has been, have been,* or *had been*). In the passive voice, the subject does not act but is *acted upon.*

Compare the passive voice with the active voice in the following pairs of sentences.

> 1. Passive voice: This newspaper *is written* by journalism students.
> 2. Active voice: Journalism students *write* this newspaper.
> 3. Passive voice: My garden *was devoured* by rabbits.
> 4. Active voice: Rabbits *devoured* my garden.

- In sentence 1, the subject, *this newspaper,* is passive; it is acted upon. In sentence 2, the subject, *students,* is active; it performs the action.
- Note the difference between the passive verb *is written* and the active verb *write.*
- However, both verbs (*is written* and *write*) are in the *present tense.*
- The verbs in sentences 3 and 4 are both in the *past tense: was devoured* (passive) and *devoured* (active).

Use the passive voice sparingly. Write in the passive voice when you want to emphasize the receiver of the action rather than the doer.

PRACTICE 6 Fill in the correct **past participle** form of the verb in parentheses to form the passive voice. If you are not sure, check the chart on pages 396–398.

1. The barn was _____ (build) by friends of the family.

2. Who was _____ (choose) to represent us at the union meeting?

3. These ruby slippers were _____ (give) to me by my grandmother.

4. These jeans are _____ (sell) in three sizes.

5. On their weekend camping trip, Sheila and Una were constantly _____ (bite) by mosquitoes and gnats.

6. It was _____ (decide) that Bill would work the night shift.

7. The getaway car is always _____ (drive) by a man in a gray fedora.

8. Her articles have been _____ (publish) in the *Texas Monthly.*

9. Harold was _____ (see) sneaking out the back door.

10. A faint inscription is _____ (etch) on the back of the old gold watch.

CHAPTER 29 The Past Participle

PRACTICE 7 Rewrite each sentence, changing the verb into the **passive** voice. Make all necessary verb and subject changes. Be sure to keep the sentence in the original tense.

Example | My father wore this silk hat.
| This silk hat was worn by my father.

1. The goalie blocked the shot.

   _____

2. The lifeguard taught us to swim.

   _____

3. The usher warned the noisy group.

   _____

4. Her rudeness hurt her reputation.

   _____

5. The campers folded up the tent.

   _____

6. The judges declared the match a draw.

   _____

7. The conductor punched my ticket full of holes.

   _____

8. The interviewer asked too many personal questions.

   _____

Part F

Using the Past Participle as an Adjective

The **past participle** form of the verb can be used as an **adjective** after a linking verb:

> 1. The window is *broken*.

- The adjective *broken* describes the subject *window*.

The **past participle** form of the verb can sometimes be used as an adjective before a noun or a pronoun.

> 2. This *fried* chicken tastes wonderful.

- The adjective *fried* describes the noun *chicken*.

PRACTICE 8 Use the past participle form of the verb in parentheses as an adjective in each sentence.

1. My _____ (use) laptop was a great bargain at only $200.

2. Bob is highly _____ (qualify) to install a water heater.

3. The _____ (air-condition) room was making everyone shiver.

4. The newly _____ (rise) cinnamon bread smelled wonderful.

5. Were you _____ (surprise) to hear about my raise?

6. He feels _____ (depress) on rainy days.

7. She knows the power of the _____ (write) word.

8. My gym teacher seems _____ (prejudice) against short people.

9. The _____ (embarrass) child pulled her jacket over her head.

10. We ordered _____ (toss) salad, _____ (broil) salmon, _____ (mash) potatoes, and _____ (bake) apple rings.

PRACTICE 9 Proofread the following paragraph for errors in past participles used as adjectives. Correct the errors by writing above the lines.

(1) To experience the food of another culture is to appreciate that culture in new ways. (2) A fine example is the traditional Chinese wedding banquet, where each beautiful dish is chosen, prepare, and presented to carry a promise for the couple's future. (3) Carefully season shark's fin soup opens the feast; this rare and expensive treat signifies health and long life to both family lines. (4) Each table receives its own glazed Peking duck to indicate the couple's fidelity. (5) In Chinese tradition, chicken represents the phoenix, a magic bird that rises from the ashes, and lobster represents the dragon. (6) Often combine and bake in a single dish,

these two foods mark the peaceful union of two families. (7) Because the Chinese word for fish sounds like "abundance," a whole steamed fish is offered to the newly marry couple—a wish for prosperity. (8) At the end of the meal, satisfy guests enjoy dessert buns filled with lotus seeds, promising fertility and future children. (9) It should come as no surprise that an old-fashion Chinese banquet can last an entire day.

PRACTICE 10 REVIEW

Proofread the following essay for past participle errors. Correct the errors by writing above the lines.

Crazy as They Want to Be

(1) *Saturday Night Live*, the wacky late-night comedy program, has entertain generations of television viewers since 1975. (2) The show has took aim at presidents, self-help experts, Olympic athletes, and current issues—as when concerns about the environment inspired a Global Warming Christmas Special. (3) The dream job of every aspiring comedian, *SNL* is credit with launching many careers. (4) Eddie Murphy, Billy Crystal, Damon Wayans, Mike Meyers, and Chris Rock are just a few of the celebrate comedians who were introduced to the public in outrageous *SNL* sketches like the Coneheads, Mr. Robinson's Neighborhood, and Wayne's World.

(5) Although men have outnumber women throughout the show's history, *SNL* recently has presented more, funny females. (6) Cheri Oteri is one of the comics whose creative energy has electrify the aging program. (7) She has made her mark with dead-on impressions of Barbara Walters, Mariah Carey, and Judge Judy. (8) Perhaps Oteri's best-knowed character is the clumsy cheerleader Arianna, who fails to make the squad but shows up optimistically at every team event. (9) Another talented comic, Molly Shannon, is recognize for her portrayal of Catholic schoolgirl Mary Katherine Gallagher, a boy-craze adolescent who falls

through walls. (10) Nominate for an Emmy, Shannon was ask to take Mary Katherine onto the big screen in *Superstar*.

(11) *Saturday Night Live* continues to update its image. (12) In 2001, Tina Fey became the first female head writer in the show's history. (13) With her trademark dark-rimmed glasses and navy suit, the bookish brunette has became hugely popular in her role as a cheery, poison-tongue anchorwoman opposite Jimmy Fallon on *SNL*'s fake news. (14) When Tom Cruise and Nicole Kidman were divorce, Fey wisecracked that their children would be returned to the studio's prop room. (15) With comics like Fey, *SNL* might have attracted a new generation of viewers.

Exploring Online

http://online.ohlone.cc.ca.us/~mlieu/participles/review2.htm
Graded past participle crossword puzzle; try it.

CHAPTER 30

Nouns

PART A Defining Singular and Plural
PART B Signal Words: Singular and Plural
PART C Signal Words with *Of*

Part A

Defining Singular and Plural

Nouns are words that refer to people, places, or things. They can be either singular or plural. **Singular** means one. **Plural** means more than one.

Singular	Plural
the glass	glasses
a lamp	lamps
a lesson	lessons

- As you can see, nouns usually add *-s* or *-es* to form the plural.

Some nouns form their plurals in other ways. Here are a few examples:

Singular	Plural
child	children
crisis	crises
criterion	criteria
foot	feet
goose	geese
man	men
medium	media
memorandum	memoranda (memorandums)
phenomenon	phenomena
tooth	teeth
woman	women

407

These nouns ending in -f or -fe change endings to -ves in the plural:

Singular	Plural
half	halves
knife	knives
life	lives
scarf	scarves
shelf	shelves
wife	wives
wolf	wolves

Hyphenated nouns form plurals by adding -s or -es to the main word:

Singular	Plural
brother-in-law	brothers-in-law
maid-of-honor	maids-of-honor
passer-by	passers-by

Other nouns do not change at all to form the plural; here are a few examples:

Singular	Plural
deer	deer
equipment	equipment
fish	fish
merchandise	merchandise

If you are unsure about the plural of a noun, check a dictionary. For example, if you look up the noun *woman* in the dictionary, you may see an entry like this:

woman, women

The first word listed, *woman,* is the singular form of the noun; the second word, *women,* is the plural.

Some dictionaries list the plural form of a noun only if the plural is unusual. If no plural is listed, that noun probably adds -s or -es.* *Remember:* Do not add an -s to words that form plurals by changing an internal letter. For example, the plural of *man* is *men,* not *mens;* the plural of *woman* is *women,* not *womens;* the plural of *foot* is *feet,* not *feets.*

---

* For more work on spelling plurals, see Chapter 38, "Spelling," Part H.

PRACTICE 1   Make these singular nouns plural.

1. man _____
2. half _____
3. foot _____
4. son-in-law _____
5. moose _____
6. life _____
7. tooth _____
8. medium _____
9. woman _____
10. crisis _____
11. passer-by _____
12. criterion _____
13. shelf _____
14. mouse _____
15. child _____
16. father-in-law _____
17. knife _____
18. deer _____
19. secretary _____
20. goose _____

Part B
Signal Words: Singular and Plural

A **signal word** tells you whether a singular or a plural noun usually follows.

These signal words tell you that a singular noun usually follows:

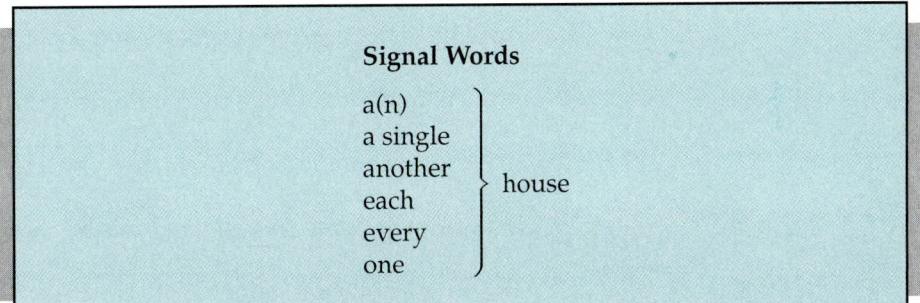

These signal words tell you that a plural noun usually follows:

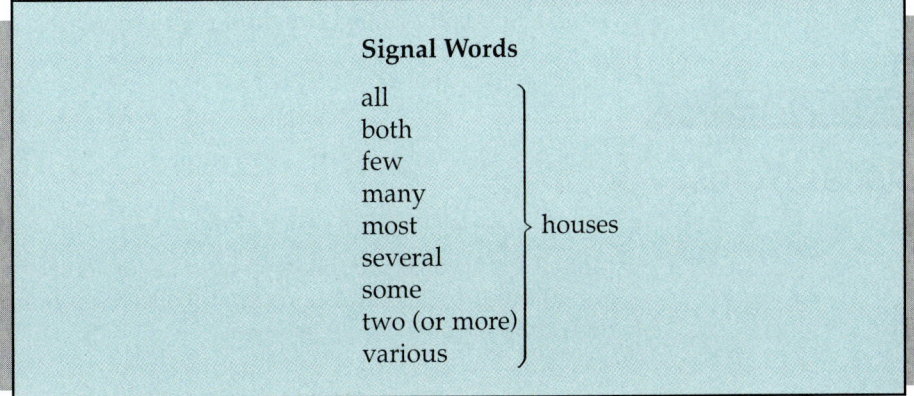

PRACTICE 2 Some of the following sentences contain incorrect singulars and plurals. Correct the errors. Put a C after correct sentences.

1. By three years old, most children have firm ideas about how men and woman should behave.
2. Children develop their concepts about gender differences through *conditioning,* a process of learning that reinforces certain behaviors while discouraging other.
3. Conditioning occurs through the messages delivered by parents, peer, and the media.
4. Research shows that parents begin to treat their childrens differently as early as 24 hour after birth.
5. Fathers hold their infant girls gently and speak softly to them, but they bounce baby boys, playing "airplane" and tickling their feets.
6. Mothers, too, condition gender roles; they reward little girls who play quietly and help with chores, while excusing the loud play of boys as natural.
7. Once in school, children quickly learn that certain kinds of make-believe—such as playing house or having tea parties—are girls' games; boys are encouraged by their friend to crash cars and shoot toy guns.
8. While the boundaries are less rigid for girls at this stage, most boys who show any interest in feminine clothes or activity will be mocked by their peers.
9. Many TV ad play a key conditioning role by showing boys involved in sports or jobs and girls playing indoors with toy ovens or dolls.
10. By limiting choices for most child, we ignore many talents and interest that might greatly enhance their lifes and society as a whole.

Part C

Signal Words with *Of*

Many signal words are followed by *of* . . . or *of the.* . . . Usually, these signal words are followed by a **plural** noun (or a collective noun) because they really refer to one or more from a larger group.

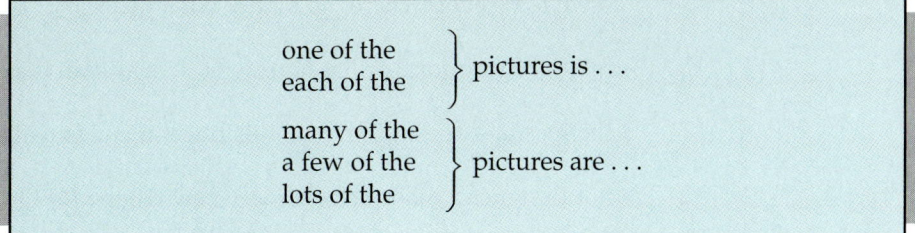

- *Be careful:* The signal words *one of the* and *each of the* are followed by a **plural** noun, but the verb is **singular** because only the signal word (*one* or *each*) is the real subject.*

> *One* of the coats *is* on sale.
>
> *Each* of the flowers *smells* sweet.

PRACTICE 3 Fill in your own nouns in the following sentences. Use a different noun in each sentence.

1. Since Jacob wrote each of his ─────── with care, the A's came as no surprise.

2. You are one of the few ─────── I know who can listen to the radio and watch television at the same time.

3. Naomi liked several of the new ─────── but remained faithful to her long-time favorites.

4. Many of the ─────── wore Walkmans.

5. Determined to win the Salesperson of the Year award, Clyde called on all his

   ─────── two or three times a month.

6. One of the ─────── was wearing a down jacket.

PRACTICE 4 REVIEW

Proofread the following essay for errors in singular and plural nouns. Correct the errors above the lines.

The Language of Color, the Color of Cash

(1) Have you ever wondered why, every year, the merchandises in different stores seems strangely color-coordinated? (2) One year, lavender man's shirts

───────
*For more work on this type of construction, see Chapter 27, "Present Tense (Agreement)," Part C.

seem to be everywhere, no matter what the brand. (3) The next year, the hot color might be turquoise or lime green. (4) It is as if all the designer met secretly to pick the season's hues. (5) In fact, this phenomena is real, but it is color-trend experts, not designers, who pick the next new colors. (6) One of the most famous color-trend company is Pantone. (7) Each year, Pantone selects several color palettes for its long list of client—DKNY, Apple Computer, Pottery Barn, Nike, Kitchen Aid, and more.

(8) Pantone is known for its 1757 colors, including 27 shade of white. (9) Chances are that the pale yellow of that kitchen mixer and matching toaster in the store window is a Pantone shade. (10) Those gray and moss green sheet and towels stacked on a department store shelves may well be colors by Pantone. (11) The company's laboratories create and standardize a formula for every shade. (12) Each of the special color that helps sell a brand is kept top-secret. (13) IBM is known as "Big Blue," after its color, mixed from two Pantone shades. (14) Barbie pink is a trademarked Pantone color, and the jewelry store Tiffany is now working with Pantone to trademark the famous robin's egg blue of its bags, box, and medium ads.

(15) At their annual meeting, Pantone's color forecasters consider many criterion. (16) Sand and pale blue are soothing earth tones in times of stress. (17) Red is exciting and daring; yellow is uplifting. (18) During war years, patriotic colors do well, as do traditional colors like colonial blue and burgundy. (19) Color is a language that peoples respond to, whether they are aware of it or not. (20) Pantone is banking on it.

Exploring Online

http://webster.commnet.edu/grammar/quizzes/cross/plurals_gap.htm
Interactive: Check your expertise at making nouns plural.

CHAPTER 31 Pronouns

PART A Defining Pronouns and Antecedents
PART B Making Pronouns and Antecedents Agree
PART C Referring to Antecedents Clearly
PART D Special Problems of Case
PART E Using Pronouns with *-Self* and *-Selves*

Part A

Defining Pronouns and Antecedents

Pronouns take the place of or refer to nouns, other pronouns, or phrases. The word that the pronoun refers to is called the **antecedent** of the pronoun.

1. *Eric* ordered *baked chicken* because *it* is *his* favorite dish.
2. *Simone and Lee* painted *their* room.
3. *I* like *camping in the woods* because *it* gives *me* a chance to be alone with *my* thoughts.

- In sentence 1, *it* refers to the antecedent *baked chicken*, and *his* refers to the antecedent *Eric*.
- In sentence 2, *their* refers to the plural antecedent *Simone and Lee*.
- In sentence 3, *it* refers to the antecedent *camping in the woods*. This antecedent is a whole phrase. *Me* and *my* refer to the pronoun antecedent *I*.

413

PRACTICE 1 In each sentence, a pronoun is circled. Write the pronoun first and then its antecedent, as shown in the example.

Example | Have you ever wondered why we exchange rings in (our) wedding ceremonies?   our   we

1. When a man buys a wedding ring, (he) follows an age-old tradition.
2. Rich Egyptian grooms gave (their) brides gold rings five thousand years ago.
3. To Egyptian couples, the ring represented eternal love; (it) was a circle without beginning or end.
4. By Roman times, gold rings had become more affordable, so ordinary people could also buy (them).
5. Still, many a Roman youth had to scrimp to buy (his) bride a ring.
6. The first bride to slip a diamond ring on (her) finger lived in Venice about five hundred years ago.
7. The Venetians knew that setting a diamond in a ring was an excellent way of displaying (its) beauty.
8. Nowadays, a man and a woman exchange rings to symbolize the equality of (their) relationship.

Part B

Making Pronouns and Antecedents Agree

A pronoun must *agree* with its antecedent in number and person.*

1. When *Tom* couldn't find *his* pen, *he* asked to borrow mine.
2. The three *sisters* wanted to start *their* own business.

- In sentence 1, *Tom* is the antecedent of *his* and *he*. Since *Tom* is singular and masculine, the pronouns referring to *Tom* are also singular and masculine.

- In sentence 2, *sisters* is the antecedent of *their*. Since *sisters* is plural, the pronoun referring to *sisters* must also be plural.

---

* For more work on pronoun agreement, see Chapter 20, "Revising for Consistency and Parallelism," Part B.

1. Indefinite Pronouns

anybody
anyone
everybody
everyone
nobody
no one
one
somebody
someone

Each of these words is **singular**. Any pronoun that refers to one of them must also be singular: *he, him, his, she,* or *her.*

As you can see from these examples, making pronouns agree with their antecedents is usually easy. However, three special cases can be tricky.

> 3. *Anyone* can quit smoking if *he* or *she* wants to.
>
> 4. *Everybody* should do *his* or *her* best to keep the reception area uncluttered.

■ *Anyone* and *everybody* require the singular pronouns *he, she, his,* and *her.*

In the past, writers used *he* or *him* to refer to both men and women. Now, however, many writers use *he or she, his or her,* or *him or her.* Of course, if *everyone* or *someone* is a woman, use *she* or *her*; if *everyone* or *someone* is a man, use *he* or *him*. For example:

> 5. *Someone* left *her* new dress in a bag on the sofa.
>
> 6. *Everyone* is wearing *his* new tie.

PRACTICE 2 Fill in the correct pronoun and circle its antecedent. Make sure each pronoun agrees in number and person with its antecedent.

1. Anyone can become a good cook if _____ tries.

2. Someone dropped _____ lipstick behind the bookcase.

3. No one in the mixed doubles let _____ guard down for a minute.

4. Everybody wants _____ career to be rewarding.

5. Everyone is entitled to _____ full pension.

6. Mr. Hernow will soon be here, so please get _____ contract ready.

7. One should wear a necktie that doesn't clash with _____ suit.

8. The movie theater was so cold that nobody took off _____ coat.

2. Special Singular Antecedents

each (of) . . .
either (of) . . .
neither (of) . . .   Each of these constructions is **singular.** Any
every one (of) . . .   pronoun that refers to one of them must also be
one (of) . . .   singular.*

> 7. *Neither* of the two men paid for *his* ticket to the wrestling match.
>
> 8. *Each* of the houses has *its* own special charm.

- The subject of sentence 7 is the singular *neither,* not *men;* therefore, the singular masculine pronoun *his* is required.

- The subject of sentence 8 is the singular *each,* not the plural *houses;* therefore, the singular pronoun *its* is required.

PRACTICE 3 Fill in the correct pronoun and circle its antecedent. Make sure each pronoun agrees in number and person with its antecedent.

1. Each of the men wanted to be _____ own boss.

2. One of the saleswomen left _____ sample case on the counter.

3. Every one of the colts has a white star on _____ forehead.

4. Neither of the actors knew _____ lines by heart.

5. Neither of the dentists had _____ office remodeled.

6. Each of these arguments has _____ flaws and _____ strengths.

7. Every one of the jazz bands had _____ own distinctive style.

8. Either of these telephone answering machines will work very well if _____ is properly cared for.

3. Collective Nouns

Collective nouns represent a group of people but are usually considered **singular.** They usually take singular pronouns.

> 9. The *jury* reached *its* decision in three hours.
>
> 10. The debating *team* is well known for *its* fighting spirit.

---

*For more work on prepositional phrases, see Chapter 24, "The Simple Sentence," Part B.

- In sentence 9, *jury* is a collective noun. Although it has several members, the jury acts as a unit—as one. Therefore, the antecedent *jury* takes the singular pronoun *its*.
- In sentence 10, why does the collective noun *team* take the singular pronoun *its*?

Here is a partial list of collective nouns:

Common Collective Nouns

class	family	panel
college	flock	school
committee	government	society
company	group	team
faculty	jury	tribe

PRACTICE 4 Read each sentence carefully for meaning. Circle the antecedent and then fill in the correct pronoun.

1. My family gave me all _____ support when I went back to school.

2. The government should reexamine _____ domestic policy.

3. The college honored _____ oldest graduate with a reception.

4. Eco-Wise has just begun to market a new pollution-free detergent that _____ is proud of.

5. The panel will soon announce _____ recommendations to the hospital.

6. The two teams gave _____ fans a real show.

7. The jury deliberated for six days before _____ reached a verdict.

8. After touring the Great Pyramid, the class headed back to Cairo in _____ air-conditioned bus.

Part C

Referring to Antecedents Clearly

A pronoun must refer *clearly* to its antecedent. Avoid vague, repetitious, or ambiguous pronoun reference.

1. Vague pronoun:	At the box office, *they* said that tickets were no longer available.	
2. Revised:	The cashier at the box office said . . .	
	or	
3. Revised:	At the box office, I was told . . .	

- In sentence 1, who is *they*? *They* does not clearly refer to an antecedent.
- In sentence 2, *the cashier* replaces *they*.
- In sentence 3, the problem is avoided by a change of language.*

4. Repetitious pronoun	In the article, *it* says that Tyrone was a boxer.	
5. Revised:	The article says that . . .	
	or	
6. Revised:	It says that . . .	

- In sentence 4, *it* merely repeats *article*, the antecedent preceding it.
- Use either the pronoun or its antecedent, but not both.

7. Ambiguous pronoun:	Mr. Tedesco told his son that *his* car had a flat tire.
8. Revised:	Mr. Tedesco told his son that the younger man's car had a flat tire.
9. Revised:	Mr. Tedesco told his son Paul that Paul's car had a flat tire.

- In sentence 7, *his* could refer either to Mr. Tedesco or to his son.

PRACTICE 5 Revise the following sentences, removing vague, repetitious, or ambiguous pronoun references. Make the pronoun references clear and specific.

1. In this book it says that hundreds of boys are injured each year copying wrestling stunts they see on TV.

    Revised: _____

    _____

2. On the radio they warned drivers that the Interstate Bridge was closed.

---

*For more work on using exact language, see Chapter 22, "Revising for Language Awareness," Part A.

Revised: _____

_____

3. Sandra told her friend that she shouldn't have turned down the promotion.

    Revised: _____

    _____

4. In North Carolina they raise tobacco.

    Revised: _____

    _____

5. The moving van struck a lamppost; luckily, no one was injured, but it was badly damaged.

    Revised: _____

    _____

6. Professor Grazel told his parrot that he had to stop chewing telephone cords.

    Revised: _____

    _____

7. On the news, it said that more Americans than ever are turning to nontraditional medicine.

    Revised: _____

    _____

8. Keiko is an excellent singer, yet she has never taken a lesson in it.

    Revised: _____

    _____

9. Vandalism was once so out of control at the local high school that they stole sinks and lighting fixtures.

    Revised: _____

    _____

10. Rosalie's mother said she was glad she had decided to become a paralegal.

    Revised: _____

    _____

Part D

Special Problems of Case

Personal pronouns take different forms depending on how they are used in a sentence. Pronouns can be **subjects, objects,** or **possessives.**

Pronouns used as **subjects** are in the **subjective case:**

> 1. *He* and *I* go snowboarding together.
> 2. The peaches were so ripe that *they* fell from the trees.

- *He, I,* and *they* are in the subjective case.

Pronouns that are **objects of verbs** or **prepositions** are in the **objective case.** Pronouns that are **subjects of infinitives** are also in the **objective case:**

> 3. A sudden downpour soaked *her.* (object of verb)
> 4. Please give this card to *him.* (object of preposition)
> 5. We want *them* to leave right now. (subject of infinitive)

- *Her, him,* and *them* are in the objective case.

Pronouns that **show ownership** are in the **possessive case:**

> 6. The carpenters left *their* tools on the windowsill.
> 7. This flower has lost *its* brilliant color.

- *Their* and *its* are in the possessive case.

Pronoun Case Chart

Singular	Subjective	Objective	Possessive
1st person	I	me	my (mine)
2nd person	you	you	your (yours)
3rd person	he	him	his (his)
	she	her	her (hers)
	it	it	its (its)
	who	whom	whose
	whoever	whomever	

(continued)

Pronoun Case Chart
(continued)

Plural	Subjective	Objective	Possessive
1st person	we	us	our (ours)
2nd person	you	you	your (yours)
3rd person	they	them	their (theirs)

Using the correct case is usually fairly simple, but three problems require special care.

1. Case in Compound Constructions

A **compound construction** consists of two nouns, two pronouns, or a noun and a pronoun joined by *and*. Make sure that the pronouns in a compound construction are in the correct case.

> 8. *Serge* and *I* went to the pool together.
> 9. Between *you* and *me*, this party is a bore.

- In sentence 8, *Serge* and *I* are subjects.
- In sentence 9, *you* and *me* are objects of the preposition *between*.

Never use *myself* as a substitute for either *I* or *me* in compound constructions.

PRACTICE 6 Determine the case required by each sentence, and circle the correct pronoun.

1. (He, Him) and Harriet plan to enroll in the police academy.
2. A snowdrift stood between (I, me) and the subway entrance.
3. Tony used the software and then returned it to Barbara and (I, me, myself).
4. The reporter's questions caught June and (we, us) off guard.
5. By noon, Julio and (he, him) had already cleaned the garage and mowed the lawn.
6. These charts helped (she, her) and (I, me) with our statistics homework.
7. Professor Woo gave Diane and (she, her) extra time to finish the geology final.
8. Between you and (I, me), I have always preferred country music.

2. Case in Comparisons

Pronouns that complete **comparisons** may be in the **subjective, objective,** or **possessive** case:

> 10. His son is as stubborn as *he*. (subjective)
> 11. The cutbacks will affect you more than *her*. (objective)
> 12. This essay is better organized than *mine*. (possessive)

To decide on the correct pronoun, simply complete the comparison mentally and then choose the pronoun that naturally follows:

> 13. She trusts him more than I . . . (trust him).
> 14. She trusts him more than . . . (she trusts) . . . me.

■ Note that in sentences 13 and 14, the case of the pronoun in the comparison can change the meaning of the entire sentence.

PRACTICE 7 Circle the correct pronoun.

1. Your hair is much shorter than (she, her, hers).
2. We tend to assume that others are more self-confident than (we, us).
3. She is just as funny as (he, him).
4. Is Hanna as trustworthy as (he, him)?
5. Although they were both research scientists, he received a higher salary than (she, her).
6. I am not as involved in this project as (they, them).
7. Sometimes we become impatient with people who are not as quick to learn as (we, us).
8. Michael's route involved more overnight stops than (us, our, ours).

3. Use of *Who* (or *Whoever*) and *Whom* (or *Whomever*)

Who and **whoever** are in the **subjective** case. **Whom** and **whomever** are in the **objective** case.

CHAPTER 31 Pronouns 423

> 15. *Who* is at the door?
>
> 16. For *whom* is that gift?
>
> 17. *Whom* is that gift for?

- In sentence 15, *who* is the subject.
- The same question is written two ways in sentences 16 and 17. In both, *whom* is the object of the preposition *for*.

Sometimes, deciding on *who* or *whom* can be tricky:

> 18. I will give the raise to *whoever* deserves it.
>
> 19. Give it to *whomever* you like.

- In sentence 18, *whoever* is the subject in the clause *whoever deserves it*.
- In sentence 19, *whomever* is the object in the clause *whomever you like*.

If you have trouble deciding on *who* or *whom*, change the sentence to eliminate the problem.

> 20. I prefer working with people *whom* I don't know as friends.
> or
> I prefer working with people I don't know as friends.

PRACTICE 8 Circle the correct pronoun.

1. (Who, Whom) will deliver the layouts to the ad agency?

2. To (who, whom) are you speaking?

3. (Who, Whom) prefers hiking to skiing?

4. For (who, whom) are those boxes piled in the corner?

5. The committee will award the scholarship to (whoever, whomever) it chooses.

6. (Who, Whom) do you wish to invite to the open house?

7. At (who, whom) did the governor fling the cream pie?

8. I will hire (whoever, whomever) can use a computer and speak Korean.

Part E

Using Pronouns with -Self and -Selves

Pronouns with -self or -selves can be used in two ways—as reflexives or as intensives.

A reflexive pronoun indicates that someone did something to himself or herself:

> 1. My daughter Miriam felt very grown up when she learned to dress *herself*.

- In sentence 1, Miriam did something to *herself*; she *dressed herself*.

An intensive pronoun emphasizes the noun or pronoun it refers to:

> 2. Anthony *himself* was surprised at how relaxed he felt during the interview.

- In sentence 2, *himself* emphasizes that Anthony—much to his surprise—was not nervous at the interview.

The following chart will help you choose the correct reflexive or intensive pronoun.

Antecedent		Reflexive or Intensive Pronoun
Singular	I	myself
	you	yourself
	he	himself
	she	herself
	it	itself
Plural	we	ourselves
	you	yourselves
	they	themselves

Note that in the plural -self is changed to -selves.

- **Be careful:** Do not use reflexives or intensives as substitutes for the subject of a sentence.

> Incorrect: Harry and *myself* will be there on time.
>
> Correct: Harry and *I* will be there on time.

PRACTICE 9

Fill in the correct reflexive or intensive pronoun. Be careful to make pronouns and antecedents agree.

1. Though he hates to cook, André _____ sautéed the mushrooms.

2. Rhoda found _____ in a strange city with only the phone number of a cousin whom she had not seen for years.

3. Her coffee machine automatically turns _____ on in the morning and off in the evening.

4. The librarian and I rearranged the children's section _____.

5. When it comes to horror films, I know that you consider _____ an expert.

6. They _____ didn't care if they arrived on time or not.

7. After completing a term paper, I always buy _____ a little gift to celebrate.

8. Larry _____ was surprised at how quickly he grew to like ancient history.

PRACTICE 10   REVIEW

Proofread the following essay for pronoun errors. Then correct the pronoun error above the line, in any way you choose.

The Many Lives of Jackie Chan

(1) Few movie stars can claim a career as unusual as him. (2) For one thing, Jackie Chan performs his death-defying stunts hisself. (3) Although he was a huge star in Asia for more than twenty years, fame eluded him in the United States until recently.

(4) Chan was born in Hong Kong in 1954. (5) Because him and his parents were so poor, he was sent to live and study at the Peking Opera School. (6) There, they trained him in acting, dancing, singing, sword fighting, and kung fu. (7) When the school closed in 1971, their lessons paid off for Chan in an unexpected way.

(8) Chan worked as a stuntman and fight choreographer and landed acting roles in several films, including Bruce Lee's *Enter the Dragon*. (9) Lee, he died in

1973, and Chan was the natural choice to fill Lee's shoes. (10) In several films, Chan tried to imitate Lee, but the films were unsuccessful. (11) In 1978, however, Chan came up with the idea of turning Lee's tough style into comedy. (12) *Snake in the Eagle's Shadow* and *Drunken Master* were hilarious hits; it established "kung fu comedy." (13) Jackie Chan became one of Hong Kong's most popular stars.

(14) However, Hollywood directors did not appreciate Chan as a stuntman, actor, comedian, director, and scriptwriter all in one, and its early American films flopped. (15) Chan understood his own strengths better than them. (16) He returned to Hong Kong, but him and his fans always believed he could make a U.S. comeback. (17) This happened when *Rumble in the Bronx*, China's most popular film ever, was dubbed in English. (18) Finally, they began to appreciate this manic, bruised, and battered action hero who films were refreshingly nonviolent. (19) Since then, Chan's U.S. films, like *Rush Hour, Rush Hour 2,* and *Highbinder,* are being received almost as well as its Hong Kong counterparts.

Exploring Online

http://webster.commnet.edu/cgi-shl/quiz.pl/pronouns_add1.htm
Interactive pronoun quiz.

CHAPTER 32 Prepositions

PART A Working with Prepositional Phrases
PART B Prepositions in Common Expressions

PART A

Working with Prepositional Phrases

Prepositions are words like *about, at, behind, into, of, on,* and *with*.* They are followed by a noun or a pronoun, which is called the **object** of the preposition. The preposition and its object are called a **prepositional phrase.**

> 1. Ms. Fairworth hurried *to the computer lab.*
> 2. Students *with a 3.5 grade average* will receive a special award.
> 3. Traffic *at this corner* is dangerously heavy.

- In sentence 1, the prepositional phrase *to the computer lab* explains where Ms. Fairworth hurried.

- In sentence 2, the prepositional phrase *with a 3.5 grade average* describes which students will receive a special award.

- Which is the prepositional phrase in sentence 3 and what word does it describe?

_____

---

* For more work on prepositions, see Chapter 24, "The Simple Sentence," Part B.

In/On for Time

Two prepositions often confused are *in* and *on*. Use *in* before months not followed by a specific date, before seasons, and before years that do not include specific dates.

> 1. *In March,* the skating rink will finally open for business.
> 2. Rona expects to pay off her car *in 2008.*

Use *on* before days of the week, before holidays, and before months if a date follows.

> 3. *On Sunday,* the Kingston family spent the day at the beach.
> 4. *On January 6,* Bernard left for a month of mountain climbing.

In/On for Place

In means *inside* a place.

> 1. Tonia put her DVD player *in the bedroom.*
> 2. Many country groups got their start *in Nashville.*

On means *on top of* or *at a particular place.*

> 3. That mess *on your desk* needs to be cleared off.
> 4. Pizza Palace will be opening a new parlor *on Highland Avenue.*

PRACTICE 1 Fill in the correct prepositions in the following sentences. Be especially careful of *in* and *on*.

1. _____ a little town _____ the coast of the Dominican Republic, baseball is a way of life.

2. Once known for cattle and sugar, San Pedro de Macoris has been exporting world-class baseball players _____ the major leagues _____ fifty years.

CHAPTER 32 Prepositions 429

3. Hall-of-Famer Juan Marichal and homerun hitter Sammy Sosa are just two Dominicans who have made names _____ themselves _____ the majors.

4. Other stars born in or _____ San Pedro de Macoris are Pedro Martinez, Felipe Alou, Rico Carty, and Manny Ramirez.

5. Baseball was first introduced _____ the island _____ American mill and plantation owners, who encouraged their workers to learn the game.

6. Because equipment was expensive, boys from poor families often batted _____ a tree branch, using a rolled-up sock _____ place _____ a ball.

7. Each young man dreamed that he would be discovered _____ the baseball scouts and sent to play _____ *las ligas mayores.*

8. Amazing numbers of these players succeeded, and many Dominican athletes later returned to invest _____ the local economy.

9. For example, Sammy Sosa owns office buildings _____ San Pedro, and Jose Rijo is building a baseball academy _____ youngsters.

10. Major league teams, including the Dodgers, Giants, and Expos, now operate year-round training camps _____ the island, hoping to cultivate the athletes _____ tomorrow.

PART B

Prepositions in Common Expressions

Prepositions are often combined with other words to form fixed expressions. Determining the correct preposition in these expressions can sometimes be confusing. Following is a list of some troublesome expressions with prepositions. Consult a dictionary if you need help with others.

Expressions with Prepositions

Expression	Example
according to	*According to* the directions, this flap fits here.
acquainted with	Tom became *acquainted with* his classmates.
addicted to	He is *addicted to* soap operas.
afraid of	Tanya is *afraid of* flying.
agree on (a plan)	Can we *agree on* our next step?
agree to (something or another's proposal)	Roberta *agreed to* her secretary's request for a raise.
angry about or at (a thing)	Jake seemed *angry about* his meager bonus.
angry with (a person)	Sonia couldn't stay *angry with* Felipe.
apply for (a position)	By accident, the twins *applied for* the same job.
approve of	Do you *approve of* bilingual education?
argue about (an issue)	I hate *arguing about* money.
argue with (a person)	Edna *argues with* everyone about everything.
capable of	Mario is *capable of* accomplishing anything he attempts.
complain about (a situation)	Patients *complained about* the long wait to see the dentist.
complain to (a person)	Knee-deep in snow, Jed vowed to *complain to* a maintenance person.
comply with	Each contestant must *comply with* contest regulations.
consist of	This article *consists of* nothing but false accusations and half-truths.
contrast with	The light blue shirt *contrasts* sharply *with* the dark brown tie.
correspond with (write)	We *corresponded with* her for two months before we met.
deal with	Ron *deals* well *with* temporary setbacks.
depend on	Miriam can be *depended on* to say the embarrassing thing.
differ from (something)	A DVD player *differs from* a VCR in many ways.
differ with (a person)	Kathleen *differs with* you on the gun control issue.
different from	Children are often *different from* their parents.
displeased with	Ms. Withers was *displeased with* her doctor's advice to eat less fat.
fond of	Ed is *fond of* his pet tarantula.

(continued)

Expressions with Prepositions
(continued)

Expression	Example
grateful for	Be *grateful for* having so many good friends.
grateful to (someone)	The team was *grateful to* the coach for his inspiration and confidence.
identical with	Scott's ideas are often *identical with* mine.
inferior to	Saturday's performance was *inferior to* the one I saw last week.
in search of	I hate to go *in search of* change at the last moment before the toll.
interested in	Willa is *interested in* results, not excuses.
interfere with	That dripping faucet *interferes with* my concentration.
object to	Martin *objected to* the judge's comment.
protect against	This heavy wool scarf will *protect* your throat *against* the cold.
reason with	It's hard to *reason with* an angry person.
rely on	If Toni made that promise, you can *rely on* it.
reply to	He wrote twice, but the president did not *reply to* his letters.
responsible for	Kit is *responsible for* making two copies of each document.
sensitive to	Professor Godfried is *sensitive to* his students' concerns.
shocked at	We were *shocked at* the graphic violence in that PG-rated film.
similar to	Some poisonous mushrooms appear quite *similar to* the harmless kind.
speak with (someone)	Geraldine will *speak with* her supervisor about a raise.
specialize in	This disc jockey *specializes in* jazz of the 1920s and the 1930s.
succeed in	Oscar *succeeded in* painting the roof in less than five hours.
superior to	It's clear that the remake is *superior to* the original.
take advantage of	Celia *took advantage of* the snow day to visit the science museum.
worry about	Never *worry about* more than one problem at a time.

PRACTICE 2 Fill in the preposition that correctly completes each of the following expressions.

1. The number one goal of 76 percent of college freshmen today is making a lot of money, according _____ the annual American Freshman survey.

2. Every year since 1966, the Higher Education Research Institute has been responsible _____ this survey of hundreds of thousands of college students.

3. The fascinating results show what students each year hope for, worry _____, complain _____, depend _____, and hold dear.

4. In sharp contrast _____ today's freshmen, freshmen surveyed in the 1970s cared most about finding "a meaningful philosophy of life."

5. The majority of today's freshmen are more interested _____ politics, activism, and volunteer work than students in recent years, but they are less interested _____ religion.

6. Students of different races are more sensitive _____ the problem of racism and more likely to be closely acquainted _____ someone of a different race.

7. Just 30 percent of students today call themselves "liberal," but their more liberal opinions on certain social issues contrast _____ those of students in the past.

8. For example, students who object _____ the death penalty have increased to 32.2 percent in the last 20 years, and 57.9 percent believe that same-sex couples should have the right to marry.

9. Dealing _____ many pressures, college students report that their physical and emotional health is at a record low.

10. Experts expect students to rely even more _____ finding sources of strength—people and beliefs _____ which they can depend.

PRACTICE 3 REVIEW

Proofread this essay for preposition errors. Cross out the errors and write corrections above the lines.

Dr. Daniel Hale Williams, Pioneer Surgeon

(1) On a lifetime of many successes, Dr. Daniel Hale Williams's greatest achievement was to pioneer open-heart surgery.

(2) Young Williams, an African American who grew up in the mid-1800s, knew poverty. (3) He relied to his wits to get by, becoming in turn a shoemaker, musician, and barber. (4) At the age of twenty-two, he met Dr. Henry Palmer, who soon saw he was capable on becoming a physician. (5) Williams's medical education, the usual one at the time, consisted in a two-year apprenticeship with Dr. Palmer, followed by three years at the Chicago Medical College, where he specialized on surgery.

(6) It was an exciting time in medicine, for surgeons had just started using antiseptics to protect patients for infection. (7) "Dr. Dan," as he was now called, became an expert on the new surgical techniques and a leader in Chicago's medical and African-American communities. (8) In 1891, he succeeded with opening Provident Hospital, the first interracial hospital in the United States. (9) There, African Americans were assured first-rate medical care; moreover, black interns and nurses received thorough professional training.

(10) It was to Provident Hospital that frightened friends brought James Cornish in July 9, 1893. (11) Near death, the young man had received a deep knife gash near his heart during a fight. (12) Sensitive to the dangerous situation, Dr. Williams decided to operate immediately. (13) According with eyewitnesses, he first made a six-inch incision and removed Cornish's fifth rib. (14) Then he repaired a torn artery and stitched up the punctured sac surrounding the heart. (15) Fifty-one days later, Cornish left the hospital, recovered and deeply grateful for Dr. Williams to his life. (16) The age of open-heart surgery had begun.

(17) Much lay ahead for Dr. Williams. (18) He was responsible to reorganizing the Freedmen's Hospital at Howard University from 1894 to 1898; on 1913, he accepted an invitation from the American College of Surgeons and succeeded on becoming its only African-American charter member. (19) The high point of his life, however, remained that night in 1893.

Exploring Online

http://webster.commnet.edu/grammar/quizzes/preposition_quiz1.htm
Graded preposition quiz.

http://www.pacificnet.net/~sperling/quiz/prep4.html
Graded preposition quiz.

CHAPTER 33 Adjectives and Adverbs

PART A	Defining and Using Adjectives and Adverbs
PART B	The Comparative and the Superlative
PART C	A Troublesome Pair: *Good/Well*

Part A

Defining and Using Adjectives and Adverbs

Adjectives and **adverbs** are two kinds of descriptive words. **Adjectives** describe or modify nouns or pronouns. They explain *what kind*, *which one*, or *how many*.

> 1. A *black* cat slept on the piano.
> 2. We felt *cheerful*.
> 3. *Three* windows in the basement need to be replaced.

- The adjective *black* describes the noun *cat*. It tells what kind of cat, a *black* one.
- The adjective *cheerful* describes the pronoun *we*. It tells what kind of mood we were in, *cheerful*.
- The adjective *three* describes the noun *windows*. It tells how many windows, *three*.

Adverbs describe or modify verbs, adjectives, and other adverbs. They tell *how*, *in what manner*, *when*, *where*, and *to what extent*.

> 4. Joe dances *gracefully*.
> 5. *Yesterday* Robert left for a weekend of sky diving.
> 6. Brigit is *extremely* tall.
> 7. He travels *very* rapidly on that skateboard.

- The adverb *gracefully* describes the verb *dances*. It tells how Joe dances, *gracefully*.
- The adverb *yesterday* describes the verb *left*. It tells when Robert left, *yesterday*.
- The adverb *extremely* describes the adjective *tall*. It tells how tall (to what extent), *extremely* tall.
- The adverb *very* describes the adverb *rapidly*, which describes the verb *travels*. It tells how rapidly he travels, *very* rapidly.

Many adjectives can be changed into adverbs by adding an *-ly* ending. For example, *glad* becomes *gladly*, *hopeful* becomes *hopefully*, *awkward* becomes *awkwardly*.

Note the pairs on this list; they are easily confused:

Adjectives	Adverbs
awful	awfully
bad	badly
poor	poorly
quick	quickly
quiet	quietly
real	really
sure	surely

> 8. The fish tastes *bad*.
> 9. It was *badly* prepared.

- In sentence 8, the adjective *bad* describes the noun *fish*.
- In sentence 9, the adverb *badly* describes the verb *was prepared*.

PRACTICE 1 Circle the correct adjective or adverb in parentheses. Remember that adjectives modify nouns or pronouns; adverbs modify verbs, adjectives, or adverbs.

1. Have you ever seen (real, really) emeralds?

2. Try to do your work in the library (quiet, quietly).

3. We will (glad, gladly) take you on a tour of the Crunchier Cracker factory.

4. Lee, a (high, highly) skilled electrician, rewired his entire house last year.

5. She made a (quick, quickly) stop at the photocopy machine.

6. It was (awful, awfully) cold today; the weather was terrible.

7. The fans from Cleveland (enthusiastic, enthusiastically) clapped for the Browns.

8. Are you (sure, surely) this bus stops in Dusty Gulch?

9. He (hasty, hastily) wrote the essay, leaving out several important ideas.

10. It was a funny joke, but the comedian told it (bad, badly).

11. Tina walked (careful, carefully) down the icy road.

12. Sam swims (poor, poorly) even though he spends as much time as he can posing on the beach.

13. Sasha the crow is an (unusual, unusually) pet and a (humorous, humorously) companion.

14. The painting is not (actual, actually) a Picasso; in fact, it is a (real, really) bad imitation.

15. It is an (extreme, extremely) hot day, and I (sure, surely) could go for some (real, really) orange juice.

Part B

The Comparative and the Superlative

The **comparative** of an adjective or adverb compares two persons or things:

> 1. Ben is *more creative* than Robert.
> 2. Marcia runs *faster* than the coach.

- In sentence 1, Ben is being compared with Robert
- In sentence 2, Marcia is being compared with the coach.

The **superlative** of an adjective or adverb compares three or more persons or things:

> 3. Sancho is the *tallest* of the three brothers.
> 4. Marion is the *most intelligent* student in the class.

- In sentence 3, Sancho is being compared with the other two brothers.
- In sentence 4, Marion is being compared with all the other students in the class.

Adjectives and adverbs of one syllable usually form the **comparative** by adding *-er*. They form the **superlative** by adding *-est*.

Adjective	Comparative	Superlative
fast	fast*er*	fast*est*
smart	smart*er*	smart*est*
tall	tall*er*	tall*est*

Adjectives and adverbs of more than one syllable usually form the **comparative** by using *more*. They form the **superlative** by using *most*.

Adjective	Comparative	Superlative
beautiful	*more* beautiful	*most* beautiful
brittle	*more* brittle	*most* brittle
serious	*more* serious	*most* serious

Note, however, that adjectives that end in *-y* (like *happy, lazy,* and *sunny*) change the *-y* to *-i* and add *-er* and *-est*.

Adjective	Comparative	Superlative
happy	happ*ier*	happ*iest*
lazy	laz*ier*	laz*iest*
sunny	sunn*ier*	sunn*iest*

PRACTICE 2 Write the comparative or the superlative of the words in parentheses. Remember: Use the comparative to compare two items; use the superlative to compare more than two. Use *-er* or *-est* for one-syllable words; use *more* or *most* for words of more than one syllable.*

1. The ocean is _____ (cold) than we thought it would be.

2. Please read your lines again, _____ (slowly) this time.

3. Which of these two roads is the _____ (short) route?

4. Which of these three highways is the _____ (short) route?

5. Belkys is the _____ (busy) person I know.

---

* If you have questions about spelling, see Chapter 38, "Spelling," Part G.

CHAPTER 33   Adjectives and Adverbs   439

6. That red felt hat with feathers is the _____ (outlandish) one I've seen.

7. Today is _____ (warm) than yesterday, but Thursday was the _____ (warm) day of the month.

8. The down coat you have selected is the _____ (expensive) one in the store.

9. Each one of Woody's stories is _____ (funny) than the last.

10. As a rule, mornings in Los Angeles are _____ (hazy) than afternoons.

11. Is Pete _____ (tall) than Louie? Is Pete the _____ (tall) player on the team?

12. If you don't do these experiments _____ (carefully), you will blow up the chemistry lab.

13. This farmland is much _____ (rocky) than the farmland in Iowa.

14. Therese says that Physics 201 is the _____ (challenging) course she has ever taken.

15. Mr. Wells is the _____ (wise) and _____ (experienced) leader in the community.

PRACTICE 3   Proofread the following paragraph for comparative and superlative errors. Cross out unnecessary words and write your corrections above the lines.

(1) Every ten weeks through 2008, the U.S. Mint will put a new state quarter into circulation. (2) In fact, this 50 States Quarter Program, which began in 1999, has become the most popularest program in the Mint's history. (3) Although the front of each new quarter still bears the familiar image of George Washington, the reverse imprint celebrates one of the fifty states with a design that honors its unique history and traditions. (4) Some designs are least surprising than others, like New York's Statue of Liberty or Georgia's peach. (5) However, other designs are more bolder. For example, the Indiana coin features a race car from the Indianapolis 500, and the Ohio quarter pictures an astronaut, in honor of Ohio-born space pioneers Neil Armstrong and John Glenn. (6) The quarters are released in the order in which each state joined the union and will conclude in 2008 with the

appearance of Hawaii's still-secret design. (7) At last survey, 100 million adults were collecting the quarters, the most highest number of coin enthusiasts ever recorded. (8) Most people think the new quarters are more pretty and more interesting than before. (9) And the U.S. Mint assures concerned taxpayers that changing the quarter five times a year won't cost them a cent.

Part C

A Troublesome Pair: *Good/Well*

Adjective	Comparative	Superlative
good	better	best
bad	worse	worst

Adjective	Comparative	Superlative
well	better	best
badly	worse	worst

Be especially careful not to confuse the adjective **good** with the adverb **well**:

1. Jessie is a *good* writer.
2. She writes *well*.

- *Good* is an **adjective** modifying *writer*.
- *Well* is an **adverb** modifying *writes*.

PRACTICE 4 Fill in either the adjective *good* or the adverb *well* in each blank.

1. Corned beef definitely goes _____ with cabbage.
2. How _____ do you understand Spanish?
3. He may not take phone messages very _____, but he is _____ when it comes to handling email.
4. Exercise is a _____ way to stay in shape; eating _____ will help you maintain _____ health.
5. Tony looks _____ in his new beard and ponytail.

CHAPTER 33   Adjectives and Adverbs   441

6. This is a _____ arrangement: I wash, you dry.

7. On a rainy night, Sheila loves to curl up with a _____ book.

8. The old Persian carpet and oak desk are a _____ match; they go _____ together.

9. At the finals, both teams played _____; it was a _____ game.

10. They are _____ neighbors and are _____ liked in the community.

PRACTICE 5   Fill in the correct comparative or superlative of the word in parentheses.

1. Lucinda is a _____ (good) chemist than she is a mathematician.

2. Bascomb was the _____ (bad) governor this state has ever had.

3. When it comes to staying in shape, you are _____ (bad) than I.

4. Of the two sisters, Leah is the _____ (good) markswoman.

5. You can carry cash when you travel, but using a credit card is _____ (good).

6. Our goalie is the _____ (good) in the league; yours is the _____ (bad).

7. When it comes to bad taste, movies are _____ (bad) than television.

8. Your sore throat seems _____ (bad) than it was yesterday.

9. Gina likes snorkeling _____ (good) than fishing; she loves scuba diving _____ (good) of all.

10. A parka is the _____ (good) protection against a cold wind; it is certainly _____ (good) than a scarf.

PRACTICE 6   REVIEW

Proofread the following essay for adjective and adverb errors. Correct errors by writing above the lines.

Julia Morgan, Architect

(1) Julia Morgan was one of San Francisco's most finest architects, as well as the first woman licensed as an architect in California. (2) In 1902, Morgan became

the first woman to finish successful the program in architecture at the School of Fine Arts in Paris. (3) Returning to San Francisco, she opened her own office and hired and trained a very talented staff that eventual grew to thirty-five full-time architects. (4) Her first major commission was to reconstruct the Fairmont Hotel, one of the city's bestest-known sites, which had been damaged bad in the 1906 earthquake. (5) Morgan earned her reputation by designing elegant homes and public buildings out of inexpensively and available materials and by treating her clients real good. (6) She went on to design more than 800 residences, stores, churches, offices, and educational buildings, most of them in California.

(7) Her bestest customer was William Randolph Hearst, one of the country's most rich newspaper publishers. (8) Morgan designed newspaper buildings and more than twenty pleasure palaces for Hearst in California and Mexico. (9) She maintained a private plane and pilot to keep her moving from project to project. (10) The most big and famousest of her undertakings was sure San Simeon. (11) Morgan worked on it steady for twenty years. (12) She converted a large ranch overlooking the Pacific into a hilltop Mediterranean village composed of three of the beautifullest guest houses in the world. (13) The larger of the three was designed to look like a cathedral and incorporated Hearst's fabulous art treasures from around the world. (14) The finished masterpiece had 144 rooms and was larger than a football field. (15) San Simeon is now one of the most visited tourist attractions in California and seems to grow popularer each year.

Exploring Online

http://owl.english.purdue.edu/handouts/esl/esladjadvEX1.html
Paper quiz: Choose the adjective or adverb; check your answers.

http://ccc.commnet.edu/grammar/adjectives.htm
Everything you wanted to know about adjectives but were afraid to ask.

CHAPTER 34 The Apostrophe

PART A The Apostrophe for Contractions
PART B The Apostrophe for Ownership
PART C Special Uses of the Apostrophe

Part A

The Apostrophe for Contractions

Use the **apostrophe** in a **contraction** to show that letters have been omitted.

1. *I'll* buy that coat if it goes on sale.
2. At nine *o'clock* sharp, the store opens.

- *I'll*, a contraction, is a combination of *I* and *will*. *Wi* is omitted.
- The contraction *o'clock* is the shortened form of *of the clock*.

Be especially careful in writing contractions that contain pronouns:

Common Contractions

I + am = I'm	it + is or has = it's
I + have = I've	we + are = we're
I + will or shall = I'll	let + us = let's
you + have = you've	you + are = you're
you + will or shall = you'll	they + are = they're
he + will or shall = he'll	they + have = they've
she + is or has = she's	who + is or has = who's

443

A photograph by Ansel Adams of Half-Dome and Merced River in Yosemite National Park

PRACTICE 1 Proofread these sentences and, above the lines, supply any apostrophes missing from the contractions.

1. Ansel Adams wasnt only a great photographer; he was also a conservationist who helped save wildlife areas and establish national parks.

2. Hes best known for his dramatic scenes of the wilderness, but he also made huge technical contributions to the field of photography.

3. Because of Adams, theres now a film-exposure system that controls light and dark contrasts in every part of a photograph.

4. Adams was a talented musician who had planned to become a concert pianist; he hadnt expected a career in photography at all.

5. Its a well-known fact that the fourteen-year-old Adams took his first photo while on a family vacation trip to Yosemite National Park in 1916.

6. His decision didnt happen overnight, but he eventually realized that music wouldnt be as satisfying a field for him to work in as photography.

7. People werent surprised when he transferred the great attention to detail that he had given his piano technique to developing sharp, clear prints.

8. Whats most unusual is how Adams worked with light, space, and mood when he photographed storms, mountains, and other natural scenes.

9. Before Adams, many people couldnt believe that photography would become an art form.

10. Theyve been proven wrong: Adams published books about photography as well as books of his own photographs, and he established photography departments in museums and universities throughout the United States.

Part B

The Apostrophe for Ownership

Use the apostrophe to show ownership: Add an *'s* if a noun or an indefinite pronoun (like *someone, anybody,* and so on) does not already end in *-s:*

> 1. I cannot find my *friend's* book bag.
> 2. *Everyone's* right to privacy should be respected.
> 3. *John and Julio's* apartment has striped wallpaper.
> 4. The *children's* clothes are covered with mud.

- The *friend* owns the book bag.
- *Everyone* owns the right to privacy.
- Both John and Julio own one apartment. The apostrophe follows the compound subject *John and Julio.*
- The *children* own the clothes.

Add only an apostrophe to show ownership if the word already ends in -s:*

> 5. My *aunts'* houses are filled with antiques.
>
> 6. The *knights'* table was round.
>
> 7. *Mr. Jonas'* company manufactures sporting goods and uniforms.

- My *aunts* (at least two of them) own the houses.
- The *knights* (at least two) own the table.
- *Aunts* and *knights* already end in -s, so only an apostrophe is added.
- *Mr. Jonas* owns the company. *Mr. Jonas* already ends in -s, so only an apostrophe is added.

Note that *possessive pronouns never take an apostrophe:* his, hers, theirs, ours, yours, its:

> 8. *His* car gets twenty miles to the gallon, but *hers* gets only ten.
>
> 9. That computer is *theirs*; *ours* is coming soon.

PRACTICE 2 Proofread the following sentences and add apostrophes where necessary to show ownership. In each case, ask yourself if the word already ends in -s. Put a C after any correct sentences.

1. Bills bed is a four-poster.

2. Martha and Davids house is a log cabin made entirely by hand.

3. Somebodys cell phone was left on the sink.

4. During the eighteenth century, ladies dresses were heavy and uncomfortable.

5. Have you seen the childrens watercolor set?

6. Mr. James fried chicken and rice dish was crispy and delicious.

7. The class loved reading about Ulysses travels.

8. The Surgeon Generals latest report was just released.

9. Our citys water supply must be protected.

10. He found his ticket, but she cannot find hers.

---

*Some writers add an 's to one-syllable proper names that end in -s: James's bike.

11. Every spring, my grandmothers porch is completely covered with old furniture for sale.

12. Jacks car is the same color as ours.

13. Celias final, a brilliant study of pest control on tobacco farms, received a high grade.

14. The mens locker room is on the right; the womens is on the left.

15. The program is entering its final year.

Part C

Special Uses of the Apostrophe

Use an apostrophe in certain expressions of time:

> 1. I desperately need a *week's* vacation.

- Although the week does not own a vacation, it is a vacation of a week—*a week's vacation*.

Use an apostrophe to pluralize letters, numbers, and words that normally do not have plurals:

> 2. Be careful to cross your *t*'s.
> 3. Your *8*'s look like *F*'s.
> 4. Don't use so many *but*'s in your writing.

Use an apostrophe to show omitted numbers:

> 5. The class of '72 held its annual reunion last week.

PRACTICE 3 Proofread these sentences and add an apostrophe wherever necessary.

1. Cross your *t*s and dot your *i*s.

2. I would love a months vacation on a dude ranch.

3. Too many *and*s make this paragraph dull.

4. Those *9*s look crooked.

5. You certainly put in a hard days work!

PRACTICE 4   REVIEW

Proofread the following essay for apostrophe errors. Correct the errors by adding apostrophes above the lines where needed and crossing out those that do not belong.

The True Story of Superman

(1) Sometimes, things just dont work out right. (2) That's how the creators of Superman felt for a long time.

(3) Supermans first home wasnt the planet Krypton, but Cleveland. (4) There, in 1933, Superman was born. (5) Jerry Siegels story, "Reign of Superman," accompanied by Joe Shuster's illustrations, appeared in the boys own magazine, *Science Fiction*. (6) Later, the teenagers continued to develop their idea. (7) Superman would come to Earth from a distant planet to defend freedom and justice for ordinary people. (8) He would conceal his identity by living as an ordinary person himself. (9) Siegel and Shuster hoped their characters strength and morality would boost peoples spirits' during the Great Depression.

(10) At first, the creators werent able to sell their concept; then, Action Comics' Henry Donnenfield bought it. (11) In June of 1938, the first *Superman* comic hit the stands. (12) Superman's success was immediate and overwhelming. (13) Finally, Americans had a hero who wouldnt let them down! (14) Radio and TV shows, movie serials, feature films, and generations of superheroes' followed.

(15) While others made millions from their idea, Siegel and Shuster didnt profit from its' success. (16) They produced Superman for Action Comics for a mere fifteen dollars a page until they were fired a few years later when Joe Shusters eyes began to fail. (17) They sued, but they lost the case. (18) For a long time, both lived in poverty, but they continued to fight. (19) In 1975, Siegel and Shuster

finally took their story to the press; the publicity won them lifelong pensions. (20) The two mens long struggle had ended with success.

Exploring Online

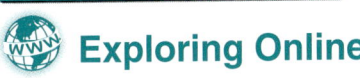

http://webster.commnet.edu/grammar/quizzes/apostrophe_quiz2.htm
Graded practice: Apostrophe or no apostrophe? This is the question.

CHAPTER 35 The Comma

PART A   Commas for Items in a Series
PART B   Commas with Introductory Phrases, Transitional Expressions, and Parentheticals
PART C   Commas for Appositives
PART D   Commas with Nonrestrictive and Restrictive Clauses
PART E   Commas for Dates and Addresses
PART F   Minor Uses of the Comma

Part A

Commas for Items in a Series

Use commas to separate the items in a series:*

> 1. You need *bolts*, *nuts*, and *screws*.
> 2. I will be happy to *read your poem*, *comment on it*, and *return it to you*.
> 3. *Mary paints pictures*, *Robert plays the trumpet*, but *Sam just sits and dreams*.

Do not use commas when all three items are joined by *and* or *or*:

> 4. I enjoy *biking* and *skating* and *swimming*.

---

* For work on parallelism, see Chapter 20, "Revising for Consistency and Parallelism," Part C.

PRACTICE 1 Punctuate the following sentences:

1. At the banquet, Ed served a salad of juicy red tomatoes, crunchy green lettuce, and stringless snap beans.
2. As a nursing assistant, Reva dispensed medication, disinfected wounds, and took blood samples.
3. Ali visited Santa Barbara, Concord, and Berkeley.
4. Hiking, rafting, and snowboarding are her favorite sports.
5. The police found TV sets, blenders, and blow dryers stacked to the ceiling in the abandoned house.
6. I forgot to pack some important items for the trip to the tropics: insect repellent, sunscreen, and antihistamine tablets.
7. Don't eat strange mushrooms, walk near the water, or feed the squirrels.
8. Everyone in class had to present an oral report, write a term paper, and take a final.
9. We brought a Ouija board, a Scrabble set, and a Boggle game to the party.
10. To earn a decent wage, make a comfortable home, and educate my children—those are my hopes.

Part B

Commas with Introductory Phrases, Transitional Expressions, and Parentheticals

Use a comma after most introductory phrases of more than two words:*

> 1. *By four in the afternoon,* everybody wanted to go home.
> 2. *After the game on Saturday,* we all went dancing.

---

* For more work on introductory phrases, see Chapter 21, "Revising for Sentence Variety," Part C.

Use commas to set off transitional expressions:

> 3. Ferns, *for example*, need less sunlight than flowering plants.
> 4. Instructors, *on the other hand*, receive a lower salary than assistant professors.

Use commas to set off parenthetical elements:

> 5. *By the way*, where is the judge's umbrella?
> 6. Nobody, *it seems*, wants to eat the three-bean salad.

- *By the way* and *it seems* are called parenthetical expressions because they appear to be asides, words not really crucial to the meaning of the sentence. They could almost appear in parentheses: *(By the way) where is the judge's umbrella?*

Other common parenthetical expressions are *after all, actually, as a matter of fact,* and *to tell the truth.*

PRACTICE 2   Punctuate the following sentences:

1. Frankly I always suspected that you were a born saleswoman.

2. All twelve jurors by the way felt that the defendant was innocent.

3. On every April Fools' Day he tries out a new, dumb practical joke.

4. In fact Lucinda should never have written that poison-pen letter.

5. Close to the top of Mount Washington the climbers paused for a tea break.

6. To tell the truth that usher needs a lesson in courtesy.

7. Near the end of the driveway a large lilac bush bloomed and brightened the yard.

8. He prefers as a rule serious news programs to the lighter sitcoms.

9. To sum up Mr. Choi will handle all the details.

10. During my three years in Minnesota I learned how to deal with snow.

Part C
Commas for Appositives

Use commas to set off appositives:*

> 1. Yoko, *our new classmate*, is our best fielder.
> 2. *A humorous and charming man*, he was a great hit with my parents.
> 3. This is her favorite food, *ketchup sandwiches*.

- Appositive phrases like *our new classmate*, *a humorous and charming man*, and *ketchup sandwiches* rename or describe nouns and pronouns—*Yoko, he, food*.

> 4. The poet *Shelley* wrote "Ode to the West Wind."
> 5. Shelley's wife, *Mary*, wrote *Frankenstein*.

- A one-word appositive is not set off by commas when it is essential to the meaning of the sentence. Without the appositive *Shelley*, we do not know which poet wrote the ode.
- A one-word appositive is set off by commas when it is not essential to the meaning of the sentence. The name *Mary* does not affect the meaning of the sentence.

PRACTICE 3 Punctuate the following sentences.

1. The Rock the popular wrestler and actor starred in movies and made a video with musician Wyclef Jean.

2. Long novels especially ones with complicated plots force me to read slowly.

3. David a resident nurse hopes to become a pediatrician.

4. I don't trust that tire the one with the yellow patch on the side.

5. Tanzania a small African nation exports cashew nuts.

6. Watch out for Phil a man whose ambition rules him.

7. Sheila a well-known nutritionist lectures at public schools.

---

*For more work on appositives, see Chapter 21, "Revising for Sentence Variety," Part D.

8. A real flying ace Helen will teach a course in sky diving.

9. We support the Center for Science in the Public Interest a consumer education and protection group.

10. My husband Bill owns two stereos.

Part D

Commas with Nonrestrictive and Restrictive Clauses

A **relative clause** is a clause that begins with *who, which,* or *that* and modifies a noun or pronoun. There are two kinds of relative clauses: **nonrestrictive** and **restrictive.***

A **nonrestrictive relative clause** is not essential to the meaning of the sentence:

> 1. Raj, *who is a part-time aviator,* loves to tinker with machines of all kinds.

- *Who is a part-time aviator* is a relative clause describing *Raj*. It is a nonrestrictive relative clause because it is not essential to the meaning of the sentence. The point is that *Raj loves to tinker with machines of all kinds.*
- **Commas** set off the nonrestrictive relative clause.

A **restrictive relative clause** is essential to the meaning of the sentence:

> 2. People *who do their work efficiently* make good students.

- *Who do their work efficiently* is a relative clause describing *people*. It is a restrictive relative clause because it is *essential* to the meaning of the sentence. Without it, sentence 2 would read, *People make good students.* But the point is that certain people make good students—*those who do their work efficiently.*
- Restrictive relative clauses *do not* require commas.

PRACTICE 4   Set off the nonrestrictive relative clauses in the following sentences with commas. Note that *which* usually begins a nonrestrictive relative clause and *that* usually begins a restrictive clause. Remember: Restrictive relative clauses are *not* set off by commas. Write a C after each correct sentence.

---

*For more work on nonrestrictive and restrictive clauses, see Chapter 21, "Revising for Sentence Variety," Part D.

1. Olive who always wanted to go into law enforcement is a detective in the Eighth Precinct.
2. Employees who learn to use the new computers may soon qualify for a merit raise.
3. Polo which is not played much in the United States is very popular in England.
4. A person who always insists upon telling you the truth is sometimes a pain in the neck.
5. Statistics 101 which is required for the business curriculum demands concentration and perseverance.
6. Robin who is usually shy at large parties spent the evening dancing with Arsenio who is everybody's favorite dance partner.
7. This small shop sells furniture that is locally handcrafted.
8. His uncle who rarely eats meat consumes enormous quantities of vegetables, fruits, and grains.
9. Pens that slowly leak ink can be very messy.
10. Valley Forge which is the site of Washington's winter quarters draws many tourists every spring and summer.

Part E

Commas for Dates and Addresses

Use commas to separate the elements of an address. Note, however, that no punctuation is required between the state and ZIP code if the ZIP code is included.

1. Please send the books to *300 West Road, Stamford, CT 06860*.
2. We moved from *1015 Allen Circle, Morristown, New Jersey*, to *Farland Lane, Dubuque, Iowa*.

Use commas to separate the elements of a date:

> 3. The sociologists arrived in Tibet on *Monday, January 18, 1999,* and planned to stay for two years.
> 4. By *June 20, 2007,* I expect to have completed my B.A. in physical education.

Do not use a comma with a single-word address or date preceded by a preposition:

> 5. John DeLeon arrived *from Baltimore in January* and will be our new shortstop this season.

PRACTICE 5   Punctuate the following sentences. Write a C after each correct sentence.

1. The last few decades have seen the growth of an ancient Native American custom—the *powwow,* a gathering where tribal members dance to celebrate the circle of life.

2. At hundreds of powwows across the United States and Canada families and friends reaffirm their heritage, socialize, and compete for prize money.

3. Thirty-three powwows and festivals were held in September 2002 alone, for example, each one with singing, chanting, drumming, and dancing.

4. On Saturday September 28 2002 the Permian Basin Intertribal Powwow began in Odessa Texas.

5. On the weekend of September 6 to September 8 2002 Native Americans and visitors could choose between the Great North Winds Powwow in Manistique Michigan and the Stillwater Powwow in Redding California.

6. The Indian Summer Festival was held in the Community Center Bartlesville Oklahoma on September 13 14 and 15 2002.

7. Some families even spend June to September going from powwow to powwow or traveling "the Red Road."

8. The Red Road is a path of commitment to living without alcohol and drugs and embracing a healthier lifestyle.

9. Each year, thousands attend the powwows to dance admire the spectacular traditional costumes meet interesting people, or just feel part of the circle of life.

10. For more information on powwows, you can contact the American Indian Heritage Foundation 6051 Arlington Blvd. Falls Church VA 22044.

Part F
Minor Uses of the Comma

Use a comma after answering a question with *yes* or *no:*

> 1. *No,* I'm not sure about that answer.

Use a comma when addressing someone directly and specifically naming the person spoken to:

> 2. *Alicia,* where did you put my law books?

Use a comma after interjections like *ah, oh,* and so on:

> 3. *Ah,* these coconuts are delicious.

Use a comma to contrast:

> 4. Harold, *not Roy,* is my scuba-diving partner.*

---

* For help using commas with coordinating and subordinating conjunctions—and help avoiding run-ons, commas splices, and fragments—see Chapters 25 and 26.

PRACTICE 6   Punctuate the following sentences.

1. Yes I do think you will be famous one day.
2. Well did you call a taxi?
3. The defendant ladies and gentlemen of the jury does not even own a red plaid jacket.
4. Cynthia have you ever camped in the Pacific Northwest?
5. No I most certainly will not marry you.
6. Oh I love the way they play everything to a salsa beat.
7. The class feels Professor Molinor that your grades are unrealistically high.
8. He said "March" not "Swagger."
9. Perhaps but I still don't think that the carburetor fits there.
10. We all agree Ms. Crawford that you are the best jazz bassist around.

PRACTICE 7   REVIEW

Proofread the following essay for comma errors—either missing commas or commas used incorrectly. Correct the errors above the lines.

The Pyramids of Giza

(1) The pyramids of Giza, Egypt a wonder of the ancient world still inspire awe. (2) Built nearly 5,000 years ago the largest of these tombs, was ordered by Khu-fu, a powerful pharaoh of ancient Egypt. (3) The two smaller pyramids nearby belonged to his successors his son Khafre and his grandson Menkaure. (4) The three pyramids—together with the Sphinx many temples and causeways—comprised a ceremonial complex for the dead not far from the Nile River.

(5) We marvel today at the ability of this ancient people to build such colossal structures without the benefit of work animals or machinery not even the wheel. (6) The Great Pyramid for instance is 750 square feet and 480 feet high, roughly the size of Shea Stadium filled in with solid rock to a height of forty stories. (7) More than 100,000 workers, who were probably peasants forced into service

cut two-and-a-half-ton limestone blocks from quarries on the other side of the Nile ferried them across the river, and then dragged them up ramps to be fitted exactly in place. (8) Experts estimate that 2.3 million blocks had to be moved over a period of more than twenty years, to complete the project.

(9) Perhaps the greatest wonder, however is that these structures have lasted. (10) Countless other buildings statues, and monuments have been constructed and admired, yet they have fallen into ruin while these magnificent structures remain. (11) The pyramids are considered all but indestructible. (12) It has been said, in fact that they could withstand a direct hit by an atomic bomb.

Exploring Online

http://owl.english.purdue.edu/handouts/grammar/g_commaEX1.html
Paper quiz with answers: Revise for commas.

http://webster.commnet.edu/grammar/quizzes/commas_fillin.htm
Interactive quiz: Where have all the commas gone?

CHAPTER 36 Mechanics

PART A   Capitalization
PART B   Titles
PART C   Direct Quotations
PART D   Minor Marks of Punctuation

Part A

Capitalization

Always capitalize the following: *names, nationalities, religions, races, languages, countries, cities, months, days of the week, documents, organizations,* and *holidays.*

> 1. The *Protestant* church on the corner will offer *Spanish* and *English* courses starting *Thursday, June 3*.

Capitalize the following *only* when they are used as part of a proper noun: *streets, buildings, historical events, titles,* and *family relationships.*

> 2. We saw *Professor Rodriguez* at *Silver Hall*, where he was delivering a talk on the *Spanish Civil War*.

Do not capitalize these same words when they are used as common nouns:

> 3. We saw the professor at the lecture hall, where he was delivering a talk on a civil war.

460

Capitalize geographic locations but not directions:

> 4. The tourists went to the *South* for their winter vacation.
> 5. Go south on this boulevard for three miles.

Capitalize academic subjects only if they refer to a specific named and numbered course:

> 6. Have you ever studied psychology?
> 7. Last semester, I took *Psychology* 101.

PRACTICE 1 Capitalize wherever necessary in the following sentences. Put a C after each correct sentence.

1. Barbara Kingsolver, a well-known novelist, nonfiction writer, and poet, was born on april 8, 1955, in annapolis, maryland.

2. She grew up in rural kentucky and then went to college in indiana; after graduating, she worked in europe and since then has lived in and around tucson, arizona.

3. In college, Kingsolver majored first in music and then in biology; she later withdrew from a graduate program in biology and ecology at the university of arizona to work in its office of arid land studies.

4. Kingsolver's first novel, *The Bean Trees*, has become a classic; it is taught in english classes and has been translated into more than sixty-five languages.

5. The main character, named taylor greer, is considered one of the most memorable women in modern american literature.

6. In a later novel, *The Poisonwood Bible*, Kingsolver follows the family of a baptist minister in its move to the congo.

7. The fanaticism of reverend price brings misery to his family and destruction to the villagers he tries to convert to christianity.

8. Kingsolver's writing always deals with powerful political and social issues, but her novels don't sound preachy because she is a wonderful storyteller.

9. She has won awards and prizes from the american library association and many other organizations; she also has earned special recognition from the united nations national council of women.

10. This gifted writer, who plays drums and piano, performs with a band called rock bottom remainders; other band members are also notable writers—stephen king, amy tan, and dave barry.

Part B

Titles

Capitalize words of a title except short prepositions, short conjunctions, and the articles *the, an,* and *a.* Always capitalize the first and last words of the title, no matter what they are:

> 1. I liked <u>The Color Purple</u> but found <u>The House on the River</u> slow reading.

Underline the titles of long works: *books,* newspapers and magazines, television shows, plays, record albums, operas,* and *films.*
Put quotation marks around shorter works or parts of longer ones: *articles, short stories, poems, songs, paintings, scenes from plays,* and *chapters from full-length books.*

> 2. Have you read Hemingway's "The Killers" yet?
> 3. We are assigned "The Money Market" in <u>Essentials of Economics</u> for homework in my marketing course.

- "The Killers" is a short story.
- "The Money Market" is a chapter in the full-length book <u>Essentials of Economics.</u>

---

*The titles and parts of sacred books are not underlined and are not set off by quotation marks: Job 5:6, Koran 1:14, and so on.

CHAPTER 36   Mechanics   463

Do not underline or use quotation marks around the titles of your own papers.

PRACTICE 2   Capitalize these titles correctly. Do not underline or use quotation marks in this practice.

1. inside women's college basketball
2. the genius of frank lloyd wright
3. breath, eyes, memory
4. an insider's guide to the music industry
5. the orchid thief
6. dave barry's guide to marriage and/or sex
7. power point made easy
8. a history of violence in american movies
9. harry potter and the sorcerer's stone
10. currents from the dancing river

PRACTICE 3   Wherever necessary, underline or place quotation marks around each title in the sentences below so that the reader will know at a glance what type of work the title refers to. Put a C after any correct sentence.

Example | Two of the best short stories in that volume are "Rope" and "The New Dress."

1. African-American writer Langston Hughes produced his first novel, Not Without Laughter, when he was a student at Lincoln University in Pennsylvania.

2. By that time, he had already been a farmer, a cook, a waiter, and a doorman at a Paris nightclub; he had also won a prize for his poem The Weary Blues, which was published in 1925 in the magazine Opportunity.

3. In 1926 Hughes wrote his famous essay The Negro Artist and the Racial Mountain, which appeared in the Nation magazine; he wanted young black writers to write without shame or fear about the subject of race.

4. Because he spoke Spanish, Hughes was asked in 1937 by the newspaper the Baltimore Afro-American to cover the activities of blacks in the International Brigades in Spain during the Spanish Civil War.

5. For the rest of his life, he wrote articles in newspapers such as the San Francisco Chronicle, the New York Times, and the Chicago Defender.

6. In fact, for more than twenty years he wrote a weekly column for the Chicago Defender, in which he introduced a character named Simple, who became popular because of his witty observations on life.

7. The stories about Simple were eventually collected and published in five books; two of those books are Simple Speaks His Mind and Simple Takes a Wife.

8. In 1938, Hughes established the Harlem Suitcase Theater in Manhattan, where his play Don't You Want to Be Free? was performed.

9. Because Hughes's poetry was based on the rhythms of African-American speech and music, many of his poems have been set to music, including Love Can Hurt You, Dorothy's Name Is Mud, and Five O'Clock Blues.

10. Few modern writers can rival Hughes's enormous output of fine poems, newspaper articles, columns, sketches, and novels.

Part C

Direct Quotations

1. He said, "These are the best seats in the house."

- The direct quotation is preceded by a comma or a colon.
- The first letter of the direct quotation is capitalized.
- Periods always go *inside* the quotation marks.

> 2. He asked, "Where is my laptop?"
> 3. Stewart yelled, "I don't like beans!"

- Question marks and exclamation points go inside the quotation marks if they are part of the direct words of the speaker.

> 4. "That was meant for the company," he said, "but if you wish, you may have it."
> 5. "The trees look magnificent!" she exclaimed. "It would be fun to climb them all."

- In sentence 4, the quotation is one single sentence interrupted by *he said*. Therefore, a comma is used after *he said*, and *but* is not capitalized.
- In sentence 5, the quotation consists of two different sentences. Thus a period follows *exclaimed*, and the second sentence of the quotation begins with a capital letter.

PRACTICE 4 Insert quotation marks where necessary in each sentence. Capitalize and punctuate correctly.

1. The sign reads don't even think about parking here.
2. Alexander Pope wrote to err is human, to forgive divine.
3. Well, it takes all kinds she sighed
4. He exclaimed you look terrific in those jeweled sandals
5. The article said Most American children do poorly in geography.
6. These books on ancient Egypt look interesting he replied but I don't have time to read them now.
7. Although the rain is heavy she said we will continue harvesting the corn.
8. Give up caffeine and get lots of rest the doctor advised.
9. The label warns this product should not be taken by those allergic to aspirin.
10. Red, white, and blue Hillary said are my favorite colors

Part D

Minor Marks of Punctuation

1. The Colon

Use a colon to show that a direct quotation will follow or to introduce a list:*

> 1. This is the opening line of his essay: "The airplane is humanity's greatest invention."
> 2. There are four things I can't resist in warm weather: fresh mangoes, a sandy beach, cold drinks, and a hammock.

Use a colon to separate the chapter and verse in a reference to the Bible or to separate the hour and minute:

> 3. This quotation comes from Genesis 1:1.
> 4. It is now exactly 4:15 P.M.

2. Parentheses

Use parentheses to enclose a phrase or word that is not essential to the meaning of the sentence:

> 5. Herpetology (the study of snakes) is a fascinating area of zoology.
> 6. She left her hometown (Plunkville) to go to the big city (Fairmount) in search of success.

3. The Dash

Use a dash to emphasize a portion of a sentence or to interrupt the sentence with an added element:

> 7. This is the right method—the only one—so we are stuck with it.

The colon, parentheses, and the dash should be used sparingly.

---

*Avoid using a colon after any form of the verb *to be* or after a preposition.

CHAPTER 36 Mechanics

PRACTICE 5 Punctuate these sentences with colons, dashes, or parentheses.

1. Calvin asked for the following two light bulbs, a pack of matches, a lead pencil, and a pound of grapes.

2. They should leave by 1130 P.M.

3. The designer's newest fashions magnificent leather creations were generally too expensive for the small chain of clothing stores.

4. Harvey the only Missourian in the group remains unconvinced.

5. She replied, "This rock group The Woogies sounds like all the others I've heard this year."

6. If you eat a heavy lunch as you always do remember not to go swimming immediately afterward.

7. By 9:30 P.M., the zoo veterinarian a Dr. Smittens had operated on the elephant.

8. Note these three tips for hammering in a nail hold the hammer at the end of the handle, position the nail carefully, and watch your thumb.

9. Whenever Harold Garvey does his birdcalls at parties as he is sure to do everyone begins to yawn.

10. Please purchase these things at the hardware store masking tape, thumbtacks, a small hammer, and some sandpaper.

PRACTICE 6 REVIEW

Proofread the following essay for errors in capitalization, quotation marks, colons, parentheses, and dashes. Correct the errors by writing above the lines.

The Passion of Thomas Gilcrease

(1) Thomas Gilcrease, a descendent of creek indians, became an instant Millionaire when oil was discovered on his homestead in 1907. (2) He spent most of his fortune collecting objects that tell the story of the american frontier, particularly of the Native American experience. (3) The Thomas Gilcrease institute of american history and arts in Tulsa, oklahoma, is the result of his lifelong passion.

(4) This huge collection more than 10,000 works of art, 90,000 historical documents, and 250,000 native american artifacts, spans the centuries from 10,000 B.C. to the 1950s. (5) Awed visitors can view nearly 200 George Catlin paintings of Native American life. (6) They can walk among paintings and bronze sculptures by Frederic Remington with names like The Coming And Going Of The Pony Express that call up images of the West. (7) Museumgoers can admire Thomas Moran's watercolors that helped persuade congress to create yellowstone, the first national park. (8) In addition, visitors are treated to works by modern Native Americans, such as the display of wood sculptures by the cherokee Willard Stone.

(9) The museum also houses many priceless documents an original copy of the declaration of independence, the oldest known letter written from the new world, and the papers of Hernando Cortés. (10) A new glass storage area even allows visitors to view the 80 percent of the holdings that are not on display. (11) Thousands of beaded moccasins and buckskin dresses line the shelves, and a collection of magnificent war bonnets hangs from brackets.

(12) When the Gilcrease Institute opened its doors on May 2, 1949, *Life* magazine declared "it is the best collection of art and literature ever assembled on the American frontier and the Indian. (13) Thousands of visitors agree.

Exploring Online

       http://webster.commnet.edu/cgi-shl/par_numberless_quiz.pl/caps_quiz.htm
       Graded capitalization practice.

CHAPTER 37

Putting Your Proofreading Skills to Work

After you have written a paragraph or an essay—once you have prewritten, drafted, and revised—you are ready for the next step—**proofreading.**

Proofreading, which takes place at the sentence level, means applying what you have learned in Units 5 and 6. When you proofread, carefully check each sentence for correct grammar, punctuation, and capitalization. Is every sentence complete? Do all verbs agree with their subjects? Are there any comma errors? Do all proper nouns begin with a capital letter?

This chapter gives you the opportunity to put your proofreading skills to work in real-world situations. As you proofread the paragraphs and essays that follow, you must look for any—and every—kind of error, just as you would in the real world of college or work. The first four practices tell you what kinds of errors to look for; if you have trouble, go back to those chapters and review. The other practices, however, contain a random mix of errors and give you no clues at all.

PROOFREADING PRACTICE 1

Proofread this paragraph, correcting any errors above the lines. To review, see these chapters:

Chapter 26   run-ons, comma splices, fragments
Chapter 27   present tense problems, subject-verb agreement
Chapter 28   past tense problems
Chapter 29   past participle problems

(1) Mount Everest is the tallest mountain in the world. (2) The highest point on Earth, and the dangerous dream of every mountain climber. (3) Everest set in the Himalaya Mountains of central Asia and rise 29,028 feet. (4) The deadliest threat to climbers are not the steep, icy slopes or even the bitter cold and ferocious

469

winds it is the lack of air. (5) Air at the top of Everest has only one-third the oxygen of air below, so without preparation, the average person would live less than an hour at the summit. (6) In fact, altitude sickness begin at 8,000 feet, with headache, nausea, and confusion. (7) At 12,000 feet, the brain and lungs starts filling with fluid, which can lead to death. (8) How, then, has anyone ever climbed Everest, the answer is acclimatization. (9) Mountaineers climb slowly, about 2,000 feet a day, and they drink huge amounts of water. (10) They also carry oxygen. (11) Amazingly, in 1980, the first person to climb Everest solo was also the first to climb it without oxygen. (12) That was Reinhold Messner from Italy. (13) Who later wrote in *Climbing* magazine that the lack of air "saps your judgment and strength, even your ability to feel anything at all. I don't know how I made it." (14) Over 145 climbers have died scaling Mount Everest, nonetheless, this danger keeps tempting others to try their skills and their luck.

PROOFREADING PRACTICE 2

Proofread this paragraph, correcting any errors above the lines. To review, see these chapters:

Chapter 20	inconsistency of number or person, parallelism problems
Chapter 26	run-ons, comma splices, fragments
Chapter 27	present tense problems, subject-verb agreement
Chapter 29	past participle problems
Chapter 34	apostrophe errors

(1) American culture emphasizes quick results we pick up fast food and do our banking in drive-through lanes. (2) We buy gadgets that promise to save you time. (3) We even call ahead for restaurant seating, so we wont have to wait for a table. (4) Now a new trend know as *speed dating* becoming popular in big cities like Los Angeles, Chicago, and Boston. (5) Also called pre-dating or "McDating." (6) This activity is suppose to reduce the time that busy single people spend getting to know each other. (7) Speed dating events are arranged by companies like

HurryDate and 8MinuteDating. (8) At these events, even numbers of men and women are paired off, each couple chats for eight to ten minutes while trying to determine potential compatibility. (9) Then a bell rings, and everyone switch partners. (10) At the end of the session, participants who are interest in each other are provide with each other's phone and email contacts. (11) Some say that speed dating is ideal for people who are busy, who dislike the bar scene, or who hope to lessen the pain of rejection. (12) Others calls it drive-through dating, just another crazy American fad.

PROOFREADING PRACTICE 3

Proofread this paragraph, correcting any errors above the lines. To review, see these chapters:

Chapter 26	run-ons, comma splices, and fragments
Chapter 28	past tense errors
Chapter 29	past participle problems
Chapter 33	adjective and adverb errors

(1) Lea Salonga, a talented Broadway performer, has became a role model for aspiring young actors, both in the United States and her native Philippines. (2) Born in Manila, Salonga began performing at age seven. (3) After she won a small part in a local production of *The King and I*. (4) Her poularity grew quickly. (5) She acted in many theater productions, recorded a number of albums. (6) And even star in her own children's television show, called *Love, Lea*. (7) Through it all, Salonga's parents focused on her education and good manners rather than her fame. (8) When British talent scouts arrived in Manila, they were charm by the gracious young woman with the beautiful soprano voice and cast her immediate as the lead in their new musical *Miss Saigon*. (9) Salonga was only 20 when she winned a Tony award for her sensitive portrayal of a Vietnamese woman who sacrifices her own life to give her child a more better one. (10) Since then, Salonga

has starred in some of the popularest Broadway musicals, landed a role in *As the World Turns*, and singing the soundtrack for the female leads in the Disney films *Aladdin* and *Mulan*. (11) Despite her success, Salonga remains close to her family and her traditional upbringing. (12) Her first kiss occurred on the set of *Miss Saigon* she was chaperoned on dates until she turned 21. (13) Salonga's parents have encouraged her to complete her college education. (14) With her balanced lifestyle and much achievements, Lea Salonga encourages other young people to follow their dreams without loosing sight of their roots.

PROOFREADING PRACTICE 4

Proofread this paragraph, correcting any errors above the lines. To review, see these chapters:

Chapter 21	relative clause problems
Chapter 26	run-ons, comma splices, fragments
Chapter 27	present tense problems, subject-verb agreement
Chapter 30	noun errors
Chapter 31	pronoun errors
Chapter 36	capitalization errors

(1) In french, its name means "Circus of the Sun," but don't expect Cirque du Soleil to have old-fashioned lion tamers, elephants on parade, or clowns with orange hair. (2) Instead, this innovative Quebec-based company draws on the ancient traditions of chinese acrobat. (3) And feature strangely beautiful sets and costumes. (4) Dramatic lighting and eerie live music sets the mood. (5) Then a bare-chested man fly through the darkness above the stage, 40-foot wings of red silk flowing from his arms. (6) Four young asian woman contort their tattooed bodies so they resemble flowers, figure eight, or spirals. (7) A giant wheel with human spokes rolls across the stage while acrobats perform. (8) Dangling from an open door who swings high in the air. (9) In a show called "O," after the french word for "water," a 1.5-million-gallon pool of water appears in the stage, under-

water swimmers rise magically from the stage floor, and acrobats near the ceiling dive and disappear into the water. (10) Cirque has grown from a tiny group of street performers in 1984 to an Entertainment Empire of 500 acrobats which perform in six shows on three continents. (11) The secret of Cirque du soleil's success lies in its ongoing spirit of teamwork. (12) Despite their large numbers, performers from forty different countries still create the shows together. (13) Proposing ideas and designing their own roles. (14) The result is a show that dazzles even those whom think they have seen it all.

PROOFREADING PRACTICE 5

This paragraph contains many of the errors you have learned to avoid in Unit 6. Proofread each sentence carefully, and then correct each error above the line.

(1) If you want to eat well and do our planet a favor become a Vegetarian. (2) Most vegetarian's eat eggs, milk, dairy products and fish. (3) All youre giving up are leathery steak's and overcooked chicken. (4) A vegetarian dinner might begin with a greek salad of, crisp cucumbers, sweet red onion black olives, and a sprinkling of feta cheese. (5) Youll think you're sitting in a little café overlooking the mediterranean sea. (6) For the main course, head to mexico for tamale pie. (7) A rich, flavorful dish made of pinto beans's, brown rice, green peppers and tomatoes. (8) On the table of course is a loaf of warm bread. (9) Do you have room for dessert how about some ben and jerrys ice cream, made in vermont? (10) As you linger over a cup of french espresso coffee think how your vegetarian meal was delicious, nutritious, and a help to our planet. (11) If more people ate vegetarian the land given to raising cattle and crops to feed cattle could be used for raising grain, many of the worlds hungry people could be fed. (12) To read about vegetarianism, get the best-known guide *laurels kitchen: a handbook for vegetarian cookery and nutrition.*

PROOFREADING PRACTICE 6

This paragraph contains many of the errors you have learned to avoid in Unit 6. Proofread each sentence carefully, and then correct each error above the line.

(1) Since ancient times, the Zunis of New Mexico have used *fetishes*. (2) Small objects carved from stone or wood that are believed to have magical powers. (3) The Zuni religion have a complex tradition of fetishes based on the six directions. (4) North, south, east, west, above, and below. (5) Each of the directions are associated with special forces and a guardian animal. (6) The East, for example, where the sun rises, is the source of all life, truth, and new ideas it is represented by a white wolf. (7) Because wolfs are highly intelligent, social, and loving as parents, they are good to adopt as a personal fetish if you feel you share these qualities. (8) Likewise, someone facing a big decision or a family problem might seek the help of their wolf fetish. (9) The other five guardian animals are the mountain lion, black bear, badger, eagle, and mole. (10) Additional fetish animals include coyotes, owls, snakes, deers, and rabbits. (11) The Zunis still holds fetishes sacred in its religion and continues to carve them. (12) In fact, some Zunis are famous for their distinctive carving, their fetishes sell all over the world as works of art.

PROOFREADING PRACTICE 7

This essay contains many of the errors you learned to avoid in Unit 6. Proofread each sentence carefully, and then correct each error above the line.

In the Market for a Used Car?

(1) For several year's now, used car sales have exceeded new car sales. (2) Good used cars can be founded at dealers. (3) And through newspaper ads. (4) You might also let your friends know your in the market for a used car, they might know of someone who wants to sell their car. (5) Wherever you look for a used car keep the following tips in mind.

(6) First shop before you need the car. (7) This way you can decide exactly what type of car suit you most best. (8) Do you want a compact. (9) Or a midsize car? (10) What features are important to you? (11) Should you get an american-made car or a japanese, german, or other import? (12) If you shop when you are'nt desperate, you are more likely to make a good choice and negotiate good.

(13) Second narrow your choices to three or four cars, and do some research. (14) Start with the *kelley blue book used car price manual,* online at http://www.Kbb.com. (15) The blue book as its called for short gives the current value by model year and features. (16) Its also a good idea to check *consumer reports* magazine. (17) Every april issue lists good used car buys and cars to avoid. (18) Based on what you learn go back and test-drive the cars that interest you the mostest. (19) Drive each for at least an hour, drive in stop-and-go traffic in the highway, in winding roads, and in hills.

(20) When you do decide on a car ask your mechanic to look at it. (21) Be sure to get a written report that include an estimate of what repair's will cost. (22) Money spent at this point is money spent wise, if the seller wont allow an inspection take your business elsewhere.

(23) When you buy a used car you want dependability and value. (24) Follow these tip's youll be able to tell a good buy when you see it.

PROOFREADING PRACTICE 8

This essay contains many of the errors you learned to avoid in Unit 6. Proofread each sentence carefully, and then correct each error above the line.

Gators and Crocs

(1) With their scaly bodies slit eyes and long tails, alligators and crocodiles look a lot like dinosaurs. (2) In fact alligators and crocodiles descended from the same family as dinosaurs. (3) While its true that alligators and crocodiles look a lot alike, they differ in three ways.

(4) First alligators and crocodiles are found in different parts of the world. (5) Alligators be found in china, central america, and south america. (6) On the other hand, crocodiles are found in africa (especially around the nile river), australia, southeast asia, india, cuba, and the west indies. (7) Only in the southern united states is both alligators and crocodiles found. (8) In all cases however alligator's and crocodile's live in hot, tropical regions. (9) Reptiles are cold-blooded, so at temperatures below 65 degrees, alligators and crocodiles gets sluggish and cannot hunt.

(10) Alligators and crocodiles also differ in appearance. (11) Alligators has broader flatter snouts that are rounded at the end. (12) Crocodiles has narrower almost triangular snouts. (13) The best way to tell the difference is to view both from the side when they have their mouths closed, you can see only upper teeth on an alligator, but you can also see four lower teeth on a croc. (14) If you get really close you can see that alligators have a space between they're nostrils while the nostrils of crocs are very close together.

(15) Finally alligators and crocodiles are temperamentally different. (16) Alligators are not aggressive they are even a bit shy. (17) They will lie in wait along a river bank for prey when on land, they move slow and uneven. (18) Crocodiles, however, are much more aggressive. (19) They are fast, mean, and often stalk they're prey. (20) The australian freshwater crocodile and the nile crocodile can even run on land, with their front and back legs working together like a dog. (21) Nile crocodiles kill hundred's of people every year.

(22) Alligators and crocodiles have outlived the dinosaurs, but they might not survive hunters who want to turn them into shoes wallets briefcases and belts. (23) In 1967, the u.s. government declared alligators an endangered species. (24) Fortunately american alligators have repopulated and are now reclassified as threatened. (25) Importing crocodile and alligator skins are banned worldwide,

but some species is still threatened. (26) These frightening and fascinating ancient creatures need help worldwide if they are to survive.

Exploring Online

http://www.unc.edu/depts/wcweb/handouts/proofread.html
Proofreading instruction and practice.

http://ccc.commnet.edu/grammar/
Interactive grammar and writing help. Explore, learn, review!

Writers' Workshop

Adopt a New Point of View

No matter how excellent the content of an essay, report, or business letter, grammatical errors will diminish its impact. Ironically, errors call attention to themselves. Learning to proofread your writing might not seem terribly exciting, but it is an all-important skill.

When this student received the interesting assignment to *write as if you are someone or something else,* he decided to see what it's like to be a roach. His audience: humans. His tone: wacky. In your group or class, read his essay, aloud if possible. Underline details or sentences that are especially effective or humorous, and **proofread** as you go. If you spot any errors, correct them.

It's Not Easy Being a Roach

(1) It's not easy being a roach. My life consist of the constant struggle to survive. We have existed for millions of years, yet we still do not get the respect that we deserve. We have witnessed the dawn of the dinosaur and the coming of Jesus. We have experienced two world wars, enjoyed the benefits of cable television, and feasted our eyes on many women taking showers. Being small has its advantages, and it doesn't hurt to be quick either. Because we have live so long. You would think that respect would be ours, but that is not the case.

(2) We are looked upon as pests rather than pets, we are quieter than household pets. We don't eat much, and contrary to popular belief, we are very clean. Sure, some of us prefers the wild life of booze, drugs, and unprotected sex with other insects, but that doesn't mean that most of us are not seeking a happy life that includes love and affection from you humans. I think it's high time that you appreciated our value as insects, pets, and potential lifelong companions.

(3) I might have six legs, but that doesn't mean I can handle all the burdens that come with being a roach. My wife is pregnant again, which means 10,000 more mouths to feed. It's bad enough that I have to find a meal fit for thousands, I also live in fear of becoming a Roach McNugget. For some strange reason, rodents consider us food. Do I look scrumptious to you? Does my body ignite wild fantasies of sinful feasting? I think not. Mice and rats refuse to respect us because they see us as midnight munchies.

(4) I don't ask for much—a home, some food, and maybe an occasional pat on the head. If I can't have these simple things, I would prefer

> somebody simply step on me. A fast, hard crunch would do—no spraying me with roach spray, no Roach Motel. I may be on the lower end of the species chain, but that doesn't mean I'm not entitled to live out my dreams. I am roach and hear me roar!
>
> (5) When you humans kill each other off with nuclear bombs, we will still be around. With luck on our side, we will grow into big monsters because of exposure to radiation. Then I don't think those of you who remains will enjoy being chased around by giant, glowing roaches—all because you humans didn't want to hug a roach when you had the chance.
>
> (6) One more thing: Stop trying to kill us with that pine-scented roach spray. It doesn't kill us it just makes us smell bad. If I want to smell like pine trees, I will go and frolic in some wood, naked and free. You people really tick me off.
>
> —Israel Vasquez (Student)

1. How effective is Mr. Vasquez's essay?

   _____ Strong thesis statement?   _____ Good supporting details?

   _____ Logical organization?   _____ Effective conclusion?

2. Discuss your underlinings. What details or lines in the essay did you like the most? Explain as exactly as possible why you like something or why it made you laugh.

3. Mr. Vasquez's sense of humor comes through to readers. Does he also achieve his goal of presenting a roach's point of view?

4. Would you suggest any revisions? Is this essay effective or offensive? Why? Does the final paragraph provide a strong and humorous conclusion, or does it seem like an afterthought?

5. This essay contains several serious grammar errors. Can you find and correct them? What two error patterns does this fine writer need to watch out for?

Group Work

In writing as in life, it is often easier to spot other people's errors than our own. In your group or class, discuss *your* particular error patterns and how you have learned to catch them. Do you have problems with comma splices, *-ed* verb endings, or prepositional phrases? Discuss any proofreading tricks and techniques you have learned to spot and correct those errors successfully in your own papers. Have someone jot down the best techniques that your group mates have used, and be prepared to share these with the class.

Writing and Revising Ideas

1. Adopt a new point of view; discuss your life as a bird, animal, insect, or object.

2. Write as a person of another gender, ethnic group, or period in history.

UNIT 7

Strengthening Your Spelling

CHAPTER 38 Spelling

CHAPTER 39 Look-Alikes/Sound-Alikes

CHAPTER 38 Spelling

PART A	Suggestions for Improving Your Spelling
PART B	Computer Spell Checkers
PART C	Spotting Vowels and Consonants
PART D	Doubling the Final Consonant (in Words of One Syllable)
PART E	Doubling the Final Consonant (in Words of More Than One Syllable)
PART F	Dropping or Keeping the Final *E*
PART G	Changing or Keeping the Final *Y*
PART H	Adding *-S* or *-ES*
PART I	Choosing *IE* or *EI*
PART J	Spelling Lists

Part A

Suggestions for Improving Your Spelling

Accurate spelling is an important ingredient of good writing. No matter how interesting your ideas are, if your spelling is poor, your writing will not be effective.

Some Tips for Improving Your Spelling

- **Look closely at the words on the page.** Use any tricks you can to remember the right spelling. For example, "The *a*'s in *separate* are separated by an *r*," or "*Dessert* has two *s*'s because you want two desserts."

- **Use a dictionary.** Even professional writers frequently check spelling in a dictionary. As you write, underline the words you are not sure of and look them up when you write your final draft. If locating words in the dictionary is a real problem for you, consider a "poor speller's dictionary."

- **Use a spell checker.** If you write on a computer, make a habit of using the spell-check software. See Part B for tips and cautions about spell checkers.

- **Keep a list of the words you misspell.** Look over your list whenever you can and keep it handy as you write.

- **Look over corrected papers for misspelled words** (often marked *sp.*). Add these words to your list. Practice writing each word three or four times.

- **Test yourself.** Use flash cards or have a friend dictate words from your list or from this chapter.

- **Review the basic spelling rules explained in this chapter.** Take time to learn the material; don't rush through the entire chapter all at once.

- **Study the spelling list on pages 490–491,** and test yourself on these words.

- **Read through Chapter 39, "Look-Alikes/Sound-Alikes,"** for commonly confused words (*their, there,* and *they're,* for instance). The practices in that chapter will help you eliminate some common spelling errors from your writing.

Part B

Computer Spell Checkers

Almost all word-processing programs are equipped with a spell checker. A spell checker picks up spelling errors and gives you alternatives for correcting them. Get in the habit of using this feature as your first and last proofreading task.

Depending on your program and the paper you are writing, determine the best ways to use the spell checker. For example, if your paper repeats an unusual name, use the "ignore all" feature rather than check the name each time it appears. If the name appears when you're using "ignore all," you've spelled the name differently that time.

What a spell checker cannot do is think. If you've mistyped one word for another—*if* for *it,* for example—the spell checker cannot bring it to your attention. If you've written *then* for *than,* the spell checker cannot help. Proofread your paper after using the spell checker. For questions about words that sound the same but are spelled differently, check Chapter 39, "Look-Alikes/Sound-Alikes." Run spell check again after you've made all your corrections. If you've introduced a new error, the spell checker will let you know.

PRACTICE 1 With a group of four or five classmates, read this poem, which "passed" spell check. Can your group find and correct all the errors that the spell checker missed?

Eye halve a spelling check her,

It came with my pea see.

It clearly marques four my revue,

CHAPTER 38 Spelling 483

Miss steaks eye can knot sea.

I've run this poem threw it.

Your Shirley please too no

Its letter perfect in it's weigh.

My checker tolled me sew.

Part C

Spotting Vowels and Consonants

To learn some basic spelling rules, you must know the difference between vowels and consonants.

> The **vowels** are *a, e, i, o,* and *u*.
>
> The **consonants** are *b, c, d, f, g, h, j, k, l, m, n, p, q, r, s, t, v, w, x,* and *z*.
>
> The letter *y* can be either a vowel or a consonant, depending on its sound:
>
> daisy   sky
> yellow   your

- In both *daisy* and *sky, y* is a vowel because it has a vowel sound: an *ee* sound in *daisy* and an *i* sound in *sky*.
- In both *yellow* and *your, y* is a consonant because it has the consonant sound of *y*.

PRACTICE 2 Write *v* for vowel and *c* for consonant in the space on top of each word. Be careful of the *y*.

Example

```
c v c v c
h o p e d
```

1. _ _ _ _
   r e l y

2. _ _ _ _ _ _ _
   p e r h a p s

3. _ _ _ _ _ _ _
   i n s t e a d

4. _ _ _ _
   y a w n

5. _ _ _ _ _
   f o r g e

6. _ _ _ _ _ _ _ _
   b y s t a n d e r

Part D

Doubling the Final Consonant (in Words of One Syllable)

When you add a suffix or an ending that begins with a vowel (like *-ed, -ing, -er, -est*) to a word of one syllable, double the final consonant *if* the last three letters of the word are *consonant-vowel-consonant* or *c-v-c*.

> plan + ed = planned   swim + ing = swimming
> thin + est = thinnest   light + er = lighter

- *Plan, swim,* and *thin* all end in *cvc*; therefore, the final consonants are doubled.
- *Light* does not end in *cvc*; therefore, the final consonant is not doubled.

PRACTICE 3 Which of the following words should double the final consonant? Check to see whether the word ends in *cvc*. Then add the suffixes *-ed* and *-ing*.

	Word	Last Three Letters	-ed	-ing
Example	drop	cvc	dropped	dropping
	boil	vvc	boiled	boiling
1.	tan			
2.	brag			
3.	mail			
4.	peel			
5.	wrap			

PRACTICE 4 Which of the following words should double the final consonant? Check for *cvc*. Then add the suffixes *-er* or *-est*.

	Word	Last Three Letters	-er	-est
Example	wet	cvc	wetter	wettest
	cool	vvc	cooler	coolest
1.	deep			
2.	short			
3.	red			

Word	Last Three Letters	-er	-est
4. dim			
5. bright			

Part E

Doubling the Final Consonant (in Words of More Than One Syllable)

When you add a suffix that begins with a vowel to a word of more than one syllable, double the final consonant *if*

(1) the last three letters of the word are *cvc*, and

(2) the accent or stress is on the *last* syllable.

begin + ing = beginning   **control + ed = controlled**

- *Begin* and *control* both end in *cvc*.
- In both words, the stress is on the last syllable: *be-gin'*, *con-trol'*. (Pronounce the words aloud and listen for the correct stress.)
- Therefore, *beginning* and *controlled* double the final consonant.

listen + ing = listening   **visit + ed = visited**

- *Listen* and *visit* both end in *cvc*.
- However, the stress is *not* on the last syllable: *lis'-ten*, *vis'-it*.
- Therefore, *listening* and *visited* **do not** double the final consonant.

PRACTICE 5 Which of the following words should double the final consonant? First, check for *cvc*; then check final stress. Then add the suffixes -ed and -ing.

	Word	Last Three Letters	-ed	-ing
Example	repel	cvc	repelled	repelling
	enlist	vcc	enlisted	enlisting
	1. happen			
	2. admit			
	3. offer			
	4. prefer			
	5. compel			

Part F

Dropping or Keeping the Final *E*

When you add a suffix that begins with a vowel (like *-able*, *-ence*, *-ing*), drop the final *e*.

When you add a suffix that begins with a consonant (like *-less*, *-ment*, *-ly*), keep the final *e*.

move + ing = moving   pure + ity = purity

- *Moving* and *purity* both drop the final *e* because the suffixes *-ing* and *-ity* begin with vowels.

home + less = homeless   advertise + ment = advertisement

- *Homeless* and *advertisement* keep the final *e* because the suffixes *-less* and *-ment* begin with consonants.

Here are some exceptions to memorize:

| argument | courageous | knowledgeable | truly |
| awful | judgment | simply | manageable |

PRACTICE 6 Add the suffix indicated for each word.

Example hope + ing = *hoping*

hope + ful = *hopeful*

1. love + able = _____
2. love + ly = _____
3. pure + ly = _____
4. pure + er = _____
5. complete + ing = _____
6. complete + ness = _____
7. enforce + ment = _____
8. enforce + ed = _____
9. arrange + ing = _____
10. arrange + ment = _____

PRACTICE 7 Add the suffix indicated for each word.

Example come + ing = *coming*

rude + ness = *rudeness*

1. guide + ance = _____
2. manage + ment = _____
3. dense + ity = _____
4. polite + ly = _____
5. motive + ation = _____
6. sincere + ly = _____
7. like + able = _____
8. response + ible = _____
9. judge + ment = _____
10. fame + ous = _____

Part G

Changing or Keeping the Final Y

When you add a suffix to a word that ends in -y, change the y to i if the letter before the y is a consonant.
Keep the final y if the letter before the y is a vowel.

happy + ness = happiness   **portray + ed = portrayed**

- The y in *happiness* is changed to i because the letter before the y is a consonant, p.
- The y in *portrayed* is not changed because the letter before it is a vowel, a.

However, when you add *-ing* to words ending in y, always keep the y:

copy + ing = copying   **delay + ing = delaying**

Here are some exceptions to memorize:

day + ly = daily   pay + ed = paid
lay + ed = laid   say + ed = said

PRACTICE 8 Add the suffix indicated for to each of the following words.

Example marry + ed = __married__

buy + er = __buyer__

1. try + ed = _____
2. vary + able = _____
3. worry + ing = _____
4. pay + ed = _____
5. enjoy + able = _____
6. wealthy + est = _____
7. day + ly = _____
8. duty + ful = _____
9. display + s = _____
10. occupy + ed = _____

PRACTICE 9 Add the suffix in parentheses to each word.

1. beauty (fy) _____
   (ful) _____
   (es) _____
2. lonely (er) _____
   (est) _____
   (ness) _____
3. betray (ed) _____
   (ing) _____
   (al) _____
4. study (es) _____
   (ous) _____
   (ing) _____

Part H

Adding -S or -ES

Nouns usually take an -s or an -es ending to form the plural. Verbs take an -s or -es in the third person singular (*he, she,* or *it*).

Add -es instead of -s if a word ends in *ch, sh, ss, x,* or *z* (the -es adds an extra syllable to the word):

> box + es = boxes   crutch + es = crutches   miss + es = misses

Add -es instead of -s for most words that end in *o*:

> do + es = does   hero + es = heroes
> echo + es = echoes   tomato + es = tomatoes
> go + es = goes   potato + es = potatoes

Here are some exceptions to memorize:

> pianos   sopranos
> radios   solos

When you change the final *y* to *i* in a word,* add -es instead of -s:

> fry + es = fries   marry + es = marries   candy + es = candies

PRACTICE 10   Add -s or -es to the following nouns and verbs, changing the final *y* to *i* when necessary.

Example | sketch _sketches_

echo _echoes_

1. watch _____
2. tomato _____
3. reply _____
4. company _____
5. bicycle _____
6. piano _____
7. donkey _____
8. dictionary _____
9. boss _____
10. hero _____

Part I

Choosing IE or EI

Write *i* before *e*, except after *c* or in an *ay* sound like *neighbor* or *weigh*.

> achieve, niece   deceive   vein

---

* See Part G of this chapter for more on changing or keeping the final *y*.

- *Achieve* and *niece* are spelled *ie*.
- *Deceive* is spelled *ei* because of the preceding *c*.
- *Vein* is spelled *ei* because of its *ay* sound.

However, words with a *shen* sound are spelled with an *ie* after the *c*: ancient, conscience, efficient, sufficient.

Here are some exceptions to memorize:

either   seize
neither   society
foreign   their
height   weird

PRACTICE 11

Pronounce each word out loud. Then fill in either *ie* or *ei*.

1. bel __ __ ve
2. __ __ ght
3. effic __ __ nt
4. n __ __ ther
5. cash __ __ r
6. th __ __ r
7. ch __ __ f
8. soc __ __ ty
9. rec __ __ ve
10. fr __ __ nd
11. consc __ __ nce
12. h __ __ ght
13. ach __ __ ve
14. v __ __ n
15. for __ __ gn
16. perc __ __ ve

PRACTICE 12 REVIEW

Test your knowledge of the spelling rules in this chapter by adding suffixes to the following words. If you have trouble, the part in which the rule appears is shown in parentheses.

	Part		Part
1. nerve + ous _____	(F)	6. occur + ed _____	(E)
2. drop + ed _____	(D)	7. carry + ing _____	(G)
3. hope + ing _____	(F)	8. tomato + s/es _____	(H)
4. busy + ness _____	(G)	9. believe + able _____	(F)
5. radio + s/es _____	(H)	10. day + ly _____	(G)

PRACTICE 13   REVIEW

Circle the correctly spelled word in each pair.

1. writting, writing
2. receive, recieve
3. begining, beginning
4. greif, grief
5. relaid, relayed
6. piece, peice
7. resourceful, resourcful
8. argument, arguement
9. marries, marrys
10. thier, their

Part J

Spelling Lists

Commonly Misspelled Words

Following is a list of words that are often misspelled. As you can see, they are words that you might use daily in speaking and writing. The trouble spot, the part of each word that is usually spelled incorrectly, has been put in bold type.

To help yourself learn these words, you might copy each one twice, making sure to underline the trouble spot, or copy the words on flash cards and have someone test you.

1. across
2. a**dd**ress
3. ans**w**er
4. arg**u**ment
5. **athl**ete
6. **begin**ning
7. beha**v**ior
8. calend**a**r
9. ca**r**eer
10. cons**c**ience
11. crow**ded**
12. defin**i**te
13. d**e**scribe
14. desp**e**rate
15. di**ff**erent
16. dis**a**ppoint
17. dis**a**pprove
18. doesn't
19. eigh**th**
20. embarra**ss**
21. envir**o**nment
22. exa**gg**erate
23. famil**i**ar
24. fina**ll**y
25. govern**m**ent
26. gra**mm**ar
27. hei**gh**t
28. **ill**egal
29. immedi**ately**
30. import**ant**
31. int**e**gration
32. intel**l**igent
33. **int**erest
34. int**er**fere
35. je**w**elry
36. jud**g**ment
37. kno**w**ledge
38. mainta**in**
39. math**e**matics
40. mea**nt**
41. nece**ss**ary
42. nerv**ous**
43. o**cc**asion
44. opin**ion**
45. optim**ist**
46. partic**ular**
47. **per**form
48. **per**haps

49. perso**nn**el	58. **re**ference	67. su**r**prise
50. po**ss**ess	59. r**hy**thm	68. taught
51. po**ss**ible	60. rid**i**culous	69. temperature
52. **pre**fer	61. separate	70. thorough
53. pre**ju**dice	62. sim**i**lar	71. thought
54. privi**lege**	63. **s**ince	72. tire**d**
55. pro**bably**	64. speech	73. until
56. **ps**ychology	65. stren**gth**	74. wei**gh**t
57. pu**r**sue	66. su**cc**ess	75. written

Personal Spelling List

In your notebook, keep a list of words that *you* misspell. Add words to your list from corrected papers and from the exercises in this chapter. First, copy each word as you misspelled it, underlining the trouble spot; then write the word correctly. Study your list often. Use this form:

As I Wrote It   **Correct Spelling**

1. probly   probably

2. _____   _____

3. _____   _____

PRACTICE 14   REVIEW

Proofread the following essay for spelling errors. (Be careful: There are misspelled words from both the exercises in this chapter and the spelling list.) Correct any errors by writing above the lines.

Man's Best Clone

(1) Ever since the sucessful cloning of Dolly the sheep in 1996, scientists have experimented with cloning other animals. (2) Now a Texas company is offering cloning services to people who want to copy their favorite cat or dog. (3) Losing a beloved pet is dificult for anyone, so it should come as no suprise that some greiving pet owners are hurrying to resurrect their furry friends.

(4) Genetic Savings & Clone already has preserved the tissue of hundreds of pets whose owners hope one day to cuddle a clone. (5) Freezing a DNA sample

from Fido or Fluffy costs over a thousand dollars, with yearly maintenance around $100. (6) Once the cloning process is perfected, creating the replacment animal will cost $10,000 more—making Fluffy II one expensive little cat!

(7) Ironically, experts tell owners of pricy purebred animals to forget about cloneing. (8) The bloodlines that produce the look and behavor of pure breeds work nearly as well as cloning. (9) On the other hand, if Fido has four or five breeds in his blood, he truly is a unique mutt and a good posibility for cloning.

(10) Critics say cloning pets is ridiclous. (11) Because both genes and enviroment determine animal behavior, puting a piece of Fido in the fridge will not guarentee good results. (12) Owners who beleive thier copycat will have the same adoreable personality as the original kitty are bound to be disapointed. (13) The Humane Society opposes cloning, urging lonely pet owners to adopt an abandoned animal at their local shelter instead. (14) With thousands of strays needing homes, creating a copy cat or dog seems like a waste of money and scientific resources. (15) But people are so tyed to their pets that Genetic Savings & Clone might well remain a booming busyness.

Exploring Online

http://webster.commnet.edu/cgi-shl/quiz.pl/spelling_quizl.htm Interactive spelling test.

http://grammar.uoregon.edu/examples/Equiz8.html Challenging spelling test. Raise your level.

CHAPTER 39

Look-Alikes/Sound-Alikes

A/an/and

1. *A* is used before a word beginning with a consonant or a consonant sound.

   a **man**   *a* **house**   *a* **union** (here *u* sounds like the consonant *y*)

2. *An* is used before a word beginning with a vowel (*a, e, i, o, u*) or silent *h*.

   an **igloo**   *an* **apple**   *an* **hour** (*h* in *hour* is silent)

3. *And* joins words or ideas together.

   Edward *and* **Ralph are taking the same biology class.**
   She is very honest, *and* **most people respect her.**

PRACTICE 1   Fill in *a*, *an*, or *and*.

1. The administration building is _____ old brick house on top of _____ hill.

2. _____ artist _____ two students share that studio.

3. The computer in my office has _____ flat screen _____ _____ CD burner.

4. For lunch, Ben ate _____ tofu sandwich, _____ apple, _____ two bananas.

Accept/except

1. *Accept* means to receive.

   That college *accepts* **only women.**   **I** *accepted* **his offer of help.**

2. *Except* means other than or excluding.

   Everyone *except* **Marcelo thinks it's a good idea.**

493

PRACTICE 2   Fill in *accept* or *except*.

1. Jan has read all of Shakespeare's comedies _____ one.
2. Please _____ my apologies.
3. Unable to _____ defeat, the boxer protested the decision.
4. Sam loves all his courses _____ chemistry.

Affect/effect

1. *Affect* (verb) means to have an influence on or to change.

    Her father's career as a lawyer *affected* her decision to go to law school.

2. *Effect* (noun) means the result of a cause or an influence.

    Careful proofreading had a positive *effect* on Carl's grades.

3. *Effect* is also a verb that means to cause.

    The U.S. Senate is attempting to *effect* changes in foreign policy.

PRACTICE 3   Fill in *affect* or *effect*.

1. You are mistaken if you think alcohol will not _____ your judgment.
2. Attractive, neat clothing will have a positive _____ on a job.
3. Hot, humid summers always have the _____ of making me lazy.
4. We will not be able to _____ these changes without the cooperation of the employees and the union.

Been/being

1. *Been* is the past participle form of *to be*. *Been* is usually used after the helping verb *have, has,* or *had*.

    She *has been* a poet for ten years.

2. *Being* is the *-ing* form of *to be*. *Being* is usually used after the helping verb *is, are, am, was,* or *were*.

    They *are being* helped by the salesperson.

PRACTICE 4   Fill in *been* or *being*.

1. Have you _____ to Rib Heaven yet?
2. Pete thinks his phone calls are _____ taped.
3. Are you _____ secretive, or have I _____ imagining it?
4. Yoko has never _____ to Omaha!

Buy/by

1. *Buy* means to purchase.

   My aunt *buys* new furniture every five years.

2. *By* means near, by means of, or before.

   He walked right *by* and didn't say hello.

   ***By* sunset, we had finished the harvest.**

PRACTICE 5 Fill in *buy* or *by*.

1. You can't _____ happiness, but many people try.

2. Lee _____ sand _____ the ton for his masonry business.

3. Please drop _____ the video store and _____ some blank tapes; I want to tape the football game.

4. _____ _____ out his partners, Joe became sole owner of the firm.

It's/its

1. *It's* is a contraction of *it is* or *it has*. If you cannot substitute *it is* or *it has* in the sentence, you cannot use *it's*.

   ***It's* a ten minute walk to my house.**   ***It's* been a nice party.**

2. *Its* is a possessive and shows ownership.

   Industry must do *its* share to curb inflation.

PRACTICE 6 Fill in *it's* or *its*.

1. Put the contact lens in _____ case, please.

2. _____ about time H.T. straightened up the rubble in his room.

3. The company offered some of _____ employees an early retirement option.

4. You know _____ cold when the pond has ice on _____ surface.

Know/knew/no/new

1. *Know* means to have knowledge or understanding.

   Carl *knows* he has to finish by 6 P.M.

2. *Knew* is the past tense of the verb *know*.

   I *knew* it.

3. *No* is a negative.

   He is *no* longer dean of academic affairs.

4. *New* means recent, fresh, unused.

   I like your *new* hat.

PRACTICE 7 Fill in *know, knew, no,* or *new.*

1. I _____ he's _____ in town, but this is ridiculous.
2. If I _____ then what I _____ now, I wouldn't have made so many mistakes when I was young.
3. Abe and Gabe _____ that they have _____ chance of winning the marathon.
4. _____, I don't _____ the way to Grandma's house, you hairy weirdo.

Lose/loose

1. *Lose* means to misplace or not to win.

   Be careful not to *lose* your way on those back roads.
2. *Loose* means too large, not tightly fitting.

   This shirt is not my size; it's *loose*.

PRACTICE 8 Fill in *lose* or *loose.*

1. When Ari studies in bed, he _____ the _____ change from his pockets.
2. Several layers of _____ clothing can warm you in winter.
3. Don't _____ any sleep over tomorrow's exam.
4. If you _____ that _____ screw, the handle will fall off.

Past/passed

1. *Past* is that which has already occurred; it is over with.

   Never let the *past* interfere with your hopes for the future.
2. *Passed* is the past tense of the verb *to pass.*

   The wild geese *passed* overhead.

PRACTICE 9 Fill in *past* or *passed.*

1. As Jake _____ the barn, he noticed a man talking to the reindeer.
2. To children, even the recent _____ seems like ancient history.

3. Mia _____ up the opportunity to see a friend from her _____.

4. This Bible was _____ down to me by my mother; it contains records of our family's _____.

Quiet/quit/quite

1. *Quiet* means silent, still.

   The woods are *quiet* tonight.

2. *Quit* means to give up or to stop doing something.

   Last year I *quit* drinking.

3. *Quite* means very or exactly.

   He was *quite* tired after playing handball for two hours.

   That's not *quite* right.

PRACTICE 10 Fill in *quiet*, *quit*, or *quite*.

1. The stone cottage is a _____ place in which to study.

2. Nora is _____ dedicated to her veterinary career.

3. Don't _____ your job, even though you aren't _____ happy with the working conditions.

4. Each day when he _____ work, Dan visits a _____ spot in the park.

Rise/raise

1. *Rise* means to get up by one's own power.
   The past tense of *rise* is *rose*.
   The past participle of *rise* is *risen*.

   The moon *rises* at 9 P.M.

   Daniel *rose* early yesterday.

   He has *risen* from the table.

2. *Raise* means to lift an object or to grow or increase.
   The past tense of *raise* is *raised*.
   The past participle of *raise* is *raised*.

   ***Raise* your right hand.**

   She *raised* the banner over her head.

   We have *raised* one thousand dollars.

PRACTICE 11 Fill in the correct form of *rise* or *raise*.

1. The loaves of bread have _____ perfectly.

2. The new mayor _____ his arms in a victory salute.

3. Once the sun has _____, Pete _____ the shades.

4. We all _____ as the bride walked down the aisle.

Sit/set

1. *Sit* means to seat oneself.
   The past tense of *sit* is *sat*.
   The past participle of *sit* is *sat*.

   ***Sit* up straight!**

   He *sat* down on the porch and fell asleep.

   She has *sat* reading that book all day.

2. *Set* means to place or put something down.
   The past tense of *set* is *set*.
   The past participle of *set* is *set*.

   Don't *set* your workout clothes on the dining room table.

   She *set* the package down and walked off without it.

   He had *set* the timer on the stove.

PRACTICE 12 Fill in *sit* or *set*.

1. Please _____ your briefcase here. Would you like to _____ down?

2. Have they _____ in on a rehearsal before?

3. Tom _____ the chair by the window and _____ down.

4. Sorry, I wouldn't have _____ here if I had known you were returning.

Suppose/supposed

1. *Suppose* means to assume or guess.
   The past tense of *suppose* is *supposed*.
   The past participle of *suppose* is *supposed*.

   Brad *supposes* that geology will be interesting.

   We all *supposed* she would win first prize.

   I had *supposed* Dan would bring his trumpet.

2. *Supposed* means ought to or should; it is followed by *to*.

   You were *supposed* to wash and wax the car.

   Remember: When you mean *ought to* or *should*, always use the *-ed* ending—*supposed*.

PRACTICE 13
Fill in *suppose* or *supposed*.

1. Why do you _____ wolves howl at the moon?

2. I _____ you enjoy reggae.

3. Detective Baker is _____ to address the Citizens' Patrol tonight.

4. Wasn't Erik _____ to meet us at five?

Their/there/they're

1. *Their* is a possessive and shows ownership.

   They couldn't find *their* wigs.

2. *There* indicates a direction.

   I wouldn't go *there* again.

   There is also a way of introducing a thought.

   ***There* is a fly in my soup.**

3. *They're* is a contraction: *they* + *are* = *they're*. If you cannot substitute *they are* in the sentence, you cannot use *they're*.

   If *they're* coming, count me in.

PRACTICE 14
Fill in *their*, *there*, or *they're*.

1. If _____ not _____ on time, we will leave without them.

2. _____ two of the most amusing people I know.

3. _____ are two choices, and _____ both risky.

4. Two mail carriers left _____ mail bags _____ on the steps.

5. The motorcycles roared _____ way into town.

6. Don't worry about _____ performance in the race because _____ both tough.

Then/than

1. *Then* means afterward or at that time.

   First we went to the theater, and *then* **we went out for a pizza and champagne.**

   I was a heavyweight boxer *then*.

2. *Than* is used in a comparison.

   She is a better student *than* **I.**

PRACTICE 15 Fill in *then* or *than*.

1. First, Cassandra kicked off her shoes; _____ she began to dance.
2. Jupiter's diameter is eleven times larger _____ Earth's.
3. If you're more familiar with this trail _____ I, _____ you should lead the way.
4. Fran lived in Chicago _____; now she lives in Los Angeles.

Through/though

1. *Through* means in one side and out the other, finished, or by means of.

   The rain came *through* **the open window.**

   Through **practice, I can do anything.**

2. *Though* means although. Used with *as*, *though* means as if.

   Though **he rarely speaks, he writes terrific letters.**

   It was *as though* **I had never ridden a bicycle before.**

PRACTICE 16 Fill in *through* or *though*.

1. _____ study and perseverance, Charelle earned her degree in three years.
2. Dee usually walks to work _____ she sometimes rides the bus.
3. Julio strode _____ the bank as _____ he owned it.
4. Clayton is a Texan _____ and _____.

To/too/two

1. *To* means toward.

   We are going *to* **the computer lab.**

   To can also be combined with a verb to form an infinitive.

   Where do you want *to go* **for lunch?**

2. *Too* means also or very.

   Roberto is going to the theater *too*.

   They were *too* bored to stay awake.

3. *Two* is the number 2.

   There are *two* new nursing courses this term.

PRACTICE 17 Fill in *to, too,* or *two*.

1. Please take my daughter _____ the movies _____.

2. Dan, _____, took _____ hours _____ complete the exam.

3. Luis went _____ Iowa State for _____ semesters.

4. This curry is _____ hot _____ eat and _____ good _____ resist.

Use/used

1. *Use* means to make use of.
   The past tense of *use* is *used*.
   The past participle of *use* is *used*.

   Why do you *use* green ink?

   He *used* black-and-white film for the project.

   I have *used* that brand of cell phone myself.

2. *Used* means in the habit of or accustomed to; it is followed by *to*.

   I am not *used* to getting up at 4 A.M.   **They got *used* to the good life.**

Remember: When you mean *in the habit of* or *accustomed to*, always use the *-ed* ending—*used*.

PRACTICE 18 Fill in *use* or *used*.

1. Marie _____ to drive a jalopy that she bought at a _____ car lot.

2. We will _____ about three gallons of paint on this shed.

3. Can you _____ a _____ laptop?

4. Pam _____ to _____ a pick to strum her guitar.

Weather/whether

1. *Weather* refers to atmospheric conditions.

   In June, the *weather* in Spain is lovely.

2. *Whether* implies a question.

Whether or not you succeed depends on you.

PRACTICE 19 Fill in *weather* or *whether*.

1. In fine _____, we take canoe rides on the lake.

2. _____ or not you like Brazilian food, you'll love this dish.

3. The _____ person never said _____ or not it would snow.

4. In 1870 a national _____ service was established.

Where/were/we're

1. *Where* implies place or location.

   Where have you been all day?

2. *Were* is the past tense of *are*.

   We *were* on our way when the hurricane hit.

3. *We're* is a contraction: *we* + *are* = *we're*. If you cannot substitute *we are* in the sentence, you cannot use *we're*.

   Since *we're* in the city, let's go to the zoo.

PRACTICE 20 Fill in *where*, *were*, or *we're*.

1. _____ going to Hawaii _____ the sun always shines.

2. _____ you standing _____ we agreed to meet?

3. There _____ two high-rise apartment houses _____ the ballpark used to be.

4. _____ determined to attend college though we don't yet know _____.

Whose/who's

1. *Whose* implies ownership and possession.

   Whose term paper is that?

2. *Who's* is a contraction of *who is* or *who has*. If you cannot substitute *who is* or *who has*, you cannot use *who's*.

   Who's knocking at the window?

   Who's seen my new felt hat with the red feathers?

PRACTICE 21 Fill in *whose* or *who's*.

1. _____ convertible is this?

2. Tanya, _____ in my history class, will join us for dinner.

3. We need someone in that position _____ dependable, someone _____ abilities have already been proven.

4. _____ biology textbook is this?

Your/you're

1. *Your* is a possessive and shows ownership.

   Your knowledge astonishes me!

2. *You're* is a contraction: *you + are = you're*. If you cannot substitute *you are* in the sentence, you cannot use *you're*.

   You're the nicest person I know.

PRACTICE 22 Fill in *your* or *you're*.

1. _____ sitting on _____ hat.

2. When _____ ready to begin _____ piano lesson, we'll leave.

3. Let _____ adviser help you plan _____ course schedule.

4. When _____ with _____ friends, _____ a different person.

Personal Look-Alikes/Sound-Alikes List

In your notebook, keep a list of look-alikes and sound-alikes that *you* have trouble with. Add words to your list from corrected papers and from the exercises in this chapter; consider such pairs as *adapt/adopt, addition/edition, device/devise, stationery/stationary,* and so forth.

First, write the word you used incorrectly; then write its meaning or use it correctly in a sentence, whichever best helps you remember. Now do the same with the word you meant to use.

Word	Meaning
1. though	means although
through	We hiked through the woods.
2.	

PRACTICE 23 Write a paragraph using as many of the look-alikes and sound-alikes as possible. Exchange paragraphs with a classmate and check each other's work.

PRACTICE 24 REVIEW

The following essay contains a number of look-alike/sound-alike errors. Proofread for these errors, writing the correct word above the line.

Isabel Allende

(1) Possibly the best-known female writer of Latin-American literature, Isabel Allende has survived many political and personal tragedies. (2) Most of those events have found there way into her books. (3) Born in 1942, Allende was raise by her mother in Chile after her parents' divorce. (4) When her uncle, President Salvador Allende, was killed during a military coup in 1973, she fled. (5) For the next seventeen years, she lived in Venezuela, were she was unable to find work and felt trapped in a unhappy marriage.

(6) One day, learning that her grandfather was dying in Chile, Allende began to write him a long letter; that letter grew until it became her first novel. (7) Still her most famous book, *The House of the Spirits* established Allende's style of writing, which combines political realism and autobiography with dreams, spirits, an magic. (8) The novel, which was banned in Chile, was translated into more then twenty-five languages and in 1994 was made into a movie.

(9) Buy 1988, Allende had divorced, moved to northern California, remarried, and written her fourth novel, *The Infinite Plan,* which is her second husband's story. (10) Her next book traced the profound affect on Allende of the death of her daughter, Paula. (11) The book *Paula*, like *The House of the Spirits,* was suppose to be a letter, this time too her daughter, who lay in a coma in a Madrid hospital.

(12) After *Paula* was published, Allende stopped writing for several years. (13) She started again in 1996, on January 8, the same day of the year that she had begun every one of her books. (14) The result was *Aphrodite,* a nonfiction book about food and sensuality that was quiet different from Allende's passed work.

(15) With renewed energy to right again, Allende spun the tale of an independent woman who leaves her home in Chile to move to San Francisco during the Gold Rush. (16) Two novels, *Daughter of Fortune* and *Portrait in Sepia*, complete her story.

(17) Isabel Allende is famous for been a passionate storyteller who's writing captures both the Latin-American and the universal human experience. (18) As the first Latina to write a major novel in the mystical tradition, she not only created a sensation, but she paved the way for other female Hispanic writers, including Julia Alvarez and Sandra Cisneros.

 **Exploring Online**

http://webster.commnet.edu/cgi-shl/quiz.pl/spelling_add2.htm Graded look-alikes quiz. Test your skills.

http://webster.commnet.edu/cgi-shl/quiz.pl/spelling_add4.htm Interactive spelling and look-alikes test.

Writers' Workshop

Discuss a Time When Diverse People Were United

Some writers are naturally good spellers, and others are not. If you belong to the latter group, this unit has given you some techniques and tools for overcoming your spelling problems.

In your group or class, read this student's essay, aloud if possible. Underline the ideas and sentences you find especially effective. If you spot any spelling errors, correct them.

> **A Community of Fishermen**
>
> (1) Although City Island is probably best known for it's seafood restaurants, it's just before dinnertime that I most enjoy the island. That's when the fishing boats leave: The *Riptide, Apache,* and *Daybreak* all cruise out of their slips and head for the hot spot of the day. These large vessels can pack up to a hundred passengers on board, and the crowd is usualy more diversifyd than all the fish being hoisted over the railing.
>
> (2) Anglers from all walks of life compete for the prize money that is awarded for catching the biggest fish. The anglers are black, white, brown, and yellow, but they leave any thoughts about their skin pigment back at the dock alongside there problems. What these fishermen do for a living, where they come from, and what kind of car they'll drive home that night are concepts of little importance. The things that count now are catching big fish, learning new tricks to catch them, and above all, having a good time. Men of all diffrent races and religions now have something in common; they are all fishermen.
>
> (3) The passengers might be culturally diverse, but with the exception of an ocasional girlfriend or wife, they're all men. Grandfathers show sons and grandsons the ropes. Veterans give tips to the newer guys next to them, and as they hold their fishing poles over the side of the boat, elbow to elbow, they link together in a chain of masculinity.
>
> (4) It's an eight-hour trip, and with a couple of hours down, you'll actually observe the passengers coming together. Almost everyone is drinking beer, and everyone likes to team up and tease landlubbers who get seasick. Salty old men swap fish tales and complain that the fishing is not what it used to be. Fathers talk shop and exchange jokes and busness cards. Younger men play pranks, like sliping bait into an old-timer's

> pocket when he's not looking. Naturally, they'll take things too far and get found out, but old-timers were not always old and will usually find humor in the gag. Toward the end of the trip, everyone congratulates the winner of the pool and slips in the last few jokes. Clearly, the conflicts that are so common in life are almost nonexistant when your out on a boat in the middle of Long Island Sound.
>
> (5) Something about sharing close quarters and a passion for the same sport makes men feel like equals. The unity seen on a fishing boat is proof that people can blend without having problems as long as they have something in common. As Anna Quindlen writes in her essay "Melting Pot," "We melt together, then draw apart."
>
> —Paul La Valle (Student)

1. How effective is Mr. La Valle's essay?

    _____ Strong thesis statement?   _____ Good supporting details?

    _____ Logical organization?   _____ Effective conclusion?

2. Discuss your underlinings. What details or lines in the essay did you like the most? Explain as exactly as possible why something struck you as interesting or moving.

3. What is the main idea of paragraph 2? Which sentence, if any, is the topic sentence? What is the main idea of paragraph 3? What is the main idea of paragraph 4?

4. This student ends his essay with a correctly punctuated quotation. Who is the source of the quotation? Does it provide a strong conclusion for the essay? Why or why not?

5. Give examples of times when or places where diverse people have united to become a true community.

6. This student's spelling errors are distracting in an otherwise thoughtful and very well written essay. What suggestions would you make to him for improving his spelling?

Group Work

In your group, find and correct the spelling errors in this essay. See if your group can find every error. Hint: There are eleven misspelled or confused words.

Writing and Revising Ideas

1. Discuss a time when diverse people were united.
2. Write an essay that concludes with a quotation. Use Anna Quindlen's words, "We melt together, then draw apart," or choose another quotation from the Quotation Bank at the end of this book or elsewhere.

UNIT 8

Reading Selections

Reading Strategies for Writers

The fifteen enjoyable and thought-provoking reading selections that follow deal with many of the concerns you have as a student, as a worker, and as a member of a family. Your instructor may ask you to read and think about a selection for class discussion or for a composition either at home or in class.

The more carefully you read these selections, the better you will be able to discuss and write about them. Below are ten strategies that can help you become a more effective reader and writer:

1. **Note the title.** A title, of course, is your first clue as to what the selection is about. For example, the title "Strike Out Little League" lets you know that the selection will discuss negative aspects of organized sports for children.

    A title may also tell you which method of development the author is using. For instance, a selection entitled "Husbands and Wives: Different as Night and Day" might be a comparison/contrast essay; one entitled "Using the Library—Electronically" might be a process piece explaining how to use a computerized library catalogue.

2. **Underline main ideas.** If you read a long or difficult selection, you may forget some of the important ideas soon after you have finished the essay. However, underlining or highlighting these key ideas as you read will later help you review more easily. You may wish to number main ideas to help you follow the development of the author's thesis.

3. **Write your reactions in the margins.** Feel free to express your agreement or disagreement with the ideas in a selection by commenting "yes," "no," "Important—compare with Alice Walker's essay," or "Is he kidding?" in the margins.

    You will often be asked to write a "reaction paper," a composition explaining your thoughts about or reaction to the author's ideas. The comments that you have recorded in the margins will help you formulate a response.

4. **Prepare questions.** As you tackle more difficult reading selections, you may come across material that is hard to follow. Of course, reread the passage to see if a second reading helps. If it does not, put a question mark in the margin.

    Ask a friend or the instructor to help answer your questions. Do not be embarrassed to ask for explanations in class. Instructors appreciate careful readers who want to be sure that they completely understand what they have read.

5. **Note possible composition topics.** As you read, you may think of topics for compositions related to the ideas in the selection. Jot these topics in the margins or write about them in your journal. They may become useful if your instructor asks you for an essay based on the selection.

6. **Note effective writing.** If you are particularly moved by a portion of the selection—a phrase, a sentence, or an entire paragraph—underline or highlight it. You may wish to quote it later in class or use it in your composition.

7. **Circle unfamiliar words.** As you read, you will occasionally come across unfamiliar words. If you can guess what the word means from its context—from how it is used in the sentence or in the passage—do not interrupt your reading to look it up. Interruptions can cause you to lose the flow of ideas in the selection. Instead, circle the word and check it in a dictionary later.

8. **Vary your pace.** Some essays can be read quickly and easily. Others may require more time if the material is difficult or if much of the subject matter is

unfamiliar to you. Be careful not to become discouraged, skimming a particularly difficult section just to get through with it. Extra effort will pay off.

9. **Reread.** If possible, budget your time so you can read the selection a second or even a third time. One advantage of rereading is that you will be able to discuss or write about the essay with more understanding. Ideas that were unclear may become obvious; you may even see new ideas that you failed to note the first time around.

    Another advantage is that by the second or third reading, your responses may have changed. You may agree with ideas you rejected the first time; you may disagree with ones you originally agreed with. Rereading gives you a whole new perspective!

10. **Do not overdo it.** Marking the selection as you read can help you become a better reader and writer. However, too many comments may defeat your purpose. You may not be able to decipher the mass—or mess—of underlinings, circles, and notes that you have made. Be selective.

The following essay has been marked, or annotated, by a student. Your responses might be different. Use this essay as a model to help you annotate other selections in this book—and reading material for your other courses as well.

How Sunglasses Spanned the World

Could be a process essay

1   Like many of the world's inhabitants, you probably own at least one pair of sunglasses, chosen as much for the image they project as for their ability to protect your eyes from the sun. In fact, sunglasses have become a staple in almost every country; it is no longer surprising to spot sunglasses on robed Arabian sheiks, Bolivian grandmothers, or Inuit fishermen tramping Arctic snows. The process by which sunglasses have gained worldwide popularity is a fascinating one that began, surprisingly, in the justice system of medieval China.

staple—standard item

Inuit—Eskimo

2   Dark glasses with smoke-tinted quartz lenses existed for centuries in China prior to 1430, but they were not used for sun protection. Chinese judges wore the darkened lenses in court to conceal their eye expressions and keep secret their reactions to evidence until the end of a trial. In 1430, when vision-correcting glasses were introduced into China from Italy, these lenses, too, were smoke-tinted, but almost entirely for judicial use. Some people wore the darkened lenses for sun protection, but the idea never really caught on.

Step 1—really Stage 1

This is a great idea. judicial—relating to court

3   Five hundred years passed before the popularity of sunglasses began to grow. In the 1930s, the U.S. Army Air Corps asked the optical firm of Bausch & Lomb to produce a highly effective spectacle that would protect pilots from the dangers of high-altitude glare. Company scientists perfected a special dark-green tint that absorbed yellow light from the spectrum. They also designed a slightly drooping metal frame to protect the aviator's eyes, which repeatedly glanced down at the plane's instrument panel.

Stage 2—aviator glasses invented

I wonder why . . .

I own a pair just like this!

spectrum—range or band (light breaks into a series of colors)

Stage 3

4   Soon this type of sunglasses was offered to the public as Ray Ban aviators, scientifically designed to ban the sun's rays. For the

first time in history, large numbers of people began to purchase sunglasses.

Stage 4—sunglasses are chic

The next step in the process—making sunglasses chic—was the result of a clever 1960s advertising campaign by the firm of Foster Grant. Determined to increase its share of the sunglass market, the company began to feature the faces of Hollywood celebrities wearing sunglasses above a slogan that read, "Isn't that . . . behind those Foster Grants?" Big stars of the day like Peter Sellers, Anita Ekberg, and Elke Sommer posed for the ads, and the public love affair with sunglasses took off. Behind those Foster Grants, everyone now could feel like a movie star.

5 *Ah, yes. What makes anything span the world? Advertising.*

Stage 5—designer shades

In the 1970s, the trend escalated further when well-known fashion designers and Hollywood stars introduced their own brand-name lines, charging high prices for status sunglasses in the latest styles. A giant industry developed where only a few decades earlier none had existed, and shades became big business.

6 *True. I know people who spend $200 for wrap-arounds to wear dancing—at night!*

Stage 6

parasol—umbrella for the sun

Today sunglasses—like blue jeans and Coca-Cola—circle the globe. Protection against solar radiation is just part of their appeal. As women in ancient times had hidden seductively behind an expanded fan or a tipped parasol, modern women and men all over the world have discovered the mystery, sex appeal, and cosmopolitan cool of wearing sunglasses.

7

Writing ideas—
- *Research the development or origin of another popular item.*
- *Think more about the power of advertising to influence us.*
- *Observe sunglass wearers and write about them.*

Homeward Bound

Janet Wu

At age 12, American-born Janet Wu learned that her grandmother was still alive in China. From their first meeting, despite the miles and differences separating them, the two developed a powerful bond. Their story underscores the importance of staying connected to our ancestors and our heritage. Janet Wu is Television News Anchor/Reporter for WHDH-TV, Boston.

1   My grandmother has bound feet. Cruelly tethered[1] since her birth, they are like bonsai trees,[2] miniature versions of what should have been. She is a relic[3] even in China, where foot binding was first banned more than 80 years ago when the country could no longer afford a population that had to be carried. Her slow, delicate hobble betrays her age and the status she held and lost.

2   My own size 5 feet are huge in comparison. The marks and callouses they bear come from running and jumping, neither of which my grandmother has ever done. The difference between our feet reminds me of the incredible history we hold between us like living bookends. We stand like sentries[4] on either side of a vast gulf.

3   For most of my childhood, I didn't even know she existed. My father was a young man when he left his family's village in northern China, disappearing into the chaos of the Japanese invasion and the Communist revolution that followed. He fled to Taiwan and eventually made his way to America, alone. To me, his second child, it seemed he had no family or history other than his American-born wife and four children. I didn't know that he had been writing years of unanswered letters to China.

4   I was still a young girl when he finally got a response, and with it the news that his father and six of his seven siblings had died in those years of war and revolution. But the letter also contained an unexpected blessing: somehow his mother had survived. So 30 years after he left home, and in the wake of President Nixon's visit, my father gathered us up and we rushed to China to find her.

5   I saw my grandmother for the very first time when I was 12. She was almost 80, surprisingly alien and shockingly small. I searched her wrinkled face for something familiar, some physical proof we belonged to each other. She stared at me the same way. Did she feel cheated, I wondered, by the distance, by the time we had not spent together? I did. With too many lost years to reclaim, we had everything and nothing to say. She politely listened as I struggled with scraps of formal Chinese and smiled as I fell back on "Wo bu dong" ("I don't understand you"). And yet we communicated something strange and beautiful. I found it easy to love this person I had barely met.

6   The second time I saw her I was 23, arriving in China on an indulgent[5] post-graduate-school adventure, with a Caucasian boyfriend in tow. My grandmother sat on my hotel bed, shrunken and wise, looking as if she belonged in a museum case. She stroked my asymmetrically[6] cropped hair. I touched her feet, and her

---

1. tethered: tied
2. bonsai trees: dwarf trees forced to grow in small pots
3. relic: an object or fragment from the past
4. sentries: guards
5. indulgent: whimsical, unnecessary
6. asymmetrically: unevenly

face contorted with the memory of her childhood pain. "You are lucky," she said. We both understood that she was thinking of far more than the bindings that long ago made her cry. I wanted to share even the smallest part of her life's journey, but I could not conceive of surviving a dynasty[7] and a revolution, just as she could not imagine my life in a country she had never seen. In our mutual isolation of language and experience, we could only gaze in wonder, mystified that we had come to be sitting together.

I last saw her almost five years ago. At 95, she was even smaller, and her frailty frightened me. I was painfully aware that I probably would never see her again, that I would soon lose this person I never really had. So I mentally logged every second we spent together and jockeyed with my siblings for the chance to hold her hand or touch her shoulder. Our departure date loomed like some kind of sentence. And when it came, she broke down, her face bowed into her gnarled[8] hands. I went home, and with resignation[9] awaited the inevitable news that she was gone.

But two months after that trip, it was my father who died. For me, his loss was doubly cruel: his death deprived me of both my foundation and the bridge to my faraway grandmother. For her, it was the second time she had lost him. For the 30 years they were separated, she had feared her son was dead. This time, there was no ambiguity,[10] no hope. When she heard the news, my uncle later wrote us, she wept quietly.

When I hear friends complain about having to visit their nearby relatives, I think of how far away my grandmother is and how untouched our relationship remains by the modern age. My brief handwritten notes are agonizingly slow to reach her. When they do arrive, she cannot read them. I cannot call her. I cannot see, hear or touch her.

But last month my mother called to tell me to brush up on my Chinese. Refusing to let go of our tenuous[11] connection to my father's family, she has decided to take us all back to China in October for my grandmother's 100th birthday. And so every night, I sit at my desk and study, thinking of her tiny doll-like feet, of the miles and differences that separate us, of the moments we'll share when we meet one last time. And I beg her to hold on until I get there.

Discussion and Writing Questions

1. Why does the author start her essay by contrasting her grandmother's feet and her own? What other differences between the two women's lives are revealed through this comparison (paragraphs 1 and 2)?

2. A language barrier exists between the author and her grandmother, yet they communicate "something strange and beautiful" (paragraph 5). What would you say this *something* is?

3. Paragraph 6 describes the author's visit to China with her boyfriend. Did you find any details especially strong or moving? How do these details help us understand what the grandmother means when she says, "You are lucky"?

---

7. dynasty: a family or group that rules for generations
8. gnarled: twisted, bumpy
9. resignation: hopeless acceptance
10. ambiguity: uncertainty
11. tenuous: weak, slender

4. Do you ever complain, like the author's friends, about having to visit relatives? What do you think the author would say to those who do not seek out or appreciate time with family members? What benefits do these relationships offer? What can we learn from older relatives?

Writing Assignments

1. Do you and a family member have a special relationship in spite of distance, age, or other barriers? Describe this relationship and what makes it unique. You might begin as Wu does with a single contrast that reveals other differences between you.

2. Are any of your cultural traditions or customs being lost through immigration or the passage of time? Write an essay describing one special tradition or custom that is being lost in your family—or a special tradition that your family keeps alive.

3. How do people in the United States tend to regard the elderly? How do these attitudes and beliefs compare with what you were taught—or with the views of some other culture? For ideas on America's increasingly negative view of aging, visit http://www.cps.unt.edu/natla/web/changing_attitudes_handout.htm.

Cell Yell: Thanks for (Not) Sharing

Eric A. Taub

Once considered a luxury, cell phones have become a common and sometimes obnoxious presence in our daily lives—whether we own one or not. In this *New York Times* article, Eric Taub considers the reasons why cell phones—and their users—so often intrude on the people around them.

1 With just five minutes to takeoff, the young man across the aisle on the Baltimore-bound flight whipped out his cellphone and began a hurried and boisterous conversation, explaining the fine points of marketing his new Christmas-gift Web site to an unseen underling. With glazed eyes staring at the seat in front of him, the executive unconsciously pounded his foot in rhythm to his conversation, oblivious[1] to the 15 surrounding passengers glaring at this human loudspeaker in seat 23B.

2 The harried young executive was engaged in one of the more despised forms of mobile-phone behavior. In the industry it is called cell yell—a tendency of many cellphone users to speak into their phones more loudly than necessary, unwittingly involving surrounding strangers in their personal business.

3 Cell yell has created a subculture of cell-yell haters. The phenomenon has given rise to a Web site (www.cellmanners.com). An artist, John Detrich, offered a cell-yell-themed illustration for sale online. And The Register, a British Web site devoted to technology, reported that a mobile phone user in Germany died two years ago after a beer-garden brawl over his lack of cellular civility.

4 It is too simplistic to put the blame for this antisocial behavior strictly on technology, social scientists say, because the way society uses new inventions both defines and reflects the existing culture. In the 1950's, people were used to the privacy of enclosed phone booths when making calls in public places. If cellphones

---

1. oblivious: unaware

had been invented then, people would probably have jumped into those same booths to use them. Today, with more mobile, informal and open societies, many in Western countries relish the idea of speaking in open spaces, oblivious to the presence of others, and often in too loud a voice.

Mobile phone design doesn't help temper that arch behavior. Unlike standard corded phones, cellphones provide little in the way of aural[2] feedback; it has long been known that if you can hear yourself through the earpiece, you are better able to keep your voice properly modulated. (That's why the hard of hearing often speak more loudly than others.) Because the mouthpiece of the typical cellphone barely extends to the cheek, many users act, consciously or not, as if they have to shout to be heard.

"Cellphones are so small that people don't trust the technology to work," said Timo Kopomaa, a social scientist at the University of Technology in Helsinki and author of a study on cellphone behavior. That is one reason Motorola makes phones that flip open, according to a company executive: to give people the illusion that the phone is bigger and the microphone is closer to the mouth.

Add to that loud street sounds, plus the relative novelty of being able to speak to anyone anywhere, and suddenly throngs[3] are shouting above the ambient[4] noise in public squares, restaurants and post offices as they become engrossed in personal conversations, consequently "privatizing the public space," Dr. Kopomaa said. By doing so, he said, they ignore the needs of the nonphoning public, "denying others the privacy they selfishly appropriate for their own use."

Perversely, many onlookers find it difficult to withdraw attention from the unwanted cellular intrusion. The ringing phone has long taken precedence over a conversation between two people in the same physical space; an unanswered phone expresses urgency and creates tension for the listener.

A ringing cellphone is perceived as even more important than a ringing traditional phone. Sounding in public, it "spreads tension to all those within earshot, yet because it's not for them, they're powerless to answer the call," said Dr. Sadie Plant, a researcher in Birmingham, England, who was commissioned by Motorola to study cultural differences in cellphone use.

Some cellphone owners prominently display even cellphones not in use, for their presence alone creates tension, as bystanders wonder if they are soon going to ring, Dr. Plant said. Users also often engage in "stage-phoning," making unimportant calls in public just to impress others.

Dr. Plant found individuals who actually enjoyed listening to strangers' cell calls; a soap opera was created, but one with only half the information available. It was up to the eavesdropper to fill in the unheard party's responses with fantasy dialogue. Others found it obnoxious, since they are neither fully admitted to nor excluded from that cellphone user's world.

The public cellphone user creates what Dr. Kopomaa calls a "black hole" as the user psychologically withdraws from his immediate surroundings to focus on the call. At the same time, others are forced to suspend their own activities, whether they were talking with the cellphone user or trying to concentrate on their own affairs.

"People are forced to remain present both physically and mentally," Dr. Kopomaa wrote in "The City in Your Pocket," a Finnish study of cellphone culture. Since a phone conversation by its nature is the opposite of public speaking, surrounding people are "disgusted by this forced eavesdropping," he theorized.

---

2. aural: heard
3. throngs: crowds
4. ambient: surrounding

Cellphone users tend to answer their phones quickly, but not because they are concerned about annoying their fellow citizens. Rather, a rapid response to a ring shows bystanders that the users have "telecredibility," Dr. Kopomaa said. They have mastered this new technology, and they do not have to fumble to figure out how to answer it.

When Dr. Kopomaa recently discussed the implications of his study in an interview on his cellphone while riding a ferry from Finland to Sweden, he did what few other cellphone users do: he retreated into the ship's bathroom for privacy. In doing so, Dr. Kopomaa, 45, betrayed his age; studies indicate that young Western people see the cellphone, and the receipt of cellphone calls, as a symbol of virility and social importance, and therefore something to be flaunted.

In Dr. Plant's view, the cellphone has become a psychosexual[5] symbol of performance. When mixed couples dine in restaurants, for example, it is more likely that the male will place his phone on the table and the female will leave hers in her purse, according to Dr. Plant. When two women dine together, both tend to keep them out of sight. But if one woman places her phone on the table, the other will probably follow suit.

Dr. Plant found this tendency toward display to be as true in Chicago as in London. Indeed, while cell boorishness[6] is not confined to one country, certain practices are culture-specific. In China, cellphone owners prominently carry them in crocheted or silk bags, Dr. Plant said, while Japanese users often customize their phones with stick-on designs and graphically distinctive cases. In many countries, texting—sending short, coded text messages to another cell user—has become the communication method of choice, especially for adolescents. It offers the socially shy the anonymity and immediacy of e-mail.

"Boys can ask girls out by sending a text message, without having to hear the disappointment in their voices," Dr. Plant said. "And I've observed many noncommunicative teenage boys become much more communicative thanks to texting."

But even where texting is used as a nonintrusive way to communicate, it seems it is not being used enough, judging from the anti-cellphone backlash. A bagel shop in Westlake Village, Calif. banned the use of cellphones while ordering last year because customers routinely asked for the wrong food when they were busy jabbering. To stem the jangle of ringing cellphones, Cingular Wireless is erecting kiosks[7] at 100 Loews movie theaters as a sort of lobby-based cellphone purgatory where users will be encouraged to place and receive any calls.

"People are very upset when they're forced to hear the results of a stranger's medical tests," said Carol Page, a Boston public relations consultant and founder of CellManners.com. The site has so far recruited three "cell spies," volunteers in Boston, San Francisco and Washington who report on bad cellular behavior—like the man who insisted on phoning while using the urinal, or the wedding guest whose phone went off between the words "I" and "do."

As a new consensus[8] develops over the use of cellphones, perhaps the fear of stigma,[9] rather than rules and laws, will do the most to turn the disruptive tide. In Finland, Dr. Kopomaa has noticed that people already use cellphones more often in casual restaurants than in expensive ones. And when they do, they now call not from their table but from outside the establishment, sharing the space with society's other shunned antisocial group of addicts, cigarette smokers.

---

5. psychosexual: perceived as sexual
6. boorishness: rudeness
7. kiosks: small booths
8. consensus: general agreement
9. stigma: a mark of disgrace

Discussion and Writing Questions

1. How does the author define "cell yell" (paragraph 2)? What changes in society since the 1950s does the author suggest account for the way people use cell phones today?

2. How does mobile phone design contribute to bad cell phone manners? What part does the cell phone user's sense of self-importance play?

3. Eavesdroppers on cell phone conversations experience various reactions, both positive and negative. According to the author, what are some of these reactions and how do people listening against their will handle their strong feelings?

4. Based on the author's examples, what are the rude cell behaviors that bother people the most? What behaviors bother *you* the most? To read other people's humorous and outrageous illustrations of bad cell manners, visit www.cellmanners.com; enter and click "cell wars" or "news."

Writing Assignments

1. Write an essay in which you argue for or against having a "designated outcast zone" for cell talkers in restaurants, theaters, or other places—the way many establishments now isolate smokers. Develop your thesis with two or three clear supporting points.

2. Is the rudeness of cell phone users just a symptom of a society that has become less considerate and more self-centered? With a group of classmates, brainstorm other possible "symptoms" of this trend. Some ideas might include rude clerks and customers, aggressive drivers, or the dying art of thank-you notes. Then select one of these and write an essay in which you suggest ways to reverse the trend.

3. Email is another technology that some people use inconsiderately or even abusively. For instance, some people forward jokes many times a day, and many advertisers send "spam"—ads and email junk. Write an essay in which you suggest rules of etiquette for online mail. If you have access to a computer, you may wish to look up "netiquette"—the new word for rules to govern online behavior. Try www.albion.com/netiquette/.

A Brother's Murder

Brent Staples

Brent Staples grew up in a rough, industrial city. He left to become a successful journalist, but his younger brother remained. Staples's story of his brother is a reminder of the grim circumstances in which so many young men of the inner city find themselves today.

It has been more than two years since my telephone rang with the news that my younger brother Blake—just twenty-two years old—had been murdered. The young man who killed him was only twenty-four. Wearing a ski mask, he emerged from a car, fired six times at close range with a massive .44 Magnum, then fled. The two had once been inseparable friends. A senseless rivalry—beginning, I think, with an argument over a girlfriend—escalated[1] from posturing,[2] to threats, to violence, to murder. The way the two were living, death could have come to either of them from anywhere. In fact, the assailant had already survived multiple gunshot wounds from an accident much like the one in which my brother lost his life.

As I wept for Blake I felt wrenched backward into events and circumstances that had seemed light-years gone. Though a decade apart, we both were raised in Chester, Pennsylvania, an angry, heavily black, heavily poor, industrial city southwest of Philadelphia. There, in the 1960s, I was introduced to mortality, not by the old and failing, but by beautiful young men who lay wrecked after sudden explosions of violence. The first, I remembered from my fourteenth year—Johnny, brash lover of fast cars, stabbed to death two doors from my house in a fight over a pool game. The next year, my teenage cousin, Wesley, whom I loved very much, was shot dead. The summers blur. Milton, an angry young neighbor, shot a crosstown rival, wounding him badly. William, another teenage neighbor, took a shotgun blast to the shoulder in some urban drama and displayed his bandages proudly. His brother, Leonard, severely beaten, lost an eye and donned a black patch. It went on.

I recall not long before I left for college, two local Vietnam veterans—one from the Marines, one from the Army—arguing fiercely, nearly at blows about which outfit had done the most in the war. The most killing, they meant. Not much later, I read a magazine article that set that dispute in a context. In the story, a noncommissioned officer—a sergeant, I believe—said he would pass up any number of affluent, suburban-born recruits to get hard-core soldiers from the inner city. They jumped into the rice paddies with "their manhood on their sleeves," I believe he said. These two items—the veterans arguing and the sergeant's words—still characterize for me the circumstances under which black men in their teens and twenties kill one another with such frequency. With a touchy paranoia born of living battered lives, they are desperate to be *real* men. Killing is only machismo taken to the extreme. Incursions[3] to be punished by death were many and minor, and they remain so: they include stepping on the wrong toe, literally; cheating in a drug deal; simply saying "I dare you" to someone holding a gun; crossing territorial lines in a gang dispute. My brother grew up to wear his manhood on his sleeve. And when he died, he was in that group—black, male and in its teens and early twenties—that is far and away the most likely to murder or be murdered.

I left the East Coast after college, spent the mid- and late 1970s in Chicago as a graduate student, taught for a time, then became a journalist. Within ten years of leaving my hometown, I was overeducated and "upwardly mobile," ensconced[4] on a quiet, tree-lined street where voices raised in anger were scarcely ever heard. The telephone, like some grim umbilical, kept me connected to the old world with news of deaths, imprisonings and misfortune. I felt emotionally beaten up. Perhaps to protect myself, I added a psychological dimension to the physical distance I had already achieved. I rarely visited my hometown. I shut it out.

As I fled the past, so Blake embraced it. On Christmas of 1983, I traveled from Chicago to a black section of Roanoke, Virginia, where he then lived. The desolate public housing projects, the hopeless, idle young men crashing against one another—these reminded me of the embittered town we'd grown up in. It was a place where once I would have been comfortable, or at least sure of myself. Now,

---

1. escalated: increased
2. posturing: trying to appear tough
3. incursions: attacks, violations
4. ensconced: settled comfortably

hearing of my brother's forays[5] into crime, his scrapes with police and street thugs, I was scared, unsteady on foreign terrain.[6]

I saw that Blake's romance with the street life and the hustler image had flowered dangerously. One evening that late December, standing in some Roanoke dive among drug dealers and grim, hair-trigger losers, I told him I feared for his life. He had affected the image of the tough he wanted to be. But behind the dark glasses and the swagger, I glimpsed the baby-faced toddler I'd once watched over. I nearly wept. I wanted desperately for him to live. The young think themselves immortal, and a dangerous light shone in his eyes as he spoke laughingly of making fools of the policemen who had raided his apartment looking for drugs. He cried out as I took his right hand. A line of stitches lay between the thumb and index finger. Kickback from a shotgun, he explained, nothing serious. Gunplay had become part of his life.

I lacked the language simply to say: Thousands have lived this for you and died. I fought the urge to lift him bodily and shake him. This place and the way you are living smells of death to me, I said. Take some time away, I said. Let's go downtown tomorrow and buy a plane ticket anywhere, take a bus trip, anything to get away and cool things off. He took my alarm casually. We arranged to meet the following night—an appointment he would not keep. We embraced as though through glass. I drove away.

As I stood in my apartment in Chicago holding the receiver that evening in February 1984, I felt as though part of my soul had been cut away. I questioned myself then, and I still do. Did I not reach back soon enough or earnestly enough for him? For weeks I awoke crying from a recurrent dream in which I chased him, urgently trying to get him to read a document I had, as though reading it would protect him from what had happened in waking life. His eyes shining like black diamonds, he smiled and danced just beyond my grasp. When I reached for him, I caught only the space where he had been.

Discussion and Writing Questions

1. Staples says that he was "introduced to mortality" in Chester, Pennsylvania, in the 1960s (paragraph 2). What does he mean?

2. What does the author mean when he says his brother grew up to "wear his manhood on his sleeve" (paragraph 3)? Does he imply that there are other ways of expressing masculinity?

3. Staples speaks of a dream in which he holds a document for his brother to read (paragraph 8). What do you suppose that document might say? What does this dream seem to say about communication between the two brothers?

4. Staples begins his narrative by describing the moment at which he hears of Blake's death. Why does he *start* with this event, instead of moving toward it?

Writing Assignments

1. Write a narrative about a shocking incident that took place in your neighborhood. Like Staples, you may want to start with the incident, and then narrate the smaller events in the story that led up to it. Or you can follow time order and end with the incident.

---

5. forays: undertakings, trips
6. terrain: ground

2. Do you think Brent Staples could have done more to change his brother? Can we really influence others to change their lives?

3. In a group with three or four classmates, discuss the most significant problem facing young people in the inner city today. Is it crime? Drugs? Lack of educational or employment opportunities? Choose one problem and decide how it can be solved. Your instructor may ask you to share your solution with the class. Then write your own paper, discussing the problem you think is most significant and proposing a solution.

Only Daughter

Sandra Cisneros

Sandra Cisneros is the author of *The House on Mango Street* and other books. She often writes about the experience of being bicultural, bilingual, and female. Here, she explores the ways in which her birth family helped define who she is—and is not.

Once, several years ago, when I was just starting out my writing career, I was asked to write my own contributor's note for an anthology I was part of. I wrote: "I am the only daughter in a family of six sons. *That* explains everything."

Well, I've thought about that ever since, and yes, it explains a lot to me, but for the reader's sake I should have written: "I am the only daughter in a *Mexican* family of six sons." Or even: "I am the only daughter of a Mexican father and a Mexican-American mother." Or: "I am the only daughter of a working-class family of nine." All of these had everything to do with who I am today.

I was/am the only daughter and *only* a daughter. Being an only daughter in a family of six sons forced me by circumstance to spend a lot of time by myself because my brothers felt it beneath them to play with a *girl* in public. But that aloneness, that loneliness, was good for a would-be writer—it allowed me time to think and think, to imagine, to read and prepare myself.

Being only a daughter for my father meant my destiny would lead me to become someone's wife. That's what he believed. But when I was in the fifth grade and shared my plans for college with him, I was sure he understood. I remember my father saying, "*Que bueno, mi'ja,* that's good." That meant a lot to me, especially since my brothers thought the idea hilarious. What I didn't realize was that my father thought college was good for girls—good for finding a husband. After four years in college and two more in graduate school, and still no husband, my father shakes his head even now and says I wasted all that education.

In retrospect, I'm lucky my father believed daughters were meant for husbands. It meant it didn't matter if I majored in something silly like English. After all, I'd find a nice professional eventually, right? This allowed me the liberty to putter about embroidering my little poems and stories without my father interrupting with so much as a "What's that you're writing?"

But the truth is, I wanted him to interrupt. I wanted my father to understand what it was I was scribbling, to introduce me as "My only daughter, the writer." Not as "This is only my daughter. She teaches." *Es maestra*—teacher. Not even *profesora*.

In a sense, everything I have ever written has been for him, to win his approval even though I know my father can't read English words, even though my father's only reading includes the brown-ink *Esto* sports magazines from Mexico City and the bloody *¡Alarma!* magazines that feature yet another sighting of *La*

Virgen de Guadalupe on a tortilla or a wife's revenge on her philandering[1] husband by bashing his skull in with a *molcajete* (a kitchen mortar made of volcanic rock). Or the *fotonovelas*, the little picture paperbacks with tragedy and trauma erupting from the characters' mouths in bubbles.

My father represents, then, the public majority. A public who is uninterested in reading, and yet one whom I am writing about and for, and privately trying to woo.

When we were growing up in Chicago, we moved a lot because of my father. He suffered bouts of nostalgia. Then we'd have to let go our flat, store the furniture with mother's relatives, load the station wagon with baggage and bologna sandwiches and head south. To Mexico City.

We came back, of course. To yet another Chicago flat, another Chicago neighborhood, another Catholic school. Each time, my father would seek out the parish priest in order to get a tuition break, and complain or boast: "I have seven sons."

He meant *siete hijos*, seven children, but he translated it as "sons." "I have seven sons." To anyone who would listen. The Sears Roebuck employee who sold us the washing machine. The short-order cook where my father ate his ham-and-eggs breakfasts. "I have seven sons." As if he deserved a medal from the state.

My papa. He didn't mean anything by that mistranslation, I'm sure. But somehow I could feel myself being erased. I'd tug my father's sleeve and whisper: "Not seven sons. Six! and *one daughter*."

When my oldest brother graduated from medical school, he fulfilled my father's dream that we study hard and use this—our heads, instead of this—our hands. Even now my father's hands are thick and yellow, stubbed by a history of hammer and nails and twine and coils and springs. "Use this," my father said, tapping his head, "and not this," showing us those hands. He always looked tired when he said it.

Wasn't college an investment? And hadn't I spent all those years in college? And if I didn't marry, what was it all for? Why would anyone go to college and then choose to be poor? Especially someone who had always been poor.

Last year, after ten years of writing professionally, the financial rewards started to trickle in. My second National Endowment for the Arts Fellowship. A guest professorship at the University of California, Berkeley. My book, which sold to a major New York publishing house.

At Christmas, I flew home to Chicago. The house was throbbing, same as always; hot *tamales* and sweet *tamales* hissing in my mother's pressure cooker, and everybody—my mother, six brothers, wives, babies, aunts, cousins—talking too loud and at the same time, like in a Fellini[2] film, because that's just how we are.

I went upstairs to my father's room. One of my stories had just been translated into Spanish and published in an anthology of Chicano writing, and I wanted to show it to him. Ever since he recovered from a stroke two years ago, my father likes to spend his leisure hours horizontally. And that's how I found him, watching a Pedro Infante movie on Galavisión and eating rice pudding.

There was a glass filmed with milk on the bedside table. There were several vials of pills and balled Kleenex. And on the floor, one black sock and a plastic urinal that I didn't want to look at but looked at anyway. Pedro Infante was about to burst into song, and my father was laughing.

I'm not sure if it was because my story was translated into Spanish, or because it was published in Mexico, or perhaps because the story dealt with Tepeyac, the

---

1. philandering: unfaithful
2. Fellini: an Italian movie director whose films were full of strange, unforgettable characters

colonia my father was raised in and the house he grew up in, but at any rate, my father punched the mute button on his remote control and read my story.

I sat on the bed next to my father and waited. He read it very slowly. As if he were reading each line over and over. He laughed at all the right places and read lines he liked out loud. He pointed and asked questions: "Is this So-and-so?" "Yes," I said. He kept reading.

When he was finally finished, after what seemed like hours, my father looked up and asked: "Where can we get more copies of this for the relatives?"

Of all the wonderful things that happened to me last year, that was the most wonderful.

Discussion and Writing Questions

1. In what two ways can the title of this essay, "Only Daughter," be interpreted?

2. What expectations did the author's father have for his daughter? Did his limited expectations create any advantages for her? Why did the father's comment "I have seven sons" bother her so much?

3. In paragraphs 16 through 18, Cisneros describes one of her trips home. She includes vivid details that help the reader "see" and "feel" life inside her parents' house. Which details do you find especially effective? Although the home is in Chicago, which details capture the family's Mexican heritage?

4. For years, the author wanted her father's attention and approval. Why do you think he finally appreciated her achievement as a writer?

Writing Assignments

1. In a group with three or four classmates, share statements about your personal history like those in Cisneros's opening paragraphs. First, take five minutes working on your own, and then define yourself, using a two- or three-sentence pattern: "I am _____

_____. That explains everything."
Revise your sentences until you feel they capture a truth about you. Now share and discuss these statements with your group. What is most and least effective or intriguing about each? Use your definition as the main idea for a paper to be written at home.

2. Have you (or has someone you know) wanted another person's approval so badly that it influenced how you conducted your life? Who was the person whose approval you sought, and why was that approval so important? What did you do to please him or her and what happened? Was it worth it?

3. What were your family's expectations for you as you grew up, and how did those expectations affect your life choices? Were the expectations high or low? Did your gender or place in the family (oldest, middle, youngest) affect them? Did you accept or reject the family's vision for you?

The Case for Torture

Michael Levin

Leaders like Martin Luther King and Mahatma Ghandi have preached nonviolence no matter what, and many people agree that deliberately injuring another person is wrong. However, philosophy professor Michael Levin argues in this startling essay that torture is sometimes necessary.

It is generally assumed that torture is impermissible,[1] a throwback to a more brutal age. Enlightened societies reject it outright, and regimes suspected of using it risk the wrath of the United States.

I believe this attitude is unwise. There are situations in which torture is not merely permissible but morally mandatory. Moreover, these situations are moving from the realm of imagination to fact.

Suppose a terrorist has hidden an atomic bomb on Manhattan Island which will detonate at noon on July 4 unless . . . (here follow the usual demands for money and release of his friends from jail). Suppose, further, that he is caught at 10 A.M. of the fateful day, but—preferring death to failure—won't disclose where the bomb is. What do we do? If we follow due process—wait for his lawyer, arraign him—millions of people will die. If the only way to save those lives is to subject the terrorist to the most excruciating possible pain, what grounds can there be for not doing so? I suggest there are none. In any case, I ask you to face the question with an open mind.

Torturing the terrorist is unconstitutional? Probably. But millions of lives surely outweigh constitutionality. Torture is barbaric? Mass murder is far more barbaric. Indeed, letting millions of innocents die in deference[2] to one who flaunts his guilt is moral cowardice, an unwillingness to dirty one's hands. If *you* caught the terrorist, could you sleep nights knowing that millions died because you couldn't bring yourself to apply the electrodes?

Once you concede that torture is justified in extreme cases, you have admitted that the decision to use torture is a matter of balancing innocent lives against the means needed to save them. You must now face more realistic cases involving more modest numbers. Someone plants a bomb on a jumbo jet. He alone can disarm it, and his demands cannot be met (or if they can, we refuse to set a precedent[3] by yielding to his threats). Surely we can, we must, do anything to the extortionist[4] to save the passengers. How can we tell 300, or 100, or 10 people who never asked to be put in danger, "I'm sorry, you'll have to die in agony, we just couldn't bring ourselves to . . ."

Here are the results of an informal poll about a third, hypothetical,[5] case. Suppose a terrorist group kidnapped a newborn baby from a hospital. I asked four

---

1. impermissible: not allowed
2. deference: respectful submission
3. precedent: a possible example in similar situations
4. extortionist: one who gets something by force or threat
5. hypothetical: assumed to be true for the purposes of argument

mothers if they would approve of torturing kidnappers if that were necessary to get their own newborns back. All said yes, the most "liberal" adding that she would administer it herself.

I am not advocating torture as punishment. Punishment is addressed to deeds irrevocably[6] past. Rather, I am advocating torture as an acceptable measure for preventing future evils. So understood, it is far less objectionable than many extant[7] punishments. Opponents of the death penalty, for example, are forever insisting that executing a murderer will not bring back his victim (as if the purpose of capital punishment were supposed to be resurrection, not deterrence[8] or retribution).[9] But torture, in the cases described, is intended not to bring anyone back but to keep innocents from being dispatched.[10] The most powerful argument against using torture as a punishment or to secure confessions is that such practices disregard the rights of the individual. Well, if the individual is all that important—and he is—it is correspondingly important to protect the rights of individuals threatened by terrorists. If life is so valuable that it must never be taken, the lives of the innocents must be saved even at the price of hurting the one who endangers them.

Better precedents for torture are assassination and preemptive[11] attack. No Allied[12] leader would have flinched at assassinating Hitler[13] had that been possible. (The Allies did assassinate Heydrich.[14]) Americans would be angered to learn that Roosevelt could have had Hitler killed in 1943—thereby shortening the war and saving millions of lives—but refused on moral grounds. Similarly, if nation A learns that nation B is about to launch an unprovoked attack, A has a right to save itself by destroying B's military capability first. In the same way, if the police can by torture save those who would otherwise die at the hands of kidnappers or terrorists, they must.

There is an important difference between terrorists and their victims that should mute talk of the terrorists' "rights." The terrorist's victims are at risk unintentionally, not having asked to be endangered. But the terrorist knowingly initiated his actions. Unlike his victims, he volunteered for the risks of his deed. By threatening to kill for profit or idealism, he renounces civilized standards, and he can have no complaint if civilization tries to thwart him by whatever means necessary.

Just as torture is justified only to save lives (not extort confessions or recantations),[15] it is justifiably administered only to those *known* to hold innocent lives in their hands. Ah, but how can the authorities ever be sure they have the right malefactor?[16] Isn't there a danger of error and abuse? Won't We turn into Them?

Questions like these are disingenuous[17] in a world in which terrorists proclaim themselves and perform for television. The name of their game is public

---

6. irrevocably: impossible to change
7. extant: existing
8. deterrence: preventing similar acts
9. retribution: punishment
10. dispatched: killed
11. preemptive attack: striking first, before the enemy does
12. Allied: in World War II, the Allied Powers included the United States, Britain, France, the Soviet Union, and China
13. Hitler: dictator of Nazi Germany who ordered the murder of millions of Jews and others
14. Heydrich: a Nazi organizer of mass executions
15. recantations: taking back of previous statements
16. malefactor: evildoer
17. disingenuous: falsely innocent-seeming

recognition. After all, you can't very well intimidate a government into releasing your freedom fighters unless you announce that it is your group that has seized its embassy. "Clear guilt" is difficult to define, but when 40 million people see a group of masked gunmen seize an airplane on the evening news, there is not much question about who the perpetrators are. There will be hard cases where the situation is murkier. Nonetheless, a line demarcating[18] the legitimate use of torture can be drawn. Torture only the obviously guilty, and only for the sake of saving innocents, and the line between Us and Them will remain clear.

There is little danger that the Western democracies will lose their way if they choose to inflict pain as one way of preserving order. Paralysis in the face of evil is the greater danger. Some day soon a terrorist will threaten tens of thousands of lives, and torture will be the only way to save them. We had better start thinking about this.

Discussion and Writing Questions

1. What is the author's main point—his thesis? According to Levin, in what specific circumstances should torture be used? Do you agree that someone who refuses to torture a terrorist is guilty of moral cowardice?

2. What arguments *against* torture does the author answer in paragraph 4? Are his answers convincing? His introduction also answers the opposition (paragraphs 1 and 2). Why do you think Levin spends so much time answering the opposition in this essay?

3. Levin first argues that torturing one person to save millions of lives would be acceptable; then he works down from millions to 300, 100, 10, and finally, a single infant (paragraphs 3–6). Would you, like the four mothers, approve of torturing someone who kidnapped your newborn if this would get your infant back?

4. Why does Levin argue that torture should never be used as punishment (paragraph 7)?

Writing Assignments

1. Write a reply to Michael Levin's essay. Develop an argument against torture under any circumstances. For ideas visit the United Nations web site on torture at http://www.unhchr.ch/html/menu2/i2civtor.htm or Amnesty International's site at http://www.stoptorture.org.

2. Write an essay called "A Case for (or against) Racial Profiling." Consider whether authorities should use racial or ethnic profiling to identify possible terrorists at airports and elsewhere. What about profiling on highways (where African Americans are sometimes stopped for DWB, "driving while black")? Carefully plan your argument before you write.

3. Conduct an informal poll of mothers based on a hypothetical kidnap case, as Levin does in paragraph 6. Ask at least five mothers whether they would support torture of the kidnapper and why. Organize your findings and write a paper presenting them.

---

18. demarcating: setting boundaries

Let's Get Vertical

Beth Wald

At age sixteen, backpacking in Canada, Beth Wald fell in love with the wilderness. Today she is a writer and photographer of wild places. In this article, she shares her passion for rock climbing—a "vertical dance" up cliffs and mountains.

Here I am, 400 feet up on the steep west face of Devil's Tower,[1] a tiny figure in a sea of petrified[2] rock. I can't find enough footholds and handholds to keep climbing. My climbing partner anxiously looks up at me from his narrow ledge. I can see the silver sparkle of the climbing devices I've jammed into the crack every eight feet or so.

I study the last device I've placed, a half-inch aluminum wedge 12 feet below me. If I slip, it'll catch me, but only after a 24-foot fall, a real "screamer." It's too difficult to go back; I have to find a way up before my fingers get too tired. I must act quickly.

Finding a tiny opening in the crack, I jam two fingertips in, crimp[3] them, pull hard, and kick my right foot onto a sloping knob, hoping it won't skid off. At the same time, I slap my right hand up to what looks like a good hold. To my horror, it's round and slippery.

My fingers start to slide. Panic rivets[4] me for a second, but then a surge of adrenaline[5] snaps me back into action. I scramble my feet higher, lunge with my left hand, and catch a wider crack. I manage to get a better grip just as my right hand pops off its slick hold. My feet find edges, and I regain my balance. Whipping a chock (wedge) off my harness, I slip it into the crack and clip my rope through a carabiner (oblong metal snaplink). After catching my breath, I start moving again, and the rest of the climb flows upward like a vertical dance.

I've tried many sports, but I haven't found any to match the excitement of rock climbing. It's a unique world, with its own language, communities, controversies, heroes, villains, and devoted followers. I've lived in vans, tepees, tents, and caves; worked three jobs to save money for expenses; driven 24 hours to spend a weekend at a good rock; and lived on beans and rice for months at a time—all of this to be able to climb. What is it about scrambling up rocks that inspires such a passion? The answer is, no other sport offers so many challenges and so many rewards.

The physical challenges are obvious. You need flexibility, balance, and strength. But climbing is also a psychological game of defeating your fear, and it demands creative thinking. It's a bit like improvising[6] a gymnastic routine 200 feet in the air while playing a game of chess.

---

1. Devil's Tower: a 900-foot rock formation in Wyoming
2. petrified: turned to stone
3. crimp: press, pinch, or bend
4. rivets: holds
5. adrenaline: hormone released in response to stress or fear
6. improvising: inventing without preparation

Climbers visit some of the most spectacular places on earth and see them from a unique perspective—the top! Because the sport is so intense, friendships between climbers tend to be strong and enduring.

Kids playing in trees or on monkey bars know that climbing is a natural activity, but older people often have to relearn to trust their instincts. This isn't too hard, though. The ability to maintain self-control in difficult situations is the most important trait for a beginning climber to have. Panic is almost automatic when you run out of handholds 100 feet off the ground. The typical reaction is to freeze solid until you fall off. But with a little discipline, rational thinking, and/or distraction tactics such as babbling to yourself, humming, or even screaming, fear can change to elation[7] as you climb out of a tough spot.

Contrary to popular belief, you don't have to be superhumanly strong to climb. Self-confidence, agility,[8] a good sense of balance, and determination will get you farther up the rock than bulging biceps. Once you've learned the basics, climbing itself will gradually make you stronger, though many dedicated climbers speed up the process by training at home or in the gym.

Nonclimbers often ask, "How do the ropes get up there?" It's quite simple; the climbers bring them up as they climb. Most rock climbers today are "free climbers." In free climbing, the rope is used only for safety in case of a fall, *not* to help pull you up. (Climbing without a rope, called "free soloing," is a *very* dangerous activity practiced only by extremely experienced—and crazy—climbers.)

First, two climbers tie into opposite ends of a 150-foot-long nylon rope. Then one of them, the belayer, anchors himself or herself to a rock or tree. The other, the leader, starts to climb, occasionally stopping to jam a variety of aluminum wedges or other special gadgets, generically[9] referred to as protection, into cracks in the rock. To each of these, he or she attaches a snaplink, called a carabiner, and clips the rope through. As the leader climbs, the belayer feeds out the rope, and it runs through the carabiners. If the leader falls, the belayer holds the rope, and the highest piece of protection catches the leader. The belayer uses special techniques and equipment to make it easy to stop falls.

When the leader reaches the end of a section of rock—called the pitch—and sets an anchor, he or she becomes the belayer. This person pulls up the slack of the rope as the other partner climbs and removes the protection. Once together again, they can either continue in the same manner or switch leaders. These worldwide techniques work on rock formations, cliffs, peaks, even buildings.

Some of the best climbing cliffs in the country are in the Shawangunk Mountains, only two hours from New York City. Seneca Rocks in West Virginia draws climbers from Washington, D.C., and Pittsburgh, Pennsylvania. Chattanooga, Tennessee, has a fine cliff within the city limits. Most states in the U.S. and provinces in Canada offer at least one or two good climbing opportunities.

Even if there are no large cliffs or rock formations nearby, you can climb smaller rocks to practice techniques and get stronger. This is called bouldering. Many climbers who live in cities and towns have created climbing areas out of old stone walls and buildings. Ask someone at your local outdoor shop where you can go to start climbing.

---

7. elation: joy
8. agility: quick and easy movement
9. generically: generally

There's no substitute for an expert teacher when it comes to learning basic techniques and safety procedures. One of the best (and least expensive) ways to learn climbing is to convince a veteran climber in your area to teach you. You can usually meet these types at the local crag[10] or climbing shop.

As another option, many universities and colleges, some high schools, and some YMCAs have climbing clubs. Their main purpose is to introduce people to climbing and to teach the basics. Other clubs, such as the Appalachian Mountain Club in the eastern U.S. and the Mountaineers on the West Coast, also provide instruction. Ask at your outdoor shop for the names of clubs in your area.

If you live in a place completely lacking rocks and climbers, you can attend one of the fine climbing schools at the major climbing area closest to you. Magazines like *Climbing, Rock & Ice,* and *Outside* publish lists of these schools. Once you learn the basics, you're ready to get vertical.

In rock climbing, you can both lose yourself and find yourself. Life and all its troubles are reduced to figuring out the puzzle of the next section of cliff or forgotten in the challenge and delight of moving through vertical space. And learning how to control anxiety, how to piece together a difficult sequence of moves, and how to communicate with a partner are all skills that prove incredibly useful back on the ground!

Discussion and Writing Questions

1. How effective is the opening of this essay (paragraphs 1–4)? Does the author's description of her climb up Devil's Tower grab and hold your attention?

2. The author uses many vivid verbs in paragraphs 3 and 4. How many can you spot, and which ones are especially strong?

3. What benefits of rock climbing make it the author's favorite sport? Does this article make you want to try rock climbing? Why or why not?

4. Can a person learn to "defeat fear" even if he or she does not climb rocks or jump out of planes? Give examples from the lives of famous people, your friends, or family members to illustrate.

Writing Assignments

1. The author has "lived in vans, tepees, tents, and caves; worked three jobs; driven 24 hours to spend a weekend at a good rock; and lived on beans and rice for months—all of this to be able to climb." Is there a hobby or activity for which you would make great sacrifices? Describe the sacrifices you would make (or have made) in order to do this thing.

2. What do you think are the causes of the recent rise in "extreme" sports—rock climbing, snowboarding, mountain biking, and so forth? For ideas, you might visit http://www.expn.go.com/.

3. Dr. Richard Carmona, the first Latino Surgeon General of the United States, was once a high school dropout who turned his life around in the Army Special Forces. He has said that the person who "takes a chance, gives his all, does not let the past dictate the future, will succeed." Think of the greatest challenge you have overcome, and describe the process by which you did it.

---

10. crag: a mass of rock forming part of a rugged cliff

On the Rez

Ian Frazier

Do you think a single act of courage or heroism can reverse decades of misunderstanding? In his book *On the Rez*, Ian Frazier tells the true story of SuAnne Marie Big Crow, who faced a taunting crowd and decided to answer its jeers with a surprising gift.

Some people who live in the cities and towns near reservations treat their Indian neighbors decently; some don't. In Denver and Minneapolis and Rapid City police have been known to harass Indian teenagers and rough up Indian drunks and needlessly stop and search Indian cars. Local banks whose deposits include millions in tribal funds sometimes charge Indians higher interest rates than they charge whites. Gift shops near reservations sell junky caricature[1] Indian pictures and dolls, and until not long ago beer coolers had signs on them that said INDIAN POWER. In a big discount store in a reservation-border town a white clerk observes a lot of Indians waiting at the checkout and remarks, "Oh, they're Indians—they're used to standing in line." Some people in South Dakota hate Indians, unapologetically, and will tell you why; in their voices you can hear a particular American meanness that is centuries old.

When teams from Pine Ridge play non-Indian teams, the question of race is always there. When Pine Ridge is the visiting team, usually the hosts are courteous and the players and fans have a good time. But Pine Ridge coaches know that occasionally at away games their kids will be insulted, their fans will feel unwelcome, the host gym will be dense with hostility, and the referees will call fouls on Indian players every chance they get. Sometimes in a game between Indian and non-Indian teams the difference in race becomes an important and distracting part of the event.

One place where Pine Ridge teams used to get harassed regularly was the high school gymnasium in Lead, South Dakota. Lead is a town of about 3,200 northwest of the reservation, in the Black Hills. It is laid out among the mines that are its main industry, and low, wooded mountains hedge it around. The brick high school building is set into a hillside. The school's only gym in those days was small, with tiers of gray-painted concrete on which the spectator benches descended from just below the steel-beamed roof to the very edge of the basketball court—an arrangement that greatly magnified the interior noise.

In the fall of 1988 the Pine Ridge Lady Thorpes[2] went to Lead to play a basketball game. SuAnne was a full member of the team by then. She was a freshman, fourteen years old. Getting ready in the locker room, the Pine Ridge girls could hear the din from the Lead fans. They were yelling fake Indian war cries, a "*woo-woo-woo*" sound. The usual plan for the pre-game warm-up was for the visiting team to run onto the court in a line, take a lap or two around the floor, shoot some baskets, and then go to their bench at courtside. After that the home team would come out and do the same, and then the game would begin. Usually the Thorpes lined up for their entry more or less according to height, which meant that senior Doni De Cory, one of the tallest, went first. As the team waited in the hallway leading from the locker room, the heckling got louder. Some fans were waving food stamps, a reference to the reservation's receiving federal aid. Others yelled, "Where's the cheese?"—the joke being that if Indians were lining up, it must be to

---

1. caricature: cartoon
2. Lady Thorpes: named for Native American Jim Thorpe, one of the greatest athletes of all time

get commodity cheese. The Lead high school band had joined in, with fake Indian drumming and a fake Indian tune. Doni De Cory looked out the door and told her teammates, "I can't handle this." SuAnne quickly offered to go first in her place. She was so eager that Doni became suspicious. "Don't embarrass us," Doni told her. SuAnne said, "I won't. I won't embarrass you." Doni gave her the ball, and SuAnne stood first in line.

She came running onto the court dribbling the basketball, with her teammates running behind. On the court the noise was deafening. SuAnne went right down the middle and suddenly stopped when she got to center court. Her teammates were taken by surprise, and some bumped into each other. Coach Zimiga, at the rear of the line, did not know why they had stopped. SuAnne turned to Doni De Cory and tossed her the ball. Then she stepped into the jump-ball circle at center court, facing the Lead fans. She unbuttoned her warm-up jacket, took it off, draped it over her shoulders, and began to do the Lakota shawl dance. SuAnne knew all the traditional dances (she had competed in many powwows as a little girl), and the dance she chose is a young woman's dance, graceful and modest and show-offy all at the same time. "I couldn't believe it—she was powwowin', like, 'Get down!'" Doni De Cory recalls. "And then she started to sing." SuAnne began to sing in Lakota, swaying back and forth in the jump-ball circle, doing the shawl dance, using her warm-up jacket for a shawl. The crowd went completely silent. "All that stuff the Lead fans were yelling—it was like she *reversed* it somehow," a teammate says. In the sudden quiet all they could hear was her Lakota song. SuAnne dropped her jacket, took the ball from Doni De Cory, and ran a lap around the court dribbling expertly and fast. The audience began to cheer and applaud. She sprinted to the basket, went up in the air, and laid the ball through the hoop, with the fans cheering loudly now. Of course, Pine Ridge went on to win the game.

• • •

For the Oglala, what SuAnne did that day almost immediately took on the status of myth. People from Pine Ridge who witnessed it still describe it in terms of awe and disbelief. Amazement swept through the younger kids when they heard. "I was, like, '*What* did she just do?'" recalls her cousin Angie Big Crow, an eighth grader at the time. All over the reservation people told and retold the story of SuAnne at Lead. Anytime the subject of SuAnne came up when I was talking to people on Pine Ridge, I would always ask if they had heard about what she did at Lead, and always the answer was a smile and a nod—"Yeah, I was there," or "Yeah, I heard about that." To the unnumbered big and small slights of local racism that the Oglala have known all their lives SuAnne's exploit made an emphatic reply.

Back in the days when Lakota war parties still fought battles against other tribes and the Army, no deed of war was more honored than the act of counting coup. To "count coup" means to touch an armed enemy in full possession of his powers with a special stick called a coup stick, or with the hand. The touch is not a blow, and serves only to indicate how close to the enemy you came. As an act of bravery, counting coup was regarded as greater than killing an enemy in single combat, greater than taking a scalp or horses or any prize. Counting coup was an act of almost abstract courage, of pure playfulness taken to the most daring extreme. Very likely, to do it and survive brought an exhilaration to which nothing else could compare. In an ancient sense that her Oglala kin could recognize. SuAnne counted coup on the fans of Lead.

And yet this coup was an act not of war but of peace. SuAnne's coup strike was an offering, an invitation. It gave the hecklers the best interpretation, as if their silly, mocking chants were meant only in good will. It showed that their fake

Indian songs were just that—fake—and that the real thing was better, as real things usually are. We Lakota have been dancing like this for centuries, the dance said; we've been doing the shawl dance since long before you came, before you got on the boat in Glasgow or Bremerhaven, before you stole this land, and we're still doing it today. And isn't it pretty, when you see how it's supposed to be done? Because finally what SuAnne proposed was to invite us—us onlookers in the stands, namely the non-Lakota rest of this country—to dance too. She was in the Lead gym to play, and she invited us all to play. The symbol she used to include us was the warm-up jacket. Everyone in America has a warm-up jacket. I've got one, probably so do you, so did (no doubt) many of the fans at Lead. By using the warm-up jacket as a shawl in her impromptu shawl dance she made Lakota relatives of us all.

"It was funny," Doni De Cory says, "but after that game the relationship between Lead and us was tremendous. When we played Lead again, the games were really good, and we got to know some of the girls on the team. Later, when we went to a tournament and Lead was there, we were hanging out with the Lead girls and eating pizza with them. We got to know some of their parents, too. What SuAnne did made a lasting impression and changed the whole situation with us and Lead. We found out there are some really good people in Lead."

America is a leap of the imagination. From its beginning people have had only a persistent idea of what a good country should be. The idea involves freedom, equality, justice, and the pursuit of happiness; nowadays most of us probably could not describe it much more clearly than that. The truth is, it always has been a bit of a guess. No one has ever known for sure whether a country based on such an idea is really possible, but again and again we have leaped toward the idea and hoped. What SuAnne Big Crow demonstrated in the Lead high school gym is that making the leap is the whole point. The idea does not truly live unless it is expressed by an act; the country does not live unless we make the leap from our tribe or focus group or gated community or demographic[3] and land on the shaky platform of that idea of a good country which all kinds of different people share.

Discussion and Writing Questions

1. How was the Pine Ridge girls' basketball team usually treated when they played games at Lead? What larger problem between Indians and non-Indians in South Dakota was reflected in this behavior?

2. SuAnne's performance of the Lakota shawl dance to a silent gymnasium full of people is described in powerful detail. What descriptive details does the author include to make that scene come alive for the reader?

3. What did the students at Lead discover during SuAnne's dance that caused them to change their opinions about Lakota Indians? What made the Pine Ridge players decide that "there are some really good people in Lead" (paragraph 9)?

4. The author calls SuAnne's dance an act of courage. What was courageous about her dance that day? Consider in your answer her age, the history between Pine Ridge and Lead, and the behavior of the audience before the game.

---

3. demographic: group of similar people

Writing Assignments

1. SuAnne Marie Big Crow's actions that day made her a hero for the people of the Pine Ridge reservation. With a group of classmates, brainstorm the qualities that make someone a hero. Then, select two or three of these qualities and write an essay defining heroism. You may wish to illustrate with an anecdote of your own about someone who performed like a hero in a difficult situation.

2. How can we promote tolerance in the world? Think of a conflict that you have experienced or heard about—perhaps between two ethnic groups, gangs, families, or individuals. What specific actions would you recommend to help promote understanding and tolerance between the two sides? If you have access to a computer, explore the web site www.tolerance.org for more ideas.

3. Frazier says that equality and justice do not live until they are expressed in action—until "we make the leap from our tribe or group" into a larger community that "different people share" (paragraph 10). Write an essay in which you describe someone who has made such a leap, such as reaching out to an outsider, standing up against a stereotype, or moving to a new country or community.

Bam! Crash! Kapow! Girls Are Heroes Now

Susan Hopkins

Until recently, most superheroes were male—think Spiderman, Superman, and Batman. Today, however, many new superheroes are not only female but very aggressive. Here, Australian feminist Susan Hopkins discusses examples of this trend. She is the author of *Girl Heroes: The New Force in Popular Culture.*

It used to be that not even girls wanted to be girls—being "girly" was associated with weakness and cowardice. Since about the mid-1990s, however, girlhood has become "cool". Today's female action heroes, who are more direct, physical, aggressive and assertive than their predecessors, are also much younger. They are girls, or at least identify as such. Buffy the Vampire Slayer was a superhero while she was still in high school and the animated Powerpuff Girls haven't yet left kindergarten. It appears that after decades of feminist critique[1] media images of weak girls are finally losing currency.[2]

To behave aggressively is no longer considered unfeminine and unattractive. Girl characters are expected to be assertive and achievement-oriented. Empowered sex objects like Buffy, Xena and Charlie's Angels not only know what they want, they are willing and able to fight for it. There is nothing secondary about the girl action hero; she is frequently portrayed as more powerful, intelligent and violent than her male co-stars. She appeals to a generation of young women who want it all—including the kind of violence which used to be reserved for men.

Even the notoriously sexist Walt Disney company has made some concession[3] to changing times. Like other cultural industries, Disney has been infiltrated by a

---

1. critique: critical discussion
2. currency: general acceptance
3. concession: acknowledgment

new breed of writers, producers and promoters sensitive to identity politics. Traditional Disney features depicted women as weak, helpless and incapable of independent action. Today, Disney heroines like Pocahontas and Mulan reject marriage in order to pursue their destiny as warriors, leaders and (pseudo)[4] historical legends. The modern Disney heroine is not looking for love but searching for herself and her sense of personal accomplishment.

The hugely successful Powerpuff Girls also represent the reversal of negative gender stereotypes. Blossom, Bubbles and Buttercup are a trio of animated supergirls who fly, kick, punch and generally destroy monsters, mutants[5] and villains. In an interview for *Billboard* magazine, creator Craig McCracken has claimed he originally intended to call them "the Whoop-Ass Girls" but the network wouldn't allow it. Despite the fact that they are only five years old, the girls fight fearlessly to rid the world of evil. "Saving the world before bedtime" is their celebrated motto. The cartoon works on the apparent contradiction between "cute little girl" and "awesome superhero"—one moment the girls are enjoying a slumber party, the next they are smashing evil genius monkey Mojo Jojo.

Learning from the Spice Girl "girl power" phenomenon of the 1990s, the *Powerpuff* show relies on assertive girly appeal. The characters are drawn in a manner that exaggerates their girlhood—huge eyes, hair bows, pigtails, pastel dresses, heart-shaped clips and black school shoes on tiny feet. Blossom, the leader of the group, has the power to breathe ice and fire and plays lead guitar in the Powerpuff girl "band." Bubbles, the Baby Spice of the group, is drawn to sugar and everything sweet. The short-tempered Buttercup is the tough one. She is also the best fighter and invariably wears a determined expression. Buttercup is loud, combative, selfish and smelly—yet loveable. In the episode "Down and Dirty," Buttercup refuses to take a bath, stinking up the Pokey Oaks Kindergarten. Buttercup is pleased when she discovers her overpowering odour is causing the villains she battles to choke and retreat. In the "Collect Her" episode, Buttercup is seen using a side of meat as a punching bag (in a reference to the film *Rocky*). Like a masculine hero, she rarely smiles and despises wimps and cry babies.

It's no accident that *Powerpuff* apparel and merchandise are marketed to girls through action sports like snowboarding, surfing and skateboarding. For better or worse, girl heroes are now aggressors—they have laid claim to a masculine alliance with action. In pop culture representation and in real life, too, girls are releasing their anger, frustration, and aggressive impulses.

Today, "fighting like a girl" is something to be proud of. Girls are fighting back, not just against male violence but also against restrictive stereotypes of feminine passivity. Today's girls don't just want the tough action hero—they want to be the tough action hero. They might play at being "girly," but they have become all they ever wanted in a man.

Discussion and Writing Questions

1. The author writes that female superheroes like Buffy the Vampire Slayer and Xena are reversing negative stereotypes about girls and women. What are these negative stereotypes?

2. Hopkins develops her essay with examples of female action heroes. What examples from TV and movies does she give in paragraph 2? What kinds of examples does she discuss in paragraph 3? Paragraph 4?

---

4. pseudo: false or deceptive
5. mutants: biologically altered individuals

3. Do you have a favorite superhero? What qualities do you admire in him or her? What is the appeal of superheroes to many young people and adults?

4. Today's "girl hero" is often aggressive to the point of violence. Is this a change for the better or worse? Why?

Writing Assignments

1. Female celebrities in music, movies, and other media have a major impact on many young girls—through their clothes, behavior, and language. Choose one such celebrity *or* a child you know who is influenced by a celebrity and discuss this influence—positive, negative, or both.

2. Hopkins refers to female action heroes as "empowered sex objects" (paragraph 2). For example, Charlie's Angels fight fiercely in high heels and tight leather pants without even mussing their hair. Do these impossible media images empower real women or just make them feel inferior?

3. What is the difference between a superhero and a hero? What qualities does each possess? Is one more human than the other? Write an essay contrasting the two, giving specific examples. For ideas, see http://www.cwrl.utexas.edu/~tnelson/309k_s02/dictionary/patrick/.

My Outing[1]

Arthur Ashe

Arthur Ashe was the first African-American male to become a great tennis champion. After a heart attack ended his career, he contracted AIDS through a blood transfusion. He kept his illness private for years while he pursued many business interests and human-rights projects. Then the possibility of a newspaper report forced him to reveal his condition to the public. The press conference he refers to was held in April 1992. Ashe died of AIDS in 1993.

The day after my press conference, I made sure to keep the two appointments on my calendar because I was anxious to see how people would respond to me after the announcement. I was thinking not only about the people I knew personally, even intimately, but also about waiters and bartenders, doormen and taxi drivers. I knew all the myths and fears about AIDS. I also understood that if I hadn't been educated in the harshest possible way—by contracting the disease and living with it—I would probably share some of those myths and fears. I knew that I couldn't spread the disease by coughing or breathing or using plates and cups in a restaurant, but I knew that in some places my plates and cups would receive special attention, perhaps some extra soap and hot water. Perhaps they would be smashed and thrown away.

That morning, I accompanied Donald M. Stewart, head of the College Board Testing Service, on a visit to the offices of the New York Community Trust. We were seeking a grant of $5,000 to support the publication of a handbook aimed at student-athletes. The appointment went well; we got the money. And in the

---

1. "Outing" someone usually means revealing publicly, without permission, that he or she is homosexual. Although Ashe was not gay, he was "outed" as a person with AIDS.

evening, I went in black tie to a gala dinner to celebrate the eightieth birthday of a man I had known for thirty years and regarded as one of my key mentors in New York City, Joseph Cullman III, a former chairman of Philip Morris. At the event, which took place at the Museum of Natural History in Manhattan, I felt anxiety rising as our taxi drew up to the curb. How would the other guests respond to me? The first person I saw was an old friend, John Reese. An investment banker now, in his youth John had been an up-and-coming star with me in junior tennis. He saw me, and hurried over. There was no mistaking the warmth of his greeting, his genuine concern but also his understanding of my predicament. We walked inside together and I had a fine time at the celebration.

3   I was glad, in this context, that I had not concealed my condition from certain people. I had reminded myself from the outset that I had an obligation to tell anyone who might be materially hurt by the news when it came out. I have been both proud of my commercial connections and grateful to the people who had asked me to represent them or work for them in some other way. Several of them had taken a chance on me when they knew full well, from the most basic market research in the early 1970s, that having an African American as a spokesman or an officer might cost them business.

4   Among these organizations, the most important were the Aetna Life and Casualty Company, where I was a member of the board of directors; Head USA, the sports-equipment manufacturer that had given me my first important commercial endorsement, a tennis racquet with my very own autograph on it; the Doral Resort and Country Club in Florida, where I had directed the tennis program; Le Coq Sportif, the sports-clothing manufacturer; Home Box Office (HBO), the cable-television network for which I worked as an analyst at Wimbledon;[2] and ABC Sports, for which I also served as a commentator.

5   Not one of these companies had dropped me after I quietly revealed to their most important executives that I had AIDS. Now those executives had to deal with the response of the public. I would have to give them a chance to put some distance between their companies and me because I now carried the most abominable and intimidating medical virus of our age. In business, image is everything. And one would have to go back to leprosy, or the plague, to find a disease so full of terrifying implications as AIDS carries. AIDS was a scientific mystery that defied our vaunted[3] claims for science, and also a religious or spiritual riddle—at least to those who insisted on thinking of it as possibly a punishment from God for our evil on earth, as more than one person had publicly suggested.

6   I waited for the phone calls and the signs that my services were no longer needed. None came.

7   I read somewhere that in the two weeks following his announcement that he was HIV-positive, Earvin "Magic" Johnson received thousands of pieces of mail, and that months later he was still receiving hundreds of letters a week. Well, I received nothing approaching that volume of correspondence following my press conference, but I certainly had a mountain of reading and writing to do in its aftermath. And every time I appeared on one of the few television interview shows I agreed to do, such as with Barbara Walters or Larry King, there was another surge of correspondence. I heard from the famous and the completely unknown, people I knew and people I had never met.

8   The most moving letters, without a doubt, came from people who had lived through an AIDS illness, either their own or that of a loved one. Often the loved

---

2. Wimbledon: London, England, district where a major tennis tournament is held each year
3. vaunted: boastful

one was now dead. These writers, above all, understood why I had made such a fuss about the issue of privacy. Many probably understood better than I did, because they were more vulnerable than I am, and had suffered more. One Manhattan woman wrote to tell me about her father, who had received HIV-tainted blood, as I had, through a blood transfusion following heart surgery. Without knowing it, he had passed the infection on to her mother. For some years, they had kept their illness a secret from their daughter. After they could keep the secret from her no longer, she in turn had worked to keep their secret from other family members and friends, and from the world. Although both parents were now dead, she wrote, "I share your anger at that anonymous person who violated either your trust or their professional ethics."

A grandmother in New England, HIV-positive after a transfusion, shared with me her terror that the company she worked for would dismiss her if they found out; she was awaiting the passage of a law that might protect her. From Idaho, a mother told me about her middle-aged son, who had tried to keep his AIDS condition a secret even from her. "My son kept it to himself for six months before he told me and I'll never forget that day as we cried together." His ordeal included dementia,[4] forced incarceration in a state asylum, and ostracism[5] by relatives and friends. But mother and son had spent his last "four difficult months" together. "I'm so thankful to have had those days with him."

I heard from people whom I had not thought of in years, and some of them had been touched by their own tragedy. A woman I remembered as a stunningly beautiful UCLA coed, as we called them in those days, told me about her younger brother, who had been diagnosed with full-blown AIDS about five years before. "He is gay," she reported, "and I saw how he lost so much self-esteem and hope" because of intolerance. "No one can speak as eloquently[6] as you and Magic to allow the stigma[7] to disperse[8] regarding this situation." Another letter illustrated the power of the stigma. Signed simply, "Sorry I can't identify myself, but you understand," it came from a man who had been diagnosed with HIV three years ago. "I'm the father of six children and many grandchildren. I'm not into needles or the gay life. Don't know where it came from (really)."

As for my daughter, Camera, more than one writer underscored my fears about what she might have to undergo from insensitive people in the future. A woman whose son had died of AIDS about a year before, following the death of his wife, was now bringing up their young son: "I struggle with how this little child is going to deal with the insults and rejections that people will inflict on him when they find out that his father died from AIDS." . . .

Needless to say, I am grateful to all those who have taken the trouble to write. Most of the letters left me humbled.

Discussion and Writing Questions

1. In paragraph 3, Ashe says that he had told some business associates about his illness early on. Why had he done that? How had they reacted? Why, then, was Ashe concerned about the business community's reaction to his *public* announcement?

---

4. dementia: insanity
5. ostracism: exclusion, banishment
6. eloquently: skillfully, persuasively
7. stigma: mark of disgrace
8. disperse: disappear

2. How did the general public react to Ashe's announcement? Which letters did Ashe find most moving? Why?

3. The privacy issue was extremely important to Ashe, who felt that he had been forced by the press to make an announcement he had not wanted to make. One letter he received said, "I share your anger at that anonymous person who violated either your trust or their professional ethics" (paragraph 8). What did the letter writer mean by this statement?

4. Arthur Ashe called his life story *Days of Grace*. On the basis of this essay, why do you think he chose that title? What example or examples of "grace" did he tell about?

Writing Assignments

1. Have you ever prepared yourself for the worst—the ending of a relationship, a frightening medical test result, or other bad news—only to find that the worst did not happen? Discuss such a time: why you expected the worst, what you did to prepare, and what really happened.

2. Serious illness can force people to reevaluate their lives—their aspirations and their goals. Have you, or has someone you know, looked at life differently because of an illness or accident? Write a short account of your own or the other person's experience.

3. In a group with three or four classmates, discuss Ashe's belief that no newspaper had the right to tell the world that he had AIDS. Do you think the press was justified in revealing Ashe's condition? Why or why not? Ashe believed that his right to privacy was greater than the public's need to know. The press argued that Ashe was a public figure and that whenever a public figure is ill, his or her condition is legitimate news. Write your own essay about this issue, based on the conclusions you come to after your group's discussion.

Build Yourself a Killer Bod with Killer Bees

Dave Barry

Humorist Dave Barry writes that he was "born in Armonk, NY, in 1947 and has been steadily growing older ever since without ever actually reaching maturity." He is a Pulitzer Prize–winning columnist with the *Miami Herald*. Although Barry's columns and books often make us laugh out loud, his humor always has a point. Here he takes on America's obsession with the "perfect" body.

If there's one ideal that unites all Americans, it's the belief that every single one of us, regardless of ethnic background, is fat.

It was not always this way. There was a time, not so long ago, when Americans did not obsess about fat. In those days, a man could be portly[1] and still be considered attractive. The standards were also more lenient[2] for women: Marilyn Monroe, whom nobody ever called skinny, was a major sex goddess.

---

1. portly: somewhat stout or fat
2. lenient: tolerant; not strict

By today's beauty standards, of course, Marilyn Monroe was an oil tanker. Today's beauty ideal, strictly enforced by the media, is a person with the same level of body fat as a paper clip. Turn on your TV, and all you see are men and women who would rather have both eyeballs removed via corkscrew than eat a slice of pizza. These are genetic mutants:[3] You can see their muscles, veins, and neck bones almost bursting through their fat-free skin. I don't know who decided that the see-through look was attractive; I, personally, have never heard anybody express lust for anybody else's internal organs. But we normal humans are constantly exposed to the zero-fat mutants in the media, and we naturally assume that we're supposed to look like them. This is of course impossible, but we try. We diet constantly, especially young women, many of whom now start dieting while still in the womb.

And of course we spend millions of dollars on "exercise," defined as "activity designed to be strenuous without accomplishing anything useful." For example, we drive our cars to health clubs so we can run on treadmills. But we do NOT run to the health club, because then we would be accomplishing something useful. We pedal furiously on exercise bicycles that do not go anywhere. We take elevators every chance we get, but we buy expensive machines that enable us to pretend we're climbing stairs. It would not surprise me if yuppies started paying potato farmers for the opportunity to go into the fields and burn fat by pretending to conduct a harvest, taking great care not to dig up any actual potatoes.

If you think that's ridiculous, then you haven't seen "Tae-Bo." This was a recent hot fad, advertised extensively on TV by perspiring mutants. As I understand it, Tae-Bo is based on martial arts; the difference is that martial artists actually learn to defend themselves, whereas Tae-Bo people throw pretend punches and kicks strictly for fitness purposes. While they're busy kicking air and checking their abdominals, an actual mugger could walk right up and whack them with a crowbar.

But never mind practicality. The point is that Tae-Bo was briefly very, very hot, which means that soon everybody got bored with it. That's what always happens with exercise trends: People realize that, after countless hours of pretending to climb stairs or punching the air, they still bear a stronger resemblance to the Michelin Tire Man than to the TV mutants. So they give up on that particular trend and look for a new one.

Will this craziness ever end? Will Americans ever come to their senses and stop wasting millions and millions of dollars on hopeless efforts to look like people who don't really look like people? I hope not, because I'm planning to cash in on this. I got my idea from a wonderful newspaper article, sent in by alert veterinarian Steven Berry, from the *Leader News* of Central City, Kentucky. The article, written by Paul Camplin, is headlined "Cobbs Invented Odd Sport of Bee Fighting as Family Entertainment." It concerns the descendants of Bunn and Betty Cobb of Calhoun, Kentucky, who have gotten together annually for about 70 years to fight wild bees for fun. The article states:

"Without use of protective gear, one of the group approaches the bumble-bee hive and whacks it with a stick. When all of the now angry bees come flying out the group of bee fighters simply fight off the bees as best they can with large clumps of maple leaves."

---

3. mutants: individuals who have been biologically changed or altered

The article, which I am not making up, is illustrated by photos of members of the extended Bunn family, including grandparents, wildly waving branches at bees.

When I saw those photos, I knew I was looking at a gold mine. I'm talking about the Next Big Fitness Trend: "Tae-Bee." I'm going to make a 30-minute TV infomercial wherein enthusiastic hired mutants stress the benefits of bee-fighting (". . . and while you're OUCH burning fat, your arm motion is also OUCH building those OUCH . . .").

In no time millions of Americans will be ordering the Tae-Bee workout videotape, along with the Official (Accept No Substitutes!) Tae-Bee Maple Leaf Clump and of course the Official Tae-Bee Box o' Really Mad Bees. And if you don't think Americans will pay good money to get stung. I have one word for you: "ThighMaster."

So laugh if you want: I'm going to get rich on this thing. And then I'm going to hire a personal trainer. His sole job will be to order my pizza.

Discussion and Writing Questions

1. The first sentence of Barry's essay is funny, but it makes a serious point. What is Barry's opinion of the American obsession with weight and fitness?

2. "Today's beauty ideal is a person with the same level of fat as a paper clip," writes Barry (paragraph 2). What humorous details and comments in this paragraph underscore this point? Why does Barry call people who represent today's ideal of beauty "mutants"?

3. Do you know someone who is truly happy in his or her body, even if it's not perfect? What is the secret of this person's self-acceptance?

4. Is Barry serious about creating a Tae-Bee video and spin-off products? How do you know? What point is he making about the fitness industry and those who buy its products and services?

Writing Assignments

1. Have you ever tried a diet or fitness fad? Did it work? Write a paragraph or essay about your attempt, or that of someone you know, to build a killer bod. Your approach could be serious or humorous.

2. Do you agree that the media are responsible for fostering unrealistic beauty ideals? Write about the cause (or causes) of Americans' obsession with thinness and fitness.

3. According to the U.S. Centers for Disease Control and Prevention, over half of all Americans really do have a weight problem. About 35 percent are slightly or moderately overweight, and 26 percent are obese, or grossly overweight. Write an essay discussing either the causes of this national epidemic or effective ways to lose weight. For ideas and information, visit http://www.niddk.nih.gov/health/nutrit/pubs/unders.htm#whatcausesobesity/.

Follow the Leader to the Next Fad

Karen Castellucci Cox

Do you like to keep up with the latest styles and fads? In this essay, Karen Castellucci Cox, a professor of English at City College of San Francisco, explains the rating system that some marketers use to analyze—and sell products to—young consumers. Just how cool a customer are you? The answer might surprise you.

Rubik's Cube, step aerobics, Dove bars, grunge fashion, Pokémon—sound vaguely familiar? These are just a few of the hundreds of fads that have come and gone in the last twenty years. Different from a long-term marketing trend, such as the gradual move from compact cars to massive SUVs, a fad is characterized by the explosive popularity of a product that saturates the market and then disappears as rapidly as it arrived. The making of a fad involves a mysterious combination of invention, timing, skill, and luck. In fact, marketing analysts have spent millions trying to discover the factors that cause one product to reap[1] millions while another gathers dust on the closeout shelves.

One such company, a youth marketing consulting firm called Xtreme, studies the buying habits of those fad ringleaders called teenagers. Xtreme's president Irma Zandl believes that the key to profiting from the life cycle of a fad or fashion lies in understanding the four basic types of consumers. Adapting an earlier classification of consumers by Everett Rogers and F. Floyd Shoemaker, Zandl identifies the four types as alphas, early adopters, fast followers, and late adopters.

The first group consists of a risk-taking, innovative kind of consumer with the self-assurance to slip into a mini-skirt when the look is ankle-length or sport a purple Mohawk in a sea of sun-bleached bobs. Labeled alphas, these daring consumers stand alone in their willingness to try new products, their keen eye for potential fashion, and their insatiable[2] appetite for creating what comes next. It was an alpha who first thought to purchase jeans three sizes too big and slip them well below his hips. It was an alpha who contemplated her belly button one day and decided that might be just the place for a diamond-stud earring. But an alpha alone cannot create a genuine, raging fad.

The next group of consumers to pick up on a potential fad or fashion is comprised of early adopters. Like alphas, early adopters have the confidence to stand out from their peers. While they may not initiate the newest dance, clothing style, or haircut, these consumers are quick to imitate it, often becoming the first in their school or office to model the latest fashion. An early adopter breaks from the crowd to follow an alpha into new territory, be it hip-hop dancing, roller-blading, or body piercing. Because fads get their momentum from increased familiarity, early adopters play an important role in spreading the would-be fad throughout the wider culture.

It is at this point that the fad receives its true test, as mainstream consumers, called fast followers, decide to pass by or plunge in. Here, Zandl notes, is where fad fortunes are made. If the majority of consumers respond positively to a product, they will fall right into line—quite literally. Caught in a fad frenzy, shoppers will wait for hours in snaking queues[3] to acquire Tickle Me Elmo in time for Christmas or to purchase the latest 'N Sync CD before their friends. To exploit the

---

1. reap: gather
2. insatiable: impossible to satisfy
3. queues: lines of waiting people

herd mentality[4] fueling this multimillion dollar phenomenon, marketing experts often advise that a product be pulled from the shelves during its "hot" period, thus creating an artificial shortage, stimulating consumer interest, and lengthening the life of the fad. Despite these tricks, every fad inevitably wanes,[5] but not before attracting the attention of one last type of consumer.

This final group Zandl labels late adopters, but they could as easily be thought of as fad laggards,[6] those shoppers who find themselves attracted to a craze just as others are dropping it for something new. These belated consumers are just growing comfortable with the return of 1950s Capri pants when everyone else has moved on to retro '70s bell-bottoms. Late adopters decide to get a Furbie when the fuzzy electronic toys have been marked down to $5.99 at a liquidation outlet. Likewise, they finally find the courage to lace up their roller blades just as the masses zip past them on shiny new razor scooters. Needless to say, the late adopter's embrace of a fad signals its rapidly approaching demise.[7]

The intricate factors that propel a fad from the fringe to the mainstream and then back into obscurity again may puzzle marketing analysts forever. Yet one aspect of consumer behavior is clear: as Americans, we may treasure our individuality, but at the mall we prefer to play "follow the leader."

Discussion and Writing Questions

1. How does the author classify consumers in this essay? That is, what four categories of consumers does she identify? What is the source of these categories?

2. What kind of consumer are you? Give a specific example that reveals your type. Do you know people who might be classified in each of the four categories?

3. Why do people pay so much attention to fads and fashion trends? Is it just because advertisers assault us with propaganda, or are there other reasons?

4. How do you feel about the fact that manufacturers create artificial shortages when demand for a product is highest? Is this ethical? Why or why not?

Writing Assignments

1. Write a humorous essay about the type of consumer you know best—the alpha or the laggard, for instance. Use yourself or other people as examples and describe experiences with specific fads or products to support your points.

2. The author accuses many consumers of having a "herd mentality" (paragraph 5). Do other behaviors besides shopping reveal the herd mentality? Write an essay in which you discuss the possible causes and consequences of another form of herd mentality—peer pressure, for example.

3. Visit and explore the Bad Fads Museum online at http://www.badfads.com/home.html. Choose one of the fads listed, and write a paper arguing that it should be revived. *Or* pick a fad you know about—like the pager or belly shirt—and explain why it should be included in the Bad Fads Museum.

---

4. herd mentality: tendency to follow the crowd
5. wanes: decreases
6. laggards: those who hang back or fall behind
7. demise: death

Beauty:
When the Other Dancer Is the Self

Alice Walker

Being physically injured can be terrifying; coming to terms with a permanent disability can be a painful, difficult process. Alice Walker, a noted fiction writer, poet, and author of *The Color Purple*, tells of her feelings and experiences before, during, and after an injury that changed her life.

It is a bright summer day in 1947. My father, a fat, funny man with beautiful eyes and a subversive wit,[1] is trying to decide which of his eight children he will take with him to the county fair. My mother, of course, will not go. She is knocked out from getting most of us ready: I hold my neck stiff against the pressure of her knuckles as she hastily completes the braiding and then beribboning of my hair.

My father is the driver for the rich old white lady up the road. Her name is Miss Mey. She owns all the land for miles around, as well as the house in which we live. All I remember about her is that she once offered to pay my mother thirty-five cents for cleaning her house, raking up piles of her magnolia leaves, and washing her family's clothes, and that my mother—she of no money, eight children, and a chronic earache—refused it. But I do not think of this in 1947. I am two and a half years old. I want to go everywhere my daddy goes. I am excited at the prospect of riding in a car. Someone has told me fairs are fun. That there is room in the car for only three of us doesn't faze[2] me at all. Whirling happily in my starchy frock, showing off my biscuit-polished patent-leather shoes and lavender socks, tossing my head in a way that makes my ribbons bounce, I stand, hands on hips, before my father. "Take me, Daddy," I say with assurance; "I'm the prettiest!"

Later, it does not surprise me to find myself in Miss Mey's shiny black car, sharing the back seat with the other lucky ones. Does not surprise me that I thoroughly enjoy the fair. At home that night I tell the unlucky ones all I can remember about the merry-go-round, the man who eats live chickens, and the teddy bears, until they say: that's enough, baby Alice. Shut up now, and go to sleep.

It is Easter Sunday, 1950. I am dressed in a green, flocked, scalloped-hem dress (handmade by my adoring sister, Ruth) that has its own smooth satin petticoat and tiny hot-pink roses tucked into each scallop. My shoes, new T-strap patent leather, again highly biscuit-polished. I am six years old and have learned one of the longest Easter speeches to be heard that day, totally unlike the speech I said when I was two: "Easter lilies / pure and white / blossom in / the morning light." When I rise to give my speech I do so on a great wave of love and pride and expectation. People in the church stop rustling their new crinolines. They seem to hold their breath. I can tell they admire my dress, but it is my spirit, bordering on sassiness (womanishness), they secretly applaud.

"That girl's a little *mess*," they whisper to each other, pleased.

Naturally I say my speech without stammer or pause, unlike those who stutter, stammer, or, worst of all, forget. This is before the word "beautiful" exists in people's vocabulary, but "Oh, isn't she the *cutest* thing!" frequently floats my way. "And got so much sense!" they gratefully add . . . for which thoughtful addition I thank them to this day.

---

1. subversive wit: sarcastic, sharp sense of humor
2. faze: discourage

It was great fun being cute. But then, one day, it ended.

I am eight years old and a tomboy. I have a cowboy hat, cowboy boots, checkered shirt and pants, all red. My playmates are my brothers, two and four years older than I. Their colors are black and green, the only difference in the way we are dressed. On Saturday nights we all go to the picture show, even my mother; Westerns are her favorite kind of movie. Back home, "on the ranch," we pretend we are Tom Mix, Hopalong Cassidy, Lash LaRue (we've even named one of our dogs Lash LaRue); we chase each other for hours rustling cattle, being outlaws, delivering damsels from distress. Then my parents decide to buy my brothers guns. These are not "real" guns. They shoot "BBs," copper pellets my brothers say will kill birds. Because I am a girl, I do not get a gun. Instantly I am relegated to[3] the position of Indian. Now there appears a great distance between us. They shoot and shoot at everything with their new guns. I try to keep up with my bow and arrows.

One day while I am standing on top of our makeshift "garage"—pieces of tin nailed across some poles—holding my bow and arrow and looking out toward the fields, I feel an incredible blow in my right eye. I look down just in time to see my brother lower his gun.

Both brothers rush to my side. My eye stings, and I cover it with my hand. "If you tell," they say, "we will get a whipping. You don't want that to happen, do you?" I do not. "Here is a piece of wire," says the older brother, picking it up from the roof; "say you stepped on one end of it and the other flew up and hit you." The pain is beginning to start. "Yes," I say. "Yes, I will say that is what happened." If I do not say this is what happened, I know my brothers will find ways to make me wish I had. But now I will say anything that gets me to my mother.

Confronted by our parents we stick to the lie agreed upon. They place me on a bench on the porch and I close my left eye while they examine the right. There is a tree growing from underneath the porch that climbs past the railing to the roof. It is the last thing my right eye sees. I watch as its trunk, its branches, and then its leaves are blotted out by the rising blood.

I am in shock. First there is intense fever, which my father tries to break using lily leaves bound around my head. Then there are chills: my mother tries to get me to eat soup. Eventually, I do not know how, my parents learn what has happened. A week after the "accident" they take me to see a doctor. "Why did you wait so long to come?" he asks, looking into my eye and shaking his head. "Eyes are sympathetic,[4]" he says. "If one is blind, the other will likely become blind too."

This comment of the doctor's terrifies me. But it is really how I look that bothers me most. Where the BB pellet struck there is a glob of whitish scar tissue, a hideous cataract, on my eye. Now when I stare at people—a favorite pastime, up to now—they will stare back. Not at the "cute" little girl, but at her scar. For six years I do not stare at anyone, because I do not raise my head.

Years later, in the throes[5] of a mid-life crisis, I ask my mother and sister whether I changed after the "accident." "No," they say, puzzled. "What do you mean?"

What do I mean?

I am eight, and, for the first time, doing poorly in school, where I have been something of a whiz since I was four. We have just moved to the place where the "accident" occurred. We do not know any of the people around us because this is a different

---

3. relegated to: assigned
4. sympathetic: closely connected
5. throes: a condition of struggle

county. The only time I see the friends I knew is when we go back to our old church. The new school is the former state penitentiary. It is a large stone building, cold and drafty, crammed to overflowing with boisterous,[6] ill-disciplined children. On the third floor there is a huge circular imprint of some partition that has been torn out.

"What used to be there?" I ask a sullen girl next to me on our way past it to lunch.

"The electric chair," says she.

At night I have nightmares about the electric chair, and about all the people reputedly[7] "fried" in it. I am afraid of the school, where all the students seem to be budding criminals.

"What's the matter with your eye?" they ask, critically.

When I don't answer (I cannot decide whether it was an "accident" or not), they shove me, insist on a fight.

My brother, the one who created the story about the wire, comes to my rescue. But then brags so much about "protecting" me, I become sick.

After months of torture at the school, my parents decide to send me back to our old community, to my old school. I live with my grandparents and the teacher they board. But there is no room for Phoebe, my cat. By the time my grandparents decide there *is* room, and I ask for my cat, she cannot be found. Miss Yarborough, the boarding teacher, takes me under her wing, and begins to teach me to play the piano. But soon she marries an African—a "prince," she says—and is whisked away to his continent.

At my old school there is at least one teacher who loves me. She is the teacher who "knew me before I was born" and bought my first baby clothes. It is she who makes life bearable. It is her presence that finally helps me turn on the one child at the school who continually calls me "one-eyed bitch." One day I simply grab him by his coat and beat him until I am satisfied. It is my teacher who tells me my mother is ill.

My mother is lying in bed in the middle of the day, something I have never seen. She is in too much pain to speak. She has an abscess in her ear. I stand looking down on her, knowing that if she dies, I cannot live. She is being treated with warm oils and hot bricks held against her cheek. Finally a doctor comes. But I must go back to my grandparents' house. The weeks pass but I am hardly aware of it. All I know is that my mother might die, my father is not so jolly, my brothers still have their guns, and I am the one sent away from home.

"You did not change," they say.

Did I imagine the anguish of never looking up?

I am twelve. When relatives come to visit I hide in my room. My cousin Brenda, just my age, whose father works in the post office and whose mother is a nurse, comes to find me. "Hello," she says. And then she asks, looking at my recent school picture, which I did not want taken, and on which the "glob," as I think of it, is clearly visible, "You still can't see out of that eye?"

"No," I say, and flop back on the bed over my book.

---

6. boisterous: rowdy and noisy

7. reputedly: supposedly

That night, as I do almost every night, I abuse my eye. I rant and rave at it, in front of the mirror. I plead with it to clear up before morning. I tell it I hate and despise it. I do not pray for sight. I pray for beauty.

"You did not change," they say.

I am fourteen and baby-sitting for my brother Bill, who lives in Boston. He is my favorite brother and there is a strong bond between us. Understanding my feelings of shame and ugliness he and his wife take me to a local hospital, where the "glob" is removed by a doctor named O. Henry. There is still a small bluish crater where the scar tissue was, but the ugly white stuff is gone. Almost immediately I become a different person from the girl who does not raise her head. Or so I think. Now that I've raised my head I win the boyfriend of my dreams. Now that I've raised my head I have plenty of friends. Now that I've raised my head classwork comes from my lips as faultlessly as Easter speeches did, and I leave high school as valedictorian, most popular student, and *queen*, hardly believing my luck. Ironically, the girl who was voted most beautiful in our class (and was) was later shot twice through the chest by a male companion, using a "real" gun, while she was pregnant. But that's another story in itself. Or is it?

"You did not change," they say.

It is now thirty years since the "accident." A beautiful journalist comes to visit and to interview me. She is going to write a cover story for her magazine that focuses on my latest book. "Decide how you want to look on the cover," she says. "Glamorous, or whatever."

Never mind "glamorous," it is the "whatever" that I hear. Suddenly all I can think of is whether I will get enough sleep the night before the photography session: if I don't, my eye will be tired and wander, as blind eyes will.

At night in bed with my lover I think up reasons why I should not appear on the cover of a magazine. "My meanest critics will say I've sold out," I say. "My family will now realize I write scandalous books."

"But what's the real reason you don't want to do this?" he asks.

"Because in all probability," I say in a rush, "my eye won't be straight."

"It will be straight enough," he says. Then, "Besides, I thought you'd made your peace with that."

And I suddenly remember that I have.

I remember:

I am talking to my brother Jimmy, asking if he remembers anything unusual about the day I was shot. He does not know I consider that day the last time my father, with his sweet home remedy of cool lily leaves, chose me, and that I suffered and raged inside because of this. "Well," he says, "all I remember is standing by the side of the highway with Daddy, trying to flag down a car. A white man stopped, but when Daddy said he needed somebody to take his little girl to the doctor, he drove off."

I remember:

I am in the desert for the first time. I fall totally in love with it. I am so overwhelmed by its beauty, I confront for the first time, consciously, the meaning of the doctor's words years ago: "Eyes are sympathetic. If one is blind, the other will likely become blind too." I realize I have dashed about the world madly, looking at this, looking at that, storing up images against the fading of the light. *But I might have missed seeing the desert!* The shock of that possibility—and gratitude for over twenty-five years of sight—sends me literally to my knees. Poem after poem comes—which is perhaps how poets pray.

On Sight

I am so thankful I have seen
The Desert
And the creatures in the desert
And the desert Itself.

The desert has its own moon
Which I have seen
With my own eye.
There is no flag on it.

Trees of the desert have arms
All of which are always up
That is because the moon is up
The sun is up
Also the sky
The stars
Clouds
None with flags.
If there *were* flags, I doubt
the trees would point.
Would you?

But mostly, I remember this:
    I am twenty-seven, and my baby daughter is almost three. Since her birth I have worried about her discovery that her mother's eyes are different from other people's. Will she be embarrassed? I think. What will she say? Every day she watches a television program called "Big Blue Marble." It begins with a picture of the earth as it appears from the moon. It is bluish, a little battered-looking, but full of light, with whitish clouds swirling around it. Every time I see it I weep with love, as if it is a picture of Grandma's house. One day when I am putting Rebecca down for her nap, she suddenly focuses on my eye. Something inside me cringes, gets ready to try to protect myself. All children are cruel about physical differences, I know from experience, and that they don't always mean to be is another matter. I assume Rebecca will be the same.
    But no-o-o-o. She studies my face intently as we stand, her inside and me outside her crib. She even holds my face maternally between her dimpled little hands. Then, looking every bit as serious and lawyerlike as her father, she says, as if it may just possibly have slipped my attention: "Mommy, there's a *world* in your eye." (As in, "Don't be alarmed, or do anything crazy.") And then, gently, but with great interest: "Mommy, where did you *get* that world in your eye?"
    For the most part, the pain left then. (So what, if my brothers grew up to buy even more powerful pellet guns for their sons and to carry real guns themselves. So what, if a young "Morehouse man" once nearly fell off the steps of Trevor Arnett Library because he thought my eyes were blue.) Crying and laughing I ran to the bathroom, while Rebecca mumbled and sang herself to sleep. Yes indeed, I realized, looking into the mirror. There *was* a world in my eye. And I saw that it was possible to love it: that in fact, for all it had taught me of shame and anger

and inner vision, I *did* love it. Even to see it drifting out of orbit in boredom, or rolling up out of fatigue, not to mention floating back at attention in excitement (bearing witness, a friend has called it), deeply suitable to my personality, and even characteristic of me.

That night I dream I am dancing to Stevie Wonder's song "Always" (The name of the song is really "As," but I hear it as "Always"). As I dance, whirling and joyous, happier than I've ever been in my life, another bright-faced dancer joins me. We dance and kiss each other and hold each other through the night. The other dancer has obviously come through all right, as I have done. She is beautiful, whole and free. And she is also me.

Discussion and Writing Questions

1. When did the author stop being "cute"? Is she happy about this change?
2. Why do you think her family insists that she did not change after the shooting?
3. Until her operation at age fourteen, Walker speaks of hating her injured eye. By the end of the essay, she dances with another "dancer," who is "beautiful, whole and free. And she is also me." What makes the author change her mind about her "deformity"?
4. The author uses particular words and phrases to indicate time or chronological order in her narrative. Find the words that indicate time order. At one point in her narrative, she breaks this time order to skip back into the past. In which paragraph does this flashback occur?

Writing Assignments

1. Write about an unpleasant event or experience that resulted in personal growth for you. Your writing need not focus on something as painful as Alice Walker's injury. What is important is how you came to terms with the experience and what you ultimately learned from it.
2. Tell a story about being thrust into a completely unfamiliar situation. You might describe your reaction to attending a new school, starting a new job, or moving to a new city. Present concrete details of your experience. Organize the story around your most vivid memories, like meeting new classmates for the first time, or your first few days on the new job.
3. In a group with three or four classmates, discuss the accident that injured Walker's eye and the children's cover-up (paragraphs 8–11). Her brothers, ten and twelve, were given BB guns. How did these guns change the relationships among siblings even before the accident? Why did this happen? Are BB guns "real guns"? Have you known someone injured by "gun play"? How can such accidents be prevented? Write a paper on your own in which you present one to three ways in which Walker's injury—or one that you know about—could have been prevented.

A Smoker's Right

Mario Vargas Llosa

More and more fatally ill smokers—and their families—are suing tobacco companies for damaging their health. Mario Vargas Llosa is a Peruvian novelist and former three-pack-a-day smoker. In this article, he takes a strong, perhaps surprising, stand on just who is to blame for smoking-related illness.

Although, since I stopped smoking 30 years ago, I have detested cigarettes and their manufacturers, I have not been as pleased as other ex-smokers to see damage awards in lawsuits against tobacco companies reach the hundreds of billions of dollars, for reasons I would like to try to explain.

In Cochabamba, Bolivia, when I was 7 or 8, my cousins Nancy and Gladys and I invested our allowances in a packet of Viceroys and smoked them all. Gladys and I survived, but the weakling Nancy began vomiting, and her grandparents had to call the doctor. This first smoking experience greatly disgusted me, but my passion for being grown up was stronger than the disgust, and I went on smoking.

My adolescence at university is inseparable from the oval-shaped Nacional Presidente brand with its black tobacco, which I smoked incessantly[1] while reading, watching movies, arguing, falling in love, conspiring or attempting to write. Drawing in the smoke and blowing it out, in rings or as a cloud that dissolved into dancing figures, was a great felicity:[2] a companion, a support, a distraction, a stimulus.

When I arrived in Paris in 1958, the discovery of Gitanes catapulted[3] my tobacco habit, and soon I was smoking three packs a day. After a strong coffee and a croissant, the first drag of thick smoke had the effect of the true awakening, the start-up of the organism. A lighted cigarette in the hand was an indispensable prerequisite for any action or decision: opening a letter, answering a telephone call, requesting a loan at the bank. I took the last drag of the day when already halfway asleep.

A doctor warned me that cigarettes were harming me; I was tormented by bronchial problems, and the Parisian winters kept me sneezing and coughing incessantly. I paid no attention to him, convinced that without tobacco my life would be terribly impoverished and that I might even lose my urge to write. But, on moving to London in 1966, I tried a cowardly compromise, trading the beloved Gitanes for the blond Players No. 6, which had a filter and less tobacco and which I never really liked.

It was my neighbor, a medical professor, in the town of Pullman, Wash., who finally made me decide to stop smoking. I was in that remote place of snowstorms and red apples as a visiting professor, and he asked me one day to go with him to his office. I warned him that I was allergic to conversions, but went. For three or four hours he gave me a practical lecture against cigarettes. I returned convinced that human beings are even more stupid than we seem, because smoking constitutes an unmitigated[4] cataclysm[5] for any organism. Perhaps what most impressed me was the absolute disproportion[6] which, in the case of the cigarette, exists between the pleasure obtained and the risk run, unlike other practices, also danger-

---

1. incessantly: without stopping
2. felicity: happiness
3. catapulted: hurled upward
4. unmitigated: not lessened
5. cataclysm: violent and destructive upheaval
6. disproportion: lack of balance

ous to health, but infinitely more succulent[7] than breathing smoke in and out. Still, I went on smoking for at least a year more, in fear and remorse every time I lit up.

I quit the day in 1970 that I left London to go and live in Barcelona. It was less difficult than I had feared. The first weeks I did nothing else but not smoke—it was the only activity in my head—but it was a great help, from the first moment, to begin to sleep like a normal person and to wake up in the morning feeling fresh. It was most amusing to discover there were different smells in life—that the sense of smell existed—and above all, flavors, that is, that a steak did not taste the same as a plate of chick peas.

Quitting smoking did not at all affect my intellectual work; on the contrary, I was able to work longer hours without the chest pains that used to wrench me away from the writing desk. The negative consequences were appetite, which burgeoned[8] obliging me to exercise, diet and even fast; and a certain allergy to the odor of tobacco, which, in countries where people still smoke a lot and smoke everywhere, as in Spain or Latin America, may complicate life for the ex-smoker.

As often occurs with converts of the tiresome sort, for a while I became an anti-tobacco apostle. In Barcelona, one of my first conquests was Gabriel García Márquez[9] who, one night, livid with horror at my missionary stories about the havoc[10] wreaked[11] by nicotine, threw a packet of cigarettes on the floor and swore he would never smoke again. He kept his promise.

My zeal waned over the years, especially when, in much of the world, campaigns against cigarettes proliferated[12] and the matter began, in certain countries like Britain and the United States, to assume a complexion of witch-hunting.

It is, of course, quite fair that the tobacco companies should be penalized if they have concealed information or have used prohibited substances to increase addiction. But is it not hypocrisy[13] to consider them enemies of humanity while the product they offer has not been the object of a specific prohibition by law? Nor should there be such a prohibition.

The obligation of the state, in a democratic society, is to make citizens aware that tobacco is harmful, so that they can decide with adequate knowledge whether to smoke. This, indeed, is what is happening in most Western countries. If a person in the United States, France, Spain or Italy smokes, it is not out of ignorance of what this means for health, but because he does not wish to know, or does not care.

To commit suicide by degrees is a choice that ought to figure on the list of basic human rights. This is the only possible approach if we wish to preserve the freedom of the individual, which must include the freedom to opt not only for what is beneficial to him, but also for what harms or injures.

And so, though at first sight, the decision of juries to impose astronomical[14] penalties on the tobacco companies may seem a progressive measure, it is not so. What sort of freedom would it be that allowed us only to choose what is good for us?

---

7. succulent: juicy
8. burgeoned: increased
9. Gabriel García Márquez: famous Colombian novelist
10. havoc: destruction
11. wreaked: caused or inflicted
12. proliferated: multiplied
13. hypocrisy: pretense of being moral or virtuous
14. astronomical: extremely high

Discussion and Writing Questions

1. What is the author's thesis, or main point? What reasons does he give for his point of view?

2. Llosa describes his own smoking addiction at length. What vivid details show the importance that smoking had in his life and daily routines (paragraphs 3–4)? Why does he spend so much time describing his own habit?

3. Why did Llosa finally quit smoking? What effects did quitting have on his life?

4. The author argues that the individual must be free "to opt not only for what is beneficial to him, but also for what harms or injures" (paragraph 13). Do you agree or disagree?

Writing Assignments

1. Llosa says he began smoking as a child because his "passion for being grown up was stronger than his disgust." Write a paper discussing three reasons why so many children and teens smoke (or engage in another high-risk behavior). Illustrate with examples from your life or the lives of people you know.

2. The author points out that tobacco products are not prohibited by law, and he does not believe they should be. Write an essay explaining why cigarettes (or marijuana, unprotected sex, or other risky substance or behavior) should or should not be outlawed.

3. The author kicked his habit a year after his neighbor, a doctor, lectured him about the disaster smoking visits on the human body. What are the most effective ways for an addict to break a habit? Lectures? Groups? Hitting bottom? If you know an addict who was able to stop using, analyze how this happened.

Some Thoughts About Abortion

Anna Quindlen

Since the *Roe vs. Wade* Supreme Court decision of 1973, the issue of abortion has been the center of passionate debate in the United States. In this essay, novelist and Pulitzer Prize-winning journalist Anna Quindlen describes her own mixed feelings about the subject and at the same time gives persuasive reasons for keeping abortion legal.

1. It was always the look on their faces that told me first. I was the freshman dormitory counselor and they were the freshmen at a women's college where everyone was smart. One of them would come into my room, a golden girl, a valedictorian, an 800 verbal score on the S.A.T.'s, and her eyes would be empty, seeing only a busted future, the devastation of her life as she knew it. She had failed biology, messed up the math; she was pregnant.

2. That was when I became pro-choice.

3. It was the look in his eyes that I will always remember, too. They were as black as the bottom of a well, and in them for a few minutes I thought I saw myself the way I had always wished to be—clear, simple, elemental, at peace. My child looked at me and I looked back at him in the delivery room, and I realized

that out of a sea of infinite possibilities it had come down to this: a specific person, born on the hottest day of the year, conceived on a Christmas Eve, made by his father and me miraculously from scratch.

Once I believed that there was a little blob of formless protoplasm[1] in there and a gynecologist went after it with a surgical instrument, and that was that. Then I got pregnant myself—eagerly, intentionally, by the right man, at the right time—and I began to doubt. My abdomen still flat, my stomach roiling with morning sickness, I felt not that I had protoplasm inside, but, instead, a complete human being in miniature to whom I could talk, sing, make promises. Neither of these views was accurate; instead, I think, the reality is something in the middle. And that is where I find myself now, in the middle—hating the idea of abortions, hating the idea of having them outlawed.

For I know it is the right thing in some times and places. I remember sitting in a shabby clinic far uptown with one of those freshmen, only three months after the Supreme Court had made what we were doing possible, and watching with wonder as the lovely first love she had had with a nice boy unraveled[2] over the space of an hour as they waited for her to be called, degenerated[3] into sniping[4] and silences. I remember a year or two later seeing them pass on campus and not even acknowledge each other because their conjoining had caused them so much pain, and I shuddered to think of them married, with a small psyche in their unready and unwilling hands.

I've met fourteen-year-olds who were pregnant and said they could not have abortions because of their religion, and I see in their eyes the shadows of twenty-two-year-olds I've talked to who lost their kids to foster care because they hit them or used drugs or simply had no money for food and shelter. I read not long ago about a teenager who said she meant to have an abortion but she spent the money on clothes instead: now she has a baby who turns out to be a lot more trouble than a toy. The people who hand out those execrable[5] little pictures of dismembered fetuses at abortion clinics seem to forget the extraordinary pain children may endure after they are born when they are unwanted, even hated, or simply tolerated.

I believe that in a contest between the living and the almost living, the latter must, if necessary, give way to the will of the former. That is what the fetus is to me, the almost living. These questions began to plague me—and, I've discovered, a good many other women—after I became pregnant. But they became even more acute after I had my second child, mainly because he is so different from his brother. On two random nights eighteen months apart the same two people managed to conceive, and on one occasion the tumult[6] within turned itself into a curly-haired brunet with merry black eyes who walked and talked late and loved the whole world, and on another it became a blond with hazel Asian eyes and a pug nose who tried to conquer the world almost as soon as he entered it.

If we were to have an abortion next time for some reason or another, which infinite possibility becomes, not a reality, but a nullity?[7] The girl with the blue eyes? The improbable redhead? The natural athlete? The thinker? My husband, ever at

---

1. protoplasm: living matter
2. unraveled: came apart
3. degenerated: became worse
4. sniping: bickering, arguing
5. execrable: disgusting
6. tumult: energetic movement
7. nullity: nonexistence

the heart of the matter, put it another way. Knowing he is finding two children somewhat more overwhelming than he expected, I asked if he would want me to have an abortion if I accidentally became pregnant again right away. "And waste a perfectly good human being?" he said.

Coming to this quandary[8] has been difficult for me. In fact, I believe the issue of abortion is difficult for all thoughtful people. I don't know anyone who has had an abortion who has been casual about it. If there is one thing I find intolerable about most of the so-called right-to-lifers, it is that they try to portray abortion rights as something that feminists thought up on a slow Saturday over a light lunch. That is nonsense. I also know that some people who support abortion rights are most comfortable with a monolithic[9] position because it seems the strongest front against the smug and sometimes violent opposition.

But I don't feel all one way about abortion anymore, and I don't think it serves a just cause to pretend that many of us do. For years I believed that a woman's right to choose was absolute, but now I wonder. Do I, with a stable home and marriage and sufficient stamina and money, have the freedom to choose abortion because a pregnancy is inconvenient just now? Legally I do have the right; legally I want always to have that right. It is the morality of exercising it under those circumstances that makes me wonder.

Technology has foiled[10] us. The second trimester has become a time of resurrection; a fetus at six months can be one woman's late abortion, another's premature, viable[11] child. Photographers now have film of embryos the size of a grape, oddly human, flexing their fingers, sucking their thumbs. Women have amniocentesis[12] to find out whether they are carrying a child with birth defects that they may choose to abort. Before the procedure, they must have a sonogram, one of those fuzzy black-and-white photos like a love song heard through static on the radio, which shows someone is in there.

I have taped on my VCR a public television program in which somehow, inexplicably,[13] a film is shown of a fetus *in utero*[14] scratching its face, seemingly putting up a tiny hand to shield itself from the camera's eye. It would make a potent weapon in the arsenal of the antiabortionists. I grow sentimental about it as it floats in the salt water, part fish, part human being. It is almost living, but not quite. It has almost turned my heart around, but not quite turned my head.

Discussion and Writing Questions

1. Quindlen describes two positions she has taken about abortion. What are they?

2. In which paragraph does the author begin to express doubts about abortion? Why does she have these doubts?

3. By the end of her essay, how does Quindlen feel about abortion?

4. What types of proof does the author use in her argument?

---

8. quandary: tough spot, predicament
9. monolithic: unified and solid
10. foiled: blocked, confused
11. viable: able to live
12. amniocentesis: a medical procedure for checking the amniotic fluid in the uterus
13. inexplicably: unexplainably
14. *in utero*: in the mother's uterus

Writing Assignments

1. Write on an issue about which you are, like Quindlen, undecided. Choose a topic you know fairly well so that you can present solid arguments for both sides. Be objective, but let your reader know which side you finally find more persuasive.

2. Do you believe that teenagers should be required to inform their parents before obtaining an abortion? Argue in favor of or against this position.

3. Quindlen first gained experience with the abortion issue as a freshman dorm counselor. Write about a time that you once counseled, or gave advice to, a friend in need. Your friend might have been contemplating an abortion, like some of the young women Quindlen describes. She or he may have been fighting with a mate or having a problem with money, career decisions, or school.

Road Rage

Andrew Ferguson

Although the term *road rage* only recently entered our language, many of us have experienced it firsthand—either in ourselves or in another driver who has targeted us as the enemy. In this *Time* magazine story, Andrew Ferguson examines the causes of this tragedy—and insanity—on our highways.

It's a jungle out there. Well, not really: it's worse than a jungle. It's a stretch of roadway anywhere in America, and in place of the ravenous tigers and stampeding rhinos and slithery anacondas are your friends and neighbors and co-workers, that nice lady from the church choir and the cheerful kid who bags your food at the local Winn Dixie—even Mom and Dad and Buddy and Sis. They're in a hurry. And you're in their way. So step on it! That light is not going to get any greener! Move it or park it! Tarzan had it easy. Tarzan didn't have to drive to work.

It may be morning in America—crime down, incomes up, inflation nonexistent—but it's high noon on the country's streets and highways. This is road recklessness, auto anarchy,[1] an epidemic of wanton[2] carmanship. Almost everyone from anywhere has a story about it, as fresh as the memory of this morning's commute. And no wonder. Incidents of "road rage" were up 51% in the first half of the decade, according to a report from the AAA Foundation for Traffic Safety. Some occurrences are grisly enough to make the headlines. Last year a high-speed racing duel on the George Washington Memorial Parkway outside Washington killed two innocent commuters, including a mother of two, traveling in the opposite direction.

More often the new road anarchy manifests itself in the mundane:[3] the unsignaled lane change by the driver next to you, the guy who tailgates you if you go too slow, and the person ahead who brakes abruptly if you go too fast—each transgression[4] accented by a flip of the bird or a blast of the horn. Sixty-four percent of respondents to a recent Coalition for Consumer Health and Safety poll

---

1. anarchy: chaos, disorder
2. wanton: reckless
3. mundane: common, everyday
4. transgression: a violation of law

say people are driving less courteously and more dangerously than they were five years ago.

And the enemy is us. Take a ride with "Anne," a 40-year-old mother of three who would rather we not use her real name, as she steers her 2½-ton black Chevy Suburban out of her driveway on a leafy street in residential Washington. The clock on the dashboard reads 2:16. She has 14 minutes to make it to her daughter's game. Within a block of her house she has hit 37 m.p.h., taking stop signs as suggestions rather than law. She has a lot on her mind. "I'm not even thinking of other cars," Anne admits cheerfully as she lays on the horn. An oldster in an econo-box ahead of her has made the near fatal mistake of slowing at an intersection with no stop sign or traffic light. Anne swears and peels off around him.

Anne has a clean driving record with scarcely even a fender bender to her name. But when she takes to the highway, even her kids join the fun. "Make him move over!" they shout as she bears down on a 55-m.p.h. sluggard in the fast lane. She flashes her headlights. The kids cheer when the unlucky target gives in and moves aside. Back in town, Anne specializes in near misses. "Jeez, I almost hit that woman," she chirps, swinging the Suburban into the right lane to pass a car turning left at an intersection. She makes the game two minutes late. "I don't think I'm an aggressive driver," Anne says. "But there are a lot of bad drivers out there."

Residents of late 20th century America are arguably the luckiest human beings in history: the most technologically pampered, the richest, the freest things on two legs the world has ever seen. Then why do we drive like such jerks? The most common answer: What do you mean we, Kemo Sabe? Of course, you don't drive like a jerk. Very few drivers admit to being an obnoxious road warrior. There seem to be only three types of people on the road these days: the insane (those who drive faster than you), the moronic (those who drive slower than you) and . . . you. But this merely confuses the issue. Surely someone is doing all that speeding, tailgating, headlight flashing and abrupt lane changing, not to mention the bird flipping and horn blasting.

Aggressive driving, of course, has been around since the early decades of this century, from the moment when the average number of automobiles on any given roadway rose from 1 to 2. It is partly a matter of numbers. There are 17% more cars in America than there were 10 years ago, while the number of drivers is up 10%. More to the point: the number of miles driven has increased 35% since 1987, while only 1% more roads have been built.

But as the quantity of cars has risen, the nature of the problem has changed qualitatively as well. Maybe the congestion is making everyone cranky. Americans are famously attached to their cars; it's just the driving they can't stand. "Driving and habitual road rage have become virtually inseparable," says Leon James, a professor of psychology at the University of Hawaii who specializes in the phenomenon.

In the most comprehensive national survey on driving behavior so far, a Michigan firm, EPIC-MRA, found that an astounding 80% of drivers are angry most or all of the time while driving. Simple traffic congestion is one cause of irritation, but these days just about anything can get the average driver to tap his horn. More than one-third of respondents to the Michigan survey said they get impatient at stoplights or when waiting for a parking space; an additional 25% can't stand waiting for passengers to get in the car. And 22% said they get mad when a multi-lane highway narrows.

So not only are roads more crowded than ever, but they are crowded with drivers whom science has now discovered to be extremely touchy. Modern life offers plenty of ready-made excuses for bad driving, and here as elsewhere time seems to be of the essence: there's just not enough of it.

So many miles, so little time. For Ron Remer, 47, a soft-spoken salesman, offensive driving was simply part of the job. From his home in New Haven, Conn., he logged 30,000 miles a year selling promotional products. "People on the road were an impediment[5] to my progress," he says. "If I was late, it would reflect badly on me. Maybe the customer wouldn't want the products, and I'd be out of a sale. Getting there was the only thing that was important. If I met you in person, I might invite you for coffee or something. But on the road, you were in my way."

Remer says he's reformed now. He was stopped one night on the narrow and unlighted Merritt Parkway in Connecticut after a high-speed race with another car, and soon thereafter he enrolled in a seminar for aggressive drivers. "I was lucky to recognize my problem and try to fix it," he says.

Other road warriors are unrepentant. Alan Carter, 43, a computer specialist from North Carolina and a self-described "aggressive driver," has his own vision of a perfect commute: one with no other cars in sight. "I don't want anyone in front of me. Any time. I think maybe this type of thinking has its roots in the minutiae[6] of territorial rights and typical American individualism. But I don't really think about the deeper meanings. I just know that someone else is in my space or in the space I want."

Carter doesn't have to search for deeper meanings; that is a job for paid professionals, of whom, in America, there are many. Their theories range from the sociological to the psychological to the quasi political. "There is a greater diversity of road users now than at any other time in history," says Hawaii's James. "Therefore streets are not reserved for the optimum, skilled driver but accommodate a variety of driver groups with varying skill, acuity[7] and emotional control"—jerks, in nontechnical lingo. And unlike in previous generations, the willingness to be a jerk on the road is no longer confined to a single sex.

Ed Sarpolus, the head researcher for the Michigan study of driving behavior, was struck by the gender breakdown of aggressive drivers: 53% of them are women. "There is a tremendous cultural shift taking place," he says. "Men still outnumber women in pure numbers, but women are not only increasing, they are not falling off as they get older. Women have fought to be equal in the workplace and in society, and now they're fighting to be equal behind the wheel. [Our] data are full of soccer moms."

This democratization of the highway has occurred simultaneously [with] a decline in traditional driver's education, once a near universal part of the curriculum in America's secondary schools—and a course beloved by generations of high schoolers, since the only way you could fail was by running over the instructor's cat. Some states have backed off mandatory driver training altogether, and elsewhere most courses demand no more than six hours behind the wheel.

Driving is a curious combination of public and private acts. A car isolates a driver from the world even as it carries him through it. The sensation of personal power is intoxicating. Sealed in your little pod, you control the climate with the touch of a button, from Arctic tundra to equatorial tropic. The cabin is virtually soundproof. Your "pilot's chair" has more positions than a Barcalounger. You can't listen to that old Sammy Davis Jr. tape at home because your kids will think you're a dweeb, but in the car, the audience roars as you belt out I've Gotta Be Me. Coffee steams from the cup holder, a bag of Beer Nuts sits open at your side, and God knows you're safe. The safety belt is strapped snugly across your body, and if that fails, the air bag will save your life—if it doesn't decapitate you. Little bells and

---

5. impediment: blockage, obstruction
6. minutiae: small details
7. acuity: sharpness of vision

lights go off if you make a mistake: don't forget to buckle up! Change your oil, you sleepyhead! The illusions—of power, of anonymity,[8] of self-containment—pile up. You are the master of your domain. Actually driving the car is the last thing you need to worry about. So you can pick your nose, break wind, fantasize to your heart's content. Who's to know?

The fantasies are shaped not only by the comforts of the cars but by their sheer tonnage as well. Affluent Americans of the 1990s—so responsible at home, so productive in the workplace—want a car designed for war. With its four-wheel drive and tons of torque and booster-rocket horsepower, today's sports-utility vehicle would have come in handy at the Battle of the Bulge. "There is a real illusion of anonymity combined with potency because you have a machine you can command," says Jack Levin, a sociologist at Northeastern University's Program for the Study of Violence. "Top it off with the stress of work and people perhaps feeling insecure there, or with troubles at home, and it can make for a dangerous combination."

Road-rage experts have come up with various solutions to the anarchy of our streets and highways. We could legislate it (lower speed limits, build more roads to relieve congestion), adjudicate it (more highway cops, stiffer penalties), regulate it (more elaborate licensing procedures) or educate it away (mandatory driver's ed). Others suggest an option perhaps more typical of America circa 1998: therapize it.

"The road-rage habit can be unlearned," says James of the University of Hawaii, "but it takes more than conventional driver's ed." He calls for a new driver's ed program from kindergarten on—to teach "a spirit of cooperation rather than competition"—and grass-roots organizations called Quality Driving Circles. These, he told a radio station, would be "small groups of people meeting regularly together to discuss their driving problems and help one another do driving-personality makeovers."

Will it work? A better question might be, Do we want it to? Road-rage therapists come perilously close to calling for a transformation of the national character—remaking our rough-and-tumble, highly individualistic country into a large-scale version of a college town where everyone recycles kitty litter, drinks latte, listens to Enya[9] and eats whole grains. Is that really what we want? For all its dangers, road rage may simply be a corruption of those qualities that Americans have traditionally, and rightly, admired: tenacity,[10] energy, competitiveness, hustle—something, in other words, to be contained and harnessed by etiquette and social censure rather than eradicated[11] outright. Until then, alas, anyone braving the streets and highways of America would be well advised to employ a technique older than therapy: prayer.

Discussion and Writing Questions

1. According to Andrew Ferguson, what kinds of people are affected by road rage? Do they consider themselves dangerous drivers?

2. What are the main causes of road rage?

---

8. anonymity: the state of being unknown, unnamed
9. Enya: New Age singer
10. tenacity: persistence, refusal to give up
11. eradicated: eliminated

3. Ferguson uses illustration well to strengthen and humanize his argument; examples of drivers include "Anne," Ron Remer, Alan Carter, and others. Which examples did you find most effective? Explain why, as specifically as possible.

4. Paragraphs 17 and 18 skillfully describe driving as a "curious combination of public and private acts." What details does Ferguson include that especially capture the isolation, enjoyment, and power of driving alone in one's car? Do you agree with Ferguson that Americans "want a car designed for war"?

5. What kinds of solutions have been proposed for road rage? Will they work?

Writing Assignments

1. Have you or has someone you know experienced road rage? Describe what happened. Were you or was that person able to control the anger? If so, how?

2. Ferguson says that cars give drivers a dangerous and false sense of control and power. Guns too can give a false sense of control and power, with similarly deadly results. Does wielding a deadly weapon give us real power? Many religions tell us that real power lies in kindness, forgiveness, and serenity. Who is right?

3. In a group with three or four classmates, discuss how you and others you know have handled road rage. Discuss any programs you know of and their procedures and results. Then write your own paper on solutions for road rage. You can use information you learned from your group, as well as anecdotes, examples, or research (studies, experts' opinions, statistics, and so on). Or visit http://dmoz.org/Society/Issues/Violence_and_Abuse/Road_Rage/Prevention/.

Quotation Bank

This collection of wise and humorous statements has been assembled for you to read, enjoy, and use in a variety of ways as you write. You might choose quotations that you particularly agree or disagree with and use them as the basis of journal entries and writing assignments. Sometimes when writing a paragraph or an essay, you may find it useful to include a quotation to support a point you are making. Alternatively, you may simply want to read through these quotations for ideas and for fun. As you come across other intriguing statements by writers, add them to the list—or write some of your own.

Education

1. Knowledge is power.
   —Francis Bacon

2. Everyone is ignorant, only on different subjects.
   —Will Rogers

3. The children need the bread of the mind.
   —Rafael Cordero y Molina

4. Never be afraid to sit awhile and think.
   —Lorraine Hansberry

5. A mind stretched by a new idea can never go back to its original dimensions.
   —Oliver Wendell Holmes, Jr.

6. The contest between education and TV . . . has been won by television.
   —Robert Hughes

7. Our minds are lazier than our bodies.
   —François, Duc de la Rochefoucauld

8. This thing called "failure" is not the falling down, but the staying down.
   —Mary Pickford

9. Tell me what you pay attention to, and I will tell you who you are.
   —José Ortega y Gasset

Wisdom consists of anticipating the consequences.
—Norman Cousins

We learn something by doing it. There is no other way.
—John Holt

Work and Success

He who does not hope to win has already lost.
—José Joaquin de Olmedo

The harder you work, the luckier you get.
—Gary Player

Float like a butterfly, sting like a bee.
—Muhammad Ali

All glory comes from daring to begin.
—Anonymous

Have a vision not clouded by fear.
—Old Cherokee saying

Show me a person who has never made a mistake, and I'll show you a person who has never achieved much.
—Joan Collins

To me, success means effectiveness in the world, that I am able to carry out my ideas and values into the world—that I am able to change it in positive ways.
—Maxine Hong Kingston

Nice guys finish last.
—Leo Durocher

Do as the bull in the face of adversity: charge.
—José de Diego

Life is a succession of moments. To live each one is to succeed.
—Corita Kent

Should you not find the pearl after one or two divings, don't blame the ocean! Blame your diving! You are not going deep enough.
—P. Yogananda

It is good to have an end to journey towards, but it is the journey that matters in the end.
—Ursula K. LeGuin

Nothing is really work unless you would rather be doing something else.
—J.M. Barrie

I merely took the energy it takes to pout and wrote some blues. 25
—Duke Ellington

I write when I'm inspired, and I see to it that I'm inspired at nine o'clock 26
every morning.
—Peter De Vries

Love

If you want to be loved, be lovable. 27
—Ovid

After ecstasy, the laundry. 28
—Zen saying

The first duty of love is to listen. 29
—Paul Tillich

The way is not in the sky. The way is in the heart. 30
—Dhammapada

A successful marriage requires falling in love many times, always with the 31
same person.
—Mignon McLaughlin

Love is a fire, but whether it's going to warm your hearth or burn down 32
your house, you can never tell.
—Dorothy Parker

The old Lakota was wise. He knew that man's heart away from nature 33
becomes hard.
—Standing Bear

The way to love anything is to realize that it might be lost. 34
—G. K. Chesterton

It's like magic. When you live by yourself, all your annoying habits are gone! 35
—Merrill Marko

Love does not consist in gazing at each other but in looking together in the 36
same direction.
—Antoine de Saint-Exupéry

The story of a love is not important—what is important is that one is capable 37
of love. It is perhaps the only glimpse we are permitted of eternity.
—Helen Hayes

To deserve a people's love, you must know them. You must learn to 38
appreciate their history, their culture, their values, their aspirations for
human advancement and freedom.
—Jesus Colon

Friends and Family

Love is blind; friendship closes its eyes. — 39
—Anonymous

Friendship with oneself is all important because without it one cannot be friends with anyone else in the world. — 40
—Eleanor Roosevelt

What is a friend? A single soul dwelling in two bodies. — 41
—Aristotle

You do not know who is your friend and who is your enemy until the ice breaks. — 42
—Eskimo proverb

What's more important? Building a bridge or taking care of a baby? — 43
—June Jordan

Your children need your presence more than your presents. — 44
—Jesse Jackson

The peace and stability of a nation depend upon the proper relationships established in the home. — 45
—Jade Snow Wong

How times change: it used to be kids would ask where they came from. Now they tell you where to go. — 46
—Ann Landers

Children need love, especially when they do not deserve it. — 47
—Harold S. Hulbert

Ourselves in Society

America is not a melting pot. It is a sizzling cauldron. — 48
—Barbara Ann Mikulski

When spider webs unite, they can tie up a lion. — 49
—Ethiopian proverb

We can do not great things, only small things with great love. — 50
—Mother Teresa

A smile is the shortest distance between two people. — 51
—Victor Borge

Whether we're laughing or crying, the reality of the streets persists. — 52
—Roberto Santiago

Freedom does not always win. This is one of the bitterest lessons of history. 53
—*A. J. P. Taylor*

If you think you're too small to have an impact, try going to bed with a mosquito. 54
—*Anita Koddick*

Courage isn't the absence of fear; it is action in the face of fear. 55
—*S. Kennedy*

Racism is still a major issue because it is a habit. 56
—*Maya Angelou*

What women want is what men want: they want respect. 57
—*Marilyn Vos Savant*

The same heart beats in every human breast. 58
—*Matthew Arnold*

Basically people are people . . . but it is our differences which charm, delight, and frighten us. 59
—*Agnes Newton Keith*

I can think of no greater honor than to help others fight to survive. 60
—*Helen Cahlakee Burgess*

Wisdom for Living

Look within! The secret is inside you! 61
—*Hui Neng*

One who wants a rose must respect the thorn. 62
—*Persian proverb*

To live a creative life, we must lose our fear of being wrong. 63
—*Joseph Chilton Pearce*

Laughter can be more satisfying than honor, more precious than money, more heart cleansing than prayer. 64
—*Harriet Rochlin*

People who keep stiff upper lips find that it's damn hard to smile. 65
—*Judith Guest*

The way to get things done is not to mind who gets the credit of doing them. 66
—*Benjamin Jowett*

Self-pity in its early stages is as snug as a feather mattress. Only when it hardens does it become uncomfortable. 67
—*Maya Angelou*

When three people call you a donkey, put on a saddle. 68
—Spanish proverb

Never criticize a man until you have walked a mile in his moccasins. 69
—Native American proverb

Everyone is a moon and has a dark side which he never shows to anybody. 70
—Mark Twain

Self-examination—if it is thorough enough—is always the first step towards change. 71
—Thomas Mann

If you can't change your fate, change your attitude. 72
—Amy Tan

Time is a dressmaker specializing in alterations. 73
—Faith Baldwin

Money can't buy friends, but you can get a better class of enemy. 74
—Spike Milligan

Living in the lap of luxury isn't bad, except you never know when luxury is going to stand up. 75
—Orson Welles

Egoist. A person of low taste, more interested in himself than me. 76
—Ambrose Bierce

Envy is a kind of praise. 77
—John Gay

What doesn't destroy me strengthens me. 78
—Friedrich Nietzsche

Life shrinks and expands in proportion to one's courage. 79
—Anaïs Nin

I'm not afraid to die. I just don't want to be there when it happens. 80
—Woody Allen

Acknowledgments

(continued from copyright page)

Pages 514-516: "Cell Yell: Thanks for (Not) Sharing" by Eric A. Taub, *New York Times,* November 22, 2001, pp. G1, G5. Copyright © 2001 by the New York Times Co. Reprinted by permission.

Pages 517-519: "A Brother's Murder: by Brent Staples, *New York Times,* 3/30/86 ("About Men" Column). Copyright © 1986 by the New York Times Co. Reprinted by permission.

Pages 520-522: "Only Daughter" by Sandra Cisneros from *The House on Mango Street.* Copyright © 1990 by Sandra Cisneros. First published in *Glamour,* November 1990. Reprinted by permission of Susan Bergholz Literary Services, New York. All rights reserved.

Pages 523-525: "The Case for Torture" by Michael E. Levin, *Newsweek,* June 1982. Reprinted by permission of the author.

Pages 526-528: "Let's Get Vertical" by Beth Wald. Originally published in *Listen* Magazine, June 1999. Reprinted by permission of the author.

Pages 529-531: Excerpts from ON THE REZ by Ian Frazier. Copyright © 2000 by Ian Frazier. Reprinted by permission of Farrar, Straus and Giroux, LLC.

Pages 532-533: "Bam! Crash! Kapow! Girls Are Heroes Now," by Dr. Susan Hopkins, *Sydney Morning Herald.* Reprinted by permission of the author.

Pages 534-536: "My Outing" from DAYS OF GRACE by Arthur Ashe and Arnold Rampersad, copyright © 1993 by Arthur Ashe and Arnold Rampersad. Used by permission of Alfred A. Knopf, a division of Random House, Inc.

Pages 537-539: "Build Yourself a Killer Bod with Killer Bees" from DAVE BARRY IS NOT TAKING THIS SITTING DOWN by Dave Barry, copyright © 2000 by Dave Barry. Used by permission of Crown Publishers, a division of Random House, Inc.

Pages 540-541: "Follow the Leader to the Next Fad" by Susan C. Fawcett and Karen Castellucci Cox. Copyright © 2002 by Susan C. Fawcett and Karen Castellucci Cox. Reprinted by permission of the authors.

Pages 548-549: "A Languid Sort of Suicide" by Mario Vargas Llosa, *New York Times* (Op-Ed), 9/1/00, p. A27. Copyright © 2000 by the New York Times Co. Reprinted by permission.

Pages 550-552: "Some Thoughts About Abortion" from LIVING OUT LOUD by Anna Quindlen, copyright © 1987 by Anna Quindlen. Used by permission of Crown Publishers, a division of Random House, Inc.

Pages 553-556: "Road Rage" by Andrew Ferguson, *Time,* January 12, 1998, vol. 151, no. 1. © 1998 TIME Inc. reprinted by permission.

ESL Reference Guide

a/an/and, 493
accept/except, 493–494
Adjectives, 403–405, 435, 436–440
Adverbs, 286–288, 351–352, 435–436, 437, 438–440
affect/effect, 494
Agreement
  subject-verb, 374–376, 381–383
an/a/and, 493
Apostrophes, 443–449

be, 376, 389–390, 402–403
been/being, 494
buy/by, 495

can/could, 390–391
Capitalization, 460–462, 464
Clauses, 301–305, 343–353, 362–363, 380, 382–383, 454–455
Collective nouns, 416–417
Colons, 464, 465–466
Commands, 285–286
Commas, 450–459, 464, 465
Concise language, 318–321
Conjunctions, 343–349, 353
Conjunctive adverbs, 351–352
Consistency
  of number, 272–274
  of person, 274–277
  of tense, 267–272
Consonants
  final, doubling, 484–485
  identifying, 483
Coordinating conjunctions, 343–345, 353
could/can, 390–391

Dashes, 466
Dependent clauses, 346–349, 353, 362–363
Direct quotations, 224–225, 235–239, 464–466
do, 377

-e, final, spelling with, 486
-ed/-d verb endings, 385
effect/affect, 494
ei/ie, spelling words with, 488–489
-er/-est endings, 438
-es noun ending, 407, 488
Exact language, 312–317

except/accept, 493–494
Exclamation points, 464

Figurative language, 323–325
Fresh language, 321–323

good/well, 440–441

have, 377, 400–401
Helping verbs, 340–341

ie/ei, spelling words with, 488–489
Illustration paragraphs
  topic sentences and, 67, 68, 75
Importance, order of, 51–53, 184
Independent clauses, 301–305, 343–345, 350–352, 353, 363, 382–383
Indirect quotations, 235
Infinitive phrases, as sentence fragments, 366–367
-ing modifiers, joining ideas with, 293–295
-ing sentence fragments, 363–364
Interruptions, dashes for, 466
Irregular verbs, 396–400
it's/its, 495

know/knew/no/new, 495–496

Language
  concise, 318–321
  exact, 312–317
  figurative, 323–325
  fresh, 321–323
Linking verbs, 340, 403–405
Look-alikes, 493–505
lose/loose, 496
-ly ending, 436

Metaphors, 324

no/new/know/knew, 495–496
Nonrestrictive clauses, 302–303, 454–455
Nouns, 407–412, 460

Order
  of importance, 51–53, 184
  space, 47–50, 184
  time, 44–47, 78, 96, 184

Parallelism (parallel structure), 277–282
passed/past, 496–497
Passive voice, 402–403
Past participles, 296–298, 394–406
past/passed, 496–497
Past perfect tense, 401
Past tense, 385–393
Person
  consistency of, 274–277
  pronoun-antecedent agreement in, 414–417
Phrases
  prepositional. *See* Prepositional phrases
Prepositional phrases, 288–290, 338–339, 365, 427–429
Prepositions, 288, 338–339, 427–434
Present perfect tense, 400–401
Present tense, 374–384
Pronouns, 53–55, 413–426

Questions, 13–14, 226–227, 228, 253, 255–258, 285, 381–382, 457, 509
quiet/quit/quite, 497
Quotations, 235
  direct. *See* Direct quotations
  indirect, 235

raise/rise, 497–498
Regular verbs, 385–386, 394–395
Relative clauses, 301–305, 363, 382–383
Religions, capitalization of, 460
Repetition
  for coherence, 53–55
  for linking paragraphs in essays, 186
Restrictive clauses, 303, 454
rise/raise, 497–498
Run-on sentences, 358–362

Semicolons, 350–352
Sentence fragments, 362–373
set/sit, 498
Signal words, for singular and plural nouns, 409–411
Similes, 323
sit/set, 498
-s noun ending, 407, 446, 488
Sound-alikes, 493–505
Space order, 47–50, 184
Spelling, 480–492

A9

Subordinate clauses, 301–305, 343–345, 350, 353, 363, 382–383
Subordinating conjunctions, 346–349, 353
suppose/supposed, 498–499

Tense
  consistency of, 267–272
  past. *See* Past tense
  past perfect, 401
  present. *See* Present tense
  present perfect, 400–401
than/then, 500
their/there/they're, 499
then/than, 500
there, sentences beginning with, 381
they're/their/there, 499

through/though, 500
Time order, 44–47, 78, 96, 144, 184
to be, 376, 389–390, 402–403
to do, 377
to have, 377, 400–401, 401
to/too/two, 500–501
Transitional expressions, 58–63, 70, 78, 86, 96, 120, 135, 144–145, 152, 187–188, 452
two/to/too, 500–501

use/used, 501

Verbs, 296–298, 337, 340–342, 374–406
Voice, passive, 402–403
Vowels, identifying, 483

weather/whether, 501–502
well/good, 440–441
where/were/we're, 502
whether/weather, 501–502
whom/whomever, 422–423
whose/who's, 502–503
who/whoever, 422–423
will/would, 391
Wordiness, avoiding, 318–321
would/will, 391

-y, final, spelling with, 487
your/you're, 503

Index

a/an/and, 493
Academic subjects, capitalization of, 461
accept/except, 493–494
Action verbs, 340
Addresses, commas in, 455–456
Adjectives, 435, 436
  changing into adverbs, 436
  comparatives of, 437, 438–440
  definition of, 435
  past participles as, 403–405
  superlatives of, 437, 438–440
Adverbs, 435–436
  beginning sentences with, 286–288
  changing adjectives into, 436
  comparatives of, 437, 438–440
  conjunctive, 351–352
  definition of, 435
  superlatives of, 437, 438–440
affect/effect, 494
Agreement
  pronoun-antecedent agreement, 414–417
  subject-verb, 374–376, 381–383
an/a/and, 493
Answers, to opposition, in persuasive paragraphs, 151, 153
Antecedents of pronouns, 413–419
  agreement with pronouns, 414–417
  clear reference to, 417–419
APA style, 249
Apostrophes, 443–449
  for contractions, 443–445
  in expressions of time, 447
  for ownership, 445–447
  in plurals, 447
  for possession, 445–447
  with -s noun ending, 446
  to show omitted numbers, 447
Appositive phrases, as sentence fragments, 366
Appositives
  commas with, 453–454
  joining ideas with, 298–301
Audience
  for persuasive paragraphs, 154
  in prewriting phase, 5
Authority, reference to, in persuasive paragraphs, 151, 153

be. See to be
been/being, 494
Biblical citations, punctuation of, 466
Body of essay, 170, 177–183
  idea generation for, 177–183
Body of paragraph, 22–26
  idea generation for, 31–32
Books
  capitalization and punctuation of titles of, 462–464
  in Works Cited list, 248
Brainstorming, 11–12
  for body of essay, 178–179
  for body of paragraph, 31–32
Budgeting time, for essay questions, 253–255
Buildings, capitalization of, 460
buy/by, 495

Calls to action, ending essays with, 226
can/could, 390–391
Capitalization, 460–462
  of direct quotations, 464
  of titles, 462
Case, of personal pronouns, 420–423
Category, definition by, 103–105
Causation, confusing with time order, avoiding, 144
Cause and effect essays, 215–217
Cause and effect paragraphs, 141–149
  plan for, 142–144
  problems in, avoiding, 144
  topic sentences for, 141–142
  transitional expressions for, 144–145
  writing process for, 148–149
Causes, confusion with effects, avoiding, 144
Chronological order. *See* Time order
Cities, capitalization of, 460
Class, definition by, 103–105
Classification essays, 212–215
Classification paragraphs, 132–140
  plan for, 133–134
  topic sentences for, 132
  transitional expressions for, 135
  writing process for, 139
Clauses, 343
  dependent. *See* Dependent clauses
  independent. *See* Independent clauses
  joining, 343–345
  nonrestrictive, 302–303, 454–455
  relative. *See* Relative clauses
  restrictive, 303, 454
  subject and verb separated by, 380
  subordinate. *See* Subordinate clauses.
Clichés, 321
Clustering, 12–13
Coherence, 44–63
  order of importance for, 51–53
  repetition for, 53–55
  space order for, 47–50
  substitutions for, 55–58
  synonyms for, 55–58
  time order for, 44–47
  transitional expressions for, 58–63
Collective nouns, pronoun-antecedent agreement with, 416–417
Colons, 464, 465–466
Commands, beginning sentences with, 285–286
Commas, 450–459
  in addresses, 455–456
  with appositives, 453–454
  with contrast, 457
  in dates, 456
  with direct address, 457
  with direct quotations, 464, 465
  with introductory phrases, 451
  minor uses of, 457–458
  with nonrestrictive clauses, 454
  with parenthetical elements, 452
  in series, 450–451
  with transitional expressions, 452
Comma splices, 358–362
Common nouns, 460
Comparatives, of adjectives and adverbs, 437, 438–440
Comparison-contrast paragraphs, 126–131
  writing process for, 130
Comparison essays, 210–212
Comparisons
  pronoun case in, 422
  transitional expressions for, 120
Compound constructions, pronoun case in, 421
Compound predicates, joining ideas with, 291–293
Compound subjects, 337

Computer spell checkers, 482–483
Concise language, 318–321
Conclusions of essays, 170, 225–227
Confusing modifiers, 305–307
Conjunctions. *See* Coordinating conjunctions; Subordinating conjunctions
Conjunctive adverbs, 351–352
Consequences, prediction of in persuasive paragraphs, 151, 153
Consistency
 of number, 272–274
 of person, 274–277
 of tense, 267–272
Consonants
 final, doubling, 484–485
 identifying, 483
Contractions, apostrophes in, 443–445
Contradictions, beginning essays with, 224
Contrast, commas with, 457
Contrast essays, 210–212
Contrast paragraphs, 115–131. *See also* Comparison-contrast paragraphs
 plan for, 116–120
 topic sentences for, 115–116
 transitional expressions for, 120
 writing process for, 125–126
Controlling ideas
 in thesis statements, 174–175
 in topic sentences, 27–31
Coordinating conjunctions
 joining clauses with, 343–345, 353
 list of, 344
could/can, 390–391
Countries, capitalization of, 460

Dangling modifiers, 305–307
Dashes, 466
Dates
 capitalization in, 460
 commas in, 456
Days of the week, capitalization of, 460
Declarative sentences, 285
Definition essays, 208–210
Definition paragraphs, 107–114
 plan for, 108–110
 topic sentences for, 108
 writing process for, 113–114
Definitions, 102–107
 by category or class, 103–105
 by negation, 105
 by synonym, 102–103
Dependent clauses
 joining with subordination, 346–349, 353
 as sentence fragments, 362–363
Descriptive essays, 203–205
Descriptive paragraphs, 84–91
 plan for, 85–86
 topic sentences for, 84–85
 transitional expressions for, 86
 writing process for, 91
Descriptive titles, for essays, 228
Details, definition by class and, 103–105
Dictionaries, for spelling, 482
Direct address, commas with, 457

Directions, capitalization and, 461
Direct quotations, 235–239
 beginning essays with, 224–225
 punctuation of, 464–466
Distinguishing characteristics, definition by class and, 103–105
do, present tense of, 377
Documentation, 246–252
 summarizing or quoting in essays, 246–247
 in Works Cited list, 248–249
Documents, capitalization of, 460
Doubling final consonant, 484–485
Drafts. *See* Final drafts; First drafts; Revising

-e, final, spelling with, 486
-ed/-d verb endings, 385
effect/affect, 494
Effects, confusion with causes, avoiding, 144
ei/ie, spelling words with, 488–489
Electronic sources, in Works Cited list, 248
Emphasis, dashes for, 466
-er/-est endings, 438
-es noun ending, 407, 488
Essay examinations, 253–263
 budgeting time for, 253–255
 choosing pattern for answers to, 258–260
 instruction words in, 258–259
 process of answering, 262–263
 questions on, 253, 255–258
 reading and understanding questions on, 255–258
 topic sentences or thesis statements for, 260–262
Essays, 168–265
 body of, 170, 177–183
 cause and effect, 215–217
 classification, 212–215
 comparison, 210–212
 conclusions of, 170, 225–227
 contrast, 210–212
 definition, 208–210
 definition of, 169
 descriptive, 203–205
 final draft of, 193–194
 first draft of, 190
 illustration, 198–201
 introduction of, 222–225
 introductory paragraph of, 170
 linking paragraphs in, 186–188
 narrative, 201–203
 ordering paragraphs in, 184–185
 outlines of, 177–178
 persuasive, 217–221
 process, 205–208
 proofreading, 191
 research for. *See* Research
 revising, 190–191, 193
 thesis statement in, 170, 173–177
 title of, 227–229
 topic of, narrowing, 173–177, 223
 writing process for, 196

est/er, endings, 438
Evaluating sources, 243
Exact language, 312–317
Examinations. *See* Essay examinations
Examples, in persuasive paragraphs, 152, 153
except/accept, 493–494
Exclamation points, with direct quotations, 464
Exclamations, beginning sentences with, 285–286
Explanation paragraphs, 92, 94–95

Facts
 in persuasive paragraphs, 151, 153
 surprising, beginning essays with, 224
Family relationships, capitalization of, 460
Figurative language, 323–325
Final consonant, doubling, 484–485
Final drafts
 of essays, 193–194
 of paragraphs, 39–40
Final points, ending essays with, 226
First drafts
 of essays, 190
 of paragraphs, 34
 revising. *See* Revising
Focused freewriting, 1011
Freewriting, 8–11
 focused, 1011
Fresh language, 321–323

Geographic locations, capitalization of, 461
good/well, 440–441

have. See to have
Helping verbs, 340–341
here, sentences beginning with, 381
Historical events, capitalization of, 460
Holidays, capitalization of, 460
How-to paragraphs, 92, 93–94

Ideas
 arranging in body of paragraph, 33–34
 controlling
  in thesis statements, 174–175
  in topic sentences, 27–31
 generating
  for body of essay, 177–183
  for body of paragraph, 31–32
 joining. *See* Joining ideas
 main, underlining while reading, 509
 selecting and dropping, 32–33
 surprising, beginning essays with, 224
ie/ei, spelling words with, 488–489
Illustration essays, 198–201
Illustration paragraphs, 67–75
 plan for, 68–70
 topic sentences and, 67, 68, 75
 transitional expressions for, 70
 writing process for, 75
Illustrations, beginning essays with, 223
Imperative sentences, 285–286

Importance, order of
  for ideas in paragraphs, 51–53
  for paragraphs in essays, 184
in, for place or time, 428
Indefinite pronouns, agreement with antecedent, 415
Independent clauses, 343–345
  joining with coordination, 343–345, 353
  joining with semicolons, 350–352
Indirect quotations, 235
Infinitive phrases, as sentence fragments, 366–367
-ing modifiers, joining ideas with, 293–295
-ing sentence fragments, 363–364
Instruction words, in essay questions, 258–259
Interjections, commas with, 457
Internet, research on, 244–246
Interruptions, dashes for, 466
Introductions
  of essays, 222–225
  for quotations, 235
Introductory paragraphs, of essays, 170
Introductory phrases, commas with, 451
Irregular verbs
  past participles of, 396–400
  past tense of, 386–389
it's/its, 495

Joining clauses, 343–349, 353
Joining ideas, 291–305
  with appositives, 298–301
  with compound predicates, 291–293
  with *-ing* modifiers, 293–295
  with past participles, 296–298
  with relative clauses, 301–305
Journals, for prewriting, 15–17

Key words, selecting and dropping ideas using, 32–33
know/knew/no/new, 495–496

Language
  concise, 318–321
  exact, 312–317
  figurative, 323–325
  fresh, 321–323
Languages, capitalization of, 460
Length of sentences, 283–285
Library research, 243–244
Linking paragraphs, in essays, 186–188
Linking verbs, 340
  past participles as adjectives following, 403–405
Lists, punctuation of, 465–466
Logical order, for paragraphs in essays, 184–185
Logical sequence, for classification paragraphs, 134
Look-alikes, 493–505
lose/loose, 496
-ly ending, 436

Main ideas, underlining while reading, 509
Mapping, 12–13

Metaphors, 324
Misplaced modifiers, 305–307
MLA style, 246–252
Modifiers. *See also* Adjectives; Adverbs
  misplaced, confusing, and dangling, 305–307
  past participial, joining ideas with, 296–298
Months, capitalization of, 460
Multimedia sources, in Works Cited list, 249

Names, capitalization of, 460
Narration paragraphs, 76–83
  order for, 78
  plan for, 77–78
  topic sentences for, 76
  transitional expressions in, 78
  writing process for, 83
Narrative essays, 201–203
Narratives, as examples for illustration paragraphs, 69
Narrowing topics
  for essays, 173–177, 223
  for paragraphs, 26–27
Nationalities, capitalization of, 460
Negation, definition by, 105
no, commas with, 457
no/new/know/knew, 495–496
Nonrestrictive clauses, 302–303
  commas with, 454–455
Nouns, 407–412
  collective, 416–417
  common, 460
  plural, 407–409
  proper, capitalization of, 460
  signal words for, 409–411
  singular, 407–411
Number
  consistency of, 272–274
  pronoun-antecedent agreement in, 414–417
  subject-verb agreement in, 374–376
Numbers, omitted, apostrophes to show, 447

Objective case, of personal pronouns, 420, 422–423
Objects of prepositions, 288, 338–339, 427
of, signal words followed by, 410–411
Omissions, apostrophes to show, 443–445, 447
on, for place or time, 428
Opposition, answers to, in persuasive paragraphs, 151, 153
Order
  of importance. *See* Importance, order of
  logical, for classification paragraphs, 134
  for narration paragraphs, 78
  of paragraphs in essays, 184–185
  space, 47–50
  time (chronological). *See* Time order
Organizations, capitalization of, 460

Outlines
  for arranging ideas, 33–34
  of essays, 177–178
Outside sources
  adding and documenting, 246–252
  finding and evaluating, 243, 246
  plagiarism and, 230–231, 236–237
  quoting. *See* Quotations
  summarizing, 231
Oversimplification, in cause and effect paragraphs, avoiding, 144
Ownership, apostrophes to show, 445–447

Paragraphs, 20–167
  body of, 22–26, 31–32
  cause and effect, 141–149
  classification, 132–140
  coherence in. *See* Coherence
  comparison-contrast, 126–131
  contrast, 115–131
  definition, 107–114
  definition of, 21
  description of, 24–26
  descriptive, 84–91
  explanation, 92, 94–95
  final drafts of, 39–40
  first drafts of, 34
  how-to, 92, 93–94
  illustration, 67–75
  linking in essays, 186–188
  narration, 76–83
  order in essays, 184–185
  persuasive, 150–165
  process, 92–101
  proofreading, 40–41
  revising, 35–39
  topic of, narrowing, 26–27
  topic sentence in, 22–26
  writing process for, 43
Parallelism (parallel structure), 277–282
Parentheses, 466
Parenthetical documentation, 246
Parenthetical elements, commas with, 452
Participles, past. *See* Past participles
passed/past, 496–497
Passive voice, 402–403
Past participles, 394–406
  as adjective, 403–405
  of irregular verbs, 396–400
  joining ideas with, 296–298
  in passive voice, 402–403
  past perfect tense of, 401
  in present perfect tense, 400–401
  of regular verbs, 394–395
past/passed, 496–497
Past perfect tense, 401
Past tense, 385–393
  to be in, 389–390
  can/could in, 390–391
  irregular verbs in, 386–389
  regular verbs in, 385–386
  will/would in, 391
Peer reviewers, 190–191
Peers, revising using feedback from, 38–39

Periodicals, in Works Cited list, 248
Periods, with direct quotations, 464, 465
Person
   consistency of, 274–277
   pronoun-antecedent agreement in, 414–417
Personal look-alikes/sound-alikes lists, 503
Personal pronouns, case of, 420–423
Personal spelling lists, 491
Persuasive essays, 217–221
Persuasive paragraphs, 150–165
   audience for, 154
   building blocks of, 154
   plan for, 151–152
   support for, 153–154
   topic sentences for, 150
   transitional expressions for, 152
   writing process for, 164
Phrases
   appositive, as sentence fragments, 366
   infinitive, as sentence fragments, 366–367
   introductory, commas with, 451
   prepositional. *See* Prepositional phrases
   subject and verb separated by, 380
Place, transitional expressions indicating, 86
Plagiarism, 230–231, 236–237
Plans, for arranging ideas, 33–34
Plural nouns, 407–412
   signal words for, 409, 410–411
Plurals
   apostrophes in, 447
   consistency of number and, 272–274
Possession, apostrophes to show, 445–447
Possessive case, of personal pronouns, 420, 422
Predicates, compound, joining ideas with, 291–293
Prediction, of consequences, in persuasive paragraphs, 151, 153
Prepositional phrases, 338–339, 427–429
   beginning sentences with, 288–290
   as sentence fragments, 365
Prepositions, 338, 427–434
   in common expressions, 429–432
   list of, 288, 339
   objects of, 288, 338–339, 427
Present perfect tense, 400–401
Present tense, 374–384
   to be, to have, and *to do* in, 376–378
   sentences beginning with *there* and *here* in, 381
   separation of subject and verb and, 380
   singular constructions in, 378–379
   subject-verb agreement and. *See* Subject-verb agreement
Prewriting, 3, 4, 8–17
   brainstorming for, 11–12
   clustering (mapping) for, 12–13
   freewriting for, 8–11
   journals for, 15–17
   questions for, 13–14
   subject, audience, and purpose in, 4–7

Process essays, 205–208
Process paragraphs, 92–101
   explanation, 92, 94–95
   how-to, 92, 93–94
   plan for, 93–95
   topic sentences for, 92–93
   transitional expressions for, 96
   writing process for, 100–101
Pronoun-antecedent agreement, 414–417
Pronouns, 413–426
   antecedents of. *See* Antecedents of pronouns
   case of, 420–423
   definition of, 413
   indefinite, agreement with antecedent, 415
   personal, case of, 420–423
   possessive, case of, 420, 422
   reflexive, 424–425
   repetition of, for coherence, 53–55
   with *-self* and *-selves,* 424–425
Proofreading, 4, 328, 469–479
   of essays, 191
   mixed-error proofreading, 473–477
   of paragraphs, 40–41
Proper nouns, capitalization of, 460
Punctuation, 464–467
   apostrophes, 443–449
   commas, 450–459
   of direct quotations, 464–465
   of titles, 462
Purpose, in prewriting phase, 5

Question marks, with direct quotations, 464
Questions
   answers with *yes* or *no,* commas in, 457
   beginning sentences with, 285
   ending essays with, 226–227
   essay, 253, 255–258. *See also* Essay examinations
   preparing while reading, 509
   for prewriting, 13–14
   reporter's, 13–14
   for revising, 328
   rhetorical, as essay titles, 228
   subject-verb agreement in, 381–382
quiet/quit/quite, 497
Quotation marks
   around titles, 462
   with direct quotations, 464, 465
Quotations
   direct. *See* Direct quotations
   indirect, 235
   introducing, 235

Races, capitalization of, 460
raise/rise, 497–498
Reading essay questions, 255–258
Reading strategies, 509–510
Reference to authority, in persuasive paragraphs, 151, 153
Reflexive pronouns, 424–425

Regular verbs
   past participles of, 394–395
   past tense of, 385–386
Relative clauses
   joining ideas with, 301–305
   as sentence fragments, 363
   subject-verb agreement in, 382–383
Religions, capitalization of, 460
Repetition
   for coherence, 53–55
   for linking paragraphs in essays, 186
Reporter's questions, 13–14
Rereading, 510
Research, 240–252
   improving essays with, 240–242
   on Internet, 244–246
   in library, 243–244
   process, 240–252
   sample student essay with, 251–252
   using and documenting sources and, 246–252
   Works Cited list, 248–249
Restrictive clauses, 303, 454
Revising, 4, 328–333
   for consistency. *See* Consistency
   of essays, 190–191, 193
   of paragraphs, 35–39
   parallelism and, 277–282
   with peer feedback, 38–39
   questions for, 328
   for sentence variety. *See* Sentence variety
   for support, 35–36
   for unity, 36–38
Rhetorical questions, as essay titles, 228
rise/raise, 497–498
Run-on sentences, 358–362

-s noun ending, 407, 488
   apostrophes with, 446
-self/-selves, pronouns with, 424–425
Semicolons, joining clauses with, 350–352
Sentence fragments, 362–373
   appositive phrase, 366
   dependent clause, 362–363
   infinitive phrase, 366–367
   -ing, 363–364
   prepositional phrase, 365
   relative clause, 363
Sentences, 337–342
   compound predicates in, 291–293
   declarative, 285
   imperative, 285–286
   length of, 283–285
   prepositional phrases in, 338–339
   punctuating. *See* Punctuation; *specific punctuation marks*
   run-on, 358–362
   simple. *See* Simple sentences
   subjects of. *See* Subjects of sentences; Subject-verb agreement
   subject-verb agreement in. *See* Subject-verb agreement
   topic. *See* Topic sentences

transitional, for linking paragraphs in essays, 188
variety of. *See* Sentence variety
verbs in, 337, 340–342
Sentence variety, 283–311
commands for, 285–286
exclamations for, 285–286
lengths and, 283–285
methods of joining ideas for. *See* Joining ideas
modifier use and, 296–298
questions for, 285
sentence beginnings for, 286–290
Sequence. *See* Order
Series, commas separating items in, 450–451
set/sit, 498
Sexist language, avoiding, 415
Signal words, for singular and plural nouns, 409–411
followed by *of*, 410–411
Similes, 323
Simple sentences
independent clauses written as, 343
prepositional phrases in, 338–339
subjects of, 337–338
verbs in, 337, 340–342
Singular constructions, special, 378–379
Singular nouns, 407–409
signal words for, 409
sit/set, 498
Sound-alikes, 493–505
Sources
documenting, 246–252
evaluating, 243
research to gather. *See* Research
summarizing or quoting in essays, 246–247
Space order, 47–50
for paragraphs in essays, 184
Special singular constructions, 378–379
Specificity, of thesis statements, 174–175
Spell checkers, 482–483
Spelling, 480–492
commonly misspelled words and, 490–491
computer spell checkers and, 482–483
doubling final consonants and, 484–485
with final *e*, 486
with final *y*, 487
with *ie* and *ei*, 488–489
improving, tips for, 481–482
personal spelling lists for, 491
with *-s* or *-es* endings, 488
vowels and consonants and, 483
Streets, capitalization of, 460
Subjective case, of personal pronouns, 420, 422
Subjects (topics). *See* Topics
Subjects of sentences, 337–338
compound, 337
separated from verb, 380
Subject-verb agreement, 374–376, 381–383

Subordinate clauses
joining with subordination, 346–349, 353
relative. *See* Relative clauses
Subordinating conjunctions
joining clauses with, 346–349, 353
list of, 346
Substitutions, for coherence, 55–58
Summaries, 231–235
preparing to write, 232–234
writing process for, 234–235
Superlatives, of adjectives and adverbs, 437, 438–440
Support
for persuasive paragraphs, 153–154
revising for, 35–36
suppose/supposed, 498–499
Surprising facts/ideas, beginning essays with, 224
Synonyms
for coherence, 55–58
definition by, 102–103

Tense
consistency of, 267–272
past. *See* Past tense
past perfect, 401
present. *See* Present tense
present perfect, 400–401
than/then, 500
their/there/they're, 499
then/than, 500
there, sentences beginning with, 381
there/their/they're, 499
Thesis statements, 222–223
for cause and effect essays, 216
for classification essays, 213
for comparison essays, 211
for contrast essays, 211
controlling idea in, 174–175
for definition essays, 209
for descriptive essays, 204
for essay examination answers, 260–262
in essays, 170, 173–177
for illustration essays, 200
for narrative essays, 202
narrowing topic of, 173–177
for persuasive essays, 219
for process essays, 207
specificity of, 174–175
they're/their/there, 499
through/though, 500
Time
apostrophes in expressions of, 447
budgeting, for essay questions, 253–255
punctuation of, 466
Timed papers, 253
Time order, 44–47
confusion with causation, avoiding, 144
for narration paragraphs, 78
for paragraphs in essays, 184
for process paragraphs, 96

Titles
capitalization of, 460, 462–464
of essays, 227–229
punctuation of, 462–464
to be
passive voice with, 402–403
past tense of, 389–390
present tense of, 376
to do, present tense of, 377
to have
past perfect tense with, 401
present perfect tense with, 400–401
present tense of, 377
Topics
for essays, narrowing, 173–177, 223
for paragraphs, narrowing, 26–27
in prewriting phase, 4–5
in topic sentences, 27–31
Topic sentences, 22–26
for cause and effect paragraphs, 141–142
for classification paragraphs, 132
for contrast paragraphs, 115–116
for definition paragraphs, 108
for description paragraphs, 84–85
for essay examination answers, 260–262
in illustration paragraphs, 67, 68, 75
for narration paragraphs, 76
for persuasive paragraphs, 150
for process paragraphs, 92–93
writing, 27–31
to/too/two, 500–501
Transitional expressions
for cause and effect paragraphs, 144–145
for classification paragraphs, 135
for coherence, 58–63
commas with, 452
for comparison, 120
for contrast, 120
for descriptive paragraphs, 86
for illustration paragraphs, 70
indicating place, 86
introducing examples, 70
for linking paragraphs in essays, 187–188
list of, 60
for narration paragraphs, 78
for persuasive paragraphs, 152
for process paragraphs, 96
Transitional sentences, for linking paragraphs in essays, 188
Triteness, avoiding, 321–323
Two-part titles, for essays, 228
two/to/too, 500–501

Unbiased language, 415
Underlining
of titles, 462
while reading, 509
Understanding, of essay questions, 255–258
Unity, revising for, 36–38
use/used, 501

Vagueness, avoiding, 312–317
Verbs
   action, 340
   agreement with subject, 374–376, 381–383
   helping, 340–341
   irregular. *See* Irregular verbs
   linking. *See* Linking verbs
   passive voice of, 402–403
   past participles of. *See* Past participles
   past perfect tense of, 401
   past tense of. *See* Past tense
   present perfect tense of, 400–401
   present tense of. *See* Present tense
   regular. *See* Regular verbs
   in sentences, 337, 340–342
   separated from subject, 380
Voice, passive, 402–403
Vowels, identifying, 483

weather/whether, 501–502
well/good, 440–441
where/were/we're, 502
whether/weather, 501–502
whom/whomever, 422–423
whose/who's, 502–503
who/whoever, 422–423
will/would, 391
Wordiness, avoiding, 318–321
Words
   key, selecting and dropping ideas using, 32–33
   look-alikes and sound-alikes, 493–505
   repetition of, for coherence, 53–55
   spelling. *See* Spelling
   unfamiliar, circling while reading, 509
Works Cited list, 248–249
would/will, 391
Writing process, 3–7
   for cause and effect paragraphs, 148–149

   for classification paragraphs, 139
   for comparison-contrast paragraphs, 130
   for contrast paragraphs, 125–126
   for definition paragraphs, 113–114
   for descriptive paragraphs, 91
   for essay examination answers, 262–263
   for essays, 196
   for illustration paragraphs, 75
   for narration paragraphs, 83
   for paragraphs, 43
   for persuasive paragraphs, 164
   for process paragraphs, 100–101
   steps in, 3–4. *See also* Prewriting; Revising
   for summaries, 234–235

-y, final, spelling with, 487
yes, commas with, 457
your/you're, 503

Rhetorical Index

The following index first classifies the paragraphs and essays in this text according to rhetorical mode and then according to rhetorical mode by chapter. (Those paragraphs with built-in errors for students to correct are not included.)

Rhetorical Modes

Illustration

Louis Pasteur is revered, 51
El Niño, an unusual, 51–52
I have always considered my father, 54–55
According to sports writer, 56
Great athletes, 68
Many schools in the twenty-first century, 69
Aggressive drivers, 69–70
Random acts of kindness, 70–71
There are many quirky variations, 71
Sunlight, 170–171
Libraries of the Future—Now, 199–200
Winning, 208–209
Lisette Flores-Nieves, 223
In most cultures, 237
In her second year of college, 247
Madame Tussaud's, 276
Dr. Alice Hamilton, Medical Pioneer, 320–321
Cell Yell: Thanks for (Not) Sharing (Eric A. Taub), 514
Bam! Crash! Kapow! Girls Are Heroes Now (Susan Hopkins), 532
My Outing (Arthur Ashe), 534
Build Yourself a Killer Bod with Killer Bees (Dave Barry), 537
Some Thoughts About Abortion (Anna Quindlen), 550
Road Rage (Andrew Ferguson), 553

Narration

In 1905, a poor washerwoman, 45
When Lewis and Clark, 57
In the annals of great, 63
The crash of a Brinks truck, 77
A birthday gift, 79
Bottle Watching, 172–173
Maya Lin's Vietnam War Memorial, 201–202

In the late afternoon light, 270
On the night of December 2, 1777, 270–271
Vincent Van Gogh, 281–282
Little Richard, the King of Rock'n'Roll, 308
Dr. Alice Hamilton, Medical Pioneer, 320–321
Visiting my grandparents, 331
Homeward Bound (Janet Wu), 512
A Brother's Murder (Brent Staples), 517
Only Daughter (Sandra Cisneros), 520
Let's Get Vertical (Beth Wald), 526
On the Rez (Ian Frazier), 529
My Outing (Arthur Ashe), 534
Beauty: When the Other Dancer Is the Self (Alice Walker), 542

Description

Mr. Martin, the reason, 10
Noises in My Village, 18
The summer picnic gave ladies, 21
Visiting the house of poet, 48
Just inside the door, 48
The first time a student, 54
Mrs. Zajac seemed to have, 63
On November 27, when archaeologist, 85
The woman who met us, 87
The Day of the Dead, 203–204
In the late afternoon light, 270
I recall being told, 284
Little Richard, the King of Rock'n'Roll, 308
It is called the suburbs now, 313, 314
Mornings, a transparent pane, 324
You have to know the feel of a baseball, 326
Visiting my grandparents, 331
Homeward Bound (Janet Wu), 512
Let's Get Vertical (Beth Wald), 526

A17

A18 Rhetorical Index

Process

Most Westerners are fascinated, 45
Luck is preparation, 93
Many experts believe, 94
If your dog barks too much, 96
Skin Deep, 188–189
How to Prepare for a Final Exam, 206
Fido may be cute, 231
It was 1850, 269
A Quick History of Chocolate, 271–272
In order to give my best performance, 330
How Sunglasses Spanned the World, 510
Let's Get Vertical (Beth Wald), 526
Follow the Leader to the Next Fad (Karen Castellucci Cox), 540
A Smoker's Right (Mario Vargas Llosa), 548

Definition

These people often stay late, 23
A grand jury is an investigative body, 53
A *flashbulb memory* can be defined, 108–109
A feminist is not a man-hater, 110–111
Induction is reasoning, 111–112
Would you rather, 187
Winning, 208–209
Binge drinking, 238
Only Daughter (Sandra Cisneros), 520
Road Rage (Andrew Ferguson), 553

Comparison and Contrast

A new rival to the Barbie doll, 36
Christopher Reeve's story, 57
Zoos in the past, 58–59
Although soul and hip-hop, 116, 117–118
In my family, 119
Certain personality traits, 120–121
Either a cold or the flu, 121–122
Although contemporary fans, 127
No meal eaten in the Middle East, 128–129
The house where I grew up, 187
E-Notes from an Online Learner, 210–211
Millions of parents, 224
Speech is silver, 225
Homeward Bound (Janet Wu), 512
A Brother's Murder (Brent Staples), 517
Bam! Crash! Kapow! Girls Are Heroes Now (Susan Hopkins), 532

Classification

Gym-goers can be classified, 133
Judges can be divided, 135
The Potato Scale, 213
Follow the Leader to the Next Fad (Karen Castellucci Cox), 540

Cause and Effect

El Nino, an unusual, 51–52
Oldest Child, Youngest Child—Does It Matter? 62
What killed off the dinosaurs, 142
For Christy Haubegger, 143
Sadly, this college, 145
Bottle Watching, 172–173
Dee Kantner and Violet Palmer, 188
Why I Stayed and Stayed, 215–216
As alpine glaciers, 239
Inexperienced hikers, 240, 241
Drastic Plastic: Credit Card Debt on Campus, 251
One cause of the falling crime rate, 284
Why did I become, 285
Cell Yell: Thanks for (Not) Sharing (Eric A. Taub), 514
Only Daughter (Sandra Cisneros), 520
A Smoker's Right (Mario Vargas Llosa), 548
Road Rage (Andrew Ferguson), 553

Persuasion

Eating sugar can be worse, 23
Passengers should refuse to ride, 151
American women should stop buying, 155
This state should offer, 155–156
Writer's Workshop: *English Students, Listen Up!* 166
Sunlight, 170–171
Stopping Youth Violence: An Inside Job, 218
Millions of law-abiding Americans, 224
Single-gender schools, 226
Illness related to, 226–227
Writer's Workshop: The television commercial, 238
It's Great to Get Old, 264
In a job interview, 276
Try to imagine using failure, 285–286
Writer's Workshop: *It's Not Easy Being a Roach*, 478
The Case for Torture (Michael Levin), 523
Build Yourself a Killer Bod with Killer Bees (Dave Barry), 537
A Smoker's Right (Mario Vargas Llosa), 548
Some Thoughts About Abortion (Anna Quindlen), 550
Road Rage (Andrew Ferguson), 553

Mixed Modes

Two weeks ago, 15
I allow the spiders, 22
Pete's sloppiness, 40
The main building, 55
Much evidence shows, 57–58
The blues is the one truly American, 62
Writer's Workshop: *Young Immigrant Translators*, 64
Writer's Workshop: *English Students, Listen Up!* 166
Bottle Watching, 172–173
The house where I grew up, 187
Skin Deep, 188–189
Portrait of a Bike Fanatic, 191, 193–194
Fido may be cute, 231
Writer's Workshop: *Family Secrets: Don't You Go Talking*, 334–335
Writer's Workshop: *A Community of Fishermen*, 506–507

Rhetorical Modes by Chapter

2 Prewriting to Generate Ideas

Description
Mr. Martin, the reason, 10
Noises in My Village, 18

Mixed Modes
Two weeks ago, 15

3 The Process of Writing Paragraphs

Description
The summer picnic gave ladies, 21

Definition
These people often stay late, 23

Comparison and Contrast
A new rival to the Barbie doll, 36

Persuasion
Eating sugar can be worse, 23

Mixed Modes
I allow the spiders, 22
Pete's sloppiness, 40

4 Achieving Coherence

Illustration
Louis Pasteur is revered, 51
El Niño, an unusual, 51–52
I have always considered my father, 54–55
According to sports writer, 56

Narration
In 1905, a poor washerwoman, 45
When Lewis and Clark, 57
In the annals of great, 63

Description
Visiting the house of poet, 48
Just inside the door, 48
The first time a student, 54
Mrs. Zajac seemed to have, 63

Process
Most Westerners are fascinated, 45

Definition
A grand jury is an investigative body, 53

Comparison and Contrast
Zoos in the past, 58–59
Christopher Reeve's story, 57

Cause and Effect
El Niño, an unusual, 51–52
Oldest Child, Youngest Child—Does It Matter? 62

Mixed Modes
The main building, 55
Much evidence shows, 57–58
The blues is the one truly American, 62
Writer's Workshop: *Young Immigrant Translators* (persuasion and cause and effect), 64

5 Illustration

Illustration
Great athletes, 68
Many schools in the twenty-first century, 69
Aggressive drivers, 69–70
Random acts of kindness, 70–71
There are many quirky variations, 71

6 Narration

Narration
The crash of a Brinks truck, 77
A birthday gift, 79

7 Description

Description
On November 27, 1922, when archaeologist, 85
The woman who met us, 87

8 Process

Process
Luck is preparation, 93
Many experts believe, 94
If your dog barks too much, 96

9 Definition

Definition
A *flashbulb memory* can be defined, 108–109
A feminist is not a man-hater, 110–111
Induction is reasoning, 111–112

A20 Rhetorical Index

10 Comparison and Contrast

Comparison and Contrast
Although soul and hip-hop, 116, 117–118
In my family, 119
Certain personality traits, 120–121
Either a cold or the flu, 121–122
Although contemporary fans, 127
No meal eaten in the Middle East, 128–129

11 Classification

Classification
Gym-goers, 133
Judges can be divided, 135

12 Cause and Effect
What killed off the dinosaurs, 142
For Christy Haubegger, 143
Sadly, this college, 145

13 Persuasion

Persuasion
Passengers should refuse to ride, 151
American women should stop buying, 155
This state should offer, 155–156

14 The Process of Writing an Essay

Illustration
Sunlight, 170–171

Narration
Bottle Watching, 172–173

Process
Skin Deep, 188–189

Definition
Would you rather, 187

Comparison and Contrast
The house where I grew up, 187

Cause and Effect
Bottle Watching, 172–173
Dee Kantner and Violet Palmer, 188

Persuasion
Sunlight, 170–171

Mixed Modes
Bottle Watching, 172–173
The house where I grew up, 187

Skin Deep, 188–189
Portrait of a Bike Fanatic, 191, 193–194
Writer's Workshop: *English Students, Listen Up!* (process and persuasion), 166

15 Types of Essays

Illustration
Libraries of the Future—Now, 199–200
Winning, 208–209

Narration
Maya Lin's Vietnam War Memorial, 201–202

Description
The Day of the Dead, 203–204

Process
How to Prepare for a Final Exam, 206

Definition
Winning, 208–209

Comparison and Contrast
E-Notes from an Online Learner, 210–211

Cause and Effect
Why I Stayed and Stayed, 215–216

Classification
The Potato Scale, 213

Persuasion
Stopping Youth Violence: An Inside Job, 218

16 The Introduction, the Conclusion, and the Title

Illustration
Lisette Flores-Nieves, 223

Comparison and Contrast
Millions of parents, 224
Speech is silver, 225

Persuasion
Millions of law-abiding Americans, 224
Single-gender schools, 226
Illness related to, 226–227

17 Special College Skills: Summary and Quotation

Illustration
In most cultures, 237

Process
Fido may be cute, 231

Definition
Binge drinking, 238

Cause and Effect
As alpine glaciers, 239

Persuasion
The television commercial, 238

Mixed Modes
Fido may be cute, 231

18 Strengthening an Essay with Research

Illustration
In her second year of college, 247

Cause and Effect
Inexperienced hikers, 240, 241
Drastic Plastic: Credit Card Debt on Campus, 251

19 Writing Under Pressure: The Essay Examination

Persuasion
Writer's Workshop: *It's Great to Get Old* (persuasion), 264

20 Revising for Consistency and Parallelism

Illustration
Madame Tussaud's, 276

Narration
In the late afternoon light, 270
On the night of December 2, 1777, 270–271
Vincent Van Gogh, 281–282

Description
In the late afternoon light, 270

Process
It was 1850, 269
A Quick History of Chocolate, 271–272

Persuasion
In a job interview, 276

21 Revising for Sentence Variety

Narration
Little Richard, the King of Rock'n'Roll, 308

Description
I recall being told, 284
Little Richard, the King of Rock'n'Roll, 308

Cause and Effect
One cause of the falling crime rate, 284
Why did I become, 285

Persuasion
Try to imagine using failure, 285–286

22 Revising for Language Awareness

Illustration
Dr. Alice Hamilton, Medical Pioneer, 320–321

Narration
Dr. Alice Hamilton, Medical Pioneer, 320–321

Description
It is called the suburbs now, 313, 314
Mornings, a transparent pane, 324
You have to know the feel of a baseball, 326

23 Putting Your Revision Skills to Work

Description and Narration
Visiting my grandparents, 331

Process
In order to give my best performance, 330

Mixed Modes
Writer's Workshop: *Family Secrets: Don't You Go Talking* (mixed modes), 334–335

37 Putting Your Proofreading Skills to Work

Persuasion
Writer's Workshop: *It's Not Easy Being a Roach* (persuasion), 478

38 Look-Alikes/Sound-Alikes

Mixed Modes
Writer's Workshop: *A Community of Fishermen* (mixed modes), 506–507

Rhetorical Modes in the Reading Selections

Illustration

Cell Yell: Thanks for (Not) Sharing (Eric A. Taub), 514
Bam! Crash! Kapow! Girls Are Heroes Now (Susan Hopkins), 532
My Outing (Arthur Ashe), 534
Build Yourself a Killer Bod with Killer Bees (Dave Barry), 537
Some Thoughts About Abortion (Anna Quindlen), 550
Road Rage (Andrew Ferguson), 553

Narration

Homeward Bound (Janet Wu), 512
A Brother's Murder (Brent Staples), 517
Only Daughter (Sandra Cisneros), 520
Let's Get Vertical (Beth Wald), 526
On the Rez (Ian Frazier), 529
My Outing (Arthur Ashe), 534
Beauty: When the Other Dancer Is the Self (Alice Walker), 542

Description

Homeward Bound (Janet Wu), 512
Let's Get Vertical (Beth Wald), 526

Process

How Sunglasses Spanned the World, 510
Let's Get Vertical (Beth Wald), 526
Follow the Leader to the Next Fad (Karen Castellucci Cox), 540
A Smoker's Right (Mario Vargas Liosa), 548

Definition

Only Daughter (Sandra Cisneros), 520
Road Rage (Andrew Ferguson), 553

Comparison and Contrast

Homeward Bound (Janet Wu), 512
A Brother's Murder (Brent Staples), 517
Bam! Crash! Kapow! Girls Are Heroes Now (Susan Hopkins), 532

Classification

Follow the Leader to the Next Fad (Karen Castellucci Cox), 540

Cause and Effect

Cell Yell: Thanks for (Not) Sharing (Eric A. Taub), 514
Only Daughter (Sandra Cisneros), 520
A Smoker's Right (Mario Vargas Llosa), 548
Road Rage (Andrew Ferguson), 553

Persuasion

The Case for Torture (Michael Levin), 523
Build Yourself a Killer Bod with Killer Bees (Dave Barry), 537
A Smoker's Right (Mario Vargas Llosa), 548
Some Thoughts About Abortion (Anna Quindlen), 550
Road Rage (Andrew Ferguson), 553

Evergreen with Readings, Seventh Edition

To the instructor:

One of the best ways to improve the next edition of this textbook is to get reactions and suggestions from you, the instructor. You have worked with *Evergreen with Readings*, Seventh Edition, and I would appreciate knowing what you like about the book and what can be improved. Please answer the questions below. Tear out this page and mail it to

Susan Fawcett
c/o Marketing Services
College Division
Houghton Mifflin Company
222 Berkeley Street
Boston, MA 02116

Be honest and specific in your comments. Tell me both what is good about *Evergreen with Readings* and what could be better. Thank you.

1. Overall, how would you rate *Evergreen with Readings?* (Check one.)
   ☐ excellent   ☐ average
   ☐ good   ☐ poor

2. Which chapters or features did you find especially helpful? Why? _____
   _____
   _____

3. Which chapters or features did you find least helpful? Why? _____
   _____
   _____

4. Were any chapters too difficult or confusing for your students? Which ones?
   _____
   _____
   _____

5. Do any chapters need more explanation or practices? Which ones and why?

   _____
   _____
   _____

6. What material would you like to see added to or deleted from future editions of *Evergreen with Readings*? _____
   _____
   _____

7. Do you have any more suggestions for improving *Evergreen with Readings*?
   _____
   _____

8. How can I improve the Instructor's Annotated Edition or *Evergreen*'s ancillaries?
   _____
   _____

9. Please rate the Reading Selections.

Reading	Excellent	Good	Fair	Poor	Didn't read
How Sunglasses Spanned the World	☐	☐	☐	☐	☐
Homeward Bound, Janet Wu	☐	☐	☐	☐	☐
Cell Yell: Thanks for (Not) Sharing, Eric A. Taub	☐	☐	☐	☐	☐
A Brother's Murder, Brent Staples	☐	☐	☐	☐	☐
Only Daughter, Sandra Cisneros	☐	☐	☐	☐	☐
The Case for Torture, Michael Levin	☐	☐	☐	☐	☐
Let's Get Vertical, Beth Wald	☐	☐	☐	☐	☐
On the Rez, Ian Frazier	☐	☐	☐	☐	☐
Bam! Crash! Kapow! Girls are Heroes Now, Susan Hopkins	☐	☐	☐	☐	☐
My Outing, Arthur Ashe	☐	☐	☐	☐	☐
Build Yourself a Killer Bod with Killer Bees, Dave Barry	☐	☐	☐	☐	☐
Follow the Leader to the Next Fad, Karen Castellucci Cox	☐	☐	☐	☐	☐
Beauty: When the Other Dancer Is the Self, Alice Walker	☐	☐	☐	☐	☐
A Smoker's Right, Mario Vargas Llosa	☐	☐	☐	☐	☐
Some Thoughts about Abortion, Anna Quindlen	☐	☐	☐	☐	☐
Road Rage, Andrew Ferguson	☐	☐	☐	☐	☐

Revising and Proofreading Symbols

The following chart lists common writing errors and the symbols that instructors often use to mark them. For some errors, your instructor may wish to use symbols other than the ones shown. You may wish to write these alternate symbols in the blank column.

Standard Symbol	Instructor's Alternate Symbol	Error	For help, see Chapter
adj		Incorrect adjective form	32
adv		Incorrect adverb form	32
agr		Incorrect subject-verb agreement	26; 23
		Incorrect pronoun-antecedent agreement	30, Parts A and B
apos		Missing or incorrect apostrophe	33
awk		Awkward expression	3, Part F; 21
cap		Missing or incorrect capital letter	35, Parts A and B
case		Incorrect pronoun case	30, Part D
⊙		Missing or incorrect comma	34; 24, Parts A and B
coh		Lack of coherence	4
⊙		Missing or incorrect colon	35, Part D
con d		Inconsistent discourse	18, Part C
con p		Inconsistent person	19, Part B
con t		Inconsistent verb tense	19, Part A
coord		Incorrect coordination	24, Part A
cs		Comma splice	25, Part A
⊖		Missing or incorrect dash	35, Part D
dev		Incomplete paragraph or essay development	3, Parts C, D, and E; 14, Parts C, D, and E
dm		Dangling or confusing modifier	20, Part D
ed		Missing -ed, past tense or past participle	27, Part A; 28, Part A
frag		Sentence fragment	25, Part B; 20, Part D; 24, Part B
¶		Missing indentation for new paragraph	3, Part A
( )		Missing or incorrect parenthesis	35, Part D
‖		Faulty parallelism	19, Part C
pl		Missing or incorrect plural form	29
pp		Incorrect past participle form	28
⊙!?		Missing or incorrect end punctuation	20, Part B
quot		Missing or incorrect quotation marks	35, Part C
rep		Unnecessary repetition	3, Parts D and F
ro		Run-on sentence	25, Part A
⊙		Missing or incorrect semicolon	24, Parts C and D
sub		Incorrect subordination	24, Part B
sp		Spelling error	37
		Look-alike, sound-alike error	38
sup		Inadequate support	3, Part F
title		Title needed	16, Part C
trans		Transition needed	3, Part E; 14, Part D
trite		Trite expression	21, Part C
ts		Poor or missing topic sentence or thesis statement	3, Parts A and B; 14, Part B
u		Lack of paragraph or essay unity	3, Part F; 14, Parts C, D, and E
w		Unnecessary words	21, Part B
○		Too much space	
⌒		Words or letters to be deleted	
?		Unclear meaning	21, Part A
∧		Omitted words	
~		Words or letters in reverse order	

There's more than one way to *succeed* this semester...

SMARTHINKING.com

○ SMARTHINKING's online academic support service is available for purchase with your new textbook. It allows access to support from a real person or study resources from wherever you are, whenever you need help.

- o Connect immediately to live help
- o Submit a question for a 24-hour response from an e-structor
- o Pre-schedule time with an e-structor

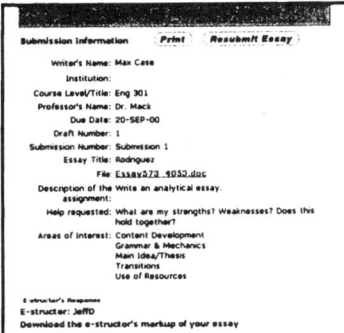

PLUS SMARTHINKING™ offers an **Online Writing Lab** so you can work on writing assignments with an e-structor and other real-time tools, like a whiteboard for math, that will help you work out difficult problems.

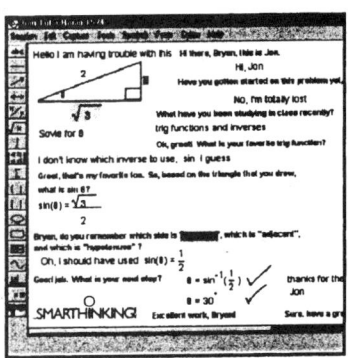

More good stuff
- Choose from live help, 24-hour submission turnaround, or scheduled appointments
- View past online sessions, questions, or essays in an archive on your personal academic home page
- View your tutoring schedule
- Access content posted by instructors in any class
- Work on other projects while waiting for help

Get help in any of the following areas:
- Mathematics (basic–calculus II)
- Statistics (introductory)
- Accounting (introductory)
- Economics (introductory macro and micro)
- Spanish
- Writing
- Grammar
- Pre-writing brainstorming
- Chemistry
- Student Success/College Survival

Getting Started with your Houghton Mifflin SMARTHINKING Tutoring Account

Thanks to your professor and Houghton Mifflin, you'll have free unlimited access to online tutoring in the subject area of your textbook from SMARTHINKING. Live help is available Sunday to Thursday, 9pm to 1am Eastern time; 8pm to midnight Central; and 6pm to 10pm Pacific.

When you're studying, doing homework or preparing for exams, don't forget that you've got an experienced tutor online ready to help. You can either go live using the virtual whiteboard in the evening or submit a question for a response, usually within 24 hrs.

If you've got a Writing text, you'll also get one submission to our Online Writing Lab (OWL). Select "Submit my writing" and follow the directions. Students with College Survival texts get live math and writing help, and one submission to the OWL. To get the help you need when you need it, simply:

STEP 1: CHECK YOUR TECH
SMARTHINKING has the following minimum requirements:
Processor: Pentium 100 processor (or Mac equivalent)
Browser: For IBM PC Compatibles users - Netscape Navigator or Communicator 4.07 or better, or Internet Explorer 4.01 or better. For Apple Mac OS users - Internet Explorer required.
Connection: A 56K modem is recommended, but a 28.8K modem is acceptable.

STEP 2: CREATE / UPDATE YOUR ACCOUNT
** TO CREATE A NEW ACCOUNT**
1. Go to www.smarthinking.com/houghton.html
2. Enter the username and password found in the envelope in your new textbook. Each one will start with an Hou. You may also have a single username starting with Miff.
3. Complete the Registration Form, choosing a new Username and Password, and check your browser settings as the directions suggest. Remember this combination, because you will use it the next time you log in.
4. The next time you login, please use the personal Username and Password you entered during registration, and hit the Login button. This will take you to your personal Academic Home Page.

TO UPDATE AN EXISTING ACCOUNT
If you currently have a SMARTHINKING account, please complete the following steps:
1. Go to www.SMARTHINKING.com and log in to your homepage.
2. Click on "My Account"
3. Click on the first Icon on the left side that says "If you received a new username and password from your school, please click here to add it to your account."
4. Enter the new username and password shown above for your school.

STEP 3: GET HELP
SMARTHINKING offers many ways for you to get the help you need:
- Connect With an e-structor Now and interact LIVE with a tutor on our interactive whiteboard. Note: The first time you run the whiteboard, you may get a plug-in notice. You must click "Yes" when asked if you will accept the plug-in. If you are having trouble loading the whiteboard you may need to change a setting on your browser. Please go to: http://www.smarthinking.com/static/fix/fix.htm for more information.
- Submit a Question and a tutor will reply, usually within 24 hours.
- Search the Schedule and search our database of tutors to find the one who is right for you.
- Submit your Writing to our Online Writing Lab and a writing tutor will give you feedback on your essay. Available only for students with College Survival and English textbooks.